DOROTHY ROWE was born in Australia and worked as a teacher and child psychologist before coming to England, where she obtained her PhD at Sheffield University. From 1972 until 1986 she was head of the North Lincolnshire Department of Clinical Psychology. She is now engaged in writing, lecturing and research, and is world-renowned for her work on how we communicate, and why we suffer.

www.dorothyrowe.com.au

Visit www.AuthorTracker.co.uk for exclusive information on your favourite HarperCollins authors.

From the reviews of *Beyond Fear*:

'This is the most extraordinary and valuable book and Dorothy Rowe is a most extraordinary and valuable person. Not only is she phenomenally wise but she also imparts her wisdom in a kind of prose poetry that moves, enlightens, reforms, beguiles and educates, all at once'   FAY WELDON

'Dorothy Rowe's is the calm voice of reason in an increasingly mad world'   SUE TOWNSEND

'Dorothy Rowe has a unique ability to tackle our most fundamental emotions and issues with her innate wisdom, common sense and quiet compassion'   MEERA SYAL

By the same author

Choosing Not Losing
The Courage to Live
Depression: The Way Out of Your Prison
Living With the Bomb: Can We Live Without Enemies?
The Successful Self
Breaking the Bonds
Wanting Everything
Time On Our Side: Growing in Wisdom, Not Growing Old
The Real Meaning of Money
Dorothy Rowe's Guide to Life
Friends and Enemies: Our Need to Love and Hate
My Dearest Enemy, My Dangerous Friend:
The Making and Breaking of Sibling Bonds

DOROTHY ROWE

Beyond Fear

20th Anniversary Edition

HARPER PERENNIAL

London, New York, Toronto and Sydney

Harper Perennial
An imprint of HarperCollins*Publishers*
77–85 Fulham Palace Road,
Hammersmith, London W6 8JB
www.harperperennial.co.uk

This edition published by Harper Perennial 2007

3

First published in Great Britain by
Fontana 1987

ISBN-13 978 0 00 724659 5
ISBN-10 0 00 724659 5

Set in PostScript Times by
Rowland Phototypesetting Ltd, Bury St Edmunds, Suffolk

Printed and bound in Great Britain by
Clays Ltd, St Ives plc

To my dear friends
Helen, Galen, Marc and Naomi

Contents

Contents

Acknowledgements

The author and publishers would like to thank the following for permission to reproduce copyright material:

American Psychiatric Association: *Diagnostic and Statistical Manual of Mental Disorders*. Ashgate Publishing: *Living with Drugs*/Michael Gossop. Basil Blackwell: *Schizophrenia and Human Value*/P. Barnham (1984). Bloomsbury Publishing Plc: *Cannabis Culture*/Patrick Matthews (1999). BPS Books: *Let's Drink to That*/Nick Heather (1996); *Recent Advances in Understanding Mental Illness and Psychotic Experiences* (2000). *British Journal of Clinical Psychology*: Mary Boyle and Anne Farmer. *British Journal of Psychiatry*: Richard Harrington, Dr Robert Hirschfeld, Professor Ian Reid and Dr Caroline Steward, Joseph Mendels. Depression Alliance: *A Single Step* (1999). *Guardian*: Nikki Sheehan, Nick Davies, Jerome Burne. Farrar Straus and Giroux Inc: *The Story of Junk*/Linda Yablonsky. Farrar Straus and Giroux Inc and Faber & Faber Ltd: *For Your Own Good*/ Alice Miller (1983). Free Association Books: *Recovery Beyond Psychiatry*/David Whitwell. Handsell Publishing: *Recovery: An Alien Concept*/Ron Coleman (1999). Harcourt Brace & Co. and Faber & Faber Ltd: *The Elder Statesman*/T.S. Eliot (1958). Harper-Collins Publishers: *Closure*/Sarah Harris (2000); *Sunbathing in the Rain*/Gwyneth Lewis. M.J. Hobbs in association with Michael Joseph: *Where Have All the Bullets Gone?*/Spike Milligan (1985). Hogarth Press: *Through Pediatrics to Psychoanalysis*/Donald Winnicott (1982). Henry Holt Inc and Jonathan Cape: 'The Welsh Marshes' in *The Shropshire Lad*/A.E. Housman. *International*

Journal of Risk and Safety in Medicine and Peter R. Breggin: 'Psychostimulants in the treatment of children diagnosed with ADHD: risks and mechanism of action'. Macmillan Publishers: *The Brain*/Jack Challoner (2000). Liz Mayne and WISH: WISH Newsletter. Mind Publications: *Accepting Voices*/ed. Marius Romme and Sandra Escher (1993). Phil Mollon: *Remembering Trauma*. Craig Newnes. *Newsday* and Peter R. Breggin: Peter R. Breggin. *Observer*: Miriam Gross, Hugh O'Shaunessy. *Openmind*: David Healy, Pat Bracken and Phil Thomas, John Vile, Dominic Beer and Bill Fulford, Vanessa Lloyd-Jones, Joanne Chambers, Linda Hart, Amanda Harris, Rachel Perkins, David Taylor. Oxford University Press: *Obsessive-Compulsive Disorder, the Facts*/ Padmal de Silva and Stanley Rachman; *Problem Drinking*/Nick Heather and Ian Robertson; *The Music of Life*/Denis Noble. PCCS Books: *This Is Madness* Vol. 1/Ron Coleman (1999); *This Is Madness* Vol. 2/Vivian Lewis and Sara Cureton (2001). Penguin Putnam Inc: *Everything in its Place*/Marc Summers. *Psychiatric Bulletin*: Maurice Lipsedge, Sam Forshall and David Nutt, David Healey, George Szmukler, Dr A.M. Mortimer, Professor Paul Bebbington. Routledge: *Wounded Healers*/ed. V. Rippere and R. Williams (1985); *The Thin Woman*/Helen Malson (1998); *Users and Abusers of Psychiatry*/Lucy Johnstone (2000); *Images of Destruction*/David Widoger (1987); *Voices of Reason, Voices of Insanity*/Ivan Leudar and Phil Thomas (2000). Scribe Publications Pty Ltd: *Punishing the Patient*/Richard Gosden. C.R. Snyder: *Excuses: Masquerades in Search of Grace*. The University of Chicago Press: *Holy Anorexia*/Rudolph Bell (1985). Virago Press and James Hale: *The Art of Starvation*/Sheila Macleod (1984). *Voices Magazine*: Sandra Esher and Marius Romme and Karina Livinstill. Weidenfeld and Nicolson: *Sick and Tired: Healing the Illnesses that Doctors Can't Cure*/Nick Read.

Introduction

Ideas about mental health and mental illness have changed over the last twenty years. Some old ideas like 'chemical imbalance' and 'a gene for this and a gene for that' linger on despite the fact that research has shown that these ideas are not hypotheses but myths. There is now a general acceptance of the idea that mental distress can be relieved by talking to a listener who has no vested interest in the situation which gave rise to the distress. The media take this idea for granted, but many members of the media fail to grasp what the talking therapies are, and speak of counselling as being a kind of unguent which is poured over some unfortunate person, as in 'the victims were counselled'. No one would willingly talk to the media about being psychotic because the media, and many members of the public, still regard anyone diagnosed as schizophrenic as being a potential axe murderer. Yet prominent figures now speak openly of their depression, and pop stars seem to regard as obligatory a drug habit followed by a period in a fashionable psychiatric clinic. Politicians speak most sympathetically about the necessity for good mental health care, though the money for such a service rarely follows through. But, in all, when it comes to mental illness, everyone's heart is in the right place.

Or is it? Despite all the changes for the better, the notion that madness is some strange thing that can fall upon an unwitting individual at any time is as strongly held as ever. The language in which we talk about madness might have changed, but the belief in that strange, wilful, sinister, mysterious force is still in the minds of most people, including the minds of those who ought to know better. To be seen to be mad is still regarded as being alien, no longer a full member of the human race. The Royal College of Psychiatrists and MIND, the National Association for Mental Health, have run a campaign aimed at removing the stigma of madness, or, in current terminology, 'having a mental health problem', while some sections of the media have a stylebook setting out what language may or may not be used (the *Guardian* stylebook bans 'offensive and unacceptable terms such as "loony, nutter, psycho and schizo"'). However, little seems to have changed in private attitudes. Despite the courageous work by members of the user/survivor movement, the term 'mental health problem' is taking on all the negative connotations of 'mentally ill'. Writing about the report issued by the National Institute for Clinical Excellence (NICE) following their study 'Mental Health and the National Press',[1] the journalist Lynne Eaton summed up NICE's results with, 'Some of the reports about people suffering mental illness, particularly news stories, contain a level of discrimination that would be deemed unacceptable for most other social groups (except, perhaps, Gypsies and asylum seekers).'[2]

In their report, NICE recommended that mental health professionals be prepared to inform the press about mental health issues. However, the language used by the majority of mental health professionals is itself suspect. In 1987, when the first edition of *Beyond Fear* was published, psychiatrists spoke of mental illness. In the intervening years the word 'illness' has disappeared from the diagnoses used by psychiatrists, though not from their general discourse, to be replaced by the word 'disorder'. When I first came to England in 1968 and worked in psychiatric hospitals there were only five basic mental illnesses, namely, schizophrenia, manic-depression, anxiety and phobias, obsessions and compulsions, and depression. The behaviours associated with these diagnoses are very distinctive and found in all societies and throughout recorded history. Many of the psychiatrists I worked with had their own idiosyncratic diagnoses for people who could not be fitted into any of these categories. At Middlewood Hospital (a Sheffield psychiatric hospital now mercifully closed) a favourite diagnosis was 'Irish'. Over the years the idiosyncratic diagnoses of American psychiatrists were pooled and the more popular ones were presented in what is now a vast tome, the *Diagnostic and Statistical Manual* (DSM – Revision IV) which covers all the ways we can behave when faced with a very difficult situation. We are all in the DSM, at least once. Psychiatrists have medicalized life, and, in so doing, joined forces with an international business comparable in size, wealth and power with the arms trade and the oil business – the pharmaceutical industry.

Psychiatric ideas of mental illness and mental disorder are based on 'the oversimplified medical model that forms part of the culture of psychiatry, the ''illness-treatment-recovery model'' ' which the retired psychiatrist David Whitwell calls 'naïve psychiatry'. This 'focuses on short-term improvements in symptoms as a main target for intervention. Although its origins are over fifty years old, and it reflects an outdated concept of what it is to recover from mental illness, it is still very much in evidence.' In his many years of work in acute psychiatry, David Whitwell came to see that, 'The claims made by professors of psychopharmacology and the drug companies for their products were never fulfilled in practice. The new clever therapies never seemed to produce the transformations they promised. And as time went on I could see less and less value in the elaborate systems of diagnosis and classification that are so central to psychiatry . . . I became more aware of the power and effectiveness of the non-specific factors which help people recover.'[3]

'Naïve psychiatry' may still be flourishing but so is naïve psychology. If this psychology were water it wouldn't wet the soles of your feet. When I read much of the work of my colleagues, whether academic papers in learned journals or self-help books for the general public, I get the feeling that most members of my profession have led extraordinarily sheltered lives, or perhaps in their teens they encountered life in all its crudity and messiness. Recoiling in horror, they comforted themselves with a fantasy of a pleasant, technicolour world where all problems are soluble. To maintain this fantasy into adulthood they had to ignore anything to do with politics. Traditionally, the British Psychological Society

(BPS) has viewed politics as distasteful. More recently psychologists in the UK, along with those in the USA and Australia, have come to fear that any interest in the political aspects of their work could threaten their livelihood in a highly competitive market. Such timidity has led to the BPS's professional journal, *The Psychologist*, reading like a high-school magazine written by diligent, unquestioning students. Psychologists feel sorry for their clients, but the way most of them talk about their clients, both publicly and privately, reveals that they do not see their clients as fellow adults but as wayward children whom they can teach to live in sensible ways. They present their advice to these children briskly and with authority because they feel it would lessen their standing in their profession and in the eyes of the public to admit to doubt and inadequacy. They seem to have no measure of how naïve they are.

There are those academic psychologists who live in a world of very long words, all of them abstract nouns. To them people are but containers for traits such as 'sociability', 'religiosity', 'extraversion' and 'introversion'. (In much the same way naïve psychiatrists see people as mere containers for 'depression' or 'schizophrenia'.) Psychologists discover these abstract nouns by giving groups of people questionnaires about what they do. Their answers are reduced to numbers, and these numbers are put through some statistical processes to see how the answers clump together in different groups. These groups are given abstract nouns as names, and these names are regarded as being 'factors' or 'traits' which explain why people behave as they do. Thus, these psychologists know that you don't have dinner with your friends because you like to see them but because you have a trait of sociability. They have not noticed that two people can do exactly the same thing but for totally different reasons, and that it is our reasons which impel us into action.

There are those clinical psychologists who aim to replace their client's 'dysfunctional cognitions' with 'functional cognitions' which bear a remarkable similarity to their own eminently 'functional cognitions'. Cognitive behavioural therapists who are in close contact with real life know quite well that there is no set of ideas or beliefs that will invariably lead to us being secure and happy, because all the interpretations we make of what is happening have both good and bad implications. For instance, seeing yourself as being competent has the good implication that you will be able to face new situations with confidence, but the bad implication that, seeing you as competent, people are less likely to help you. Naïve psychologists seem not to understand this. Psychologists who practise positive psychology, the psychology of happiness, advocate, amongst other things, that each day we should count our blessings. *Psychologies* magazine asked me to take part in a debate on happiness with Professor Christopher Peterson, an American psychologist well known for his work in positive psychology. The features editor of the magazine sent me an unedited copy of what Professor Peterson had written. He concluded his argument with,

> Should we eradicate sadness from the world? Yes. This is not to say that we should eradicate challenge and difficulty, not that we could really do that. Challenge and difficulty are the stuff of life: they make innovation and accomplishment possible. But what we should do is to encourage people to respond to setbacks not with despair but with good cheer, hope and perseverance. Happiness makes this possible.
>
> Should we pursue happiness? Yes.

This was written in August 2006 while world governments dithered over what, if anything, they should do to stop the death and destruction in Lebanon following the invasion by the Israeli army. It seems to be very naïve not to understand that there were many Lebanese and Israelis who were suffering the kind of losses which create a sadness that would stay with them till the end of their days. When we lose something which is an essential part of our being, be it a person, a home, a livelihood, or a future, we are left with an empty space inside us that no amount of blessings can ever fill.

Also in August 2006, an Austrian girl, Natascha Kampusch, who had been kidnapped when she was ten by a man, Wolfgang Priklopil, managed to escape after eight years' captivity in a cellar under Priklopil's house. This must have been a terrible experience, but worse was to come. According to those psychologists and psychiatrists who are experts on such things, at some point Natascha was struck by a terrible disease, Stockholm syndrome. This disease caused Natascha to sympathize with her captor.

Stockholm syndrome resides nowhere but in the minds of these psychologists and psychiatrists. They believe that diagnosing Natascha as having this illness shows that they are great experts. They also avoid having to explain to the public what happens to us all when we are imprisoned on our own for an indefinite period. We all need contact with other people just as much as we need food. Lacking contact with people, we become unable to distinguish our thoughts and feelings from what is going on around us. This is well known from the accounts of people who have spent long periods in solitary confinement and from sensory deprivation experiments. When we are starving we will take the vilest of nourishment, and, rather than be completely isolated, we will create a relationship with whoever is on offer, no matter how vile that person may be. Hostages like Brian Keenan and John McCarthy, who spent five years in captivity in Lebanon, much of that time on their own, have described this in detail. Psychologists who have studied how a baby forms a bond with a mothering adult have shown how the nature of the bond is very much determined by the way the mother responds to the child. Simply put, when the mother is unfailingly pleasant and kind, the child assumes that the mother will always be available and thus can bear being separated from her; when the mother is unfailingly unpleasant and unkind, the child forms only the slightest of bonds. When the mother alternates between being kind and pleasant and being unkind and unpleasant the child forms an anxious attachment to the mother, a bond which is very strong because, even though the child is frightened of her, he always hopes to be rewarded by her. To survive as a person Natascha had to form a relationship with Priklopil. Because he was sometimes kind and sometimes unkind Natascha became anxiously attached to him, and so she was distressed when she learned that he had killed himself. Placed in a similar situation, we all would have done much the same as Natascha, and none of us, including Natascha, would have been struck by the dreaded Stockholm syndrome.

Diagnoses like this put a security fence between the professional and the person who is suffering. It is the professional who is being kept safe from the horrors and the pain of real life while pretending to be an expert on people. Very little of the theory and practice of psychology and psychiatry relates to real, lived experience. Psychoanalysts have always tried to describe real, lived experience, but their desire to be special and different, as marked by their special language and by the difficulties in acquiring a ticket of entry to their group, has always overridden their desire to give a generally comprehensible account of what it is to live. Much the same can be said of the existential therapists. I have always tried to describe through the stories I tell what it is to be human, but I take things apart, while the great writers, artists and composers encompass life in all its complexity. Denis Noble, in his book *The Music of Life*, said of his colleagues, 'Scientists and others tend to be quite fond of neat, clear-cut patterns. Nature is not. Nature is inherently messy . . . For some scientists reductionism functions as a security blanket. It avoids the need to ask too many questions, to stare into the abyss of uncertainty.'[4]

For most psychiatrists and psychologists, DSM diagnoses function as a security blanket, saving them from having to confront the messiness of life and its great uncertainties. Diagnoses also allow them to see other people, not as agents, but as puppets. The theories which picture people as puppets are about behaviour being the outcome of the actions of genes, biochemistry, disorders, traits, or the movements of the planets. Such theories are far removed from what we actually do. Neuroscientists have now put beyond doubt the fact that we cannot see reality directly but know only the constructions of our brain which come from our past experience. Developmental psychologists who understand this have applied this knowledge to their studies of babies and toddlers, and have shown that babies are born, not as passive puppets, but as agents, eager to make relationships and to act on their world.

Since no two people ever have the same experience, no two people ever see anything in exactly the same way. *What determines our behaviour is not what happens to us but how we interpret what happens to us.* In every moment of our life we are engaged in interpreting what is going on. We are, in effect, meaning-creating creatures. This is what it is to be human.

All the meanings we create form a kind of structure, and out of this structure comes our sense of being a person. Because we cannot see reality directly, every interpretation we make is a guess about what is going on. Thus, what we experience as 'I', 'me', 'myself' is a set of guesses about ourselves and our world. Our guesses are also predictions. When we find that our predictions are proving to be reasonably accurate we feel secure. However, the world can often surprise us, not always in pleasant ways, and when this happens some of our ideas fall apart. This is a very common experience. Unless we know that what we are experiencing is a necessary collapse of our ideas, we feel ourselves to be falling apart. If we are full of self-confidence we can say to ourselves, 'I've got through things like this before and I'll do so again,' but, if we lack all self-confidence, we feel that our very self is crumbling, shattering, even disappearing. We feel a terror greater than our fear of death. Facing death, we can tell ourselves that some important part of ourselves will continue on, perhaps our soul or spirit, or the memories others have of us. Facing the annihilation of our sense of being a person, we feel that we are about to disappear like a wisp of smoke in the wind. In such terror we can resort to those desperate defences which psychiatrists call mental disorders. They are not illnesses but defences which serve to hold us together when we feel ourselves falling apart. We can relinquish these defences once we come to understand that what is falling apart is not our self but some of our ideas. These ideas must fall apart so we can build new ones that better reflect what is going on in our life. We are not puppets, victims of our genes, traits, or star signs, but agents, interpreting our world, making decisions and acting on our world.

If we do not value and accept ourselves, if we believe that our ideas about ourselves and our world are absolute truths, and if we try to force the world to be what we want it to be, we will be unhappy. If we value and accept ourselves, if we know that everything we know is but a set of ideas which we can choose to change, and that our ability to change the world in the way we want is extremely limited, we will be able to survive the worst that life can throw at us. There is a good chance that sometimes we will be happy.

Fear and the Fear of Fear

Chapter One

The Nature of Fear

Fear comes to us in many guises. It can come as a shiver in the delight of anticipation; or as the drenching, overwhelming, annihilating terror known by the inadequate names of existential anxiety or dread. It can come suddenly, life-savingly, in situations of danger, when it is known purely as fear; or it can gnaw away endlessly with little apparent cause, and we call it anxiety; or it can come with a sense of having the eyes of the world upon us when we are naked and alone, and we call it shame; or it can loom darkly, threatening punishment, and we call it guilt.

Fear, like death, is the great unmentionable. We maintain a conspiracy of silence so as to pretend we are not afraid. In the aftermath of great physical danger or terrible disaster everyone claims that everyone was brave and no one panicked. In 1985, when I was living in Sheffield and writing this book, at nearby Manchester airport a British Airways plane loaded with holidaymakers caught fire as it was about to take off. Those passengers who survived spoke of terror and panic and the rush for the exits as smoke filled the rear of the plane, but they soon ceased to be reported in the newspapers as other people, important people who were not aboard the plane, made their statements commending the passengers for their bravery. These important people would have had us believe that everyone aboard that plane acted with courage and decorum. Yet would not anyone, trapped in the narrow space of a crowded plane, watching the flames and breathing the acrid smoke, feel afraid and try desperately to escape?

Sixteen years on and another, even more immense, tragedy occurred in New York on 11 September 2001. Across the world

3

millions of people watched the television pictures of these events that day and over the next few days. We saw how again fear became the great unmentionable. When the two planes flew into the World Trade Center and the buildings collapsed, television crews filmed and interviewed some of the people who had escaped death. These people showed their fear and spoke about it, and such interviews were repeated in news bulletins later that day and evening, but by the next day such interviews had disappeared from our television screens. They were replaced by stories about the bravery of the firefighters and other rescue workers. The courage of the Mayor of New York, Rudy Giuliani, was praised, as was the courage of Americans generally. By then Americans had turned to patriotism and religion. The symbol of the USA, the Stars and Stripes, became a badge of courage and determination, while churches, synagogues and mosques were overflowing with worshippers. Americans were still afraid, very afraid, but this fear could not be mentioned.

The memory of such fear can stay with us for the rest of our lives, leaving us unable to enter any place which will remind us of our fear, or returning in dreams of terror when we find ourselves re-enacting, helplessly, the scenes where we once successfully escaped destruction. Some people, to give themselves freedom to go and do what they wish, put themselves through the painful process of therapy, in the hope that relearning a skill or talking about the events will remove the fear, and with that the shame of being afraid. Most people, however, adapt their lives to avoid certain situations and activities, by never entering an enclosed space or flying again, or they fog their sleeping brains with drugs to blot out dreams, or become what is known as 'a light sleeper', someone who is often awake while others sleep. They invent all sorts of excuses for not doing certain things – proneness to illness, or allergies, logical reasons for following one course of action rather than another – all to hide the fact that they are afraid. They must do this because they know, correctly, that to be afraid is to be scorned.

The fear we feel when faced with an external danger – fire or flood or a terrorist bomb – is bad enough, but what is far, far worse is the fear we feel when the danger is inside us. When the danger is outside us we know that at least some people will understand how we feel, but when the danger is inside us, when we live our lives in a sweat of anxiety, shame and guilt, we find ourselves in the greater peril that if we tell other people about our fear they will think that we are weak, or, worse, mad. So we take drugs to drown our fear and maintain the conspiracy of silence.

Edith was a very good woman who had devoted her life to others. She often acted as chauffeur for one of my clients, and while this client was talking to me Edith would visit some of the elderly patients in the hospital. One day she phoned me and asked whether, when she came the next day, she could have a quick word with me. I agreed, and so the next day she came into my room, apologizing for taking up my time and sitting nervously on the edge of her chair. What she wanted to know was whether she was going mad. The evidence that she might be was that she would often wake at 2 a.m. and lie worrying. The fear that pervaded her being manifested itself as the fear that no one would look after her when she was old. What if she became senile and incontinent, like the old women she visited on the psychiatric ward? She had done enough nursing to know that I could not truthfully say that her old age would not bring indignities and inadequacies, but there is one truth I could tell her.

Waking in the early hours of the morning in a sweat of terror is an extremely common experience. All across the country people are experiencing that terrible loneliness of being. They have woken suddenly to the greatest uncertainty a human being can know. There is no shape or structure to hold them. They are falling, dissolving; totally, paralysingly helpless without hope of recovery or of rescue. Sickening, powerful forces clutch at their hearts and stomachs. They gasp for breath as wave after wave of terror sweeps over them.

We all knew such terror when, as small children, we found ourselves in a situation which filled us with pain and helpless rage. We screamed in fear and in the hope that our good parents would rescue and comfort us. Now grown up, we know the extent of our loneliness and helplessness. Some of us wake, like Edith, completely alone. Some of us have another form sharing our bed, but it is effectively insensate, a log refusing to acknowledge our misery. Others of us, more fortunate, share our bed with a kindly person who switches on the light, makes us a cup of tea, and holds us close. Such love can make our terror recede like the tide, but, like the tide, it can return, and there is no good parent there to pick us up and cuddle us and assure us that the world is a safe place and there is no reason to be afraid. We are grown up now, and, try as we might to deny it, we know the loneliness of being. We long for good parents who will rescue and love us, but we know that there are no good parents and, while we might believe in God the Father, in these times of terror He is far away.

For some people the waves of terror and the sense of annihilation last for many minutes. Some people move very quickly to turn the terror into all kinds of manageable worries – manageable not because the worries are about problems which can be solved but because they turn a nameless terror into a named anxiety. Thoughts like 'Who will look after me when I get old?', 'I can't manage the tasks I have to do at work today', 'The lump on my groin is certain to be cancer', 'If my daughter goes to that school she'll get mixed up in drugs', 'I won't be able to meet this month's bills', 'I should have done more for my parents before they died' are indeed terrible, but they give a sense of structure and have a common, everyday meaning. With these common, everyday meanings we can pretend that the terror we felt did not happen, and that we belong to the everyday world.

However, not everyone can do this. For some people, lying there in the dark, the terror goes on and on. When Edith described to me how this happened to her she said, 'It gets so bad I think I shall run outside the house in my nightie and stand in the middle of the road so I'll get run over and that'll stop it.'

'Not in your street at 2 a.m. you won't,' I said, knowing how empty her town was at night. I went on to tell her that the terror she felt is called 'existential angst'. She laughed at this ridiculously pretentious name. 'I'll remember that next time,' she said, 'I'll lie there and think, "I'm experiencing existential angst."'

I do hope she does, and finds her laughter in the midst of her terror. It would be so monstrously unfair if Edith followed the path of a woman whose inquest was reported in the paper recently. She was an elderly patient, not long discharged from a psychiatric hospital. A nurse told the coroner that she had looked in the patient's room at midnight and seen her sound asleep. When she returned at 6 a.m. she found her floating in the bath. The coroner returned an open verdict. There was no mention of the terror which the poor woman could bring to an end only by filling the bath with water and, all alone, immersing herself in it. When fear is terrible, all we can do is run away.

Fight or Flight

Fear has a vital life-saving function. It is the means by which our body mobilizes itself to move swiftly and efficiently to protective action. When we interpret the situation we are in as dangerous, adrenaline, which is produced by the adrenal glands just above the kidneys, as well as at the ends of the neurones in the brain, is pumped into our system, thus causing our heart rate, blood pressure and blood sugar level to increase, and so preparing the body to fight or flee. If we act physically, by striking out at the source of the danger or by taking to our heels and running away, then we make use of our body's preparations. But if we neither fight back nor run away we are left with the effects of these preparations and they can be most unpleasant.

Our heart beats fast and we feel shaky, sweaty and tingly. Some people experience severe headaches, some feel nauseous, some feel dizzy and close to fainting. Some people do faint. When these reactions occur in company, where we need to be calm and collected, we can feel very ashamed of ourselves. When they occur and we do not know why, we can feel frightened and so start on the sickening cycle of fearing fear itself.

Faced with an external danger, such as a man carrying a gun, or an oncoming monstrous tsunami, we can stand and fight or flee. However, sometimes the people around us will not let us do either. Children who are frightened of their parents or teachers may be prevented from either fighting to protect themselves or running away. Lacking the means to support themselves or their children, women may be unable to flee from husbands who frighten them. Needing to support their families, men may be unable to fight or flee from employers who frighten and mistreat them.

Thus it is very easy to find ourselves in a situation where we wish to fight or to flee but feel that we can do neither. Such a conflict leaves our mind in a turmoil and our body reacting appropriately to our reading of the situation (danger) and inappropriately to our reaction to our reading of the situation (neither fighting nor fleeing).

If we can make such a conflict explicit, by thinking about it very clearly and honestly and by discussing it with understanding friends and counsellors, then we can often find a way to solve the conflict or to live with it more easily. But if we dare not make the conflict explicit to others or even to ourselves, then we cannot resolve it and our misery goes on.

Shirley came to see me because she was nervous. She had given up driving because she was frightened she would have an accident and hurt someone.

'I'm not worried about hurting myself. It's other people that I worry about.'

She felt nervous when she had to go into a room where there were other people.

'I worry that they'll all look at me. Yet I like going out and having a social life. It's just I sort of feel ashamed. I don't know why. I do go out, like we go out for a drink, and I find my hands shaking.'

She said that what she wanted was to feel more confident.

'I've never felt confident.'

Her brothers, all older than her, used to tell her that, as she was a girl, she could not play with them. At school her teachers told her that she was not bright.

'I mightn't be brainy but I'm intelligent. That's what I'm always telling my husband. He treats me like I'm stupid and don't know anything. But you can't tell him. He's one of those men who always have to be right. Don't get me wrong, he's a wonderful husband and thinks the world of me, but he does put me down.'

She spoke of how important it was to her to be herself, to have a small job so she had some money of her own, and how annoyed she got with herself when she became too nervous to do the things that she wanted to do. Yet, when she spoke of being confident, there was some sense of reservation. She would not want to be totally confident.

Why was that? Well, a great deal is expected of totally confident people. People expect them to be able to cope with everything. Shirley's problem was that if she became totally confident she would be asked to do things which she could not or would not do, and she did not want to say no to people.

'I don't like to upset people. I want to be liked.'

If Shirley's problem had been simply that she lacked self-confidence, then she could have solved that problem by taking steps to increase her self-confidence, but if she also believed that if she was self-confident she would upset people and they would dislike her, she could not afford to become self-confident.

Unavoidable Conflicts

Shirley's conflict is one which many people experience. We want to be ourselves, but we fear that if we do express our own wishes, needs and attitudes, then people will not like us. For some people being liked is not their top priority, but for many people it is a matter of life and death. More of this later. Here I want to point out that all of us, whatever we feel about being liked, are always involved in finding a balance somewhere between

Being an individual	....	Being a member of a group

If we live completely as an individual pursuing our own interests and taking no account of other people's needs and wishes, we soon become extremely lonely. If we live completely on our own, lacking the checks and balances that other people place on our interpretation of what goes on in the world, we become an extremely idiosyncratic person whom other people regard as odd, even mad. On the other hand, if we merge ourselves completely with a group we cease to be the person we are. We become a nothing. Rather than face either of these fates we have to find a balance, day by day, between being an individual and maintaining relationships with other people.

In finding a practicable balance between being an individual and being a member of a group, you have to arrive at a balance between regarding yourself as

Completely valueless and imperfect	....	Completely valuable and perfect

The more we regard ourselves as valueless and imperfect, the more we fear, hate and envy other people, the more we feel frightened of doing anything, and the more we fear the future. Regarding ourselves as bad brings a lot of troubles. Yet if we regard ourselves as perfect we delude ourselves and make it difficult for other people to get along with us. No one is perfect. We all make mistakes, get things wrong, irritate other people, and fail to make the most of our talents.

So we have to arrive at a realistic assessment of ourselves, with no false modesty, seeing ourselves as ordinary people, like all other people, yet at the same time as individuals who are valuable to ourselves and to other people, even though other people may not value us in the way that we want them to value us.

It can take us many years to arrive at an assessment of ourselves which provides a realistic and hopeful balance between imperfection and perfection. We can be plagued by doubt, confused by the conflicting demands that people make on us, and hurt by criticism.

To find out who we are and how we should assess ourselves we need to explore, to meet new people, to try out new situations and to see how we feel and react to and deal with the strange and the new. But to do this, we need freedom, and to have freedom we have to give up security.

From the moment of our birth, we have to find a balance between

Freedom .... Security

The more freedom we have, the less security. The more security, the less freedom. Total freedom means total uncertainty and great danger. Total security means total certainty and total hopelessness, for hope can only exist where there is uncertainty.

We all try to hold on to a measure of security. Most of us do this by having possessions (what is that line from a song – 'Freedom's just another word for nothing left to lose'?), just as most of us find security by keeping close to a group of people (why else would we put up with awful relatives?). Some people seek security not just in possessions and people but in a set of beliefs which makes everything that happens part of a pattern. The pattern may be in terms of heaven and hell, or Allah's will, or karma, or fate, or a constellation of stars, or the eventual victory of the proletariat, but whatever the pattern is, it gives us a sense of fixity in what would otherwise seem to be a meaningless chaos.

However, while having a belief in some kind of grand design can give a sense of security, it can make the person who holds the belief feel hopeless. If the pattern of your life is already determined by God or by your stars, or by your genes, or by your parents, or by a series of rewards and punishments called conditioning, then there is nothing you can do to change it. You are helpless and hopeless.

On the other hand, if nothing is fixed, if anything can happen, at any time, then you have an infinite number of choices about what you do with your life. Such freedom can be exciting if you have lots of confidence in yourself, but if you do not, then such freedom is very scary. So, somehow, we all have to achieve a balance between

An	Having no
infinite	choice
choice	at all

Along with the question of choice comes the question of responsibility. How much are we responsible for what happens? If we are just acting out a pattern which was determined and fixed in our stars or in our genes before we were born, then we are not responsible if we turn out to be murderers or thieves, and it is not our fault if our children turn out badly or millions of people starve. Such a release from responsibility can seem quite attractive, but, equally, if we are not responsible for when things turn out badly, we cannot take the credit for when they turn out well. You cannot take the credit when you become rich, famous and powerful, when your children lead happy, successful lives, and when you solve the problems of world hunger and nuclear war. So, being responsible does have its benefits.

But where does that responsibility end? You might be responsible for doing your work properly but are you responsible when the firm you work for goes bankrupt and you lose your job? You might be responsible for looking after your children, but are you responsible when your daughter's marriage breaks up or your son gives up his job to go surfing in California? You might be responsible for organizing your finances so that you have some money to give the charities, but are you responsible for those world events which give rise to hunger, terrorism and war?

So we have to find a balance between being

Not	Totally
responsible	responsible
for anything	for everything

Even though from the moment of birth we need other people, as small children we soon learn that other people can reject and punish

us, and this can be very painful. We protect ourselves from this
pain by becoming very careful in our relations with other people.
We withdraw from them, and when we deal with them we put on
some sort of social front. When I was researching for my book
Friends and Enemies[1] I questioned a large number of people about
the part friendship played in their lives. Many of these people spoke
of how, while they valued their friends and dreaded loneliness, they
feared being rejected or abandoned or betrayed by their friends.
Being close to other people is risky, but then we also run the risk
of loneliness.

So we have to find a balance between

The risk		The risk
of	....	of
rejection		loneliness

Thus in these six vital aspects of our lives we are for ever trying
to achieve a balance between two opposites. There is no textbook
we can consult which will tell us what is the right balance, because
what is right for one person is wrong for another. We cannot, when
we are, say, fifteen, arrive at a set of balances which will suit us
for the rest of our lives and stick with that, because what is a good
balance at fifteen is not so good at twenty and quite disastrous at
forty. So we have to keep trying to find the right balance, and we
always run the risk of getting it wrong. We are always in the
position of the juggler who is trying to keep eight oranges in the
air while balancing on a ball which is on a chair which is resting
on a plank which is supported by two rolling drums which are on
a raft floating in deep water. Any minute, something could go
wrong. It is no wonder that we often feel frightened.

We struggle on, meeting what seems an endless stream of difficulties and problems. When we encounter yet another setback, we
often look at other people and see them being like those people in
the television advertisements who are always beautiful, knowledgeable, organized, intelligent, happy, loved, admired and suffering no
greater problems than choosing the right margarine and coping

with the weather. Then we can feel just like Alice when she met a couple at a dinner party.

'They've got three children,' she told me, 'and they're all brilliant, marvellously musical, getting excellent degrees, entering wonderful careers. He's done terribly well, she's got this marvellous part-time job and she's got paintings in this new exhibition. Everything that family does is just right. Urgh!'

It is hard not to feel envy for people whose lives seem to go along more easily, more successfully than ours. However, this is the price we pay for clinging to the hope that it is possible for us to find a way of life where we are happy, trouble free and never make a mess of things. Without this hope many of us would find life very difficult indeed. The alternative version of life, in which all of us suffer one way or another, have heavy burdens and often make a mess of things, can rob us of hope and make us feel very frightened.

Many of us, as we get older, come to agree with Samuel Johnson that 'Human life is everywhere a state in which much is to be endured and little to be enjoyed', and try to meet this view of life with courage and hope. However, those of us who have read about Johnson know that during his life he was often depressed and that he was always afraid of dying.

Fear of Life and Death

Most of us go through a large part of our lives not thinking about death. 'When it comes, it comes,' we say, and secretly think that it will not. Other people die in earthquakes or car accidents or of cancer or of old age, but not me. I am the exception. Then one day something happens and we know. Death means me.

Then all the careful security we have built up comes crashing down. We are all alone, without protection, open to great forces which we cannot and do not understand. We ask in our anguish, 'Why me?' 'Why death?' 'Why life?' 'What is it all about?' There are no satisfactory answers.

From the moral and religious education we received in childhood many of us drew the comforting conclusion 'If I'm good nothing bad can happen to me or to my loved ones'. When death becomes imminent, or some other terrible disaster strikes, our belief in the protective power of virtue is swept away.

Rose's lawyer asked me to prepare a report on how Rose had been affected by her accident. She was having difficulty in getting back to work.

Rose said to me, 'The car pulled out of the driveway and hit me as I was cycling past. My bike was caught under the front of the car and I was pushed across the road. I could see the lights of other cars coming towards me. I remembered how, when I was eight, we left our beautiful home in the country and moved to London. And then I thought, "I won't have any more holidays." I ended up in the gutter on the other side of the road. A man came to pick me up and I thought he was the driver of the car. I gave him a mouthful. I was angry and then I found that he wasn't the driver . . . I feel so guilty about all of this, putting all you people to so much trouble. You've got people who need your help far more than I do. I'm all right, really, just my back's a little sore and I get a bit weepy now and then. I usen't to be like that. Always self-controlled, really. Now I think, why me? Why do I go on living and those babies die?'

Rose was not all right. She was shaken to the very core and guilty that she was alive. That sounds crazy, but it is what many people think when they have survived a terrible disaster. 'Survivors' guilt' is now a common term, derived from studies of the people who survived the concentration camps of the Second World War, or Hiroshima and Nagasaki (the *hibakusha*), or the fighting in the Vietnam War.[2] Such people feel, not joy at being alive, but fear, fear that they have done something wrong, for they *ought* to have died like their companions, fear that they have been given something they do not deserve and that they will be punished for holding on to it or that it will be suddenly taken away from them. They may have survived, but death as retribution is imminent.

Rose's question 'Why me?' was that of an ordinary woman nearing sixty who had worked diligently all her life, looking after her family, being competent in her office work, enjoying a quiet life in a country town, never expecting that her life would have any other significance than the pattern of the lives of her family and friends.

Then suddenly she was flung, not just across a road in the path of oncoming cars, but into the vast mysterious universe of being. Why me? In all this vastness, why me? Alone in all that vastness, she trembles with fear. Has she been saved for some purpose? Is there some pattern, some Grand Design, in which she has to play a significant role? If there is, why is she, an ordinary woman, chosen to play it? Will something be asked of her that she cannot perform, where she will fail and be punished for her failure? Has the Grand Designer got it wrong? Was she saved by mistake? Has she been given something that she doesn't deserve? Should she be dead, and some little baby, now dead, be alive? Or is there no design, just a random universe where some people live and others die, with no justice or fairness or reward for goodness and punishment for badness? Just randomness, chance without significance, life without meaning? Is 'Why me?' a question flung at the stars, and the stars shine coldly back with no answer?

To contemplate the significance of one's life against the limitlessness of space and the infinity of time is to create a powerful sense of awe and dread. Sometimes this is a very sensible thing to do. It certainly helps in keeping a sense of proportion about our own anxieties and ambitions, but at other times such a contemplation brings a sense of powerlessness and insignificance which can be quite overwhelming.

We all first had this experience when we were children and learning about space and time. By then we had all come across death through the demise of grandparents or pets, or stories on television, or simply the unspoken threat of death in the instruction 'Be careful crossing the road'. As young children we puzzled over the problem of what death is and we arrived at an answer.

Over the centuries of human life, death has been given many meanings. Yet in all, such explanations fall into two categories. Death is either the end of the person's identity or it is a doorway into another life. 'Another life' can be described in a multitude of ways, but whatever the description given, it implies that some significant part of the person goes on existing after death.

The curious part of arriving at an answer to the question 'What will happen to me when I die?' is that even though we may use scientific methods in seeking an answer ('Has anyone come back from death to tell us about it?' 'Are there such things as ghosts?' 'How many people could fit in heaven?') the answer we arrive at is in terms of *meaning*. We discover a meaning for death which then gives meaning to our life. We say, 'There has to be something after this. Otherwise, what's the point?' or 'This life's all we've got. It doesn't make sense, the idea of an afterlife.'

In giving death a meaning, the end of identity or the doorway to another life, we fix the purpose of our life.

If death is the end of your life, then to be able to accept your death you have to live your life in a way that you feel is satisfactory. There are a multitude of ways of seeing life as satisfactory – by becoming rich, or famous, or having a good marriage, or having children, or having done most of the things you wanted to do, or just getting by without too much trouble.

If you see death as the end of life and find yourself failing to make your life satisfactory in the way that you want it to be, you feel fear. Death looms menacingly, you see time running out, and you feel the pain and guilt we all feel when we know that we have wasted our talents and thrown away our opportunities.

If you see death as a doorway to another life you are immediately confronted with the problem of justice. If the afterlife means that there is the possibility of going somewhere better than this present world with its troubles and pain, then our likely questions are 'Does everyone go there? Is it fair that everyone goes somewhere better irrespective of the kinds of lives they lead? Should Hitler enjoy the same kind of afterlife as Mother Teresa?' The answer that most people give to these questions is no. So the idea of an afterlife, whatever form it takes, contains some notion of justice. If you see your life as a doorway to another life you then feel that you have to achieve a certain standard of goodness and excellence which will allow you entry to a better life. When you see yourself as failing to meet the standards and rules of life beyond death's doorway, you feel great fear.[3]

Seeing death as the end of existence or seeing it as a doorway to another life are ways of trying to understand, not just our own life, but our life in relation to space and time. When we contemplate the vastness of the ocean or the immensity of the heavens, we feel great awe, a mixture of respect, fear and incomprehension. To reduce our fear and increase our understanding, we develop theories to explain, in the words of the *Hitchhiker's Guide to the Galaxy*, 'Life, the universe and everything'.[4]

Some of us frame our explanation in scientific terms, and are left with puzzling things like curved space, a flat universe, black holes, and the question of whether there is life in other parts of the universe. A scientific description of life, the universe and everything is just as strange as a metaphysical or magical description. It gives rise to many fantasies, as the popularity of science fiction shows. In the end, a scientific explanation of life gives neither comfort nor security. To hold such beliefs and not be afraid requires courage and the ability to tolerate much uncertainty.

Not everyone can manage this, and so they turn to metaphysical or magical beliefs in order to find greater comfort and security. The scientific view of life and the universe sees us humans as just a small part of a vast complexity which will go on being itself with no more special regard for human life than it has for asteroids, atoms and the fifth dimension. Metaphysical and magical views of life place human beings at the centre of the universe where everything that happens relates to us and where we can influence vast forces and powers by our prayers, rituals and virtues.

Holding beliefs which place us at the centre of the universe under the control of a beneficent power can create a sense of security, and increased pride and self-confidence. Knowing that God loves you, or that your ancestors are watching over you, or that you are party to the forces of goodness which rule the world, can make day-to-day living simple and secure. However, the trouble is that everything in life has both good and bad implications.

You win a lot of money in a lottery, which is good, and then all your impecunious, greedy relatives want to share your good fortune, which is bad. As an adolescent you look forward to being an independent adult, which is good, but as an independent adult you will have no one to look after you, and that can be quite bad. In the same way, our beliefs about the nature of life and death, whatever they may be, have good and bad implications. To rest secure in God's love, or in the approbation of our ancestors, or in the power of the forces of goodness, we have to live our lives following certain rules, and if we fail to follow those rules then we are in great danger. The power which we perceived as protecting us can be turned against us and can threaten us with death and damnation.

In a group discussion about the experience of depression one woman described how when she was badly depressed she would wake during the night with the conviction that she should check whether her children were safe in their beds. She would get out of her bed to do this, but as she entered the hallway, all familiarity vanished and she found herself faced with a vast black hole. She was sure that if she took a step forward she would plunge into the hole, so she would stand there frozen with terror. The group discussed this in terms of how easy it is in the dark to lose contact with the most familiar of surroundings, and how the image of being depressed (frequently expressed as falling down into a bottomless pit) is experienced as something real and palpable. The woman listened to this and then said, 'I think that your feelings summon up powers – good powers or evil powers – out there. If you feel terrible, inside you, then you somehow draw this terrible blackness towards you. If you feel good and happy, then you draw this goodness out there to you.'

This woman's belief in supernatural powers was a comfort to her when she was happy, because happiness, she believed, attracted the benevolent power, but her belief also harmed her because when she was depressed she felt that she attracted the malevolent power.

We may try to deal with our fear of death by imagining that it will not occur for a long, long time. But if that is the case we have to travel through old age to meet death, and the prospect of old age can be full of terrors. No one likes the idea of becoming deaf, weak sighted, forgetful, frail and incontinent. No one wants to be treated like a foolish child by patronizing doctors and nurses and disrespectful relatives. Yet that is the fate which awaits many of us, and no matter what plans we may make to avert such a fate – by looking after our health, or making financial provision for a place in a superior nursing home, or threatening our relatives with guilt and retribution if they do not look after us properly – we can still be frightened.

Sometimes our fear of old age is more than just a fear of the practical problems it creates. Sometimes there is a magical dimension to our ideas about youth and old age.

Sylvia came to see me distraught after her husband of fourteen years had left her for another woman. All her conversation was about him. If her description of him was in any way accurate I would not have given him houseroom, but Sylvia desperately wanted him back.

They had met and married when she was thirty-four and he was twenty. I asked her what had made her fall in love with him.

'Chemical reaction. He made me feel so good. Young. Some women don't get older, do they? Like in those films, you've seen them, haven't you, where there's this woman and she's young and very beautiful but really she's hundreds of years old, and then something happens and she gets old, real old, suddenly, and her body starts to break up, ugh, it's horrible, and she just crumbles up and her body sort of falls in on itself.'

If this is what she feared old age would be, then it was no wonder that she wanted to hang on to a man who had the power to preserve her, even though he did beat her when he got angry.

When I was researching for my book *Time on Our Side*[5] I asked a large number of people how they felt about time passing and growing old. All agreed that growing old was frightening, but what made growing old an experience to be feared was different for each person and related to how they saw themselves. Those who had built their identity on achievement feared the time when they could achieve nothing. Those who had built their identity on being needed by others feared being of no use. Those who had built their identity on their sexual attractiveness or sexual prowess feared the fading of their beauty or their loss of vigour.

What people saw as the beginning of the descent into old age depended on how old each person was. People in their twenties saw thirty as the peak of their life, and after that was nothing but decrepitude and decay. People in their thirties saw forty as the turning point, people in their forties saw fifty as the turning point, and so on. I have now turned seventy. Old age, I know, starts at eighty.

Old age does have some actual deficits. Being ill in whatever form is no fun, and we live in a society where old people are not valued, except by politicians when they need the pensioners' vote, but most of our fears about growing old arise from our ideas about old age. Fearing being ill or losing our physical and mental capacities is bad enough, but if we add to those fears our own prejudices about old people, if we see old people as being ugly, stupid and of no importance, then old age becomes something we dread. However, we are free to change our ideas and thus reduce our fears.

Those of us who enjoy a relatively serene old age have certainly changed our ideas. When we were young many things mattered enormously to us. Now we know how little really matters, but we concentrate on that little which is of immense importance to us, be it those we love, or music, or stories as told on radio, television or film, or simply our garden.

The serenity I enjoy can be interrupted when a chronic lung disease, bronchiectasis, a legacy from childhood, flares up and brings me low. Then I feel frightened, but at the same time I am ruthless in a way I was not when younger in protecting myself from too many demands on my strength. I can achieve this easily because one of the ideas I have discarded is that I must work hard to be good, because no matter how good I am it is never enough. Now, if occasionally I am good, it is solely because it pleases me to be so.

Fear of Not Being Good Enough

When we came into the world as babies we were quite pleased with ourselves and did whatever we wanted to do. We slept when we were sleepy, cried when we were hungry or uncomfortable, and, when offered a nipple, sucked only if we wanted to suck. We had no notion of good or bad. We just were. Then society stepped in and said, 'This won't do. You are not satisfactory as you are. You have to be different.'

This all came as a terrible shock to us. We discovered that we were not masters of our own universe. There were greater powers out there and they were insisting that we had to be what they wanted us to be. We had to eat when they wanted and not just when we were hungry. We had to empty our bowels and bladder at the time and place they wanted and not just when we felt the need. We resented this interference, but we knew that the powers that demanded this from us were also the people on whom we depended for survival, and so we acquiesced. We became obedient, and, even more than that, we accepted our family's definition of us as not being good enough and needing to improve.

Having accepted this as a child, we moved into adult life fearing that we were still not good enough and ready to react with shame and guilt whenever some parental figure chided us for not doing well enough. The editor of *Good Housekeeping* saw nothing wrong with writing, 'The other visual treat is the second in our series of Norman Parkinson spectaculars photographed in Tobago. This time it's summer evening clothes – silky, slinky, sexy numbers. The models look wonderful, very Fifties, very Parkinson and should inspire many of us to take stock and try a little harder.'[6] This was written in 1985, but women's magazines have not changed, except to increase the range of matters in which women must try harder. It is not enough for a woman to look beautiful and wear beautiful clothes. She must also have a successful career, have a great social life, and be the perfect mother, cook and lover. Women readers react by making an even greater effort to lose weight or else sink deeper into a feeling of inadequacy and despair.

Men do not escape this sorry state of forever trying to do better to justify one's existence. They have, in some way, to 'make it', and when they do not, or when what they have 'made' is taken away from them, they become very frightened. Some young men set themselves the goal of having 'made it' by the time they are thirty, and so, if they fail, enter their thirty-first year in a state of rage and despair. Others set the vital age at forty, and when the failure to be rich and famous combines with a lessening of sexual performance, they sink into depression, or seek denial in alcohol or in the arms of a much younger woman. Forty is indeed a dangerous age.[7]

When we were small babies we had no concept of ourselves as separate entities. We were contiguous with the rest of our world, which presented itself to us as a continuously changing phantasmagoria. Then, by about eight months, most of us made that curious transition to the belief that what we saw was not a display of an infinite range of spectacles, coming fresh to our eyes every moment, but a limited range of spectacles which came and went and then returned. We acquired the understanding that we did not have an infinite number of mothers but just one who came and went and then returned and who was somewhere else when we could not see her. When a favourite toy disappeared, we had some idea of where to look to see it reappear. Making things disappear and reappear became a great delight as we rejoiced in our power to control our universe. We were not always successful at this. Sometimes Mother disappeared and did not reappear, no matter how hard we tried to get her back.

With the belief that objects go on existing even if they are out of sight came the understanding that if objects do this, then it is worth the bother of having some sign that stands for them when they are out of sight. There is no point in having a system of signs if there is an infinite number of things in our universe and their appearance is never repeated, but if events are repeatable then we may as well have some sort of language which we can use in reference to them. So babies who acquire 'object permanence', as Piaget called it, go on to acquire language.

As we went through this extraordinary process, something which seems to be to a large extent peculiar to the human species, we were learning that our world consisted not just of ourselves but of ourselves and other objects. Some of these objects were very important to us, especially our mother, in whose warm and loving gaze we bathed in ease and delight. Then one day, when we were absorbed in some activity, we discovered this loving gaze had vanished and had been replaced by something cold and rejecting. Suddenly we were wrested out of the state of being ourselves and we became an object in another person's eyes, an object of disgust and contempt. We were exposed, vulnerable and frightened. We had discovered *shame*.

Few of us can remember our first experience of shame, but we know when a small child has discovered it. The child ceases to be frank and open in all situations and to all people. He squirms and hides his face. If he does not look, then perhaps no one will look at him.

Experiences of shame which end with affirmations of love and reconciliation – a good cuddle – can be extremely helpful to the small child who is in the process of creating his sense of being a person, but when there are too many such experiences, or when such experiences never end with affirmations of love and reconciliation, the child can be left with the belief that he is, in his very essence, bad and unacceptable. Shame is about our identity, what kind of person we are, and when we are small and having the world defined for us by our parents, then if we are shown over and over again that we are unacceptable, that we should be ashamed of ourselves, we come to believe that this is one of the facts of the universe, as immutable and unchangeable as the pattern of night and day. As we get older such a belief about ourselves can be confirmed again and again by other events.

Margaret could not bear to be touched. She could not bear to be alone, but when she was with people she could not bear them to come too close. When she first came to see me she told me that she knew she was a bad person. She had known this ever since she was a small child. She knew that she was bad through and through.

She spoke of herself as a child without any sympathy or concern, because, as she told me when I asked, she did not deserve any. She said that as a child she had done something terrible but she would not tell me what it was. It was so bad that the children in her street had been forbidden to play with her. If she told me what it was I would see how bad she was and then I would not want to have anything to do with her.

This was the theme of our meetings, every fortnight for more than two years. She would sit, head down, saying nothing, or speaking so softly that I could not hear what she was saying. She wore glasses which darkened in the light, but when I eventually challenged her on this she changed them to lighter ones so I could at least see where she was looking.

Again and again she would say, 'If you knew what I was like you wouldn't want to know me.' Sometimes I would mock her gently, saying, 'That's right, I'd throw you out – tell you never to darken my door again.' But most times I would say, 'That's just how you feel about yourself.'

For the first year she resisted fiercely my idea that no one is intrinsically bad but that we can learn through what happens to us to experience ourselves as bad. Then she started to experiment with this idea. She would say to me, 'I say to myself, "Margaret, you're all right," but it doesn't work.'

She found our sessions together very painful. Silences forced her to writhe in embarrassment and say, 'I don't know what to say.' If I had to travel it caused her tremendous anxiety. When I discovered that she was one of those worriers who believe that worrying about something prevents it happening, I would ask her to be sure to worry about me when I was away and I would be sure to be safe. Postcards from me in faraway places with the message 'Keep worrying' would make her laugh, but still she worried that I might leave her.

One day Margaret risked telling her friend Sue about a childish misdemeanour about which she was very ashamed. Sue surprised her by not rejecting her. Margaret told Sue how her schoolfriend Betty had given her twopence to mind but she had spent it. Once she had told Sue about this, and how ashamed she had been when her act had been discovered, she found that the memory of this deed and the shame which accompanied it were not so painful.

Now she wanted to risk telling me about the greatest crime, the most shameful, terrible deed. But this was not easy. She looked at the clock and said, 'It's time to go.' It was lunch-time, when I had planned to do some shopping, but I sat still and silent. Such a moment for Margaret might never come again.

Head down, speaking softly, with many hesitations, she said, 'We lived on the corner, the end of the terrace. Then there was Shirley and Peter, then Betty and her brothers, then Carol and Mary and Ann – they were Betty's cousins – and then the Smiths, and then my grandmother's house, at the other end of the terrace. We all used to play together. They all went to the Protestant school and I went to the Catholic school. At school my best friend was Bernadette. I thought she was my best friend. She had a boyfriend, Barry, and I thought I'd like to have a boyfriend, but there wasn't anyone, only Paul, and he was awful. I didn't like him at all. He lived in a big house. We used to go there. He used to do things to me. I didn't like it but I let him. He said I'd like it but I didn't. We weren't the only ones, all of them did it – together – all of them.'

She remembered all their names. A roll-call of former playmates.

There was one boy, George, he used to tease me, and I didn't like it. I told Paul and he said he'd get George. He did, he got him, he tied him up and he did terrible things to him. I watched him – I didn't stop him – and afterwards, when George's parents found out, and the police came, I saw George's mother put her arms around him, and I thought, 'My mother won't do that to me.' When I got home, and the police took me home, my mother did put her arms around me, but I knew she didn't mean it. There was a policewoman and she took me and asked me lots of questions. She asked me who else did it, and I knew they all did but I couldn't say. She went on and on at me and I had to give her one name. I told her Betty and then they went to see

26

her. Then we had to go up to the police station and there was this policeman there and he told me I was wicked. And afterwards, the parents, they wouldn't let their children play with me. Betty could play with them but I couldn't. I'd go and watch them, but I couldn't play with them. Sometimes Bernadette would let me play with her and her sisters, but if anyone came I had to hide. And if I had to go down the street to my grandmother's, they'd all call out to me, say things to me, it was terrible. They never played with me, not ever again. And they told other people about me. When I went to secondary school, some of the boys from the boys' high school knew, and they'd say things. That's why, when I left, I went right away. But I'm always frightened they'll find out where I am and they'll tell people and I'll lose my job and nobody will talk to me.

She was crying. I gave her a tissue and said, 'That's the saddest story I've ever heard. That poor little girl.'

Margaret did not believe me. For her the shame was never ending.

But the pain for Margaret was not simply the shame she continued to feel for a misdemeanour the like of which many children at that age commit. If it is not sexual exploration it is stealing, or joy-riding, or, more dangerously, glue-sniffing. It would be a rare adult who could put their hand on their heart and swear that between the age of six and sixteen they had never broken the law or transgressed the moral code. For Margaret there was a greater problem.

One day she took me to task for never using her name when I was talking to her. I had to admit this. My style was never to use the name of the person I was talking to except when I wanted to attract their attention. I apologized to Margaret, and asked her why it was important that I use her name.

She said that it showed that I had not forgotten it and thus had not forgotten her. She told me how she felt that when she vanished from a person's sight she vanished from that person's memory. Whenever she returned to work she was surprised to find that the people there remembered her.

I said, 'I always remember who you are when you arrive,' and she responded, 'That's because you've written it in your diary.'

It was not just that she believed she was so insignificant that people did not remember her. Behind her anxiety was the fear that if everyone forgot her then her existence would cease. Most of the time she knew that believing that she existed only because other people thought of her and that she could vanish at any time was nonsense, but being left alone and forgotten was a fate she dreaded. Shame may have made her want to hide away, but shame also gave her the feeling that other people were observing her, and their gaze meant that she continued to exist. Shame strengthened her sense of existence and so she dared not relinquish it.[8]

In 1985 I wrote this story in the present tense. Now it must be told in the past tense, because for many years Margaret has led a happy life. She now has her own home and a loving partner, and she travels extensively worldwide. I have told the story of how she took charge of her life and changed in my book *Breaking the Bonds*.[9]

Many of us define ourselves in terms of our sense of guilt. A feeling of impending punishment can hang over us, like a Damoclean sword, ready to smite us for deeds done or which we have failed to do. While shame relates to our identity, the person that we are, and guilt to what we do, we can come to believe that everything we do is wrong and that we can never do anything properly, so that a sense of guilt, a pervasive sense of fear, can absorb our being to the extent that it becomes one of the structures by which we define ourselves. If we did not feel guilty we would not know what to do. As Constance once said to me, 'I was born guilty'.

Some children acquire this sense of guilt when they come to feel that it was their fault that their mother died or their parents split up, even though these events occurred when the children were far too young to understand them. Most of us acquired our sense of guilt when, as small children, we found ourselves locked in combat with a parent over where and when we should defecate, or whether and what we would eat, or because our parent was punishing us and we did not understand why. We defended our-selves with anger and protest against a parent whom we saw as interfering and unjust. However, we could not win the battle and bring it to an end. We went on battling, and, as we did, we recog-nized that the situation was becoming increasingly dangerous. We felt very keenly that our parent was wicked to do this, but if that were so it meant that the person on whom we depended was wicked. This was terrible. We had to find some way of making ourselves safe.

Our solution was to accept our parent's definition of the situ-ation. Power is always about who does the defining and who accepts the definitions. So we acquiesced. We decided that we were wrong to see the situation as 'I am being unfairly punished by my wicked parent'. The correct way to define the situation was 'I am bad and am being justly punished by my good parent', which was how our parent saw it.

This acceptance of our parent's definition may have extricated us from that dangerous situation, but the price we paid was a life-long sense of guilt. The sins of commission and omission became an integral part of our relationships with others and, knowing our badness, we have to strive to be good. Or else what will happen to us if we are not good? We shall be punished and abandoned.

This, as small children, is what we feared most of all, that our parents would abandon us and leave us alone, weak and defenceless in an alien world. We had learned what this was like when we were abandoned in our cot through a long, dark night and no one came to comfort us, or our mother left us with strangers and did not return for a long time. We heard the threat of abandonment when our parents told us of bad children being sent to children's homes or of parents being driven to leave or even to die by their children's wickedness. The most loving of parents can say in a moment of exasperation, 'I can't stand you a moment longer,' or 'You'll be the death of me.'

Threats of abandonment do not diminish as a child gets older. A friend told me how, when he was nine and causing his mother some bother, she had packed a bag with his clothes and ordered him out of the house. He spent the day sitting at the front gate, hoping to be let back in again and promising to be very good. He is a man of unsurpassed goodness.

The fear of abandonment can underlie the whole of our experience of our existence, and because it is always there, allowing no contrast with periods without it, we do not conceptualize it clearly and consciously. Thus we do not ask why we have this fear now and whence it came.

Lorna had a nasty, life-threatening disease, cystic fibrosis, but she showed that by bravely and sensibly following a strict health regime this disease need not cut short one's life nor prevent one from leading an ordinary existence. She had had to give up her work as a nurse but she had a loving, supportive husband, a wonderful daughter, a pleasant home, and a strong Christian faith which assured her that there was no reason to fear death. She could not understand why she should wake during the night consumed with panic, nor why a black depression should immobilize her in a way that her illness never did.

Nor could she understand why her GP wanted her to talk to me. But she dutifully came along, and discovered that talking to me gave her something important that was missing from her life. At home she was addressed as wife, mother, daughter, daughter in-law. Nobody talked to *her*. Now she had found someone who talked to her as *her*.

We talked about many things – the worry of her illness, the peculiarities of the medical profession, the responsibilities she carried for her family because she had always been the 'sensible, well-organized, reliable one'. We talked a great deal about her need to do everything perfectly. Visitors had to be entertained with hot meals and home-made cakes. The garden must be trim and neat, the house immaculate. 'I wouldn't dream of going out and leaving the washing up not done or a bed unmade,' she said.

I argued that she should let visitors fend for themselves and that housework should be kept to a minimum so that she had time and energy to do things which she found interesting and pleasant. At first she was doubtful, but one morning she told me, with triumph and laughter, 'I went to church on Sunday without making the bed first but I closed the curtains so the neighbours couldn't see.'

Why did she set herself such high standards and always strive to meet them? True, she had a mother who always expected her daughter to be perfect and a credit to her, but why had she accepted the enormous demands that her mother made on her?

One day, when she was telling me how fiercely she resisted going into hospital whenever her illness produced some complication, and how miserable she felt when she was there, she mentioned going into hospital when she was a child. I asked her about this and she described how she had been sent to a hospital when she was about seven. It was housed in a castle and run with military efficiency. Parents were not allowed to visit and children had to do what they were told. They had to be neat and tidy, obedient and reliable, and there were punishments if they were not. When her parents left her there she dared not cry because her mother disapproved of tears. She thought that she might never see her parents again, but when, at last, after many months, she did go home, she worried that she might be sent away again, to be abandoned and alone. So she tried very hard to be good.

Until we talked about these events in her childhood and uncovered the meaning they had for her, Lorna had not seen the connection between these childhood experiences and her drive for perfection, her fear of hospitals and the terrible panics which came whenever she felt that she was completely and absolutely alone. Buried farther was her anger towards her parents, who had abandoned her in the hospital, and towards her family, who expected her to give up being herself and to be what they wanted her to be. She had not acknowledged this anger, lest it burst forth and her family, who would not tolerate anger, reject her.

In the womb we were securely held. Being born brings us the first experience of being abandoned. We are no longer confined within secure limits, and instead a limitless world stretches around us. This uncertainty is frightening but necessary. All through our lives we cannot change anything about ourselves unless we go through a period of uncertainty. If we are wise we teach ourselves to tolerate the uncertainty of change, but, even as we do this, we retain the longing for the comfort and security of being securely held.

The ways in which this need can be met range from being physically held to knowing ourselves to be an accepted and loved member of our group. Important though this need is to all of us, there is no word for it in English. The closest word is 'dependence', from the Latin 'to hang from', but in our society to be dependent is not an admirable quality. Only weak, despicable people are dependent; strong, admirable people are independent. So we have to keep hidden our longing to be held secure in loving arms.

Not so in Japan. The Japanese language contains an important word, *amae,* which has the root 'sweet'.[10] Sweet it is to rest secure in loving arms. Sweet it is to *amaeru,* to presume upon the secure and indulgent love given by another person. It is that sense of snuggling up, of coming home, not to shouts and yells and coldness and criticism, but to welcome, allowed to be yourself and knowing that the people around you accept you as you are. The toddler who climbs on to an adult's lap, confident of a cuddle, the teenager who throws his dirty football shorts on the bathroom floor, confident that they will reappear in his drawer, clean and pressed, the wife who snuggles up to her husband in bed and confidently places her cold feet on his – all *amaeru.* We all long to *amaeru,* but so often we cannot do this. Sometimes we have no one to hold us, and sometimes the people who hold us do so too tightly and threaten to smother us.

Adults who care for babies need to find a balance between keeping the baby securely held and allowing the baby the freedom to stretch, kick and act upon the environment by exploring it. In western Europe until the eighteenth or nineteenth centuries and to this day in eastern Europe, babies were wrapped tightly from birth in swaddling sheets to form a rigid bundle and left tightly held, but not in human arms, for the first six to eight months of their life. The theory behind swaddling was, according to the historian Lloyd de Mause, 'If it [the baby] were left free it would scratch its eyes out, tear its ears off, break its legs, distort its bones, be terrified at the sight of its own limbs, and even crawl on all fours like an animal.'[11]

Nowadays good mothering practice includes both tucking the baby securely in a cot or carrying him in a sling held firmly against the adult's body *and* freeing the baby from all physical restraints in a warm, safe environment. These two kinds of condition are necessary for the baby, not just to encourage physical growth and health but to help him develop as a person who can tolerate the closeness of being in a secure group and the uncertainty of being an individual acting upon the world.

Unfortunately, some parents believe that they must teach the baby that they and not the baby are in charge, and so they do not respond to cries of hunger or distress. Some parents are too tired, or too busy, or too depressed to play with or talk to the baby. To learn, to develop our intelligence, we need to be able to act upon the world. Doing this, we develop the idea that 'I am the kind of person who can act successfully upon the world'.

The idea 'I am the kind of person who can act successfully upon the world' is one of the possibilities that can be contained in an individual's sense of being a person. If I asked you, 'Who are you?', you could list your gender, your age, nationality, religion, race, occupation and family connections. If I asked you, 'What kind of a person are you?', you could list your virtues and vices, strengths and weaknesses, alliances and enmities, your interests, wishes, needs, passions and beliefs, and all the things you know about yourself but find hard to put into mere words, but everything that you could tell me about yourself is made up of *ideas*. The sum total of these ideas *is* you, what you call I, me, myself. There is no little you sitting inside you, adding to and maintaining this sum total of ideas. You *are* your sum total of ideas, or what I call your meaning structure, because this sum total of ideas has a structure where every part is connected to every other part.

Your meaning structure is not a static structure but a feedback process in constant movement. Nowadays we are all familiar with feedback processes in objects like refrigerators and heating systems. Many refrigerators freeze and defrost themselves, and many heating systems change themselves with changes in outside temperature. There is no little engineer sitting in your refrigerator or heating system pressing the right buttons as needed. The process processes itself. It is the same with you. Denis Noble, Emeritus Professor of Cardiovascular Physiology at Oxford University, calls the self 'an integrative process'.[12] If you happen to speak Japanese or Korean you will have no difficulty in understanding this because, as Denis Noble said, 'What these languages do is to emphasise the ''doing-ness'' of things, the processes that occur, that is, the verb rather than the subject who is the possessor of the being-ness or doing-ness.' If Descartes had been Japanese or Korean he would not have said 'cogito ergo sum', 'I think, therefore I am', but 'thinking, therefore being'.[13]

Thinking of yourself as an active process can be somewhat disturbing, but think about it a bit more. Isn't that how you experience yourself, with thoughts that come and go, memories bobbing to the surface, along with ideas, images, wishes and needs? The feedback in your process operates all the time as you see the results of what you have done, and you modify what you do next time. The process which is you reflects upon itself and so it can change. If you had been born with a bit of your brain marked ME, a bit that just sits there unchanging, you would have been stuck with you for the rest of your life.

Feedback processes like those in our refrigerator and heating system and in us, our meaning structure which gives us a sense of being a person, do not operate in a vacuum. These three kinds of processes operate in relation to their environment. Deprive us of our environment, and our sense of being a person begins to disintegrate. Sensory-deprivation experiments, where an individual is deprived of sight, sound, movement, smell and touch, have shown that, under these conditions, people begin to lose the ability to distinguish what is around them from what is inside them, their thoughts and feelings. These become increasingly bizarre. There is no lack of evidence of what happens to babies and children who are deprived of loving care, while all gaolers know that the quickest way to break the toughest man is to put him in solitary confinement for an indefinite period.

Our meaning structure starts to take shape while we are still in the womb, where babies hear sounds and experience pleasure and pain. A newborn baby looks around at the world with intense interest, and so his meaning structure grows and changes. Our meaning structure grows out of the functioning of our brain, and so, like all living things, its first purpose is to stay alive.

'Staying alive' for a meaning structure means staying as one coherent whole. The aim of all the functions of the meaning structure is to keep the structure whole and not let it fall apart. If the meaning structure starts to fall apart the sense of being a person will start to dissipate. We experience this whenever we discover that we are mistaken in our judgement. Mislaying our house keys makes us anxious; discovering that the world is not what we thought it was can threaten to annihilate us as a person. Whenever we discover that we have made a serious error of judgement – say, that the person we loved has abandoned or betrayed us, or that being a good person does not protect us from disaster – we feel ourselves to be shattering, crumbling, even disappearing, and with this comes the greatest terror, the fear that we shall be annihilated as a person.

Our sense of being a person *is* our meaning structure, and this meaning structure grows out of the functioning of the brain. While we are far from understanding just how brain and mind are linked, our increasing knowledge of how the brain functions shows that there can be no scientific doubt that the brain and mind are one.

Chapter Two

Understanding the Nature of Fear

Brains and Minds

The brain is the most complex object known to us. Perhaps there are more complex objects in other parts of the universe but we have yet to encounter them. Over the last fifteen years, how scientists talk about the brain has changed dramatically. Two words have entered their language – neuroscience and neuroscientist. Anyone called a neuroscientist could be a neurologist, a physiologist, a biologist, a chemist, a psychologist, an electrical engineer or even a quantum physicist. People skilled in all these different bodies of knowledge are needed in the attempt to understand this most complex object.

There has been a subtle but important shift in how neuroscientists talk about the brain. They used to talk in terms of how the brain functions, in vision, hearing and the other senses – that is, in terms of perceiving the world. Now they talk, not in terms of the brain looking at reality, but in terms of how the brain creates a picture of reality. Our brain does not show us reality. It creates a picture of reality, and the kind of picture it creates depends on the kind of experiences we have each had. No two brains ever create exactly the same picture.

The importance of experience in what individual brains do has led neuroscientists to look more closely at what individuals do. Neuroscientists used to be concerned with simple actions, such as how we distinguish different shades of colour or two different pitches of sound. Now scientists are interested in complex behaviour. They have even ventured to discuss the problem of consciousness, something which up till recently had been banned from scientific discourse because it was 'subjective', and scientists should always be 'objective'. This was why psychologists and psychiatrists studied what people did, not what people thought about what they did and why they did it.

The study of complex behaviour immediately raises the question of how humans and animals learn. Psychologists have always favoured very mechanical explanations. They described learning in terms of reward and punishment, and assumed that what they saw as a reward or a punishment would pertain for all their subjects, whether human or animal. They thought that for all rats a sweet substance would be a reward, sour a punishment. For all children a gold star would be a reward, being deprived of sweets a punishment. Rewards and punishments were seen as levers which propelled humans and animals in certain ways. It did not occur to these psychologists that a reward was a reward and a punishment a punishment only if the person or animal receiving them thought that this was so. Some children think that gold stars are rubbish, and some children do not like sweets. From his studies of how rats learn, Dr Anthony Dickenson, of Cambridge University, concluded that rats, though they are probably not self-aware, do operate with schemas – that is, ideas about what they want. These desires, said Dr Dickenson, have to be learnt. They are not innate mechanisms in the brain.[1]

One of the excuses which some people use when they do not want to take responsibility for their actions is that they cannot help doing something because they have been 'conditioned' to act in this way. Such an excuse has no scientific basis. Whatever we do follows from a wish, a desire, a need, perhaps to possess or to avoid something. We may not be consciously aware of these wishes, needs and desires, but they are ideas which we have learnt from our experience.

Whenever we learn something, the structure of our brain changes – that is, the connections between some of the neurones in our brain change. Jack Challoner, in his fascinating book *The Brain*, explained:

The neurone is the fundamental unit of the brain. Neurones produce or conduct electrical impulses that are the basis of sensation, memory, thought and motor signals that make muscles work to produce movement. There are other types of cell present but they only give support and nourishment to these cellular workhorses. Neurones are like other cells in many ways: they have a nucleus and a membrane, for example. However, they differ in the way they function. A neurone has long fibres, called axons, coming from its cell body. Emanating from the axons or from the cell body itself are other, smaller fibres called dendrites. Neurones communicate with each other: electrical signals pass along the axon and dendrites, and the brain is constantly buzzing with these signals.[2]

These signals are actually both electrical and chemical, but just how they operate is not yet understood. This is why the statement, 'Depression is caused by a chemical imbalance in the brain' is a nonsense, or, as David Healy, Reader in Psychiatry, University of Wales, called it, 'a myth'. He added in an endnote, 'There are variations in serotonin levels and serotonergic receptors from person to person, and these may make us more or less sensitive to the effects of SSRIs [drugs] and even to stress. SSRIs do act on serotonin, but there is no evidence of a serotonergic abnormality in depression.'[3] David Wallis, Professor of Physiology at Cardiff University, explained:

Classical theory has it that the brain uses chemicals – neurotransmitters – to convey 'information' between nerve cells. These chemical messages have either a positive or negative effect on the nerve cell receiving them, dictating whether or not it will become momentarily excited.

But over the past twenty years or so, we've discovered [that] chemical interactions between nerve cells are far more varied and subtle than we thought. A whole second level of communication exists, in which chemicals change the properties of nerve cells or synapses in ways other than simple fast excitation. For instance they might alter the protein in a nerve cell. These types of interaction, known as neuromodulation, are much harder to pin down than classical neurotransmission.[4]

We are born with almost as many neurones as we are ever going to have but all these neurones have a vast array of possible connections with each other. What changes and develops over time is the connections between the axons and dendrites of the neurones. Just what connections are made, and whether a connection remains and strengthens or disappears, depends on our experience – that is, on what we learn. As Susan Greenfield wrote in her book *The Private Life of the Brain*, 'The degree of meaning that we covertly apportion to each person, object, event as we blunder around in the outside world will, in turn, be matched by a corresponding degree of neurone connections.'[5]

No two people ever have the same experience. Thus no two brains have identical patterns of connections between neurones. 'It is the personalization of the brain,' wrote Susan Greenfield, 'crafted over the long years of childhood and continuing to evolve throughout life, that a unique pattern of connections between brain cells creates what might be called a "mind".' She went on, 'My particular definition of *mind* will be that it is the seething morass of cell circuitry that has been configured by personal experiences and is constantly being updated as we live out each moment.'[6]

This seething morass of cell circuitry is the physiological basis of what we experience as our thoughts and feelings, our memories, our desires, needs and fears, our beliefs, attitudes, prejudices and opinions. All of these are ideas, some of which we can put into words, some of which we know only as visual, auditory or bodily images. Some of these ideas are conscious, some are not. All of these ideas form a picture of ourselves, our world and our life in its past, present and future, and give us our sense of being a person.

Very few of these ideas we can rightly hold with absolute certainty. We can be absolutely certain of the feelings we are experiencing in the here and now – provided we do not lie to ourselves. We can be sure that right now we are angry or right now we are sad, but if we feel that these emotions are unacceptable we can tell ourselves that we feel frightened when actually we are angry, or we can deny our sadness and pretend to ourselves and others that we are happy.

Doing this, we lose the only absolute certainty we can ever have. All the other ideas we have about what happened in our past and what will happen in our future, what the world is like, what other people think and feel, and what they do when we cannot see them, are guesses, theories about what is going on.

To live safely in the world we have to try to construct theories which represent a reasonably accurate picture of what is actually going on. Every time you drive a car or cross a busy street you have to form a reasonably accurate theory about the traffic on the road, or else you are likely to come to grief. When we daydream we can form the most fantastical theories, but if we want to turn our daydreams into reality we have to take account of what actually goes on in our world.

When our meaning structure is a reasonably accurate picture of what is actually happening, we feel secure. As soon as we discover that a part of our meaning structure is not reflecting sufficiently accurately what is going on, we feel anxious. Sometimes we can delineate precisely which bit of what is going on we could be wrong about. We can be anxious that we have not predicted accurately enough what questions will be on our forthcoming exam paper, or whether the people we are about to meet will like us. Sometimes we cannot name a reason for our anxiety because we suspect that some disaster is about to befall us but we do not know what it will be. Amplified, this kind of anxiety becomes angst or dread. When a great disaster does befall us and everything in our life becomes uncertain, we feel terror.

Whether anxiety, angst, dread or terror, all these states of fear are states of uncertainty, and uncertainty is what we cannot bear. Uncertain, we feel helpless, a prey to forces we cannot control. We want to be secure and in control.

Yet in fact there is very little over which we do have control. We can work hard and take sensible care of the money we earn, but we have no control over the worldwide financial forces which, amongst other things, determine exchange and interest rates and levels of employment.[7] We can eat sensible food and exercise regularly, but our body can still betray us. We can try in all kinds of different ways to get other people to behave as we want them to behave, but they will still fail to meet our expectations. We can try to see ourselves and our world as clearly and accurately as possible, and yet we will still get it wrong. Things are rarely as they appear to be.

The only way to cope with all this uncertainty is to accept that it is so. This is the ancient wisdom of Lao Tzu and Buddha. Lao Tzu advised:

> *True mastery can be gained*
> *By letting things go their own way.*
> *It can't be gained by interfering.*[8]

Suffering, Buddha taught, was our attempt to make something permanent in a world where nothing remains the same. Such wisdom can be hard to acquire when we are intent on surviving as a person – that is, on keeping our meaning structure whole.

If we understand that our sense of being a person is a meaning structure made up of ideas, then when events surprise us we know that we have to go through what can be a painful, unsettling period until our meaning structure can reorganise itself in a way more in keeping with what is actually going on. If we do not understand that we are our meaning structure, then when the unexpected happens we feel ourselves falling apart and are terrified lest we be annihilated as a person. Not understanding, we build up all kinds of defences to hold ourselves together when we feel ourselves in danger of falling apart.

The tool we use in building these defences is a very cunning one and represents one of the functions of the meaning structure. It is the tool of pride. How pride functions has interested me for quite a long time.

By the late seventies, through listening carefully to what

depressed people were telling me, I realised that the essence of depression was the sense of being alone in some kind of prison where the walls were as impenetrable as they were invisible. I could see that the depressed person had certain attitudes or beliefs which served to cut him or her off from other people and from everything that makes life worth living. These attitudes and beliefs preceded the person's depression, and they provided the person with all the building blocks necessary to build the prison of depression. I wrote about this in my first book, which is now called *Choosing Not Losing*.[9] I came to realize that the many and various beliefs which depressed people held could be summarised as six attitudes which, if held as absolute, unquestionable truths, would create the prison of depression. These beliefs were:

1. No matter how good and nice I appear to be, I am really bad, evil, valueless, unacceptable to myself and other people.

2. Other people are such that I must fear, hate and envy them.

3. Life is terrible and death is worse.

4. Only bad things have happened to me in the past and only bad things will happen to me in the future.

5. It is wrong to get angry.

6. I must never forgive anyone, least of all myself.[10]

These are not bizarre, idiosyncratic beliefs but are held at least in part by many members of every society, and are often taught by parents to children. They are pessimistic beliefs, but not unreasonable because life is far from easy. However, it seemed to me at first that it could be possible to help a depressed person moderate these beliefs, to be less harsh on themselves and to find it easier to take other people on trust. However, this proved not to be the case. Depressed people, I found, even though they were suffering dreadfully, resisted any suggestion that they might change their beliefs because such a change meant going from certainty to uncertainty. Indeed, they took pride in these beliefs, even though they caused them to suffer. I wrote:

> But you want absolute certainty and you have too much pride to admit that you could be wrong. You take pride in seeing yourself as essentially bad; you take pride in not loving and accepting other people; pride in the starkness and harshness of your philosophy of life; pride in the sorrows of your past and the blackness of your future; pride in recognizing the evil of anger; pride in not forgiving; pride in your humility; pride in your high standards; pride in your sensitivity; pride in your refusal to lose face by being rejected; pride in your pessimism; pride in your martyrdom; pride in your suffering.
>
> Pride, so Christian theology teaches, is the deadliest of the seven sins since it prevents the person from recognizing his sins and repenting and reforming. Sin or not, it is pride that keeps you locked in the prison of depression. It is pride that prevents you from changing and finding your way out of the prison.[11]

It is not just depressed people who possess a pride that prevents them from changing. All of us, to some greater or lesser extent, allow pride to prevent us from changing. To change in some particular way or other would put our sense of being the person that we want to be at risk. We hang on to political or religious beliefs which are clearly not in our interests, or we think of ourselves fondly as being a great singer or a great golfer even though there is much evidence to show that we are not. Moreover, the world is full of people who would rather be right than happy. It is this particular preference which creates most of the suffering in the world, both the suffering we inflict on other people and the suffering we inflict on ourselves.

This became the subject of my book *Wanting Everything*,[12] and here I returned to the question of pride. I described the pride that some people take in their high standards. Anything less than perfection is not acceptable to them. Their world has to be perfect and they have to be perfect. When the world fails to be perfect they become angry and try to force people and events to do and be what they want. When they fail themselves to live up to their own impossible standards, they turn against themselves and hate themselves. I pointed out that:

> Pride will allow us to believe all kinds of nonsensical things, and the belief in perfection is one of these. It overlooks the fact that we can perceive anything only when there is some kind of contrast or differential. We know light only because there is dark, heat only because there is cold, life only because there is death, and perfection only because there is imperfection. If we lived in a perfect world we would not know it was perfect.[13]

Pride can operate in very subtle ways. It can provide an assumption on which we can build beliefs about being humble and unselfish, such as are involved in feeling responsible for everybody and everything. Just what the extent of our responsibility is can often be hard to decide, but in general we can be responsible only for those things over which we have control. When we say we are responsible for something we are implying that we have control over that thing. Claiming to be responsible for everybody and everything is a claim to great power, and such a claim is an act of pride.[14]

When we feel responsible for certain matters but fail to prevent disaster we feel guilty. Guilt is the fear of punishment, and, uncomfortable though it may be, many people prefer to feel guilty than to feel helpless. Guilt implies that you could have kept these matters under control but you failed to act. Helplessness is a recognition of how little in the world we do in fact control and how chance-filled life can be, and this understanding can be very frightening because through it we know that we can be struck by disaster at any time and that our ideas about what is happening can be proved wrong.

Thus, when disaster strikes and we ask, 'Why in the whole scheme of things has this happened?' we seek an answer which will show a clear pattern of cause and effect. Such an answer will remove uncertainty and keep our meaning structure whole. As a result the answer 'It was my fault' can be preferable to the answer 'It happened by chance'.

Many of us begin our struggle with such questions when we are young. In a television series a mother, Nicky Harris, described the guilt she felt when her second child, a baby boy called Jordan, suddenly died. She discovered that her four-year-old daughter Jessica was also struggling with questions of guilt and responsibility. Nicky said:

> I realized soon after he died that she was feeling the same guilt that I was feeling. We always talked, and about a month after he died she said to me, 'Mummy, I know why Jordan died,' and I said, 'Why?' and she said, 'I bounced the bouncy chair too hard. Do you remember when you told me not to do that?' And I felt the guilt flowing out and I was able to deal with it. I just totally knocked that theory on the head. It had nothing to do with it. I thought I'd got that over with, and then a couple of weeks later she came back to me and she said, 'Mummy, I think I've definitely worked it out now.' This is a four-year-old child talking to me. She said, 'When Grandma was sitting over there and you were sitting over here, and I was hugging Jordan, and Grandma said, 'Don't hug him too tight, you'll kill him.' She said, 'That was it. I must have hugged him too tightly.' Inside I was crying for her for I felt the same way.[15]

Here was a four-year-old prepared to take responsibility for her brother's death because she saw that as being preferable to knowing that terrible things can happen at any time and that neither she nor her mother could prevent them. Yet, even though pride may have provided her with an explanation which showed that this event did not happen by chance, this explanation would ensure that she could never be happy. Happiness, she would have come to believe, was something she did not deserve.

I continued to study the functions of pride, and by the time I came to write *Friends and Enemies*[16] I was thinking in terms of two kinds of pride – moral pride, which is a way of thinking which develops as we create a conscience, and primitive pride, which is an integral part of the functioning of the meaning structure. Both kinds of pride aim to maintain the integrity of the meaning structure and thus prevent us from changing, and both can work together and enhance each other, but, while moral pride can be a spur to unselfishness, tolerance and a love of truth, and be amenable to logic and reason, primitive pride is always utterly selfish, utterly ruthless and impervious to the demands of reason. Nicky Harris described how, while she knew quite well that she was not responsible for her son's death, she could not help expecting and indeed wanting the police to arrest and punish her.[17]

Any working system has within it certain forms or mechanisms which enable the system to function. I wrote:

The meaning structure is a self-regulating system. All self-regulating systems have within their structure some mechanism which maintains the integrity of the system, preventing it from grinding to a halt or shattering to pieces. Our body, a self-regulating system, has a number of such mechanisms. The mechanism which forms blood clots to stem the flow of blood through a wound is one. In the meaning structure primitive pride is the form of thought or mechanism which selects from within the individual meaning structure a collection of meanings; when put together, these meanings serve to give immediate protection to the integrity of the meaning structure. This collection of meanings may have little relationship to what is actually happening or in the long term be an adequate defence. Indeed, it usually creates more problems than it was assembled to solve. Its importance is that it can be assembled immediately, in the blink of an eye.[18]

In psychology no one ever discovers anything which is completely new. Many people have noticed pride's function in survival as a person, though they may not have called it pride. Psychoanalysts have described the defence of rationalization, and one analyst, Karen Horney, wrote about what she called 'pride systems'. More recently two American psychologists, Daniel Gilbert and Timothy Wilson, uncovered what they called a 'psychological immune system', which was 'an army of rationalizations, justifications and self-serving logic'.[19] Many psychologists working with people who are experiencing a psychosis now see hallucinations and delusions as methods of trying to maintain 'self-esteem'.[20]

'Self-esteem' is a jargon term for a complex of ideas concerning how we feel about ourselves – that is, how much we care for and care about ourselves, how much we value ourselves, on what values we judge ourselves and how harshly we judge ourselves. When we are fond of ourselves, look after ourselves, when we value ourselves and judge ourselves reasonably and in a kindly manner, we feel self-confident, and so when we encounter a crisis or disaster we see it as a challenge which we shall master. When we do make a mistake both moral and primitive pride can comfort us. If, for example, you make some arithmetical errors in your income tax return and someone points this out to you, you can comfort yourself by thinking, 'Well, I mightn't be good at maths but I really know how to put words together.' Or, when someone is unpleasant to you, instead of trying to work out why, you can simply assume that actually, underneath, that person really does like you.

The more we despise and hate ourselves the greater the degree of comfort pride has to create, and the greater the degree of comfort we need the less realistic that comfort becomes. Thus we can take pride in having impossibly high standards, or we can take pride in being the object of a worldwide conspiracy of influential people, or in possessing some vast mystical power which controls the universe. Our pride can indeed comfort us, but we can become so attached to that comfort that we refuse to give up our comforting delusions, even though these are the very ideas that create great distress for us because they are so removed from a realistic appraisal of ourselves and our world. We hang on to our comforting delusions, not just because they comfort us, but because they protect us from our greatest fear.

47

Our Greatest Fear

We experience our existence in such a way that it seems to us that we live in two separate realities. One is the reality of what goes on outside us, what we call the world. The other is what goes on inside us, our thoughts, feelings, images, sensations and perceptions. To cope with living we have to be able to distinguish what goes on inside us from what goes on outside us, and then to knit together, in some consistent way, our internal and external realities so that we can find a meaning which enables us to carry our life forward and communicate with other people. We have to relate our thoughts and feelings to our perception of the outside world, and we have to relate our perception of the outside world to our thoughts and feelings. This two-way process is what psychologists call 'reality testing'. If we do not do this very well we are considered by others to be mad, or at least very strange.

Knitting these two realities together is not easy because they do not appear to be equally real. One of these realities seems to be 'really real': the other is 'kind of' real. For some of us our internal reality is more real than our external reality. For some of us our external reality is more real than our internal reality. This 'more real' relates to what it is we sometimes doubt. Some people never doubt what is going on around them but at times they doubt their own thoughts and feelings, and such doubt can lead them to say, 'I don't know who I am,' or, 'I don't know what I feel.' Other people never doubt their thoughts and feelings; indeed, their sense of existence is the one thing they never doubt, but the appearance of the world around them, or even that it exists, is something they do doubt, particularly when they lose confidence in themselves or they encounter a sudden crisis.

Whichever reality appears to be the less real for us is the reality which contains a great danger.

For those people for whom external reality is more real than internal reality, internal reality contains a danger which is felt as an emptiness, a vacancy from which all kinds of unknown and unknowable things can arise. Such people will express this by saying, 'It's not wise to introspect too much,' or 'I spend too much time trying to understand myself.' For them the embrace of external reality is not dangerous. What is dangerous is for external reality to drop away and for them to be left alone and isolated, an emptiness in an emptiness. For these people, being left alone, completely abandoned and rejected, is the greatest fear.

For those people for whom internal reality is more real than external reality, external reality contains a danger which is felt as an unknown and unknowable territory from which all kinds of uncontrolled and uncontrollable forces can arise. Such people have no anxiety about introspection, for within themselves is where they live their life, but they often speak of needing peace, which means a quietening down of, or distancing oneself from, external reality. For them external reality dropping away and leaving them isolated is not dangerous, for they live within their internal reality. What is dangerous is the embrace of external reality, because out of external reality can come the forces which confuse, overwhelm and destroy. For these people, chaos is the greatest fear.

When we are coping with our lives and having no difficulty in knitting the external and internal realities together, we can be unaware of the differences in the qualities of the realities we perceive. But once we come under stress the differences in the two realities become more pronounced, and if the stress continues and increases we become less and less effective in knitting our internal and external realities together. Some of us run away from the emptiness we find within and busy ourselves with the outside world, while some of us withdraw into ourselves and shut out the confusion outside.

A simple way of discovering which reality is more real and how we experience our existence and our annihilation of our sense of being a person is to go through a procedure of questions and answers which is called 'laddering'. This is a technique which I used in teaching, and only in a limited way in therapy. For a television programme, *The Mind Box*, I demonstrated this method with Sandy, a psychiatric nurse. While Sandy and I were seen looking at and driving cars in some dashing and bizarre sequences of film made on an empty airstrip, our conversation went as follows:

DOROTHY: Sandy, we're going to play a little game. It's called laddering, and in this we'll start with something quite trivial, and then go on to something very important, but the first thing I'm going to ask you is, can you give me the names of three kinds of cars?

[This conversation took place in the days when the UK had a large car industry.]

SANDY: Yes, Rover, Triumph and Ford.

DOROTHY: Now can you tell me one way in which two of them are the same and the other one is different?

SANDY: Yes, Rover and Triumph are all part of British Leyland and Ford is an independent company.

DOROTHY: And which would you prefer, a car from British Leyland or one from an independent company?

SANDY: I'd prefer a Ford from an independent company.

DOROTHY: Why is it important to you to have a car from an independent company?

SANDY: I think I prefer something that's somewhat unusual, something different.

DOROTHY: And why is it important to you to have something that's different?

SANDY: In some way, I suppose, I get admiration from other people.

DOROTHY: Why is it important to you to have the admiration of other people?

SANDY: The admiration of other people makes me feel good. I suppose it makes me feel . . . it helps to establish my existence.

DOROTHY: What would you do if there wasn't anyone to give you admiration, if you were completely isolated?

SANDY: Completely isolated? I can't actually foresee myself in total isolation at all.

DOROTHY: But suppose you were completely and absolutely isolated for an indefinite period?

SANDY: In that case I should think I would be withered up, I'd die away. That would be the end of my existence, I think.[21]

Now Sandy was seen alone in a vast empty space. He looked miserable, but that was because he found making a television programme a nerve-racking experience. In ordinary life he knew he needed people, and he was effective in meeting this need by having a talent for friendship and doing a job which involved people.

We use the term 'laddering' because in this process of question and answer we begin with a trivial decision and value judgement and proceed to more and more general, abstract value judgements until we reach the top of the ladder, the ultimate value judgement, which is how we experience our existence and how we experience our annihilation.

Being annihilated as a person is our greatest fear. It is worse than bodily death, for after death we can imagine ourselves, or some important aspect of ourselves – our children, our work, the memories our friends have of us – continuing, but after annihilation there is nothing of our person to carry on. We have gone, brushed aside like chalk off a blackboard, engulfed like a raindrop in an ocean, consumed like a dead leaf in a fire, swirled away like a puff of smoke when the wind blows. After annihilation our body may continue to function but that which was our person has gone.

Sandy was one of those people who experience their existence as being part of a group and their annihilation as isolation. His external reality was more real for him than his internal reality. Had Sandy been one of those people for whom internal reality is more real than external reality, our producer, Angela Tilby, would have had greater difficulty in finding images to accompany our words. Sandy may have made the same choice of cars on the same grounds of wanting something unusual, but he would have gone on from there to talk in terms of personal development and achievement. I would have asked him what would happen to him if he were unable to fulfil his ambitions, and he would have spoken about himself (not his body) being overwhelmed and destroyed by chaos. Not easy images for television to supply, but a fate very real for those of us who experience our existence as the continual development of individual achievement, clarity and authenticity, and our annihilation as chaos.

All of us fall into one or other of these groups. We are either, as my friend Sue Llewellyn refers to herself, a 'people junkie', or we are absorbed in the study and development of our internal experience. The words that are used to distinguish these groups are most unsatisfactory. Those people who experience their existence as the development of individual achievement, clarity and authenticity I called What Have I Achieved Today Persons, or introverts, and those who experience their existence as being part of a group and their annihilation as isolation I called People Persons or extraverts. 'Introvert' and 'extravert' are words which are used in many different connections, but here it is well to remember that introverts can acquire excellent social skills and can appear to be greatly 'extraverted', while there are many lonely and shy extraverts. Thus introverts can behave in ways which would be described as extroverted while extraverts can behave in ways which would be described as introverted. An extravert and an introvert can do exactly the same thing, but they each do it for different reasons. To determine whether you are an introvert or an extravert you need to look not at *what you do* but *why you do it*.

I was certainly not the first psychologist to discover that we divide into two groups, those people who turn outward to the world around them and who have as their first priority their relationships with other people, and those people who turn inward and who have as their first priority a need for organization and a sense of personal development. Freud saw this difference and labelled the two groups 'hysterics' and 'obsessionals'. Jung saw the difference and similarly called the two groups 'extraverts' and 'introverts'. The arch-critic of psychoanalysis Hans Eysenck worked in an entirely different way, using questionnaires with large groups of people, and found what he called the traits of 'extroversion' and 'introversion'. He was interested in the physiology of the brain which underlies these traits. His research team found that the two groups of people could be distinguished by the habitual arousal level of the cortex. Introverts, they found, had higher levels of arousal than extraverts. Thus introverts need an environment which is relatively calm, peaceful and organised while extraverts, in Hans Eysenck's words, are 'stimulus seeking' and enjoy an environment where there is much going on and which contains a great deal of what introverts would call 'clutter' and extraverts would describe as comforting and reassuring objects.[22]

While the majority of his fellow psychiatrists in the USA saw depression as a purely physical disease, Aaron Beck became aware in the 1960s that his depressed patients had a particular way of thinking, or what he called 'a depressive cognitive style'. He developed a way of investigating this style, and out of this initial work has come a vast body of theory, research and practice called Cognitive Therapy.[23,24]

A depressive cognitive style was made up of 'schemas' or structures which were stable and enduring and developed from early life experience.[25] By 1983 Beck and his colleagues had discovered that each depressed person's schemas had one of two distinctive superordinate schemas. They named these superordinate schemas sociotropy and autonomy. The person who used a sociotropy schema placed high value on a positive interchange with other people and was extremely concerned with being accepted, being intimate and being supported and guided by others. The person who used the autonomy schema placed high value on and was extremely concerned with achieving their goals, maintaining their high standards, being independent and maintaining what has been called 'the integrity of one's domain'.[26] A later statistical study using factor analysis found further evidence for the existence of these two distinctive cognitive styles.[27]

Some years ago, when I was running a seminar for an international group of managers, the Japanese managers in the group told me that in Japan there was a series of popular psychology books which divided people into two groups in the same way as I had described dividing people into extraverts and introverts. They could not supply me with an English translation of these books but they were totally unsurprised by what I had said.

No matter how diverse the theories and the jargon these different psychologists used, it does seem that they were all commenting on an enduring feature of all human beings – namely that, individual though our interpretations of events might be, they all seem to fall into one of two groups, one where the person is turned outward to external reality, and one where the person is turned inward to internal reality.

Over the years that I have been writing about extraverts and introverts, quite a number of people have told me that, though they have read my books or listened to me lecture, they cannot work out whether they are an introvert or an extravert, or they insist to me that 'I'm a bit of both'. I have found that such people are invariably extraverts. Introverts find what I have to say mildly interesting, but I am not telling them anything they have not always known about themselves. One of my introvert friends told me that in his teens and twenties he had wanted to think of himself as an extravert and had tried to act as such, but somehow he never got the knack of it. He resigned himself to recognizing himself as an introvert who enjoys good company. Some extraverts admire what they see as the superior qualities of an introvert, and either persuade themselves that they are an introvert or that they feel inferior to introverts. Neither attitude is wise because there is nothing to choose between being one or the other. Extraverts and introverts both enjoy certain advantages and labour under certain disadvantages.

It is not surprising that introverts usually know that they are introverts. Introverts introspect. They know that they need a peaceful environment, that chaos upsets them, and that every day they have to feel that they have achieved something, however small. Knowing that they have tidied a kitchen cupboard will allow them to feel that the day has not been wasted. They work out theories about anything that attracts their interest. (This is not to say that all such theories are clever. Some are stupid, some bizarre.) Just working out a theory about why something is so can seem to them an achievement which gives them satisfaction. Extraverts are more interested in doing than in working out why. Their thoughts are not so much concerned with theories as with fantasies that involve much activity. Extraverts can be keen and observant critics of what goes on around them, but they are not impelled to work out in any detail why such things happen.

Some extraverts, busy focusing on what they do, find the question of why they do what they do impossible to answer. A friend of mine, a delightful extravert and the author of a number of highly successful romantic novels, asked my advice about a story she was developing. When I asked her why her heroine wanted to pursue a certain investigation my question completely flummoxed her. She knew that her heroine wanted to obtain certain information but she did not know why having this information was important to her. She knew what her heroine would do but she did not know why. Yet if we do not know why we do what we do, how can we ever understand ourselves?

Of course, we all want to achieve and to have good relationships, and when our lives go well we can usually fulfil both aims, but in the final analysis we are either an extravert or an introvert, and when, our backs are to the wall, in the extremes of danger, there is only one construction of our existence and potential annihilation that we know. In ordinary life we have to make conscious attempts to learn the skills in which we are naturally deficient, and if we are wise we do this. Many introverts learn to be highly skilled in social interactions; many extraverts learn to be highly skilled in experiencing, labelling and understanding their internal reality.[28]

Unless we come across a psychologist who is keen on laddering, we rarely make conscious and explicit how we experience our existence and our potential annihilation. We simply use our experience of our existence and potential annihilation as the basis of everything we do. Sometimes it is hidden. Sometimes it comes out clearly in what we say about ourselves.

Linda Evans, who was once a very famous television star, revealed herself as an extravert when she said:

> My main purpose as a child, and as a young adult, was to be loved. I was passive and submissive at any cost. The idea of rejection was frightening to me. I've broken out of that mould by now; but I still have this feeling for anyone who is *warm*.
>
> There's an old Chinese saying, which I apply in my everyday life, that 'everyone you meet is your mirror'.[29]

In contrast, the writer Edna O'Brien, when interviewed by Miriam Gross, revealed herself as an introvert. Miriam Gross asked to what extent she felt that writing was a way of explaining oneself, of making up for the failure to communicate fully in ordinary life.

> It's a stab at it. I think it was Beckett who said – I'm paraphrasing – that you write in order to say the things you can't say. It's a cry, or a scream, or a song. Whatever form it takes, it is definitely an attempt to explain things and put them right.

Did she feel that if women had more confidence and a more active role in the affairs of the world, they would invest less energy in their emotional life?

> I do. But, ironically, I think that much as our longings might hurt us, they also enrich us. Because finally, when the curtain

is down, I mean, when one is dying, what really matters is what took place inside, in one's own head, one's own psyche. And people who acknowledge the relative failure or paucity in areas of their lives – either in love or in work – are in a way more blessed than the others who pretend or who put on masks. Though you suffer by not being confident and you suffer by not being befriended or loved as you might like to be, you are the sum of all that need and at least you're alive, you are not a robot and you are not a liar.[30]

These are two successful people, successful not only in terms of fame and wealth but in developing a way of life which allows them to be themselves, to live within and to extend that which gives them their sense of existence. Linda Evans was eminently lovable, on screen and off, as they say. Edna O'Brien used everything that came to her, whether it caused her pain or not, to develop her own clarity and understanding in ways which meet with enormous public approval. However, when we do not develop a way of life which allows us to be ourselves, when we cannot live within and extend that which gives us our sense of existence, we suffer great fear.

Ken had come to be cured. As soon as he sat down he announced, 'I have a good, secure job. I've got my own house and no money worries. I'm forty-two and I'm in good health. There is no logical reason why I should be anxious.'

He had been off work for six months. He was so overwhelmed by anxiety that he could not attempt the simplest task. He spent most of his time going over in his mind technical work he had done in past years in the homes of neighbours and friends, trying to convince himself that he had not made any mistakes and that the people living there were not in danger.

He was an engineer, a practical problem-solver. 'That's my job,' he said. 'When there's a problem, they come to me to solve it.' He liked people looking to him to solve their problems. I asked him why. He said, 'It gives me satisfaction.'

At that time the UK was in the midst of a huge strike by coal miners, and this had created a series of problems at his place of work. As he would solve one, another would be created. There was no way all these problems could be solved simultaneously. He felt that he could not afford to let his staff and his superiors see that there were practical problems which he could not solve because that, he feared, would diminish him in their eyes.

A friend, 'the most logical and competent chap I know', had committed suicide. Ken had found him. 'It didn't upset me particularly,' he said. But, in fact, inside he was greatly upset.

In later discussions Ken told me how his mother, a very strong-willed woman, had insisted that he achieve and that he help people. He had to accept what she said because she had ways of enforcing her orders. He told me how one day, when she discovered that he had lost his best sweater on his way home from school, she had come to the cinema where he was happily watching a film and, in front of all those people, had hauled him home to look for his sweater. The shame he felt then was the shame he feared if, through his own carelessness, he caused the people he had tried to help any suffering.

He had come on his own. I asked after his wife.

'She says I'm getting her down.' No, they didn't discuss things much.

At that first meeting it was not until he was near to leaving that he said, 'My sons have their own friends now. They don't need me any more.'

Ken was unable to say, 'I feel that I am alone, abandoned and rejected. I fear I shall disappear.' In contrast, Ella was able to describe her fear.

Ella nearly died in a road accident. Four years later she was still weak and shaky and prone to tears. She had not returned to work, and she found driving a car a frightening experience.

'I just want to hide myself away,' she said. 'I don't want people to see me like this. I used to be so confident and in control.'

She had always had to be competent, but only in the feminine skills of housekeeping. 'My mother thought that a girl didn't need an education. A woman's fulfilment was to be a wife and mother. I won a scholarship to grammar school but she wouldn't let me take it up. I got married and had a family, but I've always done something more. I've always worked. But now, I'm back to where I started. I've achieved nothing. I'm weak and frightened, and I'm just what my mother wanted, a wife and mother and nothing else. No personal achievement. And that's what life's about, isn't it?'

Ella's statement that life is about personal achievement is just what an introvert would say, though introverts cover a wide range of activities in what they call personal achievement. Extraverts say that life is about other people, though they cover a wide range of possible relationships with other people. Both extraverts and introverts need to achieve and they both need other people, but for extraverts achievement is to strengthen their relationships with other people while for introverts achievement is what life is about. Introverts need other people to stop them disappearing into their own internal reality and losing touch with the world around them, while extraverts need other people to provide an essential part of their sense of existence.

When we are small children we are aware that we have certain talents and powers. We may not be able to put a name to them, but we know that whenever we use them we feel an enormous joy. The passionate pleasure of acting creatively and successfully in and upon the world has always given puny human beings the will and power to go on striving in a vast and dangerous universe. As children, if we are lucky, our talents and powers are approved of and encouraged by the adults around us. If so, we can then use our talents and powers to develop and make ourselves safe. If we are extraverts we use our talents and powers to gather people around us and keep them there, and to fill the empty space within us. If we are introverts we develop our talents and powers to gain clarity and personal achievement and to relate our internal reality to the external world.

However, if as children the adults around us do not recognize or approve of our talents and powers, we are forced to neglect and to deny them and to learn skills which we know are not in us. This leaves us with a sense of feeling 'not right', in some way always an impostor. We are left with a sense of longing. We may not be able to put a name to the object of the longing, or we may know the name but be too ashamed to admit it. How could this delicate wife and mother admit that all she ever wanted was to sail her own boat round the world? How could this rugby-playing company director admit that all he ever wanted was to be principal dancer in a ballet? How their families would laugh if they said these things! Perhaps they dare not even admit these longings to themselves. Then all they become aware of are certain passionate dislikes. She 'cannot stand' Clare Francis, who was such a brilliant sailor, while he refuses to accompany his wife to the ballet, saying that he has better things to do than watch 'those poofs'. The prevalence of envy in our society shows just how many children have been prevented from developing their talents and powers and being themselves.

Both extraverts and introverts need other people. Extraverts need other people to establish and maintain their existence. Introverts need other people to help them gain clarity by setting standards and giving approval. When I was discussing this with Mick McHale, I asked him which for him was the more real, his internal or external reality – what went on inside him or what went on outside him?

He said, 'Internal reality is far more real. I tend to believe that far more than my external reality.' He went on to say that while he wanted approval, when he did actually gain it it no longer meant anything to him. 'I think the difference is, if I've got things sorted out and I know I've done a good job, I can reward myself, but if it's on the periphery of that, if I'm not sure whether I've done a good job or taken the right direction, then it's very important and I really appreciate it.'

'So getting approval makes things more clear for you.'

'Yes.'

If extraverts are left in isolation they are in danger of being overwhelmed by the emptiness within them. Under stress they continue to perceive their external reality as ordinary, but it becomes dangerous. If introverts are left in isolation they are in danger of retreating into their internal reality and losing the ability to distinguish internal from external reality. Under stress they find that external reality becomes increasingly strange.

We need other people to help us structure ourselves and our world, but it is other people who threaten the structures we create. When they disappoint, leave, reject or betray us they show us that we were wrong in our expectations. When they criticize and correct us they show us that our meaning structure may not be an accurate picture of what is going on. When they press their ideas upon us or try to force us to be what they want us to be they threaten us with annihilation. We have to learn ways to defend ourselves.

A Choice of Defences

As our meaning structure establishes itself it builds defences so as to hold itself together. We create ways of conforming to society's demands while at the same time resisting such demands. If your parents sent to you to a school where each child had to wear an identical uniform you conformed but you defended yourself by wearing your skirt a fraction shorter than regulation, or you battered your hat and wore it at a rakish tilt. If you were expected to sit quietly through long, boring church services you defended yourself by escaping into fantasy or developing private games. When people criticized you you developed a nonchalant air, or a sudden and complete deafness, or a quick wit which stung your critics and amused onlookers. As an introvert you developed methods of organization and control which, when practised, gave you a sense of achievement. As an extravert you developed your charm and gathered around you a host of friends and acquaintances.

However, defences such as these require considerable self-confidence to create and use. The less self-confidence we have the more vulnerable we are to the encroachments other people make on us. The more vulnerable we are the more desperate are the defences we need. If we lose all self-confidence and we come to feel that we are irredeemably bad and utterly valueless, we have to resort to the most desperate of defences, those behaviours which psychiatrists call the mental illnesses.

Whatever defences we choose, these defences have both to ward off those encroachments which threaten annihilation and to contain our fear. To create an effective defence we need to know just what we are defending against. An army commander collects all possible information about his enemy before he decides just how he will defend his position. Similarly, we need to be clear about the nature of the threat to us before we construct a defence. However, sometimes the threat is so frightening that we cannot bring ourselves to acknowledge it. For instance, some people cannot bear to acknowledge that those they are closest to and on whom they depend are a major danger to them. More frequently, the threat that cannot be acknowledged is the fear that they feel. Many of us find fear to be too fearful to acknowledge, and so one of the defences we can choose is to deny that we are afraid.

Chapter Three

Fear Denied

We cannot live without denying. We have to shut things out. We have to say to ourselves, 'No, no, that's not there. It didn't happen. I'll take no notice.' If we did not do this we would be overwhelmed by the multitude of things going on around us and inside us.

We ignore the noise of the traffic outside our house while we concentrate on watching television. We ignore our sense of tiredness while we push on to finish an important task. We ignore our fear as we rush to save someone else from danger, and when we are commended for our bravery we say, 'It was nothing. Anyone would have done the same.'

We all know that such denial is necessary in times of stress. By denying painful facts and emotions we become brave. However, such denial is just for a brief period of time. Later we can acknowledge the noise of the traffic, or our tiredness, or, in the privacy of our own home, feel the fear unfelt at the time of danger. Now our experience accords with reality and all is well.

On the other hand, if we do not do this, if we go on and on denying what is happening, then we start to get into difficulties because our experience accords less and less with reality. Denying the aggravating noise of the traffic, we might get angry with our children for being unruly because our denied thought is 'I bought this house and I'm not going to admit I made a mistake'. Denying awareness of tiredness, we refuse to rest and so become ill, all because our rule for living is 'It is my responsibility to see that my family are perfectly happy all the time'. Denying awareness of fear, we feel pain and breathlessness, suspect a faulty heart and await imminent death, but we tell ourselves, 'My father would despise me as a coward if I admitted being afraid.'

Denying Fear as 'Character'

Long-term denial puts us further and further out of touch with reality. If we start this kind of denial early enough and practise it assiduously enough we forget that we are denying, and we see the ways in which we deny fear as fixities, part of what we call our personality or character. The long-term denial of fear produces a number of different kinds of 'character'.

There is the person who is always *practical, sensible and down-to-earth*. Such people never indulge in fantasy or consider those questions for which there are no practical answers. In my years in the National Health Service I met these characters frequently. There were the administrators who divided the number of patients attending by the number of staff in a psychotherapy unit, decided that the resulting figure was 'uneconomic' and closed the unit, all without taking the trouble to find out what actually went on in such places and without balancing the cost of such a place against the cost of each person who, deprived of his attendance at the unit for one or two days a week, became a long-term in-patient. There were the psychiatrists who would assure a frightened, depressed woman that she had a good husband, a nice home, and that she should count her blessings, without once pausing to consider what it must be like to be forced by an unwanted pregnancy and poverty to share a house with a man who beats you up on a Friday night and enjoys his marital rights on a Saturday night, and to know that such a future stretches ahead with death as the only escape. I have tried to explain the subtleties and complexities of such matters to such administrators and psychiatrists, but it is like trying to explain colour to the innately blind.

There is the person who is always *busy keeping busy*. This is not a successful denial of fear, because the busy person is well aware that stopping being busy means becoming frightened. However, rather than face this fear, the busy person keeps dashing around, doing things, often at the expense of loved ones, who would dearly like to be given a generous share of the busy person's time or be allowed to order their own lives, and their bedrooms, in their own way, not the busy person's way. Busy people dash around doing things at the expense too of their own needs and health.

Betty's husband Roy had come to see me because he could not work. Betty was surprised when I asked whether she would come along to one of our meetings. There was nothing wrong with her, but if it would help Roy she would come. So she did, and talked about herself.

'I've always got to be doing something. I can watch television, if I'm knitting, but I can't settle to reading, and I just couldn't sit doing nothing. It annoys me to see people doing nothing. I vacuum and dust right through every day. I'd feel the house isn't cleaned properly if it isn't vacuumed one day and dusted the next.'

'She's always doing housework,' said Roy, who, depressed and unemployed, often sat doing nothing.

'I've always worked,' said Betty. 'I brought home my first pay packet the week before I turned fourteen. My mother expected us to work. There were six of us. You couldn't leave one job before you had the next lined up.'

However, she should not be working so hard now. She had angina, and the doctor said she should rest.

'He says I should rest and put my feet up every afternoon. But I can't do that. It wouldn't be right.'

'Why wouldn't that be right?' I asked.

'I don't know. I've always been like that. I'm that sort of person.'

She said that she was frightened of dying, frightened of having a stroke and ending up like her mother, a helpless invalid. She was no stranger to fear. She knew what it was like to be swept by sudden, drenching fear. 'I need to be out of the house and with people.'

She spoke of her childhood. 'I was the third of three daughters and my mother didn't want me. She told me that. She said when she had me she didn't look at me for three days.'

So Betty learned early the dread of annihilation, and the way of keeping it at bay by earning her right to exist by working hard. She preferred to risk death by heart failure than face the greater fear of being annihilated by being abandoned and rejected.

Betty worried a good deal, but she dealt with her worries by working. There are many 'characters' who deny their fear by worrying. *'I'm a worrier,'* they say, in the same way as they would say 'I'm a left-hander' or 'I'm a Gemini', something you are born with, something you cannot change.

Worrying is not good for the health. A churning stomach, tense muscles and an inability to concentrate on the task in hand can produce stomach ulcers, backache and accident injuries, as well as the kind of stress which scientists now see as important in the development of cancer and heart disease. However, worrying does have advantages, and committed worriers are reluctant to give them up.

First, being a worrier allows you to concentrate on small worries rather than a big fear. A worrier can avoid thinking about her fear that her husband is being unfaithful to her by worrying about the state of the carpets in her home; a worrier can avoid thinking about the fear that the economic recession will make his firm bankrupt by worrying about the state of his car. This way of worrying uses a lot of energy, but it does allow you to shut out a great deal of unpleasant reality and saves you from having to bother about the needs of other people.

Second, a worrier usually believes that the sign that you love someone is that you worry about that person. In the worrier's way of thinking, worrying is a sign of virtue because worrying means that you care, and caring means that you are good. Thus the worrier will often say to loved ones, 'I worry about you' and then feel hurt because loved ones do not always react with warmth and affection to such statements. In fact, they often seem offended. They also become very secretive about their activities, so as to spare themselves the guilt of having made the worrier worry. Not that this makes the worrier any happier. Secrecy on the part of loved ones about their activities allows the worrier to expand the range of options about which to worry. Moreover, the worrier usually marries someone who never admits to anxiety, someone who takes pride in being imperturbable, someone who never says 'I worry about you'. So the worrier has to find more and more to worry about in order to avoid the big fear that 'Nobody loves me'.

Then the worrier might feel that the third advantage can make up for not being loved. If you feel that the people around you are too selfish and uncaring to love you, or if you suspect that you are unlovable, you can prevent yourself from becoming quite isolated by controlling the people around you and thus keeping them near you. If you cannot make your loved ones love you, you can make them feel guilty by showing them that they have given you cause to worry. Then they, trying to avoid the imposition of guilt, will carry out your wishes. They will come home early, wrap up warmly, not smoke (at least when you are around), drive carefully (with you in the car), not swear, work hard, pass their exams, and so on. A determined worrier can make the injunction 'Don't do anything which will cause me to worry' the basic and absolute moral imperative in a family, and thus become the most powerful person in that family. I recall my father showing me a cartoon from the *Saturday Evening Post*. It featured a middle-aged couple in bed. The husband is settling down to sleep but the wife is sitting bolt upright and saying, 'You go to sleep. I'm going to sit here and worry.' It was the story of his married life.

The fourth advantage extends the worrier's powers even further, into the realms of magic. There are many worriers who believe that 'If I worry about something it won't happen'. Since so many of the things we worry about never eventuate it is impossible to disprove that worrying is an effective way of controlling the universe.

Many worriers, I find, regard their habit of worrying as something they have inherited from a parent, like the colour of their eyes or the shape of their nose. It has not occurred to them that worrying was something they had learned. One thing which parents are always teaching their children is how to become aware of a particular situation, how to define it, how to identify certain elements in it, and how to predict what will follow. Thus one parent will say, 'You've been invited to a birthday party. Won't that be fun?' and another parent will say, 'You've been invited to a birthday party. Don't eat too much or you'll be ill.' The ability to identify every potential disastrous element of a situation and to worry about it is a skill which passes from one generation to another, not by a worry gene but by learning.

Regarding the ability to worry as an inherited characteristic is one example of denying fear by *keeping things the same*. 'I'm a worrier, my parents are worriers, my grandparents were worriers, my children will be worriers.' There are many 'characters' who devote their efforts to stopping life changing. Since life *is* change, such efforts achieve little success. Nevertheless, that does not stop 'characters' who want to keep everything the same from trying to do this. Such extravert 'characters' try to maintain relationships no matter how damaging or empty these relationships may be. As Rachel said, 'I can't stand severing a relationship. It wounds me.' Such introvert 'characters' try to prevent their organization and their control of situations changing. They insist that things have to be kept a certain way, that actions have to be performed a certain way. The contents of their rooms must never be changed around, or they must always dress in a particular style, or ceremonies, like the family's celebration of Christmas, must always be carried out in the same way.

The belief that by repeating our actions we prevent life from changing is as magical as the belief that if you do not talk about a thing it has not happened. This belief often underlies the thinking of those 'characters' who take great pride in *keeping things to yourself*. Such people believe that talking about worries makes them worse, or that admitting fear to yourself and to others shows you to be weak and despicable. This can end in tragedy, as the story of Willie Peacock shows. In 1985 the UK government under Margaret Thatcher wanted to close down most of the mining industry. The miners fought back with a strike in which there was much brutality on the part of the police and, on occasion, on the part of the miners.

The widow of Willie Peacock yesterday accused his fellow miners of hounding him to his death. It was his wife Elizabeth who found him when she got home from work. She opened the front door and saw him hanging from a rafter – unable, she believes, to face one more day's torment in the pit.

Yesterday, union delegate David Hamilton ordered 1,200 men at Willie's colliery to stop work for 24 hours as a 'mark of respect' but Mrs Peacock is not impressed. 'As far as I am concerned,' she said, 'the NUM can send them back.'

Willie's friends say that men who stayed out on strike for a year picked on him because he went back after nine months sickened by the murder of a Welsh taxi driver taking a miner to work. His lunch box was contaminated with urine and excrement. His safety was threatened in whispered phone calls that taunted him for 'being a scab'. His injured foot was stamped on until it was bruised. But Willie never said a word about it to his wife because he did not want to worry her. 'I knew nothing of what he was going through,' she said yesterday. 'That's the way he was.'

Only since his death, at 41, has she learned of the harassment he suffered. Willie, married 16 years, will be buried today. His last words to his wife were 'See you later' and his last present was a model of a miner pushing a coal truck.[1]

We might wonder why Mrs Peacock had not noticed that something was amiss with her husband, but then many women collude with their spouses in pretending that they are strong, imperturbable, silent men. Such a collusion relieves the wife of the responsibility of taking her husband's feelings into account. Many women believe without question the John Wayne myth that men never get frightened. Thus they can ignore the suffering that some men undergo and collude with the denial of fear which so many men try to achieve.

Denying Other People's Pain

Denying other people's pain is a popular and effective way of denying fear. If someone is in pain, then something fearful has happened. Acknowledging another person's pain can make us frightened. We fear that the disaster that has happened to the other person could happen to us. Even if we can put this fear from us, assuring ourselves that we are safe, acknowledging another person's pain arouses in us the sentiment of pity, which is itself a painful emotion. To limit the pain of our pity we rush to help the person in pain – we offer practical help, advice, money – but if there is nothing effective we can do we feel helpless, and this, too, is a painful and fearful state. We pride ourselves on being competent, and any situation which shows that we delude ourselves about our competence is indeed fearful and to be avoided.

Acknowledging another person's pain can lead us not just to pity but to empathy, that leap of imagination which allows us to immerse ourselves in another person's experience and to feel their emotions as our own. Thus we can share another person's joy, but also another person's pain and fear, and this can be undesirable. Roy, who was ashamed of the way tears would come suddenly and unbidden to his eyes when he was watching television, said, 'Sometimes I see something, somebody in pain, and I feel their pain, just for a moment.' Lonely as he was, he adamantly refused to join a self-help group for companionship. He could not bear, so Betty told me, to have to listen to people talking about their troubles.

Empathy is a precious human skill which not only prevents us from being cruel but joins us to others. When we experience empathy we are able, if only momentarily, to leave the loneliness of being and enter another person's world.

However, to enter another person's world can mean leaving the haven of safety we have built for ourselves and being forced to recognize that life is capricious, unfair and cruel. We then have to recognize that in pain we are jangled, confused, broken. Grief feels like fear, for in grief we find that the loss we have suffered has revealed that the picture of our life which we had built up was nothing but a fiction, which the loss has shattered. Our security has gone, and we do not know how to reconstruct it. Grief is painful, messy, and the people around us may not wish us to remind them of that.

If people persist in presenting their pain to us, if they will insist on crying, or looking miserable, or parading their grief or their emaciated bodies on our television screens, we can protect ourselves from the fear such sights may arouse in us by saying, 'They brought it on themselves.' *Blaming the victim* is one of the outcomes of the belief in a Just World, where invariably good people are rewarded and bad people punished. If someone is suffering, then this suffering must be the punishment the person deserves. Thus the rape victim should not have provoked her attacker, the beaten child should not have aggravated his parents, the starving tribespeople should have known that the drought would last. We are good and therefore bad things will not happen to us. However, when they do, when we become the victim, we have either to abandon our belief in the Just World and see its ways (and God's) as capricious or mysterious beyond our comprehension, or else feel very guilty because we were bad, or very resentful because we have been punished unfairly.

Many people, not wishing to feel guilty and wanting to feel self-confident and proud of themselves, refuse to acknowledge another person's anguish because they fear it will awaken their own anguish and weakness. Rhianon's husband, a soldier with a distinguished war record, came along with her one day to instruct me to make her better. She was, he said, sick. She had no reason to be miserable and angry, yet there she was moping around the house and sometimes flying into a violent temper. She had even thrown a plate at him. He could not understand her behaviour. When I asked him about his feelings for her he said, 'Of course I love her. She's a fine wife.' When I asked how they organized their domestic routine he said, 'I help her with the shopping and her housework.' He had no objection to her interest in music. It was a nice hobby, but, of course, 'it's natural for a woman to run a home and bring up children'. Rhianon wept, just as at home she wept in loneliness. He did not move to comfort her, just as at home he would never touch her. He said to me, 'The sort of chap who puts his arm around his wife when she's depressed is likely to get dragged down too. He wouldn't be in charge any more.'

If being loving and caring is seen as weakness or as a way of being contaminated by the other person's weakness, then another person's need to be loved must indeed be denied. In the process of learning to be manly, many boys learn to define the loving, caring parts of themselves as feminine, weak and despicable, and so they have to deny that they have such attributes. Such a process of denial prevents them from understanding themselves, and so when in later life they sense within themselves the darkness of depression they are terrified. Rather than face what is inside them, they rush into some kind of frantic activity. They immerse themselves in work or sport, they have affairs with younger women, they take to drink. Anything rather than face their own fear and anguish. Many men in adult life still rely on a technique learned in boyhood, in Phillip Hodson's words, 'the happy knack of making themselves feel better by making others feel worse',[2] a technique which protects them from the pain and fear of observing another person's pain.

Of course, women too can work at denying their own fear by denying other people's anguish, even though it is not a defence which society expects a woman to be seen using. Women are supposed to be sensitive and caring, easily and foolishly distressed by another person's suffering. Many women very effectively reduce the amount of suffering they allow themselves to observe and become frightened about by refusing to read newspapers or to watch the news on television, and by concentrating solely on themselves, their family and their friends. Such deliberate ignorance does not always lead to a happy life. Many women still sense the wider world as being chaotic and dangerous, threatening to destroy what they hold dear.

Women, too, do not find it easy to use the denial of fear which *being competitive* allows. Our society considers being competitive to be a masculine attribute. Fortunately there are now many women who reject this nonsense – delight in striving, competing and achieving is natural to all of us – and so both men and women can deal with their fear by putting all their energy and conscious thought into winning and defeating. Some competitive people wisely recognize that the fear is there and that striving, competing and achieving are an effective way of confronting and controlling the fear. However, some competitive people do not recognize this. They deny their fear, and then the fear returns in the guise of tension and anger which can disrupt all their relationships, competitive or not.

Just as competitive people are often irritable, so are powerful people, or those with aspirations to power. *Becoming powerful* is a much-favoured technique for denying one's fear, be it becoming the dictator of a nation or merely the dictator of a family. Power can be described in different ways, such as having wealth or the ability to punish those who do not obey, but, in terms of denying fear, power can be thought of as the ability to define. The powerful person says, 'The world is the way *I* see it and everyone has to agree with me.' People who do not agree with the powerful person's definition of reality are fought with, punished and, if defeated, silenced. Powerful people may be effective in controlling their own fear, but they establish and maintain their power by creating fear in others. We each, naturally, define reality in our own individual way, and we give up our definitions only under the threat of rejection, loss, contempt, humiliation or pain. So in the struggle for power, whether in the family or in the state, many of us suffer great fear.

However, becoming powerful does not eradicate the experience of fear. The powerful person has few friends, and so fear returns as loneliness and the fear of abandonment.

Powerful and would-be powerful people are often angry and irritable. Anger is our natural response to frustration, and when we seek to impose our own definitions on the world we often find that the world is recalcitrant and will not always conform to our wishes. Thus the more we try to impose our definitions on the world the more frustration and anger we feel. The discovery that the world does not conform to our expectations can fill us with fear, and, rather than admit that fear, we can turn it into anger. Despots are dangerous because they are frightened and will not admit their fear.

The world that refuses to conform to our wishes can be the natural world. The sun will rise, the rain will fall, and the wind will blow, all indifferent to our pleas and threats. Or the world that refuses to conform to our pleas and threats can be the world of people, and here our pleas and threats can have an effect. We can inflict pain on other people to force them to do what we want them to do. However, we are people too, and if we hurt other people we can perceive their pain, suffer and feel frightened. One way to protect ourselves from such suffering and fear is to refuse to acknowledge that the people who do not conform to our demands are really people. They are in some way subhuman. They may look like human beings but they do not have feelings as we do, and they have no right to claim such feelings. If they are black and we are white, then we may suggest that blacks do not get depressed, no matter how poor and dispossessed they may be. If we do not wish to share our country's wealth we can claim that the poor of Asia and eastern Europe have no right to want to better themselves by migrating to wealthier countries. If we are men, then we may propose that a woman is not really a person as a man is, and that all she wants and needs is to be a sex object, or our mother, or our wife. If we are adults, then we know for a fact that children soon forget their troubles. After all, childhood is the happiest time of one's life.

However, in denying that other people have feelings we have to deny our own feelings. Objects – stones, mud, cement, machines – do not have feelings. When we deny that other people have feelings we treat them as objects. When we deny that we have feelings we treat ourselves as objects. Thus we become much less the person we might have been.

Why do we do this?

How do we do this?

Chapter Four

Learning How to Deny

Newborn babies are noisy and spontaneous. What they feel they feel totally. A happy baby is happy from top to toe. A hungry baby is possessed by hunger pangs and greed. An angry baby feels total and absolute anger, unrestrained by guilt or the fear of hurting others. A baby's feelings are fully felt and fully experienced, and the baby acts with complete unselfconscious self-confidence. Yet by the time the babies become toddlers, gone is the birthright of being simply themselves. Now self-conscious, toddlers have learned how to deny their thoughts and feelings and thus who they are. All babies must enter into a relationship with their mother in order to survive both physically and as a person, yet it is through this and other relationships that babies learn how to deny themselves and their feelings.

As babies enter into their relationship with their mother they become increasingly aware of their mother's feelings. A baby does not understand causal connections – that exploring the texture of the mother's face by pinching her cheeks causes her pain – but he is sensitive to her moods. Her joy or anger or fear are part of her baby's experience.

This experience of emotions and the means by which they are expressed, in smiles and frowns, cries and words, touches and cuddles, creates and maintains the relationship that joins the baby to the human race and to life.

Babies have been around for as long as human beings have been, yet it is only in the last forty years or so that they have been systematically studied. What is clear now is that babies come into the world primed to make relationships with other people. In the womb they learn to recognize their mother's voice, and, perhaps, their father's voice. When they open their eyes and see the world, what they look for is a face. A photographic study by Lynne Murray and Liz Andrews[1] shows little Ethan being born. One minute later he is comfortable and relaxed as he is held by his mother, Julie. He opens his eyes and looks directly at her. He watches her intently, his eyes scanning the details of her face. As Julie talks to him, his face becomes more mobile and expressive. A few minutes later Ethan is handed to his father, John. He gazes intently at his father and is totally absorbed. Then John slowly and clearly protrudes his tongue, and Ethan attends closely. He appears to be concentrating completely on his mouth as he frowns and shuts his eyes, then he looks back at John and protrudes his own tongue. He is fifteen minutes old.

These photographs show that not only is a newborn baby immediately and deeply interested in faces, and able to imitate the movement of another face, but that the emotions he expresses are not random but arise directly and meaningfully out of his experience. When the midwife interrupted Ethan's first examination of his mother's face he complained vociferously, and was not satisfied until he was back looking at his mother.

At birth babies know that a happy tone of voice goes with a smile. At nine months they can tell the difference between expressions of happiness, sadness and anger, and understand something about the emotions that produce these expressions. At eighteen months they know that other people see things differently from them. By two they have that deep knowledge of other people which we call empathy.[2]

Just as we were born with the ability to breathe, so we were born with the ability to experience our emotions fully and to be aware of other people's emotions. Small children might not be able to put an accurate name to what another person is feeling, nor to understand why the person is experiencing a particular emotion, but they can see and feel what the other person is feeling. One of the most moving photographs to have emerged from the conflict in Kosovo in 1998 was one taken by Andrew Testa. In this a young woman refugee is sitting on the ground in a state of complete despair. We can see from her clothes – leather jacket, jeans, jewellery – that she has been dispossessed of a reasonably comfortable life (no Albanian had a completely comfortable life in Kosovo under the rule of President Milosevic). Her daughter, four or five years old, is squatting in front of her, her head on one side, her hands held out at body width and curved facing each other in that gesture we all use when we want to indicate compassion for the other person. We can see that the little girl is talking to her mother and we know that she is saying, 'There, there, Mummy. Don't cry. We'll be all right.'

The little girl's gesture of empathy shows that as well as her own suffering she can also feel the suffering of her mother. Empathy enables us to leave our own limited world and enter, through our imagination, the world of other people. Thus we are able to have the closest and strongest relationship with others and to expand our own world, not just in knowledge and understanding, but in developing what is best in human beings – tolerance, kindness, generosity, love. However, empathy comes at a price.

Empathy may enable us to establish and maintain good relationships with other people, but it also means that we can more than double our own suffering when we have an empathic knowledge of another person's suffering. We feel the pain of pity, and this is often multiplied by feelings of helplessness when there is nothing we can do to reduce the other person's suffering. In order to protect ourselves from the pain of pity, many of us refuse to empathize with those who suffer. We call people fleeing terrible conditions in their homeland 'bogus migrants'. We turn off the television news when pictures of war or starvation appear. We blame the victims of injustice as being the authors of their own suffering, and we claim that people of another race, religion or nationality are not fully human and therefore do not feel pain as we do. If this becomes our preferred way of dealing with the suffering of others we seriously diminish ourselves, becoming a lesser person than we might have been.

Human beings are not merely conscious. We are self-conscious

– that is, we can, as it were, stand outside ourselves and look at ourselves. We judge ourselves. We have feelings about ourselves, and these feelings can include empathy.

Empathy is a blend of identifying with, feeling sympathy for and understanding of which we can direct not just at other people but also at ourselves. Empathy with oneself is not self-pity. Self-pity reflects the theme 'Why me? It's not fair', and this complaint is based on the idea that life ought to be fair. The underlying theme of empathy with oneself is simply 'This is'. To be able to empathize with ourselves we need to accept and value ourselves, not because we measure up to some standard which we have set ourselves but simply because we exist. When we reject and hate ourselves we have no empathy with ourselves.

However, even if we do value and accept ourselves, we can refuse to empathize with ourselves. When we suffer either physical or mental pain we can reduce our conscious awareness of the pain by refusing to empathize with ourselves. We can split ourselves into two pieces – the piece that observes and the piece that suffers. We can do this, say, to reduce the pain and horror of having a tooth pulled or of being raped. As a short-term defence this can be a very effective means of surviving as a person, but if we do not reconnect ourselves when the period of suffering is over we do ourselves enormous damage. Split in two, we cannot feel whole and acceptable, and in denying our own pain we become oblivious to the pain others feel. Thus a boy who is frequently beaten by his father can, very sensibly, deal with the pain of the beating by detaching himself from it and telling himself that he feels nothing. However, if this becomes his habitual way of dealing with pain, he grows up to be a man who inflicts pain on others and feels that he does no wrong.

To empathize with ourselves and with others we have to be able to feel our feelings fully and to name our feelings truthfully. Feelings or emotions are meanings. They are our interpretations of a situation. People often talk about emotions as if they are completely separate from thoughts, but this is not how we experience emotions. We see something happen and we feel an emotion, but what we feel *is our interpretation of what is happening in relation to our-selves*. For instance, you hear a very loud sound. You interpret this as, 'That's a bomb. I'm in danger. I'm frightened.' The first two interpretations are thoughts, the third is a feeling.

The bit of our brain that emotions relate to develops earlier than our cortex which relates to language, and so the meanings we call emotions are not initially expressed as words. However, these wordless interpretations can be turned into words. The meanings we create initially in words can be about things unconnected to us, but the meanings we call emotions are always connected to us. They are meanings about the safety of and danger to our meaning structure. When something happens which confirms or validates our ideas, we feel safe. These are feelings which can range from mild satisfaction to intense joy and happiness. These meanings/feelings are versions of the meaning, 'I've got it right! It's just how I want it to be! How wonderful!' When something happens which disconfirms or invalidates our ideas we feel in danger. These are feelings which can range from mild anxiety through fear to terror, and they can be quite complex interpretations. The meanings of safety of and danger to our meaning structure are often referred to as positive and negative emotions. Positive emotions are mean-ings about being validated as a person (e.g., happy, content, satis-fied) and negative emotions are meanings about being invalidated as a person (e.g., fear, anger, shame, guilt, hate, envy, jealousy and so on). We interpret being invalidated in a multitude of ways. Pride plays an important part in our emotions, not just in the safety emotions but in the danger emotions which can act as defences. Anger is the meaning, 'How dare this happen to me!'; envy, 'He has something which I want'; jealousy, 'He has something which is rightly mine.' Hate springs to our defence when we feel weak and helpless, and revenge turns the defence of hate into what is traditionally seen as the best of defences, attack. The emotion of forgiveness is the meaning, 'I am no longer in danger from those who injured me.'

Our emotions are statements of our own truth, but such truths can themselves seem to be dangerous to us. Introverts can find that the truth 'I am afraid' threatens chaos, while extraverts can find that the truth 'I am angry' threatens to sever relationships. Hence introverts favour the defence of isolation where they separate their feelings from their awareness of a troubling event and tell themselves that they are calm, completely undisturbed by any emotion. Extraverts favour the defence of repression whereby they separate their awareness of a troubling event from the emotion it arouses and then forget that the event has occurred. They remain aware of their feelings but explain them as arising from some other event or as being an inexplicable emotion. If these feelings are of anger they are likely to tell themselves that they are not angry but frightened. They dare not risk being angry lest those who angered them reject them.

The dangers of employing either the defence of isolation or the defence of repression are well recognized in psychotherapeutic circles, but the capacity to feel our feelings fully and to name them truthfully has in recent years been burdened with two pieces of popular jargon, namely 'emotional literacy' and 'emotional intelligence'. The term 'emotional literacy'[3] quite rightly draws attention to our need to recognize and name emotions truthfully. The term 'emotional intelligence'[4] suggests that there is some kind of intelligence to do with the emotions which is the equivalent of intellectual intelligence, and thus, like intellectual intelligence, has some inherited component. Some people might seize on this to excuse their own lack of interest in trying to understand themselves and other people. Recognizing and naming our emotions is a learned, not an inherited, skill, a skill which we can constantly improve by being honest with ourselves and by observing other people closely.

Babies, like all the newborn of other species, are born with the ability to seek out the conditions necessary for their survival. Just as a hungry baby will search for something to suck for sustenance, so a lonely baby will search for someone to love, and will offer this love trustfully and hopefully to the person who offers in return care and protection. Mothers sometimes have difficulty in loving newborn babies, but we, as babies, have no difficulty in loving our mothers, and this hook remains in our hearts for ever, no matter what our mothers do to us. We may give up loving our mothers when our love is not returned, but we never give up wishing that we had had a mother who loved us as we wished to be loved. We can feel the same about our fathers. After a lecture in which I talked about friends and enemies, a man told me about how his father had always rejected him. As he did so his eyes were squinting in the way that eyes do when they are holding back tears. His father was ninety-four and he was in his sixties.

Babies are very good at being themselves, but this does not suit whatever society they have been born into. Every family has its own rules and expectations, and the baby has to learn to conform. Long before we had words to define it we were presented with the dilemma 'Shall I be an individual or a member of a group?' We knew, though we felt our knowledge only in our fear and anger and our sense of our existence, that we could not survive alone, yet it was equally dangerous to give up being ourselves. If we were lucky we had parents who understood this, treated us with respect and loved us for what we were, and not for what we might become – that is, the person our parents wanted us to be.

Before they are even born, babies start receiving messages from their parents. It is now well established that quite early in the foetal life babies distinguish sounds and prefer pleasant sounds to unpleasant sounds. In the womb babies are able to associate one event (say, a sound) with another event (say, a change of conditions in the womb), and use the occurrence of the first event to predict the second. Thus one baby may associate the sound of sweet music with the relaxation of the womb as the mother, having switched on her favourite soap opera, puts her feet up for a rest, while another may associate the sound of a man's voice shouting obscenities with a disruption to the calm of the womb as the mother flinches away from a blow. Once born, the baby discovers a world of touch, light and smell. A newborn baby can easily identify the mother's odour and prefer it to all other smells, and just as easily distinguish the firm but gentle touch of the confident, loving mother from the uncertain or sometimes painful touch of an unconfident, even rejecting, mother.

Parents give out many messages, sometimes consciously, sometimes unconsciously. The baby finds these messages to be very powerful because they are first-time events. He has little past experience to provide a contrast, and is as yet unable to translate these messages into words. Instead, the baby creates images of sound, vision, touch, taste, kinaesthesia and smell. These images become part of the baby's meaning structure and, especially when they are reinforced by later events, can remain with the baby into adulthood, sometimes having powerful consequences.

In adult life many of us find that we can be troubled by vague anxieties or an apparently inexplicable dampening of our mood when we have no reason to feel unhappy. To work out why this happens it can be useful to bring into clear consciousness the image that accompanies these feelings. If you have kept or managed to regain the confidence you had as an artist when you were small you could paint a picture of the image. Or you could simply ask yourself, 'If I could paint a picture of what I'm feeling now, what sort of picture would I paint?', and then carefully inspect the picture in your mind's eye to find what it means for you. Do not waste your time looking for meaning in terms of Freud's dream symbols or Jung's archetypes or tarot cards or the *I Ching* and the like. What is of supreme importance is what the image means to you.

As you look for what the image means for you, you are likely to see some connections which go further and further back into your childhood, even to babyhood. It can be helpful to talk to family members about events surrounding your birth and babyhood, though from what my clients have told me, it seems that there are many mothers who do not take kindly to any suggestion that they were anything less than perfect nurturers. It can be difficult to get across that you are not making enquiries in order to blame your mother for not being perfect but simply to establish what happened and, in particular, what your mother was feeling when you were a baby.

It is important to find out about your mother's feelings so you can see whether your image arises out of what was going on inside you or out of your response to what was impinging on you from outside. Thus your image might relate to your intense feelings of hunger as your family, caught up in a war, were unable to feed you, or strong feelings of pain from an essential surgical procedure. Or it might relate to your awareness of your mother's intense feelings, perhaps of anger, hostility, despair, depression, or, most frequently, anxiety. Many women who have since childhood been plagued by vague anxieties and nameless dread find a focus for their fear in their children. Achieving motherhood, they rapidly become experts in every doom or disaster, however remote, which might beset a child. They resist any attempt to apply logic and reason to their endless anxious monologue because, perhaps for the first time in their lives, they are able to take the fear from inside themselves and feel justified in projecting it on to their baby. This can be helpful for the mother but tough for the baby, who cannot distinguish what are his own burdens and what his mother has imposed on him.

However, babies thus burdened do grow up and become able to reflect upon themselves and their life. Images of hunger and pain allow us to meditate upon the implications of such hunger and pain – namely, the feelings of helplessness, of being abandoned, alone, of having no control, of losing the structure we know to be ourselves. Doing this, we are actually dealing with our present predicament, because these are the issues that often arise in our daily lives, and, in thinking about this, we become more knowledgeable and more courageous. Images of our mother's feelings allow us to discover that her feelings belong to her, not to us. We can transfer the burden back where it belongs. When, in my forties, I discovered that my image, which I had come to see clearly and named 'Old Death's Head', was of my mother's state of depression and of her hostility to me, I could then say to myself, 'That image is not an integral part of me'. With this discovery I not only felt lightened, I saw myself as infinitely more valuable and acceptable than I had thought myself to be.

Mothers and prospective mothers have often told me how frightened they become when they encounter me talking about how a mother can have such devastating effect¯ on her baby. I respond by assuring them that if, in truth, you love your baby and wish him well and do not seek to hide this from him, then he will recognize the abiding, secure current of your love and will survive the surface ripples that come with your ordinary human fallibility. Just as some babies carry into adulthood images which produce feelings of anxiety and despair, so other babies carry into adulthood images which give self-confidence and security, even when the reality of current events may suggest the opposite. There is nothing to match the self-confidence of an adult who, as a child, never had reason to doubt his parents' love.

Bringing up children is not easy. There is no one right way to do it because so much depends on finding a desirable balance between opposites. For instance, you want your child to fit into a group, but not so well that he becomes a doormat for others to walk over, and, as much as you want your child to be an individual, you do not want him to be idiosyncratic to the point of eccentricity. You want your child to understand that to be assertive can be fine in many situations but that a person who is unremittingly selfish is not liked. Moreover, in teaching that some activity is a virtue you cannot help but imply the vice that accompanies it. If cleanliness is next to godliness, then dirtiness is next to evil.

Bringing up children can never be a simple matter of just feeding and clothing them and keeping a roof over their heads. Our physiology may determine that we each live in our own individual world, but to develop and survive as a person we need other people. Hence children have to learn to fit into society. Some are not actively 'brought up' but just left to grow, perhaps because their parents think this method of child-rearing removes the danger of harming the child by imposing rules and demands, or perhaps because they are too distracted or too selfish to do anything but leave the children to bring themselves up. Some children will thrive in a relaxed environment but others will not. Even when the parents impose no rules, the children create their own in order to develop a sort of regularity which gives security. An individual child is likely to develop rules, rituals and fantasies to create an idiosyncratic order, while in a group of children the oldest will take on the parenting role. Moreover, even when the parents think they are making no demands on the child, the latter can be busy interpreting certain of the parents' words and gestures as implied instructions.

The child's interpretations of the parent form the crux of the problem of bringing up children. You can read extensively in developmental psychology, study parenting skills and draw up a plan incorporating every best practice in parenting, or you can ignore the matter of being pregnant until the midwife puts your baby in your arms, but either way the person your baby becomes will be determined not by what you do but by how your child interprets what you do. The best you can hope for is that if you always try to behave towards your children with love, support, kindness and patience, and if you try to understand your child's point of view and take it into account in making your decisions, there will be a good chance that your children will not lose the love they so readily had for you when they were born. There will even be a chance that your children will, on a few occasions, actually listen to what you have to say.

I have now seen grow to adulthood a number of babies born to various friends of mine who have always striven to bring their children up with love, support, kindness, patience and an understanding of their children's point of view. Each of these young adults is now a basically happy individual with genuine self-confidence and not merely that adolescent cockiness which hides deep uncertainty. They get on well with their parents and other people. However, I still see around me parents whose child-rearing practices may be different from those of their grandparents but who suffer the same fraught outcomes. One way or another, many children still find themselves in situations where their sense of being a person is under threat, and so they have to develop many defences in order to keep themselves safe.

A baby's sense of being a person – that is, the baby's meaning structure – develops while he is still in the womb. Different experiences lead to neural connections, the physiological substrate of the meaning structure in the brain, being set up. Once the baby is born, his meaning structure grows and is modified with every experience, and out of the substructure of neural connections consciousness evolves. Out of consciousness comes self-consciousness. Just how and when these changes take place is not understood, but current knowledge suggests that consciousness develops slowly, coming on, as the scientist Susan Greenfield once remarked, like a light turned on with a dimmer switch.

Even though a baby may not be experiencing fully what we call consciousness, he can from his past experience create expectations. When these expectations are fulfilled (e.g., a baby's version of 'There's the music. Now I'm going to feel more comfortable') that part of his meaning structure is strengthened, but when these expectations are not fulfilled his meaning structure is threatened. A baby cries not just from hunger but from the fear created when the expectation that the discomfort of being hungry will be assuaged is not fulfilled. Learning to become a member of society is a process of having expectations not fulfilled and of finding ways of coping with such threats to the meaning structure.

To enter into the life of their family and thus into society, a baby has to acquire the knowledge that in society there are limits to self-expression. These limits, the baby soon finds, apply particularly to defecation and micturation and everything to do with cleanliness, to greed, and to anger.

All families are clean. The world over, all families are clean. They each have high standards of what constitutes *cleanliness*. The trouble is there is no universal agreement as to what constitutes cleanliness. When India was part of the British Empire the fastidious English in India deplored what they saw as the lack of hygiene in Indian homes, while Indians, the Hindus especially, deplored the disgusting habit of the English of lying in their own bath water. Similarly, in one family, underclothes may be changed every day but there are no rules about teeth-cleaning, while the family next door changes underclothes less frequently but brushes their teeth without fail after every meal. If each family discovers the rules of the other family, then each regards the other as dirty, or at least as not following the proper rules of cleanliness. Dividing the world into categories of 'clean' and 'dirty' is something all human beings do. We just do not agree on what these categories should be, and each of us believes that our categories are right and everyone else's are wrong.

A baby's introduction to his family's rules about cleanliness comes when he discovers that he is no longer allowed to relieve the pressure in his body when and where he pleases, but only at certain times and places as his family decrees. Some fortunate infants do not encounter these rules until the sphincter muscles are strong enough to hold back the pressure of urine and faeces. A baby does not acquire voluntary control over his sphincter muscles until he is about three years old. If the rules of the family are imposed at a time when the infant has a good chance of complying with the rules successfully, he can enjoy the great pleasure of basking in his family's praise and approval. However, in our society there are still a great many babies who are sat on pots and ordered to perform long before they can possibly understand what is expected of them, much less carry it out. Even more are there babies whose performance of their natural functions is treated by the adults around them with disgust and rejection. Many parents whose own toilet training left them feeling great disgust for their own excreta find that they cannot cope with their baby's. Other parents, who have followed a plan of patience and praise in toilet-training their babies, suddenly become extremely anxious when their three-year-old is in danger of failing to gain admittance to a nursery which will not take an untoilet-trained toddler.

There are sound reasons why the waste products of our body should be kept separate from other objects in our environment. Such waste products can contain elements and processes which can bring about illness and death. But our reactions to these substances are more than a sensible response to possible physical danger. There is another danger there, something so terrible that we cannot utter its name. Fire is dangerous, but we still just call it 'fire'. Whereas these waste products are never spoken of directly by well-brought-up people. All kinds of circumlocutions are used. However, if one wishes to be extremely vulgar or express great disgust and rejection, then there are a multitude of words and phrases referring to these products which can be used. 'Shit' means much more than 'faeces'.

Every infant has to learn far more than the practical procedures for the disposal of one's faeces and urine. All the magical and fantastical meanings which the members of the infant's family hold have to be learned and reacted to. There are meanings which relate to the sense of having within oneself something bad and contaminating which has to be expelled. These meanings link with a sense of being disgusted with oneself when one is the object of other people's disgust. A mother may not express disgust and rejection as she bathes her smelly baby and dresses him in clean clothes, but the contrast with dirt and disgust is implied as she says, 'Don't you feel better now? Aren't you a lovely clean baby?'

There are meanings which relate to the sense of having within oneself something which is powerful and destructive which can be used against other people or retained so that other people are not injured or such power is not lost. Infants soon discover how to take revenge on a parent by interrupting the parent's meal and demanding to be put on the pot. However, revenge against parents can be dangerous because they are giants who hold all the power.

There are meanings which relate to the need for privacy and the danger of intrusions on this privacy. Such intrusions may be in terms of being the butt of other people's humour, as when others laugh at our discomfiture when we are discovered emptying our bowels and bladder, or in terms of other people's curiosity, as when others want to inspect what we produce and to assist in its production with enemas and emetics. Such intrusions can take on a sexual quality, so that the anus can become partly or even wholly the location of the person's sexual feeling and interest. It is no wonder that so many of us are incapable of letting our body perform its functions of digestion and elimination but are forever caught in a painful oscillation between diarrhoea and constipation.

For many of us simple cleanliness is a source of fear. We have to defend ourselves against this fear. Dirt we see as danger. We divide our world into the categories of clean and dirty, categories which become fixed and impenetrable. We learn our society's methods of dealing with dirt and establishing cleanliness, and we adapt these methods to create our own rules which seem to us unbreakable, absolute laws of the universe. Every one of us operates with such a set of laws.

Often our rules go beyond their function of ordering the universe and become rituals, regular patterns of behaviour which have a magical quality. To protect our meaning structure, primitive pride, with its lack of interest in reality and reason, can easily suggest rituals which we deem capable of influencing our good fortune and keeping death at bay. The obsessions and compulsions of someone considered to have obsessive-compulsive disorder are not symptoms which present themselves at the onset of disease but are simply an extension of the rules, rituals and ideas which the individual has long held.

Our notions about dirt and cleanliness do not form one distinct part of our meaning structure, separate from all other parts. Rather, these notions connect to other ideas, and are reinforced by other ideas. Many of us have abandoned the idea that a dirty person is necessarily a wicked person, but most of us see clean as beautiful. Then we can call cleanliness purity. Robyn Davidson wrote:

A couple of years before [my journey in the desert] someone had asked me a question: 'What is the substance of the world in which you live?' As it happened, I had not slept or eaten for three or four days and it struck me at the time as a very profound question. It took me an hour to answer, and when I did, my answer seemed to come directly from the subconscious: 'Desert, purity, fire, air, hot wind, space, sun, desert desert desert.' It had surprised me, I had no idea those symbols had been working so strongly within me.[5]

Purity can also mean the absence of excess, and this was certainly the way Robyn saw it. Her camel journey across the Western Australian desert was one of shedding burdens both literally and metaphorically. However, even before this journey she had learnt in childhood that she must not be greedy.

A healthy baby is born greedy, and so it needs to be, for only greedy babies will suck. Without greed a baby would not survive. Being greedy, a baby wishes to feed when hungry and sleep when satisfied. Some lucky babies are allowed to do so. But many are not. Many millions of babies have mothers who are too poorly fed themselves to be able to feed their babies whenever they are hungry. Such babies have to make do with what is offered to them and, if they survive, they may be haunted for the rest of their lives by images of hunger and greed. These images may be immensely powerful. I have never been in danger of starving, but images of hunger have been handed down to me by earlier generations of my family. My father, who, as a soldier in France in the First World War, had often gone hungry, would at home consume scraps of food and stale crusts of bread rather than have the food thrown away. Messages about hunger came to me from other family members who had gone hungry in the bush when food was scarce, or had been told by their relatives about the famines that beset the poor in Ireland and Scotland. Living alone in London now, I buy less food than I might consume and can easily afford because I cannot bear food to be wasted. My father would be proud of me.

In affluent countries where no baby need go hungry, many do because their mothers, intent on being 'good mothers' obeying the dicta of their own mothers or the child-rearing 'experts', feed their babies according to schedules which relate to the adults' needs rather than the child's. Being hungry and being left to cry until the clock reaches a certain hour were for many of us our first lesson in learning that we were of little importance in the scheme of things. We learned that saying 'I want' is greedy, and being greedy is bad. Whenever we feel a desire that we cannot fulfil and perhaps cannot even articulate, and we see other people enjoying the fulfilment of this desire, we feel envy. Envy is a natural response, and a common one, because we can always imagine more than we can ever do or own, and if it is acknowledged and accepted it can become part of the motivation which urges us on to greater things.

However, if we feel envious and cannot do anything about it, if we feel helpless and frustrated, and the frustration goes on and on, then our envy becomes mixed with rage and a fierce desire to destroy both what we want and the person who has what we want. Babies are helpless, and, when their desires are not met, they can feel a destructive rage which they express not just in crying and flailing limbs but also in biting the breast which is offering to feed them. Some mothers, pitying their baby's helplessness, accept their baby's greed, envy, frustration and rage, and so patiently hold, soothe and feed their baby. But other mothers see this violent rage as evidence of the baby's inherent evil. They become frightened of their baby and seek to drive the evil out with stronger rules and punishments. The baby must learn obedience. What he learns is that envy is always accompanied by fearful impotence and murderous rage. Such envy is common in our world, and usually underlies the destruction and terror which one group of people can inflict on another.

Children who are taught that greed is bad are also taught that envy is bad, and so they are condemned to a life of struggling with their impulses of greed and envy, either sacrificing themselves to others, never daring to ask for anything for themselves, or resorting to devious, dishonest ways of trying to gain more for themselves and to hinder and destroy the people they envy.

In families and in society anger is always a problem. It is our natural response to frustration, and without it we, a physically weak species compared to those which competed with us for food, would not have been able to use our intelligence to establish ourselves as a viable species. Anger can make us creative and brave, but we need to live in groups, and anger within the group is always a threat to its cohesion. In a family, when the father becomes angry, whether he beats his wife and children or merely retires to his room in icy silence, the other members of the family feel frightened. As they did when they were children, many adults devote their lives to doing nothing to make their mother or father angry. A baby being angry can frighten the parents because they fear that they will not be able to control this new member of the family. For such parents the psychoanalyst Donald Winnicott wrote:

We all know what it is to lose our tempers and we all know how anger, when it is intense, sometimes seems to possess us so that we cannot for the time being control ourselves. Your baby knows about being all-out angry. However much you try, you will disappoint him at times, and he will cry in anger; according to my view you have one consolation – that angry crying means that he has some belief in you. He hopes he may change you. A baby who has lost belief does not get angry, he just stops wanting, or else he cries in a miserable, disillusioned way, or else he starts banging his head on the pillow, or on the wall or the floor, or else he exploits the various things he can do with his body.

It is a healthy thing for a baby to get to know the full extent of his rage. You see, he certainly will not feel harmless when he is angry. You know what he looks like. He screams and kicks and, if he is old enough, he stands up and shakes the bars of the cot. He bites and scratches, and he may spit and spew and make a mess. If he is really determined he can hold his breath and go blue in the face, and even have a fit. For a few minutes he really intends to destroy or at least to spoil everyone and everything, and he does not mind if he destroys himself in the process. Don't you see that every time a baby goes through this process he gains something? If a baby cries in a state of rage and feels as if he has destroyed everyone and everything, and yet the people round him remain calm and unhurt, this experience greatly strengthens his ability to see that what he feels to be true is not necessarily real, that fantasy and fact, both important, are nevertheless different from one another. There is absolutely no need for you to try to make him angry, for the simple reason that there are plenty of ways in which you cannot help making him angry whether you like it or not.

Some people go about the world terrified of losing their tempers, afraid of what would have happened if they had experienced rage to the fullest extent when they were infants. For some reason or other this never got properly tested out. Perhaps their mothers were scared. By calm behaviour they might have given confidence, but they muddled things up by acting as if the angry baby was really dangerous.[6]

Donald Winnicott wrote this about forty years ago but his wise lesson has not been learned by many people. Over the past few years I have run a number of workshops on the topic of 'Anger, Revenge and Forgiveness'. My idea for this workshop was that in the morning session we would discuss how this trinity was handled in our childhood families, and in the afternoon session our discussion would concern our present families, with the emphasis on looking for parallels and contrasts in each pair of families. So much for a great idea. In each workshop the participants, who came from a wide range of backgrounds, had so much they wanted to talk about in connection with the way anger was handled in their childhood family that little time was left for the remaining topics.

In all these workshops each of the participants fell into one of two groups with regard to their childhood experience. Either they had grown up in a family where anger was expressed with great emotion and noise, even violence, or they had grow up in a family where anger was never revealed directly. There were cold silences, sulking and icy withdrawals from family life. I asked all the participants whether their parents had even discussed with them, in the way they might have discussed with a child road safety or being unselfish, how anger ought to be handled. Not one participant said that their parents had done this. Indeed, the idea that anger could be a topic of discussion between parents and children was to some participants shocking in its novelty.

Anger is integral to the way we live. Events and people constantly frustrate us, and we respond to frustration with anger. How best to express that anger is always a problem. Anger is another aspect of our lives where we have to find a balance. An angry response can save us from death or injury, and can ward off the disconfirmation of our meaning structure. Anger is pride in action, warning us that we are in danger. When someone insults us our immediate response of 'How dare you!', whether said aloud or not, can do more for our self-confidence than any amount of positive self-talk. Yet our anger can put us in danger. Other people may respond with anger or reject us for our unacceptable behaviour. In dealing effectively with our own and other people's anger we need to see it as something which is basically natural and valuable but which needs to be tended carefully, in the same way that fire is natural and valuable but needs to be handled with care.

My workshop participants showed very clearly that the two parental styles of dealing with anger had been a poor preparation for their future life. Both groups were frightened of anger. Those who had grown up in a family where anger was unrestrainedly expressed were frightened of anger because they saw it as unpredictable, dangerous and destructive. Those who had grown up in a family which pretended that they did not feel anger were frightened of anger because it was a silent, unpredictable, hidden danger. Being frightened of anger for whatever reason prevents a person from developing flexible and adaptive ways of dealing with it. Some people deny that they ever get angry, but they find themselves plagued with inexplicable fears and with headaches or stomach and bowel disorders. Other people are aware that they are angry but they are so frightened of their anger and feel so guilty about being angry that they cannot express their anger in any effective way. If we cannot deal sensibly with anger we have difficulty in all our relationships, and if we see anger as always being wicked and unworthy we condemn ourselves as being wicked instead of understanding how anger is a necessary defence which can hold us together when events and other people threaten to annihilate us as a person.

In the first three years of their life babies learn a great deal about those aspects of the world which are dangerous and about how they can defend themselves against these dangers, including how to deny their fear and how to deny those aspects of themselves which the people around them will not accept. Adults usually treat babies with some degree of tolerance, but when babies turn into toddlers and then into children, much of this tolerance is withdrawn. As children we discover that, whatever childhood is, it is not the happiest time of our lives.

The Perils of Childhood

In 1621, Robert Cleaver and John Dod, in their book *A Godly Form of Household Government*, advised parents:

> The young child which lieth in its cradle is both wayward and full of affections; and though his body be but small, yet he hath a reat [wrong-doing] heart, and is altogether inclined to evil . . . If this sparkle be suffered to increase, it will rage over and over and burn down the whole house. For we are changed and become good not by birth but by education . . . Therefore parents must be wary and circumspect . . . they must correct and sharply reprove their children for saying or doing ill.[7]

Cleaver and Dod were making explicit the model of the child which is still very prevalent in our society today. This is the model of the child being intrinsically bad. The Christian image of the child being born in sin is an example of this model. If children are seen as being intrinsically bad then their upbringing must be concerned with inhibiting, controlling and moulding the child. Many educational systems are based on this model, including the educational system, which sets a national curriculum and demands that every child must be educated totally in terms of this curriculum. However, there is another model of the child which we can use, that of the child being intrinsically good. This second model is implied in our word 'education', which has its root in 'leading into the light'.[8] Alas, most children become victims of an education based on the idea that children are basically bad and have to be inhibited, controlled and moulded. The belief that children are not actually people but objects to be used by adults is still very prevalent in most societies, including our own.

This idea is part of the tradition that the child's point of view is of no importance, that the parents' point of view must prevail, that the parents must teach the child everything of value and that the child must sacrifice himself for the parents. This is an essential part of our culture, for this is what the Bible teaches. As the psychoanalyst Alice Miller has described it:

> It is always the Isaacs whose sacrifice God demands from the Abrahams, never the other way around. It is daughter Eve who is punished for not resisting temptation and not suppressing her curiosity out of obedience to God's will. It is the pious and faithful son Job whom God the Father continues to mistrust until he has proved his faithfulness and subservience by undergoing unspeakable torments. It is Jesus who dies on the Cross to fulfil the words of the Father. The Psalmists never tire of extolling the importance of obedience as a condition of each and every human life. We have all grown up with this cultural heritage, but it could not have survived as long as it has if we had not been taught to accept without question the fact that a loving father has the need to torment his son, that the father cannot sense his son's love and therefore, as in the story of Job, requires it.[9]

This tradition arose out of necessity. When life was 'nasty, brutish and short', a child was of little value. Adults, whose life expectancy might be no more than twenty or thirty years, were the tribe members who could maintain the tribe by having the skills to secure the food supply and by producing future generations of the tribe. A dependent child was a burden. The child had to be grateful for being allowed to exist – unsatisfactory babies were left to die – and had to prove his gratitude to his elders. As soon as the child was big enough to carry out some tasks, he or she had to begin working, and to work effectively the child had to learn the tribe's rules of conduct. If the child and the tribe were to survive, then the children had to give up their desires to play and to be irresponsible, and had to learn to conform to the rules of the tribe. Physical survival of all, children and adults, depended on obedience. Even today, in most African societies the child, even when an adult, is forbidden to correct an elder, even if the elder's ideas are leading to disaster.[10]

The lowly status of children and the necessity of children learning obedience in order to survive continues to this day where families live in poverty and near-starvation. Over the past two decades, in each of the famines in Africa, aid workers from the West saw their task as that of feeding the starving children, but for many of the tribal Africans this was not their first priority. For them, the adults should be fed before the children, and this is what they did, even if it meant that the children starved.

If the early generations of the human race had not followed the rule that children should be sacrificed in order to secure the continuation of the tribe, many of us would not be here today, benefiting from a lifestyle which does not demand that a child dies because there is insufficient food or that a child has to begin working as soon as its little hands can carry a burden or its little legs can toddle. In the West we no longer send five-year-olds into the factory to tend the machines, or seven-year-olds down the mine to pull the coal trucks, but we still demand that the parents' interests are paramount. An example of this can be seen in the Family Court in NSW, Australia. The journalist Adele Horin wrote:

A few years ago the Family Court published research on separated fathers that vividly exposed the pain and sadness many felt . . . But lawmakers got it into their mind a few years ago that all fathers (the neutral term is non-resident parent) had a right, and a duty, to be involved in their children's lives, post separation – although they framed it in terms of the child's rights. And so the Family Law Act was reformed in 1995 to shift the emphasis towards a 'right of contact' and 'shared parental responsibilities'. A major study, released this week, shows how naïve the hopes that legal changes could turn bad fathers and husbands into co-operative, involved parents post-divorce, or end the war between men and women who can't agree on the children.

The three-year study, based on interviews with judges, solicitors, parents, counsellors and written judgements, is sobering reading. It shows that the reforms have created an environment where the concern for fathers' rights has increasingly taken precedence over concern with children's rights.

It shows also the futility of trying to impose shared parenting patterns – which require a great deal of communication and co-operation – on bitterly divided couples who are slogging it out in court; and it shows the dangers of giving men who are violent greater leverage over their ex-wives and children. . .

What the Family Court increasingly deals with – its core business – are cases where violence, abuse and harassment are alleged. And thanks to the legal reforms, more children are being forced to spend time with fathers who turn out to be as dangerous as their ex-wives allege. Contact with fathers is not always good for children.[11]

As ever, children must sacrifice themselves for their parents. Peda-gogical texts from the Bible to the present day extol this tradition, while it is implicit in the arguments supporting the physical punish-ment of children.

I was once invited to talk to a meeting of the National Childbirth Trust about depression. My experience of National Childbirth Trust people was that they were well educated, concerned, aware and critical women and men. In the part of my talk where I was out-lining the links between childhood experiences and adult depression I was suddenly interrupted by a young woman, nursing a small baby, who was sitting near me.

She said, 'Can I ask you a question? It's going back to something you said. I didn't want to stop you in full flow.'

I detected a note of hostility.

'It's what you said about not beating children. Don't you think children need to be hit. How else will they learn?'

She went on, passionately, to describe how she disciplined her two elder children. (I assumed, hopefully, that she was not talking about the baby as well.) She had a wooden spoon called 'Mr Henry' with which she hit them whenever they misbehaved. 'You can't reason with young children,' she said, and then she described to us how Mr Henry accompanied them wherever they went. If the children misbehaved in public she would take them to some place where they could not be seen and there Mr Henry would do his work. 'I wouldn't hit them in front of other people. That would embarrass them. Usually I don't have to hit them. They know that if they are naughty Mr Henry will come out.'

I asked her whether she had been beaten as a child.

She said, 'I was very unruly as a child, especially when my mother's marriage was breaking up. I wasn't beaten, just hit. I caused my mother a great deal of trouble.'

Some of the people in the room shared my sadness as she gave her detailed account of the punishments her small children received, but others supported her, claiming that all children were too wild and unruly to be brought up without some form of corporal punishment. One woman, who had earlier identified herself as someone who suffered greatly with depression, assured us that *all* the children who misbehaved themselves in the school where she taught came from homes where corporal punishment was never used.

The amount of physical violence used against children is greatly underestimated. I found that many of my clients regarded hitting their children as both normal and necessary. If I commented upon this, they usually said that they hit their children only when their children needed it and that they did not hit them as much as they themselves had been hit by their parents. I hoped that this was indeed so, for some of the troubled people I saw had been brutally treated by their parents. Nevertheless, I suspect that Alice Miller was right when she wrote, 'Parents who beat their children very often see the image of *their* parents in the infant they are beating.'[12] Many people find that one very effective way of getting rid of your own pain is to inflict pain on others. If it were not so, where would dictators find the people to man their concentration camps, death squads and torture chambers?

Many men see it as their prerogative to beat their wives and children whenever they wish to do so. Sometimes women thrash their children, but often it is the woman who stands helplessly by while her husband takes his temper out on the children. In such families the children often regard their mother as a saint, a woman who suffered at her husband's hands for her children's sakes. However, it is a truism in psychotherapy that it is not possible to have one good and one bad parent. If the good parent does not protect you from the bad parent, then you have two bad parents.

Parents often justify the violence they do to their children on the incompatible grounds that a) it is necessary in order to make the children good, and b) children do not remember what is done to them. If children do not remember what was done to them for being bad, how can they remember to be good?

As the law stands in the UK, Australia and the USA adults are protected from assault but children are not protected from assault by their parents and, in the majority of schools in Australia and the USA, by their teachers. Children Are Unbeatable, an alliance of organizations and individuals committed to changing the law so that children are protected, has fought long and hard for this to be achieved. The UK Children's Commissioners, themselves appointed by the government, issued a statement on 22 January 2006, where they said in part

Children are the only people in the UK who can still be hit without consequence. The current and previous governments have made welcome progress by prohibiting all corporal punishment of children in schools, other institutions and forms of alternative care. In relation to parental corporal punishment, in England, Wales and Scotland the ancient common law defence of 'reasonable chastisement' has been limited, but not removed completely; and in Northern Ireland the government has indicated that it plans to bring the law into line with that in England and Wales.

Children have the same right as adults to respect for their human dignity and physical integrity and to equal protection under the law, in the home and everywhere else. There is no room for compromise, for attempting to define 'acceptable' smacking. This has been confirmed by United Nations and Council of Europe human rights monitoring mechanisms, and by the Westminster Parliamentary Joint Committee on Human Rights.

The UK has been told repeatedly since 1995 that to comply with its human rights obligations, the reasonable punishment defence must be removed completely in all four countries of the UK.[13]

The strongest opposition to any change in the law comes from some of the Christian churches whose members believe in following the Old Testament injunction, 'Spare the rod and spoil the child'. Adults who beat children protect themselves with a set of self-serving lies, typically, 'This hurts me more than it hurts you', 'It's for your own good', and 'I don't beat my children, I just give them a tap'.

Yet this is not how young children experience a 'tap'. In a study conducted by the National Children's Bureau and Save the Children seventy-six five- to seven-year-olds were asked their definition of a smack. 'The message from children is that a smack is a hit: on 43 occasions children described a smack as a hit, a hard hit, or a very hard hit.' When a child described a smack as a hard hit her questioner asked, 'Can it be a soft hit?' The child replied firmly, 'No'. A seven-year-old girl observed, 'A smack is parents trying to hit you, but instead of calling it a hit they call it a smack.' When asked why children usually get smacked a five-year-old girl said, 'When I'm very naughty my mum smacks me'. Her questioner asked, 'What is being very naughty?' The little girl replied, 'When you hit people a lot.' Apparently her questioner refrained from asking whether her mother was being naughty when she hit her but no doubt the little girl had considered this question.

When asked what it felt like to be smacked, the children were clear that it was very unpleasant. A six-year-old boy said, 'It feels like someone's punched you or kicked you.' A seven-year-old girl said, 'It hurts and it's painful inside – it's like breaking your bones.' Another seven-year-old girl said, 'You feel like you don't like your parents anymore.' When asked how children feel after they have been smacked, only one child said that he learnt from his mistake.[14]

The knowledge that they are being harmed by the person who should be looking after them creates a conflict that children have to resolve in some way. Some children bravely face the truth that they have parents who are not the perfect parents they would wish for, but others choose to lie to themselves and to deny their own pain and fear. They tell themselves that they are bad and deserve to be punished, and they deny that the physical punishment actually hurts. The first choice destroys the child's belief that she (and it is often a she) is valuable and acceptable, while the second destroys the child's capacity for empathy. Boys who are repeatedly beaten tell themselves that they feel nothing, and they are rewarded for this lie by being admired by their peers for being tough. Seeing yourself as being wicked and deserving punishment, and destroying your capacity for empathy, has many bad outcomes. The research carried out by Murray Straus at the Family Research Laboratory, University of New Hampshire, showed that, regardless of race, socio-economic status, the gender of the child and the quality of the support given to the child by the mother, the tendency to antisocial behaviour increases after corporal punishment. Straus also found links between corporal punishment in childhood and adult violence, masochistic sex, depression and alcohol abuse.[15]

A study which revealed how children who are physically abused lose their capacity for empathy took the form of a survey of 11,600 adults in the USA, and found that 74 per cent of those who had been punched, kicked or choked by their parents did not consider this type of behaviour abusive.[16] In Britain at least one child dies every week from injuries inflicted by an adult, usually a parent or step-parent. Yet in Sweden, where all forms of corporal punishment have been illegal for twenty years, only four children have died at the hands of an adult over that time and, of these four, only one died at the hands of a parent. A study published in 1999 on the effects of the ban on smacking in Sweden showed that the number of reports of assaults on children increased, with the result that any child at risk of serious injury was identified early, thus preventing anything like the tragic cases found all too often in Britain where, even though healthcare workers and neighbours often knew that a child was being savagely beaten, no one acted to prevent the child's brutal murder. In Britain young people's drug use and alcohol intake have increased over the past twenty years, while in Sweden these have decreased.[17]

In Britain surveys show that many more people want to ban fox-hunting than want to ban parents smacking their children. It is often said that the British prefer animals to children, but harsh, uncaring attitudes to children are found in every society. Those who want to retain the right of parents to inflict physical punishments argue that a ban would turn the parents into criminals. The Swedish government introduced many measures concerned with improving the skills of the parents and with providing good professional support.

Physical punishment gives parents no cause to think about their actions. A slap can be inflicted instantly. Over recent years psychiatrists and the pharmaceutical industry have provided parents with another method of controlling their children which requires no thought on the part of the parents except to remember when to administer a pill.

Kirsty, a social worker, told me how she had gone to visit her younger brother Tim, his wife Cora and their three-year-old son Peter. Peter was being his usual rumbustious self, rushing around, climbing on chairs and tables, enjoying rough games with his father, noisily arguing with his aunt over a jigsaw. The only time he was quiet was when he sat, transfixed, in front of the television watching his favourite programme, *Bob the Builder*.

As Kirsty watched her strong, healthy, active nephew, she remembered Tim at that age, behaving just like Peter, and wearing their parents out with his antics. She remembered too how surprised she had been when her grandmother had talked about Kirsty's father being the same at that age. Kirsty knew her father only as a very staid accountant, just like Tim had become. Over dinner, when Peter had finally gone to bed, Kirsty wanted to reminisce about the generations of boys in her family who had been such lively three-year-olds, but she was forestalled by Cora saying, 'There's something we want to ask you,' and Tim enquiring, 'Do you think Peter's got ADHD?'

ADHD, or Attention Deficit Hyperactivity Disorder, is currently a fashionable syndrome. Physical illnesses do not have fashions, only epidemics when some virus or bacillus is on the loose, or

103

when some deleterious environmental conditions prevail. Physical illnesses have some identifiable physical basis, but mental disorders do not. Some psychiatrists claim that a brain dysfunction underlies ADHD, but no such dysfunction has been found.

In the early 1960s, before ADHD was invented, I was working in Sydney, Australia, as an educational psychologist with special responsibility for children with emotional problems. Part of my work was to advise teachers about pupils whose behaviour was causing them concern. The kind of children who were most frequently referred to me were seven- or eight-year-old boys who would not or could not settle into the classroom routine. When I examined these boys and their family background I found that they fell into two groups.

The first and largest group was those boys whom school did not suit. Many such children have good performance abilities – that is, they have good hand-eye co-ordination, they can think in spatial terms, and can analyse and construct patterns but their verbal skills – either through inborn limitations or early education – have not developed to the same degree as their performance skills. However, schools use and value verbal skills much more than performance skills, and thus many boys come to feel alienated from the educational process. Consequently, if they are bored in class, they seek to entertain themselves, and if they feel rejected and undervalued they seek to protect and to assert themselves by getting attention through being naughty. If you cannot be famous you might as well be notorious.

To a casual observer this first group of boys was no different from the second group, who were also inattentive, restless and inclined to get into mischief. However, these boys were not bored and seeking attention. They were frightened, and their fear made them unable to concentrate and to keep still. The family background of these boys was one which created the child's fears. Some of these families were deeply unhappy. The mother may have been depressed and threatening suicide, or the father may have been a brutal tyrant. Some were migrants and the parents were still suffering the effects of their experiences in the Second World War. Often the adults were unable to adapt to a strange country. One young lad told me how at home his grandmother would punish him if he spoke English, yet he now thought in English and wanted to be accepted as an ordinary Australian boy.

It was not a happy time for any of these boys, but in one way they were lucky. They could not be diagnosed as having ADHD and be medicated with Ritalin.[18]

Ritalin and Equasym are the brand names of two drugs based on the generic drug methylphenidate hydrochloride, used in the treatment of ADHD. Both have been approved by the UK National Institute for Clinical Excellence (NICE), which advises that the drugs should not be given to children under six and should be used only as part of a comprehensive treatment programme. In the USA several million children have been prescribed these drugs, including large numbers of children under six, even toddlers. Ritalin is so well known in the USA that my word-processing program includes it in its dictionary. In the USA and Australia it is known as 'kiddie cocaine'. A survey of child psychiatrists and paediatricians across Australia showed that 80 per cent have prescribed stimulant drugs like Ritalin for children. In 1999 this type of drug was prescribed for 5,819 children under six, of whom 67 were aged two and 715 aged three.[19] In the UK the number of children prescribed these drugs is now in the thousands and is doubling each year. The literature supplied by the pharmaceutical companies which make the drugs speaks of 'psycho-stimulant therapy' but does not explain why children who are hyperactive are given a drug that is known for its capacity to stimulate adults.

Drugs that are prescribed for babies and children both in medicine and psychiatry are not tested on babies and children. Drugs are tested only on adults. All doctors can do is extrapolate from the recommended adult dose. Babies and children have died from some such extrapolations.[20] Recently the National Institute of Mental Health in the USA set up the Research Units on Pediatric Pharmacology (RUPP). The first report issued by one of these was that from the Johns Hopkins Medical Children's Center, where a large, randomised double-blind study showed that the drug fluvoxamine was an effective treatment for anxiety in children. This drug is a selective serotonin reuptake inhibitor (SSRI), which causes the neurotransmitter serotonin to accumulate in the synapses in the brain. Supplies of the drug were provided by Solvay Pharmaceuticals, who also gave research support (i.e., money) to the RUPP centres. The trial ran for only eight weeks, which does not make it a measure of the long-term effects of such a drug on the developing brains of children.[21]

Methylphenidate hydrochloride is a core member of the group of drugs called amphetamines, whose street name is 'speed'. It is not understood why amphetamines cause adults to feel energetic and excited while the same drug slows children down. Obviously the drug works differently on a developing brain than it does on a mature brain. What has been known for some decades now is that amphetamines are addictive. Indeed, amphetamines are so addictive, toxic and dangerous that adults cannot take them legally without prescription anywhere in the world.

Pharmaceutical companies dislike the word 'addictive'. In the prescribing information given by Medeva for their drug Equasym it says, 'Chronic use can lead to tolerance and dependence with abnormal behaviour.' 'Chronic use' is not defined. It could be six years or six months. Such companies do not like to reveal the adverse effects of any of their drugs and try to meet the legal requirements for disclosure while saying as little as possible. Adverse effects are minimized by calling them 'side effects' and by listing as few of them as possible. Medeva list for Equasym 'nervousness, insomnia, decreased appetite, headache, drowsiness, dizziness, dyskinesia, abdominal pain, nausea, vomiting, dry mouth, tachycardia, palpitations, arrhythmias, changes in blood pressure and heart rate, rash, pruritis, urticaria, fever, arthralgia, scalp hair loss'.

Peter Breggin, the American psychiatrist who has devoted his life to researching the deleterious effects of the drugs used in psychiatry, pointed out that the list of behaviours given as symptoms of ADHD in the *Diagnostic and Statistical Manual* (DSM-IV) focuses on behaviours which interfere with an orderly, quiet, controlled classroom. 'The first criterion under *hyperactivity* is "often fidgets with hands or feet or squirms in seat". The first criterion given under *impulsivity* is "often blurts out answers before questions have been completed" and the second is "often has difficulty in waiting turn". None of the ADHD criteria is relevant to how the child feels. Mental and emotional symptoms, such as anxiety or depression, are not included.' In his book *Talking Back to Ritalin*[22] Peter Breggin 'catalogued dozens of "causes" for ADHD-like behaviour. Most commonly it is the expression of the normal child who is bored, frustrated, angry, or emotionally injured, undisciplined, lonely, too far behind in class, too far ahead of the class, or otherwise in need of special attention that is not being provided. More rarely, the child may be suffering from a genuine physical disorder, such as a head injury or thyroid disorder, that requires special medical attention rather than stimulant medication.'[23]

In his book *Naughty Boys* consultant child psychiatrist Sami Timimi told how he would ask his colleagues 'to explain to me what diagnoses like attention deficit hyperactivity disorder (ADHD), conduct disorder and Asperger's syndrome were, what was going on physically in these children, and how they "knew" which child had a conduct disorder caused by family problems as opposed to ADHD caused by an immature frontal lobe (in other words a physical problem in the development of the brain). They couldn't explain this to me and didn't know how to differentiate physical from emotional or other environmental causes. The best they could come up with was "it must be so". Shockingly, I realized that the whole profession is built on subjective opinion masquerading as fact.'[24] Writing about the psychiatric conferences supported by the drug companies, he said, 'All too often I leave these mainstream events feeling like I had attended a cult convention, not a scientific conference, so bad has the lack of democratic debate or interest in non-drug-industry-driven perspectives become.'[25] Sami Timimi was born in Iraq and came to England when he was fourteen. He could see very clearly how different his upbringing was from that of his English fellow students. Later, as a child psychiatrist, he could relate this understanding to the problem of ADHD, which is a problem only in countries which have a western culture. Outside these places it is unknown. Of course in these places there are some naughty boys, but haven't there always been? What is it that happens to boys particularly in western societies that does not happen to boys elsewhere?

Sami Timimi pointed out that, 'Early in the twenty-first century we in the West are living in the bizarre paradox of Western governments spending billions every year to fight a war on drugs with the right hand whilst the left hand hands out millions of prescriptions for cocaine-like stimulants to its children.'[26] Peter Breggin explained the long-term significance of these 'therapeutic' effects in an article which he called 'The New Generation Gap: Today's Kids Suffer Legal Drug Abuse'. He wrote:

> We are the first adults to handle the generation gap through the wholesale drugging of our children. We may be guaranteeing that future generations will be relatively devoid of people who think critically, raise painful questions, generate productive conflicts, or lead us to new spiritual and political insights. Growing up on psychiatric drugs, millions of children are developing little sense of their own personal responsibility. Instead of discovering their own capacity to improve their lives and transform the world for the better, they are being taught they are brain-defective – and require lifetime treatment with psychiatric drugs.[27]

When I was a child my family gave me to understand that there was something intrinsically wrong with me as a person because I had a chronic lung disease, bronchiectasis. This so undermined my self-confidence that it is only in recent years that I have been able to talk to people, other than the doctors I consulted, about the effects this disease had on my life. How much worse it must be to be told that you have a defective brain, that the way you behave is unacceptable, that you are incapable of controlling your behaviour, and that only by depending on a drug will you be in any way acceptable to your family and to society. A number of studies looking at what children on Ritalin thought of the drug confirmed this. One child said, 'I think it is a kind of sickness, because it, it kind of takes over, I know it takes over my body . . . it's like you don't have that much control . . . I kind of feel weird, because you need a pill to control yourself.'[28]

The child psychiatrist Sandra Scott, writing in *New Scientist*, said, 'Contrary to what some parents presume, drugs do not treat bad behaviour directly. Using drugs to treat conduct disorder exposes the child to unnecessary side effects and makes it harder to apply more effective methods such as cognitive behavioural therapy – getting the child to understand why he behaves in the way he does – or therapy involving the child's family.'[29] The 'comprehensive treatment programme' recommended by NICE includes both cognitive behavioural therapy and family therapy.

Another consultant psychiatrist, Felicity, told me how, while she did prescribe Ritalin, she was well aware that many of the mothers of children diagnosed with ADHD had little idea how to use praise in getting a child to behave well. These women relied solely on criticism and punishment, often physical punishment. The multidisciplinary team of which Felicity was a member used group methods to help the mothers learn how to praise their children. One sticking point was often the mother's inability to see that praise which is followed immediately by criticism is in effect not praise at all. There is no point in saying to a child, 'You behaved really well then,' if this is immediately followed by, 'Why didn't you behave like that yesterday?'

However, using praise effectively to encourage a child to behave well is not simple. Over the past century much of the research carried out by psychologists has been devoted to proving the obvious, but then the obvious is only what people are prepared to see. For many people what was obvious was that children will learn to behave correctly if all their errors are punished. This 'obvious' fact psychologists have shown not to be true. We all learn best when our correct behaviour, or even just-approaching-correct behaviour, is rewarded and our errors ignored. This has been shown to be the case not just with our own species but with a wide range of other species.

The idea that rewards, not punishments, should have primacy was gradually, though not completely, taken up by teachers and education specialists. However, knowing what response to reward can be tricky. What nearly right answers should be rewarded? Is $6 + 4 = 11$ less wrong than $6 + 4 = 13$, and thus deserving some modest praise?

The question of what behaviour to reward is even more difficult when it comes to more general achievements and social relationships. A continuing problem for those of us who try to help people change and thus lead happier lives is that a good but relatively complex idea, if taken up enthusiastically but uncritically by people seeking fame and fortune, becomes oversimplified and is applied lavishly without any careful thought. The Freudian psychoanalytic idea that sexual repression can lead in complex ways to neurotic misery, when taken up enthusiastically and uncritically by advocates of free love, became the source of fame and wealth for a few and the source of great misery for many, with an immense increase in the number of people suffering from sexually transmitted diseases. Similarly the idea that children should be praised for right responses was linked to the idea that adults should treat children with respect, and together they were turned into one oversimplified notion called 'self-esteem'. A person was deemed to have, or not to have, self-esteem, in the same way that a person might have, or not have, a car. Or a person was deemed to have high or low self-esteem, in the same way that a car might have a nearly full or nearly empty petrol tank. What followed was competition between therapists in a scramble to win fame and fortune out of 'self-esteem' and its spin-offs, like 'the inner child'. In the USA, where self-confidence is usually ranked as the highest virtue (being sure that God is actively engaged in supervising your welfare is a mark of supreme self-confidence), parents began praising their children as enthusiastically and uncritically as they used to beat them.

Fashions have their day. Now some psychologists in the USA are saying that too much praise lowers children's motivation and can turn them into 'praise junkies'. Nikki Sheehan, writing in the parents section of the *Guardian*, said:

Dr Ron Taffel, author of *Nurturing Good Children Now*, described watching children sledding in Central Park. 'Their parents were screaming, "Great job! Phenomenal sledding! That's the best I've ever seen,"' said Taffel in the *New York Times*. As he points out, the children were being praised for obeying the laws of gravity. 'It cheapens the praise, and children may become dependent.'

Lilian Katz, from the University of Illinois, claims that saying, 'good painting' will keep children at task while you are watching, but, once adult attention is withdrawn, many lose interest in the task. She believes that demotivation may occur as the child's focus moves from enjoyment of the task in hand to the search for more praise: the more we reward, the more likely the child is to lose intrinsic interest in whatever they were doing to get the reward ...

Research in the classroom by Mary Bud Rowe, at the University of Florida, found that students who were praised lavishly were more hesitant in their responses, less likely to persist with difficult tasks and did not share their ideas with fellow students. Creativity may also be affected as they take fewer risks with their work.

One explanation for the loss of confidence and motivation is that over-praised children feel under pressure to keep it up. 'What kids need is unconditional support,' avers Alfie Kohn, author of *Hooked on Praise*. 'That's not just different from praise – it's the opposite of praise. "Good job!" is conditional. It means we're offering attention and acknowledgement and approval for jumping through our hoops.' Kohn suggests instead that a simple, evaluation-free description of what the child is doing tells them that you have noticed, and lets them take pride in their actions.[30]

Unconditional support means that the parent is on the child's side even when the child get things wrong. Occasionally the parent does praise, but, in deciding when to do this, the parent discriminates between what the child is well capable of doing and what requires some special, new effort by the child. Just as a parent needs to separate the act from the actor in correcting the child ('That was a bad thing you did', instead of 'You are a bad child') so the parent needs to separate the act from the actor in praising the child. 'That was a clever thing you did' allows the child to conceive of cleverness as a choice of how to behave, say, cleverly or stupidly, whereas 'You are a clever child' could lead the child to make one of three unhelpful assumptions. The child could overestimate his innate ability and thus come to feel that he need not try to make an effort in anything he does; he could doubt that he is as clever as his parent says he is because he doubts the veracity of his parent's praise, and so come to feel that he is an impostor who will one day be found out; he could worry that he might not always be able to demonstrate his cleverness as his parent expects, and so come to feel that he will often disappoint his parent.

Life is never as simple as an examination with mutually exclusive right and wrong answers. Most of the things we do are both right and wrong. Everything we do has good and bad consequences. Parents need to think carefully about what they should praise in a child's behaviour and when and where they should offer praise.

What an adult chooses to praise in a child's behaviour reveals as much about the adult as it does about the child. Here is a fictional incident which has the hallmarks of being taken from real life. Anna is the protagonist in Sarah Harris's novel *Closure*, which is about a group of middle-class thirty-year-olds in London in the 1990s. Roo is Anna's long-time friend.

Anna agreed to drive over to Roo's house, although she was not in the mood for Roo's five-year-old daughter, Daisy, who, last week, had laughed at Anna's shoes.

'They're ridiculous,' she had said, as if trying out a new word for size. 'Mummy says you dress like you're a teenager and if you leave it much longer you won't have any children.' She had paused, as if to allow Anna to reflect on her words, before saying, with horrified indignation, 'Why is your hair all straggly?'

Roo had praised Daisy for the proper use of the word 'straggly'.[31]

Closure is not a deep psychological novel but Sarah Harris does show how her heroine Anna is still struggling with the questions of who she is and to what degree she should value and accept herself. A five-year-old child could threaten her with annihilation. She had tried to deny her fear by indulging herself in foolish, romantic fantasies about a man, a radio agony uncle, whom her commonsense should have told her was a poseur.

Sexual activity and sexual fantasies are an extremely popular defence against the fear of annihilation, but they are a defence which wounds us because in childhood our experiences relating to our sexuality gave us much that we had to deny.

The Perils of Sexuality

I have often felt envious of women younger than myself, simply because they were born, as I see it, into an easier age than I was. I envied the young girls of the sixties who did not have to struggle, and fail, as I did, with the inappropriate and sophisticated clothes of the fifties. I envied the choices which the sexual revolution of the sixties and seventies gave to young women. Yet, as I watch what happens to girls and women nowadays, even the educated women who handle work, children, husbands and lovers with such flair and competence, I can see that the same sacrifices are demanded of girls as have always been demanded if they are to join the group called women. Boys too are still sent down a path which leads to a truncated, inadequate manhood, the man denying so much of himself that he becomes much less than he might have been.

Life in the second half of the twentieth century offered people in the developed world many more opportunities for satisfaction, enjoyment and progress, yet from 1946 there was a steady rise in the number of young people killing themselves. In recent years the suicide rate for young men has continued to rise while that for young women has levelled out.

The problem is that boys are still being educated for a society which no longer exists. The Industrial Revolution of the nineteenth century created a society in which a young man who conformed to society's rules had a place. He could secure an apprenticeship in an industry and rise steadily through the ranks. If better educated, he could join a bank, go into trade, or join a profession. Whichever, he had a job for life and the respect of the society that had created a place for him. The end of the Second World War and the dropping of the atomic bombs in 1945 ended the old certainties. My generation was the last which could safely assume that it would have a job for life. As the old certainties crumbled, many young people struggled to find a place in society. Young women could still find a place as a mother, but where was the place for a young man brought up to be a real man in the old tradition? Being a coalminer, or a steelworker, or a deep-sea fisherman was a real man's job. Working in a call centre is not.

To maintain our meaning structure we need the people around us, not just friends and family but society generally, to confirm who we know ourselves to be. Lacking such confirmation, and lacking the self-confidence to confirm ourselves, we feel threatened with annihilation. If we believe that we cannot change ourselves or society, the threat of annihilation can become so great that we turn to the most desperate of defences. We destroy our body in order to survive as the person we know ourselves to be. Many young men have said to themselves, 'If I can't live as a man I'll die as a man.'

Meanwhile women were now required to enter the competitive workplace but still exhibit the old necessary attributes of femininity and beauty. This was a daunting task, and to relieve their anxiety many young women took up smoking, a slow form of suicide. Educated young women, holding responsible positions and competing successfully with men, smoke for the same reasons that schoolgirls of limited education, ability and opportunity smoke. Smoking is a way of denying the fear of annihilation. These young women believe that to be allowed to exist they must be attractive; that to be attractive they must be slim; that smoking dulled their appetite and made them look sophisticated and in control. Unfortunately, nicotine is more addictive than heroin, and thus many women who have lost their youthful slimness find themselves trapped in an addiction which, even if it does not kill them, wrinkles and yellows their skin. In our society the old, if they are noticed at all, are not regarded as attractive.[32]

Although the roles for men and women have changed, the methods of child-rearing have changed very little. Consequently, many girls and boys are still finding that the best way of surviving their childhoods is to become traditional women and men.

My garden borders on one side a row of large Victorian houses which have been turned into a hotel used by the council to house homeless families. My garden wall is topped by a trellis where jasmine and clematis grow riotously. A great profusion of growth developed on the hotel side of the trellis and, with this weight on one side, the strong autumn winds pushed the trellis away from the wall. I took my garden shears and a roll of plastic bags into the hotel garden and began cutting back the bundles of intertwining branches.

The garden was empty and all was quiet. Then there was the sound of a woman's voice raised in anger. She was yelling, 'Stay in or get out! Just close the bloody door.'

I could not hear anyone reply, but the woman screamed at this person, 'I don't care what you want. Get out.'

A door slammed. Round the corner of a hedge came a fair-haired boy of about six. Although the day was chilly he had no jacket on. He saw me and headed straight at me. 'What are you doing?' he demanded.

I described what I was doing. He eyed my shears enviously. 'Can I have a go?'

'Wait till I've cut some more, then you can do some cutting while I put all this stuff in these bags.'

He waited impatiently while telling me about some fantastic garden where he cut things down, and then grabbed the shears as soon as I offered them. He clipped a few pieces and for one moment I thought he might prove to be actually helpful, but his interest soon waned. He tried out bigger and bigger branches and, even though his attempts were unsuccessful, kept boasting to me how great he was at cutting things down. 'I'm the best at this,' he said. 'Aren't I the best cutter you've ever seen?'

Ordinarily I would not have agreed, but, knowing that he needed some help in recovering from the onslaught his mother had made on him, I said that he was doing an excellent job.

A little girl of about four was watching us from a balcony. She was the daughter of a couple I had taken to be Kosovan refugees. She never attempted to speak English but her mother would struggle with a few phrases when she and I exchanged pleasantries over the wall. The little girl came down the steps from her flat and stood watching the boy, who had now lost all interest in my task and was wandering around the garden trying to cut down different kinds of unlikely branches. The little girl's gaze inspired him to greater feats of strength, all unsuccessful, but which he passed off as brilliant.

As all women know, the duty of watching a male while he demonstrates his prowess in some masculine endeavour is a tedious one, and we soon find more interesting things to do. The little girl came over to see what I was doing. When I tore a fresh black bag off the roll and opened it, she reached out her hands, grasped the top of the bag, and held it up in exactly the position needed for me to put the greenery into it. It was precisely the kind of help I needed. Obviously she had done this many times before. Perhaps she had held the plastic bags open when her parents were hastily packing a few possessions as they tried to escape from what seemed like certain death.

The little girl helped me gather the last scraps of greenery and we both stood back to admire a job well done. By this time her mother had come out on to the balcony and was watching us. Now I come to the saddest part of the story. I was very sorry for the little boy, and I was sorry for the women who, one day, would bear the brunt of his anger against the mother who had so humiliated and threatened him, but now I tried to convey to the little girl's mother how clever and wise her daughter was. I wanted her to agree with me, but she did not. She believed that it was wrong to accept praise, and praise for her child was to be negated just as she would negate praise for herself. Moreover, she had to teach her daughter womanly modesty. 'No, no,' she said, and with her hands she pushed away my words. Secretly she might have been proud of her daughter, but neither I nor her daughter were allowed to know this. 'No, no,' she said, 'it was nothing.'

Girls and boys are brought up differently, but the message each gets is the same. As you are you are not acceptable. You must become what your parents want you to be.

Girl babies are not all that different from boy babies. True, there are anatomical differences, and some researchers say that boy babies are more active than girl babies, although other researchers say that adults see in babies what they expect to see, but all babies come into the world as themselves, curious about the world, and wanting to act upon it, but for little girls it is not to be. Neither is it for little boys.

Every society, every family, has very clear ideas about what is masculine and what is feminine. There is considerable overlap in these ideas throughout the world, even though practices vary. Orthodox Jews and Muslims regard women's hair as something dangerous which can snare and incite a man to sexual fervour, the expression of which he is not responsible for, while in most Christian countries virtuous women no longer have to keep their hair covered. (My mother was one of the last generation of women who felt it a necessary modesty to wear a hat. She and I battled over whether I should wear one. I prevailed, but only after considerable humiliation whereby I was told that it was impossible for me to be properly dressed because my head was so big that no hat would fit me.) However, the idea that women have to keep themselves covered and/or secluded because their sexuality is a danger to men is common to all cultures. Even in countries where women are allowed to leave their homes unescorted by a man, it is the custom that if a man who is attacking and raping women has not been caught by the police, it is the women who are instructed to stay at home, not the men.

The fear of women's sexuality is based not simply on the belief that the woman may passively, simply by her presence, arouse a man to passion, but on the belief that she may use her sexuality in an aggressive, assertive way. A feminine woman is not assertive. Little girls are taught this with great efficiency; they are taught and shown that assertive, aggressive women are not loved or even liked. Nowadays a woman can appear to be strong and assertive, but there is still an expectation that she will not go too far.

Going too far means being so strong, assertive and clever that the woman robs men of their rightful status. When, in 2000, the A-level results in the UK showed girls doing much better than boys, these girls were not allowed to enjoy their success publicly. The media told them a) that the A-level examinations were getting easier, b) that girls did easy subjects like languages while boys did the hard subjects of mathematics and physics, and c) that girls were causing the boys to do badly because their success humiliated the boys. David Blunkett, then the Secretary of State for Education, agreed with this last point. Blunkett showed himself to be a man of tradition. In discussions about corporal punishment he would say that he had slapped his sons when they were children, and he knew that they had suffered no harm.

Being assertive means standing up for oneself, and standing up for oneself is usually a response to a situation which leads one to be angry. If a woman feels that she cannot afford to be seen to be angry, she may try to give up feeling angry.

However, giving up anger is as sensible as giving up breathing, and just as easily done. Women may give up the social expression of anger, and they may even deny its existence to such an extent that they never consciously feel angry, but the unexpressed anger is there, and it takes its toll. The preponderance of depressed women has more to do with what they do with their anger than what their hormones do to them. Many men prefer to explain a woman's depression in terms of hormones rather than anger, for the second explanation involves a recognition that women have a right to anger, just as a man has. Of course, there are many women who feel, and express, a powerful anger, but, as they cannot direct this anger at its true source, the conditions of their lives, they express it against the only objects available to them, their children. Many of us come to adulthood bearing on our soul, if not our body, the scars of the blows our mother's anger dealt us, and many of us, unable to retaliate when we were children, take out our anger with our mother on our own children. Thus do the sins of the mother get visited on the children.

In dealing with her children in this way, a mother treats them simply as objects, something with which she can express her passion, like the door she slams or the plate she hurls at the wall. One way in which children can survive these painful, frightening, unjust events is to turn themselves into objects. 'Sticks and stones may break my bones but names will never hurt me', we might have chanted defiantly to ourselves in order to summon the courage to survive, encasing ourselves in a metal box, on the outside of which the wicked witch's blows and curses rained without effect.

Girls are not as efficient as boys in turning themselves into objects so as to protect themselves from a parent's anger. Since boys are encouraged from their earliest days to take part in rough-and-tumble games, while girls are discouraged from climbing, jumping and fighting, boys have more experience in how to develop techniques for avoiding or minimizing physical pain. Some years ago many Australian girls became weary of being expected to sit on the beach admiring the boys' prowess on their surfboards and instead acquired their own boards and learned to surf. Similarly in the UK many girls got weary of having to cheer the boys' football teams and instead got their own football kit and formed their own teams. However, research shows that, while girls on the whole are keen on sport in junior school, once they enter secondary school their interest wanes. They believe that girls who play sport are not seen to be feminine. This view reflects that of society. Women's sport receives only a fraction of the government finance and sponsorship deals that men's sport receives, while the media show scant interest in reporting it.

Since an essential part of femininity is being sensitive to what another person says and does, girls remain vulnerable to their mother's angry abuse and insults, while a boy who is learning how

119

to be a traditional man is learning to devalue such sensitivity. At around five or six a boy usually develops a peculiar functional deafness which renders him incapable of hearing his mother's voice except for certain phrases, ranging from 'Do you want an ice cream?', through 'How much money do you need?' to 'Here's my keys. You drive.' Many boys who receive a great deal of physical punishment learn to take great pride in the amount of punishment they can take without showing any pain or fear. Many boys not only make their closest relationships with machines, but they come to think of themselves as a machine – hard, logical, efficient, powerful, unaffected by emotional confusion and doubt.

The processes by which a girl learns to be feminine and a boy masculine require that each gives up vital parts of his or her self. Boys must give up those parts of themselves which might be labelled feminine, and girls those parts of themselves which might be labelled masculine. Having been forced to relinquish parts of ourselves which we valued (we begin our lives by valuing every part of us, and we no more want to give up part of our potentiality than we want to give up an arm or a leg), we envy those people who have what we have lost. Thus men envy women, and women envy men not their penises, those curious appendages which always make women laugh, but the power and freedom which men have. Many men, however, long for what they see as the security and gentleness of a woman's life, but are afraid to claim this as their own, clinging instead to women and hoping to share their good fortune. The woman may similarly be clinging to a man in the hope of sharing his power and freedom. On such misunderstandings are so many marriages made.

These are the ordinary patterns of life for most boys and girls, but for some children the extraordinary occurs.

On the whole, life for a child in the developed world is the best it has ever been in human history. Children are no longer required to work at a very early age, schooling is relatively humane, and most children are reasonably well fed, clothed and housed, and are not routinely beaten. However, the history of childhood is one of misery and tragedy. Adults have always regarded children as possessions which they could use and abuse.[33] This abuse was both physical and sexual. Physical abuse was seen as essential for the education of the child, while the sexual abuse was hidden by a conspiracy of silence.

When Freud embarked upon the unusual method of actually listening to his patients, he found that many of them recounted stories of sexual abuse in their childhood. He developed his theory that sexual abuse lay at the root of much neurosis, but later he revised his ideas and said that the prime cause of neurosis was the young child's sexual fantasies directed at its parents. So attached did Freud become to this theory that he not only ignored actual sexual abuse but also the physical abuse his patients suffered in childhood.[34] When Jeffrey Masson, who had access to the Freud archives, wrote about Freud's change of theory and described the reasons for this change as politic, not scientific,[35] all hell broke loose in the psychoanalytic community. Jeffrey Masson and all his works became anathema for all Freudian disciples. But what better way was there to protect abusive adults than to say that anyone who told of being abused in childhood was merely reporting childish fantasies?

A number of members of the women's liberation movement in the 1970s were very critical of psychoanalysis, saying that Freud had not understood women and consequently belittled them. Some women now felt strong enough to speak publicly about their experiences of sexual abuse in childhood, and a number of books were published in which the writers revealed their experiences and described the long-term effects of these experiences.[36] However, it was not until the late 1980s that the seriousness of sexual abuse began to be recognized by the mental health professions. Many mental health professionals were reluctant to change their theories about mental illness because to do so meant changing significant parts of their meaning structure, and this required courage. Other mental health professionals who were highly critical of the psychiatric system quickly saw how important it was to acknowledge the seriousness of the problem. Lucy Johnstone, in her excellent book *Users and Abusers of Psychiatry*, wrote:

Surveys indicate that about one in eight women are victims of sexual abuse in childhood, with the figure rising to as much as 50 per cent in women who use psychiatric services. Among the recognised long-term consequences are eating disorders, substance abuse, self-harm, anxiety and depression, as well as more general difficulties with relationships, self-esteem and sexuality. Women with a diagnosis of borderline personality disorder often report a history of child sexual abuse as well.[37]

Therapists had to find a new way of working with clients who had been sexually abused. Some therapists in the USA developed the practice of advising a client who had been sexually abused by a parent to confront the offending parent. Therapists can argue the pros and cons of this method and never come to a conclusion, but the immediate effect of this method was that the client's family was thrown into turmoil. Jack's story, which I shall recount later on, tells of a family who accepted the truth of one such revelation. Other families did not, and ferocious battles in and out of the law courts followed. In the USA, where every problem in life is turned into a medical condition, False Memory Syndrome was discovered. Whole forests of trees were sacrificed as arguments raged between those who said that all accusations of sexual abuse were completely true and those who said that all accusations of sexual abuse were completely false. Quiet voices of reason were lost in the clamour.

Eventually the dust settled and quiet voices of reason can now be heard saying that stories of sexual abuse in childhood may come from three sources:

1. Where the person has always clearly remembered the events of sexual abuse.

2. Where the person repressed memories of sexual abuse in childhood but certain events in later life triggered recall of these memories.

3. Where the person had not been sexually abused by the

parent but in other ways had been hurt by the parent, thus
leading them to harbour a deep hatred and a need for
revenge on the parent.

With sources two and three it is safe to assume that the person has
suffered such a threat to their sense of being a person that a desperate defence, that of massive repression or a passion for revenge,
is seen as necessary. When the person clearly remembers the abuse
it can be that as a child they found the abuse extremely threatening
and shameful. As an adult the person still feels besmirched, guilty
and worthless. Or it may be that the person as a child did not find
the actions of the abusive adult personally threatening. The child
may merely have been intrigued with what went on, in the way
that children can be intrigued by strange or bizarre scenes which
an adult might find unpleasant, even revolting. As an adult I do not
want to see any living thing killed, but as a child I would not miss
seeing my father dispatch a chicken with an axe and proceed to
pluck and eviscerate it. Or it may be that, for the child, the abuse
brings comfort and pleasure, as the story of Jack will show, but
this reaction can have the unhappy outcome that the child identifies
with the abuser and goes on to become an abuser himself. Often
the damage that is done to a child comes not from the actual abuse
but from the behaviour of adults when they discover the abuse.
The child may discover that adults see him as damaged or dirty, or
as being responsible for the abuse. I was not sexually abused as a
child, but, when I was fourteen, a man inveigled me into witnessing
him exposing himself. I was amazed and somewhat disconcerted,
because in our prudish household penises were certainly not on
view, but not for a moment did I consider telling my mother about
this event. I knew full well that she would blame me for what had
happened. I should not have been on my bicycle, on that road,
coming straight home from a swim on a hot Saturday afternoon. If
I were not such a bad child this event would not have happened.

These three possible sources of the accounts of sexual abuse
seem straightforward, but the stumbling block is a clear and agreed
definition of sexual abuse. Some of the fathers accused of sexual

abuse by their daughters insisted that they were lying and defined sexual abuse as sexual penetration. They would have agreed with Bill Clinton's assertion that he did not have sex with Monica Lewinsky. However, all women know that there is more to sex than penetration. For a girl, a father's lewd comments about her developing bosom or her sexual potential, or the father's refusal to recognize the boundaries a girl creates to maintain her privacy, can seem to the girl as threatening and dangerous as a full sexual onslaught. A girl can clearly distinguish the warm, loving, sexual gaze of a man who accepts her as the person she is from the hard, sexual, threatening gaze of a man who sees her as an available sexual object. To women the first gaze is delightful; the second terrifying.

It was this second kind of gaze on the part of the father of a fourteen-year-old girl which made me certain that there was something seriously amiss in the family of this girl, who had been brought halfway across Britain to be a research patient in the psychiatric unit where I was working. This happened thirty years ago, in the early 1970s, when psychiatrists were completely convinced that there were such things as mental illnesses, and that these illnesses had a physical cause. My psychiatrist colleagues were researching what was called the biological basis of mood change, and this young girl, Karen, was deemed to be a suitable patient for a physiological study.

At that early stage in my career I was prepared to accept the psychiatric theories of mania and depression, and so I took part in the research by being a proper psychologist who administered tests. Karen seemed to exhibit only one mood, that of terrified shyness, but she submitted patiently to my demands and to those of the psychiatrists who were measuring certain physiological changes.

Karen's degree of shyness suggested that she was frightened to do anything in case she made a mistake and displeased someone. This came out clearly in my tests, during which, if she made a response at all, it was guarded and extremely limited to the point of seeming childish, far below the level of intellect and maturity she had shown before she became ill. However, as the weeks went by, she gradually relaxed, though she remained shy, and this relaxation was reflected in her test responses, which became more able, various and creative.

There were a number of young patients in the unit, and I took it upon myself to try to make their time with us more interesting. The unit, an old house set in large grounds, was reasonably pleasant and comfortable, infinitely better than the traditional asylum where Karen had first been incarcerated, but there was little for patients to do except sit in the dayroom or carry out a few very simple tasks in occupational therapy. I helped to bring the young patients together so they could get to know one another, and occasionally we went for walks or into town to shop and to go to the cinema.

When I worked in Sydney as an educational psychologist, the only office I had was my car. I worked in schools and often visited a child's family at home. This I found invaluable, because it allowed me to discover aspects of the child's life which the family either kept secret or simply did not think to mention to me. Accordingly, though I had met Karen's parents when they came to visit her, I wanted to see the family home.

Karen's parents made me welcome. Her mother was quiet and undemonstrative, not given to hugging or kissing her daughter. Her father was much more lively and demonstrative. I felt that the parents had secrets, but it was not until one particular visit, when I was getting into the father's van while he stood holding the door, that I had a clue as to what these secrets might be. I glanced up and saw him looking at me. He did not look away. He wanted me to see him looking at me with a searing sexual gaze that was both a threat and an invitation. Now I knew that the family secrets were, in part at least, sexual.

My psychiatrist colleagues did not think that my concerns about the family were in any way significant. Months passed. Karen started at a school close to the unit. She studied successfully and fitted into the school routine. Her physiological tests showed nothing of significance and so, eventually, she went home.

Karen and I kept in touch by cards and letters. Thirty years went by. Every Christmas she sent me a card and a letter with a summary of her year's events. She left school, got a job, met and married a fine man. She continued working and had children who did well academically. We met socially sometimes when I was in her part of the UK, but it was not until after her father died that she phoned me and asked whether she could talk to me. Over the years she had suffered periods of depression, but she and her husband had learned to recognize the danger signs and deal with it effectively. Now, however, what was happening was different.

Karen remembered remarkably little of her childhood, and she did not speculate about the significance of what she did remember. She had not linked one memory of her father forcing her to eat baked beans with the fact that her choice of diet was extremely limited and not based on any theory of nutrition. There was a wide range of ordinary foods she could not bring herself to eat, just as she could not possibly eat baked beans.

Karen had a similar problem with sex. She loved her husband and she wanted to respond fully to him, but, while she could approach him with passion, at the critical moment she would pull back, frightened and not knowing why she was afraid. It seemed that from early childhood she had been operating under four internalized injunctions: Don't remember, don't ask questions, be afraid, know that you can never be good enough.

Karen had remained close to her parents and, when her father became seriously ill, she shared her mother's anxiety. However, very shortly after her father died her mother spoke of him being a wonderful man who had devoted himself to his family. Karen suddenly felt very angry. This was not like her. She did not get angry with people. Whenever something went wrong she always blamed herself. She should have tried harder, been a better person. However, now not only was she angry, she was *not* blaming herself for getting angry.

Karen had always found it difficult to talk about herself, so when she came to see me after her father's death she spoke haltingly, sidling up to something rather than confronting it head on. Thus we sidled up to the question of what her father had or had not done when she was a child and a teenager. I knew that this could not be a conversation between client and therapist because I was part of Karen's past, just as her father had been. Our conversation had to be like that of two family members who were trying to remember and understand the past. So I told Karen what I remembered of my visit to her family, and how her father had looked at me. She smiled sadly and shook her head. 'That's what he did to all my girlfriends. I didn't like to invite them home.'

I did not feel it was necessary for Karen to dig in her memory for particular events and lay them out like the contents of a trunk that had stood unopened for many years. If she had had no one to talk to she and I might have done that, but she and her husband did talk to one another. They knew each other very well.

How very different Karen's life would have been had the first doctor who saw her said to himself, 'I wonder what's going on in this child's home that makes her so frightened she can hardly move?' Nowadays most doctors would ask themselves this question, and most child psychiatrists would know that to understand why a child behaves as he does he must be looked at in the context of the family. Many, though not all, child psychiatrists and clinical psychologists know the truth of the advice I was given back in 1961. It was: 'The presenting problem is never the real problem.' Family therapists are no doubt well aware that the real problem has something to do with the family member who refuses to attend discussions with the therapist.

Karen's main interest seemed to be to fill in the gaps in her family story. Until she knew the full story she would feel incomplete and thus inadequate. I gave her some of my papers from all those years ago, and she spoke to several family members whom she felt could bear the burden of uncovering family secrets. She would not speak about these matters to her mother because she did not feel that her mother, now old, could bear to be forced to remember the past.

Karen's principal problem, as I saw it, was that her propensity to blame herself for every disaster turned the natural sadness she felt into depression. Otherwise she managed her life very well. Had she been having greater and more diverse difficulties I would have recommended that she read Carolyn Ainscough and Kay Toon's book *Breaking Free: Help for Survivors of Child Sexual Abuse*,[38] and perhaps join a self-help group of adult survivors. This kind of group has enabled many men and women to confront the demons from their past and defeat them. Alas, such groups are sparse, and few are a regular part of mental healthcare.

For all the people who have suffered sexual abuse in childhood to receive appropriate help, governments would have to recognize and deal with the incidence of abuse not just in families but in certain institutions. A great deal of fuss is made about strangers who prey upon children. When the *News of the World* printed the photographs of a number of convicted paedophiles now living in the community, there were noisy demonstrations and the homes of suspected paedophiles were attacked. What was ignored in all this was that the majority of children who suffer abuse do so at the hands of a parent or someone they know and trust. It is far worse to be abused by someone you know and trust than by a stranger. Recovery from abuse by a stranger can be relatively straightforward, though not easy, by seeing it as a chance event for which you are not responsible and do not deserve, and the offender as being completely in the wrong and meriting punishment. However, when the offender is someone in whom you have placed your trust, someone whom you love and you hope loves you, recovery is not simple. We all long for a parent who loves us and looks after us, and when our parent falls far short of the mark the longing we have for the parent they might have been can tie us to the parent who harms us. Our longing for the perfect parent can prevent us from seeing the parent who harms us as a mere human-sized human being. Instead we see this parent as looming over us, wielding massive parental power which we dare not ignore or disobey.

Powerful though a parent may seem to be, how much more powerful is a man who has access to God's power. The Catholic Church demands from its clergy and its flock obedience and silence. Any institution which operates on principles of obedience and silence creates the conditions for the abuse of power. Catholic children were, and sometimes still are, fiercely and brutally beaten.

When I was a child in Australia the Christian Brothers' schools for boys were notorious for the priests' brutality against the pupils. Martin McGuinness, now Minister for Education in Northern Ireland, and Conor McPherson, the brilliant young Irish playwright, have spoken of the beatings they received at Catholic schools. In recent years some Catholics have broken the order of silence and have spoken, not just of physical abuse, but of sexual abuse at the hands of priests. What started as a trickle of accounts of sexual abuse by the clergy turned into a torrent in the USA, the Netherlands, the UK, Australia and Ireland. These accounts showed how the clergy used their priestly power to coerce and silence their victims. An eleven-year-old girl told how a priest would follow an act of abuse by saying: 'This is our *secret* and you mustn't tell anybody. You are very special Sarah, very *special* indeed. Secrets can never be *broken*. However, if you do tell anyone, then *God* will know what you have done. Because I am a *priest*, God will inform me of your deed, and as a consequence you will need to be punished. I want you to *remember*, Sarah, if God tells me *you* have been naughty, I will kill you. Do you understand? I will *kill* you.'[39]

The Catholic Church was extremely slow to acknowledge that harm had been done by priests to those in their care. Following legal action by some victims, the Church has made some modest remunerations, and some dioceses have created the post of child protection officer, but the ethos of the institution has not changed. How can it when a cardinal, in the process of inauguration, 'takes a vow of secrecy to the Pope which states: ''I promise to keep secret anything confided in me in confidence that if revealed will cause scandal or harm to the Roman Catholic Church.'' '[40]

When Monsignor James Joyce was child protection officer for the Catholic diocese of Portsmouth from 1994 to 1999, he met victims of abuse and their families. He wrote, 'Most were in shock, stunned not only by what had happened and its effect on them, but also by the silence and denial by the Church. Many victims of abuse had their lives destroyed. They found relationships with their families and friends distorted, their sexuality confused and their whole being affected. They couldn't understand why it had happened to them.'[41]

Monsignor Joyce found that the system whereby child protection officers were priests or deacons who, as the Church requires, had made a vow of obedience to their bishop rendered them powerless. A priest or deacon cannot tell a bishop what to do. He wrote, 'The climate in the Church is still one of denying abuse and minimising its effect, because to accept it is to open up issues about power. Parishes and dioceses can still be run on the whim of a priest or a bishop, and there is no appeal or grievance procedure in the law of the Church.'[42]

Media stories of abusive priests have been matched by stories about workers in care homes for children who physically and sexually abused the children in their care, and by stories of international paedophile rings whose members entrap, abuse and even murder children for their own amusement and for the creation of pornography which is now a multibillion-dollar industry. Some care home assistants and some paedophiles have been charged, and some of these have been convicted for their crimes. Terrible though all these stories are, however, they do not arouse the kind of public passion that forces governments to take some major action to deal with the perpetrators, protect children and compensate those who have suffered. Nick Davies, whose investigations into care home abuse and the activities of paedophiles have won awards, noted that 'The political reality is that the Home Office continues to steer police resources into dealing with reported crime. In its major 1996 inquiry, Childhood Matters, the NSPCC concluded: "The legal system, designed to provide justice and redress for the victims of abuse, is failing to do so consistently." '[43]

Nick Davies wrote about the work of Rob Jones, who, as a young detective sergeant, moved to Avon and Somerset's Child Protection Team, where he developed a way of working which resulted in the successful prosecution of many of the members of a paedophile ring who preyed on teenage boys. In 2000, wrote Nick Davies, 'Rob Jones devised his own package of proactive child protection to safeguard children from abuse, particularly in the world of sport. He called it Child Safe. His chief constable supported him. It was the only such scheme in the country and he set out to spread it to other forces and recruited footballing stars, including Gary Lineker and Kevin Keegan, to help him. Some forces have adopted it. Others are not so keen. They say it's women's work.'[44]

'Women's work' is something such men belittle and scorn because what men call women's work involves caring for others. Caring for others calls for the tender emotions which many men in the course of their upbringing are forced to learn to deny. For the majority of women feelings of affection, kindness, sympathy and tenderness are linked to sexual feelings, but when men deny these feelings and their link to sexual feelings, sex becomes an activity no different from driving a fast car or winning a game of golf. Sexual feeling becomes no more than the sensation of excitement and power that can confirm the man's sense of existing as a person. To get this feeling he acts upon someone's body, or on his own, and uses it as an object, in the same way he uses a car or a golf club. Just what a man does with a sexual object is often bizarre – it is men, rarely women, who develop fetishes and perversions – and often inhuman – it is men, extremely rarely women, who commit rape.

If this attitude towards sex is the result of what is an ordinary upbringing for a boy, what happens to a boy who experiences not just the usual indoctrination about maleness but also the experience of being treated as a sexual object?

Jack and his wife Joy agreed to my recording his story, in the hope that it might be of use to other people in a similar predicament. All that Jack asked was that I should not give the name of the orphanage he lived in as a child. 'Things are different now,' he said, 'or at least I hope they are.'

We had met twelve years previously when their son Mark had been in trouble at school. He was a very bright lad, but he stayed away from school a lot, and when he was there he would not work. His headmaster wanted to expel him, but before this could be done the Education Department needed a psychologist's advice. Mark and his parents came to see me, and eventually Mark went to a boarding school. His parents came a few more times to discuss their marriage. It had become clear that much of Mark's difficult behaviour stemmed from the strain in their relationship.

Joy found it hard to criticize Jack because she knew he was a devoted, caring father. She wanted to make their relationship better and wanted to talk to me about it. Jack was not so keen, but he came back with her for several meetings. After a while they stopped coming, saying that things were better, and I lost touch with them. Over the years I often wondered what had happened to Mark. I was relieved, as we sat down in my office, when Joy said, 'Mark said that we ought to get in touch with you.' She went on, 'It's very good of you to see us, and at such short notice too.' She told me that Mark was married with two children and had his own business. Alice, their eldest, was married, their second daughter, Jenny, was working in Edinburgh, Ray was a research scientist, and Louise, the youngest, was at university.

Joy paused and looked at Jack. He looked dreadfully upset. He said, 'I've been very stupid. It's about the children . . . when they were young . . . what I did to them. I . . . interfered . . . with them . . . not all of them. I didn't think – '

His voice broke. Joy, gently, took over, and went on talking, taking responsibility for telling me what had happened. She spoke very simply and directly, explaining carefully and laying no blame, trying to be fair to everyone concerned. She described how their eldest daughter, Alice, had three children and lived a hundred miles away. Joy had noticed how infrequently Alice visited them, and how when they visited Alice the atmosphere was very strained. She knew that Alice and her husband were having difficulties and that Alice was consulting a counsellor about this. One day Alice phoned to say that she would be calling to see them. She made a special point of arranging to arrive at a time when Jack would be home from work. When she came she asked both of them to sit down so that she could tell them something very important. Joy thought Alice was going to tell them she had left her husband, and was puzzled when Alice said that she was going to leave the problem with them.

Then she told Joy, and reminded her father, how when she was twelve her father had interfered with her sexually. He had asked her to undress for him and he had fondled her breasts. She had been very frightened by this. Over the years she had tried to forget what had happened to her. She had begun to wonder whether it had really happened, especially when at college she had confided in a friend, only to be told that Freud had said that girls often had these kinds of fantasies about their fathers. She was sure that this was not a fantasy. When her marriage ran into difficulties she went to a counsellor, and her counsellor had helped her see how what her father had done to her had undermined her trust in men and so had affected her relationship with her husband.

She had asked Mark whether anything had happened to him. Mark had said that it had, and that it had gone on for a long time. She wrote to Jenny about it, but not to Louise. Alice had always been very close to her little sister, and she was sure that nothing had happened to Louise. Her counsellor had advised her that the problem was not hers but her parents', and that the only way she could rid herself of its effects was to return it to her parents. This she was doing, and, having done so, she left.

Joy did not attempt to describe the pain and confusion Alice left behind. Coming to see me was her way of trying to sort out her confusion. As to most introverts, it was important to her to see things clearly, no matter how painful they might be. She had always been like that. I found in the notes I had made twelve years earlier that I had written of Joy: 'She would puzzle over the problems our discussions raised, remember them to the next session, and try to find a solution.' I had noted, 'She said that she had a constant, nagging anxiety and a sense of imminent disaster from some unknown quarter.' I had also noted Jack's 'reluctance to enquire deeply into personal matters'.

Joy said she could not understand how it was that she had never noticed anything. Alice and Jack were always getting angry with one another, but Alice had always been an angry child, ever since she was little. Joy had spoken to Mark, and he had told her how Jack had engaged him in sexual acts for quite some while, stopping only when he thought there was a danger that she would find out. Jack defended himself. 'It was just mutual masturbation, nothing else. Just like boys playing together.'

Joy said, 'What about Ray? He told me there were times with him too.'

Jack shook his head. 'I can't remember.'

Joy said to me, 'This is what's so terrible, he can't remember. If he doesn't remember what he did, what other things has he forgotten? Will he do it again? Can we trust him? You can see why Mark and Alice worry he might with our grandchildren.'

Jack found it hard to speak. 'I wouldn't, I couldn't. I know Mark and Alice don't trust me. But I wouldn't, not with my grand-children.'

Joy pressed him, reminding him of what he had done to Mark.

Jack said, 'It started when Mark asked me about sex. I never thought much about it. Just two males together. At the orphanage, everyone did it.'

Jack went on to tell me about his life in the orphanage. After his father died his mother felt that she could not cope with him, so, at just eight years old, he was sent to a home for boys. There, he said, every new boy suffered 'virtual rape from the older boys and from the masters. Everybody was involved in it. You learned not to complain because there was no one you could complain to. When you got older you did it to the younger boys. It went on in all the boys' homes. When I got older I was sent to other homes we were shifted around a lot and I met up with boys from other homes and they did it.'

Jack said that he had never thought about his time in the orphanage at all. 'I can't remember much about that time. I don't remember anything before I was eight. I know my mother used to have lodgers. One of them used to take me out to the woods. I can remember he used to buy me ice cream. Perhaps something happened then. I don't remember.' He spoke of the terrible guilt he felt now. Before, 'I didn't think about it. I thought the children would have forgotten it.'

Joy said, 'When Alice was a child I told her not to let anyone do anything to her that she didn't want and to tell me, even if it was someone close, like an uncle. Alice reminded me of this. She said, "I couldn't tell you, Mummy, because there was someone, and you were always telling us what a good father we had."'

Joy told me how, over the past ten years, Jack had suffered several sudden, violent illnesses, sometimes necessitating him being admitted to hospital. The doctors had explained these in terms of a virus, but now she wondered whether the illnesses were connected with all this. Now these things were being discussed, the illnesses had stopped.

Some weeks later, when we were arranging the next appointment, she said that in the three weeks between this meeting and the last she had thought she might go mad. All the structures she had built to form the world she lived in had now been revealed as fictions which bore little relation to reality, and she was no longer sure of what reality was. In those weeks she had felt that she had to hold all her thoughts very carefully in her mind, otherwise everything would fall apart. Jack threatened every part of her being. She was trying to hold it all together by continuing to be the good, patient, understanding, calm, unaggressive person she had always been, and by maintaining her faith that there was something beyond this life which would offer reparation for her suffering. However, Jack threatened even this. He would shrug his shoulders and say flatly, 'This is all there is and when you're gone, you're gone.'

When we met three weeks later, Jack agreed that he needed people. 'I don't like being on my own,' he said. He didn't want to talk about what had happened. 'What's happened has happened,' he said, 'and I can't change it. I'm sorry it happened, but I can't do anything about it. If Joy could accept that we could get on with thinking about the future. That's what's important, not the past.'

Joy could not do that. She needed to think about what had happened, to reinterpret much of what she remembered of the past years, and to understand, no matter how painful that process of understanding was. 'Jack just accepts things without thinking about them,' she said. 'He just takes what someone says or what he reads in the paper without working something out for himself.'

The way Joy would sit quietly, thinking, worried Jack very much. He felt that she had withdrawn from him and that he was in danger. He could not put this feeling into words. Instead he thought about leaving himself. He said, 'Would it be best if I left? She'd be better on her own, without me.'

I said, 'We can't work out what's best to do until we understand what happened and why it happened.'

So Jack reluctantly agreed to talk some more about his past. He described how he had been conscripted into the air force and posted to the Far East where, in the absence of women, many of the men found sexual relief with one another. 'That's all it was, just relief,' he explained.

I asked whether he considered himself to be a homosexual – that is, having loving relationships with men as the most important relationships of his life.

'Oh, no,' he said, 'I wouldn't want to live with a man. I like women.'

His last sexual experience with another man had been when he came out of the air force and was living in Wales. He had later moved to the Midlands, where he had met Joy. None of these sexual encounters had been with children.

Joy said, 'Jack's always seen sex as something very surface. When the children were little and he was working very hard, I wouldn't see him until late and we'd no sooner get in the bedroom than he'd want to. I couldn't get him to understand I wasn't like that. I needed time to be with him.' It was no good if Joy offered simply to oblige him. He wanted every sexual encounter to be passionate and grand, in which he possessed Joy totally. Instant, total gratification.

We went on to talk about their children. Jack was very proud of them. All of them, except Mark, had excelled academically, and Mark was now being successful in his own business. 'I couldn't ever believe I could have such bright kids,' said Jack. 'Right from the beginning they seemed older than me.'

What did he mean, they'd always seemed older than him?

Gradually we put together an answer to this question. When the children were tiny he did not see them very much as he was working so hard, but once they started at school he became aware of how bright they were and how much they knew. He could not discipline them, but only, in Joy's words, 'quarrel with them'. He felt inferior to them, and frightened of them. There was only one area of experience where he felt his knowledge was superior to theirs – sex – and so he thought he could teach them about this. All the time he could not see anything wrong in doing this. Of course, sometimes we teach children something because we feel that it is important that they know it, and other times we teach them something so we can demonstrate our superiority over them. Sometimes we need to demonstrate our superiority because we envy them.

Joy had brought along letters from her daughters Jenny and Alice. Jenny was angry with Alice for speaking about the subject to Joy, causing Joy hurt. Jenny said she had spent years trying to forget 'the experience' and did not want to discuss the matter now. Jenny's letter implied that something very unpleasant had happened. Jack said he could remember very little, but he insisted that whatever had happened was nothing more than when he was 'fooling around with her', playing the childish games Jenny had always enjoyed. He admitted he had touched her breasts. 'I didn't expose myself or ask her to touch me,' he said. 'It was her body I wanted to see.' He was distraught with remorse. 'I didn't realize how much I had hurt her. I wouldn't want to hurt her ever. I wish I could tell her how sorry I am and ask her to forgive me.'

Jenny had always been extremely good as a child. Alice had been argumentative, and she and Jack had often clashed, but Jenny never argued with him. Jack was puzzled as to how Jenny could be so upset now about what had happened; as a teenager she had always been very friendly to him. She had won a scholarship to a boarding school of great repute, and he had often driven her to and from the school, several hundreds of miles away. Moreover, at home she would often go from bathroom to bedroom quite scantily clad. Why would she do this? I guessed that Jenny throughout her teens was trying to prove to herself that these painful events of her childhood had never happened or, if they had, that they had no untoward significance.

As Jenny was coming for Christmas I suggested that Jack write her a letter, saying what he had just told me he wanted to say to her. We spent some time discussing this proposed letter. Jack was worried that if he did what I suggested giving Jenny the letter soon after she arrived home this might spoil Christmas, and the family's ritual celebrations of Christmas were very important to Jenny (and to Jack). 'She likes everything to be exactly the same every year,' he said. 'I'll give it to her just before she leaves.'

'That won't give her time to discuss it with us if she wants to,' said Joy. She went on, 'We have to show the children that we are able to bear all this, because if we can't bear it, then they'll find it hard to bear what they have to bear.'

When they came back to see me on New Year's Eve they agreed that they had had a good Christmas. Jenny, Louise and Ray had come home, and there had been a family celebration. Jack had written the letter to Jenny, saying how sorry he was and asking for her forgiveness. He had put the letter on her bedside table on Boxing Day morning. Later Joy had looked in and seen that the letter had disappeared. Jenny did not mention it for the rest of her stay. 'Her manner didn't change at all,' said Jack. 'She was just like she's always been, all the time she was with us. Perhaps she'll write to me when she gets back home.'

Mark and Alice, spending Christmas with their own families, had phoned over the holiday. 'They didn't want to talk to me,' said Jack. 'This is my punishment.'

Joy told me how she and Ray had talked together about the sexual approaches Jack had made to his son, which Jack did not remember. They had not included Jack in this conversation because they both wanted to spare his feelings. Now, in her gentle, precise way, she told me what Ray had told her. Jack sat with his head down.

Ray described three events. The first was a simple enquiry from Jack as to whether Ray got erections. Ray had not sensed there was anything wrong with this until Jack, leaving Ray's bedroom, had said, 'Don't tell your mother.' The next time Ray and Jack were playing, just fooling around, Jack put his hand down Ray's trousers and touched his penis. Ray pulled himself away. The third occasion was no more than a look which Ray, undressed, found hard to distinguish from the close looks which parents give to children when inspecting for unwashed faces and adolescent pimples.

Jack still could not remember these events. 'Jack doesn't bother to sort things out,' said Joy. 'Something happens and he just covers it up with something else. It's like our attic. When we moved to that house he just piled things up there, just a higgledy-piggledy mess. That attic always reminded me of Jack's mind. I hated to go up there. But now I've got everything in it sorted out. We put up some shelves and changed the glass in the window to let in more light.' She smiled. 'Now we're getting his mind sorted out getting things clear and in order.'

The reason that the attic, like all the cupboards and shelves in their house, was crammed full of things was because Jack couldn't bear to throw things away.

'We weren't allowed any possessions at the orphanage. If you had something you had to carry it with you to keep it or it disappeared. When I went into the orphanage it was just after Christmas and I had all my Christmas presents. They soon disappeared. I had a billiard table and cue. The cue was the first to go. One of the masters took it and used it as a cane. He often belted me with it. I soon learned how you had to get things. You were always on the lookout for something you could exchange for something else. But it always had to be something you could carry with you. It wasn't until you were a work boy that you had a locker, just a small one, about eighteen inches square, and you were allowed to buy a lock to put on it. But even then someone would break the lock and take your things.'

Jack talked about the beatings and indiscriminate cruelty in the orphanage. The matron, he said, wore a large ring, and as she walked past a boy she would slap him across the head, often cutting his face with the ring. Even today Jack cannot bear to have his head touched.

'We would get belted for anything and nothing,' he said. 'Every fortnight we had boot inspection. We had to stand holding our boots upside down. The chap who mended our boots would allow us to lose just one stud from the sole. For every other stud missing you'd get a belting. We'd do anything to get studs for our boots. If you found one you treasured it like gold. Sometimes you'd manage to get hold of a new one and then you'd have to scratch it for ages to make it worn like the other ones. If he thought you'd put a new one in, well, you'd had it.'

The boys were beaten and whipped for all kinds of offences and often for nothing at all. 'I wet the bed every night from the time I went into the orphanage until the time I left. There was a group of us that did this, and we were always punished, every time. We'd be beaten, or wrapped up tight in the wet sheets and made to stand out in the cold. All the other boys knew what you'd done. We always had to wash our own sheets. The staff never did anything to help us.' There was no one to whom the boys could turn for help. 'No one would have believed us,' he said, 'and my mother, even if she had believed me, which she wouldn't, wouldn't have done anything anyway.'

As Jack described at length the cruelties that had been perpetrated on these helpless boys, he smiled and occasionally laughed. I asked him why he did so and he said, 'Well, it's a long time ago , and there's nothing I can do about it.'

I asked him whether he had beaten his own children. 'Nothing like the way I was beaten,' he said. 'Only when they needed it.' 'I'd stop him,' said Joy. 'I can't bear violence. It's so ugly.' 'Alice was the main one,' said Jack. 'She used to wind me up. I wouldn't belt her just slap her around the face.'

Several times in this conversation Jack remarked with some awe how he was remembering things he had never thought of before, 'not just general things, but specific things. I can remember just what happened and what I felt.' He went on, 'You know, when I remember being with someone then, I remember it as being pleasant. It was warm. You were accepted, even though it was only for a night. The masters, well, they lived two lives. If one of them said

140

to you "Come to my room at seven o'clock tonight" you knew what it was for. You weren't going to get belted. They were really nice to you then. They gave you sweets and cakes, things you hardly ever got. Then next morning if you stepped out of line they'd belt you. If a master chose you, well, it was like being taken out of the pond. We were just like fish in a pond. If one master chose you, then the other masters didn't. They each had their own group of boys. Your master might keep you for a long time, or he might get sick of you and then you'd get thrown back in the pond.'

Jack stressed that the good part was that 'you were always paired off with someone. There wasn't much group sex. Sometimes the boys in the dormitory would have, for want of a better word, a wanking party to see who could come first, and there was one master, a slimy creep, who used to get several boys in his room and make them do it while he watched, but most times, even with the boys in the dorm, even if it was only once, it was just the two of you. It made you feel special.'

Jack was very special for over a year. One master, known as the Major, singled him out. In his room Jack learned more than sex. The Major played records and introduced Jack to classical music. Music became Jack's great love. The Major would also take Jack on excursions out of the school. 'He would take me to Salvation Army meetings. Sometimes they would have concerts, really good music. And they always made a big fuss of me. They'd stuff me full of cakes and buns and give me a big bag of food to take back for my friends. I was really happy there. It was great, getting out and meeting people.'

Then, suddenly, the Major left. 'The staff were moved around the different homes a lot,' he said, 'but we usually had a few weeks' warning. With the Major, he just left in twenty-four hours. I was thrown back in the pond and I was just another boy there for, well, over a year.'

I asked Jack whether the other boys were envious when one boy was singled out by a master. 'No, they just took it for granted. Everyone did it. If you woke in the morning and saw a boy's bed empty you knew he was with so-and-so. And the boys who went with masters, they brought back sweets and things, for the other boys. If they didn't hand them out they had them taken off them.' Jack had felt envious of anyone who had something that he did not have.

Despite their continual financial difficulties, Jack and Joy had always found the money to give their children the things they needed to pursue their interests. If one was interested in music, then musical instruments were bought. If another was interested in tennis, then tennis rackets and tennis lessons were bought. Jack was proud of his children's achievements and of his hard-won ability to give them what they needed, but underneath that there must have lurked a small boy's envy of the other kids' possessions.

The conversation turned to television, and Joy remarked that Jack could not stand any programme that revealed emotions. When I enquired, 'What emotions?' it became clear that Jack could not tolerate watching the expression of realistically tender feelings. He enjoyed the violence of westerns and war films ('Well, it's only on the screen, isn't it?') but the expression of real, tender, personal feelings, with all the concomitant yearning and pain, was something he could not bear to witness.

Joy had suggested that Jack might like to come to see me on his own, and I was surprised when he agreed to do this. He spoke again of his sexual experiences at the orphanage. He described how he had been there only a few hours when a boy came to him and said he was wanted. He was taken down to the basement where the boiler was, and there he found a group of the older boys.

'They grabbed me, spread me on the table, and each of them raped me. If I struggled they hit me. They were big boys, fully developed, big enough for it [anal rape] to be very painful.'

A day or so later he was taken again, this time by just two boys. 'It wasn't as bad as the first time. I got used to it.' With most of the masters 'it was just down with the trousers and, bang, in. All you got out of it was a sore bottom.'

He told me how one master would beat boys on the bottom with a cane until their flesh was red and sore. Then he would smooth cream over the boy's buttocks very gently. Then, 'bang, in. It was pain, pleasure, pain. Funny thing, I really like smoothing cream on. I like smoothing cream over Joy's back.' He added, 'I was a skinny little kid, and I always was the passive partner, but after, when I got older, I did it to the younger kids. I wonder now what happened to them.'

Jack spoke fondly of the Major. He said, 'The Major had a great influence on me. With him, well, sometimes we just sat in front of the fire and made toast – you know, bread on toasting forks – and listened to music. Other times, well, he wasn't in a hurry. There'd be mutual masturbation, and after, well. I know I was the passive partner, but I'd got something out of it.' He described how the Major would dress up in a woman's suspender belt and stockings and would dress Jack as a schoolgirl. He said, 'I got something out of it being loved and wanted, if only for one thing.'

Jack spoke of 'men's sex and women's sex'. Men's sex, as he wanted it, was chiefly arousal and excitement, not orgasm. 'I don't put much importance on that,' he said. If, when they were making love, Joy had an orgasm first, Jack would lose interest immediately. Making love to Joy was very important to him, but so was masturbation. He also valued his collection of pornography. Reading pornography was, he said, very stimulating. He found it immensely pleasurable to spend an afternoon in his bedroom, where he would dress up, as the Major had done, in suspender belt and stockings and read what he called 'my books', his collection of pornography.

Joy accepted these activities, although she refused to watch his blue films and hated to look at his pornography. This was part of his life which was separate from her, and, as she explained to me later, when she first discovered what Jack did she did not know any other men and supposed that all men were like that. She now knew that they were not. Mark's abhorrence of Jack's collection of books made that quite clear, but she thought that she should accept this quirk of Jack's character because she loved him. 'I'm very good at loving,' she said.

Jack defended his activities to me. 'Why should I stop doing it? I'm not hurting anyone.'

When, as children, we suffer some severe trauma and discover that the world is not at all as we believed it to be, we struggle to master our experience – that is, to create a meaning for it which can fit without much difficulty into our meaning structure. However, our experience of life is so limited that we do not have many alternative meanings from which to choose our interpretation. We experiment with elements of the traumatic experience itself, perhaps believing that there is some hidden meaning which we can discover if we keep repeating in some form the experience itself. Jack was a child and therefore could respond only with the eroticism of a child. As the psychoanalyst Ferenczi said, 'The erotic life of the child remains at the level of foreplay, or knows satisfaction only in the sense of ''satiety'' but not the feeling of annihilation that accompanies orgasm.'[45] Jack's experience of the erotic remained that of a child. Moreover, as a child he had dealt with his fear of the Major by identifying with him. Anna Freud called this process 'identification with aggressor', but the old saying 'If you can't beat them, join them' would do just as well.

Joy spent a week helping Alice when one of her children was ill. It had been a painful, difficult time for both women. They knew that they should talk, but neither wanted to distress the other. Risking Alice's pain and anger, Joy told her about the discussions she and Jack had had with me and how she now understood him much better. She said to me, 'Isn't it strange, you can live with a man for thirty-five years and not know him.'

Joy talked to Alice about Alice's childhood when, as the eldest, Alice had to endure the birth of five siblings. One of these babies had lived only four days, and Jack had ordered Joy, 'You're not to cry.' Forbidden to talk about her grief, for talking brought on tears, Joy withdrew into a depression. She struggled on with performing her duties as wife and mother but, as she told me, 'I can't remember Alice then. She was the schoolgirl in the family. It's no wonder she was argumentative and demanding.'

Alice, as she told her mother later, did not want her to talk about those times. 'I thought you were going to criticize me and tell me what a great trouble I was to you.' Joy was not placing the blame on Alice. She was reviewing what she herself had done and was feeling the pain that loving parents feel when they realize that what they have done to their children, often with the best of intentions, has hurt and harmed them.

Alice told Joy of her encounters with Jack when she was just blossoming into womanhood. 'He said that he wanted to undress me. This made me feel that I was supposed tō respond, like the ball was in my court. I had to put up a barrier, but at the same time I felt that because I had refused him he rejected me. I still feel he's rejecting me.' Joy hastened to reassure her that Jack had not rejected her and that he loved her very much. Alice said, 'I wish he'd write and tell me that.'

Jack felt very discomfited at the prospect of writing another letter, but his face lit up with happiness as he told me how, when he had phoned Joy recently, Alice had answered the phone, and instead of immediately calling Joy had asked him how he was. He was delighted too that, as Jenny was leaving after Christmas, she had invited them to visit her.

His face was again alight with pleasure as Joy told me about her visit to Mark and his family, and about Mark's little daughter. Jack longed to see his granddaughter, but, as he told me with great sadness, 'Mark won't talk to me.' A few weeks later Jack told me that he had written a second letter, this time to Alice. Mark, too, had phoned and taken the time to talk to him.

Jack's story shows how the sexual abuse of children can be handed down from generation to generation, like the family jewels. It seems likely, from Jack's memory of the trip to the woods and the ice cream, and the fact that he retrieved this memory and wondered about its significance, that he had had some sexual encounter when he was small. However, the events of his early life (he said he remembered almost nothing of his first eight years) and many of the events of his childhood he hid in the deepest recesses of his memory. When he said that he did not expect his children to remember what he had done to them, he was speaking truthfully, for he did not remember what had been done to him.

This forgetting was not just because he was the kind of person for whom repression is the most favoured form of defence. In those situations where he had been the victim of sexual and physical abuse he was completely helpless. There was no one to whom he could turn for help, and he was a small child in a world of powerful and dangerous adults. He did not want to remember what had been done to him, because with those memories would come that feeling of terrible helplessness and abandonment.

Jack's story shows, too, how a child, needing a personal relationship in the way he needs food, will, in the way that a starving man will eat anything, accept affection in whatever form it is offered. Children should never be put in a position where they have to accept love at any price but, alas, many of them are.

Denying Who You Are

The price that Jack had to pay did not seem to him at the time too high. He was in the business of surviving, so learning to laugh at cruelty instead of being shocked by it did not seem significant; nor did learning to ignore his grief at the loss of the tenderness and love which should have been his by rights. He did not see that learning to laugh at cruelty to yourself means that you are no longer shocked at the cruelty inflicted on others, and that you might now be as cruel to others as others were to you. He could not possibly see, as a child, that in not allowing himself to grieve for himself he would, in later life, not allow his wife to show her grief for the child she had lost, and that this would cause great hurt to the person he loved and needed so much.

Deciding as a child not to allow yourself to grieve over the cruelty that has been done to you may mean that in adult life you cannot assess or appreciate the sufferings of others. Or you may become the kind of person who sees nothing wrong with persecuting the people whom you dislike. Quentin Crisp, himself no stranger to persecution, was asked on Irish television, 'Are you accepted more now you are successful?' He replied:

I think people misunderstand the principle of persecuting homo-sexuals, or, indeed, of persecution in general. It is not directed at a person, it is directed at anybody who is not likely to find defenders. During the course of your life you pile up a great deal of bitterness – your wife does not love you, there are your children who do not obey you, there is your boss who does not give you any preferment – and one day you see someone whom no one will blame you for attacking, and then all your bitterness pours out. And it doesn't matter who it is, as long as you can lash out at somebody without anyone reproaching you later. This is why people attack the weak, homosexuals, but especially effeminate homosexuals.[46]

Or you may become the kind of person who is plagued by depression. You have no sympathy for the child that you once were. It is very striking in therapy how depressed people will talk with great sympathy about, say, the starving children of Africa, but when they speak of the child they once were there is not a trace of sympathy or concern for that little frightened person. 'I was a very bad child,' they will say, 'and deserved to be punished by my parents.'

Among those people who devote their lives to helping others are many who show enormous sympathy for other people's suffering but are remarkably tough and unpitying towards themselves. They can recognize that as a child they had a difficult time, and can acknowledge that they suffered a great deal, but they refuse to give to themselves in adult life what, as a child, they lacked. Instead, they lavish this love and concern on others, and draw satisfaction from that. This is the defence mechanism of projective identification, the means by which we can identify with another person, and then give to that person what we would like to be given to us. Many of the people who are devoted to animals, even to the point of giving up their own lives to save animals from slaughter or of murdering those who appear not to care for animals, are engaged in this kind of identification. This is a kind of second-hand self-love, and it is the equivalent of eating thin gruel rather than a decent meal. However, those people who have never been loved properly as children can find it very difficult to love themselves to the degree which their humanness requires in adulthood.

Children try to rebel against adults who treat them badly, but the adults can punish them by regarding them as being mad and/ or bad. To avoid this fate children learn to conform, and they endure the pains and humiliations of childhood because they know that as well as the threat there is a promise. If you are disobedient as a child bad things will happen to you, but if you are good you will be rewarded, and the reward is that when you grow up you will have the power and privileges that adults have. One of the privileges of adulthood is that you can not only take your bad feelings out on the children in your charge, but you can feel virtuous while doing it. 'I'm only beating you for your own good, darling.' Some parents do not indulge in such hypocrisy, but what we all do as we grow up and encounter life's difficulties is try to feel good about ourselves. We need to think well of ourselves so as to find the courage to face life. If we suspect that we may have been damaged during our upbringing we shall think less well of ourselves, and our courage may fail.

In order not to feel sad and uncertain some adults say, 'I had a good childhood and my parents were wonderful,' and maintain this view by remembering very little of their childhood. Other people, less successful in forgetting the painful events of their childhood, insist that what happens to us in childhood has little effect in adult life. Despite the intense interest in recent years in therapy and counselling, there are still many people who maintain this view. Yet such people will work hard as parents, worrying about their children's education, teaching them good manners and healthy eating habits, all the things which they believe will help the child in adult life. If I comment, as I often do, that if what parents do has no effect on their children then a lot of parents have wasted an awful lot of time, they look pained and confused. They had been demonstrating the wonderful ability we all have of holding two opposing beliefs at one and the same time.

By denying that bad things happened to us in childhood, or by denying that what happens to us in childhood has any significance in our later life, we create disjunctions, gaps in what should be the coherent story of our life. This has many serious consequences;

one is that because we cannot see the connections between the events of our childhood and our adult life we continue to do to our children what was done to us. Thus do the sins of the fathers continue to be visited upon the children. To recognize that what was done to us in childhood has damaged us and prevented us from fulfilling our potential requires great bravery and an endurance of pain.

To recognize that what was done to you in childhood has profoundly affected you means that you have not only suffered in childhood but that you cannot enjoy the power and privileges of being an adult in charge of children. The privileges of parenthood are considerable. I remember how my mother and my sister, six years older than me, used to urge me to obedience as a child by telling me not to be selfish. They would, for instance, tell me to carry out some task and save them the trouble of doing it themselves. I would observe that by my acting unselfishly they were enabled to do what they wanted to do – that is, to be selfish. If I pointed this out they would say that I was a difficult, ungrateful child. I found this very unpleasant, but fortunately I did not decide to tell myself that these things did not happen.

If we learn to deny our experiences we fail to become the person we know we could have been. Some of us understand this very clearly, but most of us do not. We are all haunted by a sense of loss because all of us have denied something of ourselves, but only some of us can name this sense of loss. Sarah Kane in her last play before she killed herself, named her sense of loss. The play is a monologue in which she often speaks of searching for someone she has never met. The penultimate line of the play is 'It is myself I have never met, whose face is pasted on the underside of my mind.'[47]

For most of us, all that we know of the myself we have never met is an ache and a longing. Because we cannot name it we find it frightening. We try to ignore this pain, or obliterate it with indulgences of food or drugs or alcohol, or gifts to ourselves, or by prodigious feats of self-denial, or we try to run away from it by immersing ourselves in continuous hard work, or frantic,

149

competitive play, or we try to expel it in our works of art, or bury it in depression, or belittle it in contempt for another's weakness, or destroy it in violent, murderous rage. However, it remains a painful vacancy, there to trouble and frighten us just when we thought we were safe.

To be safe in any situation we need to know just what the dangers are. To keep ourselves safe from disease we need to assess the factors in each disease which could harm us and how able we are to ward off each threat. In so doing we have to take into account how physically strong we are and what practical measures we can take to avoid infection.

Just as we are surrounded by threats to our physical safety, so we are surrounded by threats to our sense of being a person. We need to assess the dangers realistically, and not run away from them or tell ourselves that they do not exist. We need, too, to assess how able we are to counter the dangers and to deal with the effects. The more we value and accept ourselves the better able we are to deal with threats to our meaning structure. However, every act of lying to ourselves – for that is what denial is – undermines our sense of being valuable and acceptable, and having the right to exist as the person we are. The less we value and accept ourselves the greater every threat to our meaning structure becomes, and the more and more desperate the defences we devise to hold ourselves together as a person.

That multitude of behaviours which gets labelled as neurotic or psychotic, or as mental illness or mental disorder, or as simply mad, has one common cause. It is the loss of confidence in ourselves. We see ourselves as valueless, unacceptable, even wicked, and, in the face of a threat to our meaning structure, we feel ourselves falling apart, shattering, crumbling, even disappearing. We seek to defend ourselves, and the less we value ourselves the more desperate the defence we need to construct.

Whatever defence we construct is a means of interacting with or fending off the people around us. They, and society generally, evaluate and respond to the defence we choose to use. If we use the defence of working hard and achieving to avoid having to deal with the pain of denial, society is likely to reward us because we live in a society which regards hard work and achievement as virtues. But what happens when our defence conflicts with society's norms and values? How does society respond to our need to defend ourselves with a desperate defence?

Chapter Five

How Society Responds to Mental Distress

Plus ça change, plus c'est la même chose. The more things change, the more they remain the same. Survivors of the psychiatric system, both the patients who suffered at the hands of the system and those members of staff who were appalled by the cruelty of the system and struggled against it, can only agree that the more things change the more they remain the same. Some aspects of the psychiatric system are much better than they were twelve years ago, but much of the system, and the ideas on which it was based, remain. Administrators of a health service became managers of a health business, and psychiatry, which had rejected Freud and Jung and all that followed them, discovered psychotherapy. Such changes brought a vast increase in the psychiatric and managerial jargon that may try to sound thoughtful and efficient but of which Craig Newnes, one of the founders of the critical psychology movement, said, 'The new National Health Service has embraced a culture of militarism, business jargon, and meaningless soundbites. The militarism is typified by a new language of targets or objectives and sometimes more pointedly; in a recent NHS marketing seminar group leaders discussed ''Principles of Marketing Warfare'', ''Attack Strategies (including guerrilla attacks)'' and ''Principles of Guerrilla Marketing Warfare''. And all of this presented to nurses and other staff quite explicitly pacifist in their politics or nature. The business agenda is reflected in a preoccupation with business plans and similar documents concerned with tendering, purchaser risk and efficiency improvements.'[1] Miller Mair, a psychologist who has seen the changes in the psychiatric system over the last thirty years at close quarters, commented, 'The language of marketed

152

care degrades people and contributes to a cruder understanding of ourselves.'[2]

Many psychiatrists use the jargon of therapy, but this jargon, as well as military and marketing jargon, is naught but a smokescreen to hide the fact that the system remains the same, and for the same reasons that the system in France remained the same – namely that the people who hold the wealth, prestige and power in the system do not want to relinquish what they hold, and are prepared to sacrifice those who have no power, prestige or money in order to keep what they hold.

'Twas ever thus. Throughout history no privileged group has ever voluntarily given up its privileges. The privileged always manipulate their society in order to keep their privileges, and much of this manipulation is aimed at keeping the society stable, for only in a stable society are their privileges safe. For a society to be stable it must be made up of people who conform to its rules and customs. Anyone who does not conform is a threat to society and to those who hold power.

Those who do not conform in terms of race, nationality or religion are easily dealt with. They become strangers, enemies, and are easily persecuted.[3] Such persecution can be carried out in many different ways, but always the persecutors try to justify their cruelty. It is not unknown for psychiatry to supply such justifications. During the Second World War German troops were stationed in Norway, and a number of these soldiers had liaisons with Norwegian women. Children from these liaisons were classed by Hitler as Aryans, the highest possible classification in the Third Reich. As such they had to be taken from their Norwegian mothers and placed in special homes reserved for such privileged children. At the end of the war the Norwegians transferred their hatred of the Germans to these children. They were put in orphanages and asylums where they were sexually and physically abused and not educated. As justification for this a leading Norwegian psychiatrist explained that these children were mentally subnormal and insane because their mothers must have been insane to have consorted with German men. Only recently have a few of these children, now quite elderly, been able to speak publicly about their cruel treatment.[4]

Those who do not conform to the laws and customs of society, but who cannot be expelled as strangers and enemies, are deemed to be bad or mad, if not both, but in any event they are punished because they are feared. For their hundredth issue the journal *Openmind* ran a survey to find the heroes and villains of mental health. (A most distinguished group, Freud, R. D. Laing, Peter Breggin and myself, appeared in the survey as both heroes and villains, thus supporting my contention that different people see things differently.) The nominations for the villains category were submitted by a reader, Terry Simpson. His first nomination was 'fear'. He explained: 'Fear of ''madness'' is second only to fear of death in our society. Distressed people have been abused, isolated, assaulted and killed in a systematic way since the term ''mad'' was invented.'[5]

Our fear of madness stems from our fear of annihilation as a person. If we do not understand our own fear, then when we find ourselves falling apart, crumbling, shattering, disappearing, we fear that we are going mad, and indeed our reaction to the threat of annihilation as a person *is* what society calls madness. *Madness is our fear of annihilation and our defences against that fear.* If we understand what our fear is – that is, that events have shown us that there is a serious discrepancy between what we thought our life was and what it actually is – we can, despite our sadness and distress, act sensibly and effectively. If we do not understand what the fear of annihilation is, we become frightened of it. We then deny this fear in ourselves and we reject those whose behaviour may remind us of the fear we want to deny. This is why people suffering mental distress are rejected.

Terry Simpson's second villain was greed and his third ignorance. Greed, he said, dominated society and created many of the conditions which led to mental distress. Our fear of madness arises out of our ignorance, and so it is fear and ignorance which ensure that many people suffering mental distress find themselves rejected by family and friends. A large survey by the Mental Health Foundation found that 56 per cent of people suffering mental distress reported being discriminated against by their family and 51 per cent reported discrimination by friends. One person commented, 'I've always been asked if the way I'm feeling is due to my mental health problems. I'm not allowed to express emotions good or bad like "normal" people.'[6] Such a response to distress serves only as yet another threat of annihilation to the distressed person.

Those people who reported that it was possible to discuss their distress with their family and friends described them as being close, supportive and understanding. Clearly these families and friends were not frightened of non-conformity, or of any threat to the privileges they might possess. Many families, my own included, would put the reputation of the family ahead of the distress a family member may feel. The desire to preserve the good name of the family ensured the success and the profitability of the lunatic asylums.

Popular media, in order to make money, reflect public opinion and do not try to change it. Consequently, the theme of any news story concerning a person suffering mental distress is always 'madness equals danger'. Whenever a person is murdered by a stranger who is described as being psychotic, the story becomes front-page news. The British government usually responds to the clamour to lock up mad people with promises to do just that. Yet Home Office statistics continue to show that murder, like incest, is a family affair. There has been no increase in homicides by psychiatric patients since the closing of the large psychiatric hospitals. George Szmukler, one of the psychiatrists who has studied the Home Office figures, commented, 'Especially frightening to the public is the prospect of being killed by a stranger with psychosis. In fact the risk of this is around the same as that of being killed by lightning – about one in ten million.'[7]

However, as George Szmukler commented, 'Mental health services are becoming increasingly coercive. There has been a substantial increase in the use of compulsory admissions to psychiatric hospitals in England and Wales . . . the government press release announcing a review of the Mental Health Act states: "new legislation is needed to support our new policies, for example, to provide extra powers to treat patients in a range of clinical settings, including where necessary in the community, and to ensure a proper balance between the interests of the public and the rights of the individual.'' Note the order in the final clause.'[8]

A survey by the psychiatrist Stephen M. Lawrie compared how newspapers covered psychiatric and physical illness. In nine daily newspapers over a one-month period he found that '213 article headlines about various aspects of medicine and 47 on psychiatry were identified. Ninety-nine (46%) of the former were critical in tone compared with 30 (64%) of the latter. We gained the impression that negative articles about physical medicine tended to criticize doctors whereas negative articles about psychiatry tended to criticize patients. Tabloid and broadsheet newspapers did not differ in their rates of negative coverage.'[9]

For some years now the Mental Health Media Council has given annual awards to programmes on television and radio which present mental health issues realistically and well.[10] However, though many people in the media are keen to receive these awards, good television programmes on mental health issues are seen by the men who hold the power in television as worthy, dull and of interest only to women, and so such programmes, if they are made at all, are not shown at popular viewing times. MIND, along with its annual award for a book on mental health issues, gave a Bigot of the Year award. Strangely, winners of this award never turned up at the award ceremony to collect their prize. MIND stopped awarding it, partly because bigoted journalists and editors seemed to have mended their ways, and partly because MIND wanted to concentrate on something really positive. So they nominated a yearly MIND Champion to honour the person who had made the most positive contribution to increasing public awareness of mental health issues.

In 2000 the Royal College of Psychiatry joined with MIND in a campaign to combat the stigma of mental illness. Many fine words were uttered and many trees sacrificed to this endeavour. A website, supported by the pharmaceutical companies Lundbeck Ltd and Pfizer Ltd UK, was set up.[11] In all this the public were admonished for their intolerance and urged to change their ways. However, while for MIND such a campaign involves no conflict of interest – after all, to combat the stigma of mental illness is one of the reasons why MIND exists – for psychiatrists there is a conflict which renders all their fine words in their documents concerning good practice[12] about listening to their patients, respecting their privacy and dignity, treating them politely and considerately highly dubious.

Lucy Johnstone, in her book *Users and Abusers of Psychiatry*, summed up this conflict on interests as follows: 'Psychiatry is required to be the agent of society while purporting to be the agent of the individual; and its main function is not treatment but social control.'[13]

For psychiatrists this conflict of interests may have been difficult enough, but to this is now added the requirement that psychiatrists be the agent of the pharmaceutical industry, whether or not their drugs are helpful to the individual. To understand how this conflict of interests came into being and how it operates now, we need to understand the history of psychiatry. It is in this history that we can find many of the reasons why so little changes in the psychiatric system.

What Has Stayed the Same?

In the history of Western thought it is only comparatively recently that madness has been seen as illness, and thus appropriately the concern of the medical profession. Originally, and still in many societies, madness was seen as a sign that the person was possessed by evil spirits and was thus the concern of priests. The priests were the most powerful people in society. They had unearthly powers, they could grant forgiveness of sins, and they could excommunicate even the King – that is, they could prevent the King from communicating with God. In the Middle Ages theories about madness were concerned with possession by the Devil and damnation by God. Although the Church was a most powerful institution, it did not lay claim to all the people who might be considered mad. Up to the eighteenth century 'mad people for the most part were not treated even as a separate category or type of deviant. Rather, they were assimilated into the much larger, more amorphous class of the morally disreputable, the poor, and the impotent, a group which also included vagrants, minor criminals, and the physically handicapped.'[14]

So wrote Andrew Scull, who, in his study of the history of lunatic asylums, showed how in the late eighteenth century certain members of the medical profession had realized that money could be made out of providing accommodation (asylums) for those whom the doctors could diagnose as insane. There already existed a number of such institutions operated by kindly, and not so kindly, people, not members of the medical profession, who offered, according to their advertisements, a protected and health-giving environment, sometimes with 'moral therapy'. Such a service could be provided at a profit to the landlord of a small asylum.

To justify their taking over the care of the insane, doctors needed to show that they had some special expertise. So they set about showing that insanity was a physical illness and that they were the only people with the necessary expertise to cure such an illness. They invented many different theories about how madness was the result of some purported bodily change. However, such a claim to the territory of insanity might not have been accepted by the rest of society had not other major changes in society been taking place.

During the eighteenth century the population of Britain, like that of other industrialized countries, had increased. The enclosure of the shared public lands by the powerful landowners forced many people to leave their villages. The population of urban areas grew, and British society became increasingly unstable. The government created hugely punitive laws, and then dealt with the large numbers of people who broke the laws by transporting them, first to the American colonies, and then, after the American Revolution, to Australia. By 1840, however, the Australian states were refusing to take any more convicts.

The idea of collecting all the people who could not or would not work and putting them in one secure place was appealing to a government that felt more secure when most of the population were law abiding, obedient and hard working. The Protestant work ethic, flourishing in the success of nineteenth-century British industry, defined the inability or refusal to work as bad or mad. So those who could not or would not work were tidied away into the asylums for the lunatic poor which the Lunatics Acts of 1842 and 1845 required to be built in every county and borough. There was an immediate rise in the number of insane people, as good citizens disposed of those who were an embarrassment or an annoyance.[15]

The practice was adopted by all industrialized countries. Labour was needed for industry, and those who refused to be part of the workforce were a nuisance which had to be confined and controlled. However, the amount of labour needed at any one time varies with the state of the economy. When the economy flourishes, more labour is needed, and when the economy slumps many people in the workforce lose their jobs. A large number of unemployed people can be a threat to the stability of the economy, but here psychiatry can help. Richard Warner, in his book *Recovery from Schizophrenia*, shows how there is a close relationship between the state of the economy and the recovery rates for schizophrenia. When there is a labour shortage psychiatrists talk about schizophrenia in terms of social causes and rehabilitation, but when there is a labour surplus they talk about biological causes, which means that no recovery is possible.[16]

Fulbourn Hospital in Cambridge was opened as the Cambridgeshire and Isle of Ely Pauper Lunatic Asylum in 1858. Its history was not dissimilar to that of the other pauper lunatic asylums in England. When Dr David Clark was appointed as superintendent there in 1953 he found that the back wards

were overcrowded with people, with scrubbed floors, bare wooden tables, benches screwed to the floor, people milling around in shapeless clothing. There was a smell of urine, paraldehyde, floor polish, boiled cabbage and carbolic soap – the asylum smell . . . The women were in 'strong clothes', shapeless garments made of reinforced cotton that couldn't be torn. Many of them were in 'locked boots' which couldn't be taken off and thrown. There was nothing movable. There were no knives. Spoons were taken in and counted every meal. The women all had their hair chopped off short giving them identical grey mops. At the back of the ward were padded cells, in which would be one or two naked women smeared with faeces, shouting obscenities at anyone who came near. Then there were the airing courts. Grey, big courts, paved with tarmac, surrounded by a wall twelve feet high and a hundred men milling around. A few of them walking, some running, others standing on one leg, posturing, with the urine running out of their trouser leg, some sitting in a corner masturbating. A couple of bored young male nurses standing on 'point duty', looking at them, ready to hit anybody who got out of line, but otherwise not doing anything. A scene of human degradation.[17]

The large asylums which were built to house the lunatic poor have now been closed or are in the process of closing, though some remain and are even growing bigger, but the ideas and practices which determined their creation and operation have not changed.

The government policy developed in the 1980s of closing the largest psychiatric hospitals and putting the inhabitants of these hospitals into the community with teams of professionals to support them seemed wise and humane. And so it would have been had the policy been followed, but this would have required the government to support it with adequate funding. However, politicians, like most of the constituents who vote for them, fear madness, and so mental health receives a multitude of fine words from politicians but little money or true concern. Thus only a few people received the support necessary for them to live securely and well in the community. The majority were, as Andrew Scull wrote, 'assimilated into the much larger, more amorphous class of the morally disreputable, the poor and the impotent.' History came full circle.

When we contemplate some great cruelty in the past it is usual to express horror that such terrible things should happen and imply by the expression of horror that nothing like that could happen today. 'They', those unnamed people who allowed such cruelty to exist or who caused such cruelty, are quite different from *us*, who are so wise, compassionate and caring.

Yet if we do enquire who 'they' were, and the records are there for us to see, 'they' turn out to be not some strange breed of evil men and women but ordinary people, not unlike us, going about their business and trying to be good. They were husbands, wives, parents, responsible employers and employees. The doctors, nurses, administrators and members of the hospital boards in the nineteenth century were virtuous men and women, just as the doctors, nurses, administrators and members of the health authorities are today.

The problem is that the processes whereby children learn to be good and to deny who they are can also be the processes whereby they learn to be blind to the suffering of other people. When the extremes of pain force a child to change his perception of the situation from 'I am being unjustly punished by my bad parent' to 'I am bad and am being justly punished by my good parent', the child not only sacrifices himself to preserve his parent as good, but he damages or even destroys his ability to perceive evil in the here and now. He is no longer able to view with a clear, perceptive, steady gaze the pain, cruelty and injustice which people suffer in this world. He may be able to see it in far-off lands, in places unconnected with his personal life, but when the evil is close by, part of the world where he has responsibilities, he has to turn away, to hide his eyes, pretend that nothing has happened, or wrap up what he sees in all kinds of sentimentalities, pretences, moralities and lies. The people who crammed thousands of helpless, disturbed men and women into the bare, locked wards of a pauper lunatic asylum were no different from those who now put helpless, disturbed people into small, miserable rooms or let them wander the streets, homeless, cold, and hungry, and call this cruelty 'community care'. When we lose part of our spirit in learning to be good, we usually have no compunction in then trying to destroy the spirit of other people.

Psychiatric hospitals are monuments to the destruction of the human spirit. Many of these monuments still exist but have been turned into what estate agents call desirable properties. These monuments always had imposing façades, built to impress the worthy, sane citizens and to intimidate the mad and those who feared that within them the seeds of madness lay. Behind the façades were the long, echoing corridors, laid out in a pattern where corridor mirrored corridor, turning inward, a maze without an exit rather than a path with a goal. Along the corridors were sly little doors whose secrets were known only to the staff, and large, heavy doors, fitted with big locks, which opened into rooms not built to any human scale but simply as storage space, cold and dead. When I worked in such places in the 1970s and 1980s these vast spaces where people were once herded were 'cubicalized', furnished with single beds with matching small dressing table and wardrobe, each cubicle given the illusion of privacy by a curtain or a thin partition, while other rooms were given an illusion of homeliness with a carpet, easy chairs and a television. The bare cells where once recalcitrant and dangerous patients were imprisoned were now 'side rooms', containing a bed and a wardrobe, but the narrow window and the slit in the door, through which the nurses could cast a watching eye, prevented any sense of personal space and belonging. The attempts to turn these hospitals into places where people could feel comfortable and at home were as successful as turning the Pyramids into bungalows by putting a white picket fence round them would be.

I had visited psychiatric hospitals in Sydney, but it was not until I came to England in 1968 that I had to work in them. Eighteen years of knowing such places has not reduced my horror at the inhumanity they represent.

The people whose mental distress leads them to become inmates of psychiatric hospitals differ in the kinds of problems they have and in the way they behave, but the one thing they all have in common is that they have a very low opinion of themselves. The psychiatric hospital, in the past and in the present, does nothing to change this, but rather serves to decrease the patients' self-confidence even further. The buildings still stress the patients' insignificance and unworthiness. The procedures and practices of the staff, despite their care and concern for the patients, prevent the resurgence of the spirit and the recovery of self-confidence which are necessary if the person is to find the courage necessary to return to ordinary life.

As the old psychiatric hospitals closed, certain wards in general hospitals were delineated as psychiatric wards. Some of these wards were part of the general hospital; others were new buildings constructed specially for that purpose. Initially these wards with their new décor seemed to send a message that the nasty old system had disappeared and a new therapeutic system had taken its place, or at least all the rhetoric accompanying their opening said so. However, as time passed it became clear that the old system was still operating.

The new wards are of two kinds – acute, for people who are acutely distressed, and rehabilitation, for people whose distress has been numbed and contained but who cannot manage in the community. Not all general hospitals have rehabilitation wards, but such that exist are little different from the long-stay wards of the old psychiatric hospitals. When my colleague Craig Newnes was talking to me about changes in the psychiatric system he mentioned the hospital in the area where he was in charge of psychological services. He said, 'This place has wards that are identical to the wards I first worked on in 1971, thirty years ago. They're absolutely the same: people shuffle about, they're not all massively over-medicated but on the whole they shuffle about, they do mad things; the men assault the women – that hasn't changed at all. Although the décor's better.'

Craig mentioned another change in the system, but not one for the better. This change has been brought about through managers and computers. He said:

There's a tidal wave of so-called information that exists about people in the system, and what's remarkable about it is that none of it's confidential. In the old days there may or may not have been information, and it wouldn't have been on computer, but the chances were that the only people who got to hear about

Mrs Bloggs being admitted to Ward 5 would be the consultant, several nurses, a social worker and a psychologist, if there was one involved – and occasionally the patient's GP. But that would be about it. Now what happens is the information comes into the system, you still have ward meetings, and most meetings will now be attended by up to five additional students, and these students are just there for the day, and they go off again, having heard about Mrs Bloggs and her depression. Then all of that information is passed to our information centre, where there are fifteen non-clinicians, any one of whom can read this stuff if they want to, and then all of that is passed to our purchasers and the GPs and the community nurses. So when the client says, 'If you write down what I'm telling you who will know?' what you actually have to say is, 'I haven't a clue. I honestly can't tell you. For all I know, the Secretary of State himself will read it.'

Much information is collected, not to improve patient care, but to protect the staff, should there be an inquiry, an inquest or a court case. Patients and their families are now more inclined to sue should anything go wrong with their care, and inquiries, inquests and litigation usually attract media attention, all of which can have a deleterious effect on the careers of the staff involved.

In November 2000 MIND published its report on a survey of 343 people who had experienced life on an acute ward. The survey showed that 'wards are not always therapeutic environments for many people in distress: the atmosphere on the wards was depressing: decoration was basic: access to food and drinks was often denied; illegal drugs were being used on the wards.'[18]

Vanessa Lloyd-Jones described her stay on a psychiatric ward when she was deeply depressed as devastating. She wrote:

Some staff showed great kindness and patience. However, they were in the minority and I suffered and witnessed some truly dreadful treatment from so-called professional health-care staff. Some patients, for no other reason than a raised voice, were roughly handled – pinned down by four male staff, given an injection and sent to the infamous seclusion room. I realize that in very extreme cases this is necessary, but 99 per cent of the time this was not so, and was nothing but power-crazed staff laying down the 'law'. This is happening in psychiatric hospitals all over the country and is Dickensian. Often the ward was run by agency staff who a) had no rapport with the patients and b) frequently dispensed the wrong drugs. The latter was an occasional source of amusement in our dull lives, but could also result in serious consequences.[19]

A survey of patients with experience of acute and rehabilitation wards showed that 'Patients expressed gratitude to staff who were approachable, kind and sympathetic; who made an effort to talk to them; who appeared happy; who treated them as one might treat a friend. Conversely, staff who showed little interest; who were ''hard faced'' or never smiled; who came across as dismissive; who did not notice or ignored them when they were upset, were felt to be unhelpful and made patients worse.'[20]

Vanessa Lloyd-Jones did not name the ward she was on, but Linda Hart named hers. She wrote:

[In Stretton Ward attached to Leicester General Infirmary] the twelve female patients share one bath and a shower – except the shower can't be used if there's a patient in the seclusion suite situated next door. There are washing facilities in each dorm but no curtain to offer even basic privacy. None of the drawers or cupboards in which patients store their personal possessions have locks. Communal areas on Stretton consist of one large day-room where a semicircle of chairs is arranged around a television (no video) which is constantly on. I have a problem with TV, in that it gets caught up in some of my symptoms, so this room is out of bounds for me. The other two rooms are the 'quiet' room and the 'smoke' room. These were deplorably small, and while I was there the quiet room was inhabited by Kenny, who played records of military music and Vic Reeves, or it was commandeered by doctors wanting to speak to patients, or new arrivals awaiting admission. Never was it quiet.

The smoke room was where I (having little alternative), and the majority of male patients, spent the time. Nine dilapidated chairs lined the nicotine stained walls and a copper-topped table (an old pub throw-out) was the repository for drinks, ashtrays, food, tobacco, cigarettes and feet. Commercial radio, at just too high a volume, kept up one source of constant noise, only to be outdone by the extractor fan. This resembled the droning of a jet engine – only we were going nowhere. 'I wouldn't put a pig in that room,' said Alice, one of my visitors, looking at the filthy stained carpet, dirty curtains and bleak walls. I would gladly have cleaned up the mess myself, but patients are denied access to cleaning materials and the vacuum cleaner.[21]

Psychiatric wards are the only part of a hospital where people are allowed to smoke, and that is what patients do, all day every day, because they are anxious and there is nothing else to do. Linda Hart wrote that on the ward there was 'an absence of stimulation and occupation. Those confined to the ward have no opportunity for fresh air and exercise and, as Shane was fond of pointing out, at least you got that in prison. There is an occupational therapy department, but very rarely was there a place for anyone on the ward to attend. And somehow I can't see Shane attending ''creative activities'' where the main occupations are painting garden gnomes and colouring in pictures. I don't think it would match his dreams of owning a string of nightclubs and being high on vodka and whiz.'

Vanessa had attended occupational therapy. She wrote, 'For day treatment centre read primary school. Patients are patronized and made to play games that resemble those of childhood car journeys. Art, which I do consider therapeutic, is relegated to painting by numbers. Contrary to professional opinion, patients have not lost the use of their brains, and most therapies offered simply serve to perpetuate this myth.'

However, most psychiatric wards are keen to advertise what therapeutic activities they offer. When my friend Sarah accompanied her niece Ruth, who was being admitted to a psychiatric unit, she found that the unit supplied a little information book for patients and carers. In this book were listed under 'Therapies and Activities' the following: counselling, relaxation and anxiety management, daily living skills, complementary therapies, leisure activities, dramatherapy, assertiveness training, and coping with depression. This proved to be nothing but a wish list. There was one occupational therapist for the ward and she was on leave. I have written about Sarah and Ruth and their experience of the psychiatric system in the introduction to Lucy Johnstone's *Users and Abusers of Psychiatry*. Suffice it to say that if Ruth had not had her Aunt Sarah, a well-educated, middle-class woman who could find her way around any institution and was utterly fearless, to fight for her, today she would be either dead from suicide or confined for life to a long-stay ward. Instead, though she still lacks self-confidence, she is leading an ordinary life in society.

The study of acute wards carried out by the Sainsbury Centre in 1998 showed that 40 per cent of patients did not take part in any social or recreational activity, and that only 5 per cent received any of the psychological therapies. By contrast, junior doctors, not consultants, were seen relatively frequently, eleven contacts during an average thirty-eight-day stay, though it is likely that such contacts were concerned only with medication. The Nuffield Institute for Health study in 1996 found that patients spent 4 per cent of their time with staff and 28 per cent doing nothing or watching television. Summing this up in the *Psychiatric Bulletin*, Matt Muijen said, 'All this suggests an atherapeutic environment, a care vacuum, rather than a place offering the most intensive therapeutic interventions to the most vulnerable and unwell people.'[22]

Matt Muijen pointed out that 'This intense pressure on beds has changed the profile of patients on psychiatric wards. In-patient units are filled with highly disturbed people with diagnoses of schizophrenia, and growing proportions have complex problems, whether social, psychological or physical. Hospital wards are a bizarre and illogical mixture, probably uniquely so, of old and young, male and female, psychotic and depressed, retarded and agitated and voluntary and detained.' Hardly a place of safety, which is what an asylum is supposed to be.

One striking difference between the old psychiatric hospitals and the new psychiatric wards is the prevalence of illegal drugs which the staff seem to be powerless to control. In the hospitals where I worked patients had no difficulty in smuggling in alcohol, and there was a brisk trade in prescribed drugs. Some patients hoarded prescribed drugs for a suicide bid while others traded them with users of illegal drugs in and out of the hospital, but, while cannabis was popular with younger patients and members of staff, heroin and cocaine were not generally available. Now the picture is very different. Linda Hart said, 'Street drugs pose serious problems on the ward, as they do in the outside world. One seventeen-year-old lad stole £60 from another patient, bought heroin with it, overdosed and spent some time in intensive care. He was eventually discharged with brain damage that left him semi-paralysed. Another patient, Mike, had been a heroin addict for seventeen years. Prior to his detention on the ward, he'd been clear of drugs for three years. Being on Stretton Ward, with little to occupy him or help him feel good, he started using heroin again.'

The mixing of the sexes on these wards brings great danger to the women there. As Jeannette Copperman said in *Society Guardian*:

Government watchdog the National Patient Safety Agency published a report revealing reported sexual incidents, including 19 reported rapes, in mental health care settings between November 2003 and September 2005. This is almost one reported rape a month. In 11 of the 19 reported rapes, the alleged perpetrator was a member of staff. The NHS litigation authority has also received three claims for compensation following unwanted pregnancies. The report, which the Department of Health initially tried to suppress, also states that the problem is being significantly under reported.

To make matters worse, over half the women who come in to patient wards have had previous experiences of violence, rape, domestic violence or child sexual abuse . . .

In 2000, the Department of Health pledged to abolish mixed sex wards and bring in separate sleeping, bathroom and day facilities. Guidance to raise the profile of gender-sensitive services more broadly was published but only one target was set, on women's sleeping areas. No extra money was made available.

In 2005, the government reported that 95% of health authorities were complying with the guidance on women-only wards. Yet this is far from the experience of many mental health service users. Implementation has been patchy, and the mental health charity MIND has called for a national audit. While in some areas real change and improvement have taken place, in others the change has been largely semantic. Many health trusts have simply put a curtain between the male and female sleeping bays and claimed to comply with the guidance.[23]

The old asylums had been divided into two completely separate sections, one for men and one for women. Changes in the sixties brought the walls between these two sections down, and men and women patients could mingle easily in the hospital grounds. For some patients this was a welcome comfort, but the psychiatrists did little to protect vulnerable girls and women from the men, and some treated the whole matter as a joke. However, at the very least the women had their dormitory to retreat to, but then the managers who put money before all else stepped in. They worked out that if women and men patients shared a ward building running costs would be reduced. To give a psychiatric gloss to what was an economic ploy, psychiatrists talked of the benefits men and women patients would gain from socializing together on one ward. They took no account of what was becoming more and more apparent – that a significant number of women who become psychiatric patients, perhaps the majority, have suffered sexual abuse. To be put on a ward with men, let alone disturbed men, was torture, not treatment. The Campaign for Women-Only Psychiatric Wards finally reached the ear of the government. Single-sex wards were promised, but government ministers still did not realize that, as Jolie Goodman of the Campaign said, 'Single sex accommodation should mean, simply, that women should have the right to be treated in a ward where there are no men, seven days a week, twenty-four hours a day.'[24]

Psychiatric wards are persistently understaffed. The way that nurses' pay is graded means that nurses earn more for working in the community than on psychiatric wards. Consequently these wards are largely staffed by nurses on overtime, and they are often extremely tired. Many temporary agency nurses are used, despite the fact that agency nurses cannot supply the continuity which patients need if they are to build up a relationship with one or two nurses. All this also means that patients who need supervision because they are a danger to themselves do not always get it.

About 180 psychiatric in-patients commit suicide each year. Almost half of those suicides happen on the ward itself, or in hospital grounds, and the rest while patients are on leave, according to an ongoing national confidential inquiry into suicide and homicide by people with mental illness. Hanging, usually from shower or curtain rails, is the most common method. A quarter of the wards where suicides happen have nursing shortages. One in five patients is under special observation – 3 per cent constantly – at the time they kill themselves. Psychiatric services appear slow to learn the lessons. Since 1971 repeated reports have recommended that wards could reduce suicides by replacing fixed curtain and shower rails with collapsible versions. Yet data to the ongoing confidential inquiry reveal that such deaths are still happening. At the same time, other means of committing suicide are readily available while obvious preventative measures are ignored.[25]

When suicides occurred in the psychiatric hospitals in which I worked I was often left with the impression from the way the hospital inquiry was conducted that many managers and doctors saw suicide as inevitable and a benefit to an overstretched psychiatric service. However, fear of litigation has now led to more detailed inquiries. All that such inquiries seem to have achieved is to have induced paranoia in doctors and nurses. Though working in the health service is now very difficult, what is abundantly clear to anyone who works in mental health is that the psychiatric system is there for the benefit and convenience of the staff, not the patients. Rachel Perkins, who knows the psychiatric system both as staff and patient, had some wise advice for service users. 'If you want something, ask for the opposite.' She explained, 'If you want the attentions of a professional, refuse to see them, then you stand a fair chance of being "assertively outreached". If you don't want to be seen, then persistently phone and demand a visit, and then you can be ignored as "attention seeking". This way the services can remain "in charge" and dictate what you do. Beliefs run deep that the expressed opinions of mad people should be discounted as manifestations of madness.'[26]

Rachel would also advise anyone caught up in the system to insist on regular case conferences. That way you might be able to avoid what Erving Goffman, in his study of life within a psychiatric hospital,[27] called 'the degradation ceremony'. Such conferences have not changed over the years. If you are an in-patient you will find yourself summoned to the consultant's office or a large meeting room where you will wait outside the door until the consultant calls for you. On entering, you will be confronted by a group of people, perhaps five, perhaps twenty, of whom you might have met no more than one or two. The ground rule of such a meeting is that anyone in the group can ask you any question they wish about yourself, no matter how personal, yet you are not allowed to ask members of the group any questions. The consultant may at the end ask you whether you would like to ask a question, but do not be so foolish as to think he means this. You are allowed to ask when you can go home, but you are not allowed to protest if the consultant's answer is not to your liking. You cannot leave until you are dismissed, but if you behave badly – that is, argue, or show anger or distress – the consultant will order a nurse to remove you. The fact that such an experience would be disturbing for the most strong-minded individual, let alone someone in a state of mental distress, seems never to have occurred to most psychiatrists.

I have witnessed many of these ceremonies, and the greatest horror I felt was at the way so many of the doctors and nurses did not see anything questionable in what they were doing. In 1985, in a television programme about long-stay patients going into the community, a case conference was shown where the consultant psychiatrist and the nurses were seated in a circle in the consultant's office. A woman patient, carelessly dressed and hair unbrushed, was brought in and seated in the centre of the circle. The consultant questioned her about her weekend outside the hospital, when she had quarrelled with her lover. The woman began to cry – huge, wrenching sobs.

I was not surprised that no one moved to comfort her. The doctor and nurses just sat, stony faced. This is what would have happened in most case conferences. The doctors and nurses would have let her cry until she stopped, or the consultant, discomfited or irritated, would have asked one of the nurses to take her out of the room. What did surprise me was that they did not move to comfort her when the camera was watching. Many of us, under the eye of a television camera, 'fake good' in order to win the approval of our unseen audience, but it did not occur to these people that among their unseen audience might be someone who would consider their inaction to be cruel and insensitive.

In 1995 I was a member of the Mental Health Media Council and part of the team of judges for the MHM awards. One television documentary submitted to us impressed us greatly. It was a fly-on-the-wall programme where the camera team simply followed a psychiatric team as they enquired into the welfare of a young man who went by the name of John Baptist. John was a beautiful, happy young man. His face glowed with energy and enthusiasm. His flat was neat and organized, just as he and his life were neat and organized. Lucy Johnstone takes up the story.

John Baptist is the adopted name of a black man who believes that he was born white, is descended from the royal family, and that his sister has been cannibalised, but is apparently coping perfectly well with his life. He does not see *himself* as mentally ill and does not want medication, being extremely unhappy about his previous experiences of psychiatry. However, his beliefs are causing concern to the psychiatric team, who see him as 'very ill and need(ing) treatment', and arrange a police escort to hospital. Articulate and assertive, John is not prepared to accept his (white, male, middle-class) consultant's view without challenge. He angrily describes how last time he 'came out of this hospital hardly able to brush my teeth, hardly able to eat, hardly able to stand . . . I was less than a baby. Now, what sort of medicine is that?' He demands to know what proof the consultant has that his beliefs are untrue, and forces the consultant to admit that this is in fact a matter of personal judgement: 'Well you're right in a way there . . . the only way I make that diagnosis is on people's thoughts and feelings.' However, in this unequal power battle there is little doubt whose delusion is going to carry the day, and we see the consultant telling the camera that 'I've no doubt this is a schizophrenic illness', while John is threatened with a locked ward if he tries to leave. The rest of the programme charts John's determined but unsuccessful attempts to gain his freedom, while insisting on retaining his beliefs. His assertiveness and refusal to compromise about his ideas clearly count against him, for the chief evidence against him at a tribunal hearing is that he used to be 'angry, irritable, shouting at people, verbally aggressive' and that he still has 'inappropriate beliefs', that he is 'more of a whole person' and has therefore improved. In one of the final scenes, we see a team member persuading John, in ultra-caring tones, to set the seal on his degradation and defeat by signing a form to confirm that he is 'permanently and substantially disabled' by mental illness, in return for a bus pass. John's mental illness is at last being properly treated; or, to put it another way, he has now been permanently and substantially disabled as a punishment for obstinately refusing to regulate his thoughts according to white cultural norms.[28]

Lucy Johnstone told John Baptist's story in the context of her examination of the treatment that black people receive in a white psychiatric system. Black people are far more likely to receive the diagnosis of schizophrenia than white people. Various complex theories have been put forward to explain this phenomenon, but plain racism may well be the reason. A study by M. Loring and B. Powell in the USA, in which 290 psychiatrists were shown case histories identical in every way except gender and race, found that black and white psychiatrists gave a diagnosis of schizophrenia more frequently to black clients than to white.[29]

Roland Littlewood and Maurice Lipsedge have made their life's work the study of what happens to black people in a white psychiatric system. Their fine book *Aliens and Alienists*, now in its third edition, shows how black people express their mental distress in terms of the ideas and beliefs of their culture. They wrote, 'The assumption running throughout this book is that all individuals try to make sense of their predicament. They are driven by a quest for *meaning*. We believe that even the mentally ill are making meaningful statements. Dismissing these as totally mad (meaningless) is characteristic perhaps of only a few cultures, including Britain.'[30]

Since white psychiatrists are unlikely to have a detailed knowledge of the wide variety of black cultures represented in a multicultural country, such psychiatrists are unlikely to recognize the symbols and metaphors of such alien cultures and so are liable to class the utterances of the black person in a state of distress as mad. When we do understand the symbols of a culture we can see as ordinary behaviour what other people would call madness. Littlewood and Lipsedge tell the story of how two Hasidic parents asked them for help with their fourteen-year-old son Chaim, whom the parents considered to be insane. The Weinberg family from north London were Orthodox Jews, the men dressing in traditional black clothes, their hair in ringlets, while their womenfolk wore wigs. The family eschewed all the trappings of modern society, including radio, television and record player, and the children devoted themselves to the study of the Torah. When the two psychiatrists arrived at the house to see Chaim, the boy was very embarrassed, but took them up to his room. Much to their surprise, the room was decorated in the way most fourteen-year-old boys in the UK decorate their bedrooms, with football paraphernalia. Through one of his friends Chaim had encountered football and quickly became besotted. All these decorations were just the ordinary symbols of British society, but to the Weinberg parents they were evidence of madness. These parents expected the psychiatrists to use their powers of social control to force their son to conform to their wishes.

Lucy Johnstone points out that, admirable though their book is, it 'falls down, in my view, in its reluctance to take its arguments to their logical conclusion and challenge the whole concept of ''mental illness'', and to admit that psychiatry's primary function is to regulate social norms not just for immigrants and ethnic minorities, but for all of us.'[31]

It is hardly ever possible to be an advocate for an individual's rights and for society's rights at one and the same time. This is why the legal system operates with two kinds of advocacy, one for the plaintiff and one for the defendant, or, in criminal cases, one for the Crown and one for the defendant. Whenever we attempt to be the advocate for two opposing ideas, for instance, when we try to befriend both partners in an acrimonious divorce, we can choose either to be completely truthful about each side, perhaps by saying 'In marriage break-up there's faults on both sides', whereupon the couple unite in hating us, or, in cowardice and confusion, we act in bad faith, dissembling, lying and pretending. Clerics get into this kind of a mess whenever a disaster raises the question of why bad things happen to good people. If God is all good, how can He let good people suffer? The best explanation the clerics can manage is that the faithful have to take God on trust, which is a fudge of an answer for a Church that claims to be in possession of the Absolute Truth. (The Evangelicals do not have this problem. They take the view that if bad things happen to you it is because you are a bad person.)

However, the problem of bad things happening to good people arises only occasionally, and the rest of the time clerics can give a fairly consistent message about God's love and forgiveness, but for psychiatrists the necessity of appearing to be the advocate for both sides defines every aspect of their work.

The rights of the individual and the rights of society are not always opposed. I find that in the UK my right to be safe in my own home and on the streets does not usually conflict with society's right to uphold the rule of law, but in cases of mental distress the rights of the individual and the rights of society are nearly always in conflict.

The final path of causes which leads to the mental distress is the way that the individual interprets his situation, but there is always the question of the nature of the situation which the person has to interpret. When, in 1967, I interpreted my situation as utterly intolerable and I decided to leave Australia for England I was able to take advantage of one of the most effective therapies, the geographical therapy of putting half a world between me and my tormentors. I could do this because I had an education and a profession, and I could raise the money for my son and me to travel to England. There are many people for whom geographical therapy would be their salvation, but for the fact that society had perhaps denied them the rights to an education, the acquisition of a marketable skill and enough money to travel, or perhaps denied them the legal right to leave their country. For many people decent housing and a regular wage would effect more cures of mental distress than any amount of psychiatric drugs or hours of therapy.

Psychologists have not had to look after society's interests but simply the interests of the individual, though this may change if psychologists are to be given powers to detain patients. However, they still have to struggle with the question of how much they should devote themselves to individual clients and how much they should try to change aspects of society which harm their clients. Some psychologists, like Sue Holland in White City, London, have used psychological methods to help a disadvantaged community achieve considerable improvements in their situation. But with a few exceptions, psychiatrists have been remarkably absent from the struggle for beneficial change.

Perhaps this is why, over the years of its existence, psychiatry has changed so little. Craig Newnes said to me:

If you compare the change in communication, information technology, simple heating systems, the quality of cars – if you compare what's happened in the last twenty years in virtually any other field, then psychiatry should have changed to that extent. And what makes me really angry about it is it has no right not to have changed. Why on earth couldn't it pull itself out of the nineteenth century? That's the scary bit. Basically what's happened is that people just get much more toxic medication, which has to be monitored much more closely. On décor, if you look at our hospital, the only difference between our hospital and St John's, where you and I used to work, is that ours is much better decorated. That's it. But the redecoration programme is still on a five-year cycle and the wards get pretty shabby pretty quickly. So even they're not much better. Why is it that psychiatry hasn't changed? There's something deeply wrong about that.

The history of psychiatry reminds me of the history of the communist leaders in the USSR. After the success of the revolution in 1917, Lenin and his co-conspirators did not to try to sort out the terrible problems of the country of which they were now in charge. Instead they set about consolidating their power. Even before Lenin's death the conspirators jostled for power, and those who looked as if they would make trouble, like Trotsky, were disposed of. Stalin emerged as a leader who presented himself as a wise, kindly man devoted to his people. As schoolchildren during the Second World War we were taught to call him Uncle Joe and feel pleased because he was on our side, but in fact he despised his people and readily had millions murdered, or put in concentration camps, or reduced to penury, all to keep him in power. His successors continued the process of consolidating their power. They used the resources and the wealth of their country and its satellites to strengthen their power, and they murdered truth in order to create a propaganda which said that only they had the knowledge and skills to look after their people. The fact that so many people in Russia and other erstwhile communist countries mourn the passing of communism shows how readily people will give up their freedom and let other people take responsibility for them. In the same way many people readily give up their freedom when a psychiatrist says to them, 'You've got depression. It's a chemical imbalance of the brain. I can look after you.'

The doctors who took over from the variety of people who ran asylums in the early nineteenth century in their own small way carried out a revolution. Having gained power, they had to consolidate it, and to do this they had to find a means of justifying their position. The only claim they could make was that they knew more about bodies than other people, and so they explained mental distress in terms of the way the body functions. This became their unquestionable dogma, their Absolute Truth. Language and theories within this dogma changed with changing fashions, but the dogma as laid down by the British psychiatrist Henry Maudsley remained untouched. In 1874 he wrote, 'It is not our business, as it is not in our power, to explain psychologically the origin and nature of any of these depraved instincts; it is sufficient to establish their existence as facts of observation, and to set forth the pathological conditions under which they are produced; they are facts of pathology, which should be observed, and classified like other phenomena of disease.'[32] He defined mind and all its products as 'a function of matter, an outcome of interacting and combined atomic forces not essentially different in kind from the effervescence that follows a chemical combination or the explosion of a fulminate'.[33]

Psychiatrists were the only people who could establish what 'facts of observation' are. Eliot Slater and Martin Roth, in their influential textbook *Clinical Psychiatry*, advised the student psychiatrist: 'It is the objective world in which we live and to which the subjective world must pay deference. It is even more important to know what the facts are than what the patient makes of them.'[34] That is, if you think your mental distress is linked to your relationship with your father, and your psychiatrist thinks that your depression is caused by a chemical imbalance in your brain, then your psychiatrist must be right and you wrong.

Any system which is based on a claim to possession of an absolute truth has to expel its dissidents. This is what happened to psychiatrists who spoke out in criticism of the system. Nowadays, in public, psychiatrists speak of R. D. Laing in patronizing tones. 'Poor Ronnie,' they say, 'very bright, but misguided', but in private (I am an Associate of the Royal College of Psychiatrists and when I was working in the NHS I studied psychiatrists at very close range) Ronnie Laing is spoken of with hatred. In the USA, among psychiatrists, Thomas Szasz and Peter Breggin are the unmentionable names. In case conferences I have seen junior doctors who would like to express a mildly dissident opinion remain silent for fear of losing their livelihood, or at least a good reference, and I have seen psychiatrists who have produced competent research which questions psychiatric dogma do a Galileo and recant and repent, or at least so reframe their results that their significance is obscured. Aaron Beck and his disciples in the USA have been very careful not to let the undoubted success of cognitive therapy present a challenge to the psychiatric dogma and, perhaps more importantly, to the pharmaceutical industry which supports research.

Among British psychiatrists Henry Maudsley's view that mind was no more than an epiphenomenon of the brain – that is, of no more significance than an effervescence might be in a chemical reaction – continued to be the prevailing view. When many European psychoanalysts sought refuge in the USA from the Third Reich they influenced American psychiatrists to the extent that, by 1962, fifty-nine out of eighty-two psychiatric departments were headed by psychoanalysts. Psychoanalysts, who more often than not deem themselves to be in possession of the Absolute Truth, fitted well into the psychiatric system, but their failure to effect cures, and the discovery in the 1950s and 1960s of the major and minor tranquillizers and the first antidepressants, led to their downfall and the rise of the biological psychiatrists. David Healy, writing in the *Psychiatric Bulletin,* said:

By the 1990s, the rise of psychopharmacology and biological psychiatry was complete. The chance⌐ of a non-neuroscientist becoming a head of a psychiatric department in the USA was highly unlikely and not much more likely in the UK. The standard textbooks were heavily neuroscientific in their emphasis. Where once the APA [American Psychiatric Association] was controlled by analysts, annual meetings now generated millions of dollars – largely from pharmaceutical company sponsored satellite symposia, of which there were 40 in 1999, at approximately $250,000 per symposium in addition to fees for exhibition space and registration fees for several thousand delegates brought to the meeting by pharmaceutical companies, as well as several million dollars per annum from sales of successive versions of the DSM [Diagnostic and Statistical Manual].

The UK, which had once stood dismissive of American trends and diagnoses, increasingly followed American leads. Fashions in recovered memory therapies or fluoxetine-taking rapidly crossed the Atlantic, influenced in part perhaps by the ever-increasing attendance of British psychiatrists at APA meetings. By 1999, it was possible that greater numbers of British psychiatrists, sponsored largely by pharmaceutical companies, attended the APA meeting than the annual meeting of the Royal College of Psychiatrists, a development that would have been incredible a decade before.[35]

David Whitwell describes himself as 'a psychiatrist who has worked in acute psychiatry all his professional life'. Retired, he wrote a book, *Recovery Beyond Psychiatry*, where he summed up what his career had taught him. He had trained in the 1960s and had accepted without question that 'the aim of doctors is to diagnose the illness, deliver the correct treatment, and so bring about a recovery; it is an "illness-treatment-recovery model".'[36] However, he came to see this model did not fit what actually happened. Only a naïve psychiatrist could practise what David Whitwell called 'naïve psychiatry'. He wrote, 'The concept that has been applied in psychiatry is borrowed from medicine. It holds out the idea that people will simply "get back to normal", and then be just as they were before. This is a child's view of what happens when you become unwell.'[37] In his 'Confessions of a Naïve Psychiatrist' he wrote,

> The picture began to change for me when I started to get to know my patients better, and to remain in touch with them for long periods after they had gone back home. I was also influenced by ex-patients who took on the role of mediating between the patients and the professionals. I was now responsible for a catchment area. This meant that anyone from that area who developed a serious mental illness became my responsibility. I had to treat them as I thought best, using the resources that were available. These included a ward in a psychiatric unit, a number of nursing staff and latterly a community mental health centre. I looked after the same patch for twenty years – so I got to know the patients from that area very well. I had never been convinced that people with psychiatric illnesses followed the clear patterns described in the textbooks in psychiatry. However, the longer I was in touch with the same population, the less easy it was to fit each person with a useful diagnosis. The other casualty of this greater familiarity with people's lives was the 'illness-treatment-recovery' model. It was still possible to see symptomatic improvement during spells of treatment in hospital – but when I met people later I would question whether they had 'really' recovered.[38]

In explaining his present point of view he wrote, 'My quarrel is with the idea that *treatment* can make people recover, not with the idea that *people* can recover. I think that there is a very positive message about recovery; it is possible and attainable, but depends on the active involvement of the individual. I am not an anti-psychiatrist but I think that psychiatry needs to be kept in its place. It can do great things to support people, keep them alive, and alleviate their complaints, but it cannot give them a new life . . . there is no science that can be applied to the person as a whole, and so no substitute for the understanding that comes from looking at the person in the context of the narrative of their life.'[39]

Clearly David Whitwell has learned from his patients. However, most of his colleagues do not share his view. He wrote, 'A key issue is strategy. A person needs to have some way that they can regain the feeling that their problems are under control. With mental health there are always several ways in which symptoms can be tackled. It is a question of what helps the person. If it helps to believe that the voice that bullies you night and day is your dead mother, then it helps. It sometimes seems that in psychiatry being right has a higher priority than helping someone to get better. This is a profound problem. Doctors tend to have strong beliefs about the world, and people and science. They hold their theories as articles of faith. Things that are thought or assumed to be true are not seen as beliefs but as facts of life. This is why questioning them is not a matter for discussion and debate.'[40]

Naïve psychiatrists, and naïve psychologists of whom, alas, there are many, have great difficulty in understanding how we live in our language world, our world of ideas, as a fish lives in water, and that everything we know and do is mediated by language – that is, by our ideas. On many occasions I have tried to explain this to psychiatrists and to psychiatrists in training, and each time I have failed. Lawyers, I find, have no difficulty in understanding that 'language creates reality, and not reality language', but then, of course, language is their business.

I have often tried, and failed, to explain to doctors the process of 'reification', whereby we turn a verb into a noun, and then think that because we have a name there must in reality be a thing which possesses that name. For instance, a person is observed to be behaving strangely, and this 'behaving', a verbal form, is turned into a noun. 'This person has schizophrenia.' 'Schizophrenia' becomes a *thing* which some people have and on which millions of pounds and dollars have been fruitlessly spent. The idea that mental illnesses are things which actually exist and which exert influences is quite popular. Thus, the *Guardian* carried the headline 'Depression forced mother to jump from window',[41] as if depression crept up behind her and pushed her out of the window.

Psychiatry has always placed great emphasis on finding the

correct diagnosis. The idea is that if somehow you can isolate from the continually changing spectacle of life a particular portion and give that portion a name, you have, in some way, taken control of the passing spectacle, or at least a part of it. This is, of course, an illusion, as Hindus would say, or a fiction, as Buddhists would say, but we all do it all the time in the attempt to make sense of our experience. Wise people do not take their isolating and naming activities too seriously, but less secure people hang on to their vocabulary of names as a drowning man holds on to a lifebelt. Psychiatry is full of drowning men.

One woman I knew came into the hospital in a very distressed state. She could not, she said, cope with looking after her home and husband and children any longer. She was greatly troubled by headaches and by strange sensations in her head. She had been examined by a consultant physician and a neurologist, and numerous tests had been made, but no physical cause for her symptoms could be found. So she was sent to a psychiatrist, and he had brought her into hospital.

I met her and her husband after the junior doctor had asked me to see them. The husband was a tall, powerfully built man with a fierce temper. He had been reduced to working as a truck driver because the business venture into which they had put all their money had failed. She dared not complain that she had lost her home and her security, because she was afraid of him. It was safer to blame herself and to make her complaint against him a physical complaint which he had to take seriously and treat with concern. It was not difficult to see what was going on, as the couple were very ready to talk. The difficult part would be to get them to pay attention to what they were doing and to consider changing it. The senior nurses on the ward had come to the same conclusion about the couple, and together we tried to work out a treatment plan.

The consultant psychiatrist took no notice of our efforts. He was the clinical tutor who arranged and led the training case conferences. He instructed his junior doctor to present the woman at the case conference as an interesting case for diagnosis. So the junior doctor interviewed her and prepared a case history. The woman was taken to the case conference, where she found herself in a room with fourteen men, only two of whom she had met before. They asked her a lot of questions and she grew more and more confused.

When there were no more questions, the clinical tutor told her to leave the room. Then the doctors set to work to decide upon the correct diagnosis. 'Schizophrenia' and 'manic depression' were discussed and dismissed. 'Endogenous depression' and 'anxiety state' seemed possible, but there was no agreement. The reports of the physician and the neurologist were examined, but an organic cause could not be revealed. The clinical tutor urged his doctors to arrive at a diagnosis. The other consultants grew weary of the discussion and the junior doctors became more and more puzzled. Finally, the clinical tutor produced the answer. The correct diagnosis was, he said, 'hypochondriasis in an inadequate personality'. The junior doctor recorded it obediently in the case notes. Next day the student nurse on the ward showed it to me. 'What does it mean?' she asked.

I replied, 'It means that the woman says she's ill when she isn't and that she can't cope with her responsibilities.'

The student nurse shook her head. She could see that the diagnosis helped no one except the consultant psychiatrist.

When thoughts, feelings, images and ideas are seen as no more than the epiphenomena of the action of the brain, a psychiatrist does not try to understand what a patient tells him. Instead, he listens to the patient to determine what symptoms of mental illness are present. In an interview, Emeritus Professor Alec Jenner described how he used to work. He said, 'It struck me that another mistake I had originally made in psychiatry was to discuss psychopathology with the patients rather than discuss life with them. I was always interested in the sort of hallucination they had, and whether it fitted in with Schneider's classification, and things of that sort. Wherever I went I was The Expert and the patients were the riff-raff.'[42]

The psychiatric system certainly treated the patients as riff-raff, and some of the psychiatrists I have worked with spoke of them as such. One psychiatrist I knew used to refer to the patients on the long-stay wards as 'the dregs'. Alec always spoke of his patients with a wry concern. He had not lost his ability to see patients as people, and it was this and his respect for truth even when the results of his research did not support his theory, which led him to change. His light on the road to Damascus was not me, who was always pointing out his errors, much to his fury, but a young lad. Alec told his interviewers:

At that time a patient that impressed me was a young lad whose father had died and his mother married someone else and the step-father didn't have a lot of time for him. The lad never said anything except: 'You bastard psychiatrists.' He'd attacked a nurse with a knife, pretty viciously. Then one day he said: 'Can I go to the cinema?' He was quite isolated and I was frightened of what he might do. But he said: 'I want to see *One Flew over the Cuckoo's Nest*.' So I decided this was my chance, because this was really his first communication with anybody since we had taken him in. I said: 'OK, but you'll have to be careful, and behave.' He went with some nurses. When he came back he said: 'I can tell you now what's wrong.' So I said: 'Why don't you discuss it with one of the nurses who went with you to the film, and write it all down?' So he said, 'I'll do that. I'll bloody well show you.' The great document never appeared, but we became friends and spent quite a lot of time talking together. The story emerged about him being pushed on one side in the family as the mother struggled to know how to cope with the relationship with a second horrible husband on whom she depended financially but who discriminated grossly between his children and her children from her previous marriage. Her ability to protect her own was compromised and painful to her, and that led to a vicious and complex circle of feelings and despair. So the lad and I began to sort things out realistically, and largely his previous behaviour disappeared.

Alec told two other stories of people who seemed deeply disturbed but whose problems resolved themselves once they were listened to and treated with respect. He commented, 'Both those last two examples were probably the most frighteningly violent patients I had to deal with, and both resolved quite remarkably. Of course, I can't say I was able to help resolve everybody's problems so easily. By the time of those instances I had already lost faith in the possibility of an outright biochemical cure. They just confirmed my loss of belief. So then I became rather frightened. What the hell would I do now?'

What Alec did was to open up his department of psychiatry to a wide variety of people interested in mental health issues. He conducted research into non-biological subjects, such as the meaning hallucinations have for the person experiencing them; he incorporated the NHS art therapists into the university Department of Psychiatry, and he arranged for some new academic posts in order to have in the department two interacting wings, one psycho-therapeutic, including art therapy and a Bachelor of Arts course in Psychiatry, Philosophy and Society, and the other conducting physical studies; he founded the journal *Asylum* with some nurses and colleagues as a forum for democratic debate, and included in this debate patients and ex-patients; he brought together a diverse collection of students and supervisors for masters and doctorate degrees; he enabled the Centre for Psychotherapeutic Studies to be set up; and much more in a similar vein.

In the eyes of the senior doctors in the medical school he was the Devil incarnate. The psychiatrist Duncan Double reported, 'I have been told that the University Department in Sheffield does not have a good reputation because of its antipsychiatric stance.'[43] Alec was asked to oust staff who, as it turned out, brought large amounts of money into the university. He found the actual process of retirement very painful, and he was saddened to learn that his department was likely to return to more strictly medical structures once he had left. He did not want to deny a place for medicine in psychiatry, but he did want a shift in the priorities of those working in the field of mental health.

Psychiatry, as the agent of the state, cannot afford to take account of how individuals think and feel. Any police officer can describe how taking account of the thoughts and feelings of those they charge with an offence muddies the waters of justice. Most, if not all, criminals have had terrible things happen to them early in their lives, and they have ways of thinking which explain, though they do not excuse, their criminal behaviour. An understanding of this is now incorporated into police training. A senior police officer, interviewed on Radio 4 about a fight between groups of Muslim and Hindu young men in Bradford, talked about how these young men felt diminished by not having a job. He went on to say that every young man needs to assert his individuality and significance, or, as he expressed it, 'strut his stuff'. Far be it from me to suggest that the police have great sensitivity and psychological understanding, but at least in the police force there is some overt recognition of the conflict between the viewpoints of the individual and society. In the psychiatric system this is not the case. Instead, the viewpoint of anyone who comes into the psychiatric system as a patient is negated, denigrated and ignored, and the viewpoint of the psychiatrist, as the representative of society, is supreme.

This is abundantly clear in that vast tome, the bible of the psychiatric system, the *Diagnostic and Statistical Manual* (DSM). My copy runs to 886 pages and weighs a kilogram, and it is the paperback version. The DSM is an example of how human beings can take a simple idea and develop it out of all proportion, but all with little reference to what is actually going on. The original idea came from Carl Linnaeus, an eighteenth-century naturalist, who developed a system for classifying plants which everybody interested in botany could use. Psychiatrists in the late nineteenth century thought they could do the same with mental illnesses, but they overlooked one very important fact. When you are trying to decide what a plant in your garden is, the plant does not look at you and think, 'I don't like this person so I'm going to shut my petals tight,' or, 'This person is so keen for me to be a pink carnation that I'll pretend I am one, even though I'm really a yellow dandelion.' Plants do not lie, dissemble, get angry or resentful, or try to please when subjected to study, but people do. Psychiatrists who make use of the manuals that categorize mental illness never seem to realize this. They must think that what they see is really there, and that they have all the necessary knowledge and experience to put people into certain categories without any reference to what the person is actually thinking and feeling. They seem to be unaware that, no matter how well we know another person, we can never know that person completely because we can never get inside another person's head and see things as they see things.

Past years have seen a battle between the DSM in the USA and the International System for Classification (ICD) in Europe. The DSM, backed by the pharmaceutical and health insurance industries, has triumphed and grown bigger and bigger. The term 'mental illness' was dropped and replaced with 'mental disorder'. Look through the DSM and you will see that there is no aspect of human life which is excluded from its pages. You can only conclude that life itself is a mental disorder.

For an excellent account of the history and background of the DSM, read Herb Kutchins and Stuart A. Kirk's *Making Us Crazy*,[44] which won the MIND Book of the Year award in 2000. There you will see how homosexual disorder was suddenly and universally cured when a protest by homosexual people about being told that they were mentally ill was too powerful to be ignored by the authors of the DSM, and how the authors wanted to include the Self-defeating Personality Disorder, which strangely affects women rather than men, but rejected the Delusional Dominating Personality Disorder, which strikes so many men, put forward by the psychologist Paula Caplan.

The DSM is constructed out of agreements by groups of psychiatrists. That in itself is a kind of miracle, because all the studies of how much psychiatrists agree over diagnoses using broad categories like 'schizophrenia' and 'depression' show that what agreement occurs does so largely by chance. However, even if the DSM committee hand-picks their judges and forces them to agree (I am not for a minute suggesting that this is what they do), such agreements are not scientific. Science is about truth, or, as scientists put it, about validity. Agreements between a group of people do not establish truth. Herb Kutchins and Stuart Kirk wrote, 'Even if you found people who agreed that the earth was flat, that the moon is made of cheese, that smoking cigarettes poses no health risks, or that politicians are never corrupt, such agreements do not establish truth.'[45] Even if groups of people agree many times over that there is such a thing as a Self-defeating Personality Disorder, their agreement does not prove that such a disorder exists.

I think that the best summary of what the DSM actually is came from some Australian psychiatrists writing in the *Journal of Law and Medicine*. They said, 'The DSM is no more than the distillate of the prejudices and power plays of a group of ageing American academics, of no interest to most Europeans and only passing relevance to some Australians.'[46]

None of these ageing academics is interested in the thoughts and feelings of people suffering mental distress. Such distress can arise for many diverse reasons, and it can be expressed in many diverse ways, but the one thing that people in this distress have in common is that they have lost their self-confidence, they feel bad about themselves, they judge themselves harshly and feel worthless, all ways of thinking and feeling which are often lumped together under the jargon of 'loss of self-esteem'. The term 'self-esteem' does not feature in the index of the DSM. Neither does 'self-confidence', nor 'loss' of any kind. In the category Major Depressive Disorder one symptom is listed as 'feelings of worthlessness or excessive or inappropriate guilt (which may be delusional) nearly every day (not merely self-reproach or guilt about being sick)'.[47] It is the psychiatrist, not the patient, who decides whether the guilt felt is appropriate, and such a decision depends on the way in which the psychiatrist sees himself and his world. For instance, a patient may be expressing intense guilt over the death of his dog. If the psychiatrist loves dogs and always has one as a pet he would be likely to see such guilt as being appropriate, but if he is indifferent to or hates dogs he would be likely to see the guilt as inappropriate.

Self-esteem is mentioned in Manic Episode but as 'inflated self-esteem or grandiosity'.[48] Again the measurement of the degree of inflation is the psychiatrist's, not the patient's. I have known several exceedingly grandiose psychiatrists beside whom Louis XIV, the Sun God of France, would seem quite plebeian. They always regarded any patient with even slightly grandiose ideas as a competitor and punished him accordingly.

I have spent many years feeling angry and sad about what psychiatrists do to people, while enjoying some smug satisfaction in knowing that we psychologists are always sensitive to our clients' thoughts and feelings. I can no longer enjoy such satisfaction because so many of my colleagues have taken to the DSM like a donkey to a carrot. They use DSM categories in their research as if these categories were real entities. Their conversations are peppered with references to these categories, usually reducing them to initials and thus to the exclusivity which is the mark of a profession more interested in personal pride, power and prestige than in the search for truth. They say ever so casually, 'There's plenty of EBM that shows that CBT and DBT with BPD are cost effective, but not as much as CBT or CAT with PTSD.' Psychologists who have objected to the use of the DSM in clinical work and research have been told by those who do use it that, as Craig Newnes said, 'Psychologists have to use the DSM and have to talk about personality disorders because that's where the money is.'

Psychologists are no different from other people, so it is not surprising that for some of them a little bit of power goes to their head. But there is something else happening, and that is a crime for which my profession has been guilty from its beginnings, because numbers are so much easier to handle than people.

The difficulty in studying people is that people are diverse, messy, inconsistent and endlessly changing. They lie and dissemble. They refuse to fit into categories and they ruin theories. As a psychologist you think up all these wonderful categories and create a lovely theory to use them in. You devise elegant tests to prove your theory, and then you give these tests to various people. You expect them to behave just as you predict. Do they hell! They each go their own way and, if you give them half a chance, they argue with you. What can you do?

You take the results from your tests and run. In the peace and quiet of your office you put your figures in your computer and run a few correlations. Now you look for the correlations that are about the same size. Call this group of correlations a factor and give it a name. If the correlations suggest something nonsensical – say, that left-handed people use lots of salt on their food but enjoy bungee-jumping – you may find it difficult to explain why these attributes should cluster together. You fear that this is just a chance, and therefore meaningless, result. In that case, perform the sleight of hand which is known among statisticians as 'rotating the axes'. If you now get a cluster or two of correlations that seem to hang sensibly together, announce that you have done a principal component analysis and discovered several factors. Ignore the fact that what these factors stand for was readily apparent before you started. Perhaps you have discovered that depressed people feel miserable and do not sleep well. Now leave out all mention of people. Say that there is a strong correlation between depression, low self-esteem and insomnia. All these words are abstract nouns, and the more abstract nouns you use the more highly regarded your work will be. Wherever possible, invent abstract nouns, preferably polysyllabic. *Never* resort to saying that real people actually do something. Real people not only ruin theories, they impede your progress to the upper reaches of your profession. Remember that psychologists who stick closely to real people acquire neither money nor status. This applies to all the professions and all the staff who work in the psychiatric system. If you are really important you never encounter a patient, unless it is a grateful patient and you are both on television.

There has been discussion among some members of the British Psychological Society about whether psychologists should have the right to prescribe medication, but here there is little pressure to allow them to do this. Some American psychologists are demanding they be given this right. Either they see no conflict between telling their clients that the cause and cure of their distress lie in the way they have interpreted their situation and at the same time telling them that their problems can be solved by altering their brain chemistry, or they tell them that their distress is a result of some genetic cause or a brain chemistry imbalance but that therapy can ease the symptoms. American psychologists are usually dependent on psychiatrists for work, and so money comes to override truth. However, it is easy to overlook such discrepancies as one reaches out for the great prize of direct access to the power and wealth of the pharmaceutical industry.

What psychologists should be telling people is that drugs do not change the way we think, nor do they make anyone be nice to you or love you, nor do they solve your problems at work or in your love life, nor do they change your memories of an unhappy childhood into memories of a happy childhood. Drugs can make you richer, but only if you buy shares in drug companies. They can sometimes, in some circumstances, take the edge off your misery or calm you down, and there could be circumstances where this would be worth doing, but only if you have made sure that you have informed yourself fully about these drugs.

This is not easy to do because much of what is presented in the psychiatric system as fact is really propaganda, carefully crafted fictions.

There is the fiction that complex behaviours like depression and schizophrenia have as their root cause a gene for each condition. Many psychiatrists and psychologists state this as if it is an undisputed scientific fact, even though they know – or they should know – that geneticists and physiologists have shown that this is not how genes operate. Denis Noble wrote, 'There is no one-to-one correspondence between genes and biological functions. Strictly speaking, therefore, to speak of a gene as the "gene for x" is *always* incorrect. Many gene products, the proteins, must act together to generate biological functions at a high level. If we must use the expression "gene for x" then we should at least add the plural and speak of "the genes for x". Even this way of speaking is, however, seriously misleading. Not only do many genes co-operate in coding for the proteins that interact to produce any biological function, each gene may also play a role in many different functions, which makes it difficult to label genes with functions . . . It is patterns, not just individual genes which matter.'[49]

Knowing this but not wanting to admit it, many psychiatrists and psychologists now talk about 'a genetic component'. Of course there is a genetic component in being depressed or being psychotic. There is a genetic component in using your mobile, watching television and having lunch. There is a genetic component in everything you do. You exist. If there wasn't a genetic component you wouldn't exist.

Genes cannot account for what we become and what we do. Denis Noble pointed out, 'Much more than the genome is involved in the development of an organism . . . DNA never acts outside the context of the cell. And we each inherit much more than our DNA. We inherit the egg cell from our mother with all its machinery, including mitochondria, ribosomes, and other cytoplastic components, such as the proteins that enter the cell to initiate DNA transcription . . . Also (a mere bagatelle, I allow) we inherit the world. The peculiar chemistry of water, lipids, and many other molecules whose form and properties are not coded for by DNA – all that is given.'[50] Physiologically we are made up of 'networks of interactions at many levels'.[51] At the level of genes, 'genes are controlled by proteins. Those proteins in turn are coded for by other genes. Those other genes can in turn be switched by other proteins coded by yet more genes. The system depends on massive networks of such gene–protein–gene–protein . . . etc . . . interactions . . . These are not networks that operate independently of higher-level process.'[52]

One of the big problems we have in trying to understand ourselves and the world around us is that, in order for our brain/mind to construct a picture, it has to divide into separate chunks the ever-changing, ever-moving whole that, according to the physicists, reality seems to be. We like these chunks to be clear and distinct from one another. Men are different from women, houses are different from horses, and mad people are different from sane people. As Denis Noble said, 'Scientists and others tend to be quite fond of neat, clear-cut patterns. Nature is not. Nature is inherently messy. This should not surprise us. Natural selection has been a long, haphazard process. The fundamental drivers of the process have been random – gene mutation and gene drift, weather, and meteoric and geological events. Why, then, should the outcome have to conform to our logical ideas about how to build a living system that succeeds?'[53]

This is what makes the notion of Intelligent Design so silly. An Intelligent Designer would have known that, when our ancient ancestors decided to walk upright instead of on all fours, their sinuses would not drain properly and their spine and hip bones would have difficulty in supporting their body. Thanks to our Unintelligent Designer we suffer from sinusitis, glue ear, and low back pain.

When our Unintelligent Designer designed our brain he should have seen the difficulties which would arise out of the way we cannot perceive anything unless it stands in contrast to something else. We can't see a black cat on a black night. For us to know anything we have to know its opposite. To know 'I love you' we have to know 'I don't love you'. Sometimes we don't know that we love someone because we have never had any occasion not to love that person. This is one of the reasons why kind, loving parents can find themselves being taken for granted by their offspring. Knowing A and not-A, as the philosophers would say, means that we can want opposing things. Thus we can want company while wanting to be on our own, we can desire the person we hate, and we can be sane and mad simultaneously. To make some kind of sense of what we are experiencing we have to categorize things. However, if we make our categories rigid and then try to impose our categories on to the world, we soon find ourselves defending the indefensible. This is what has happened to psychiatrists who insist that there are clear-cut mental disorders, and that these are caused by malfunctions in the brain.

This brings us to the next fiction which is paraded as scientific fact, namely, that depression is caused by a chemical imbalance and that the SSRI drugs right this imbalance.

If an oncologist published a fact sheet intended for the general public on the cause and treatment of cancer and in it made statements purporting to be scientific facts but which were no more than unsubstantiated opinion, he would be severely reprimanded, if not struck off, by his professional body. Yet psychiatrists can do exactly the same thing and incur no censure at all. Indeed, their unsubstantiated opinion is quoted as fact, and used by the pharmaceutical companies in promoting their wares. Depression, so a great many psychiatrists still say, is caused by a chemical imbalance in the brain.

The history of this idea has been summarized by Jeffrey R. Lacasse and Jonathan Leo in their paper 'Serotonin and Depression: A Disconnect between the Advertisements and the Scientific Literature'[54] They wrote,

In 1965, Joseph Schildkraut put forth the hypothesis that depression was associated with low levels of norepinephrine, and later researchers theorized that serotonin was the neurotransmitter of interest. In subsequent years, there were numerous attempts to identify reproducible neurochemical alterations in the nervous systems of patients diagnosed with depression . . . In a recent review of these studies, the chairman of the German Medical Board and colleagues stated, 'Reported associations of subgroups of behaviour (e.g., violent suicide attempts) with low CSF-5HIAA [serotonin] concentrations are likely to represent somewhat premature translations of findings from studies that have flaws in methodology.' Attempts were made to induce depression by depleting serotonin levels, but these experiments reaped no consistent results. Likewise, researchers found that huge increases in serotonin, arrived at by administering high-dose L-trytophan, were ineffective at relieving depression.

Contemporary neuroscience research has failed to confirm any serotonergic lesion in any mental disorder, and has in fact provided significant counterevidence to the explanation of simple neurotransmitter deficiency. Modern neuroscience has instead shown that the brain is vastly complex and poorly understood. While neuroscience is a rapidly advancing field, to propose that researchers can objectively identify a 'chemical imbalance' at the molecular level is not compatible with extant science. In fact, there is no scientifically established ideal 'chemical balance' of serotonin, let alone an identifiable pathological imbalance. To equate the impressive recent achievements of neuroscience with support for the serotonin hypothesis is a mistake.

Surely all psychiatrists know that the brain does not function as a hydraulic system, yet many psychiatrists still argue that the fact that drugs that increase the amount of serotonin in the brain cure depression proves that depression is caused by a lack of serotonin in the brain. In the same way it can be argued that, since headaches are cured by aspirin, headaches must be caused by a lack of aspirin.

Over the past thirty-eight years I have observed that British psychiatrists rarely let the words, 'I was wrong' pass their lips but, when mounting scientific evidence shows them that one or other of their beliefs is unsupported by the research, they quietly, without fanfare, change what they say. While their less research-oriented colleagues are still insisting that depression is caused by a chemical imbalance, the advertisements for antidepressants in the *British Journal of Psychiatry* are now unlikely to have any mention of chemical imbalance. This is in great contrast to advertisements for antidepressants in the USA, where drugs can be advertised directly to consumers, and on the World Wide Web. Lacasse and Leo found content from consumer advertisements which included, 'When you're clinically depressed, one thing that can happen is the level of serotonin (a chemical in your body) may drop . . . To help bring serotonin levels back to normal, the medicine doctors now prescribe most often is Prozac', and, 'While the cause is unknown, depression may be related to an imbalance of natural chemical between nerve cells in the brain. Prescription Zoloft works to correct this imbalance.'[55]

The detailed fact sheet published on depression by the Royal College of Psychiatrists has no mention of chemical imbalance as a cause, though it still refers to depression running in families and personality being related to genes. This stands in stark contrast to the fact sheet *Why Do I need to Take Antidepressant Drugs?*

published by *beyondblue*, the National Depression Initiative[56], a mental health organization into which the Australian government has poured many millions of dollars. This states, 'Medical research indicates that depression is often associated with specific changes in the chemical message systems of the brain (serotonin, noradrenaline, dopamine).' Further down the page there is the statement, 'Severe depression appears to be associated with a reduction in the chemicals in the brain', followed by, 'Antidepressant medication is designed to correct the imbalance of chemical messages between nerve cells (neurons) in the brain.' Beside these statements is an outline drawing of the head and shoulders of a person with what looks like a leaking balloon in his head but presumably is meant to be the person's brain. Two straight lines from this brain go to two rectangles. The first rectangle is entitled 'Depressed', and the second 'Recovered'. Below the titles and inside the rectangles is a sketch of what could be the heads of two snakes snapping at each other but they are labelled, 'First Nerve Cell', and 'Second Nerve Cell' with the words 'electronic message' printed along each one. By rights these 'nerve cells' should be labelled either axons or dendrites of two cells, but the authors of this fact sheet obviously did not want to tax the feeble minds of their readers too much. Between the first and second nerve cell are some black dots and green arrows. There are more black dots in the Recovered rectangle than there are in the Depressed rectangle. In the Depressed rectangle an arrow points to the diminished dots to indicate that there are 'Reduced brain chemicals', while a similarly placed arrow in the Recovered rectangle indicates that there are 'Many chemicals available'. The psychiatrists who created this fact sheet either do not know that it is rubbish or they do know, but hold their patients in contempt. In either case there is no excuse for such unprofessional behaviour.

Why are so many psychiatrists resistant to changing their ideas? Partly it is laziness. When you've expended a great deal of effort in passing your examinations you do not want to be told that what you learnt is no longer regarded as being true. Partly it is the simplicity of the chemical imbalance or 'a gene for' theory. If you start to take into account what actually happens to people and what people actually do, understanding the subtlety and complexity of human experience takes great mental effort. Moreover, it is personally unsettling because accounts of other people's experiences draw your attention to the issues in your own life. No one can be an expert on the life of another person, so if you do not want to relinquish the pleasure that can come from being courted and entertained at great expense by the drug companies you have to continue promoting the chemical imbalance myth. The way in which the pharmaceutical industry seeks to seduce doctors has been described by David Healy in his book *Let Them Eat Prozac*.[57] Here too David Healy described how he fell foul of Eli Lilly, manufacturers of Prozac, when his research showed that a small but significant number of people taking SSRI drugs became suicidal and, in some cases, murderous. Because he refused to be silenced, those companies which manufacture SSRI drugs now are obliged to mention in their information sheets on these drugs the 'side effect' of suicidal and hostile thoughts.

David Healy continued to monitor all that was coming into the public domain showing an association between the SSRI drugs and hostile or homicidal thoughts and actions. SSRI drugs are now prescribed even more widely than simply for depression. For instance, children deemed to have obsessional compulsive disorder (OCD) are given paroxetine (Paxil), and women diagnosed as having 'premenstrual dysphoric disorder' are given Sarafem which is Prozac under another name. As a result, an increasing number of people are at risk of experiencing, and possibly acting upon, suicidal, hostile or homicidal thoughts. This raises an as-yet unanswered question of whether acting under the influence of a prescribed drug can be used as a defence in a court of law.[58] It is imperative that anyone being prescribed an SSRI drug be given detailed information about all the possible effects of that drug.

Getting information about prescribed drugs is not easy, but it is one of the things in the psychiatric system which has improved. Craig Newnes said:

If you're in a place like our hospital, where the patients' council has done a fantastic amount of work on the information about medication and so on, you're more likely to get some kind of truthful account of what the medication will do to you. Places like Tolgarth in Wales have a patients' council leaflet on medication, which is the only leaflet given to the patient, and it's ruthlessly honest. It lists the pros and cons of each drug. And under cons it will have anything up to a hundred side effects, including death. Under positive effects it quite literally says, 'This medication will help you sleep better.' That's it. And despite that balance, people still take the drugs. So the bottom line is the treatment isn't better, but the information about the treatment's better.

Doctors used to take the view that the less the patients knew the better, but increasing litigation by dissatisfied patients and their families has made doctors and managers more aware of the need to provide accurate information. Even so, the information provided by the psychiatric system often omits important facts. David Crepaz-Keay wrote, 'Many of the everyday things that build confidence and protect people from mental health problems can be harder to get as a result of taking the drug: it is hard to get a job when you cannot muster the energy to get out of bed; it is hard to get a girlfriend when you cannot muster an erection. Even the reparative effects of sitting in the sun may be denied to a person due to high photosensitivity and increased risk of sunburn.'[59]

For a detailed, critical account of the physical treatments used in the psychiatric system, read the chapter on this in Lucy Johnstone's *Users and Abusers in Psychiatry*. For accurate, easily digested information, see MIND's books and pamphlets on the different drugs and their effects.

All this material carries a warning. If you are already taking psychiatric drugs do not suddenly stop taking them. If you do, your body and brain will react in ways which you will find most unpleasant. What you experience is not a recurrence of your old symptoms but the effects of your body and brain suddenly being deprived of a substance they had grown used to. 'Cold turkey' is not advisable for anyone taking psychiatric drugs. If you want to stop taking the drugs you must do so very slowly, diminishing the amount you take each day or even each week by only tiny amounts. You need to give your body and brain time to adjust to the changes.

Very little is known about how psychiatric drugs operate in the body and brain. Even less is known about how electro-convulsive therapy (ECT) works. ECT, wrote Lucy Johnstone, 'is given in a designated room where the patient lies on the bed and is given a general anaesthetic and a muscle relaxant. Padded electrodes are placed on her head and an electric current, about enough to light a lightbulb, is passed through her brain, causing an epileptic seizure lasting approximately 20–90 seconds. She will probably wake up confused and with a headache, and will need to rest for about an hour afterwards. Standard length courses of ECT consist of four to twelve individual shocks given a few days apart.'[60]

Lucy used the pronoun 'she' quite accurately. Many more women than men are given ECT, and many of these women are older women. A report issued by the Department of Health in October 1999 showed that 2800 people – two-thirds of them women – were given ECT in the first three months of that year. Robert Kendall, then President of the Royal College of Psychiatrists, explained that women were more likely to be given ECT because more women than men got depressed, and that older women were given ECT because they were more prone to the side effects of drugs.[61]

When I worked in psychiatric hospitals, sharing meals, case conferences and idle chitchat with my psychiatrist colleagues, I observed that these men were firm in their belief that all a woman needed to be happy was a home, a husband and children. Therefore any woman who had all three but was depressed must have endogenous depression that is, depression which occurred without any external reason. The appropriate treatment for endogenous depression was considered to be ECT. The frequency with which women are still given ECT suggests that psychiatrists still think in this way. I found that most of the male psychiatrists did not enquire into the state of the woman's marriage. Any complaint she might make about her marriage would be discounted with 'That's your illness talking, my dear', while a chat with her husband, man to man, would establish that she had nothing to complain of. My colleagues tell me that little has changed, yet, in fact, many of the older depressed women live with men who are constantly critical, resentful of their own loss of sexual prowess, and all too keen to blame this on their wives, whom they call fat, ugly and useless. Psychiatrists who prescribe ECT do not seem to bother to consider what happens to most women as they get older. Possibly older women patients remind them of their own mother, and that is problem enough. If they looked at their older women patients they would see that as women get older they suffer a series of losses. The menopause shows them they have lost their youth, and their mirror shows them they have lost their beauty. Their children grow up and lead their own lives; their parents die; their marriage may have failed or become unsatisfying; if they work, most are forced at sixty to retire; once they are past fifty they become increasingly invisible because society does not value older women.[62] Most, if not all, of the things that gave them their sense of being a person disappear. Some women manage to retain enough self-confidence to forge a new life, but many women do not. For them the gap between what they thought their life would be and what it actually is widens dangerously. They blame themselves for everything that has gone wrong, and they become depressed.

How on earth could a few shots of electricity through the brain change all this into happiness? Only if the electricity wiped out all memory, but then, if we lose all memory of our past, we lose our sense of who we are. Patients have told me that their psychiatrist had assured them that their bad memories would be obliterated but the good memories remain. Of course, these patients found that this was not so. They certainly forgot many things, events immediately before and after the ECT, and other events that disappeared and left behind blanks in the person's life story. Lucy Johnstone wrote:

Memory loss (reported by 74 per cent of ECT patients in one study) may span all areas of life experience. Thus, people may be unable to recall educational and professional experiences;

201

films, books and plays; important social events such as birthdays and family gatherings; names and faces of friends and acquaintances; household details such as how to do the chores and where things are kept; familiar locations such as the layout of the local shops or town; what happened to them in hospital; inner thoughts and feelings; and public events such as elections and news stories. Obviously this can be extremely distressing.[63]

Lucy quoted one woman as saying, 'There are a lot of blanks that have to be pieced together for me. Sometimes when I get very frustrated and angry, I ask my husband or father to tell me different things that I've known since childhood, like my relatives and uncles, and what my children's names were, and where they were and what they did. I always had a very good knowledge of this because I had been the one in the family who kept in communication and kept the family aware of each other's doings. . . But I cannot go back and feel the feelings I had then. I told my sister one day that I don't remember the things shown in the pictures from my honeymoon, but I can see a happy female in the photographs. The experience is lost. I have the data that somebody gave me, I have the pictures, and therefore I know it did occur. But the actual physical feeling of being there – no, it's gone.'

In our memories 'the physical feeling of being there', like all our feelings, our own personal truth, is the unique meaning which people, places and objects can have for us. A shirt is just a shirt, but when it is the shirt you were wearing when you were intensely happy, or sad, or angry, or frightened, it can take on a very special meaning. One woman who had had ECT said, 'Even when I was depressed my garden was a wonderful solace. Now it's as if the flowers are cardboard cut-outs, or as if I'm watching them on TV. I can't *reach* them.'

'Reach them' refers to the connection we feel to the world around us. For most of us this connection is to nature, to trees and flowers, sky, mountains and sea. This connection can sustain us when everything else in our life is horrible. It is the one meaning which can reliably release us from the prison of our own individual world of meaning. This connection is also the one meaning which can assure us of our worth and importance when the rest of the world is grinding us down.

To have random gaps in our life story, to lose the feelings which are our own truth, to lose the sense of belonging, is to be wounded as a person. No wonder people feel diminished after ECT. No wonder the beneficial effects of ECT, if there are any, last little more than about a few weeks.

Psychiatrists argue that ECT is life saving when a person is severely depressed and unable to eat or sleep or care for themselves. David Whitwell wrote, 'Some psychiatrists think that ECT is essential for people who are refusing food and drink because of their disturbed mental state. However, this is never so clear-cut; even in extreme cases there will be a variety of options.'[64] As I have seen in psychiatric hospitals, ECT certainly blasts such people into submission, but whether good intensive nursing with lots of tender loving care would have much happier results is a question which is not asked, much less examined, in the psychiatric system. Psychiatrists and managers would say, 'We don't have the staff for that,' but there is a deeper reason. In this system being nice to patients is forbidden. Many psychiatrists have explained to me that, if there were pleasant wards and pleasant care, the patients would not want to get better and go home.

If you have turned against yourself and hate yourself, if you see a large discrepancy between what you thought your life was and what it actually is, if you feel yourself falling apart, and you try to defend yourself but in ways which other people consider to be mad, how can being put in unpleasant surroundings and being denigrated in subtle and not so subtle ways by the people who are supposed to be caring for you help you get yourself together and recover your self-confidence?

What I have written here about the psychiatric system will offend many people who work in that system. They will insist that nowadays patients are treated with dignity and respect, and that altogether the system is much, much better.

Just how much better is it?

203

What Has Changed, and for the Better?

Craig Newnes and I worked together in Lincolnshire in the 1970s. This was in the early years of Craig's career as a psychologist. He went on to build up a large psychology service in Shropshire, and to be one of the founders of the critical psychology movement. He is a man of prodigious energy, and he is extremely well informed about what goes on in the psychiatric system. When I was gathering information for this book I asked him whether I could record our conversation about changes in the psychiatric system. I began by asking him what had changed for the better since he and I had worked together.

There was a long, long pause. Craig was thinking hard. Finally, he said that patients were now less likely to become long-stay patients for the rest of their lives. Now people might spend two or three years on a rehabilitation ward, but patients on acute wards would be quickly discharged into the community. He went on:

It means you're less likely to be institutionalized. In terms of what's gone on in the community, I don't know that it's better. I think what's happened in the community is that more people have been psychiatrized. They've been labelled: they've been diagnosed, they've been given drugs and they've been told they've got this disorder or that disorder. In Shropshire ten years ago there was no community mental healthcare. Shelton was this rather obscure hospital that not many people knew about – except GPs, of course, and the people who worked there – and if you were fairly mad you'd probably be referred to a psychiatrist in Shelton. The psychiatrists were based in Shelton and they didn't therefore tend to spread the psychiatric message to all the GPs in the wilds of Shropshire. In the last ten years we've developed nine community mental health teams, and they have on average ten professionals in each. They're made up of psychiatrists, clinical psychologists, social workers, community psychiatric nurses, and all those people spread the gospel of madness. So what happens in the community is that you're more likely to get labelled, you're more likely to get diagnosed and assessed. But I don't know if that's *better*.

The story of John Baptist, told earlier, is an example of a person being psychiatrized. Community care can work very well when the team see their role as giving a person support and practical help, with medication being used only if the person and the team work out together what medication is beneficial. However, where teams are concerned only with diagnosis and medication, they take with them into the community all the punitive and destructive attitudes to the patients which dominated the old psychiatric hospitals.

One aspect of treating a person with dignity and respect is that we keep our promises to that person. Patients in psychiatric hospitals were not regarded by the psychiatrists and staff as meriting dignity and respect, and they made no attempt to keep their promises to them. A psychiatrist would promise a patient an appointment for an interview, or a nurse promise to take a patient to his bank or shopping, and the patient would wait and wait, feeling increasingly disappointed and foolish, and finally give up hope that the promise would be kept. Any patient who complained about this treatment would be fobbed off with feeble excuses or publicly shamed for being demanding. For community teams to work well they would have to abandon such attitudes to patients and learn to keep their promises. Therapists and counsellors know that it is utterly unacceptable to fail to keep an appointment with a client, and, if necessity forces this, then they must apologize and make reparation. Not all members of community teams have learnt this. Readers who write to me about the therapy they have received frequently mention how they could not place any trust in a community nurse who would make appointments and then fail to keep them.

Psychiatric nurses are likely to have other habits which they need to abandon. Craig said, 'It's only very recently that nurses have been trained not to distract people when they start talking about the voices they hear. Nurses in psychiatric hospitals had been taught that, if someone starts talking about what the voices are saying, they had to distract the patient and get him to talk about something else.' Marius Romme and the Hearing Voices Network have shown that the voices that a person hears are not merely a symptom of a psychosis but a meaningful part of the person's experience which needs to be understood by anyone who wishes to help that person.

Many psychiatric nurses have undergone additional training in counselling and various kinds of therapy, but, as Craig explained, 'If you go on to the ward for women, you'll see that at half past eight there's a drug trolley, at half past twelve there's a drug trolley, half past five there's a drug trolley, half past nine there's a drug trolley, and you would think the only thing these nurses knew how to do was to administer drugs. Actually loads of them have gone for additional training, and when they talk about what they'd like to do with people, they talk about counselling, but what they actually do is administer drugs. It doesn't matter what you teach people, if you make them work in a psychiatric hospital what they do is administer drugs. In that respect they haven't changed at all.' This also happens to community teams whose main function is seen as administering drugs.

For someone trained in the psychiatric system it is not easy to work in those ways which are essential if patients are to be treated with dignity and respect. It is not just a matter of acquiring a new set of techniques. It is a matter of overcoming the fear of committing the great sin of 'going native'. This was how Sue Aitken described her experience as a psychologist working in a psychiatric team. In an article entitled 'The Patient as Enemy: Notes from a Fifth Columnist', she described how, in a case conference, she attempted to give the team a condensed account of a woman she had been seeing for psychotherapy.

I had been wondering for some minutes what I was doing wrong. The atmosphere in the vast Georgian day room where the ward round was taking place had grown colder by the minute. The social worker's expression was glazed Rogerian [from Carl Rogers, originator of a particular therapy]. Sister was looking through me with the kind of fixed worldly wise expression I imagined she kept for learner nurses, the one she used when they asked with the layman's commonsense naivety why Mr X couldn't have his clothes back . . .

Even the consultant, who had previously offered me affable support, now shifted in his chair, uneasily trying to span the roles of progressive psychiatrist who did not want the local reputation of organic minded autocrat, and husband/father to the ward on whose domestic harmony his easy work relationship relied. He could not afford to flirt with disruptive alternatives.

The social worker kicked off. 'It sounds as if she's very *dependent* on you,' she said. Heads raised. A common denominator thought, 'Yes, that's right.'

'Of course she tries to manipulate us as well,' added sister unhelpfully, with a sideways glance at the doctor. He gave a sympathetic nod to the carpet. The implication was that not only was I being manipulated, but I had not the professional gumption to realize it. 'Manipulation' usually seems to mean that the patient is managing to stay one step ahead of the experts. . .

[From then on] feedback sessions began to be peppered with comments which I found extremely undermining: – 'She's very clever,' 'You can get too involved,' 'She *says* that she doesn't sleep,' 'Yes of course we've heard that too,' 'She's been up to her games again.'

My confidence in my understanding of my relationship with Sheila began to falter. Could so many people have got it wrong? Perhaps I was too gullible – I believed what she told me: too sympathetic, not 'confronting' enough . . .

The ward rounds grew worse, and I found myself starting to present my bit in the kind of humorous, offhand way which seemed to be the popular key-note of the proceeding: 'Well, she's still struggling along much the same, and of course she's rather suspicious of us all. Haw haw.' The art seemed to be to present her as a wayward child, whose transparent antics were a source of great amusement to us grown-ups. This created a sense of common omniscience and predictability about Sheila, which felt comfortable. If she was 'only' trying to manipulate or draw our attention, then we would not 'give her what she wanted'. She would quickly catch on to this, and mend her ways: we would be spared the trouble of working out what smashing the lavatory window actually meant.

Simple answers lightheartedly presented quickly re-established me favourably in the social whirl of the ward round. I could relax, drink my coffee and share a joke with the best of them, but it left me with a depressed sense of betrayal of Sheila. I realized that something like loyalty was in question – just whose side was I on? And amazingly I could not simultaneously be on Sheila's side and on the staff's side. Aha! The puzzle began to clear and the thing took on the atmosphere of a Graham Greene novel. The chaps down at the Club wanted to know if Aitken had gone native. I must declare myself a truly white person. I could quickly buy my way back into the approval of the Club (the ward round) by running down the natives (patients) but I could not enjoy an amicable gin and tonic (milky coffee) at the Club and then go off and consort with the house-boy.

My mistake with Sheila had been to talk about her as if she were an equal whose own view of things was important in understanding her, and this would not do at all. I couldn't just saunter into the Club and start sounding off in all seriousness about how some native thought his own country should be run: there was a trained army to do that dammit.

Sue concluded:

A hospital team of paid trained 'experts' in the care and cure of mental distress needs to have some concrete way of demonstrating their expertise – hence case conferences, interdisciplinary discussions, notetaking, itemized plans of action, and so on. The general feeling is that we should all have a clear idea of the direction things are going to take when a person is admitted, and a plan for the part each one of us will play in the process. There is strong pressure for everyone to 'take the same line', as if by presenting no alternatives we help a person to make choices; or by pretending that we do not disagree, we help her to cope with conflict.

If the patients do not get better, this approach forces us to blame them – they are manipulating, resisting, they don't want to get better – otherwise our expertise is called into question.

The values enshrined in psychotherapy demand a radically different approach, and I do not know if our institutional organizations could accommodate it. If they were to do so we might one day find ourselves being able to write in someone's case-notes or nursing process sheet: 'We have taken her in because she needs comfort, and are waiting for her to tell us what she wants to try next.'[65]

The stance of a therapist or counsellor is necessarily a modest one. Their role is to be a support and a resource to someone who is trying to elucidate what choices are available and what are the best choices to make. Of course, there are therapists who believe that they know what is best for people, but such therapists, while they can do harm, at least have no legal powers to keep their clients in thrall, though they might do this psychologically, whereas psychiatrists have considerable legal authority over their patients. The psychiatric system contains many people who believe that they are experts in their field. Such people can find it difficult to abandon the expert role and adopt the therapeutic stance needed for a community health team.

Such a team works in the community and therefore should draw on the wealth of knowledge about work in the community which has developed since the 1970s, when the idea that people can solve their own problems by working together started to gain momentum. Since then self-help groups for all manner of problems have burgeoned, and professionals drawn to working with self-help groups have to find new ways of working. Any professional wishing to work in the community must adopt a stance similar to that of a therapist, a stance which says, 'I am not an expert but I do have skills which you might find useful. I want to listen to you and so learn.' Sue Holland, a psychologist with many years of experience working in the community, was very critical of the way mental health teams moved into the community. She wrote:

> The move from hospital to community has not grown out of a real sense of communing with its residents, their histories, their struggles, their anger and desires, but merely extends the walls of the hospital ward into the community. Hospital trained staff with hospital gained status (nothing less than seniors and principals) make up the new community mental health teams, with the possible exception of the community psychiatric nurses who are expected to provide both the street credibility and the ethnicity.
>
> In moving their location from the hospital psychiatric wing to the community purpose-built centre, the team member quickly espouses the goals of positive mental health and the involvement with self-help groups. No apprenticeship seems to be deemed necessary. No long nights at tenants' meetings or long hours lobbying councillors at committee meetings. No getting out of bed at 2 a.m. to advise a neighbourhood woman worker how to cope with a suicidal incest survivor. No years of negotiating a therapeutic understanding with priests, teachers, community workers and neighbourhood police. No years of supporting black women in their struggle against day-after-day racist attacks and humiliation. If I sound bitter, it is because I am.[66]

Community teams can make the mistake of thinking that they know all they need to know about the community where they will be working. In the UK most, if not all, of the professionals in a community mental health team are likely to be middle class, while the community in which they work may be working class. The English middle class, on the whole, believe that they understand working-class people, but I, as a working-class Australian, know that they do not. Witness the pitiful attempts by politicians to align themselves with working-class constituents. In the past, Australian professionals (the word 'white' would be redundant here) have assumed that they knew all they needed to know about Aboriginal people, but no longer. Now white psychologists have had to learn a very different way of working, lessons which could well be learnt by community teams everywhere.

In Australia white psychologists have grown up in a society where the emphasis is on the individual, and so solutions to problems focus on the individual, not the community. In contrast, in Aboriginal society the emphasis is on the community. For white society the inability to control one's drinking is seen as an individual failure. The Aboriginal view is that alcoholism is a community problem. Some Aboriginal communities have developed programmes whereby the community limits or abolishes opportunities for drinking and supervises heavy drinkers closely. Such programmes have proved to be very effective.

A white psychologist who offers a service to an Aboriginal community has to work in ways very different from those he would use in a white community. He would have to take his services to the community and not expect the community to come to him. In their account of how a white psychologist should work with an Aboriginal community, David Vicary and Henry Andrews,[67] both psychologists working in Western Australia, described how a white psychologist should spend considerable time learning about how Aboriginal people see themselves and their world and in contrasting his own belief system with this. Referrals should be made informally and meetings held in places chosen by the family of the person who is in difficulties. The family will also decide who should attend the meetings and how frequent these meetings should be. In the 'white' health services doctors reveal very little of themselves to patients. Sometimes they do not even reveal their name. In the Aboriginal community a white professional has to give a full account of himself and be prepared to answer questions about himself, and the community will make its own enquiries about the professional. One aspect of the professional's work which is most important to the Aboriginal community is that the professional should keep his promises.

In Australia it took white mental health professionals a long time to learn that imposing their white psychiatric system on the Aboriginal community was at best useless and at worst harmful. What they had to do was to listen to the community and then see whether what they had to offer was relevant and useful. In the UK much of the best innovative work in mental health has been done by voluntary organizations. Such organizations get little financial support from the government and, unless the organization advocates the use of medication, it gets no support from the drug companies.

Within the NHS some community teams have developed ways of working whereby they listen to the community and try to understand each individual, not in terms of a diagnosis, but in terms of the person's own viewpoint. However, such innovations are at the mercy of the managers, who want to save money, and colleagues who get frightened when one of their number steps outside the system. Methods of listening to clients and getting to know the community take more time and require more staff than simply diagnosing, prescribing and delivering medication. In the short term medication is cheaper than therapy, but over the long term therapy proves to be cheaper. Research into the long-term use of medication in depression shows that a large proportion of patients have recurrent or unremitting depression,[68] whereas research into the long-term effects of therapy, particularly cognitive behavioural therapy, shows that 'Psychological treatment effects are more long-lasting and wide-ranging than those associated with drug therapies.'[69] Unfortunately many managers are prevented by the terms of their budget from thinking in the long term. Accordingly they purchase the treatment which in the short term is the cheapest.

The psychiatrists Patrick Bracken and Philip Thomas, founders of the Critical Psychiatry Movement, set up the Bradford Home Treatment Service whereby patients were treated in their own homes rather than in hospital. They worked in a largely migrant community, and so they strove to avoid Eurocentric notions of illness and cure. In an article in the *British Medical Journal* they showed how the symptoms of a woman who had been given the diagnosis of affective disorder were in fact defences aimed at

maintaining her sense of being a person in the face of disconfirmation from her family. They wrote:

A 53 year old married Sikh woman had had two admissions to
hospital in the previous six years with a diagnosis of affective
disorder. She was referred urgently by her general practitioner
in July 1999, and when seen at home she had pressure of speech
and labile, irritable mood and was noted to be preoccupied with
religion and past events in her life. Her family complained that
she was overactive and spending excessive amounts of money.
She was referred to Bradford Home Treatment Service where
her key nurse, a Punjabi speaker, explored a number of issues
with her and her family.

It emerged that the patient felt in conflict with her elderly
mother-in-law, with whom the family shared a house. She
believed that the elderly lady, who seemed to govern decisions
about her grandchildren's forthcoming marriages, was usurping
her position in the family. At the same time she had a duty of
care for her mother-in-law, who suffered from diabetes and
required her daughter-in-law's help to administer insulin. She
also had a bond of loyalty towards her mother-in-law, which
made it difficult for her to acknowledge the conflict, particularly
outside the family.

With her nurse's support, the patient was able to produce her
own interpretation of her psychotic behaviour:

- *Overactive behaviour and spending excessively:* to
  reclaim her role as mother and wife, to increase her
  contribution to family life, empowerment
- *Overtalkative:* seeking and demanding her husband's time
  when alone, need to discuss and influence family
  decisions, openly airing grievances
- *Hostile, irritable:* openly critical of family, challenging
  and retaliating, disagreeing
- *Preoccupation with past:* to contextualise grievances, add
  weight to her argument, and elicit understanding

213

- *Religious preoccupations:* to renew her strength, a way of coping with stress, a focus in her life.

Framing her problems in this way rather than in terms of a medical diagnosis allowed a space in which these issues could be explored gently with the patient and her family. Her husband became more accepting of his wife's grievances and her behaviour. She has kept well over the past 12 months, needing no drugs.[70]

In September 2006 MIND held a conference entitled 'Coming of Age'. The pamphlet advertising this conference read

21 years from MIND's national conference in 1985, where service users were given an equal share of the platform for the first time, this 24-hour conference has been devised, directed and will be totally comprised of delegates and speakers who are service users and survivors.

As part of the celebrations to commemorate MIND's 60th anniversary (and their ongoing commitment to promoting the voice of service users), this conference is only for people who have had direct experience of mental distress (including service users and survivors). This is to ensure an opportunity to share views and network in a space where users and survivors from all backgrounds can come together without influence from service providers or decision-makers with no personal or direct experience of mental distress.

In the ten years or so before 1985 an increasing number of psychiatric patients felt that they had to protest at the treatment they received in the psychiatric system. Out of these protests came Survivors Speak Out – 'survivors' because they had managed to survive the psychiatric system which destroyed so many people. These survivors became a force which the psychiatric system could not ignore. The term 'user' instead of 'survivor' was more acceptable to members of the psychiatric system, especially when survivors demanded the right to be involved in decision-making and practice in the system. The two great changes in the psychiatric system have come not from professionals but from survivors, namely, user advocacy and involvement in the psychiatric system, and the Hearing Voices Network (see Chapter 12).

Vivian Lewis is a consultant clinical psychologist and Sara Cureton is a service user representative for, amongst others, women who have experienced eating distress. Together they contributed a chapter on the treatment of eating disorders to Volume 2 of *This Is Madness*. They described the often brutal and usually ineffective treatment of anorexic women in psychiatric hospitals, the lack of adequate services in the UK, and the extraordinary difficulties encountered by those women who have tried to set up a service that takes as its starting point the needs and wishes of the women for whom the service is intended.[71]

They concluded their chapter:

Women need to be able to select from a range of psychological therapies, free from the constraint of a male, medical-model-dominated system. They need to be educated and empowered to be able to make fully informed choices. They need to have opportunities to collect together and combine their energies creatively for positive and constructive action. They also need to feel enabled to claim time and space for themselves to reflect on their own particular journeys. Finally, they need to develop a voice that is truly listened to without them having to shout, literally or metaphorically. Women have to rediscover their power and be enabled to develop constructive means of *ex*pression in order to be able to denounce and oppose the manifold means of their *op*pression.[72]

One such centre to meet the needs of women is the Ashcroft Project in Norfolk. It is 'a pioneering charity founded in 1986 for women suffering severe and enduring emotional distress and long term mental health problems. The project provides residential care, respite care, day services and supported housing.'[73]

Near my home in north London is a mental health project called Drayton Park, located in an ordinary house in an ordinary street, set up by women for women, and run by women. However, it was established by an NHS Trust, and shows that women-only projects with a more holistic approach to mental health problems need not rely on voluntary organizations but can be set up as part of the national mental health services. Users made a major contribution to the philosophy and procedures of Drayton Park, and they continue to work there as advocates. Drayton Park offers an alternative for women who would otherwise have been admitted to hospital. A woman may refer herself to Drayton Park, and where such a placement would not be appropriate for her she is helped to explore other alternatives. When a woman leaves the project she can still keep in touch and visit. If they wish to do so, women may bring their children with them. Each woman has her own bedroom and bathroom, which the child can share.

Drayton Park is an example of what, thirty years ago, used to be called milieu therapy. Everything that goes on in the house, from the large array of possible therapies and therapists to the supply of tea and coffee, is aimed at supporting and encouraging the women. Each woman has her own dedicated member of staff, but she can look to other members of staff for guidance and support. The staff and the women eat together in the large, airy dining room. There are a number of sitting rooms and a large garden. When I visited I found the place and the atmosphere completely un-ward-like. It was much more like the group therapy centres that were so popular in the 1970s, Esalen in California, the most famous, and the current Skyros Centre in Greece, where self-knowledge is sought in a beautiful place and a friendly, relaxed atmosphere. At Drayton Park the women are regarded not as 'cases' of some disorder or other, but as people whose lives are difficult and who need to have their worth and acceptability reaffirmed.

Writing in Volume 2 of *This Is Madness*, Jan Wallcraft, a user working for the Mental Health Foundation, and John Michaelson, a university lecturer interested in decision-making, described Drayton Park, though they did not name it, approvingly, and said,

'Although the project was not user-led, it did go some way towards demonstrating that a service model of self-advocacy discourse could be successful in meeting the needs of its users.' They gave as an example of self-advocacy discourse an explanation of intentional self-injury as 'Usually an expression of deep distress; requires sensitive treatment that does not remove personal control', whereas the standard discourse of mental illness would say, 'A sign that the person has become a danger to him- or herself; need for close supervision and control in hospital.'[74]

Another excellent example of professionals collaborating with users is the report by the Division of Clinical Psychology within the British Psychological Society, *Recent Advances in Understanding Mental Illness and Psychotic Experiences*.[75] Well set out and easy to read (for once psychologists have laid aside their usual dictum 'Never use a single-syllable word when a polysyllabic word will do'), it is interspersed with accounts by users of their own experiences. The authors of the report refer to 'experiences' rather than 'symptoms', to 'people diagnosed with schizophrenia' rather than 'people with schizophrenia', and 'people' rather than 'patients'. They avoid pejorative words like 'schizophrenic'. The report recommends that discrimination against people with mental health problems should become as unacceptable as racism or sexism.

Professionals have worked with users to set up patients' councils in psychiatric units and out-patient services, and to set up advocacy schemes whereby users work as advocates for other users who feel unable to speak for themselves. The work of the user movement has been so successful that within the mental health services it has become politically correct for professionals and managers to incorporate, or appear to incorporate, user opinion in their policy-making. In the July 2001 'College News', the Royal College of Psychiatrists reported that 'The College's Council has recently agreed that service users and carers should have more input into decisions about policy and practice.' Accordingly, the existing Patients' and Carers' Liaison Group was to become a Special Committee of Council, two members of the committee were to become members of Council (the principal College decision-making body), and members of the committee were to sit on subcommittees concerned with public policy and public education.

Meanwhile, the Department of Health National Service Framework (NSF) for Mental Health was developed, with good intentions and fine words but, as Lucy Johnstone pointed out, based on assumptions that have not been discussed, much less challenged. She wrote, 'The underlying model of mental distress that informs the document is quite clearly a biomedical one.' All the vocabulary used, entirely uncritically, is that of illness. Mention is made of social factors, but the document reveals no understanding that a medical model will require government services quite different from what is required if mental distress is seen as the outcome of social issues and the difficulties people experience in relationships. A medical model of mental distress will require the government to provide doctors, nurses and psychiatric hospitals. A model based on social and relationship factors will require the government to reduce poverty, improve education, increase support to children and families, and provide more therapists and counsellors.[76]

The present UK government under Tony Blair prefers the illusion of democracy to the real thing. In discussions about the NSF, the Department of Health invited users to take part, and then ignored or sidelined them. The NSF whole-heartedly endorses drug treatments and ECT, and sees the talking therapies as less important than medical treatment, thus showing that the people who wrote the final document had not read any of the extensive literature on users' experience of these treatments. When Premila Trividi, a black user, was invited to be involved in the development of the NSF, she 'jumped at the chance'. Two years later she wrote, 'Even the words ''National Service Framework'' make my heart sink, and I am very clear that I would never again be involved in such a disempowering and damaging consultation process.'

Premila found that there were only seven users in the whole group of over ninety people involved in the consultation. Users had no choice about which area of mental health they could work on. None was allocated to areas relevant to their experience. No attention was paid to issues of race and culture in the discussions, but the users themselves were subject to offensive and demeaning comments such as 'The users here are not representative. They are too articulate.'[77]

With a few exceptions, users' experiences of consultation by the experts might be summed up by a cartoon in *Openmind* in which a doctor is saying to a user, 'Your experiences could be *invaluable* in helping current users, which is why I'd like you to join in preliminary discussions with a provisional sub-committee looking at possible agenda items for the policy department.'[78] Not surprisingly, some user organizations have preferred to develop their own systems of care. The Hearing Voices Network and the various self-harm groups have drawn on their own experiences in the psychiatric system to develop their own kind of counselling and support techniques. Since 2005 trainees in psychiatry have been required to receive training directly from users. Again there is a gap between theory and practice. A study of 'Service user involvement in training: the trainees' view' showed that 'although many trainees have the opportunity to learn from service users, this is still patchy and not necessarily in the local in-house academic programme'. In their answers to a questionnaire about their experience with user trainers, trainee psychiatrists expressed many anxieties and doubts.[79]

Counselling, and courses in counselling, have blossomed over the last ten years. New areas in which counsellors can work have been developed in the NHS. Counsellors can be found working with patients with a physical illness and alongside clinical psychologists. Counsellors have made an impact on GP practices. In England about half of such practices now have a counsellor. One result of this puzzled the psychiatrist Michael King. In an editorial in the *Psychiatric Bulletin* he reported research which showed that 'GP practices with counsellors referred more patients to clinical psychologists, but not to psychiatry, than practices without counsellors'.[80] Perhaps this is because those GPs who see their patients not as cases of illness but as people in an environment feel more at home with psychologists and counsellors than with psychiatrists.

A study published in the *British Medical Journal* in December

2000 showed that counselling was the most effective treatment for depression that had lasted for less than a year. This study also revealed, as did a MORI poll in 1996, that people suffering from anxiety and depression preferred to see a counsellor than to take pills. Literal-minded psychiatrists and managers think of counselling and therapy as being in some way the equivalent of drugs, so that, say, one hour's counselling equals 250mg of an antidepressant. However, counselling and therapy do not work that way. Counselling undoubtedly works, but how and why is another matter.

Craig Newnes wrote about what he discovered when, in his first year in Shropshire, he and his colleague set up what they called 'Introduction to Psychotherapy and Counselling' courses. He described how these courses were concerned with 'those things called "listening skills", and what became very apparent was that we could teach people not to interrupt, and we could teach people to sit quietly with someone, and we could teach people to paraphrase what someone had said and feed it back to them so they then said it again in a different way. What we couldn't teach people is what they were meant to be listening *for*. We eventually worked out that, although they know they're meant to be listening, they don't actually know what they're meant to be listening *to*. You then get this rather weird world where people say, "I felt listened to." When you ask people who had counselling, "What was your counselling like?", they say, "Oh, I felt listened to." So you've got this paradox where the clinical counsellor or nurse has been taught to listen but they've got no idea what they're listening for, but the client still finds that helpful.'

I can confirm this from my own experience. In the course of my career I have seen great changes in depressed and anxious people when all I have done for them is listen to them telling their story. In psychiatric hospitals I have met many people whose case notes were many inches thick but who had never told their story. They had been the subject of countless clinical interviews, but a clinical interview is about what the psychiatrist, and not the patient, thinks is important. What is of prime importance to all of us is our own life story, which we want to tell in our own way.

We all want to feel that our life has some significance. It will of course seem significant to us, but we need other people to confirm that significance. For some people, getting their name in a newspaper or appearing briefly on television is utterly thrilling, even though the media may have held them up to shame and ridicule, because they have had a moment of fame and therefore their lives are now significant. Many people follow the lives of the famous, and those who are famous for being famous, because it is part of an unspoken contract whereby, if we pay attention to other people, then, when it is our turn, other people will pay attention to us.

Having the significance of our life confirmed by others is one of the best defences we can use to hold our meaning structure together. It gives us the courage to face, day by day, the slings and arrows of outrageous fortune and not be defeated. Many of the people who seek help for their mental distress have no one, no relative or friend, to confirm the significance of their life. Good friends can be hard to find, and relatives can be utterly self-absorbed and may listen only to criticize. How wonderful, then, to find yourself in a room, an uninterrupted hour ahead of you, with a sympathetic stranger who has no personal interest in you other than a commitment to listen to your story. You do not need advice. As you tell your story and the stranger listens, you find yourself feeling stronger, more confident, ready to sort out those things in your life which you know need to be dealt with.

Whenever we suffer mental distress we are experiencing conflicts between some of the ideas we hold. Whenever we are busy telling ourselves that we are bad, worthless, deserving of the ills that have befallen us, at the same time our primitive pride is coming to the defence of our meaning structure by being outraged at the insults we have had to endure. This is why people who do not value and accept themselves 'take things personally' – that is, they are offended and hurt by the remarks or actions of other people which would be seen as unintended slights or mistakes by those who value and accept themselves. 'Taking things personally' is a response to an insult to one's pride.

Another conflict arises when we confuse those things which the nature of life prevents us from having with those things we cannot have because of our own ideas.[81] For instance, the nature of life prevents us from being eternally youthful and immortal, so to rail against growing older and dying is a waste of time, though many people do just this. If we believe that it is a fact of nature that anyone over fifty is valueless and utterly unimportant, then we ensure that growing older will, for us, be nothing but misery.[82]

As we tell our story, we may become keenly aware of the conflicts between the ideas we hold. It can be extremely useful to have a counsellor or therapist who is not just listening but knows what to listen for – namely, the ways in which we can create conflicts, traps and dilemmas for ourselves out of the way we create our meanings. In drawing this to our attention, our therapist or counsellor needs to help us understand that we do not see ourselves and our world exactly as they are, but that what we see is what we have learned to see. All we can know are our interpretations, and, as we have created these interpretations, we are free to change them.

Some therapists listen, but only for that which will confirm their particular theory. They are like those psychiatrists who listen only for evidence of the symptoms of mental illness. Good therapists and counsellors listen in order to learn how the other person sees himself and his world.

Different therapists work in different theoretical frameworks and so use different words and metaphors. Very popular at present are cognitive behavioural therapy, interpersonal therapy, cognitive analytic therapy, and psychodynamic therapy. All these techniques demand that the therapist begin by discovering how the client sees himself and his world. The fact that an increasing number of psychiatrists are undergoing training in the popular therapies suggests that an increasing number of psychiatrists are paying attention to how their patients see themselves and their world.

Unfortunately, in some places the old ideas from the psychiatric system remain. Therapy is organized to suit the professionals, not the patients. Many people have been subjected to an investigation through interview or questionnaire only to be told that they are 'not suitable for therapy'. This verdict is presented as the result of scientific tests, when all that is happening is that the professionals want to reduce their waiting lists and look good to their managers. Many people have been offered a course of therapy, but for a ridiculously short period, as if the learning of a very unhappy lifetime could be understood and remedied in the course of six one-hour sessions. Again, this has to do with the waiting lists, money and professionals' convenience.

Therapy and counselling have now become big business, nowhere near as big a business as the drug industry, but big enough for some people to do quite well for themselves. Ten years ago the market in therapy and counselling seemed to be infinite, but it is now clear that the number of people who would consider therapy in times of stress is limited. Many people battle through on their own or with the help of friends; others prefer to take their bad feelings out on those around them and see no reason why they should change. Now there is competition for clients. Psychologists and counsellors in the NHS have more work than they can handle, but therapists and counsellors in private practice compete for trade.

In the USA some ambitious therapists create a niche market for themselves by inventing a disorder and them claiming to be an expert in its cure. In 2000 one such invented disorder was Sudden Wealth Syndrome (SWS), which inflicted the young men and women who became multimillionaires in the dot.com industry. Many of my friends tried to catch this disorder but regrettably it proved not to be contagious. In 2001 the dot.com industry slumped, and suddenly many of the young men and women in the industry were found to be suffering from Sudden Loss of Wealth Syndrome (SLOWS). The 'symptoms' of SWS, as listed on their website by the Money, Meaning and Choices Institute, which claims to have discovered SWS, are: marked increase in anxiety symptoms or panic attacks, money-related ruminations, anxiety and depression in response to stock market volatility, sleep disorders, irritable mood, excessive guilt, identity confusion, fear of loss of control, paranoid thinking, depression.[83] The 'symptoms' of SLOWS are similar to these. However these 'symptoms' are simply a description of how we feel when we discover that there is a serious discrepancy between what we thought our life was and what it actually is. Suddenly becoming wealthy or suddenly losing what we thought was secure create such a discrepancy. The 'anxiety symptoms', 'panic attacks' and 'fear of loss of control' refer to the terror we feel when we sense that we are shattering, crumbling, disappearing. As we lose our sense of being a person we become confused about who we are. We fluctuate between blaming ourselves, and thus becoming depressed, and blaming others, and thus becoming paranoid. We think constantly about our situation, and our fear prevents us from sleeping and makes us irritable. The therapists at the Money, Meaning and Choices Institute did not explain this to their clients, perhaps because they did not understand this themselves. The fact that some dot.com entrepreneurs actually sought treatment for the disorders which had stricken them shows that the purveyors of the emperor's new clothes are doing very well by calling themselves therapists.

In the UK the only effective advertising available to therapists is word of mouth. If you want to find a good therapist, ask among your friends and acquaintances. However, even the most glowing testimonial is not a guarantee of satisfaction. The effectiveness of therapy depends on the nature of the relationship between the therapist and the client. A good relationship is a special kind of friendship, but, as we all know, the fact that we are friends with two people does not mean that when these two people are introduced to one another they will themselves become friends.

When we suffer mental distress, finding effective help is not easy. What we need to do is to help ourselves by learning more about ourselves.

The Alternatives

Chapter Six

Choosing a Defence

Everyone needs some defences. We have to have ways of stopping people overwhelming us and intruding into our privacy. All societies have rules about public behaviour, while individuals develop their own habits of courtesy and social behaviour, not just to grease the wheels of social intercourse but to fend people off by being polite to them. We must have ways of organizing and controlling events whose potential for chaos can be threatening. All societies have laws concerning how we should respond to certain events, while people with some power, such as police officers and teachers, develop a range of techniques for keeping other people in order. As individuals we organize our homes and buy insurance against disasters.

However, all defences, whether those devised by society or those devised by individuals, are expensive. Maintaining law and order costs a great deal of money, while developing those ways of thinking and acting which protect our meaning structure also take time, effort and energy. Defending ourselves requires strength, but we weaken ourselves when we do not value and accept ourselves. The weaker we feel, the more defences we need, and the more defences we need, the more expensive they become.

The stronger we are, the fewer defences we need to hold ourselves together against the threat of being annihilated as a person. This inner strength is a matter of knowing who you are. Then everything about yourself is clear to you. You recognize when your thoughts and actions are influenced by pride because you know how important it is to see things as they are and not as you wish them to be. You are not denying parts of yourself, nor lying to yourself, nor are you torn by inner conflicts. You have met yourself and you and yourself are one.

It is not a matter of never being afraid, because no one lives without experiencing fear occasionally, but it is a matter of recognizing that you are afraid, identifying the cause, and asking yourself whether the threat is real or imaginary and how much your own ideas have contributed to the threat. For instance, being seriously ill can be a threat, but you can increase the threat by being too proud to ask for help. Inner strength means that there is a strong centre to your being even when you are experiencing a whirl of emotions provoked by a confusion of events.

This strong centre comes from not lying to yourself. You know your own truth, the only part of what you know of which you can be completely sure – provided you are not lying to yourself about your thoughts and feelings.

Some people have had this inner strength since childhood, when they were able to resist attempts by the adults around them to force them to lie to themselves, or perhaps they were brought up by people who encouraged them not to lie to themselves. Other people develop this inner strength when, in later life, they realize that the source of many of their fears and conflicts is not what has happened to them but how they have interpreted what has happened to them. They have realized that, when they suffer loss or find that their life is not what they thought it was, it is best to reconstruct their view of themselves and their world, and not to see themselves as the helpless victim of a malign fate. For such people what I say about how we create and use meaning is not profound scientific reasoning but simple common sense.

It is a matter of knowing who you are and accepting who you are. In the dialogue you have with yourself there is no constant refrain about how valueless and unacceptable you are. However, you do not see yourself as a finished work. You want to improve some of your skills and to explore some potentials, but you do not think in terms of not being good enough, of feeling shamed and guilty about your failures, of rejecting and criticizing yourself. Alas, if you do think in these terms you can never rest in your impossible task of trying to be what you think you ought to be, which is to be perfect.

People differ in what attributes they define as the good they must aspire to and the bad which they must avoid. For some people 'good' is being hard working and conscientious, for others being unselfish and generous, for others being smiling, attractive and friendly, for others being an accepted member of a team, but whatever they see as good is a goal which they strive for but which forever eludes them. What many people find the hardest to do when they are trying to change and come to value and accept themselves is to give up assessing themselves in terms of good and bad. This habit of thinking in terms of individual goodness and badness is reinforced by the belief that we live in a Just World where, ultimately, good people are rewarded and bad people punished. All religions teach that we live in a Just World, although they differ in how they define goodness and badness, rewards and punishments. Many people who would describe themselves as not at all religious still feel that, if ultimately goodness were not rewarded and badness punished, they would find life unendurable.

Keen though we may be to see the wicked punished and to get our just rewards, the belief in the Just World prevents us from being a unified person. We divide ourselves in two – the person who merits or does not merit rewards and the person who decides whether rewards or punishments are merited. This division reflects a child's view of the world where, indeed, children are judged by adults and rewarded and punished accordingly. Children always rebel against their parents and teachers. They have to do this, otherwise they will be wiped out as a person and become automatons, always obedient to the adults' bidding. However, if children internalize their relationship with adults and divide themselves into the parent who judges and the child who sometimes submits and sometimes rebels, they are forever in conflict with themselves.

Often people will not be aware that they are basing their interpretations on a belief in the Just World. Some people, such as evangelical Christians, are very clear about their beliefs in a Just World. For them to be good is to believe in the Good News of salvation through faith in Jesus Christ: to be bad is to reject the Good News. Rewards and punishments follow as appropriate. Most people do not make their belief in a Just World as overt and specific as this, but they reveal their belief in it in their reaction to the gains and losses that come their way.

The financial adviser Alvin Hall made a fascinating television series called *Your Money or Your Life*.[1] Each programme consisted of Alvin Hall visiting, at their invitation, people who were in some kind of financial difficulty. He would look at how they handled their money and work out a plan to resolve their difficulties. What was clear in each of these programmes was that the source of these financial difficulties was not a sudden and unpredictable disaster but the meanings these people had given to their money.[2]

One woman who had been enjoying what she had thought was a secure family life in a comfortable home was now facing the loss of her home in the financial settlement that her husband wanted to arrange after he had left her and their children. Women in such a situation usually suffer financial loss, but for this woman her problem was not just financial. She was greatly shocked to discover that being a good wife and mother does not guarantee that your husband will not walk out on you.

In another programme in the series a young couple wanted help with the debt they had accumulated, even though they had on a number of occasions been given generous financial help by their family, money that had been given in order to pay essential bills they had spent on treats for themselves. They agreed with Alvin Hall that they needed to create and stick to a budget, but even with a budget the wife would indulge herself and her daughter by buying clothes which they certainly did not need. As the couple talked to Alvin Hall about how they handled their money, they did not sound like adults discussing a serious problem but like children who were rebelling against their parents by spending their lunch money on sweets. They seemed to have no idea that the people they were rebelling against were themselves.

Many lottery winners reveal their belief in a Just World in their response to their win. I discovered this when I did some work on a television programme about what lottery winners were doing with their prize. The belief in the Just World means that you have to deserve any prize that may come your way. In a Just World the scales of justice must balance. If you win something you do not deserve you will have to strive to be especially good, because if you fail to increase your degree of goodness something bad will happen to you. Thus some of the lottery winners I studied had not allowed themselves to enjoy their win but instead had set up an enterprise whereby they had to work as punishingly hard as they had always done. Other lottery winners dissipated their money as quickly as possible so as to remove the source of the danger they were in, while other winners responded with relief when a catastrophe befell them and thus balanced the scales of justice.

Many of the people involved in marketing and advertising know the power of the belief in the Just World. They devise advertisements for luxury goods with slogans such as 'You deserve it' or 'Naughty but nice'. Sinning can be thrilling, but only if you believe in the Just World.

Believers in the Just World will not indulge themselves in any way unless they feel they deserve it. A friend of mine explained her inability to stop smoking, even though she was well aware of the dangers, with 'A cigarette is my treat. I deserve it'. A spoilt child is one who gets what he does not deserve. Advice to depressed people that every day they should enjoy something pleasant – have some chocolate, go for a pleasant walk, watch an amusing film, relax to some music – mostly falls on deaf ears. They believe they do not deserve any reward and doing something for yourself simply because it is enjoyable is wicked.

Belief in the Just World is a defence against insecurity and the helplessness that comes with insecurity, and it is a defence that is very difficult to give up. If urged to relinquish it many people can conceive only of its opposite – if I am not trying to be good I am trying to be bad. They cannot see that there is a multitude of alternatives to the belief in the Just World available to us, without requiring us to believe in some absolute, unquestionable system of justice.

Some people think in terms of reasonable behaviour, the assessment of such behaviour being dependent on the situation they find themselves in. There are no absolute standards to apply to what can be called reasonable behaviour, so this measure requires constant monitoring. They ask themselves questions like 'I am fond of my mother and want to help her, but is it reasonable for her to expect me to devote all my time to her and for me to feel that I should when I have responsibilities to my own family and to my job?'

I do not believe in the Just World, but I do not think I am particularly wicked. It is important to me to be kind and helpful to people, to try not to hurt them, and to try to keep my promises. When I ask myself why it is important to me to behave in this way, my answer is that whenever I feel I have failed to be kind or have hurt someone or not kept my promise, the smooth tenor of my life is disturbed. I feel jangled and upset. If I ask myself why it is important to me not to feel jangled and upset, my answer is that of an introvert. Being jangled and upset is the chaos that an introvert fears. My way of dealing with this fear is to strive to put things right. I apologize, I try to make amends, I see what I can learn from my errors.

My father was an extravert. He did not believe in the Just World, but he expressed his philosophy of life in three sayings which he often quoted. The first saying, 'You only get back what you give away', does not refer to the Just World but to relationships with other people. If you are nice to people it is likely that they will be nice to you. He did not regard this saying as an absolute rule. In his dealings with my mother he knew only too well that his niceness to her could be answered in the most unpleasant ways. Mother believed that it did not matter how she treated members of her family, though she was unfailingly polite to strangers when she encountered them, and in any family argument she would be utterly ruthless. My father also knew that if he was unpleasant to Mother the consequences would be far worse. He would say, 'You catch more flies with honey than you do with vinegar.' I never met anyone who disliked my father, so in fact he did get back what he gave away. His third saying was 'Never let the sun go down on your wrath'. He knew that relationships were of prime importance to him, and even though he got angry and other people would occasionally get angry with him, he would never sever a relationship.

My father assessed people but did not judge them except where excessive cruelty was involved, as in the behaviour of Montague Norman, the governor of the Bank of England and architect of the Great Depression, and the generals in the First World War who caused the death of millions of men. My mother, a believer in the Just World and driven by a pride that demanded perfection, judged people as harshly as she judged herself. She was always cut off from other people, always disappointed and resentful.

My mother created for herself a very isolated life, and in that isolation she allowed certain ideas to fester. She felt that, if other people spoke about her, it was to her detriment, and, since she believed she was always right, she would not attempt to check her ideas with other people. This is always a grave mistake.

Mary consulted me about how inadequate and anxious she always felt. One day, very distressed, she told me about the disaster of her uncle's visit to her home. Actually, the visit had gone much better than she had expected, despite her considerable anxiety beforehand, and when he left she allowed herself to feel a small glow of pride that she had managed a dinner and breakfast for her family and her uncle without anything going wrong. Or so she thought, until her uncle's thank-you letter arrived. In it he said all the usual things about enjoying his visit and how delightful the dinner had been. Then he wrote, 'You really ought to have a hook for dressing gowns on the bathroom door.'

With this Mary fell apart. 'That's just what my family always do to me. They come and visit and they say everything's nice, and then they go away and criticize me. It's always me. I'm always the one that's stupid, that's got it wrong, and they're going to put me right. It's always me.'

I had a sneaking sympathy for her uncle. On my travels I am always finding myself in strange bathrooms with nowhere to hang my clothes, but I would never dare mention this to my hostess, and

Mary was terribly hurt. So we spent a long time discussing the affair of the missing hook on the bathroom door.

Months later Mary arrived looking happier than I had ever seen her. She had been on holiday, 'a marvellous holiday. I've really been spoilt,' and she had met a cousin, someone she was fond of and had not seen for a long time.

'It was lovely to meet Joan again. We went sailing, just the two of us, like we did when we were girls, and we anchored for lunch, and just talked. I haven't talked like that for years and years. When we were talking, she said Uncle came to visit them – do you remember, when he came to visit me –'

'The hook on the bathroom door,' I said.

'Yes. You do have a good memory. Well, he came to visit Joan, and when he left he wrote and criticized the kind of notepaper she uses. Joan says he always does that when he stays with anyone in the family. It's because he sees himself as head of the family and he thinks it's his job to keep us all up to the mark. I'd have never known that if I hadn't gone sailing with Joan.'

When I told Mary that I had written about the bathroom hook incident as an illustration of the importance of testing one's ideas, she said, 'Yes, but if every time you check you get told that you're wrong and it's your fault, you give up checking, don't you? If you don't get anything right, you have to withdraw.' As this mirrored my experience with my mother and sister throughout my childhood, I could only agree.

Difficult though my mother was for me to live with, she certainly taught me – though not intentionally – many of the things I needed to know when I became a clinical psychologist. As well as keeping herself away from people other than close family, she cut herself off from all those parts of life of which she disapproved. Certain topics, such as sex, were never to be mentioned in her presence. As a child it struck me that my mother must have known about these matters which she refused to discuss. How could she know that something was so vile and immoral that it could not be discussed unless she had already encountered it? Years later, as my clients talked to me about their distress, and in doing so revealed the gaps and inconsistencies in their story which arise when we deny parts of ourselves, it occurred to me that we have to know what it is that we are supposed not to know in order not to know it. We are all aware of the impossibility of not thinking about an elephant when instructed not to do so. Telling ourselves that we do not know what we know takes a great deal of energy, and that kind of loss weakens us.

Knowing that we have to maintain the impossible position of denying what we know makes us fearful of exploring ourselves. Yet the one thing that we each need to understand about ourselves is how we experience our sense of existence and what we fear the most. If we do not know this about ourselves we make decisions about how we live our lives which lead to nothing but misery. Many extravert men, good team players, accept a position as a boss, and then find themselves quite unable to deal with the dislike that employees usually direct at a boss, whoever he may be. Many introvert women devote themselves to their family, only to discover that a life which gives them no sense of achievement is an unhappy one. We need to be able to answer the questions 'How do I experience my sense of existence? Is it in terms of relationships with other people, or is it in terms of my individual achievement, organization and control?' and 'What do I fear the most, complete rejection and abandonment or utter chaos?'

However, it is not just a matter of knowing what is most important to you. You have to have the self-confidence to go after it. Lacking this, both extraverts and introverts get into difficulties. Such extraverts expect to be rejected and abandoned, while such introverts expect to fail.

Betsy always lay awake at night listening to her husband's breathing. She listened carefully, fearful in case the breathing stopped. He was a healthy man, so there was no reason why he should stop breathing, but every pause in his breathing made her heart flutter.

When she was a child she used to listen to her parents' breathing, fearful that it would stop and she would be left alone. Often in the living room after dinner they would doze in front of the fire, and she, instead of reading or playing a quiet game, would sit and listen.

Betsy could not bear to be alone. She complained about having to look after her daughter's dogs, but they made being alone in the house during the day bearable. 'I can talk to them,' she said, 'and if I hit them they come back for a cuddle. They won't go away and stay away' – as her teenage children might if she chastised them. Her children knew that she was fearful of criticizing them, and so they behaved outrageously.

By contrast, Roy, when I asked him what he did with his day, would say, 'I sat in the lounge room.' He refused to join a group. 'Too much chatter,' he would say. Roy had injured his back at work. He should have received considerable compensation, but the doctor he was referred to for assessment, through laziness or incompetence, failed to carry out a proper examination. Roy should have complained, but he lacked the confidence to do so. He sat at home, blaming himself for being a failure.

Part of knowing ourselves is knowing what we do when we feel threatened, either by disconfirmation or by adverse events. Here I need to use the word 'reality', but not to refer to everything that exists, but rather to what for us is everyday reality. There is the reality of what goes on inside us, our thoughts and feelings, and the reality of what goes on around us. Each of these realities has for us a sense of being real. We have not dreamt or imagined it. When life is going well for us these two realities are equally real, but once we are under great stress, for each of us one of these realities becomes more real than the other.

Extraverts turn outward. Other people – who are what maintain their sense of existence – are in our external reality. Under stress extraverts find that external reality remains real while internal reality becomes less real. They seek the solution to their predicament in the world around them. Their motto is 'Don't sit and think. Do something.'

Introverts turn inward. A sense of achievement – which maintains their sense of existence – comes from within. Under stress, introverts find that internal reality remains real while external reality becomes less real. They seek the solution to their predicament inside themselves. Their motto is 'Withdraw, be still, work out what's happening, plan'.

By going into their more real reality, both extraverts and introverts are defending their meaning structure, but how effective their chosen defence is depends on how they feel about themselves. The less they value and accept themselves the more energy they have to use in their defence, and the more desperate the defence they have to resort to. The most desperate of defences are those ways of behaving which are called mental illnesses or mental disorders.

If we understand that our sense of being a person is our meaning structure, that we have to defend our meaning structure against disconfirmation, and that the less we value and accept ourselves the more expensive the defences we need, then all those ways of behaving which society calls mad are easy to understand. No major classificatory system like the *Diagnostic and Statistical Manual* (DSM) is needed.

However, the invention of mental disorders is now an industry in which many people, including some very powerful people, have a vested interest. Fashions in these invented mental disorders wax and wane, but before I can proceed with a discussion of desperate defences I need to talk about three currently popular disorders.

Popular but Confusing Diagnoses

There are two major differences between physical illnesses and mental illnesses. First, physical illnesses have demonstrable physical causes. No physical cause has been found for any of the mental disorders. Second, the prevalence of physical illnesses waxes and wanes according to physical conditions, while the prevalence of mental illnesses depends on the ideas that people hold.

In the eighteenth century the physical illness of scurvy was prevalent in sailors on long sea voyages, but when ships' captains followed the example of the great navigator Captain James Cook and issued lime juice or fresh fruit to their crew, scurvy disappeared. By contrast, while acute psychosis is found in the Third World, chronic schizophrenia is rare, unlike in the industrial world, where chronic schizophrenia is common. The difference arises from the way in which people with psychosis are treated. In the Third World such people are not excluded from their community, whereas in industrialized countries psychotic people are excluded from society and treated with drugs that have a deleterious effect on the brain.

Fashions change in how people express their mental distress. In the late nineteenth and early twentieth centuries a disorder called conversion hysteria was common. The victim developed an apparently physical disorder such as blindness, or an inability to feel pain and touch in a limb, or an inability to walk, but whatever the physical disorder, it did not correspond with any underlying pattern of physical functioning and no underlying impairment of physical functioning could be found. What was happening was that the person was using a physical symptom as a metaphor for some kind of mental distress. Perhaps the blindness was a metaphor for the fact that the person did not want to see what was happening before her eyes, or the anaesthesia of the arm a metaphor for not being able to be touched, or the inability to walk for a lack of confidence in standing up for herself. Most of the people given a diagnosis of conversion hysteria were women, and in that era women were greatly constrained by the conventions of society. As women gained more freedom, the incidence of conversion hysteria declined, and in its place came anorexia and more recently bulimia. Society no longer demanded that women be sexless in thought and deed, but it did demand that they be thin.

People have ideas about how they are allowed to express their distress, and psychiatrists and therapists have ideas about how mental distress ought to present itself. I have often observed that psychiatrists and therapists prefer to diagnose their patients as having a disorder that they can treat rather than a disorder that reflects what is actually going on. Schizophrenia and depression are popular disorders with psychiatrists because there is a defined drug treatment for them, but none of the multitude of personality disorders has any single and simple treatment. Insurance companies have strong views about which mental disorders they will consider for claims. Since the diagnosis of any mental disorder depends on what the patient says about himself, it is not surprising that, as David Healy noted, 'Psychotherapists no less than the pharmaceutical industry coach both their colleagues and the potentially treatable population as to the currently most appropriate clinical presentations.'[3]

Fashions in how mental distress is expressed and fashions in how psychiatrists categorize such expressions may change, but mental distress itself has been with us for ever. We are a physically puny species living on a planet that is indifferent to our existence, despite our desire to believe that the universe is keenly sensitive to our actions, needs and wishes. Sometimes we may enjoy a bountiful harvest, but drought, floods, fire and earthquakes bring us sorrow and loss. Death is inevitable, and even the most secure of us can suffer sickness and disability. Terrible though natural disasters are, we can wreak on ourselves more and greater terrors. Our capacity for war, conflict and cruelty seems to be limitless.

Few of us over a lifetime escape from being part of, or witnessing, or being affected by, some terrible event. We then have to find a way of living with the memory of that event.

Our meaning structure stores memories, but not in the way a filing cabinet stores files. Put a file in a filing cabinet and when you retrieve it a day or a year later it will be in much the same state as when you filed it. Memories are not files. They are constructions, in the same way that thoughts and feelings are constructions. We try to construct each memory in such a way that it fits comfortably into our meaning structure. This means that we forget some aspects of the event, highlight some, and alter others. We have thoughts and feelings about what we remember of the event, and these thoughts and feelings change what we remember. If a memory does fit into our meaning structure we have mastered it, and so we are not overwhelmed with emotion whenever it comes to mind. An important part of inner strength is a mastery of our memories.

We have not mastered a memory if, whenever we speak or even think of that event, we get angry, or cry, or if we dare not talk about a particular event because we feel ashamed and guilty. One of the great benefits of therapy can be that we come to master our memories.

It is easy to master those memories which fit our ideas. If you like to think of yourself as being a competent, helpful person, and you become involved in an event where without difficulty you behave successfully in a competent and helpful way, the memory of that event slips easily into your meaning structure. After the event you will spend a little time congratulating yourself, and then you will turn to the matters that lie in the present and the future, not in the past. However, if you become involved in an event where you make a fool of yourself, or someone outwits you in an argument, you cannot construct a memory which slips easily into your own meaning structure. Instead you go on thinking about the event and feeling the emotions it aroused in you. You may be so upset that you cannot eat or sleep. Perhaps you have nightmares in which you are reliving the experience.

All this thinking, feeling and dreaming is not a waste of time. You are busy working on your memory of the event, reshaping it as a carpenter shapes and reshapes a piece of wood so that it will fit into a certain space. You take the story of the event and write yourself some better lines. How deft we all are at thinking of what we would have said had we thought of it at the time! In rewriting the story you shape it into a story which you can tell to someone else. Perhaps you turn it into a drama which will elicit sympathy from a listener who, in comforting and supporting you, will help you restore your self-confidence. Perhaps you turn it into a comic story to tell your friends, who will laugh with you and let you know that they think you are a wonderful individual who leads an interesting and amusing life. By telling and retelling your story, the emotion involved in the event diminishes. Even the funniest story told two hundred times will become dull.

In reshaping your story you have been moderating those aspects of your story which were threatening to annihilate you as a person. If at the end of the event you think, 'What an idiot I am!', that thought is very threatening. You are not the person you thought yourself to be or want yourself to be. Your pride has taken a blow.

Disconfirmation threatens, and you become frightened. However, if in the process of thinking, dreaming and talking about the event you change 'What an idiot I am' into 'It's an easy mistake to make', the threat to your meaning structure is markedly reduced, even more so if you are able to add to 'It's an easy mistake to make' the pride-restoring thought 'I'll do better next time'. But what if you cannot do this? What if the threat to you as a person is your conclusion 'I am utterly wicked, useless and hopeless', and 'The world is a far worse place than I ever thought it could be'? Gordon Turnbull, a psychologist who investigated the effects of trauma, described a woman who had suffered a great trauma and who was afraid to look in the mirror because of what she might not see, thus confirming her belief that she was already dead.[4] Not dead in the physical sense, but annihilated.

People whose work involves them in dangerous and often catastrophic events – fire-fighters, accident and emergency doctors, nurses and paramedics, aid workers, the military, the police – have to develop ways of thinking which prevent them from creating identity-threatening constructions about those events. Most of them come to think of their work in terms of 'I do what I can to the best of my ability'. Rather than blame themselves for mistakes and inadequacies, they focus on the people who have caused the catastrophe – an enemy force, venal politicians, greedy entrepreneurs, or their perennial enemy, their bosses. They develop the excellent defence of a sense of humour, even a black humour, to maintain a sense of proportion and strengthen their links with their colleagues. All these defences protect their image of themselves as a competent, helpful person.

However, sometimes an event occurs which is so unusual, so outrageously cruel, that it defies a reconstruction which would allow those affected by it to create a memory which can slip easily into their meaning structure.

One such public event was the disaster that occurred in the Hillsborough football stadium in Sheffield, UK, in 1986. To prevent football supporters from running on to the field and missiles being thrown at the players, a high wire fence was built around the pitch.

In a game between Liverpool and Nottingham Forest the Liverpool fans were directed to one enclosed area, but a failure in crowd control on the part of the police and the organizers of the game meant that more and more supporters were pushed into one limited area. The fence prevented any escape, and in the crush ninety-six supporters died. Standing on the pitch, the police watched helplessly as the tragedy unfolded.

Policemen and women are trained to size up a situation in terms of a practical problem which they then set about solving. To do their job effectively they need to think of themselves as being competent problem-solvers. At Hillsborough they were forced to see themselves as helpless and incompetent. They had let people down. Even worse, they could not shore up their failing self-confidence by taking pride in the organization to which they belonged. As they stood there watching the agony of the people behind the wire barrier, they knew that a failure on the part of senior police at the ground to foresee and prevent the disaster had robbed them of the ideas that maintained their sense of identity. They could not take pride in themselves and in their police force. For some of them the disaster challenged their belief in a Just World, and that increased their sense of vulnerability and helplessness. Of course, they did not think in those terms. Rather, what they felt was the terror of the threat of annihilation. This terror, and their efforts to deal with it, went on for days, even weeks, even, for some of these police officers, for years.

Whenever we experience an event the implications of which threaten our meaning structure we cannot simply forget it. We have to go on working on our memory of the event in the hope of mastering it. We think about it, we dream about it. Our thoughts torture us. Our dreams become nightmares. Concentrate though we may on other matters, the memory of the event breaks through, sometimes so vividly that we feel we are reliving the experience. The slightest incident or the smallest object can remind us of the event, and we feel the powerful emotions we felt at the time.

Unable to master our memory, we try to get away from it. We avoid places and people that have links with the event. If asked to recall some aspect of it, a specific incident or how we felt, we sometimes find a strange gap in our memory, like a page missing from a book. Whatever this incident or feeling was, its meaning was so utterly threatening to us that, instead of trying to turn it into a retrievable memory, we have repressed it or isolated and repressed the emotion it aroused. So absorbed have we become in the battle to master our memory we have no energy left over to be involved in ordinary affairs, or even to have the feelings we once had for the people who used to matter to us. We cannot get on with our life until we master our memory, and, as we cannot do this, we have no future. All this effort put into a fruitless task leaves us unable to sleep, or control our temper, or concentrate. Robbed of our belief that we live in a world where we know how to keep ourselves safe, we wait anxiously for the next catastrophe, and every unexpected sound seems to be a confirmation of our expectation.

Whether or not you have been involved in some catastrophe, you can read my description of how we try to master our memory and recognize it as an ordinary, though terrible, experience. Such an experience is not pathological. It is an ordinary human response to an extraordinary event. Everyone going through such an experience needs comfort and support, just as we all need comfort and support when someone we love dies, but it demeans us and denies our experience when our ordinary experience is categorized as a mental disorder. Yet this is what has happened to the experience of trying to master the memory of a catastrophic event. This experience has been turned into Post Traumatic Stress Disorder, abbreviated to PTSD, and all the aspects of the experience which I have described here have been turned into the symptoms of this disorder.[5] How this ordinary experience became a mental disorder is an interesting though disheartening story.

In all wars soldiers encounter many events the memory of which defies mastery. Each man struggles as best he can to live with his memories, but often the struggle markedly reduces his effectiveness as a soldier. The institution called 'the army' always refused to recognize this. Soldiers who could not continue to fight were punished for being cowards or their condition given some derogatory label like 'shellshock' to imply madness. As the army saw it, these men had to be denigrated because, not only did they weaken the fighting force, they might reveal to civilians that war was not the noble enterprise the army presented it as being. Herb Kutchins and Stuart Kirk, in their chapter on PTSD in their book *Making Us Crazy*,[6] described how, in the Second World War, American psychiatrists returned greatly stressed soldiers back to the front line in the belief that all the soldiers were suffering from was 'battle fatigue', and all they needed was sleep and a hot meal before returning to the battlefield. The inefficiency and cruelty of this method was spotlighted during and after the Vietnam War when the Veterans Administration found itself nearly overwhelmed by veterans needing help because they were unable to return to normal life. These men could not do this because they could not master their memories of a war that was waged as much against helpless civilians as against the Vietcong. Many young Americans had gone to Vietnam inspired by President Kennedy's challenge 'Ask not what your country can do for you. Ask what you can do for your country,' and found that what their country asked them to do was to use that country's might against the weak and vulnerable and to give their own lives in an unwinnable war. To add to this horror, the returning veterans found that they were not heroes to their country and that no one wanted to hear the truth about what had happened in Vietnam.

A group of veterans, aided by some professionals who recognized the difficulties they were experiencing, began a campaign for public recognition of the problem. As part of this campaign they approached the committee that decided what should be included in the DSM. After much argument, it was agreed that the veterans' plight should have a place in the DSM, and Post Traumatic Stress Disorder appeared in the third revision in 1980. What the veterans wanted was recognition of their suffering. They did not foresee that the price they were to pay for such recognition was that they were now to be defined as being mentally ill.

Nor could they have foreseen that PTSD would become big

business. Before its invention it was assumed that when someone was involved in a catastrophic event that person suffered for a while and then gradually the suffering decreased. 'Time heals' is an ancient saying. Now the assumption is that whenever a person is involved in or witnesses a catastrophic event that person is inevitably hit by another disaster, a thing called PTSD. You do not simply suffer, you have a disorder. A disorder is a disability, and this disability was caused by someone else. PTSD quickly became a gold mine for lawyers.

Having acquired a disorder, the person has to be treated for that disorder, and there is no shortage of experts of every variety who know all about PTSD. Type the words 'Post Traumatic Stress Disorder' into an Internet search engine and you will be overwhelmed by the number of websites which offer expert advice. Along with these websites there is a library of books on PTSD. Some are self-help books, some are learned tomes written by psychologists and psychiatrists in their usual impenetrable style. Acquire PTSD and you can be a research subject for life. Professional reputations have been built on it, conferences organized, and learned discussions conducted on its symptoms and its cures. Search as you might, you are unlikely to encounter anyone who will say to you, 'What you're going through is horrible, but it is normal. This is what happens to all of us when we have an experience which challenges some of our strongest beliefs. It doesn't mean that you are a bad person or that there is nothing you can believe in. It just means that you need to think about some ideas that in the past you took for granted and perhaps some of these ideas you'll need to change so that you can come to live with your memory of a terrible event.'

The experts in mental disorders do not like plain and simple speaking because that would reveal how little they actually know. The language they use obscures and confuses both themselves and the people who come to them for help. Take, for example, the way reference is made to someone in mental distress. 'That person has schizophrenia' and 'That person is a schizophrenic' are used interchangeably, yet the underlying meanings of each are very different. If we have something – a cold, a car, a mental disorder – then that thing is separate from us, but if we are something – blue eyed, stupid, mentally disordered – then that quality is intrinsic to us.

Take me as an example. I have bronchiectasis. I am an introvert. The disease in my lungs is not intrinsic to me as a person, whereas being an introvert is intrinsic to me. I spend part of each day coughing and part of each day organizing my home and my work. However, coughing is a symptom of my illness, whereas organizing my home and my work is an essential part of me because in behaving like this I am defending my meaning structure and creating a sense of achievement. Anyone who wanted to understand me would have to distinguish between the symptoms of an illness and the outward manifestations of the person I am. To understand those outward manifestations – my behaviour – it is necessary to discover how I see myself and my world.

Professionals concerned with mental disorders do not bother to distinguish 'you have' from 'you are'. Someone with schizophrenia becomes 'a schizophrenic'; someone with the fashionable Borderline Personality Disorder becomes 'a borderline'. However, even though these professionals imply by their choice of words that the illness is intrinsic to the person, they are unlikely to be interested in how a person sees himself and his world. Psychiatric literature is concerned with what people do, not with why they do it.

This sloppy confusion of having an illness and being a person has always existed in the discourse of psychiatrists, but it became embedded in psychiatric discourse when the authors of the DSM sought to extend the territory psychiatrists controlled. Just as various European countries built up their overseas empires in the nineteenth century, so psychiatrists in the twentieth century claimed jurisdiction over every aspect of human behaviour. They were not satisfied to be the experts on the desperate defences – mental illnesses, as they called them – of schizophrenia, mania, depression, obsessions and compulsions and agoraphobia. They wanted to be the experts on every form of behaviour which manifests or causes mental distress. So they invented personality disorders.

A personality disorder is defined in the DSM as 'an enduring pattern of inner experience and behaviour that deviates markedly from the expectations of the individual's culture, is pervasive and inflexible, has an onset in adolescence or early adulthood, is stable over time, and leads to distress or impairment'. At present ten kinds of personality disorder are listed, though as Herb Kutchins and Stuart Kirk have described, there are constant battles over whether this or that supposed personality disorder should be included. The fourth revision of the DSM lists:

Paranoid Personality Disorder is a pattern of distrust and arid suspiciousness such that others' motives are interpreted as malevolent.

Schizoid Personality Disorder is a pattern of detachment from social relationships and a restricted range of emotional expression.

Schizotypal Personality Disorder is a pattern of acute discomfort in close relationships, cognitive or perceptual distortions, and eccentricities of behavior.

Antisocial Personality Disorder is a pattern of disregard for, and violation of, the rights of others.

Borderline Personality Disorder is a pattern of instability in interpersonal relationships, self-image, and affects, and marked impulsivity.

Histrionic Personality Disorder is a pattern of excessive emotionality and attention seeking.

Narcissistic Personality Disorder is a pattern of grandiosity, need for admiration, and lack of empathy.

Avoidant Personality Disorder is a pattern of social inhibition, feelings of inadequacy, and hypersensitivity to negative evaluation.

Dependent Personality Disorder is a pattern of submissive and clinging behavior related to an excessive need to be taken care of.

Obsessive-Compulsive Personality Disorder is a pattern of preoccupation with orderliness, perfectionism, and control.[7]

To this list the authors of the DSM added *Personality Disorder Not Otherwise Specified*. No one escapes. If nothing else, you and I have a personality disorder not otherwise specified.

The whole concept of personality disorder is confused. If personality disorder is an illness, something that a person has, then the illness can be cured or at least medically managed in the way that diabetes is managed. If this is so, it is appropriate that personality disorder be the province of medical doctors – that is, psychiatrists. If a personality disorder is intrinsic to the person, as being an introvert or an extravert is, then it is not a matter of cure but of learning new ways of behaving, in which case it is the province of parents, teachers, clerics, psychologists, therapists and counsellors.

The authors of the DSM are not interested in clarifying this matter. Just as the British took up the burden of empire in order to look after the ignorant natives in far-flung lands, so psychiatrists took up the burden of personality disorder in order to look after weak and ignorant humanity. In neither case had it got anything to do with making money and being powerful.

Nevertheless, Borderline Personality Disorder (BPD) has proved to be both a money-making and personally satisfying disorder. One of the disadvantages for a psychiatrist looking after people with a mental disorder is that they are not great company. Manic people can be terrifying, schizophrenic people live in a world of their own, and depressed people are not a bundle of laughs. The kind of patient that male psychiatrists have always liked is attractive women with the diagnosis of hysteria. These women talk, they are amusing, they sometimes flirt. They can be grateful for the psychiatrist's attention. They can brighten up his day. They can get a bit clingy and demanding, and they tend to get upset, but if that happens he can discharge them or get his junior doctor to see them. In case conferences he can always get a few laughs when he presents them. As for treatment, all the chaps will agree that what this woman wants is a good fuck. Then it is guffaw and snigger with a sideways glance at any woman present to see how she is taking it.

Time rolls on but nothing changes. Hysteria has now become Borderline Personality Disorder and, as ever, many more women than men are given this diagnosis. Herb Kutchins and Stuart Kirk see the use of this diagnosis as a way of discrediting patients and rationalizing the inappropriate behaviour of therapists – namely, having sex with their patients. They give a vivid example of this in an article published in 1989 in the *American Journal of Psychiatry* by a Harvard psychiatrist, Thomas Gutheil, and titled 'Borderline Personality Disorder, Boundary Violations and Patient-Therapist Sex: Medicological Pitfalls'. 'The remarkable thesis of Gutheil's article is that BDP diagnosis of *female patients* is an explanation of the inappropriate sexual behaviour of their *male psychiatrists*. Furthermore, according to Gutheil, if a female patient complains about her psychiatrist's behaviour, it is taken as additional evidence of the accuracy of the diagnosis BDP and increases the likelihood that her accusation will be perceived by others as false.'[8] Thus the age-old cure for hysteria can be applied with impunity by the psychiatrist.

According to the DSM, BPD has nine symptoms, but the presence of only five of these is necessary for a diagnosis. Richard J. Correlli, MD, at Stanford University, an expert on BDP, defined the condition as:

Relationships with others are intense but stormy and unstable with marked shifts of feelings and difficulties in maintaining intimate, close connections. The person may manipulate others and often has difficulty with trusting others. There is also emotional instability with marked and frequent shifts to an empty lonely depression or to irritability and anxiety. There may be unpredictable and impulsive behavior which might include excessive spending, promiscuity, gambling, drug or alcohol abuse, shoplifting, overeating or physically self-damaging actions such as suicide gestures. The person may show inappropriate and intense anger or rage with temper tantrums, constant brooding and resentment, feelings of deprivation, and a loss of control or fear of loss of control over angry feelings. There are also identity disturbances with confusion and uncertainty about self-identity, sexuality, life goals and values, career choices, friendships. There is a deep-seated feeling that one is flawed, defective, damaged or bad in some way, with a tendency to go to extremes in thinking, feeling or behaviour. Under extreme stress or in severe cases there can be brief psychotic episodes with loss of contact with reality or bizarre behaviour or symptoms. Even in less severe instances, there is often significant disruption of relationships and work performance. The depression which accompanies this disorder can cause much suffering and can lead to serious suicide attempts.[9]

Dr Correlli explained the fact that many more women than men are diagnosed with BPD with the statement 'This may be related to genetic or hormonal influences'. There is no form of distress which a woman at any time in her life can suffer which cannot be explained by 'It's your hormones, my dear'. Dr Correlli mentions that women have more incestuous experiences in childhood than men, and that these can have deleterious effects, but then he claims that 'There may be an innate predisposition to this disorder in some people. Because of this there may ensue subsequent failures in development in the relationship between mother and infant particularly during the separation and identity-forming phases of childhood.' That is, it is the child's fault if the mother cannot love the child.

A study reported in the *British Journal of Psychiatry* as long ago as 1984 showed that of twenty-one people diagnosed with BPD, 81 per cent were women, 81 per cent had histories of major trauma, 68 per cent had been sexually abused, 71 per cent had been physically abused, and 62 per cent had witnessed severe domestic violence.[10] These results have been replicated many times.

Louise Pembroke is very familiar with the diagnosis of BPD. Her mental distress had led her to self-harm. The appalling treatment she received in the psychiatric system led her to start a campaigning organization of and for people who self-harm. She found that many of the women who self-harm had been given the diagnosis of BPD. I asked her for her definition of BPD. She wrote:

Women with this diagnosis are viewed by staff as too much like hard work. Any non-compliance or expression of dissent by a woman will add more weight to receiving this diagnosis. My own definition is that BPD stands for: difficult, dependent and going nowhere in the eyes of psychiatrists and psychologists. Many women who get this label are justifiably afraid, because often they have been systematically let down, and then the very people who are supposed to assist end up pathologising that fear by saying that if she doesn't trust them that is part of her mistrustful, fearful condition. It's like raising a hand in front of someone who has been consistently beaten and then punishing her for flinching because she doesn't know whether the raised hand will slap her or not. BPD is one of the worst diagnoses to receive because it is total invalidation and clinical code for 'don't bother'. I call myself 'voice-hearer' because it's descriptive. I remember a friend of mine at the Maudsley emergency clinic being asked, 'What do you think your problem is?' Her response was, 'An appalling life'. I think that would be a more fitting definition of BPD, as women who get lumbered with it usually have had appalling lives that demonstrate incredible resilience in the face of coping with the uncopable.[11]

There is no cure for an appalling life. Pills will not cure it, nor take away the memories and the fear. Calling an appalling life a disorder only makes that life worse. A specific therapy, dialectical behaviour therapy, has been devised for BDP, but, like all therapies, its success is dependent on the quality of the relationship between the therapist and the client. Louise Pembroke told me that, in her experience, 'Practitioners don't have the imagination to think. They find it easier to follow the set structure of a singular deterministic model rather than be led by the individual determining what the framework of working will be. DBT predetermines the problems with universal attributes and universal solutions. The ''24 hour rule'' prohibits contacts between therapist and individual for 24 hours after the individual has self-harmed. Can you imagine the Samaritans having a rule like that! There is no humanity or support in that action. It is the epitome of punishment, something people who self-harm are all too familiar with.'[12]

Anthony Ryle has developed some special strategies for BDP in his cognitive analytic therapy (CAT),[13] which is an integration of personal construct psychology and object relations theory. Object relations theory is concerned with our relationships with our internal objects – that is, the representations of certain people which we create and store inside us. Your mother may be dead but you still have your version of her inside you, which is fine if she was the mother you wanted her to be but not so fine if she was not. Every time you read one of my books you are learning about personal construct psychology. It is concerned with how we create meaning and how the meaning we create determines our behaviour. A CAT therapist has ways of organizing each therapy session, and such organization is aimed at helping the client get a clearer understanding of how he creates meaning.

In the DSM there is nothing at all about treatment. The authors of the DSM are concerned only with observable behaviour that they can categorize as a symptom. They question a patient only in so far as such questioning elicits information about symptoms. They explain the patient's behaviour in terms of an illness. They are not concerned with the reasons why a person behaves as he does. The index of the DSM does not list self-esteem, yet an important part of mental distress, whatever form it might take, is a loss of self-confidence and self-acceptance. The authors of the DSM are not interested in how a person feels about himself. The term 'self-esteem' does not appear anywhere as being relevant to a disorder, except in connection with mania as the symptom of 'inflated self esteem or grandiosity'.[14] Nor does the index of the DSM list extravert or introvert. The authors are not interested in how a person experiences his sense of existence. As a result of this lack of interest the various disorders described are a muddle of the defences to which extraverts and introverts can resort.

BPD, being popular, gets applied to anyone, but of the nine symptoms listed five clearly refer to an extravert's greatest fear and the defences against that fear to which extraverts resort when they face a severe loss of self-confidence. Their greatest fear is the fear of being abandoned. The threat of annihilation is felt as a fear of disappearing. What the DSM calls chronic feelings of emptiness is both the emptiness of being unloved and the diminished realness of thoughts and feelings, while the impulsivity listed by the DSM is the preference for action over thought. Extraverts experience more mood changes than introverts, who are wary of emotion because emotion can create chaos and they prefer to stay calm, but extraverts enjoy emotion because it is stimulating. For them a touch of melancholy heightens their experience of happiness. However, when they lose their self-confidence their emotions give them a wild rollercoaster ride.

These are the characteristics of what used to be called hysteria. However, being given a diagnosis of BPD does not mean that you are therefore an extravert. The diagnosis of BPD tells you nothing about yourself, but a great deal about the person who gave you the diagnosis.

The symptoms listed in the DSM do not arise spontaneously. They are particular ways of behaving in response to a threat to our meaning structure. Some of these ways of behaviour are available to us all, while some are ways used primarily by either extraverts or introverts. Take, for instance, the symptom of PTSD which the DSM describes as 'inability to recall an important aspect of the trauma'.[15] Here part of the traumatic event, or the emotion aroused by the traumatic event, has implications for the person which threaten the person's meaning structure. Instead of trying to master the memory of the event or of the emotion aroused, the person builds a defence against it.

This method of dealing with a threatening memory is analogous to the way we may deal with a troublesome pet dog. When we acquire the dog we discover that it is not house trained. It rushes about the house, scrambling over the furniture, making a mess and destroying our possessions, and, worst of all, it constantly snaps at us and nips our heels. We cannot get rid of the dog, so in the garden, out of sight of the house, we build a pen with fence too high for the dog to jump over. We pay someone to feed it, and we try to forget it is there, but when the moon shines we hear the dog howling and we feel afraid.

When the dog is actually a memory of a terrible event, the pen we may put the memory in is either the defence of repression or the defence of isolation. Neither is an impermeable defence. There is always a leakage, like the howling of a dog, back into consciousness.

With the defence of repression the memory is pushed into that part of the meaning structure which is unconscious. Extraverts favour this defence, and some extraverts become extremely skilled at repressing not simply traumatic events but any event that the person finds a challenge to how they wish to see themselves. However, while the event may not come back into consciousness, the emotion aroused by the event leaks out, and the person feels anxious and irritable without knowing why.

Extraverts who rely heavily on the defence of repression are often 'nervy', impatient, unable to settle at anything for long, and unable to tolerate even the briefest period of being totally alone. Feeling the threat of annihilation, not understanding it, and not being aware of the source of the threat, they may become very demanding of their docile family in order to keep them close. Some of these extraverts keep their family close by a clever use of guilt and an indifference to truth which means they can turn every situation to their advantage. If any member of their family rejects their manipulations they respond with total outrage, and, if that fails, they suddenly become very weak and pitiable, thus provoking guilt in the offending family member and forcing him to surrender. The television comedy series *Steptoe and Son* concerned such a relationship between a manipulative father and a son who wanted to rebel but was easily provoked to guilt by his father. In contrast, some extraverts who rely heavily on the defence of repression keep their family close to them by being very lovable people, genuinely kind, loving, generous, apologetic about their neediness, and never without someone to look after them.

Extraverts who rely heavily on the defence of repression but who lack a docile family survive by creating a crowded environment for themselves with a multitude of objects with which they have the kind of relationship they have with people, thus maintaining their sense of existence. They adorn themselves with jewellery, flowing hair, scarves and eye-catching clothes, and they fill their home to the brim with interesting and exotic furniture, pictures and objects which provide a dramatic setting that friends and acquaintances find enticing. Such extraverts add much-needed spectacle and excitement to the lives of others, but they can lose the relationships they crave because their use of the defence of repression interferes with their memory of events, particularly events which are important to other people, though not to themselves. They may fail to remember the important details of other people's lives, the kind of details which we expect someone who loves us to remember. The defence of repression can ruin friendships.

With the defence of isolation the event is remembered but the emotion that went with the event is isolated and denied. Introverts favour this defence, and some introverts become extremely skilled at denying all emotion. They can describe quite calmly traumatic events which they have experienced and say, 'No, I was not upset.'

Emotion is always troubling to introverts because it challenges control and threatens chaos. Introverts always have a theory about the way things ought to be, and they try to push everything into a pattern that will confirm their theory. Emotion, the person's own truth, can challenge the introvert's theory, and such challenges are always frightening. If you pride yourself on being calm and sensible in a crisis because your theory is that this is the way people ought to behave, getting upset damages your pride and ruins your theory. But emotion denied does not cease to exist. Unacknowledged, it can have a deleterious effect on the efficient functioning of the immune system, thus making the person vulnerable to physical disorders. Moreover, as truth will out, an incident of little apparent importance can trigger a catastrophic grief or anger reaction.

Human beings, as T. S. Eliot once remarked, cannot bear too much reality. We have to repress and isolate some of our experience. However, these are expensive defences, and if we rely on them too much we get into difficulties. One such difficulty could be that we earn a diagnosis of Dissociative Disorder.

The DSM lists four kinds of Dissociative Disorder. Dissociative Amnesia, where the person forgets important personal information, and Dissociative Fugue, where the person forgets who he is and deserts his home for some other place, are examples of the massive repression used by extraverts. The third disorder, Depersonalization Disorder, seems to confuse the experiences of extraverts and of introverts when, under great stress, one of their realities becomes less real. For extraverts the experience is what psychiatrists call depersonalization, whereby the person finds that their internal reality of thoughts and feelings has become unreal. For introverts the experience is what psychiatrists call derealization, whereby the person finds that their experience of external reality, the world around them, has become unreal.

Depersonalization and derealization are experiences which most of us have had when we have been suddenly confronted with a crisis, such as the death of a loved one. Such experiences usually do not last very long, but for a small number of people depersonalization persists. A Depersonalization Research Unit has been set up at the Maudsley Hospital in London. Researchers at this unit described depersonalization as 'a psychiatric condition characterised by an alteration in perception and experience of the self . . . Imagine being constantly out of touch with your own feelings and senses: this is similar to depersonalisation disorder. Sufferers of this disorder experience a sense of unreality and detachment from various aspects of themselves, which manifests itself as a sense of disconnection from one's own body, cognition or affective state. Clinical sufferers sometimes self-mutilate in an attempt to "feel" themselves, such is the severity of the condition.'[16]

The fourth Dissociative Disorder has become extremely popular. It is Dissociative Identity Disorder (DID), which used to be known at Multiple Personality Disorder. DID has always been around – the 1957 film *Three Faces of Eve* was about a woman with three identities inside her – but it came into prominence when in the 1970s child sexual abuse became a topic for public discussion. Many of the women who gave accounts of what had happened to them in childhood described how they defended themselves as a person even though they could not defend themselves physically. They would separate themselves from their body and position themselves somewhere else in the room. They became in effect the person who was being abused and the person who watched the abuse.

An essential part of consciousness is that we are able to observe ourselves. We can observe what we are thinking and what we are doing. In watching what we do, what we actually see is just a part of our body, our arms and the front of our body below the breastbone. However, we often see ourselves in mirrors, so we are able to imagine what we look like to an observer. Also, we are able at times to disassociate ourselves from pain. If, when I am on my own, I accidentally bump my head or cut my finger I scream and yell, but when I am undergoing some small but painful medical procedure I deal with the pain by dissociating myself from it. I am a good patient.

We all have the ability to use the defence of disassociation. However, introverts use it to disassociate the emotion generated in the event from the event itself. Extraverts who do not have a strong sense of being a person – and few children have this – are able to create alternative selves because they are well practised in playing a number of roles. Indeed, extraverts whose sense of being a person is weak will often say of themselves that all they have inside themselves is nothing but a variety of roles. They choose a role to suit a particular situation.

The kind of disassociation which is needed to create alternative identities is possible only with the defence of repression. Some of the people who have been abused use repression to create alternative identities, and some simply repress their memories of abuse. However, repression is not permanent amnesia, and what has been forgotten can break through into consciousness, especially in a situation where the person is trying to remember the past. Once child sexual abuse had become a topic to be discussed in therapy, many women in therapy began to remember what had happened to them in childhood. Some therapists took the view that their clients should confront their parents with their past mistreatment. Not all parents accepted this confrontation as Joy and Jack did. Many parents protested, and soon the recovered memory or false memory controversy was in full swing.

Phil Mollon, who has written an excellent book on the false memory debate, began his *Remembering Trauma*:

> The dark and savage landscape of the recovered memory debate is dangerous territory into which to stumble and fall – a quagmire of pain, rage and fear, with threats, real and imagined, lurking in every murky shadow. People are in agony. Their injuries are childhood abuse, false accusations of abuse and false denials of abuse. Scientists and clinicians, who innocently wade in to help, find themselves lashed by those driven to fury by their anguish. Everyone is paranoid.[17]

Leaving aside the professionals who wanted to be seen as experts in child abuse and the psychiatrists, psychologists and therapists who were embarrassed about having ignored sexual abuse for so long, all the participants were paranoid because they saw themselves as victims. The women and men who had been abused were indeed victims. Parents who entered the debate saw themselves as victims because they felt they had always done their best, while fathers using the Clinton definition of sex as being nothing less than full penetrative sexual intercourse absolutely denied abuse. There were some people, how many cannot be known, who saw themselves as victims of their parents' cruelty and, even though this cruelty did not include sexual abuse, they climbed on to the bandwagon to seek revenge.

All this publicity served to make DID popular. However, I have found that the material available on the Internet on DID is markedly different from that available on BPD. It seems that BPD is a fiction which panders to prejudice, whereas DID seems to be fact presented and discussed by people who have considerable sympathy for someone whose life is so distressing that the person can deal with it only by a kind of role play.

Joan A. Turkus, MD, was medical director of the Post-traumatic and Dissociative Disorders Program at the Psychiatric Institute of

Washington. She presented her overview of diagnosis and treatment on what she called the spectrum of dissociative disorders. This spectrum ranges from the everyday 'getting lost' in a book or film through dissociative amnesia and fugue to DID. She defined dissociation as 'the disconnection from full awareness of self, time, and/or external circumstances. It is a complex psychoneurological process. . . Researchers and clinicians believe that dissociation is a common, naturally occurring defence against childhood trauma. Children tend to dissociate more readily than adults. Faced with overwhelming abuse, it is not surprising that children would psychologically flee (dissociate) from full awareness of their experience. Dissociation may become a defensive pattern that persists into adulthood and can result in a full-fledged dissociative disorder.'

The treatment Dr Turkus recommended was 'long-term psychodynamic/cognitive psychotherapy facilitated by hypnotherapy'. She and her colleagues developed what they called the Empowerment Model, which 'uses ego-enhancing progressive treatment to encourage the highest level of function, ''how to keep your life together while doing the work'' '. That is, she saw as central to therapy the person's sense of self-worth. She noted that 'Antidepressant and antianxiety medications can be helpful adjunctive treatment for survivors, but they should be viewed as *adjunctive* to the psychotherapy, not as an alternative to it.'[18]

The organization Dissociation in the UK published on the Web the Guidelines for Treatment agreed upon by the International Society for the Study of Dissociation. In the section on psychotherapy the guidelines stress that 'The DID patient is a single person who experiences himself/herself as having separate parts of the mind that function with autonomy. The patient is not a collection of separate people sharing the same body. . . Wherever possible, treatment should move the patient toward a sense of integrated functioning. . . Therapists working with DID patients generally ought to hold the whole person to be responsible for the behaviour of all the alternate personalities.'

However, the guidelines also note that 'Doctors who prescribe medication and therapists who treat patients on medication need to be aware that personality states within the person may report different responses and side effects to the same medication.'[19]

When a doctor asks a patient about the effects of medication the patient uses what psychologists call 'declarative memory' to respond. Declaratory memory concerns those memories which can be brought into consciousness. Declaratory memory is a relatively small part of our overall memory. The rest is implicit memory, the memories we acquired by experience but no longer need to bring into consciousness. As babies we had to learn how to bring our hand to our mouth and how to walk. Babies work very hard to acquire these kinds of skills, but as an adult our memory of how to perform these skills has become implicit. All our life we are learning, and much of what we learn is stored in our implicit memory. Implicit memories can be acquired by implicit awareness. We can be aware but not be aware that we are aware. Intuition is the outcome of implicit awareness and implicit memory. We know something without knowing how we came to know it.

Using their knowledge of implicit memories and implicit awareness psychologists have examined what, in a learning task, each of the alternative identities within one person actually learns and how each of them learns it. Alternative identities often deny knowledge of the others' existence. Each has his or her own store of declarative memories. However, what these learning experiments have shown is that implicit awareness appears to cross the amnesic barriers between each identity, and this implicit awareness relates to implicit memory. Phil Mollon commented, 'There may be nowhere to hide from implicit memory. Avoidance of explicit memory requires only to be kept from conscious awareness, whereas implicit memory, by definition, does not require consciousness. The phenomenon of multiple personality and dissociative identity disorder illustrates the complex ways in which the mind can contort and divide itself in an effort to restrict awareness of painful internal and external realities.'[20]

The presence of a number of identities within one individual does not mean that there are several meaning structures within the individual. There is only one meaning structure, but in order to keep itself intact it pretends to divide itself into several separate entities while not allowing knowledge of the pretence to come into consciousness. The aim of therapy is to restore a conscious sense of wholeness which reflects the unity of the meaning structure. Inner strength requires a conscious sense of wholeness.

Dissociative Identity Disorder may have become a popular disorder, but it is a desperate defence chosen by relatively few people. Let us turn now to the desperate defences resorted to by a great many people.

Choosing a Desperate Defence

Choosing a desperate defence is not a matter of considering an array of options and then saying to ourselves, 'I feel very frightened. Now, shall I deal with this by becoming depressed or shall I become manic?' Whether we become depressed or manic is a matter of which outcome becomes inevitable out of the choices we have already made concerning how we see ourselves and our world. The actual experience of a desperate defence never seems to be optional. It always seems to be inevitable, and so it is, but it is inevitable not because of our genes or our brain chemistry but because it is the inevitable outcome of the conclusions we have drawn about ourselves and our world.

For instance, if you hold the beliefs 'Smoking is the only way I can calm my nerves', 'I am a naturally anxious person just like my mother', and 'If I worry about something it won't happen but if I don't worry it will', then these beliefs make it inevitable that you cannot give up smoking. Someone who uses smoking as a defence (and if you cannot give up smoking you are using it as a defence) sees the way to deal with fear and anxiety in terms of ingesting something. Whether what is ingested is nicotine or chocolates depends on other choices you have made. If you see smoking as an effective way of keeping yourself thin and chocolate as a way of getting fat, and if you believe that if you are fat people will not like you, and that if people do not like you that will be the end of

261

you, then it is inevitable that you will keep on smoking. To give up smoking you will have to change the ideas that lead you to smoke.

Not everyone sees ingesting something as the way to deal with fear and anxiety. Some people use their body as the way to deal with these emotions. They see having a physical illness, painful and physically threatening though it may be, as explicable and acceptable while fear and anxiety are not.

Developing some kind of bodily solution and becoming depressed are defences which are available to all of us. The choice of other defences depends on which of the two realities we see as the more real.

Extraverts see external reality as the more real, and so, when their self-confidence diminishes, they may turn to the world outside them. Although the source of their fear is actually inside them, they locate it in their external reality. The danger appears to them to be outside their home, so they do not venture out. However, sometimes the fear and the unacknowledged hate inside them are too great for this defence to work. Then they feel that they must run away from what is inside them, and so they rush into external reality and get busier and busier.

Introverts see internal reality as the more real and so, when their self-confidence fails them, they withdraw into their internal reality. External reality has become unreal and therefore dangerous. It has to be kept in order, so the introvert tries to impose control, but whatever tidying up, cleaning and keeping safe he does, it is never enough, because he constantly doubts that his measures to impose order have been sufficient. When obsessions and compulsions fail, the external reality that the introvert comes to see bears little resemblance to the general image of the world which most people share. His thoughts and actions in terms of his very idiosyncratic perception of himself and his world make sense to him but not to other people.

In summary:

- We can all use our body in some way as a defence.
- We can all use depression as a defence.

- Extraverts can use phobias or mania as a defence.
- Introverts can use obsessions and compulsions or schizophrenia (psychosis) as a defence.

These defences are desperate defences, resorted to when we do not value and accept ourselves and when we have discovered that there is a serious discrepancy between what we thought our life was and what it actually is. Our choice of a defence is determined by the ideas we already hold, and each defence comes into being without any conscious thought or decision-making.

Each of these defences has some general characteristics which all the people who use it experience, but each of us becomes depressed, or agoraphobic, or manic, or obsessional and compulsive, or psychotic in our own individual way.

Chapter Seven

A Bodily Solution?

We turn other people, and ourselves, into objects in order to control our fear. To turn another person into an object, we choose to perceive that person as lacking the needs, desires and feelings that we have. To turn ourselves into an object, we choose not to perceive the needs, desires and feelings that we have.

One of the simplest ways of turning yourself into an object is to regard yourself as nothing but a body. Everything about you can be explained and understood in terms of your body. If you lash out at other people, it is because you are a man, and men have lots of testosterone which makes them aggressive. If you sink into a deep depression, it is because you are a woman, and female hormones cause depression. If you are anxious, it is because your body is prone to producing too much adrenaline. If you have diarrhoea, it is because you have an irritable bowel. If you have a stomach ulcer, it is because your stomach produces too much acid. If you have migraine, it is because your blood pressure changes. If you get bronchitis, it is because you inherited a weak chest.

These kinds of explanations, whether couched in ordinary language or in the jargon of the medical profession, are 'nothing but' explanations, the aim of which is to enclose, belittle and dismiss, rather than to understand. The circularity of their arguments ('You get a lot of colds because you have a weak chest.' 'How do you know I have a weak chest?' 'Because you get a lot of colds.') matches the way in which a part of human experience can be encircled, reduced and dismissed.

Of course, we cannot have rage, depression, anxiety, diarrhoea, ulcers, migraine or bronchitis unless we have a body to have these things in. (I am leaving aside the belief that our soul will continue after our body has disappeared. Presumably in heaven there are no afflictions, of body or soul. Descriptions of hell seem to imply that we take our bodies with us there.) However, to say that these experiences are nothing but events in an object that is a body is to fail to understand what human experience is.

There is a long tradition in western Europe and in the countries that derive their cultures from western Europe of explaining human experience in terms of bodily function. Even before Descartes' division of the person into body and soul had been seized on by the intellectuals, the tradition that a human being is basically nothing but a body was well established. The theory of bodily 'humours' described and explained people in terms of their bodies.

This kind of explanation is immensely attractive. A body is *there*. You can see it. It is contained within its skin. Its movements are like those of a machine. It can be taken apart like a machine. To understand a machine you do not have to consider its social situation. A functioning tractor will function just as well on the steppes of Russia as on the plains of the United States. To understand a machine you do not have to understand its feelings, thoughts, needs or desires, because it does not have any. A body may produce feelings, thoughts, needs or desires, but you do not have to worry about them because they are nothing but froth and bubble, the trivial foam upon the substance of life.

Moreover, there is nothing to be ashamed of if a machine breaks down. A part can break or wear out. That is the nature of a machine. So, if you are your body, and your body is a machine, then there is nothing to be ashamed of if one of your parts breaks down or wears out. There is no need to be ashamed if you are ill.

However, what if the froth goes wrong? What if all those thoughts and emotions make you feel confused and frightened? Why, then, remember how machines work. If a machine, when it is running properly, gives off white smoke as waste, and suddenly it starts giving off black smoke, then you know there is something wrong with your machine. Similarly, when your body is functioning properly, it produces nice white foam, lots of happy, contented thoughts. If something goes wrong with your body it may start producing some nasty black foam, lots of frightening, miserable thoughts. We do not have to worry about what these black thoughts mean. All we need do is discover what is wrong with our body and put it right. If, through the limitations of medical science, we cannot do that, then at least we do not have to feel ashamed if our body is not functioning properly. It is not our fault if the machine breaks down.

And, of course, since it is not our fault, then other people will feel sorry for us. What bad luck, they'll say. Never mind, dear. What can we do to help you? Take things easy. Aren't you brave! I don't know how you put up with it. I do admire you.

Jacky, stricken with osteoarthritis and a thyroid disease for some twelve years, wrote to me to say that she found my book *Depression: The Way out of Your Prison*[1] helpful. She said, 'I am not arguing that chronically sick people become depressed. Indeed, I have met many who seem to take a pride in being ill and have found that their illness brings them attention and consideration which had previously been denied them. The fact that their disease is physical, chronic, and recognized as such, seems to give them a sense of wellbeing and security which they can expect to be life-long. They have, in fact, become much happier people.'[2]

Not all people welcome an explanation of their pain and confusion in bodily terms. A senior nursing sister, writing of her experience of depression, described how she became depressed while she was a patient in hospital following an accident which badly damaged her leg. She wrote:

I know all about the importance of significant life events in the aetiology of depression, but I cannot accept other people's explanation of my depression in terms of my orthopaedic history. I found it helpful to have sympathy for my accident, but infuriating to be told time and time again that I had ample reason to be depressed. Perhaps there are patients who find it more acceptable to be depressed because of a physical ailment. For me this kind of attempted reassurance merely confirmed me in my view that people have a total lack of understanding of how much worse it was to be depressed than to have a broken leg. I found it devastating to be forced to have a physical reason for the way I felt and a belittling of my very real and overwhelming personal and emotional problems.'[3]

When you recognize that you do have 'very real and overwhelming personal and emotional problems', it is very painful when other people treat your problems as being non-existent, or as being much less important than their problems, or as being no more than everyday troubles which anyone can deal with just by being sensible or pulling themselves together. Alas, this is indeed what many people will do, because the sight of other people's personal and emotional problems can remind them of their own.

If, as a child, you have been taught that it is not permissible for you to reveal all your needs, desires and feelings, if you have slotted yourself into the role that your family and your society have decreed is yours, those of your needs, feelings and desires which you are forbidden to have do not disappear. They are still there, and you have to find some way of dealing with them, even if you do not consciously acknowledge their existence.

How can you solve this problem? *Why not try a bodily solution?*

If having a lot of frightening thoughts is a sign that there is something wrong with your body, then perhaps if you are able to make your body very healthy all these frightening, miserable thoughts will go away. Accordingly many of us develop an obsession with health.

There we all are, jogging ten miles each day, spending hours at the gym working out, or going to an aerobics class no matter how tired we are, all in the belief that if we make ourselves stronger and healthier we shall never be frightened, or overtaken by old age and death. In the early 1980s, when the threat of nuclear war between the USSR and the USA loomed large, there was a noticeable increase in the number of people who exercised regularly and took an interest in the food value of what they ate. It is a forlorn hope that you can run fast enough to outpace the waves of a nuclear warhead's destruction, or that a lean and muscled body can withstand radiation, but it is a way of feeling a fraction less helpless in the face of such immense peril. After the bombings in the London Underground in July 2005 many of the people who normally travelled by underground took to cycling instead, despite the fact that their chances of being demolished by a truck were much higher than being blown up by a terrorist bomb.

In recent years, there has been an increasing interest in choosing food to promote health and not merely to sustain life or indulge a fancy. This interest reflects a distrust and a turning away from the vast, complex food industry which is part of the even vaster industries which dominate our world. If we eat food that we know and trust, we shall be safe. Underneath this may be the hope that if we can get back to a simpler life and live close to nature, then we shall be safer. However, when people do, or did, live close to nature and depend entirely on nature, life is both dangerous and short.

One of the few ideas my parents shared was the belief that it was absolutely imperative that bowels should be emptied every day. The fear that life was full of hidden dangers and that people might have within themselves dangerous and destructive powers was transferred into bodily terms – namely, that the waste products of the body are dangerous and must be flushed out daily, or else something terrible will happen. In my childhood home the kitchen cupboard always contained a packet of Epsom salts which my mother took ritually every morning. Many of my battles for autonomy and independence centred on Epsom salts and a metal container and rubber hose which my mother regarded as absolutely essential for good health. Since then I have discovered that I was not the only child whose privacy was intruded upon in this way. The number of packets of laxatives which I see on chemists' shelves suggests to me that the belief that danger can be averted by a daily bowel movement is still powerful.

Of course, a successful evacuation of your bowels can leave you with a sense of completion and achievement. The behaviourist child experts who advise parents to give regular praise to children who pee and crap in the appropriate receptacles are themselves reinforcing this idea. The importance of this feeling of being able to act effectively on the world should not be underestimated. Acting effectively is the means whereby we knit together our internal and external realities, and feel a sense of power. Such experiences are not merely pleasurable. They give us the hope and courage we need to carry our lives forward. We can prove ourselves by acting on the world.

Such acting upon the world and proving oneself can be conceived of solely in bodily terms. Many boys, going through the process of rejecting those aspects of themselves which might be labelled 'feminine', attempt to prove themselves by carrying out feats, like gargantuan eating, or ingesting unusual objects (like live frogs), or leaping out of high windows, or climbing the tallest trees, or being the one who can pee the highest up a wall. Many men, feeling but not understanding their loss of part of themselves in the process of fulfilling their society's concept of what it is to be a man, will try to prove themselves by developing a body that is exceptionally strong, or capable of swift movement, or by carrying out some feat of bravery and peril. The desire to prove yourself by bodily means has provided leaders with an effective method of persuading men to die in battle.

To put yourself through tests of strength and endurance, or to devote much thought and effort to making yourself healthy, you have to have some notion of yourself as being of value. Of course, you are not good enough, but there is something there which you can regard as good. You are worthy of preserving.

If this sense of self-worth diminishes or has never been established, then a bodily solution to the problem of fear by making yourself healthier and stronger will not be appropriate. Instead, the bodily solution can be to become ill.

Not Frightened, Just Ill

As psychologists are wont to say, only behaviour that is rewarded is repeated. Anything which causes us nothing but pain we do once and once only. When I used to say this to my clients who

269

saw themselves as the passive victims of phobias, panic attacks, depressions, obsessions, compulsions and various physical complaints, they looked at me in disbelief and anger. Why would anyone willingly inflict pain upon themselves? Yet we do.

To explain this I usually gave the example of what each of us decided the day we first discovered what happens when you put your hand in the fire or touch something extremely hot. For most of us this was a totally unpleasant experience, one we decided to avoid for the rest of our lives. However, some of us drew different conclusions. Some of us, when we were small children, had parents who ignored us, or who noticed us only to punish us. Then one day, when we burned our hand, we discovered that we were neither ignored nor punished but loved and cosseted and given the attention we craved so much. We drew the conclusion that the pain or injury or illness was a price worth paying for love and security, and so we entered into a lifetime of being ill.

People who believe that they are not sufficiently good and valuable *in themselves* to be the centre of other people's concern can use illness as a way of gaining the kind of attention that is almost as good as being loved and wanted. When such people have been using this device from childhood as a way of dealing with fear, they do not develop a language in which to talk about emotions. If as a child you discover that when you say to your mother, 'Mummy, I'm frightened,' you are ignored, punished, or humiliated, but if you say, 'Mummy, I'm sick,' you are comforted and loved, then you do not develop a language that distinguishes degrees and kinds of fear, anger, envy, greed and love, but you do develop a language that distinguishes different kinds of bodily sensations. These names for bodily sensations come to stand for different emotions, but as the language of the emotions is never developed the person cannot translate bodily sensations into emotions. It is like having a French/English dictionary where all the English words have been removed. The person cannot translate a pain in the neck into the tension and fear we feel when we are under attack from others and cannot retaliate, or a headache into the rush of blood to the head which accompanies sudden and unexpressed anger.

Having only a language of bodily sensations to explore oneself and one's relationships through life means that all questions and answers that arise have to be framed in this language. 'Why am I afraid?' becomes 'Why does the sweat pour off me whenever I tackle a new job?' and 'Why am I lonely?' becomes 'Why do I have this terrible pain in my heart?'

Having nothing but a language of bodily sensations in which to frame questions about experience, a person has to consult other people who know this language. These are doctors, and if the doctor knows only the language of bodily sensations and does not have a language of the emotions, then the answers to his patient's questions can only be expressed in bodily terms. Some doctors do have a language of the emotions and can translate bodily sensations into emotional experience, but many doctors are as limited in their range of languages as their patient, and so the doctor and patient join together in looking for solutions in pills, potions and operations. When the X-rays and the pathology tests fail to reveal a physical cause, and the pills, potions and operations fail to remove the symptoms, the doctor may grow weary of the patient, label him hypochondriacal, and dispose of him by sending him to a psychologist.

Walter once had the opportunity to read his own medical notes and had seen himself described a hypochondriac. This had hurt him deeply, for the pain he felt in his shoulder and arm were as real and strong as any other pain he had ever felt. The fact that the doctors he had consulted could not find a cause for the pain was not his fault. He tried to be patient with them and to believe them when they said that the pain had nothing to do with his heart. When his old GP retired, a young man took over. He asked about his family (he had none) and his friends (he had two) and suggested that he join a social club where he could meet people, Walter tried not to be offended when this young doctor said he would like him to go and talk to a psychologist. He agreed to go, just as he had agreed to years of tests, examinations and medications.

Walter's face was criss-crossed with lines of unhappiness and worry, and his eyes were filled with pain. He told me about his

271

life. He had always worked hard and so had done well. Money was no problem. He could afford to travel and there was hardly an exotic or interesting place which he had not visited. His marriage had been brief and painful, and now he lived alone in considerable comfort with a daily housekeeper who kept his house immaculate, just as he wished. His hobby was buying and repairing antique clocks, which he did with consummate care and precision. Many a man would envy him his life.

That is, a man who had little need for other people and who wished to pursue his own interests would envy him. However, Walter, like all extraverts, had an immense need for other people, and he had made the immense mistake of constructing a way of life for himself which extraverts dread, a life of nearly complete isolation. For him the pain of that way of living was terrible.

Most extraverts develop in childhood the social skills that assure them a steady supply of friends and acquaintances throughout their lives. They may not be greatly interested in the hidden depths of the people they meet, but they are interested in their superficial characteristics, their names, the names of their children, the football team they support, the hairdresser they recommend, the food they are allergic to, and so on, and they flatter and please their friends and acquaintances by remembering these details and enquiring about them. Many an introvert, deficient in these skills because so much time has been spent learning the skills of keeping things in order and trying to understand why things are as they are, has had cause to bless the extravert who eases social interaction and makes everybody feel warm, comforted and loved.

However, not all extraverts learn these skills. Perhaps they grew up in a family which kept itself to itself and where visitors were not encouraged. Perhaps in their childhood they were made to feel so frightened and insecure that all their attention was on themselves and they had no time to get to know other people, especially since all the people around them frightened them so. Perhaps the people around them demanded such high standards and achievements from them that they were so busy being good they had no time just to play and so get to know other people.

Whatever had happened to Walter in his childhood, he had certainly not learned the life-saving skills that every extravert needs. He had no social skills whereby he could get to know other people. He had never learned the art of small talk – how to discuss the weather, or the best route from A to B. If a person asked him a question about something he knew a good deal about he would answer at length, perhaps at greater length than his questioner wanted, but he could not initiate a conversation unless he felt certain that what he wanted to say and to hear was of considerable importance and practical value. The delights of gossip were totally lost on him. This was not surprising. He did not find people interesting, and so the foibles of his fellows amused him not at all. He longed for companions but had no talent for companionship.

I asked him about his childhood. Just an ordinary one, he said, and went on to describe an extraordinary one. His father had died when he was little and his mother married again. His stepfather, he said, was a very fine person. He took a great interest in Walter and in everything he did. He believed in the precept 'If a job's worth doing, it's worth doing well', only in his case it was not just 'well' that he demanded. It was 'perfectly'. He was a fine craftsman and he taught Walter his skills. Walter tried hard and did well, but no matter how well he did he never earned his stepfather's praise.

'He never praised me, not once,' said Walter. 'It was always ''You could have done better''. He never accepted my excuses.'

So Walter tried harder. He did not get angry with his stepfather. That would not be right, and besides, Walter did not like any kind of anger or aggression. That always made him feel very uncomfortable. He hated it at school when the boys started fighting. He always tried to avoid fights. He did not like school much. 'I wasn't any good at sport. I had a lot of sickness, missed a bit of school.'

I did not know whether Walter's shoulder pain was caused by some physical disability or not. I had seen many ill people with a history as a psychiatric patient being dismissed by doctors as 'hysterical' or 'neurotic', yet, at a later date, their symptoms were discovered to have a basis in a menstrual disorder, or high blood pressure, or cancer, or to be a symptom of the psychiatric drugs themselves. However, it is possible to see in Walter's account of his childhood a pattern whereby he had learned to escape from the pressures of home and school by being ill. His mother, he said, always looked after him well when he was ill. Perhaps when he was ill she was allowed to show him the affection that at other times his stepfather would regard as unsuitable for a boy to receive. In his adult life he certainly got on better with women than with men, and it was to women that he looked for love and friendship.

Walter was extremely puzzled when I said that he would feel a lot better if he made the effort to meet more people and actually be interested in them. He could see no connection between his loneliness and his pain. I did not try to describe to him the real physical ache we all feel when we long to be held and there is no one there to hold us. I have never had any success in teaching the language of the emotions to people who failed to learn it in their childhood. Like all languages, it is something we can pick up with the greatest of ease when we are small and learning to speak, but to learn it later in life requires great effort and desire. Like all languages, it can only be learned and practised in relationships with other people, so perhaps if Walter concentrated on some basic social skills he might, in passing, acquire the elements of a language of emotions. He might then be able to distinguish between the pain of loneliness and the pain of a malfunctioning body.

Walter came to see me for several months, and then one day he announced that he would not be coming any more. He was starting to depend on me, and that would never do.

Some of us, when we were making the discovery that fire burns, and burnt flesh is painful, discovered something else, and this discovery made us seek out pain for the rest of our lives. Some children discover that their pain produces not love and comfort but pity, and this is welcome and acceptable, for at other times what they receive is contempt. Biographers of T.E. Lawrence have described how he was fascinated by pain and how he would punish and degrade himself in an attempt to evoke pity rather than contempt. As a child he was frequently thrashed by his mother, who was both powerful and puritanical. People like Lawrence prefer pity to love, because pity is something which comes to us from a distance, whereas love is something up close and therefore dangerous.

Both extraverts and introverts need other people. An extravert's sense of existence is dependent on the presence of other people or animals and objects which to the extravert represent people. An introvert needs other people to keep him in touch with external reality. If we value and accept ourselves we are not frightened of other people, and so we can keep ourselves in touch with other people in the ways we need. When we do not value and accept ourselves we are frightened of other people, and so we cannot keep people around us to ward off annihilation or to stop us withdrawing into ourselves. Consequently, many people find that, although they lead a basically secure life, constantly in the background is a sense of being afraid. Because they do not understand that what they are feeling is the fear of annihilation, they create an endless series of bodily explanations for this fear. They are prone to accidents such as falling off ladders and crashing their car. They catch frequent colds and never miss out on that nameless virus which is always going around. They readily accept suggestions from their doctor that this or that condition might be ameliorated by an operation. They do not get labelled 'hypochondriacal' because most of their complaints and all their accidents clearly have a physical basis, but friends and family may be bemused by the fact that this basically healthy person is always ill or recovering from an accident.

However, the mind and body are one, and fear in our mind is always fear in the body, and fear in our body can make us ill.

From Fear to Illness

Sarah described how the trouble had started two years earlier. She had been riding her moped and a lorry had pulled out suddenly, knocking her down. She was not badly hurt, just bruised, but her moped was destroyed. Next day she felt ill. She developed a high temperature with vomiting and diarrhoea. This illness persisted for a week. Her general practitioner diagnosed 'a virus'. She appeared to get better but the diarrhoea and nausea persisted. She could not eat and lost a great deal of weight. Her GP sent her to a specialist, who diagnosed 'an irritable bowel' and prescribed some medication. She put on the weight she had lost but the diarrhoea and nausea remained. Her GP sent her to me.

She came, she said, because having to rush to the toilet was spoiling her life. She would feel herself getting tense, and then she would have to dash for the toilet. She would wake up in the morning feeling fine, but then she would start to worry about whether she was going to feel tense, and so the tension and churning would start. 'It's the fear of fear,' she said.

She had not told anyone that she was coming to see me. Both her husband and her father had no time for people who were mentally ill. Her father thought that getting upset was 'a weakness'. It was all right to get angry. Her father always hit his children when they annoyed him, and that was often. 'He used to hit me around the head. Couldn't be bothered bending down, I suppose.'

I was struck by how often in her conversation she used words and metaphors to do with the stomach and bowels. In speaking of her father she said, 'I hate his guts'. To explain to me how she felt that her mother-in-law, who kept her house perfect, looked down on her, she said, 'In that house nobody farts'.

Sarah was a good talker, and in her torrent of words she scattered the significant pieces of her life with prodigal abandon. However, she could not pause and put the pieces together. She could see no connection between the nausea and diarrhoea and the conditions of her life, not even the obvious one that terror can loosen our sphincter muscles. She had always had, so she said, 'weak bowels', 'spent a lot of my time in the loo', but she did not connect this with the fear she had of other people. She said, 'A lot of people don't like me. I talk too much. I always get picked on. If my sister and I were fighting my father would blame me for starting it. If my brother was beating me I would be blamed for provoking him.' She denied that her married life was tense, even though she said, 'The children and I feel much better when he's out.' Again and again Sarah spoke of fights in her family, and most of the fights involved her father. His way of imposing his will on his family was to hit his wife and children.

When we are in a prolonged situation involving fighting, either as a participant or as an observer, whether the fighting is in a war or in a family, we have to deny that we are frightened. Soldiers learn to deny their fear by deadening it with alcohol or, as in Vietnam, drugs, or with boredom, obscenities and cruelty to others. In families fear can be ever present, and no more remarked on than the air the family breathes. Every action taken can be aimed at avoiding violence, or defending oneself, or getting one's blow in first. Soldiers may remember witnessing their first battle and the fear they felt then, but children born into a violent family may not consciously remember the first battle they witnessed. Nevertheless, the effect on small children is profound. When Sarah was small she saw her father strike her mother. She heard shouting and her mother crying. From a child's perspective such events are terrifying and inexplicable.

From our earliest days we are in the business of explaining our world to ourselves. In every moment of our experience we are explaining our world to ourselves. Most of the time our explanations are split-second activities, because everything around us and everything happening to us are familiar and already explained, but when something new happens we immediately have to find an explanation. This way we master our experience.

The explanations we create can come only from our past. We interpret every new situation in terms of our past experience. We hear a loud noise, and immediately explain it to ourselves. 'It's the back door slamming,' or 'It's Granddad falling downstairs.' But if we say to ourselves, 'What's that?' and cannot find an answer, we have to rush outside to look, or ask somebody, 'What was that?' Until we can explain the event to ourselves in some satisfactory way we feel uncomfortable, somehow not at one with our world. The explanation we give ourselves need not be true. When I was a small child, and through the sultry evening air would come a deep rumbling sound, my father would say, 'There's Jim McMahon rolling his stones.' I found the line of distant hills beautiful and mysterious, so the picture of Jim McMahon rolling big boulders above and beyond them was to me a thoroughly satisfactory explanation. To me it was true. After all, my father said so. I was never afraid of thunder. Dad's explanation allowed me to master that situation.

However, all too often we come across a situation we cannot master because we cannot explain it in any satisfactory way. It may be that the event is completely novel to us and there is nothing in our past experience which has prepared us for it. When our house disappears in an earthquake, or foreign troops take over our country, or our good and obedient child is revealed as a drug addict, we find that we cannot explain these events in terms of our past experience, and so we cannot master them. They remain in our minds as inexplicable horrors over which we had no control and over which we have to puzzle endlessly.

Sometimes something happens for which we do have explanations available from our past experience, but none of these explanations produces satisfaction and contentment, and so mastery is not possible. We are left puzzling and fretting. We may have been told, as children, that if we were good and worked hard at school, when we grew up we would get a good job and live happily and securely ever after. So we were good and worked hard, and we did get a good job and counted ourselves happy. Then, suddenly, the job disappeared. We were without work. How can we explain this? Was it because we did not work hard enough? Were we not good enough? Or had our parents and teachers lied to us? Do we live in a world where goodness is not always rewarded? To master this event we have either to denigrate ourselves or change the way we see our world and remember our past. Thus mastery can be very difficult to achieve.

A small child has very little past experience to bring to new events. Most events in an infant's life are totally new experiences, and wise parents try to restrict the number of new events an infant has to encounter each day. They try, too, to make these new events something the child can enjoy and so master. If the event is not enjoyable, then wise parents help the child master it by lots of comforting and cuddling and explanations that the child can understand and accept.

However, when a small child is presented with events that he cannot master because there are no explanations he can understand or accept, and because the parents neither recognize that the child is distressed nor seek to comfort and reassure him, then the child is in peril of being overwhelmed and his fragile sense of being a person annihilated. In this situation one desperate defence the child can use is to take the whole experience inside him. He cannot distance himself from it, for it is too vast and all encompassing, and too important, for it involves the people most important to him. It becomes part of himself, part of his fantasies and nightmares, part of his very person.

This is the process by which many of us 'inherited' depression. We took in our mother's depression, and carry within us images of darkness, despair and murderous rage – not our own but our mother's. It is the process whereby many of us first acquired the notion that we were bad. We could explain all that darkness and violence and hate inside us only by seeing it as part of us and knowing it to be bad.

Sometimes this darkness filled with violence, rage and fear is felt as something more compact than a generalized sense of badness. It is felt as an evil *thing* inside, and as a thing in our body it could, perhaps, be got rid of. If we locate this evil *thing* in our digestive system we have ways of getting rid of it. We could vomit it up, or we could void it through our bowels, but it is an evil thing over which we have no control. It stays lodged hard inside us, blocking and cramping our intestines and bowels, and, when we least expect it, it rushes to the exit, soiling and shaming us.

To discover these meanings and make them conscious the person has to return to those events which gave rise to the meanings, and that involves returning to the original fear and helplessness. This is often too perilous a journey to make, even in the company of a friendly therapist, and so many people prefer to explain much of their experience in terms of 'weak bowels'. If your powerful, terrifying and fascinating father has defined fear as weakness, then you will not risk an even more frightening situation.

If fear is a weakness, then Sarah dare not admit that she is afraid. Afraid of being ill, yes, but of a deeper, more pervasive fear, no. When I spoke of how a close brush with death, as she had experienced in the accident, can make us all too aware of our mortality, she said, 'I remember when I was twelve, lying awake at night and worrying about dying.'

It seemed that the conclusion she had drawn from this experience was that she had to be in control of every aspect of her life. She said, 'I make all the decisions in our house – where we'll live, what we'll spend our money on,' and, 'I want everything to be perfect.' She seemed to have planned every part of her future. 'My children aren't perfect. I wanted my daughter to look like me and she looks like my mother-in-law.'

Our children's looks are something we cannot control, just like death. Our bowels can be the battleground where we can fight to control fear and death, just as our bowels were the first battleground between our desire to do what we wanted and the greater powers of our family to control and punish and threaten to annihilate us. The problem about making our bowels the site of and the metaphor for this struggle is that they are no more than weak flesh, and when they are expected to do more than cope with the results of our digestion they soon suffer damage. An irritable bowel can lead to very painful and unpleasant disabilities.

Shortly after Sue Backhouse and Christine Dancy set up the IBS Network with its journal *Gut Reaction*[4] they persuaded the consultant gastroenterologist Nick Read to advise them. He knew that there was more to IBS than malfunctioning bowels. Very gently he set about persuading members of the network to accept that worry and stress played a big part in the condition. However, Nick Read's interests were wider than IBS. He was concerned with what doctors call functional illnesses, maladies which did not show any structural or pathological changes, as distinct from organic illnesses, which have a definitive pathology and cause. In 2005 his book *Sick and Tired: Healing the Illnesses that Doctors Can't*

Cure[5] was published. It is a must-read for anyone who is troubled by a physical complaint that is impervious to treatment.

He began his book by pointing out that, 'By every objective measure, people now have less disease and are living longer than at any time since records were kept . . . [Yet] like anorexics starving in the midst of plenty, more and more people seem to be feeling ill. When people were interviewed for the 2002 General Household Survey, 35 per cent of them claimed to be suffering from a chronic or long-standing illness, an increase of 13 per cent since 1972. Comparable rates of chronic illness have been reported by consumer surveys across the European Union . . . In Australia, a recent survey of self-reported health revealed that as many as 87 per cent of people over the age of fifteen had one or more long-standing health conditions, although these figures included short-sightedness and deafness as well as headaches and backaches.'[6] It seems that 'Literally millions of people are racked by back pain, tormented by abdominal gripes, alarmed by ringing in the ears, tortured by headaches, exhausted by sleep deprivation, frustrated with constipation, debilitated with nausea or faintness or anorexia, overwhelmed by the burden of obesity, terrified by shortness of breath or palpitations or just too sick and too tired to cope.'[7] With an organic illness, irrespective of who the invalids are, their symptoms are the same and their illness runs much the same course. Functional illnesses are not like this. There are as many kinds of headache, back pain, irritable bowel, and so on, as there are people to endure them. Just as we each have our own individual view of the world, so we have our own individual functional illness.

People with functional illnesses are not pretending to be ill. Nick Read wrote, 'In the whole of my medical career I have yet to meet anyone I thought was imagining their symptoms or making them up, but I *have* met thousands upon thousands of ill people who are struggling desperately to protect themselves from potentially mind-shattering effects of unbearable life situations. These people don't deserve to be dismissed with a diagnosis that cannot be treated. Their illness needs to be understood as a state of disharmony involving the whole person – mind, body, spirit – within their particular social environment. And they need to be helped to uncover its meaning and to find an appropriate resolution for what caused it.'[8]

It seems that the state of disharmony existed before the illness. 'Studies of people with chronic functional illnesses have shown that they have experienced more severe loss, more deprivation and more disruption in childhood than healthy people and patients with organic diseases. They are also more likely to report a history of physical and sexual abuse.'[9] 'Many surveys have clearly shown that patients with functional syndromes score more highly for anxiety and depression than healthy people or people with organic illness. They also tend to have experienced more threatening life events.'[10]

Experiencing 'threatening life events' can leave us fearing that worse might follow. 'People with chronic functional illness are more likely to perceive life changes as negative and worry about what may seem to others to be relatively trivial problems.'[11] People who worry enormously and see things in a negative light are likely to view themselves in the same way. They cannot accept themselves and they cannot relax and be happy. Miserable people who do not like themselves find it hard to make friends. Nick Read wrote,

So many of my patients tell me that they don't know who they are. It always seems to me such a chilling statement. Without a strong sense of their place and role in society, they lack social support and a cognitive template that would help them regulate bodily tensions induced by the challenges in their lives. Lonely people tend to suffer more tiredness, bowel upsets, muscular aches and pains, colds, heart attacks, strokes, cancer and depression. They tend to overeat and visit their doctors more frequently. And there is evidence that they have impaired stress responses that can be rectified only if they have more social contact. Loneliness may well be the most important public health risk of our time, greater than the effects of either smoking or overeating, but it is rarely considered, probably because the very idea is threatening to society.'[12]

In his book Nick Read gives the reader an account of the life story of a number of his patients. The illness can be understood only in the context of the narrative of their life. In studying these narratives he has found that 'the episodes in life that challenge a person's sense of their own identity are most likely to result in illness.'[13] We all encounter events which challenge our sense of identity. We can survive these if we look at them with a clear and steady eye, not lying to ourselves about what has happened and the consequences which follow, not telling ourselves that we are not upset or grieving or angry with those who have betrayed us. However, if we have grown up in a family where we were not allowed to express our feelings in any way other than through physical symptoms, and we come into adulthood believing that we should fulfil what other people expect of us instead of being ourselves, we create a narrative of our life that leads inevitably to us expressing our distress, regret and anger in wordless, physical ways. We need to construct another narrative, one which is as truthful as we can make it, because only such a narrative can give us the courage to face whatever life brings.

Expressing emotions through physical symptoms is painful and a waste of time, but it does show that, even though you do not like yourself very much, you at least seek a little comfort for yourself through the care and concern that others may show you. But what if you hate yourself?

Punishing the Body to Ease the Mind

Self-harm

Dave was a young man pursued, harried and punished by an implacable conscience. He expected society to punish him as harshly as he deserved, and when society failed to do that, he punished himself. Drunk and angry, he had smashed some shop windows, and for this he was fined. He told me, 'I was so disgusted at being fined I wouldn't pay it. I thought I had got off too light. I resented not being punished. I was disgusted by what I had done.'

Dave was an expert in taking punishment. As children he and his brother had frequently been thrashed by their father with their mother's agreement. Dave took great pride in the fact that, when his brother was beaten, 'He would sob his heart out. I would never cry. Because I wouldn't cry he would give me a bigger belting. They just wanted to see tears. I wouldn't cry.'

He said, 'I think my father got more satisfaction out of hitting my brother because he would cry and I wouldn't.' Dave's father was a hard man who expected instant and complete obedience from his sons. Such a parent is a major threat to a child's sense of being a person, and a child must find some way of defending himself. Dave saw his not crying as a way of defeating his father and defending himself, even though this meant that he received many brutal beatings. To survive the pain he took pride in his refusal to cry. He sympathized with people who suffered but he despised people who cried. His refusal to cry turned, as he knew, to anger, and the anger directed at himself turned to depression.

He was angry that the overdose which had brought him into hospital had failed to kill him. We talked about how he saw different ways of killing himself. He could see how every method could fail. I said, 'You want to do it properly.' He agreed and said, 'If a job's worth doing it's worth doing well.'

The hospital gave Dave no way to relieve the tension that was building up inside him, so, unable to endure any more, he cut himself. He told me, 'I could have smashed someone else, but I wasn't in the mood. I was sat at the other end of the lounge where they couldn't see me. I got the nail scissors out and just started to cut away. I was feeling fed up. I wanted to see how much pain I could stand before it actually hurt me.' If being fed up meant being fed up with himself, then by cutting himself he could show himself that he could take pride in his ability to withstand pain.

I wrote about Dave in my first book, *The Experience of Depression*.[14] Eight years later the publishers HarperCollins acquired this book and changed its name to *Choosing, Not Losing*.[15] I managed to contact Dave to tell him about the new edition. He told me that he was happily married and had a son. His wife Shirley had helped him enormously to become stable and settled. They had had four financially tough years and in that time Shirley had been ill and their son had had a serious accident. Nevertheless, Dave called these years 'the good years'. Now all was well. Dave had security and happiness, but with them his old anxiety had returned. He said, 'I feel I'm being punished for doing well. I don't deserve what I've got.'

To conclude Dave's chapter in the new edition of my book, I wrote:

> Dave's old adversary, his harsh, demanding conscience, this 'severe and speechless critic', was alive and well and wanting to do battle. Dave now stands at the crossroads of his life. He can choose to go on living his life as he has lived it up to now – a self divided, ever at war with a conscience which was formed when he was a child who, as children do, saw the world in black and white, good and bad, and who determined to punish himself as a way of avoiding being overwhelmed by his harsh and punitive parents. If Dave chooses to continue on this path, then he will go on suffering great anxiety and never enjoy to the full the success and love which are rightly his.
>
> Or he can choose to take account of what he has learned in his family life in the last ten years, that life is not a simple matter of black and white, good and bad, that we are all a mixture of strengths and weakness, and so we must learn to forgive one another and ourselves. Forgiveness enables us to enjoy our good fortune and the fruits of our labour and to face life with courage.[16]

Two years later Shirley phoned me to tell me that Dave was dead. He had walked on to the railway lines and, as an express train approached, had laid his head on a rail. A job well done.

Lord Claverton, a character in T. S. Eliot's play *The Elder Statesman*, said:

What is this self inside us, this silent observer,
Severe and speechless critic, who can
Terrorise us
And urge us on to futile activity,
And in the end, judge us more severely
For the errors into which his own reproaches
Drove us?[17]

This harsh critic, our conscience, has a secret conspirator, our primitive pride, which beguiles us into siding with the judge so that we can congratulate ourselves upon our high standards and our capacity to suffer. Dave, a good man, could be kind to everyone except himself.

When Dave was in hospital, his cutting of himself was regarded by the doctors and nurses as no more than a symptom of his mental illness. It was not a symptom with which they sympathized. People who self-harmed were regarded as manipulative and attention-seeking patients whose attempts to get attention must be ignored or punished. No one paused to consider that there must be something wrong with the psychiatric system if a patient cannot gain the attention of the doctors and nurses other than by self-harm. I once witnessed a scene at the beginning of a case conference I was attending. The consultant in charge was sitting beside the door, which was open. A nurse came to the door and told the consultant that one of his patients, a young woman, would like to see him urgently. The young woman stood just behind the nurse and witnessed the consultant refusing to see her. He could have turned around to face her and to explain that he was about to start a meeting but that he could see her briefly later, but he did not. He kept his back to the open door. With a well-practised skill, the young woman used the razor blade hidden in her hand to slice her arm from elbow to wrist. The nurses hustled her away and the consultant began the meeting.

I would like to say that this kind of event would never occur now, but I cannot. Attitudes have not changed. There are some psychiatrists and some nurses who can recognize the degree of stress that a person must feel to injure herself in brutal ways, and there are some accident and emergency doctors and nurses who treat people who self-harm with the same high degree of compassion they give to all their patients, whether they have been injured in an act of altruism or in a drunken brawl, but the attitude that people who self-harm must be shamed, punished and ignored still prevails. Phil Thomas told a conference on self-harm in March 2001 how he had accompanied a friend who had seriously wounded herself to the accident and emergency department of his local hospital. None of the staff there recognized him, a consultant psychiatrist, and behaved as they always behaved. This showed that they felt no shame in letting a member of the public watch how they made this seriously injured woman wait, bleeding profusely, in a public place, for an inordinately long period of time. When a doctor at last approached her he did not introduce himself, nor did he take her into a cubicle for examination. The treatment he gave was perfunctory and painful.

Pat Bracken and Phil Thomas wrote:

> People who self-injure find that their distress is met with overwhelming hostility. They are accused of attention-seeking, or wasting staff time. They are told that their wounds don't need suturing, or that they don't need a local anaesthetic. They are told that medical and psychiatric help is contingent upon giving up self-injury. 'Contracts' dictate that help will be withdrawn if cutting continues. No one would question the right to treatment of a rugby player injured in a game. His injuries are not stigmatised because, despite the risks, he has chosen to participate in a dangerous sport. The exercise of choice appears to confirm his rationality. Take smoking. Everyone knows that it is harmful, but no one believes that smokers are insane because they choose to smoke.[18]

No doubt Phil Thomas has always felt compassion for his patients, but it was his encounter with Sharon Lefevre which made him keenly aware that self-harm should not be denigrated as a mere symptom of mental illness. Sharon knew herself well, and recognized that self-harm was a coping strategy and as such should be accepted and managed. In her book *Killing Me Softly* she described self-harm as a coping strategy used by those with past experiences of abuse. She wrote, 'Self-harm is a way of relating to your past truth. It may appear very negative, but it is very positive. The language of self-harm is keeping the person alive.'[19]

This is the message of the self-harm movement. Self-harm is a defence used to hold yourself together as a person. More women than men self-harm, more people between teens and middle age than the elderly. The highest rates are among those aged between fifteen and twenty-nine. All kinds of methods, including cutting, scratching, burning and poisoning, may be used.

These methods of self-harm are at the far end of a continuum that begins with methods we all use. In a situation which demands that we be silent and calm, even though we are upset, we may clench our fists and dig our fingernails into the palms of our hands, thus creating enough pain to distract us from our distress. In a situation where we must not laugh but are in danger of being overcome by mirth, we may bite the inside of our cheeks, and the pain of that will stop us laughing.

Many people in prison or secure hospitals self-harm, not surprisingly since these institutions intensify feelings of helplessness and self-hatred. It is often said that people self-harm in order to relieve tension, but this is too simple an explanation. WISH, the organization for women in secure hospitals, published in its newsletter an article by the Basement Project in Wales, which is a community-based organization that provides groups and information for women who have suffered childhood abuse of any kind. The members of the project wrote:

> We see self-harm as a way of coping with overwhelming feelings that result from awful experiences. But how does it achieve this? There are lots of ways self-harm seems to 'work' and it can be different for different people or at different times. Here are some of them.

Feeling anguish and pain – expressing or distracting oneself from painful feelings
Needing to take some control – giving a sense of control over something in one's life
Exploding with anger – expressing or defusing angry feelings
Feeling guilt and shame – dealing with feelings of guilt, shame and self-hatred
Feeling empty and needy – trying to fill the emptiness inside and gain some comfort
It's who you are – a way of saying 'this is me'
Feeling unreal or panicky – a way of 'bringing oneself back' from panic or numbness
Sending a message – letting others know how you feel when words seem useless

If you are someone who self-harms you may recognize that self-harm works in some of these ways for you. It is great that you have found some way of coping. Self-harm may even have saved your life in the past. You may feel that self-harm has been a necessary friend to you. But you may also feel it has become a tyrant which you cannot do without even if you would like to. The reasons why you self-harm are special and unique to you. They may include some of those mentioned above, but this does not include everything that can lead someone to self-harm.[20]

Louise Pembroke and the organization National Self-harm Network produced the book *Cutting the Risk: Self-harm, Self-care and Risk Reduction*,[21] which gives people the necessary knowledge to avoid permanent damage or fatal injuries. Another primary expert, Dee Cox, joined Gerrlyn Smith and Jacqui Sarajian, both of whom are clinical psychologists and mothers who have fostered daughters who self-harmed, to write the book *Women and Self-Harm*.[22] This is a good source book for people who self-harm and for those who need to understand.

Another way of punishing the body is to starve.

Anorexia and Bulimia

Our body is the only object in the world which we can know both subjectively and objectively. We can look at it as an object in the world and we can know how it feels from the inside. Because we can look at our body as an object, it is easy for us to divide ourselves into mind and body. This way of thinking about ourselves has a long history. Rudolph Bell, in his book *Holy Anorexia*, wrote, 'It was Plato who expressed the dualistic basis of extreme asceticism in its fullest logical form. The human soul, he reasoned, is of divine origin and therefore destined to participate in the world to come. But this soul is trapped in the body, literally incarcerated in the world that is, a world incapable of betterment. Thus the body impedes the freedom of the soul, acting as its prison, and only by disengaging from the world of the senses can the religious spirit liberate itself to realise its divine potential.'[23]

The separation of soul and body became an essential part of Christianity. Christians strove for goodness by fasting in order to purge themselves of the evils of the flesh. It is this urge to reach an impossible goal of goodness which today drives many young women and some young men to starve themselves, but instead of this being seen as the quest for holiness it is labelled a mental disorder. Women who eat and vomit up what they have eaten are castigated and called bulimic, whereas 'Saint Teresa of Avila, the Spanish mystic and spiritual force of the Catholic Reformation who invigorated whole Orders, regularly used an olive twig to induce vomiting so that she might receive the host without fear of rejecting it.'[24]

Rudolph Bell traced the development of holy anorexia from its beginnings in the early thirteenth century until its transformation during the Catholic Reformation in the sixteenth century by studying the lives of 261 holy women. 'Holy anorexia,' he said, 'involves a need to establish a sense of oneself, a contest of wills, a quest for autonomy.'[25] Accounts of the lives of these women are patchy and are often stories which are much elaborated by the telling, but it seems that these women as children were obedient, accepting

290

their religious instruction as the literal truth. They believed that if they were good then they and their loved ones would be safe. However, as their stories show, events tested their beliefs. 'Often a death in the family seems to have been crucial. The pious and trusting girl loses someone she loves deeply; her dependency is shattered and her faith tested. Ultimately she passes the test and visualises her dead mother, father, brother, or sister in heaven or in purgatory and in need of human sacrifice and prayer. Yet the world of base desires remains; it is her body, the girl decides with no small amount of pressure from catechism lessons only she takes literally and seriously, that brings death, that brought the death of her loved ones.'[26] The girl begins a rigid programme of fasting and bodily mortifications. 'The suppression of physical urges and basic feelings – fatigue, sexual drive, hunger, pain – frees the body to achieve heroic feats and the soul to commune with God . . . Death becomes a logical, sweet, and total liberation from the flesh.'[27]

The death of her loved ones created that most serious of discrepancies between what the girl thought her life was and what it actually was. In a society totally dominated by the Church, the girl felt she could not let go of her belief in the absolute tenets of the Church. In the same way a modern young woman may feel that she cannot question the absolute truth that thin is good and fat bad. A desperate defence such as anorexia is a function of pride, and pride takes no account of what is actually going on. Pride denies that the loss which the person has suffered has actually happened. Pride tells the young woman that she has the power through denial of her bodily needs to restore what has become temporarily unavailable. While the medieval young woman might want to restore her loved ones to life, or at least to eternal life in heaven, a modern young women may want to restore her mother's unconditional love for her, or her philandering father to the sanctity of the family home. Through sacrifice and control, that which has been torn apart will be made whole. Rudolph Bell wrote of Catherine Benincasa (Catherine of Siena, 1347–80), 'The solution to the dilemma of balancing her great faith/dependency against her drive for free will/ autonomy, and to the burden of surviving in the place of her three sisters, came through sacrifice, penance, and God. She became totally His servant, and therefore refused to serve men on earth, even while she humbly attended to their worldly needs and obeyed their commands. From the three year moratorium of silence and fasting at home which she imposed on herself when she was sixteen she emerged convinced that she had achieved a direct and personal relationship with God. Once she had persuaded herself of the reality of this favoured position she was ready to take on the world. Through prayers that sounded like market transactions, including words such as ''defrauded'' and ''established terms'', she believed she had rescued her father from purgatory and her mother from hell.'[28] Pride works in wondrous ways its mission to perform.

Denying the needs of the body is still the way to virtue, because to be thin is to be acceptable and attractive – that is, good – and setting one's own standards for thinness frees one from the bonds of family and society. The aim of fasting, whether as a medieval holy woman or as a modern young woman, is to be virtuous and in control. Writing about her own relationship with food, the novelist Nicci Gerrard said, 'If I wake at night I often plan meals in my head. The gifts I will give, to bind them to me. In my head food is about pleasure, appetite, generosity, conversation, conviviality, life. But in reality it is just so often divorced from life, and is about denial, or acts as a puritanical reward for a task achieved.'[29]

Controlling yourself, controlling others, taking pride in being thin, are all defences to hold the person together in the face of the threat of annihilation. Just how these ideas are expressed depends on the ideas prevailing in society at the time. The Reformation of the Catholic Church in the sixteenth century changed the definition of a holy woman. Women could become saints by doing good works and not by punishing their bodies, so the phenomenon of holy anorexia largely disappeared. The idea that the body was gross and bad did not vanish but was expressed in different ways. By the nineteenth century the idea that superior people had a capacity for 'sensibility' and 'exquisite feelings' was popular because it fed pride. Superior people also had a capacity for suffering, and to suffer was still regarded as a sign of virtue. However, through the nineteenth century doctors were developing their claim to be the experts on madness, and mental illnesses were being 'discovered' and described with all the eagerness and lack of scientific rigour that the authors of the DSM display today. This was a splendid opportunity for misogynous doctors to denigrate women. Helen Malson, in her book *The Thin Woman*, where she explored the ideas that created the conditions for anorexia, quoted from the nineteenth-century texts on 'anorexia nervosa' and summarized the ideas contained therein with:

> The subject of 'anorexia nervosa' was thus produced as perverse, mentally weak, irrational, obstinate and childish; even as deceitful, selfish, vain and spoilt. She was still 'hysterical'. And, in construing the patient as the other of rational masculinity, these texts simultaneously constructed and consolidated a justification for asserting medical authority and force ... By constituting 'the patient' as other, as pathological, 'perverse' and childish, medical discourse thus provided its 'justification' for forcibly administering often appalling 'treatments' in utter disregard of the woman's objections. And these texts not only advocated force-feeding and/or enemas as a cure for anorexia: medical authority also asserted the need for 'moral control' 'fitted for persons of unsound mind'. Patients were often removed from their families and hospitalised to this end.[30]

By the twentieth century 'The construction of fat-as-ugly and thin-as-beauty is so dominant and normalised that it often appears to be an unquestionable prescription of some law of natural aesthetics.'[31] Moreover, thinness can imply illness and illness suffering, and those who suffer courageously are to be admired. Nicci Gerrard wrote, 'At the time of my life when I was most acutely miserable ... I rather wanted to look like a victim, made visible and heroic by my suffering. I looked frail. I was one of the walking wounded.'[32]

At the same time 'The beautiful thin body is not construed as a requirement for attracting a man who will save the woman. Rather, it *is* the state of salvation. And this ''salvation'' is achieved through the woman's efforts rather than through male intervention.'[33]

At the same time the holy anorexics did not require the ministrations of their priest or bishop for their salvation. That they achieved on their own. Medieval or modern, these women, by starving their bodies, established their sense of being a person. Helen Malson quoted one of the women she interviewed as saying, 'If I didn't have anorexia, if I wasn't thin, I wouldn't have an identity. I'd just be this big bad blob. [Being thin] made me feel good and in control.'[34]

'Being in control' means being in control of your body. This is one of the attributes of a good woman. Whatever the particulars of an anorexic woman's upbringing, she develops a sense of her body as, in Susie Orbach's words, 'a false body'. 'Where the developing child has not had a chance to experience physicality as good, wholesome and all right, it has little chance to live in an authentically experienced body.'[35]

From their earliest childhood most women are taught not to enjoy their own physicality – that is, not to explore to the limits the functions of their body and not to enjoy what their body can do. Boys can take part in rough-and-tumble games, they can run and climb and hurl themselves into the water, but girls do not do these things, or, if they do, they have to perform them according to certain rules and to aim for perfection. Nowadays many young women have honed their body to perfection through work-outs at the gym where, as a male friend told me, women work very hard while the men do little more than a few press-ups and lift a couple of weights, no more than they find pleasurable. Young girls learn to dive and swim properly, and if they want to explore the relationship of their bodies to space, they have to take up gymnastics and follow the strict rules of that sport. A friend once told me that she took up gymnastics as a girl because she wanted to prove that even in movement through the air she was perfectly controlled all the time. When she was too old for gymnastics she took up depression, another occupation which aims at perfect control all the time.

Boys, too, are allowed to explore the functions of their bodies. They can take great interest in how they pee, shit and fart. They can compare erections and the speed with which they can ejaculate. Girls are taught that curiosity about excretory functions is not permissible and that jokes about such functions are extremely vulgar. Excreting something as simple as perspiration is most indelicate. The old adage 'Horses sweat; men perspire; ladies *glow*' may no longer be fashionable, but the plethora of antiperspirants on the market shows that while horses may have disappeared from our roads the sentiments about sweat have not changed.

One aspect of their bodies which women can find hard to control is menstruation, which can still in our society arouse feelings of horror and disgust and a need for secrecy. For women alienated from their bodies it is not a badge of womanhood to be worn with pride. Sheila MacLeod, in her autobiography of her anorexic years, *The Art of Starvation*, said that in her teenage years:

> I was horrified and disgusted by menstruation rather than by sexuality. I felt that some dreadful punishment had been visited upon me, punishment for a crime which I had never committed. But I think I knew unconsciously that the crime was twofold: I was being punished for being female and for having grown up. At the same time I didn't *feel* female, in the sexual sense. Neither did I feel male, but rather neuter. And I certainly didn't feel grown-up. The crimes in question had been committed by my body, not by me.[36]

One of the advantages of fasting is that in a long fast a woman ceases to menstruate.

To treat our bodies in this way, to see them as contemptible and dangerous objects which have to be controlled, hidden and forced into a shape that they would not naturally assume (my mother's generation of women wore corsets; present generations wear the invisible corsets of exercise and diet) is to do terrible damage to how we experience our existence. Our body is the only part of our existence which occupies both our internal and our external realities. It is the bridge between our two realities. To live comfortably and bravely in our two realities, we need to live comfortably and bravely within our bodies. We should not feel ashamed and frightened of our bodies, nor should we be ignorant of them.

It is hard for a young woman in a consumer society, where pictures of women's bodies are used to sell every commodity, to feel easy about her body. 'For women themselves, the body has become a commodity in the marketplace or their own commodity, the object with which they negotiate the world.'[37] Anorexic women use their bodies 'as a vehicle for self expression'[38] but, unlike those successful actors, dancers and sportsmen and women who regard their bodies as their finest attribute, they do not regard their bodies with pride and satisfaction. (Alas, anorexia and bulimia are now well represented in the sporting world, while a number of actresses in the public eye are better known for their thinness and fragility than for their acting ability.) These women seek approval and acceptance, but they observe their bodies with contempt. Bodies are objects which can go out of control. Bodies demand food and rest; they grow fat; they excrete faeces, urine and blood.

Other people's bodies may be satisfactory, provided they are not fat, but to the anorexic woman her body is an object of profound disgust. In no way can the anorexic woman accept the humanness of her body. She has grown up in a family that has impressed on her that she is unsatisfactory and that the body she was born with is unsatisfactory. Sheila MacLeod dated the first step on her path to anorexia when she heard her aunt compare her to her mother Dolly. ' ''She's going to be stout – just like Dolly.'' All the light and colour seemed to be drained from my surroundings. I was blazingly angry with her and wanted to shout, ''No, I'm not! Why the hell should I be? And who are you to say so?'' But of course I said nothing – to retaliate would have been considered insufferably rude – and walked on, pretending not to have heard . . . it is clear that she had no idea what effect her remark could have had on me . . . she was following the family pattern of talking about children in their own presence in the third person instead of addressing them directly. This pattern implies that children have no thoughts or feelings of their own and are incapable of understanding the wider meanings of the simplest observations.'[39]

In Susie Orbach's masterly study of anorexia, *Hunger Strike*, the themes of control and acceptability constantly recur. All anorexic women want to control their bodies, but those among them who are extraverts want to do so in order to be acceptable to others, while those among them who are introverts want to control their bodies in order to keep chaos at bay. Anorexia is a defence available to us all, provided we take as an absolute truth the current fashion of regarding thin as good and fat bad, and we have come to hate ourselves.

Research into the backgrounds of women who become anorexic has not revealed the extensive physical and sexual abuse that many of the women who self-harm or are given the label of Borderline Personality Disorder have endured. Rather, most of these women have grown up in homes that to the outside observer are ordinary and pleasant. However, the ethos of the family, as it seems to the growing girl, is one of very high standards. The girl feels that to be acceptable to her parents she must achieve in every possible way as a daughter, as a student and as a member of society. She must in all ways be a credit to her family in every aspect of virtuous femininity. The parents' standards permeate every aspect of the girl's life. An eight-year-old girl is eager to please, but a thirteen-year-old feels the stirrings of rebellion. She wants some corner of her life to be hers alone. The choice of which boys' band to support or which footballer's photograph to hang on her bedroom wall is usually made in terms of how unsuitable these young men look to her mother. Teenage rebellion is essential if a girl or boy emerging from childhood is to create a sense of being a person strong enough to withstand the inevitable demands and disappointments of the teen and early adult years. Unfortunately some parents will not tolerate any rebellion, and some teenagers are too frightened to try.

When I was a teenager in the 1940s there was a clear demarcation between different age groups, and so what could be rebelled against was clearly discernible. My mother's generation of women wore corsets, hats, stockings and 'nice' dresses usually in pretty pastels. The Queen, five years older than me, has always faithfully kept to this style of dressing, but as a teenager I rebelled. No hats, stockings, corsets, but rather sunfrocks that wickedly bared my arms and, most shockingly, shorts. In those inhibited times any slightly older woman who dressed in the way young women did would be chastised with the comment 'Mutton dressed as lamb'. Now that phrase has disappeared and clothes no longer define an age group.

How can a girl be different from her mother if her mother wears what she does? In just one way, but for that the girl must be very thin. Most women, once in their thirties, see their body develop markedly womanly curves, and dieting has little effect. A mother cannot wear the clothes those skinny little models in the fashion magazines wear, but her daughter can. ·

So her daughter can rebel by becoming extremely thin, even more so if her mother rejects and punishes her rebellion or tries to compete with her in being thin. Research has shown that the mothers of bulimic girls tend to weigh less than the mothers of girls who do not resort to bulimia or anorexia. Mothers of bulimic girls tend also to be far more critical of their daughters.[40]

Sisters too can play a part in determining whether a girl turns to anorexia as a defence. A study by a team at the Eating Disorders Unit of the Institute of Psychiatry, London, found that 'Anorexic sisters perceived more maternal control and reported more antagonism towards and jealousy of their sisters than did their unaffected sisters. In addition, anorexic women reported having fewer friends and boyfriends than their sisters.'[41] Such matters may appear insignificant to an outside observer, but to the young woman they cloud her life.

We live in a society that is crowded with images. There are mirrors everywhere. We take photographs and are photographed. Our television and films are more concerned with images than with words, while our print media often rely more on pictures rather than words to tell a story. How we perceive images is a subject of constant research by psychologists. Such research has established that once we learn to see ourselves in a particular way we may find it hard to change our way of seeing ourselves, even though our common sense tells us that we have changed. It has been shown that many body-builders will compulsively exercise because, when they look in the mirror, they see themselves as small, even though they are actually large and muscular.[42] Similarly, people who compulsively starve themselves see their image in the mirror as being much fatter than they actually are.

I discovered that this was not an attribute confined to those people who set out to change their body size. I have always been plump, sometimes extremely so. In the spring of 1999 I became quite ill. I did not recognize that I had a serious lung infection. I had no fever, but I had little strength and I could not eat. The condition persisted over the summer and I lost fourteen kilograms in weight. Intellectually I knew that I was much thinner. My scales told me so, and my clothes hung on me. Yet when I looked in the mirror I appeared to be unchanged. When I went shopping for clothes I discovered that I could no longer make judgements about which clothes would fit me because those that now would fit looked to me impossibly small. I did not actually *see* what I looked like until some friends sent me a photograph taken, unbeknownst to me, at a celebration they had held. When I took the photograph out of its envelope I expected it to be a picture of my friends, but it was a photograph of a white-haired, thin woman wearing my best blue shirt. For once the way I had learned to see myself did not interfere with my seeing what was actually there.

Seeing themselves as they actually are is probably one of the things which may help a person give up the defence of anorexia. The bony angularity of the severely anorexic woman has none of the softness and curves traditionally associated with beauty. However, as with all the defences, the key to relinquishing this defence is to come to value and accept yourself. All therapy of whatever kind should be targeted on this.

Alas, this is currently not so. The tradition of cruel treatment for anorexic women continues. Under the guise of saving the woman's life now that she is dangerously thin, anorexic women are confined in hospital and forced to eat. They may no longer be force-fed, but they are subjected to a behavioural regime where the ordinary matters of life, such as getting out of bed, watching television and the like, are contingent on the woman eating and putting on weight. Lucy Johnstone summed up the effects of such a regime:

The very narrow definition of the problem [as one of weight loss] allows psychiatrists to claim success for these methods; they certainly do make people put on weight. Their wider effects are less beneficial. Anorexia is all about control; to the anorexic, the rigid control she maintains over her weight is her only defence against chaos and despair. To have this defence seized from her as large amounts of food are virtually forced down her is terrifying for her. Not surprisingly, many anorexics try to retain some control of the situation by any means left to them, such as secret vomiting or drinking large quantities of water before weighing sessions. This has earned them a reputation for being devious and manipulative patients, and persecution may result. Since the underlying issues are not resolved, anorexics often lose weight again as soon as they are discharged, and may spend months or years being shuffled in and out of hospital to be fattened up and released again.

Treatments which focus solely on weight gain are falling into the same trap as the anorexic herself, they are treating her body as an object, as something separate from her as a person, to be forced into one shape or another without any regard to what this means for the young woman herself. Rather than helping the anorexic to accept and make friends with her body, the hospital may view it as a problem, an enemy, that has to be beaten down, the only difference being that the hospital wants it to be fat whereas the anorexic wants it to be thin. This in its turn is a reflection of the way society presents women's bodies as objects to be manipulated into the correct shapes to sell consumer goods, attract men, display the latest fashions, and so on. In addition, the situation where powerful male doctors decide what is to be done to her body may echo and reinforce her fears about sexual relationships, that this is another area where she will feel used and out of control. The same attitudes underlie much of the academic research on anorexia, for which young women may be recruited to have electrodes attached to their hands, pulse and blood pressure taken, and haemoglobin and urea and cholesterol checked, in order to aid the classification of anorexics versus bulimics, dieters versus vomiters, without any regard to the person to whom the body is attached.[43]

A research team at the Section of Adolescent Psychiatry at the University of Liverpool looked at what had happened to seventy-five adolescents (seventy-one girls and four boys) two to seven years after they had been diagnosed as anorexic. The team found that two of the adolescents had died. The twenty-one who had received hospital treatment had a significantly worse outcome than the fifty-one who had never been admitted to hospital. The researchers concluded, 'Multivariate analysis suggests that admission [to hospital] to be a major predictor of poor outcome' and 'The negative consequences of in-patient treatment are neglected in research.'[44]

The therapy that offers the greatest chance of success is one which treats the person as a whole person, not just as a body that is too thin. A good example of this is the Cedars in Colchester, which has as its philosophy 'to provide an holistic supportive environment for individuals with eating disorders, their family and carers, focusing on self-help and user empowerment'. The centre offers counselling, a self-help group, group therapy, meditation and relaxation, massage, and aromatherapy. Such centres are few, but they offer the possibility that the person may gain the necessary courage to relinquish the defence of voluntary starvation.

The body offers another form of defence available to all of us, that of

Dulling the Brain to Ease the Mind

Any activity that gives us immediate pleasure can become an activity which we feel impelled to repeat over and over again. Eating glucose in one of its many forms can release energy quickly, and that can seem so immensely pleasurable that a person constantly seeks to consume more of that particular food. Chocaholics bemoan their attraction to chocolate but continue to consume it because they feel better when they eat it. One woman told me, 'I don't drink or smoke, but when I need comfort I go to one of those pick-and-mix sweets bars. It takes me back to my childhood.' Tea and coffee can give a pleasurable surge of energy which many people want to repeat regularly. Tough exercise can give a person such a pleasurable high that exercising ceases to be a health-maintaining activity and becomes a passionate obsession. The thrill of winning, or the thrill of merely having the chance to win, can bring a person again and again to the gaming tables and override common sense, which says that such losses cannot be sustained. Casino owners are the only ones who win. To all these activities and many more the word 'addiction' has been applied, so much so that it has become quite meaningless. To say that someone has an addiction is only to say that this is something which the person does very often. For the word to be meaningful it needs to be confined to those activities which have a demonstrable effect on the functioning of the brain. It is clear that the ingestion of certain drugs does this. The popular drugs that do this are the legal drugs, nicotine and alcohol, and the illegal drugs which include cannabis, heroin and cocaine.

Nicotine

Over the last fourteen years smoking has almost become a secret vice. No longer does the Marlboro Man ride the range, the epitome of everything that is manly and admirable. Now sports stars have to keep their smoking secret,[45] and a number of people suffering from the effects of the drug have sued the tobacco companies, including a lifetime smoker of Marlboro cigarettes who sued Philip Morris, the makers of Marlboro cigarettes, and was awarded US$3 billion for his incurable lung cancer.[46] Most restaurants and offices are now smoke-free zones, and pitiful little groups of smokers huddle in dank corners outside the buildings where they work. If smokers want to fly or travel by train they have to endure many hours of deprivation of their anxiety-relieving cigarettes.

Yet the total number of smokers has not diminished. The big tobacco companies are rich and powerful. They have successfully targeted children, young women and people in the developing countries, and among these groups sales are booming. The Jesuits used to say that if they educated a boy for his first seven years they had him for life. The same applies to smoking, but where an individual can reflect upon his religious beliefs and decide to change, nicotine addiction has a lasting, seductive embrace.

The Royal College of Physicians regards nicotine addiction as being similar to the addiction to hard drugs such as heroin and cocaine.[47] The National Institute on Drug Abuse in the USA gave the following account of the effects of nicotine:

Nicotine can act as both a stimulant and a sedative. Immediately after exposure to nicotine, there is a 'kick' caused in part by the drug's stimulation of the adrenal glands and resulting discharge of epinephrine (adrenaline). The rush of adrenaline stimulates the body and causes a sudden release of glucose as well as an increase in blood pressure, respiration, and heart rate. Nicotine also suppresses insulin output from the pancreas, which means that smokers are always slightly hyperglycemic. In addition, nicotine indirectly causes a release of dopamine in the brain regions that control pleasure and motivation. This reaction is similar to that seen with other drugs of abuse such as cocaine and heroin and it is thought to underlie the pleasurable sensations experienced by many smokers. In contrast, nicotine can also exert a sedative effect, depending on the level of the smoker's nervous system arousal and the dose of nicotine taken.

Chronic exposure to nicotine results in addiction. Research is just beginning to document all of the neurological changes that accompany the development and maintenance of nicotine addiction. The behavioural consequences of these changes are well documented, however. Greater than 90 percent of those smokers who try to quit without seeking treatment fail, with most relapsing within a week.

Repeated exposure to nicotine results in the development of tolerance, the condition in which higher doses of a drug are required to produce the same initial stimulation. Nicotine is metabolized fairly rapidly, disappearing from the body in a few hours. Therefore some tolerance is lost overnight, and smokers often report that the first cigarettes of the day are the strongest and/or the 'best.' As the day progresses, acute tolerance develops, and later cigarettes have less effect.

Cessation of nicotine use is followed by a withdrawal syndrome that may last a month or more; it includes symptoms that can quickly drive people back to tobacco use. Nicotine withdrawal symptoms include irritability, craving, cognitive and attentional deficits, sleep disturbances, and increased appetite and may begin within a few hours after the last cigarette. Symptoms peak within the first few days and may subside within a few weeks. For some people, however, symptoms may persist for months or longer.

An important but poorly understood component of the nicotine withdrawal syndrome is craving, an urge for nicotine that has been described as a major obstacle to successful abstinence. High levels of craving for tobacco may persist for 6 months or longer. While the withdrawal syndrome is related to the pharmacological effects of nicotine, many behavioural factors also can affect the severity of withdrawal symptoms. For some people, the feel, smell, and sight of a cigarette and the ritual of obtaining, handling, lighting, and smoking the cigarette are all associated with the pleasurable effects of smoking and can make withdrawal or craving worse. While nicotine gum and patches may alleviate the pharmacological aspects of withdrawal, cravings often persist.[48]

Professor Michael Gossop, a leading addictions researcher at the National Addiction Centre at the Institute of Psychiatry in London, wrote, 'Cigarette smoking is one of the most addictive of all drug habits. It appears to be more likely to produce dependence than using either tranquillisers or alcohol: the nearest drug habit, in terms of the risk of becoming dependent, is injecting heroin.'[49]

I asked Diana, a psychologist colleague, someone I knew to be tremendously capable and skilled at her job, how she came to take up smoking. She said, 'I was fourteen and I went to my first grown-up party. I was scared to death. I was sitting there, not talking to anyone, and this boy came over and spoke to me. He asked me if I had any cigarettes and when I said I did not he went away. So I thought, ''That's how you get boys to talk to you, smoke.'' When I went home I stole some of my mother's cigarettes – both my parents smoke heavily – and practised in secret. At first it was horrible, but I persisted because when I went to parties after that I did not feel so nervous if I was smoking a cigarette.' Pleasant physiological changes and improving how you feel about yourself make a near-irresistible combination.

It is not surprising that the simple behavioural methods of rewards for not smoking and punishment for smoking did not work. In the 1980s my friend and colleague Miller Mair grew tired of trying to treat smokers who said they wanted to give up smoking, with behavioural methods, because he found that his results were no better than what would be expected in the general population when people decide to give up smoking. Some succeed; some do not. He decided to concentrate on finding out what meaning the cigarettes had for each person. He would say to his client, 'If your cigarette was a person, what kind of person would it be?' He got some very revealing answers. One man saw his cigarette as the perfect woman, beautiful and compliant. Another man always smoked one particular brand, no matter how difficult they were to obtain. They were his mates, and he was always loyal to his mates.

I often use Miller's question when someone complains to me about not being able to give up smoking or insists that no matter how smoking affects health he (or, so often, she) will not stop. At a workshop on depression that I was running, one of the participants, a young psychologist whom I knew to be most able and aware, smoked heavily throughout. He also revealed himself to be no stranger to depression. The topic of smoking came up, and I asked him to imagine that his cigarette was a person and to describe that person to us. He described a person who gave him confidence, enthusiasm and the power to achieve. Could he not give these things to himself? I asked. He said no, he could not. Without his cigarettes he was empty and frightened. Sometimes a cigarette stands for that aspect of one's life which one is not allowed to express. Helen, who from earliest childhood had to be neat, clean and tidy, and who maintains this in her adult life as wife and mother, saw her cigarette as someone who was dirty and disgusting, yet someone to whom she had an immense loyalty.

On the Greek island of Skyros I met a young woman, Rosie, who had a most lovely singing voice. She told me how she wanted to develop her singing career but she smoked quite heavily and knew that to pursue this career she would have to give up. The actress Polly James had helped her to rediscover her singing voice and to realize that she had actually used smoking as a way of silencing herself. Smoking too was very much part of her social life, and Rosie could not imagine either restricting her social life or being with her friends and not smoking. When she met James, a hypnotherapist who had successfully given up smoking, Rosie decided to ask him for help. Once she had relaxed, James asked her to create in her imagination two films of herself, one in which she was smoking and one in which she was not. Rosie told me:

I was the projectionist in my own private cinema, running a film of myself sitting in a bar smoking a cigarette. I noted my appearance, body language, behaviour, and wasn't too impressed by them. I reeled the film backward, watched it again at double speed, then again at four times the speed, and finally watched the colours fade and the scene disappear. A new film, myself in the same bar as a non-smoker, noting again my behaviour and looking at the others in the bar who are still smokers. Again, rewinding and watching the scene again, since the first time I couldn't keep my favourite liquorice roll-up out of the picture, but this time stepping out of the projection room and into the film, experiencing the scene of being a non-smoker in my usual bar, anticipating the prospect of going somewhere else to sing. It felt good.

I talked to Rosie about seeing her cigarettes as people. She could do this easily and described three people vividly, each representing one of the kinds of cigarettes she would smoke in different situations. I could see how each of these characters related to Rosie as the person she was. The first was an elegant menthol cigarette. This for her was an inscrutable, exotic lady. The second, a roll-up with liquorice papers, was an elegant man, and the third, the Marlboro Light, was a salt-of-the earth woman. We talked about what these characters meant to her, how they represented something to which she might aspire and something that was an essential part of herself. They were old friends, but friends who were holding her back.

A few months after I had returned to England, Rosie wrote to me to say that she was going to stay in Greece with the man she loved. She enclosed an account of how she had given up smoking and copies of the letters she had written to each of the cigarette people, bidding them goodbye. She told the inscrutable exotic lady that 'I've wanted to be you, but how can I be? The reality is that I'm me and will be all the more interesting person when I express what's inside me instead of wearing your mask. You're scared to feel. You're not just inscrutable, you're unapproachable, and I don't want to be. I'm saying goodbye to you and with that my self-induced loneliness and fear of closeness.' She told the elegant man, 'What I wanted to be of you I already am, but I'm also a nice person, unlike you who is shallow and vain and not very interesting.' She told the salt-of-the-earth woman, 'It's been fine, but leaving you won't leave a gap in my life and you won't have time to miss me either. That was then, this is now, and I've forgotten your name already.'

When I had finished writing this section on nicotine I contacted Rosie and asked her to check whether there was anything she wanted me to change in her story. She wrote back to say it was fine, and went on to say that in the two years since we had met she had not smoked. She did lapse once, when an unexpected turn of events left her briefly downhearted, but she become so ill she immediately stopped smoking. She wished her husband would give up, but he considered smoking to be a proof of masculinity, and would not dream of asking himself what kind of person his cigarette was.

As I had learned when I was with Rosie in Skyros, she was an extravert whom everyone loved, but, like many extraverts, she was intrigued by the calm demeanour with which introverts can present themselves, just as introverts can be constantly amazed and envious of the apparent ease with which extraverts can deal with social situations. Both groups delude themselves. The apparent social skill of extraverts can hide a terror of social situations, while the impassivity of the introvert can be a screen for hidden shallows. Envying our opposite only makes us feel worse about our own limitations.

Smoking can appeal to both extraverts and introverts because it can be a defence against the weakness that each feels. It can be seen as a way of creating and maintaining relationships, because it can grease the wheels of social intercourse, whether it is a matter of offering a cigarette to someone you have just met or lighting someone's cigarette in what you hope is a sexually seductive manner. Or smoking can be the individual satisfaction of marking the end of a section of work, or pausing for reflection, or bringing troublesome feelings under control.

However, like the psychologist Diana, most people take up smoking to allay anxiety and to build up their self-confidence. When we fear that we are not acceptable, that we lack the ability to achieve, that other people will not like or admire us, we need a defence, and smoking can seem to provide the solution.

But it is only a short-term solution. In the long term it can kill us, and can kill other people. According to the National Institute on Drug Abuse, in the USA tobacco use accounts for one-third of all cancers, and is linked to 90 per cent of all lung cancer. In the UK deaths from lung cancer reflect the increase in the number of women smoking. Rates for women with lung cancer have risen 36 per cent in the last twenty years and now exceed the number of deaths from breast cancer. Smoking also causes lung diseases such as chronic bronchitis and emphysema. It exacerbates asthma symptoms, and is associated with cancers of the mouth, pharynx, larynx, oesophagus, stomach, pancreas, cervix, kidney, urethra and bladder. One-fifth of deaths from heart disease are attributable to smoking. Inhaling tobacco smoke from someone else is estimated to cause three thousand lung cancer deaths in the USA each year and contributes to forty thousand deaths related to heart disease. In pregnant women carbon monoxide, a lethal gas, and nicotine interfere with the oxygen supply to the foetus. Women who smoke are more likely to have premature babies and babies with low birth weight. Some physiological therapies for nicotine addiction have been developed, such as nicotine gum, nicotine patches and a nicotine inhaler. The antidepressant bupropion has been marketed under the name Zyban as a treatment for nicotine addiction, but its safety is in doubt. However, such treatments rarely work on their own.

All the behavioural methods for giving up smoking – reducing the number of cigarettes smoked each day, rolling your own cigarettes, holding a pretend cigarette, avoiding social situations where smoking occurs – have limited effect. It is essential to discover the meaning cigarettes have for you. Are they your friends, and you could not live with the guilt if you abandoned them? Are they steadfast and loyal friends, the only steadfast and loyal friends you have found and will ever find? Do you secretly despise the human race and find in a cigarette the perfection you demand? Is a burst of nicotine the only method you know for keeping in check that sense of nameless dread that comes upon you in an unguarded moment? Is it easier to smoke and risk an extremely painful death than unmask your loneliness and fear and deal with them?

Alcohol Addiction

Margaret had not told me that she drank a good deal and often, but after she had phoned me at home late at night I began to suspect that the distress and incoherence she showed during these late-night calls was a common pattern and not a chance occurrence. So I asked her about her drinking. She was very defensive. She said, 'I'm not going to stop drinking.' To justify this she told me something she had never told anyone before. She said, 'I can't stand the pain.'

'What pain?' I asked.

'In my chest, under there.'

I recognized the place and the pain. I remembered when I had made the discovery that the phrases 'a broken heart' and 'heartache' were not simply empty metaphors but referred to a real physical experience. When we lose somebody or something very important to us our hearts do ache and break. That special muscle which pumps our blood may keep on working normally, but somehow, perhaps because our anguish alters the way we breathe, a pain, sometimes dull and aching, sometimes sharp and piercing, develops behind the lower end of the breastbone, in the region of the heart.

I told Margaret about this. She was amazed to find that this pain was a common phenomenon. She had always thought that it was peculiar to her, further evidence of her essential badness. Drinking, to some extent, eased the pain.

I was quite stern with Margaret. I was not going to continue to see her unless she consulted a doctor about how her drinking was affecting her health. There was no point in my trying to help her sort out her emotional problems if meanwhile her liver was solidifying into cirrhosis.

We argued about this for some time, and eventually she agreed to have one of those complete overhauls which a private medical scheme offers as the last word in medical care. Margaret's liver proved to be all right, but her blood pressure was up, quite worryingly so. This made her realize that something potentially serious was amiss, and she made a determined effort to cut down on her drinking. When she read the first draft of this chapter she pointed out to me that she was still drinking, though not as much. Her social life was with people who drank a good deal, but by then she was following a daily exercise routine which involved regular running, something she found immensely satisfying and peaceful. This seems to have solved the problem of her high blood pressure. This was the beginning of a series of changes through which she transformed her life.

Margaret had agreed, though reluctantly, to come and see me because, while she was deeply ashamed of herself and saw her suffering as the punishment she deserved, she had some small hope that her life could be better. Without this hope she would have gone on drinking, and her doctor would have changed her diagnosis from 'depressive' to 'problem drinker' or 'alcoholic'.

Over the years I have seen many of my friends and acquaintances go through a period of heavy drinking when their life was falling apart. Then the circumstances of their life changed, or they effected a change in their life themselves, and thus a heavy consumption of alcohol became irrelevant to them. They returned to social drinking.

Some people drink heavily because their friends, colleagues and even their family do. They do not wish to be excluded from their group. Some people turn to alcohol as a defence against fear and the fear of fear, and against loneliness and heartache when the circumstances of their lives allow them to use this defence. It is very difficult to become an alcoholic if alcohol is completely unavailable where you live, or if you cannot afford to purchase it. There is ample evidence that the incidence of alcoholism in a country correlates negatively with the cost of alcohol. The cheaper alcohol is the more drunks there are. Governments can reduce the incidence of alcoholism by increasing the tax on alcohol, but, while moralistic politicians may deplore the evils of drink, raising taxation on it loses votes, and politicians prefer being elected to saving lives.

It is easy to use alcohol as a defence when you live in a society where social life is built around drinking. Heavy drinking became a very popular pastime in England during the Industrial Revolution. In the nineteenth century drinking came under attack from the evangelical Temperance Movement, which the middle class and the aspiring working class supported. Members of these classes who felt in need of some mind-relaxing drug had to turn to opium, which could be purchased legally, or drink alone and in secret. Nowadays many men see drinking as an essential characteristic distinguishing strong, masculine men, and younger generations of women no longer believe that it is shameful to be drunk.

If the circumstances that allow a person to use the defence of alcohol do not change, and if the person has no desire to change then that person continues to drink heavily. People refuse to change when they are frightened of their fear and frightened that other people will see their fear. Alcohol solves their problems in the short term. A consultant psychiatrist whose heavy drinking was a way of life called it 'a sinister but effective peacemaker, a means of securing for however short a time some way out of the prisonhouse of reality to the Golden Age'.[50] Heavy drinkers use their drinking not only as a way of avoiding their own pain but as a way of bamboozling those people who want them to stop drinking. Discussions about how much you drink or what appalling things you did when you were drunk prevent your would-be helpers from perceiving how depressed and lonely you are.

Alcohol does more than just hide pain and fear. It provides some marvellous excuses. C. R. Snyder et al., in their book *Excuses: Masquerades in Search of Grace*,[51] devote six large, tightly packed pages to all the research studies that show how useful drinking alcohol can be. For instance, people who believed that they had drunk alcohol when in fact they had not (some research psychologists have no compunction about lying to their subjects), and who also believed that you were allowed to be aggressive when you were drunk, or that alcohol made you feel less nervous in company, became aggressive when aggravated, or more relaxed (as measured by heart rate) when meeting someone new.

A number of studies in which the hapless male subjects were wired up to a machine that measured penile tumescence showed that

men whose normal sexual response is inhibited by sexual guilt or social restraints will show the greatest disinhibition effect when they believe they are drinking alcohol. There is an important payoff in this process, since the men can absolve themselves of responsibility for their actions by blaming alcohol for their disinhibited behaviour.[52]

One study found that

> those child molesters who claimed to have been intoxicated at the time of their offence expressed significantly more derogatory attitudes toward other child molesters than those who did not claim to have been intoxicated. We would suggest that those subjects who claimed intoxication may have held more derogatory attitudes because, *having the excuse of intoxication, they could deny their personal membership of the reviled fellowship of child molesters.* In effect, they could disparage child molesters without disparaging themselves. By admitting a relatively minor problem (alcohol abuse), they were enabled to simultaneously admit their crime and deny personal responsibility for it.[53]

Drinking alcohol is something we can choose to do. It is an *activity*. Nevertheless, a popular way of referring to this activity is to say, 'I have a drink problem'.

Social workers and volunteer counsellors often speak in this way of their clients. 'He has a drink problem' sounds more polite and understanding than 'He's a drunk'. Whenever I hear about 'a drink problem' I always get a vision of some ordinary person carrying a briefcase. The briefcase is the problem the person has. I always want to ask the person to show me his problem in the same way that he could show me his new, shiny briefcase.

I sometimes do this when the person who declares himself to have a drink problem is actually presenting himself to my scrutiny. My request 'Show me your problem' is like a Zen koan, aiming to demonstrate that so many of the confusions and conflicts we get ourselves into come not from what *is* but from the language we use.

English, like the other Indo-European languages, prefers nouns to verbs – that is, words which refer to objects rather than words which refer to actions. Some languages, such as the Hopi Indians' language, are not like this. They can talk about activity without having to create an object doing the activity. A Hopi Indian might observe an event which he calls 'sudden brightening' but which we, using English, have to refer to as 'the lightning flashed'. Now we have created an object, lightning, which does something, like flashing.

We might say, 'I was swimming,' but often we say, 'I had a swim.'

Where is the lightning when it is not flashing?

Where is the swim before I had it?

Where is your drink problem?

Why don't you throw it away?

Why can't you throw it away?

The only answer is that you cannot throw your drink problem away because it is not a thing you have. It is what you do. Your problem is *you*.

By claiming that you have a drink problem you are, in fact, by your choice of language, distancing yourself, splitting yourself off from part of your experience. Here you are; there is your problem.

While you split yourself in this way you cannot deal with the problems your drinking creates, much less the pain and fear which underlie your drinking. You have to own every part of yourself. You have to say not 'I have a drink problem' but 'I drink a lot'.

If you drink a lot you will get a lot of problems. In the UK, in the two years to December 1999, there was a drop in crime rates except for a 29 per cent rise in 'stranger violence', in which the person who is attacked does not know his attacker. Many of these attackers are drunk. The biennial British Crime Survey showed that 'Alcohol was involved in more than 50 per cent of the 880,000 attacks by strangers in 1999. In 1990 a Home Office report showed that 30 per cent of sex offenders were intoxicated, 33 per cent of burglars and 50 per cent of people involved in street punch-ups. A British Medical Association study suggested 50 per cent of domestic violence was alcohol related, as were 65 per cent of homicides and 75 per cent of stabbings.'[54]

If you drink heavily, then compared to light drinkers and abstainers,

- You are twice as likely to die of heart disease
- You are twice as likely to die of cancer
- You are twelve times as likely to die of cirrhosis of the liver
- You are three times as likely to die in a car crash
- You are six times as likely to commit suicide.[55]

Alcoholism is not a disease, even though it does cause a number of diseases. However, many people for different reasons like to regard alcoholism as a disease. Every month it seems some scientist or other announces that he is on the verge of discovering the gene for alcoholism, but this imminent discovery is never heard of again. The same old circular argument appears: 'Why does this person drink so much?' 'Because he has the disease of alcoholism.' 'How do you know he has the disease of alcoholism?' 'Because he drinks so much.'

The vast alcohol industry, the manufacturers, the distributors and the vendors, uphold the disease theory because they can then claim that their product is for normal drinkers. If a few unfortunate individuals develop the disease it is because they would have developed it anyway. Alcohol is not the problem. It is the individual. Nick Heather and Ian Robertson, in their definitive book *Problem Drinking*, wrote, 'The diseased alcoholic was made a scapegoat for society's inability to properly control its favourite psychotropic drug, ethyl alcohol.'[56]

The philosophy of Alcoholics Anonymous is based on the belief that alcoholism is a disease. The aim of AA is not to enable people to drink sensibly but to teach people who drink heavily that they were born an alcoholic and that they must be committed to lifelong abstention. The founders of AA, William Wilson, a stockbroker, and Robert Holbrook Smith, a physician, were involved in the Oxford Group, a popular and aggressively evangelical religious movement of the 1930s and a forerunner of Moral Rearmament, a right-wing political pressure group. AA does not present itself as a religious movement, but, as Nick Heather and Ian Robertson point out, the Twelve Steps advocated by the AA 'contains only two mentions of alcohol but five references to God'.[57]

AA describes its members as being 'in recovery'. They never actually recover from this disease but are forever in recovery and in need of AA support. In the USA psychologists, psychiatrists and therapists in private practice realized that they had stumbled on to a gold mine. What followed was that every behaviour constant repetition of which could cause problems for the person concerned was defined as an addiction, and addiction was defined as a disease. People who ate too much, or shopped too much, or gambled too much, or smoked too much, or who had too much sex, or loved too much, or played computer games or chatted in website forums too much, or who ate too much chocolate, or played the stock market too much – all these and more were addicts. What they needed was a twelve-step programme, and, once they entered the programme, they were 'in recovery'. This made the clients of these psychologists, psychiatrists and therapists happy because they could feel proud of being some distinctive person, perhaps a shopaholic or a sex addict, and they could feel virtuous because they were in recovery – that is, trying to be good. This also made these psychologists, psychiatrists and therapists happy because they had a good income for life.

Having a member of the family who drinks too much is not easy, and so AA developed groups called Al-Anon to help family members. From Al-Anon two popular movements developed separate from AA. These were Adult Children of Alcoholics (ACOA) and the Codependency movement. 'The idea that having an alcoholic parent could contribute to current emotional difficulties became transformed into the further notion that having had an alcoholic parent in the past was largely responsible for one's emotional problems now. From this basis, ACOA proliferated into a major social movement in the USA, supported by the fashionable thesis that problems in living are all caused by childhood traumas and that happiness can only be achieved by recalling and confronting these early traumatic events. Although still based on

12-step principles, ACOA went far beyond AA teaching and was disowned by the Fellowship.'[58]

Nick Heather and Ian Robertson went on:

> Unfortunately for the ACOA movement, the number of people in society with a clearly alcoholic parent is limited. It was therefore necessary to invent the concept of the near alcoholic – a parent who drank but who had few or no alcohol problems. By this means, a large proportion of the population became potential candidates for ACOA. In the bestseller describing ACOA, the author listed 13 characteristics of adult children of alcoholics, including embarrassment, self-absorption, guilt, fear, anger, lethargy, self-pity, and a single characteristic, 'false hope, disappointment, and euphoria'. These are, of course, normal human emotions that apply, at some time or other, to all of us. But by putting these things forward as defining characteristics of an abnormal upbringing by an alcoholic parent and by the further claim that anyone with these problems must by definition have had that kind of childhood, a vast untapped source of credulity was opened up for the ACOA movement to exploit. The fact that many people who experienced these emotions clearly did not have an alcoholic parent created no difficulties; at least one of their parents must have been a near alcoholic!

But Codependency went much further even than this. Whereas ACOA had confined itself to 13 sorts of emotional problems the disease of Codependency was said to show itself in nearly 250 diagnostic characteristics and even that list was not exhaustive. These characteristics refer to almost every conceivable kind of feeling or behaviour that could be construed negatively in any kind of way, including, for example, taking things personally, feeling pressured, and not feeling happy. Thus, despite the fact that they were unable to provide any clear and succinct definition of codependency, the originators of the concept could claim to be able to explain almost every aspect of everyday human malaise. No wonder that the disease of codependency was said to apply to almost 100 per cent of the population. It seems that women were especially vulnerable to the explain-all appeal of the Codependency Movement, owing no doubt to the low self-esteem many women experience in a male-dominated society.[59]

While it is possible to take pride in being born an addict but now to be in lifelong recovery, seeing yourself like this means that you can never create the solidity of inner strength which enables you to value and accept yourself to the full. You have defined yourself as having a basic flaw that is intrinsic, immovable and irreparable.

All of us are flawed in one way or another, but if we see these flaws as intrinsic, immovable and irreparable then we have decided that we cannot change, and this decision traps us in a life of dissatisfaction, inadequacy and helplessness. If we see our flaws as the result of the conclusions we have drawn from our experiences and the decisions we have made based on these conclusions, then we know that our flaws are something that we have created and that we are free to change them. Changing them may not be easy. Ideas that we have held for nearly all our lives are hard to change because so many other ideas depend on them, and our commitments to other people can make changing the circumstances of our life difficult, while a very small income or poor education can limit the range of opportunities available to us, but just knowing that we have the choice of changing or not allows us to feel free.

The philosophy underlying AA is a faith, not a science. Confession and repentance, the stock-in-trade of the revivalist preacher, do not constitute the infallible means of improving our behaviour. The reason that revivalist preachers have always flourished in the USA is because there are always many backsliders who need to be converted again and again and again. In contrast, what the research shows is that heavy drinkers can learn to moderate their drinking and become social drinkers.

In 1962 a psychiatrist at the Maudsley Hospital, London, Dr D. L. Davies, observed that seven 'alcohol addicts' whom he had followed for seven years now drank normally. His paper and other studies in the following years which found considerable evidence to support this finding were furiously rejected by the media and many members of the public. Believers in the Temperance Movement saw anyone who drank, or had a reputation of being a drunk, as the other, the stranger, the evil enemy. They had learned to see alcohol as a powerful seducer into whose clutches you would fall should you take one sip of this dangerous brew. My mother, who once had connections with the Independent Order of Rechabites, part of the Temperance Movement, forbade me as a child to drink ginger beer, lest it give me a taste for alcohol. Having demonized alcohol, those who supported the Temperance Movement protected themselves from this demon by believing that they were morally strong and that alcoholism was a disease to which morally weak people were especially prone.

If you believe that you have an inherent, unchangeable weakness which compels you with the first sip of alcohol to go on drinking until you are totally, helplessly drunk, then taking a sip of alcohol would be dangerous because, if this sip was not followed by you drinking until you were insensible, your belief would be disproved, and that would be a threat to your whole meaning structure. You are compelled by your belief to go on drinking. If you believe that how much you drink is a choice which you are free to make, then one glass of wine or beer presents you with such a choice – whether to have another drink or not. This is an easy choice to make when you drink a glass or two only to release a modest amount of tension and/or to enjoy a drink that satisfies your thirst, but it is not an easy choice when you find that alcohol reduces your keen awareness of the fear that dogs your every moment. It is not an easy choice to make when the circumstances of your life are such that drinking heavily is a readily available option and social drinking or abstinence require a marked change in your habits.

Going into a psychiatric unit or a private clinic may remove you from the opportunity to drink, though the inhabitants of the wards and clinics I have known were never short of a drink. Not drinking for several weeks or months does not prepare you to return to your usual way of life with its manifold temptations. Simply resolving not to drink does not work, because living is a day-to-day business, and what needs to change is day-to-day habits and the pattern of ideas that gave rise to those habits.

Changing day-to-day habits and ideas needs a programme, and this Nick Heather and Ian Robertson have provided in their manual *Let's Drink to Your Health: A Self-help guide to Sensible Drinking*. At the beginning of their book they point out that the manual is not aimed at the person conventionally known as an alcoholic, someone who suffers severe withdrawal symptoms if the drinking stops. Such a person needs medical treatment with sedatives and vitamins. 'Sedatives are required to prevent the symptoms of uncomplicated alcohol withdrawal, delirium tremens and withdrawal seizures, while vitamins are administered in order to prevent development of Wernicke's encephalopathy. If withdrawal is poorly treated or in an inappropriate setting, irreversible complications (for example Korsakoff's syndrome) or death may ensue.'[60]

Once the person has successfully completed their withdrawal, a careful study of *Let's Drink to Your Health* would help them reorganize their life so that it is no longer built around the defence of alcohol. With both heavy drinkers and alcoholics the need for the defence must be confronted before the defence can be relinquished, but every success the person has in not drinking at all or not drinking to excess increases their self-confidence and self-approval, and each increase makes relinquishing the defence that much easier.

In their conclusion to *Problem Drinking* Nick Heather and Ian Robertson point out that 'Drinking is indeed a matter of individual choice but it is also a matter of *collective* responsibility for shaping an environment that minimises the harm to the drinker and to others.'[61] As noted earlier, those Aboriginal communities which accepted collective responsibility for the heavy drinkers in their community have been very successful in curbing a practice that not only ruined the lives of many individuals but which severely impeded the progress of the community. Such an acceptance of community responsibility for alcoholism is rare. Alcohol and nicotine are the most destructive of the drug addictions, but, because they are the addictions of the white, middle-aged men and women who are in government, their deleterious effects are minimized and little done to help those harmed by their effects. The Temperance Movement has faded away because alcohol is no longer needed as the demon against which the virtuous can measure their virtue. The demon is now the drugs of the young, not yet powerful generations. These are what are called the illegal drugs, though in these matters distinguishing legal from illegal is not easy.

Drugs

That most mysterious organ the human brain endows us not just with consciousness but also self-consciousness. We are aware and we are aware that we are aware. Such awareness has allowed our species to do many wonderful things, but for each of us our awareness and self-awareness become at times far more than we can bear. We sleep not just enough to rest our body but also to rest our mind, and when sleep alone does not give us sufficient relief from the constant activity of our mind we turn to drugs.

Excepting the Inuit, whose bleak landscape allows few plants to flourish, every society has a traditional drug, be it wine from grapes, opium from poppies, beer from malt and hops, spirits from grain, mescaline from cactus, nicotine from tobacco, cannabis, coca or mushrooms. Every individual turns to some substance to ease the mind. Sweets and chocolates give more than a pleasant taste. They comfort and reassure. My mother, scourge of alcohol and nicotine, was passionate about her cup of tea. Tea, coffee, cocoa and chocolate contain caffeine, a drug which has a stimulant effect on the central nervous system and the heart.

Two immensely popular drugs are aspirin and paracetamol. Some 4300 million aspirin tablets are consumed each year in Britain.[62] When I was child in Australia the cure for every state of distress was 'a cup of tea, a Bex and a good lie down'. Bex was an aspirin mixture that came as a powder in a neatly folded paper. Bex addicts – that is, most housewives – could unfurl the paper wrapper, fold it into a V, and thus shake the powder into their mouth without wasting one particle. I imagine that some cocaine addicts are equally skilled in doing a line of cocaine.

The most widely prescribed drug in the world is Valium. It is one of the benzodiazepines along with Librium, Ativan and Mogadon. These drugs are called minor tranquillizers because they reduce anxiety, and many people take them rather than discover why they are anxious. People who take any of the benzodiazepines for more than a few weeks are likely to become dependent on them, and such dependence can be difficult to relinquish.[63] Research on the deleterious effects of the minor tranquillizers on people driving cars and operating machinery shows that these drugs can be as dangerous as alcohol, but the government chooses to punish the driver who drinks but not the driver who takes Valium. Michael Gossop noted, 'Tranquillizers are far from being safe drugs, and they are massively over-used. This form of drug taking is one of the hidden and more serious forms of drug abuse in our society.'[64]

Research on the effects of drugs is not simple because the effects do not depend solely on the chemical make-up of the drug. As with alcohol, the social context in which the individual takes the drug and the beliefs the individual has about the drug are very important.

Extraverts and introverts differ not only in their reasons for taking a particular drug but in their physical response to it. In his extensive research, the renowned psychologist Hans Eysenck distinguished extraverts and introverts, but he did this by using questionnaires with groups of people, not as I do by questioning individuals. He and his team identified certain characteristics of the activity of the cortex which distinguish extraverts from introverts. This suggests that there is an innate neurological basis for the distinct ways extraverts and introverts experience their existence. Hans Eysenck assumed that there were certain qualities or attributes called extraversion and introversion which could be measured. Michael Gossop wrote, 'Introverts seem to be comparatively resistant to the effects of alcohol, whereas extraverts succumb to its intoxicating influence much more readily. The opposite is true of stimulant drugs like amphetamine or caffeine. Introverts react most strongly to these drugs and extraverts least.'[65]

However, an individual's beliefs about the effect of a drug can override the drug's physiological effects. A study at the University of Stockholm showed that subjects who had been told that the drug they were being given was a sedative responded by becoming sleepy whether or not the drug they were given was actually a sedative.[66]

The history of drugs and drug use shows a remarkable repetitive pattern which has been documented by Charles Medawar in his book *Power and Dependence*.[67] Initially the new drug is seen as a wonder drug. The conditions it will cure are infinite and everyone who takes it will be happy. Thousands flock to use it. Much time elapses before the drug's deleterious effects begin to be acknowledged. The doctors who prescribe the drug and the company that makes it deny that there is any difficulty with it. Finally the problems can be denied no longer. Enthusiasm for the drug wanes, and then a new wonder drug is discovered, and the cycle is repeated. The history of wonder drugs from opium to Prozac shows that there is no such thing as a free gift and that few people learn from history.

During the Second World War the wonder drug was amphetamine, which kept people awake and active. It was some time before it was widely recognized that amphetamine was addictive and that any regular user who stopped taking the drug was likely to experience severe withdrawal reactions, while prolonged heavy use or a sudden increase in the dose could produce paranoid hallucinations.

Not surprisingly, people who took amphetamines found it hard to sleep, and so a sedative was needed. The first barbiturate was produced in 1903, but the drug did not come into prominence until the 1940s. In his book *Living with Drugs*[68] Michael Gossop remarked that barbiturates were probably the most dangerous of all the drugs he discussed.

Barbiturates assist people to sleep partly because they reduce markedly the amount of time the person spends dreaming, but when the drug is stopped more time is spent dreaming than before the drug was started. Not long after he left the army in 1946, my husband was prescribed the barbiturate Nembutal because he had difficulty sleeping. He was chronically anxious and was plagued by nightmares about some of his wartime experiences. Whenever he tried to stop taking the drug his nightmares returned even more ferociously. Nembutal left him feeling sleepy and lethargic in the morning, so his doctor prescribed amphetamines to wake him up. Many people in the 1950s and 1960s had a similar experience, and, while my husband was eventually able to break his dependence on these drugs, many other people were unable to stop taking them even though they had a most deleterious effect on their lives.

Barbiturates are highly addictive, but doctors were so slow to recognize this. Even though the number of prescriptions for barbiturates has gradually diminished, there are still many people psychologically and physically addicted to what they see as a sleeping pill. In the USA barbiturates are still the drugs most commonly mentioned in coroners' reports on drug-related deaths.[69]

It is impossible to make a clear distinction between legal and illegal drugs. Amphetamines can easily be made in a kitchen laboratory, hence 'speed' is a popular illegal drug, but it is also prescribed by doctors for hyperactive children. The hallucinogenic drug LSD was used by psychiatrists for what they hoped would be a quick path to insight and change for their patients, while the CIA ineptly explored its possibilities for mind control. In the hippie culture of the 1960s LSD was supposed to give an exalted state of consciousness where life, the universe and everything would be explained. I was a postgraduate student at Sheffield University when LSD arrived in the town. I did not try it – alcohol was my drug of choice – but I helped to mind fellow students who were on an LSD trip. My friends and I took two such hapless students along with us when we went to see *Woodstock*, but if the film and the drug produced for them any previously unknown universal wisdom they did not disclose it to us, nor did it seem to inform their subsequent work as psychologists.

Now the favourite hallucinogenic drug is Ecstasy. It was first developed in Germany in 1914 as an appetite suppressant but was never marketed. Like LSD it has been used in psychotherapy. Perhaps what research is now showing, that long-term use deleteriously affects memory, could be of use in therapy if what was forgotten was simply those bad experiences which are hard to leave behind, but unfortunately drugs and procedures that harm memory, like electroconvulsive therapy (ECT), cannot take account of the content of our memories. We lose good memories and bad.

Ecstasy is a drug very alien to older generations, and so there is ill-informed dismay, even hysteria, when someone dies after taking it. What harms and kills may not be the drug itself but the unknown constituents of the pills which are sold illegally. Drug dealers are interested in profit, not people. The journalist Nick Davies, in his study of government attitudes to illegal drugs, commented:

> The risks of consuming LSD and ecstasy are increased enormously by their illegal and unsupervised manufacture. Nobody knows what they are swallowing. Yet, when a Brighton company developed a test to check the purity of ecstasy, the government's drugs adviser, Keith Hellawell, condemned it and warned that the company risked prosecution. It is the same with black-market amphetamines: speed alone may not kill, but speed with a blindfold is likely to finish you off.[70]

Cannabis has a long history. The vast ruined Roman temples at Baalbek in the Bekaa Valley in Lebanon contain a bas-relief showing a vine and a cannabis plant growing side by side. Islam forbids alcohol but not hashish, which medieval Arabic poets celebrated in their poetry. It was by growing cannabis that the farmers of the Bekaa Valley managed to survive the long civil war in Lebanon in the 1970s and 1980s. The Lebanese government passed some draconian laws outlawing the growing of cannabis, and, as part of their invasion of Lebanon in July 2006, the Israeli forces targeted what they believed were Hezbollah strongholds in the Bekaa Valley, but the farmers, like poor farmers in other countries which grow cannabis, coca or poppies, continue with their cannabis crops because they cannot make a living without them.

I had not encountered cannabis until I went to Sheffield University in 1968. Most of my fellow students smoked it, but I did not find it an interesting drug. It killed conversation. At student parties the cannabis smokers sat silent in a darkened room while the drinkers, as ever, stayed close to the alcohol supply and engaged in noisy and, as they thought, brilliant conversation. Cannabis seemed to me to be a remarkably safe drug. The cannabis smokers did not get into fights, fall over and hurt themselves, or get smashed up in road accidents as the drinkers did. The greatest danger for the cannabis smokers came at the end of the parties when they were packed into the rear seats of the cars driven by the drinkers, all of whom were convinced that they were sober enough to drive.

Michael Gossop described the short-term physiological effects of cannabis as 'fairly unremarkable'. 'In terms of its lethal dose, cannabis is an exceptionally safe drug. It is one of the least toxic drugs known to man and there is no evidence that anyone has ever died as a direct result of taking an overdose of it.'[71] There is some evidence that cannabis use impairs the skills needed for driving a car and other vehicles, but these effects are by no means as striking as the effects of benzodiazepines or alcohol on these skills. There is some evidence that long-term use damages the lungs, but again these effects do not compare with the effects of nicotine.[72] A number of cannabis users have found that heavy use can produce short-lived psychotic states, while people diagnosed as schizophrenic may find that cannabis will provoke a relapse and aggravate existing symptoms.[73] However, such people are very likely already to be taking mind-altering prescribed drugs such as the major tranquillizers, which may not mix well with cannabis. A study commissioned by the Department of Health in 2001 found that

- Cannabis and its derivatives show promise of beneficial effects in a number of medical conditions for which standard treatment is less than satisfactory, and further controlled research is fully justified.
- Cannabis is very safe in overdose, but often produces unwanted effects which are better tolerated by patients with some conditions (e.g., multiple sclerosis, chronic pain, AIDS, cancer) than others (e.g., glaucoma).[74]

326

The British government has pledged to permit the use of cannabis-based pharmaceuticals provided they are approved by the medical control agency. However, according to the Federation of European Neuroscience Societies meeting in Vienna in July 2006, it now seems that 'even with purified cannabis extracts, changing the amount, time or place of the dose could produce completely opposite effects on the body'. Beat Lutz of the University of Mainz in Germany and David Baker at University College London, in separate studies, have found that cannabinoids (compounds in cannabis) have different effects depending on which neurones in the brain they encounter.[75]

Cannabis has other advantages. As the authorities in Amsterdam have shown, the best way to avoid football violence is to keep open the cannabis cafés, where people can smoke cannabis and drink coffee when a game is being played. Cannabis keeps the peace much more effectively than the police force.

Cannabis has been used in many countries for centuries, so any severe deleterious effects would be well known by now. However, the belief that one whiff of the weed leads inevitably to heroin, addiction and death is still held by people who refuse to accept any evidence to the contrary. They refuse to take account of the fact that the law forces cannabis users to buy their supplies from drug dealers who often wish to make a greater profit by selling cannabis users cocaine or heroin. There has been a series of detailed reports by responsible, disinterested people in the USA, the UK and Australia, and all found that cannabis use creates no serious dangers. All these reports were totally rejected, except that of the Royal Commission set up in the state of South Australia in 1978, where subsequently cannabis use and the private cultivation of ten or less cannabis plants were decriminalized and treated much as a parking offence is treated, though major cultivation and trafficking were dealt with by the criminal law. A similar approach is taken in the Netherlands.

Cannabis is simply part of their way of life for many people, just as alcohol is for others. Both produce their experts. Patrick Matthews, in his book *Cannabis Culture*, noted that, 'The way experts talk about cannabis can be not just similar but actually identical to wine-speak.'[76] Younger generations may have rejected cannabis because it was the drug of choice for their parents, but the fact that it was banned made it desirable. If only adults would remember that the most effective way to get your teenagers to do what you want is to ban them from doing it. Patrick Matthews observed, 'Dope has stayed in favour in the ''better'' English fee-paying schools because it shows that you're not trying too hard, as required by their gentlemanly code.'[77]

Cannabis is a huge industry, as Matthews pointed out. 'As a global business it's now worth at least £100 billion a year – a pot of gold that attracts the most diverse people. The fact that it's illegal means that not just growers and merchants make a living from cannabis, but customs and police officers, gangsters, drug workers, seed merchants and grow-manual authors as well.'[78] Also:

> Imperial Tobacco already makes a useful amount of money out of cannabis smoking through their recent acquisition of Rizla cigarette papers (which coincidentally are made largely out of French-grown hemp). They employ FFI, a specialist youth-oriented PR firm. This company successfully pitched the idea of taking a Rizla tent – the 'Rizla Experience' – to pop festivals, offering coffee and fruit juices. Sandra Hussey of FFI gamely tries to put a respectable spin on this: 'People who smoke rollups are expressing their individuality.' Has Ms Hussey ever seen someone make a tobacco cigarette with a Rizla King Size, which has just under 10 per cent of the market? 'Yes, I actually did once.' She asks to pass when I inquire whether she feels more comfortable with people smoking cigarettes or joints with her client's product.[79]

The weed that flourishes most profusely in the world is that of hypocrisy, grown by the people who want to appear virtuous and to deny their own weaknesses. Alas, it is very hard nowadays to find something to be holier than thou about. Sex has become so public it is boring, alcohol is so common it is dull and ordinary, and, while nicotine addicts may be persecuted, it is for the good of their health, not their morals. The only thing left to moralize about is the illegal drugs, especially cocaine and heroin. The need to demonize these drugs overrides common sense, and hence many thousands of people suffer.

Cocaine has had its supporters, notably Sigmund Freud and Conan Doyle's creation Sherlock Holmes. In the nineteenth century cocaine was sold in cigarettes, soft drinks, nose sprays, chewing gum, and various patent medicines. In 1885 a combination of extracts from the African kola nut and the South American coca leaf constituted a new soft drink, Coca-Cola. The cocaine was not removed from Coca-Cola until 1906.

For the Peruvian Indians the coca leaf is part of their culture. The drug itself was not extracted from the leaf until the nineteenth century. 'Cocaine is not physically addictive in the same way as heroin and alcohol. The important feature of cocaine is that it can produce what many people regard as a powerfully attractive experience. The drug is a central nervous system stimulant and the first site of action is the cortex. Among its effects, users describe euphoria, laughter, talkativeness and excitement.'[80] 'The effects of smoking paste, crack or freebase cocaine resemble those of intravenous cocaine injection. The blood concentration rises as fast, if not faster, causing a sudden "rush" of pleasure. This pleasant effect soon subsides, to be followed by the "down" of depression, irritability and craving.'[81] The continuous use of cocaine can lead to a feeling of persecution and a toxic psychosis, as well as the delusion that ants or insects are crawling about on or under the skin. However, studies in Canada and the Netherlands have concluded that 'the risks of cocaine use have been exaggerated by the media and that many cocaine users manage to avoid the more serious consequences'.[82]

Governments have always used an external enemy to unite the people, thus preventing the people uniting against the government. The end of the Second World War left the UK with a dearth of external enemies, and since then British governments of whatever political persuasion have used powerless minority groups – migrants, the mentally ill, drug users – as the enemy against whom the majority of the people can unite. After the Second World War the USA had the USSR and the communists to regard as the enemy, but when George Bush Senior was President the Cold War came to an end. He immediately declared war on drugs.

This war is still being fought, principally in Colombia. It has brought death and ruin to many thousands of people, but the supply of drugs has in no way diminished and the drug barons have grown wealthier. The policy of paying growers of the coca plants, mainly poor farmers, to plant another crop has degenerated into the destruction of the plants by indiscriminate aerial spraying. The chemical used is Roundup Ultra, which is made by Monsanto. The much milder form of this chemical used by domestic gardeners comes loaded with warnings about not inhaling the spray and not letting it touch bare flesh. The chemical used in Colombia is based on the compound glyphosate, which damages the human digestive system, the central nervous system, the lungs and the blood's red corpuscles. The World Health Organisation has found that glyphosate is easily transmitted through fruit and vegetables, and that traces of the chemical can be found in crops grown a year after the soil had been contaminated with it. Hugh O'Shaunessy, a journalist, described his visit to the Kofan community, which had been sprayed with a weedkiller a hundred times more powerful than that which is permitted in the USA.

Franci sits on the veranda and whimpers. The little girl is underweight. Her armpits are erupting in boils. Like most of her people, she has suffered from respiratory problems and stomach pains ever since the aircraft and helicopter gunships came over at Christmas and again at New Year dropping toxic pesticides on their villages . . .

The Kofan have been here 500 years. Now it looks as though their time is up. Pineapples are stunted and shrivelled. The once green banana plants are no more than blackened sticks. The remains of a few maize plants can be seen here and there, but the food crops have been devastated. There is hunger in Santa Rosa.

Colombian babies and children are falling ill. Peasants, already miserably poor, are getting hungrier. Indigenous tribes are being torn apart and whole communities sent into exile. The reason is the US-sponsored Plan Colombia, conceived by President Bill Clinton and roundly embraced by President George W. Bush, designed to eliminate all cocaine production in Colombia.[83]

Until 1968, when the British government began to prohibit heroin, there were fewer than five hundred heroin addicts in Britain – a few jazz musicians, some poets, some Soho Chinese. Now, according to the Home Office, there may be as many as half a million addicts. World heroin production has tripled in the past decade and cocaine production doubled. The income of the drug barons is an annual $500,000 million, greater than the American defence budget.

Yet, as Michael Gossop wrote, 'Heroin is a safe drug; it is safer, for instance, than alcohol . . . the dangers of heroin addiction owe far more to the psychology of the addict and the ways addicts use the drug rather than to any property inherent in the drug itself. Many addicts show a remarkable lack of concern for, if not deliberate disregard of, their own physical welfare.'[84] The horrors of going 'cold turkey' are exaggerated. 'The degree of discomfort that addicts experience during withdrawal can be significantly reduced by providing them with accurate information about the course of withdrawal. Most addicts can successfully complete withdrawal within a week or two. This is true even of the highest dose users.'[85]

The dangers of heroin come from the black market in the drug. Nick Davies wrote:

Heroin, so benign in the hands of doctors, becomes highly dangerous when it is cut by black market dealers – with paracetamol, drain cleaner, sand, sugar, starch, powdered milk, talcum powder, coffee, brick dust, cement dust, gravy powder, face powder or curry powder. None of these adulterants was ever intended to be injected into human veins. . . A large proportion of the illness experienced by heroin users is caused by wound infection, septicaemia and infective endocarditis, all due to unhygienic injection technique. . . Street users buy blind and so they will overdose accidentally. . . The purity of street heroin varies from 20% to 90%. . . It is peculiarly ironic that governments set out to protect their people from a drug which they claim is dangerous by denying them the safeguards and information which they insist must apply to the consumption of drugs which they know to be harmless. Compare, for example, the mandatory information on the side of a bottle of vitamin C tablets with the information available to a black-market heroin user.[86]

Michael Gossop had noted that 'Even an ordinary, safe, therapeutic dose of an opiate such as morphine or heroin can be fatal when administered to someone who has already been drinking. Many deaths might have been avoided in the past, and more could be avoided in the future, if addicts were clearly warned of this danger.'[87] Prohibition has played a major part in the spread of HIV, Aids and hepatitis C because needle exchange schemes have not been supported by governments, and this has led to the sharing of needles with subsequent infection.

The war on drugs can never be won. Many of the senior police in the UK know this, while in Australia the Illicit Drugs Report showed in 2001 that, despite the best efforts of the police, only a small percentage of heroin arriving in the country was being seized, while other drugs, such as cocaine, cannabis and amphetamines, were freely available, particularly in Sydney. The Minister for Police, Paul Whelan, said that it was 'factually accurate' to say that the war on drugs was lost because recent large drug seizures had resulted only in the price of heroin rising.[88]

Nick Davies concluded that, 'If ever [in the war against drugs] there is a war crimes trial to punish the generals who gloried in this slaughter of the innocent, the culprits should be made to carve out in stone: ''There is no drug known to man which becomes safer when its production and distribution are handed over to criminals.'''

Using drugs need not lead to lifetime addiction. 'There is', wrote Michael Gossop, 'no such thing as an addictive personality. Nor is there a single addict lifestyle. People become drug addicts for many reasons. It is futile to look for objective causes of addiction, or to talk of whether or not the addict can really give up drugs. The attitudes, beliefs and expectations of the addict are of paramount importance. If the addict believes that they are totally helpless before the power of heroin, or whatever drug it may be, then they are indeed helpless. But the origins of the helplessness lie in the psychology of the addict and not in some chemical property of the drug.'[89]

The helplessness the addict feels is akin to the helplessness we can all feel when the reward for what we do is immediate and sweet and the punishment is a long time coming. This is why the defences we acquire, whether or not they are addictions, can be so difficult to relinquish. The rewards of heroin are particularly powerful, especially when the person taking it feels unloved and powerless. Linda Yablonsky, once a heroin addict and dealer, described the experience:

I'm warm, my skin tingles. I listen to my heart beat. It's slow and easy. I don't move but I can see myself dancing. My mind races. I'm excited. It's not easy to describe this euphoria – a sublime nausea, a flushed meeting of mortal and immaterial all at once, a leap beyond fate, a divine embrace. Heroin gives the impression you've gained a level of self-knowledge closed to other pursuits, and the moment you recognize the place where you stand, it blots you out as if you've never existed. Nothing in the world can hurt you then. Nothing can touch you. And nothing can satisfy your hunger for more: more love, more pain, more sex, more excitement. More, *more*.

Everything happens, if you let it, sooner or later, all the things you've left undone come back to claim you. I feel safe here. Heroin doesn't rattle any skeletons. It's sweet. It can't get any sweeter than this. Everything is as I remember it, as I want it, as I need. I own it, the great, the pure, the impossible. All mine.

Linda Yablonsky knew only too well that 'It's all a stupid game run by creeps and fuelled by arseholes, but we accept it. The danger is part of the draw. Life isn't easy, not for anyone. Heroin is a finger up its nose. It's got a life of its own and that life is ours, we don't have to plan or think it out. There lies the beauty: I'm done with thinking. All it ever did was make me cry.'[90]

Linda Yablonsky illustrated in her autobiographical novel, *The Story of Junk*, what Michael Gossop saw as the reason why addicts find it very hard to change. He wrote:

> The slavery and helplessness of the drug user occurs regularly in junkie conversation: such comments are both a celebration of, and an apology for, the junkie life. They excuse any fault, on the grounds that, as a helpless slave to their addiction, the addict is not responsible for their own behaviour. It is a view of drug taking that combines the perverse satisfactions of martyrdom with a powerful rationalization about why it is pointless to try to give up drugs. Such beliefs are both a justification and a trap. They give meaning and significance to the addict's lifestyle, but because they attribute such invincible powers to the drug effects, they create a barrier to change. The world that addicts invent for themselves hardens and imprisons them.[91]

Drug addicts are not alone in this way of thinking.

Politicians who will not consider that prohibition has caused far more problems than it set out to cure are trapped by their own fixed beliefs. For many of them power is the delicious reward they cannot bear to abandon. Moreover, their fixed belief that a war must be waged on drugs protects them from having to tackle, as an ex-addict has had to tackle, the problem of acknowledging and living in the real world. The illegal drug industry is now a huge worldwide enterprise, intimately connected not just with the multimillion industries of money laundering, prostitution, pornography, illegal weapons, slavery and trafficking in asylum seekers, but also with the legitimate financial world. Computers now allow a trillion dollars a day to circle the world. Much of that money comes from drugs.[92] Rather than admit their fear of tackling something that is far beyond their control, politicians close their eyes, lie and dissemble.

We can all agree that life is difficult. Even when we are full of self-confidence, when we have all the money and security we need, and we are surrounded by people who love us, life is still difficult. Calamities happen, people leave us, time marches on regardless. The less self-confidence we have, the harder it is to deal with calamities, loss and the passing of time. Self-confident or not, we are all affected by events far from us and not under our control. To understand our predicament, and to make informed choices about what we should do, we need to understand not just what goes on inside us and in our immediate environment but what goes on in the wider world and how that affects our lives. Only then can we work out how to apportion responsibility for our predicament. For instance, if we choose anorexia as our desperate defence and we wish to relinquish it, we need to see how popular fads and fashions have played their part in our choice of a defence. We are not responsible for the fads and fashions of society because they have been chosen by people other than us, but we are responsible for how much we let ourselves be impressed by them.

If we do not inform ourselves so that we can apportion responsibility correctly, we find ourselves locked into one of two prisons. If we lay the blame for our predicament totally on other people, we find ourselves locked into the prison of anger, bitterness and resentment. If we lay the blame totally on ourselves, we find ourselves locked in the prison of depression.

Chapter Eight

Turning Fear into Depression

Only good people get depressed. By 'good people' I mean those who base their life on the belief that as they are they are not acceptable, and so they have to work hard to be good. The whole purpose of their life is to be good. Of course, many people do do good – in fact most of us do – but not everyone uses the measure 'good–bad' as an essential way of measuring their worth. Good people worry about not being good enough. They constantly try to do better, and they are experts in feeling guilty. Not all good people get depressed, but all the people who do get depressed are good people.

Just what constitutes being good is different for different people. Some people define good in terms of the noblest of virtues – unselfishness, kindness, generosity, reliability, truthfulness, honesty – while others define goodness in terms of meeting standards, being acceptable, achieving, bonding with and supporting one's own group, and so on. Whatever the terms, the basic belief the person holds is 'There is a standard to be met. I am far below this standard. I must always strive to reach it.' In 2006 Geoff Gallop, Premier of Western Australia, surprised everyone who knew him with an announcement that he was resigning from his post and from politics because he was depressed. Perhaps his wife was the only person who knew that all his life he had struggled with what he called 'melancholy'. In an interview six months after his resignation he described himself as 'a naturally anxious person and a perfectionist'. In his five-year premiership he had achieved a great deal, but, when his interviewer praised his record, Geoff said, 'overall I'm happy but, being a perfectionist, I think I could have done better.'[1]

Good people became good when they were small children going through the process of learning to deny both their fear and their nature. To preserve their belief that their parents were good they defined themselves as bad. To give themselves courage and hope they created a belief in the Just World. One day, they believed, their efforts to be good would be recognized. If we are born into a family where the parents seem to take for granted that virtue will inevitably be rewarded and vice punished we may grow up not realizing that we have learned to believe that we live in a Just World. Not only do all religions teach the belief in the Just World but political beliefs are often based on the belief in the Just World. A Conservative, a Communist, a Republican, a Socialist are likely to believe that, once their world is governed by the principles of their particular party, all wrongs will be righted and the world will operate as it should, as a Just World. Geoff Gallop's parents may have had very different political views, with Geoff's father staunchly supporting the Liberal (i.e. Conservative) Party and his mother being an 'uncompromising, take-no-prisoners trade unionist', but both parents were, in effect, telling Geoff that he had to work hard to be good. He interpreted this message as being that he had to make everything perfect in order to be good and receive his just reward. Geoff 'recalls being an anxious child, particularly about schoolyard life. "It was little things. I was always anxious about results and in life, being a perfectionist, always wanting to get it right. I always felt like apologising, fixing things, making them right." '[2]

No matter how virtuously good people behave, and how much they are loved and admired by others, they can never believe that they are as valuable and acceptable as other people may say they are. When life goes well for them this doubt about themselves may be no more than a feeling of humility, but, when life becomes difficult, the doubt grows to become a massive certainty. Jackie said, 'I feel as though I'm two people. One's telling me to do the good things in life and the other side's bad. And the bad always wins over the good. I feel a weak person, so I suppose character does come into it. But I feel it's not so much character, it's personality with me. I feel that along life's way I've had it all knocked out of me, which doesn't help a depressed person at all. It doesn't matter what stage of depression you're in. Lack of confidence in oneself can destroy you anyway.'

Peter said, 'I didn't like myself. I think that my self-image was very, very bad. I used to wonder why I was such an awful person. My attitude to people who appeared to like me was "If they really knew me they wouldn't like me. They wouldn't have any time for me at all."'

Good people always blame themselves. Whatever the cause of some disaster may be, good people can work out some way of blaming themselves for it. Often there are other people around who are prepared to let them take the blame. A long-lasting marriage can be based on one person always denying responsibility and the other person accepting it. For Elizabeth it was only in the safety of my room that she could explain how she felt to her husband. Bernard could not understand why Elizabeth was depressed. He was a very caring, loving husband, but what gradually emerged in our discussions was that he could not admit that he made mistakes and that he transferred the responsibility for all his mistakes on to his wife. She accepted the responsibility, blamed herself and thought even more badly of herself.

Elizabeth said, 'If something goes wrong, it's always my fault. If I write him a list of things that have to be done and he forgets one of them he says, "It's your fault. If it was important you should have underlined it." Then I think, "Yes, I should have thought of that but all the things on the list are important. I shouldn't have asked him to do so much." So then I say to him, "Well, don't you bother, I'll do it," and I do. If we have a row and he storms out of the house, I spend the rest of the day going over and over it in my mind, trying to work out what I'd done wrong and what I can do to put it right.'

This seemed to me to be one of those marriages where the wife has to appear to be weak so that she can support the husband in his role as the strong, unchanging, infallible hero. I asked Elizabeth, 'Do you feel that Bernard depends on you a great deal?'

'Yes,' she said, 'but he makes out that he doesn't.'

Bernard looked puzzled as Elizabeth and I talked. Then he said, 'We're talking at two different levels. When you said about me depending on Elizabeth, I thought that you meant I needed her, relied on her, to look after me, cooking, that sort of thing, but you're both talking about something else.'

'Yes,' said Elizabeth, 'of course I wash your shirts. That goes without saying. But that's not the kind of depending on I mean. You depend on me to take responsibility for your mistakes.'

For many good people part of being good is endeavouring always to meet other people's needs. Arthur came to see me because he had heard me on a local radio phone-in, where several callers had described their fear and depression. 'That's what happens to me,' he said.

He was a very successful man, at the top in his profession. 'I always set goals and I see that my staff achieve them.'

I asked, 'Why is it important to set goals and achieve them?' He replied, 'I don't like coming second.'

'Why set goals?'

'That's the best way to hold everything together and to move things forward.' He illustrated this by making a circle of his arms and moving slightly forward.

'Why is it important to hold things together?'

'Well, security.'

'Why is it important to have security?'

'That's hard to put into words.'

'What would happen to you if you didn't have any security, if you couldn't control things and everything fell into chaos?'

'That's what's happening to me now.'

We talked about the fear that came with early-morning waking and how this was the fear of annihilation. I said, 'I expect as a small child you were often nearly annihilated by your father. He would just about wipe you out as a person and you had to find some way of defending yourself.'

'That's where I learned to achieve. It was the only way I could please – well, nothing pleased him. By coming first, second or third, I could protect myself. Coming last, that was unthinkable.'

He would have liked to have played rugby, but his father would not let him. He had to go home straight after school and do his chores on the farm. He could not stay at school and play rugby. Yet his father would talk with great pride and interest about his schoolmate who was a good rugby player. 'He was always telling me about Bob's achievements, yet he wouldn't let me play. I couldn't understand that. I played rugby when I went to university, but that was too late to be any good.'

It was not until Arthur had talked about these things that he could recognize how all his achievements had been for his father, not for himself. He had lived his life meeting his father's needs. The poet Gwyneth Lewis, who has written the best book I have ever read about a personal experience of depression, learned to listen critically to her habitual thoughts. Writing about her depression coming to an end, she said, 'As I was feeling a lot better one day, I found myself thinking, "I'm so happy today" followed closely by, "If only Mam were this happy." I was shocked when I noticed how automatically I was willing to compromise my own wellbeing by making it conditional on someone else's. Besides, how do I know at any given time that my mother is not happy? And even if she isn't, what business is it of mine? Once I told my mother that all I wanted was for her to be happy. "What if I'm not a happy type of person?" she said, perfectly reasonably. If I want the freedom to live my own life for myself, then I have to allow it to everyone else.'[3]

Those people who spend their lives meeting other people's needs become very skilled in blaming themselves when they feel they have failed in doing this. Because women are supposed to spend much of their lives meeting other people's needs, they are usually well trained in blaming themselves.

I used to meet groups of trainee midwives to discuss any of the psychological problems they might come across in their work. Every group raised the same issue – stillbirth. What could a nurse say to a woman whose baby had just died?

In one group two of the nurses talked about one woman they had nursed who had given birth to a beautiful eight-pound dead baby. The cause of death was a separated placenta. Some weeks previously the woman had gone to a GP with a complaint of pain in her pelvic girdle. He treated her for a urinary infection. It must have been at that point the placenta had become detached, but the uterus was blocked, so there was no sign of bleeding. Thus the baby died.

One of the nurses was with the woman when, in hospital, the obstetrician and midwife tried to locate the baby's heartbeat. The nurse told us how no one spoke to the woman, but left her alone while they prodded her stomach or huddled in corners and talked in whispers. Only the student midwife sat with her and held her hand. 'What could I say to her?' she asked me.

We talked about what the woman would have been feeling then and later, when she would be trying to work out why this terrible thing had happened. Was it better to see it as a random accident or as something with an identifiable cause? We came to the conclusion that it would be better to see the death as having an identifiable cause because that made for greater safety. If we could identify the cause of that death then perhaps we could act differently in future and so avoid a similar death.

We then looked at the question of whom the woman should blame. The nurses quickly absolved the GP of blame. 'He wasn't her usual doctor,' they said. Of course she would not blame the obstetrician, they said. She would blame herself. 'She would say to herself that she should have rested more or shouldn't have lifted something heavy.'

'Women are conditioned to blame themselves,' one of them said. 'Men always blame them, and women accept this and blame themselves.'

All the nurses present agreed with this. They all seemed quite adept at self-blame. Of course, by taking the blame upon yourself you may not be happy but you do feel virtuous.

Virtue implies high standards, and the more virtuous you wish to be the higher your standards must be. There is no higher standard than perfection, and that is the standard that good people aspire to.

Jackie said, 'My world is a fantasy world where everything stays

341

the same. Clean and bright and white, and you just stare; it's just like happiness, I suppose, within a white world. I don't like a lot of change. We all, as human beings, have to accept change through our lives, but I don't like a lot of change, quick change, not that involves me anyway ... It's very hard to lower your standards; well, I find it is anyway. Because if I don't keep the standards I've already got, then I feel more depressed. So when the strength is draining, you've got no energy, you've still got to keep up those standards. Well, I have anyway, to prove to myself that I'm still around.'

Val said, 'I've always been taught that if a job's worth doing it's worth doing well, and I took that to the extreme of having to do everything perfectly, which is of course impossible, and you always fall short so that you feel you've failed, and it becomes a sort of treadmill, the more you feel you've failed the harder you've got to try to be perfect. But it's an impossible goal. You never achieve perfection ... I simply felt guilty because I couldn't achieve perfection. I constantly punished myself for not being perfect. The perfect me never made mistakes, did everything perfectly. I was completely self-sufficient. I didn't intrude on other people, kept my needs to myself, denied my own needs and thought I was doing the best thing.'

Jackie spoke of wanting certainty. If at every moment of your life you are plagued with doubt about your own worth, you long for certainty and the control that comes with it. Change cannot be tolerated. Societies that are based on maintaining extremely high and rigid standards for virtue are adamantly against change – Orthodox Jews, fundamentalist Muslims, the Amish, the Plymouth Brethren. Every Christian Church is split between those who see the world as changing and so believe that their Church should adapt, and those who believe that virtue and the path to virtue have been defined in their holy books once and for ever. It is very easy for good people to come to believe that they know what is right and what is best for other people. The less they value and accept themselves, the greater their need for certainty, and the greater their need for certainty the more they see everything in clear-cut, black-and-white terms with no shades of grey. Philip Martin wrote:

> Depression increases our usual tendency to think in extremes of black and white. Nuances escape our grasp. Things either are or they aren't. Though it may take a while to come to a decision, when we make a choice, it is usually an either/or decision. (In fact, part of the difficulty in making decisions stems from the fact that we are thinking in such stark terms, and have a hard time holding the subtleties of many possibilities in our minds.) But, though stark extremes might be comforting, they seldom describe the way things are. We need only look at ethnic, political, or religious wars to see where extreme views get us. While it is comfortable to rest in extremes, as they can give us a comfortable certainty, this certainty is ultimately a painful illusion.[4]

How we think about ourselves determines how we think about other people. We judge other people in the way we judge ourselves. If we care about ourselves, if we feel that we are valuable, if we judge ourselves according to reasonable standards and assure ourselves that when we fail we shall do better next time, then we judge others in the same way. We find it easy to like people and are surprised when someone lets us down or behaves badly. If we do not care about ourselves, if we do not feel that we are valuable, if we set ourselves impossibly high standards and judge ourselves harshly for failing, we judge other people in the same harsh way. We expect other people to let us down and to behave badly, and when they do not let us down and behave quite well we do not rejoice but believe that one day the truth as we know it will come out. Philip Martin wrote of himself:

> One of the main characteristics of my own depression was the cynical and judgemental state of mind it created. In public I was constantly looking around at other people, mentally judging them on their clothing, their manner, their speech. I had difficulty

reading, because as I read I heard myself criticizing the author, thinking I could write much better, or make a better argument. I imagined that the people I was close to lived their lives out of highly negative motives and thoughts. My judgements about myself were even more severe. I constantly upbraided myself for every thought or action. I felt that at the bottom I was defective, a shiny red apple rotting at its core.[5]

Feelings of self-hatred, a lack of confidence, self-blame, and a need to be unforgivingly judgemental while at the same time trying to live up to other people's expectations are not characteristics which suddenly appear as symptoms of depression. They are ways of thinking which have been established in childhood. All that depression does is intensify them. My depressed clients would tell me their life story, and in it these characteristics would appear again and again. There were characteristics which I had seen in my mother, and this was how she behaved when she was not depressed.

When I was a child I knew that my mother behaved oddly but I did not know why. This was a great puzzle to me since it seemed obvious that by her attitudes she created just about all of her misery. Couldn't she see this? Why didn't she change?

I had no opportunity to search for answers to these questions until I arrived in England in 1968 and went to work as a clinical psychologist in Sheffield. There I was able to talk for many hours with depressed people and to read widely in psychiatric and psycho-analytic literature.

Everyone who becomes depressed has their own individual story, but all these stories have the same theme, just as countless stories have been told all with the same theme of boy meets girl, boys loses girl, boy gets girl. Here is the story of depression.

The Story of Depression

Depression is a unique experience. It is totally different from unhappiness. When we are unhappy, even though we may have suffered the most terrible disaster, we can be comforted by other people, and we can comfort and be kind to ourselves, but when we are depressed we are surrounded by a wall as impenetrable as it is invisible. Nothing gets through that wall to comfort us, and in our solitary prison we will not comfort ourselves.

It is the sense of being alone in a prison which distinguishes depression from all other forms of unhappiness and distress. Gwyneth Lewis wrote, 'Depression isn't the same as despair, though it's easy to confuse the two. Depression's more like desolation, being alone in an uninhabited place. This isolation is the first step in self-knowledge, and the internal desert makes such learning a matter of survival . . . [Depression's] purpose is to teach you how to avoid becoming depressed again. In that sense, depression is a very kind disorder, and will return only if you refuse to learn the lessons it has to teach you.'[6] Crucially important though this isolation is, no psychiatric or psychological textbook mentions this, and few books on therapy do so. Whenever I examine a book on depression I first look for the author's definition of it, and if this is a list of symptoms with not a mention of the sense of isolation as the prime characteristic I know that this book is of limited value, because the author is writing about a mixed population of people, some of whom were depressed and some unhappy.

When I first looked at Philip Martin's book *The Zen Path through Depression* I saw right away that this man knew what depression was. He wrote:

The grey place that is depression can be frightening and disorienting. Whether or not you have been there before, each time it is different. It may sometimes seem that you are in a cold, lifeless, lonely desert. Other times it may feel like a dark, overgrown forest, filled with terrible animals lurking just out of sight in the shadows. Or you may feel you're at the bottom of the ocean; the water holds you captive, the pressure is unbearable, and you cannot breathe. Whatever the place or terrain, it feels as if there is no way out. You are truly lost.[7]

Depressed people can describe in a vivid image what they are experiencing. Geoff Gallop said, 'Being depressed is like an endless tunnel of darkness; you just can't get out of it.'[8] If I need to determine whether a person is depressed or unhappy I ask, 'If you could paint a picture of what you're feeling, what sort of picture would you paint?'

Some people will answer very simply. They'll say, 'I'm at the bottom of a black pit,' or 'I'm in a thick fog,' or 'I'm walking along an endless dark tunnel.' If you then ask the person to describe the pit, the fog or the tunnel, you will discover that each person has their own special kind of pit, or fog, or tunnel. The pit may have stainless-steel or crumbling walls, the fog may be grey or sticky and black, the tunnel may become narrower and narrower as time passes.

Some people give very elaborate, very idiosyncratic images. One man told me, 'I'm under a transparent dome and I can't get out. There's a sort of white paint running down the outside of the dome, and the people outside the dome sort of loom over me and look vague and ghostly.'

One woman, a mother of three small children, said, 'I'm in my kitchen standing at the sink. There's piles and piles of washing up. I'm looking out the window and outside it's raining and cold and horrible, and I can't get out of the kitchen until all the washing up is done, and the more I do, the more there is to be done.'

Jackie said, 'A black square – it's just blackness, and I feel as though I am in the middle of a horror movie and there is no way out. There is just dense darkness, nothing there but blackness. You feel as though you're going deeper and deeper into it, and there's no opening.'

All the images are different, but they have one common meaning. The person is alone and in some kind of prison. If unhappy people are asked to describe what they are feeling, their images are grey and miserable, but they do not contain this sense of enclosure, and other people are present, or easily available to them. Also, images of unhappiness are often described in 'as if' terms: 'I feel as if I'm walking along a rainswept street.' A depressed person will not say 'as if' but rather 'is'. I am alone in a prison. The essence of being depressed is experiencing a sense of isolation, of being utterly and completely alone.

Complete isolation in a prison for an indefinite period is the torture that will break the strongest person. Those authorities who run prisons and concentration camps know and use isolation to torture and to break a prisoner. Complete isolation affects us both physically and mentally. It is not surprising that depression has profound physiological effects on the brain and the body, and that these effects can lead to illness. However, the mental torture of depression is worse.

A doctor, writing of her experience of depression, said:

The most devastating experience was early morning waking. I experience a stomach lurch when people tell me about it in the surgery today. It is, of course, a useful symptom of physiological depression to 'elicit' from a patient, but experientially it is soul destroying. It felt like my own private torture chamber, devised to undermine every ounce of strength, and drive me under completely. Night after night, month after month, I woke up at two or three and felt lonely and hopeless, hour after hour, wishing someone else was awake to be alive and human, getting up quietly in the night to cry in the other room so as not to disturb my friend, and, worst, knowing that neither he nor anyone else could help, that I was cut off, removed from the world.[9]

Being frightened is exhausting. So is not sleeping. So is trying to fight the depression.

Val said, 'When the depression was at its worst, I felt as though I would fall into a bottomless black pit, and somehow I had to keep out of it. By my own efforts I had to pull myself out of it, but the effort of doing this day after day is a bit like trying to ride a bicycle uphill with the brakes applied, and you don't seem to get anywhere but neither do you fall backwards down the hill. But it's completely exhausting and there comes a time when you wake up and look at the day ahead and you just haven't the energy or strength to get on the bicycle, and those are the days when you just lie in bed and put the covers over your head and do nothing.'

Along with all the fear and exhaustion there is anger. Peter said, 'People in the family were aware that something was wrong. I suppose it goes back thirty or forty years before it became a crisis situation. When it got to that point I really ceased functioning externally. I couldn't go out and go to places and so on. The other side of it which was extraordinary was that if somebody came to the house, I mean, an outsider, a friend, a visitor, then I had lots of sparkle and was joking, and nobody, I'm sure, would have had the least idea that there was anything wrong at all, and when they left, down one went and became almost incommunicado with the rest of the family.'

He went on:

It was very frightening. I imagine that the fear fed the anger, because one got very angry. Never over really important things, always over trivial things like there wasn't any marmalade. That could lead to quite appalling rages. Rage where one – not one, I – became abusive, aggressive, obscene, violent, very violent indeed, which was very frightening, and it felt wrong. One sort of felt out of kilter. I used to have the most terrible sort of post-rage senses of shame and guilt and lack of understanding. Really, quite acute misery. I mean real, you know, real tears. I mean, it's not easy, I suppose, for most men, it's not easy for me certainly to say that one used to cry, and cry and cry on occasions, and I think that because one is a man, and because these expectations are put on men, certainly in my generation, that made it even worse. Where it should have been a release, a safety valve, it didn't work like that, and you felt less than a man, you felt almost castrated in a way. It was quite a dreadful feeling.

However, being depressed is also a state of great security. Jackie said:

I go very quiet. I don't want to know anybody. Very angry. I get very hurtful, not intentional hurt, but that's the only way I can get through to people, so they don't get any closer. If I hurt them, they'll stay away and therefore I can be on my own in this depression, and hide behind the mask and just solely by hurting people, being quiet, feeling angry inside and putting the barrier up, that's how I can keep people away, which I feel helps me in the state of depression ... I used to feel safe within the blackness. A fear of being with people. Being really frightened of everything and everybody around you. It's just so painful. You feel drained of everything ... Hiding behind the mask is putting yourself away from the outside world, the world you were frightened of stepping into, but people still seeing you with that smile, the joking, the laughing, and that is where the mask comes on. Behind that mask I am suffering hurt, pain, rejection, helplessness, but behind the mask and shutting myself within four walls I feel secure, because none of the outside world can come in unless I let them hurt me.

Because depression gives a feeling of security, the depressed person can feel very much in control. We are always capable of being two contrary things at once. A depressed person can feel helpless with regard to the world and completely in control of the prison, warding off people by hurting them and negating all attempts by people to help them. Anyone who tries to get near or to help the depressed person can feel the wall around the person. The cry of 'I can't get through to you!' is not an empty cliché but a reality.

A depressed person may take great pride in being in control. Val said:

I certainly felt a certain pride in carrying this depression and coping with it, living with it, not letting anyone else see that I was depressed, and I felt, from a religious point of view, that this was my cross and I would bear it, and there was a certain pride in doing that ... and I've always wanted to be in control of things so that I would know exactly what would happen and

349

I could control what would happen and avoid situations that might cause some spontaneous action on my part. It's very difficult to act spontaneously because you don't know where it's going to take you and it might lead you into some risky positions. You might get hurt. Depression is a sort of security. As I've taken some steps on the path out of depression it's been very tempting to slip back, and I can see that over the years I've used depression as security to avoid taking responsibility for myself. It's a way of avoiding making decisions.

While the prison of depression gives security it is not complete security. Bad memories keep breaking through. Chris Brewin, a psychologist who made a detailed study of the differences between people who were depressed and people suffering from Post Traumatic Stress Disorder, found that both states are troubled by intrusive memories but that they are different kinds of memories. In PTSD certain scenes from the actual trauma come suddenly and sharply into consciousness with the quality of occurring in the here and now. In depression the memories are of long ago, not so much traumatic events as events of great unhappiness, loss and painful relationships. Such memories do not simply intrude. They become the material upon which the person can muse for hour after hour, reliving and elaborating the old feelings of hurt, anger, resentment and sorrow.

At a symposium on cognitive studies in depression in 2000, Brewin expressed some puzzlement that all his research showed few features which distinguished PTSD from depression, yet it is clear from clinical encounters that depression is very different from PTSD. From what he presented it seemed to me that in his highly respected research Chris Brewin had not considered the peculiar sense of isolation which distinguishes depression from all other forms of misery. Also, it seemed that he had not considered the prime role blaming oneself has in turning sadness into depression. To carry out this particular kind of research, psychologists have to define the phenomenon they wish to study in such a way that the phenomenon, or some aspect of it, can be measured. Images of depression do not lend themselves readily to measurement, and self-blame can take many forms. Many people may not wish to speak of these experiences except in a one-to-one conversation with someone they trust or in the intimacy of a small group of people sharing similar experiences. Sadly, many psychologists, like many psychiatrists, are likely to ignore any phenomenon that does not fit their research procedures, no matter how important it may be.

Depressed people are often reluctant to talk about the strange isolation they are living in because they feel that if they tell anyone about it that person will think they are mad. That feeling of isolation is strange because when we are coping with our lives we feel that we are connected to the rest of the world. When this feeling of being connected to our environment and to other people is present all the time we forget that it is there. It is only when it stops, when we feel disconnected, that we become aware of the missing feeling of connectedness. The feeling of being disconnected can arise when we go somewhere we find very unfamiliar. Refugees feel this disconnectedness and, having no home to go back to, suffer greatly. Other people avoid this feeling of disconnectedness by never venturing into unfamiliar territory. They usually refuse to acknowledge the sense of disconnectedness and say instead, 'We never go abroad. It's full of foreigners, you know', or 'Why go away when I've got everything I need at home?'

Similarly, if we manage to stay within a circle of relatives and friends who accept and love us we may avoid that feeling of disconnectedness which we all have when we are among strangers. If we are among strangers, we seek someone with whom we can establish some sense of connectedness. When I was travelling in India I often felt that I had arrived there, not from England, but from another planet. It was amusing to observe myself and other travellers looking out for someone who resembled the people we felt connected to back home. I greeted total strangers as if they were the oldest of friends, simply because we, as Australians, Americans, Britons, Dutch, Germans, shared something, had some established connections. I found myself being welcomed by people who, back in Europe, would have passed me in the street without acknowledging my existence. What we were all trying to do, though we would not have admitted it, was to banish the pain and uncertainty that arise in us when we feel that we have no connection with the world we are in.

Because the sense of connectedness is usually omnipresent, and because the sense of disconnectedness is so painful, we have very few words for it. With regard to our feeling of connectedness to our environment, we talk of 'feeling at home', or, more pretentiously, 'being at one with nature'. However, the Western tradition is to separate ourselves from nature and see it as something which needs to be fought and conquered. Feeling connected to nature is not valued, as it is by the Japanese, the American Indians and the Australian Aborigines. The psychiatrist Takeo Doi has pointed out that the Japanese felt that their capacity to be at one with nature was one of the signs of their inherent superiority over all other races.[10]

If we want to talk about our connectedness to other people we are restricted to talking about 'relationships' and 'communications'. To describe the actual experience of feeling connected to other people we have to talk about a sense of something inside us going out and connecting with other people, and this something we can refer to only as a 'spirit' or a 'feeling'. 'Spirit' has all sorts of religious and magical connotations, which makes its use here unsatisfactory, while 'feelings' is a very overworked word with all sorts of meanings, and often with the connotation of vagueness and weakness.

Yet all the time in our relationships with other people, ourselves and our world we are making statements which serve either to connect us to these or to cut ourselves off from them. A statement like 'Isn't it a glorious day!' links us to our environment, while 'I can't stand the cold' cuts us off from it. Saying of someone 'He really pisses me off' means that we have cut ourselves off from that person, while saying to a baby, 'Aren't you just gorgeous' reflects our connection, however fleeting, to that child. Saying of yourself when you've made a mistake 'I'm a fool' cuts you off, however temporarily, from yourself, and saying 'But I'll do better next time' re-establishes the connection.

No one goes through life feeling totally connected all the time. We all know that there are dangers in our environment. We may begin our life trusting everybody, but we soon learn that every person has limitations and that total trust should not be given to other people, no matter how good they are. We learn, too, that we are not infallible and omniscient. So we all have some disconnections.

Those of us who cope with life have put up some barriers, have made some disconnections, but maintain many connections. Those people who become depressed have disconnected themselves completely, and the barriers they have built are the walls of the prison of depression.

Most of us have the capacity to be depressed because most of us in our childhood laid the first stone of depression when we learned that as we were we were not acceptable. We had to become good. The foundation of the prison of depression is the unquestioned belief that *'No matter how good I appear to be, I am bad, evil, unacceptable to myself and to other people'*.

The second building-block of the prison of depression is to believe in the Just World, however you may define it. Then, even as you berate yourself for your failings, you can believe that one day you will receive the rewards you deserve for your goodness. Often we do not realize that we do believe in the Just World until a disaster befalls us and we complain, 'Why should this have happened to me? It's not fair.' This is injured pride and a belief in the Just World speaking. No honest appraisal of the world could ever conclude that the world and anyone's life are fair and just.

The story of depression begins with the person as a child learning to be good and to believe in the Just World. These two beliefs become the assumptions underlying the life story that the child constructs. The stories we all created were not just 'When I grow up I'm going to be a doctor', or 'When I grow up I'm going to travel all around the world', but also contained plans for compensating us for the hurts and disappointments in childhood. A boy, left lonely and ignored by his parents, may make an important part of his story getting married and having a large family. A girl may plan to become famous and so receive from her father the recognition and admiration that he denied her in childhood. The comfort of a family and recognition and admiration from the father become the rewards each expects for being good.

As the boy and girl grow up their lives may proceed as each had imagined it would. The boy, now a man, marries, the girl studies and, now a woman, does well in her profession. Then disaster strikes. The man discovers that he and his wife cannot conceive, or that his wife cannot cope with married life and leaves him. The woman finds her career blocked because she lacks the ability to reach the goal she set herself, or she wins praise and recognition from everyone except her father, who dies without an encouraging word to her.

For each of them now comes the dreadful experience of discovering that there is a serious discrepancy between what they thought their life was and what it actually is. The basic assumptions of their meaning structure have been disconfirmed and they feel themselves falling apart.

As a child Gwyneth Lewis laid the foundation of her prison of depression when she decided that she was unacceptable. She wrote, 'My mother could be moody and unpredictable. Sometimes, enraged, usually by something I'd done, she'd disappear into her bedroom for a few days. I didn't understand why I had such an effect on her and caused us all so much misery. My misbehaviour caused our whole domestic world to fall apart and, because I seemed to cause these crises so often, I felt like a pariah in the family. I concluded that I must be wicked.'[11] Along with this Gwyneth was, as she said, 'an instinctively religious child', much prone to shame.[12] Having laid the foundation of her prison it took only a seemingly tiny experience to enclose her in it.

Gwyneth and her husband Leighton had made what in their situation was an eminently sensible decision not to have children. Some time later she went to visit some friends who had a farm in west Wales.

After we'd eaten and caught up on the news – they always know more of the Cardiff gossip than I do – we went out to the big shed where the sheep are wintered. I was given a pair of wellies and we embarked on the usual fiction that I was helping them with their farm work. The shed was divided so that the sheep expecting triplets were in one pen, those carrying twins in another and so forth. Our job was to separate the ewes that weren't pregnant from the rest, which we did using a system of railings and gates. Rhian explained that this had to be done so they knew which sheep needed extra rations. The 'empty' ewes wouldn't be fed.

When I heard this I felt I had been hit in the stomach. Rationally, I knew what Rhian meant was that only the pregnant sheep would be given extra food, but that's not what I heard emotionally. In my stomach, what I understood was that childless women are useless and don't deserve to be nourished. I began to starve.[13]

To understand why she had become depressed Gwyneth had to overcome her fear of criticizing her mother. Later, when she wrote her truthful account of her journey in and out of depression, she knew that this would not please her family. Many people stay depressed because they are, in effect, still children who fear their parents' wrath. Milton was one of these.

Milton had received the usual diagnosis of endogenous depression – that is, a depression that is supposed to arise without any external cause – from a psychiatrist, and he had had the usual treatment, but the depression did not go away. Taking Imiprimine made him feel a bit better and he could get back to work, but every day was a misery and a struggle. His wife phoned me and arranged an appointment, and Milton, somewhat reluctantly, came along with her.

He told me there was no reason why he should be depressed. He had a good job, a nice home, a loving wife and family. The depression came out of the blue. Well, not quite. It started soon after his son, who was doing his A-levels preparatory to going to university, announced that he was leaving school and getting a job. Nowadays this is not an unusual thing to do. Having a university degree is no longer a cast-iron guarantee of getting a job, and many young people, when they see the opportunity to get a job, abandon their studies and take the job. However, this was irrelevant to Milton. It was tremendously important to him that his son should stay at school. He should get qualifications.

Milton made 'qualifications' sound like the Holy Grail. I asked him why qualifications were important to him, and he said, 'Because I haven't got any.' Because he didn't have any qualifications he had been a disappointment to his father.

Milton's wife protested, 'Your father was proud of you and the work you do.'

Milton, who so little valued himself that he believed any praise he received was insincere, brushed this aside and explained to me, 'My father was a wonderful man. I'm not half the man he was. I've always looked up to him.'

One of Sheldon Kopp's Eternal Truths is *If you have a hero, look again; you have diminished yourself in some way.*[14] This indeed was what was happening here. Milton, as a small boy, had looked up to his father as small boys usually do. After all, fathers are taller and bigger than them. His father was an important man in their local community. He was on the council and the committees of different clubs and sporting bodies, so he was not at home most evenings. This meant that he was not there to protect Milton from his mother. Milton's parents did not get on, and his mother often took her frustration out on Milton. Milton dared not tell his father how angry and disappointed he was with him. His father would not accept his son's anger. He never let Milton win an argument, so Milton never had the joyous experience of feeling that he was the equal of his dad. Instead, Milton grew up never getting angry, but prone, as his wife said, to sulking.

The only way Milton could bury his anger with his father was to concentrate on his admiration for him. However, the only way he could maintain this uncritical, sentimental admiration of his father was to see himself as his father's inferior in every possible way. (Milton seemed surprised when I suggested to him that it is possible to admire someone without feeling inferior to that person.) Inferiors always feel obliged to give their superiors gifts, in the hope of receiving love and approval in return, and so Milton wanted to give to his father the gift of gaining his qualifications, something his father had not done for himself.

Unfortunately, National Service and other problems prevented Milton from gaining those precious pieces of paper with his name on them. So he comforted himself with the promise that his son's gaining of qualifications would be the gift he would give to his father. Now his son insisted on doing something that would mean he would not gain any qualifications. So when his son left school, Milton's world was in ruins. Being depressed was the only way he could stave off the recognition of this, but it meant going on feeling inferior, 'not half the man my father was'. Sarah Kane wrote, 'It is myself I have never met, whose face is pasted on the underside of my mind.' Milton had never met himself.

Whenever a disaster befalls us we ask, 'Why in the whole scheme of things did this happen?' There are only three possible answers – 'It was my fault', 'It was someone else's fault', 'It happened by chance'. However, in the Just World nothing happens by chance. Everything is the outcome of good or bad actions. Thus for a believer in the Just World there are only two possible answers to the question 'Why?' – 'It was my fault', or 'It was someone else's fault'. A good person feels impelled to choose 'It was my fault'. Good people are expert in blaming themselves. They know it is wrong to blame others. There is no possible disaster in the whole universe for which a good person cannot take the blame. In South American communities torn apart by earthquake or mudslides, individuals will tell visiting reporters that this disaster was God's punishment for their wickedness. When the political and economic policies of the Conservative government in the 1980s led to the closure of industries across the UK, many of those who became unemployed blamed themselves for the disaster. Many women, on discovering that their husband or partner is unfaithful, blame themselves for not trying hard enough to please him. What they should have been remembering was the harsh truth that Bill, my boss, imparted to me when I told him of my husband's faithlessness. Bill said, 'A standing cock has no conscience.'

In some proud and illogical way we may feel that it is kinder and more virtuous for us to blame ourselves than admit to ourselves the harsh truths that we have no control over nature, that rich and powerful people and organizations plunder the world and destroy livelihoods solely for their own gain, and that the sexual impulse is wayward, self-deluding and selfish.

So, there is the good person, confronted by an immense discrepancy between what they thought their life was and what it actually is, feeling the terror of annihilation, and asking, 'Why has this happened to me?' The answer comes swiftly. 'It was my fault. If I'd been a really good person this would not have happened. I must be an even wickeder person than I thought I was.'

Now everything falls into place. All is explained. The terror ebbs away. The person is now safe, but this safety has been bought at a high price – becoming disconnected from every aspect of that person's life.

The more we see ourselves as being bad and unacceptable, the more we fear other people. When we fear other people we have put a barrier between them and us lest they see how wicked we are and reject and punish us. So the good person, blaming himself for the disaster, sees himself as being even more wicked than he had thought himself to be, and immediately has to put a barrier between himself and all other people. He cannot stay connected to his past and draw comfort from that because all he can see in his past is evidence of his wickedness. He cannot stay connected to his future because all that lies ahead is punishment for his wickedness. He cannot stay connected to the world around him because he is too wicked to be part of all that. Cut off from every aspect of his life, he is in the prison of depression.

The way to turn unhappiness into depression is to blame yourself for the disaster that has befallen you.

Depression is a defence that can be used by everyone who knows how to be good. It is a very effective defence against the terror of annihilation, and so it is a very popular defence.

Whenever our meaning structure is threatened with disconfirmation, pride comes to the rescue, telling us that we alone are special. Even as we tell ourselves that we are utterly wicked, pride assures us that knowing how wicked we are shows how good we are in recognizing our wickedness. We are not content with being ordinarily wicked. Pride assures us that we are the wickedest person who has ever lived. Sarah Kane could only express the depth of her wickedness in wild exaggeration. 'I gassed the Jews, I killed the Kurds, I bombed the Arabs, I fucked small children while they begged for mercy, the killing fields are mine, everyone left the party because of me . . .'[15]

Pride creates the prison of depression and keeps us there. It is our pride in being good which allows us to blame ourselves for a disaster. It is pride which tells us that our way of seeing ourselves and our world is the right way, and, if the world insists on being different from what we think it ought to be, then the world is wrong. Sarah Kane was certain that she was right and the world was wrong. She wrote:

> *Nothing can extinguish my anger.*
> *And nothing can restore my faith.*
> *This is not a world in which I wish to live.*[16]

Pride can turn depression into an identity and a way of life. A man who always dressed in black explained on television why he remained depressed. 'I know who I am if I'm depressed. I wouldn't be myself if I wasn't depressed.'[17]

Some of the people who join depression self-help groups discover that they can become experts on being depressed, and so they make being depressed their way of life. They feel that being depressed gives them an identity, a role and purpose in life which not being depressed could never give them. They run or are part of a self-help group, they organize conferences and social events, and they help many people to lead more fulfilling lives, all of which is infinitely better than staying at home alone and miserable, but they feel that they cannot move on to a life without depression.

In depression pride can also kill us, just as it killed Sarah Kane.

Everyone at some time thinks of suicide. Most of us reject it, but very often it is the thought that we can choose to leave life which gives us the strength to stay. If we are able to accept ourselves we are able to accept our death. If we believe that our life ends in death, accepting ourselves means that we see ourselves making the best use of our lives. If we believe that our death will be a doorway to another life, we see ourselves as going to an even better life. However, if we do not accept ourselves we are not able to accept our death. If we believe that our life ends in death, not accepting ourselves means that we see ourselves as wasting our life. If we believe that our death will be a doorway to another life, we see ourselves as going on to further punishment.

The thought of the horrors of death keeps many a depressed person from suicide. Alas, as the pain of depression increases, death starts to look more attractive. When the world outside your prison looks totally unacceptable, the only escape that seems possible from the prison is into death. Jackie said, 'I think that every person that goes through a depression does think of committing suicide. It is the easiest way to get out of the fright that they are living in. There isn't another world outside the fright and the fear and the pain that one lives in, when you are depressed.'

Val said, 'When you reach a point of black despair and there seems no way out and you're threatened with being swallowed up in this black nothingness, then death is very appealing, and I believed that whatever lies beyond death has got to be better than this life that I was leading, and it seemed very attractive. . . I hadn't really decided on one particular method. I mean, one toys with all sorts of ideas. The most attractive one was to throw myself off a cliff into the sea. I love the sea, and there's something very magnetic about standing on a cliff top and watching the waves swilling, and to be sucked into that sort of spiral. I'd be part of the mass. There's something very appealing about that.'

Human beings have a wonderful capacity, as they approach death, for reconstruing it. Many people, as they get older, find that the thought of their death gets less and less frightening, until in old age it becomes a friend whose arrival is anticipated with contentment. A similar reconstruing of death can be achieved by the depressed person who looks at death as the only possible release. Such a person can change their thinking from 'I wouldn't commit suicide because I wouldn't want to upset my family' to 'If I died I would be helping my family'.

Thinking that you will be helping your family by killing yourself can seem to be very virtuous, but it is not. No family is helped by a suicide. It is not just that family members grieve and feel guilty. They may also understand that the act was deliberately intended as a blow against them, a 'See what you made me do' which allows no response. Some suicides are spur-of-the-moment, emotional acts, committed without forethought, but most are premeditated with preparations made. Successful suicides are usually preceded by suicide attempts, each attempt providing some information which assists the person in the final success. The choice of time, place and method determines who is most likely to find the body. People who choose an isolated, little-visited place know that their body is likely to be found by a stranger. Those who choose somewhere in their own home know that they are likely to be found by a family member for whom the suicide will be a message. It is not an act of love and concern to arrange for someone close to you to come upon your dead body. A family member who does so will know that the message is not 'I love you' but that of an act of revenge.

Many people contemplating or carrying out suicide think that by killing themselves they will make their life better for their children. This is never the case. When a parent suicides the child receives two messages. One is 'I don't love you enough to stay alive for you', and the second a principle for living: 'When life is difficult, give up.' A parent may feel that he or she has nothing to give a child, but there is one thing all parents can do for their children. They can show them that they have the courage to face life. They may not live their lives with grace and wisdom but they do battle on whatever the odds.

Like all desperate defences used to hold us together when we feel we are falling apart, suicide is a selfish act. It is also self-deluding. Whenever every part of us, mind and body, wants to die, we do not have to do anything. We lie down and die. Medical staff are well aware of this. Patients whose physical condition gives no cause for concern can lose interest in living and die. In tribal communities people who believe that they exist only as part of their community die when they are expelled from that community. If you cannot die without making some brutal attack upon yourself, a large part of you wants to go on living.

The tragedy of Sarah Kane was not that she died young but that she threw her precious life away. Her play *4.48 Psychosis* is a brilliant account of the experience of being deeply depressed, but it is a young writer's play. It is a monologue about what she was experiencing, not a meditation on her life. It is a scream of anguish which reveals to those who have not experienced the depths of depression just what this state is, but it does not explain why she was driven to this extreme. It does not set this experience in the context of all human life. If all we knew of Hamlet was the anguish he felt we would learn from the play nothing about ourselves and the lives of others. At twenty-four Sarah knew the *what* of the experience but she did not understand the *why*. At thirty-six, when he wrote *Hamlet,* Shakespeare knew why. If Sarah had let herself live she would, eventually, have been able to write a truly great play about depression.

When we shut ourselves into depression we do not want to come out because we do not want to discover that the things which made us lock ourselves away were really not all that important, and that if we acknowledge this people will say, 'I told you so!' When you are a child and you get so upset that you have to rush to your bedroom and slam the door, it is horrible, when you come out again, if adults laugh at you, or tell you how naughty you were to get angry, or belittle your major injuries by offering you a sweetie to make you better, or tell you to realize just how lucky you are compared with the starving children of Africa. If you feel that all you have is your hurts, then you have to hang on to them, even if this means dying.

People commit suicide in order to remain the person they, and their pride, want them to be. People commit valiant acts of heroism for the same reason. If such people survive, and afterwards are asked why they put themselves in such mortal danger, they usually say, 'If I hadn't done that I wouldn't have been able to live with myself.' People commit suicide when they feel that to live they would have to compromise with a world they do not value, even despise, and this they cannot do. They would not be able to live with themselves.

Pride, so the Church fathers taught, was the deadliest of the seven deadly sins because pride prevented us from changing. If we want to get out of the prison of depression we have to change. To do this we have to change the way we assess ourselves and our world.

Many people become depressed and go and see their GP, who prescribes a course of antidepressants, and after a few weeks they are their old selves again. Other people see their GP and are sent to a psychiatrist, who brings them into hospital. There, away from their responsibilities, and finding life in the wards comfortable and restful, they take their medication and in a few weeks they feel much better and go home. Some people, perhaps while they are in hospital, or perhaps just following the advice of their GP or a friend, find a counsellor, perhaps a marriage guidance counsellor, or a Samaritan, or a psychiatric nurse, or a social worker, and spend some time talking things over with that person. They do not go deeply into things, but they do express a lot of the feelings that they have kept bottled up and they sort out some confusions in their thinking, just by having to explain things to another person. After a few sessions, or perhaps just one session, they feel much better and can get on with their lives.

Most depressed people who do one or two of these things cease to be depressed, and, of these, most do not get depressed again. Some depressed people do not cease to be depressed because these methods do not reveal and confront the underlying feelings and attitudes for which depression is a necessary defence. Those people who cease to be depressed but who later become depressed again have been pushed back into this defence by some event which threatens their existence.

We can understand these changes if we think of them in terms of first-order change or second-order change.

All the ideas we have are in terms of pairs of contrasts. We think of up/down, in/out, here/there, good/bad, perfect/imperfect, top/bottom. We can picture these pairs of ideas as being the ends of a line or dimension, and we can give things a place on that line. For instance:

363

```
        nearly              half-              nearly
        bottom              way                top


                 *                  *                  *
bottom  ─────────────────────────────────────────────── top
```

DIAGRAM 1

The ideas and attitudes we have about ourselves we can think of as a line, and we can place ourselves on that line. If we think of ourselves as, say, an athlete, we can position ourselves on a line like this.

```
          When I've              When I've
          lost                   won


the worst                                        the greatest
athlete        *                  *              athlete
in the    ───────────────────────────────────   in the
world                                            world
```

DIAGRAM 2

Our position changes as we win or lose.

A first-order change occurs when we change our position in the dimension in which we assess ourselves.

Suppose you decide to give up thinking of yourself as an athlete and decide to think of yourself as a musician instead. You have abandoned your greatest athlete/worst athlete dimension and have acquired a new one.

```
            played                 played
            badly                  well


the worst                                        the best
musician       *                  *              musician
in the    ───────────────────────────────────   in the
world                                            world
```

DIAGRAM 3

Now you have made a second-order change.

A second-order change occurs when we give up one way of assessing ourselves and acquire another way of assessing ourselves.

It seems that the changes which take place when depressed people take a course of antidepressants, or have a few weeks in hospital, or have one or two counselling sessions, are first-order changes.

```
        depressed                          not
                                        depressed


the worst                  *            *           no worse
person in   _____  than most
in the                                               people
world



        depressed                          not
                                        depressed


never                   *              *           forgive
forgive    _____  people for
anybody                                              unimportant
anything                                             things
```

DIAGRAM 4

Here the person holds the belief that he is basically bad, but feels that this is a continuum from being the worst person in the world to being no worse than most people (and all people are basically bad). He holds the belief that it is wrong to forgive, but feels that this is a continuum from never forgiving anybody for anything to forgiving people for unimportant things. At times he experiences himself as close to being the worst person in the world and close to being totally unforgiving, and then he has shut himself off from himself and everyone else, and he is depressed. He can make a first-order change by feeling better about himself and by forgiving

365

some people. Thus he brings himself into better contact with himself and others, and so can leave the state of depression. However, he still uses these same dimensions and he can always shift on them back into depression.

To give up the defence of depression for ever the person has to make a second-order change. Thus, when he makes a mistake he no longer considers himself to be just about the worst person in the world, but simply decides that it would be best to think the matter through so he can see where he went wrong. When someone injures him he no longer refuses to forgive, but knows that by his trying to understand what happened, both forgiving and not forgiving become irrelevant.

	not depressed		not depressed	
better think this through so I can work out where I went wrong	*	———————————————	*	I'm fine

	not depressed		not depressed	
have to think this through to understand it	*	———————————————	*	forgiveness is irrelevant

DIAGRAM 5

Such beliefs render the defence of depression unnecessary.

Some people make these second-order changes by themselves. This is the ordinary human process of growing older and wiser.

Some people need a therapist to help them on the journey of self-understanding.

Whenever Lucy came to see me she would talk of her panic attacks and her physical sickness, but only sometimes, right at the end of the session, would she say something which revealed her depression. If I enquired, she did not want to talk about it. Like so many depressed people, she feared that if she talked about what she was feeling, people would think she was mad.

So I lent her a copy of my book *Depression: The Way out of Your Prison*.[18] She returned it at our next session, saying, 'Yes, I'm going to buy my own copy.'

She went on to talk about her parents. Her father had always been demanding and authoritarian. ('But he is so kind,' she would say, whenever what was being said sounded critical.) Her mother had been depressed for all of Lucy's life. At twelve, Lucy had taken on many household duties and, as she said, 'I worried about her'.

Her mother liked to visit and spend the whole day. Gavin, Lucy's husband, had to drive her home in the evening. She came, not as a friend, but as a mother to look after her sick daughter. Lucy said, 'I think Mother likes me to be sick. That way she can come and spend the day with me.'

Gavin smiled in relief. This is what had always been clear to him, but he had to wait for Lucy to see it. 'I'd get a hammering if I said it,' he said, laughing.

Lucy did not find her mother's visits a help, quite the reverse, but she dared not ask her not to come, and she dared not get better.

Often a person may see what needs to be done to leave the prison of depression but is prevented from carrying it out by another person. This may be a parent, or a husband or wife or partner. One of the reasons that so many married women stay depressed is because their husbands will not allow them to seek interests outside the home which would build up their confidence and give them a sense of being a person in their own right. I have met many a husband who cannot tolerate his wife ceasing to be depressed because then she becomes, in his eyes, argumentative and wants her own way. Similarly, a depressed husband may feel that he cannot develop those aspects of himself which he had given up in the process of becoming a good, responsible person, because if he does he would have to confront his wife, whom he sees as being much stronger than himself. Moreover, developing himself could mean becoming less of a husband and father.

When I talked to people about the events leading up to their depression I was struck by the way in which they had, over a period of a year or so before becoming depressed, given up doing those things which gave them a sense of personal value, not just those which made them feel virtuous but also those which strengthened their sense of being a person. Depressed men talked about giving up the sport they enjoyed, or leaving their smallholding for a suburban garden, or changing their sports car for a family saloon. What depressed women often mentioned was giving up work outside the home. That a job outside the home protects a woman from depression is well documented in the research literature. It is not that the work itself necessarily boosts the woman's self-confidence – so much of women's work is menial – but that in the workplace people speak to her as the person she is, and not, as at home, in one of her roles of wife, mother, daughter, daughter-in-law, sister, aunt, granddaughter, grandmother. Moreover, working means that a woman has some money of her own. It may not be much, but it is her own. If a married woman wishes to avoid being depressed there are two things she must make sure she possesses: her own bank account and a driving licence. These, combined with a sense of her own worth, such that she will always take the time to recognize and to meet her own needs, will ensure that the shades of the prisonhouse of depression never descend upon her. If she should lose her sense of self-worth, then these two possessions will help her overcome the practical problems she faces when she decides to leave the prison.

Therapists always hope that something will happen in the lives of their depressed clients which will help them gain confidence in themselves. When Jackie first came to see me she had completely lost confidence in herself and was deeply depressed. When, two months later, the producer of the BBC TV programme *The Mind*

Box, Angela Tilby, asked me whether Jackie would take part in the programme, I thought this most unlikely. I did not even want to put Angela's request to Jackie because I felt that this would be yet another burden for her, but Angela was insistent, so I complied with her request. Jackie shocked me by saying immediately, 'Yes, I'll do it,' and then put me in my place by explaining that 'I get so frightened when I come to see you that having a film crew in the room at the same time wouldn't make any difference'.

Jackie had a lot of work to do in this programme. When the filming was complete it was clear that all had gone well. Jackie came to see me, and she was no longer depressed. The making of the programme in which she was a key figure gave her the opportunity to make a statement about herself and to achieve something in her own right.

In one of her interviews with Angela, Jackie said, 'I find it very hard to forgive. I can forget but I never forgive anybody . . . I think that forgiving is getting closer to people and I don't want to get that close.' However, she was already in the process of making a second-order change. Now she thought that forgiving was a good idea, and that when you accepted yourself there was no danger in getting close to people.

Peter made a similar second-order change. He said, 'I've learned that I don't mind being emotional. I mean I can cope with being emotional, whereas at one time I used to feel guilty about it.'

When Val was reviewing the changes she had made she said to me, 'The one thing you said which I hadn't heard before was that we can change. I never thought that I could change and no one had ever suggested to me before that I could change. People sort of pulled me to pieces and said, "Well, you feel guilty, you feel as though you're not worth anything", but they never suggested that I could change the way I felt.'

Val said to Angela, 'In my experience of depression I feel as though I'm falling into a bottomless pit and if I let go I shall just disappear into the bottom of this pit. But I felt a love reaching out to me like a pair of hands. I've wanted to let go and disappear into the black hole but somehow the hands won't let me go. I used to think that I would find nothing inside me, but I've come to realize as my depression lifted, that if you let go, you don't fall into a bottomless pit, and that the hands that I thought were beyond and outside me reaching out to me in love are actually within me and supporting me from within and if I let go I fall into these hands that hold me in love.'

She went on:

I have changed from feeling that I have to suffer by trying to be perfect to earn God's love to a feeling that I only have to be still and be myself and reach within me to the . . . I suppose the soul centre you might call it, and find God there. Ever present. Loving, giving Himself and creating a sort of peace and drawing strength and confidence from that. I suppose the biggest shift is that I don't carry a burden of guilt any more in the same way. I've learned to forgive myself. I think that's the biggest shift. I used to go and pray for forgiveness, but I never really experienced forgiveness because I never forgave myself for not being what I thought I ought to be. Once you can do that and be yourself, then you live comfortably with yourself and I think that's the biggest change. . . If you start opening yourself out to relationships with other people, this is life-giving. In depression you cut yourself off, and it's death. You know, thinking of the garden, a flower opens out and can be crushed in the same way as a person. If you open yourself out you can be hurt and crushed but you've got to let this life blossom forth somehow . . . When I was depressed I sought to prove that I was good enough to be loved, and this really kept the depression going because I had to be perfect. But as I've grown spiritually and learned more about my depression I've realized that I am loved just as I am. I don't have to prove I'm lovable, and that has been an immense relief. I can stop the struggle, let go, and rest within the love I've found within me. It's nothing new. It's just something that's always been an intellectual fact to me but now has become part of my experience. Thousands of people must have discovered it in the past.

Gwyneth Lewis once asked the Australian poet Les Murray, what was the cure for depression. Les, no stranger to depression himself, said, 'The truth.' Gwyneth wrote, 'We are all the artists of our own lives. We shape them, as best we can, using our experience and intuition as guides. But we are also natural liars and we get things wrong. It's so easy for the internal commentary that forms how we live to become a forgery. Approached in a certain way, depression is a lie detector of the last resort. By knocking you out for a while, it allows you to ditch the out-of-date ideas by which you were living and to grasp a more accurate description of the terrain . . . Depression can be a great friend. It says: the way you are living is unbearable, it's not for you. And it teaches you slowly how to live in a way that suits you infinitely better. If you don't listen, of course, it comes back and knocks you out even harder the next time, until you get the point.'[19]

To leave the prison of depression all you have to do is to come to value and accept yourself and to see that we do not live in a Just World, or even an Unjust World, but simply the world. You cannot control the world by being good. The world is itself. Things happen by chance, and it is chance which gives us our freedom. If everything were certain we could not hope because hope exists only when there is uncertainty and insecurity. Only by accepting yourself and accepting insecurity can you gain the strength to deal with life's difficulties and the wisdom to be happy.

The story of depression is a simple story. It can be told without using psychiatric, psychotherapeutic or psychological jargon. No specialist knowledge is required. Everyone can understand it. Dealing with depression should be simple and straightforward, but public discussion of depression and the information given by professionals to depressed people are not straightforward. This is partly because many people, as a result of learning to deny, find it difficult to think clearly about why we do what we do (this applies to professionals as much as to everybody else), and partly because many people – the professionals and the drug companies – have their position, power and wealth to protect.

Public Discourse – Muddle and Confusion

Much of the difficulty we have in understanding why we do what we do arises from the careless way we use language. One of the reasons that the present public discourse on depression is muddled and confused is found in the way the words 'depression', 'depressed' and 'sad' are used. People will say that they are depressed when in fact what they are feeling is dispirited, or disappointed, or irritated or sad. 'Sad' has become a term of contempt. 'He's a sad guy. Why doesn't he get a life?' can be said of anyone whose interests differ from those of the speaker. With such a use of language all the important differences between sadness and depression are lost.

Every profession creates its own jargon to mystify and impress outsiders. One term much favoured by health and mental health professionals is 'clinical judgement'. It sounds so objective, and yet it is no more than the person's subjective experience, not just the experience of studying and practising in a certain profession, but all the attitudes and opinions the person has collected along the way.

Using such clinical judgement, a psychiatrist will decide whether a person is suffering from reactive or endogenous depression. These terms are not as widely used as they once were, and they are not listed in the DSM, but the ideas underlying them are still in use. The theory behind these two classifications is that *reactive depression* arises when a person has a personal reason in his life to be depressed. *Endogenous depression* arises when there is no such reason. It is seen as a physical illness which arises from within the person who, so the theory goes, usually has a 'previously normal personality'.

These two classifications have what psychologists call 'face validity'. They fit in with what can easily be observed. Some people suffer such terrible reverses in their lives that it is not surprising they become depressed in response to them. Hence reactive depression. In contrast other people appear to be living successful, contented lives when they become depressed. They will say to themselves, 'I don't know why I'm depressed. I have every reason to be happy.'

However, appearances can mislead, and no one who wants to know the truth should be content with them. Quite often we will say that we do not know why we do something – why we get headaches, or drink too much, or stay in a job we do not like, or get depressed – when in fact we do know, but we are not going to tell the person who is asking us. Many of us were brought up not to discuss family matters with strangers, and we will not do this, even if the person asking us is a doctor. We may think we *could* tell the doctor, but of course he makes notes, and we worry about who else might read them. If we have lived in a community for a few years, it is almost certain that there will be someone on the staff of the local health centre or the psychiatric hospital who knows us, so it is best to be careful.

Sometimes we know what the problem is, but it makes us feel so ashamed and embarrassed that we do not want to talk about it to someone who may not understand. When we are depressed we cannot cope with any more criticism and rejection. Even the littlest thing hurts. And then there are the things that we do not want to admit even to ourselves. We may not want to admit to ourselves that we have made bad choices and so wasted our life, or that we are bored with the person with whom we have to spend the rest of our life. So we may be very happy to collude with the doctor and say, 'There's no reason in my life why I should be depressed.'

Even if we overcome our anxiety about people knowing our secrets and our shame, we may tell the doctor about what in our lives we find very troubling, only to find that he rejects our assessment of our own lives. We may think that our marriage, or our job, or what our children do are matters which cause us so much pain that we react with depression, but those are just our personal, subjective opinions, attitudes and feelings. The doctor, in the process of arriving at a diagnosis, may dismiss them as unimportant, or simply label us as 'inadequate' or 'hysterical'. (Many psychiatrists use the term 'inadequate personality' in their formulation of the patient's disabilities. I have yet to see a definition of an 'adequate personality'. In case conferences I was often tempted to ask the consultant for such a definition, but suspected that in doing so I would reveal myself as a fool. After all, a definition of an adequate personality was right there before my eyes, in the person of the consultant himself.)

It is the doctor, not the patient, who decides whether there is anything in the patient's life which would make that person feel depressed. From my extensive observations of psychiatrists over many years, I can say that many of them make very subjective and uninformed judgements about what in a person's life could be a cause of sadness, despair or depression.

There still are, I regret to say, many psychiatrists who hold the belief that all a woman needs to feel happy and fulfilled is a home, a husband and children. Thus, when a woman who has these things presents herself in a depressed state to such a psychiatrist, he draws the conclusion that she has no reason to be depressed. Therefore the correct diagnosis is endogenous depression. This is a more serious matter than just a choice of words. Psychiatric textbooks teach that the appropriate treatment for endogenous depression is electroconvulsive therapy (ECT). Since the majority of adults who are diagnosed as depressed are married women, many more women than men receive this treatment.

However, it is not just women who are given such a diagnosis. Many good, hard-working men are so diagnosed when they become depressed in later middle age. Sometimes the diagnosis seems to have been arrived at with the psychiatrist and patient in collusion. Neither wishes to let the side down and acknowledge and reveal the pain and weakness which the depressed man is feeling. An explanation is given by the psychiatrist and accepted by the patient whereby the sterling virtues of being hard-working, conscientious and responsible are seen as creating a physical debility which allows the physical illness of depression to take hold. No mention is made of the desperate pain of feeling unloved and unwanted, as younger men rise past you to more senior positions, or as your job disappears when the firm is reorganized to achieve greater efficiency, or when your children become too grown up to take any notice of their father, or your wife treats you as a piece of old, useless furniture in the home and finds her interests elsewhere.

To uncover these hurts, to find out not just what has happened in a person's life but how that person feels about what has happened, takes a very long time. It cannot be done in a ten-minute consultation, or even in half an hour. And it requires careful listening with the attitude that what the patient has to say is of the greatest importance. This is hard work. It is much easier to ascertain what the psychiatrist calls the facts, decide whether to call the depression endogenous or reactive, and to write a prescription while reassuring the patient that his is a common problem, something that will clear up in a week or two and not to worry. The diagnosis of endogenous depression is a great labour-saving device.

Another term popular with doctors is 'clinical depression'. These words may be used with great sympathy and concern. The doctor may be saying that the person is so depressed that he should not try to continue with his ordinary life but should withdraw from the fray and take care of himself. The doctor is saying, 'This is serious and we must treat it seriously.'

Unfortunately, some doctors use the words 'clinical depression' not simply to help the patient but to stake out an area for themselves and to claim that they and they alone have expertise there. Thus used, the words are designed to mystify the patient and the public. A 'clinical depression' has to be dealt with by a psychiatrist, not a psychologist, a therapist, counsellor or social worker. These words are often used in connection with some impressive-sounding words which apparently relate to physiological processes that only a doctor could understand, and which prove that depression, or certainly 'clinical depression', is caused by some physiological or chemical change. The depressed person may have a 'chemical imbalance' in his brain. Phrases such as 'serotonin levels' can sound most scientific. All this has to be said in a mystifying way, for if the doctor explained what he was saying clearly and accurately, it would become apparent even to the non-medical listener that the physiological changes of which he speaks have been identified as occurring *while* a person is depressed. No physiological change that always *precedes* depression has been found. Since a cause has to precede an effect, the physiological changes that accompany depression cannot be the cause of the depression. Removing the physical concomitants of depression, as certain drugs do, can make a person feel better. An aspirin can remove the pain of a headache, but this does not prove that it is the lack of aspirin which causes the headache. The complex human experience that we call depression cannot possibly be fully understood and explained solely in physiological and chemical terms.

Public discourse about depression prefers to assume that there is a battle over depression with psychiatrists on one side and psychologists and therapists on the other. What is not explained is that there are many theories about the cause and cure of depression. These theories fall into two groups – those which say that depression has a physical cause, and those which say that depression arises from the way we live our life. Like all theories, each has advantages and disadvantages. The kind of theory which says that depression has a physical cause has the advantage that the depressed person is not responsible for the depression and the disadvantage that there is no cure. Psychiatrists who espouse this kind of theory do not talk of curing depression but of 'managing' it. The DSM lists some thirty-nine different kinds of depression, including 'depression in complete remission'. You may think you are happy but your psychiatrist knows that the illness is still lurking there. There are many depressed people who prefer to see their depression as a chronic physical illness and to live with it in the way people live with chronic physical illnesses such as epilepsy or diabetes. The illness is a nuisance, demanding regular pill-taking, and periods of good health can be ended abruptly, but, like epilepsy or diabetes, it is something you are born with and it is not your fault.

The theory that depression arises from the way we live our life has the disadvantage that we have to take responsibility for ourselves, and the advantage that, if depression is something which in some way we have created, we can change and cease to be depressed. Depressed people are free to choose which kind of theory suits them best.

Whether or not depression is something which comes upon us or is something we create for ourselves is a question which has been around for a long time. In the early days of Christianity, when monks would go into the desert and live in solitude, contemplating and worshipping God, they would sometimes find that their religious passion and enthusiasm drained away, and they were left feeling empty and despairing. They had expected an encounter with God and all they had found was the loneliness of the desert. This feeling was called *accidie*. Since this would often happen when the sun was high in the sky, accidie was explained as resulting from an attack by the Noonday Demon.

Being attacked by a demon was not your fault. Obviously you would have to fight the demon off, but it was not your fault the demon attacked you. So you felt ill and miserable, but you did not have to feel responsible. Then along came the theologians of the Church and they said, 'Accidie isn't caused by a demon. You do it to yourself and it's a sin.' So these poor monks had to acknowledge their responsibility for their accidie, feel guilt for their sin, and resolve to sin no more.

History is full of action replays. Now we have the psychiatrists, like the monks in the desert, saying, 'Beware of the noonday demon' (in modern terms, your genes and the chemical changes your body goes through), and the psychologists, like the theologians, saying, 'There are no demons. It's you. Acknowledge your responsibility.'

Public discourse about depression became more intense as various researchers reported that the incidence of the condition was rising significantly. A study in 1996 by the World Health Organisation looked not just at the incidence of depression but at the Disability Adjusted Life Years, which is a measure of the disease burden as reflected in the number of years lost to a person through sickness and death. This study showed that depression imposed a far greater burden than physical illnesses like cancer and heart disease and social disturbances like war.

In 2005 the National Institute for Clinical Excellence (NICE) advised that antidepressants should not be prescribed for mild to moderate depression, and that patients should be warned about the possibility that taking the SSRI drugs can result in an increase in suicidal thoughts. Richard Layard's book *Happiness: Lessons from a New Science*.[20] provoked a good deal of interest. The new science was economics which, when applied to the study of happiness, could show that it was in the government's economic interests to make radical changes in the care of depressed people. Richard Layard was the founder and director of the London School of Economics Centre for Economic Performance, and an economic adviser to the government. In June 2006 the Centre published *The Depression Report: A New Deal for Depression and Anxiety Disorders*. The summary of the report stated:

> Crippling depression and chronic anxiety are the biggest causes of misery in Britain today. They are the great submerged problem, which shame keeps out of sight. But if you mention them, you soon discover how many families are affected. According to the respected Psychiatric Morbidity Survey, **one in six of us would be diagnosed as having depression or chronic anxiety disorder**, which means that one family in three is affected.
>
> That is the bad news. The good news is that **we now have evidence-based psychological therapies that can lift at least a half of those affected out of their depression or their chronic fear**. These new therapies are not endless nor backward-looking treatments. They are short, forward-looking treatments that enable people to challenge their negative thinking and build on the positive side of their personalities and situations. The most developed of these therapies is cognitive behaviour therapy (CBT). The official guidelines from the National Institute for Clinical Excellence (NICE) say these treatments should be available to all people with depression or anxiety disorders or schizophrenia, unless the problem is very mild or recent.
>
> But the **NICE guidelines cannot be implemented** because we do not have enough therapists. In most areas waiting lists for therapy are over nine months, or there is no waiting list at all because there are no therapists. So, if you go to the GP, all

that can be provided is medication (plus at some surgeries a little counselling). But many people will not take medication, either because they dislike the side effects or because they want to control their own mood.

The result is tragic. **Only one in four of those who suffer from depression or chronic anxiety is receiving any kind of treatment**. The rest continue to suffer, even though at least half of them could be cured at a cost of no more than £750. This is a waste of people's lives. It is also costing a lot of money. For depression and anxiety make it difficult or impossible to work, and drive people onto Incapacity Benefits. **We now have a million people on Incapacity Benefits because of mental illness** – more than the total number of unemployed people receiving unemployment benefits. At one time unemployment was our biggest social problem, but we have done a lot to reduce it. So mental illness is now the biggest problem, and we know what to do about it. It is time to use that knowledge.

But can we afford the £750 it costs to treat someone? **The money which the government spends will pay for itself.** For someone on Incapacity Benefit costs us £750 a month in extra benefits and lost taxes. If the person works just a month more as a result of the treatment, the treatment pays for itself.

So we have a massive problem – the biggest problem they have for one in three of our families. But we also have a solution that can improve the lives of millions of families, and cost the taxpayer nothing. We should implement the NICE guidelines; and **most people with mental illness should be offered the choice of psychological therapy**.

Everyone who wants something done should write to their MP calling for action.[21]

The report set out a model for how therapy could be delivered, and already two pilot schemes are in operation. Although the report acknowledges the range of possible therapies that could be used in the model, psychologists and therapists who do not work in cognitive behavioural therapy have expressed their disquiet at the predominance of CBT. The government seems to view the implementation of the report favourably but those of us who are well acquainted with the scant regard that various governments have given to mental health cannot help feeling that, yet again, the money will not be available to give a decent service.

Do Pills Cure Depression?

'There's not a drug on earth that can make life meaningful.'[22]

Sarah Kane knew this only too well. Anyone who has been through the psychiatric system will laugh wryly at Sarah's account in her play *4.48 Psychosis* of the drugs she was given and the notes in her case file made by the staff about her reactions to the drugs. If drugs cured depression, then in the years following the discovery of the first antidepressants in the late 1950s depression would have all but disappeared in the way that common infectious diseases all but disappeared after the discovery of antibiotics in the 1940s.

Psychiatrists know this. In 1993 the First International Conference on Mood Disorders was held in London under the title of 'Depression: Challenge for the '90s'. When the proceedings were published the following year they were introduced by Joseph Mendels, Medical Director of the Philadelphia Medical Institute. He wrote:

> Depression has been essentially regarded as a short-term illness with some tendency to recurrence, in sharp contrast with schizophrenia, which was viewed as a largely chronic condition. There is now clear evidence that, for a substantial number of the millions of people who suffer from a major depressive disorder, the condition is often chronic or recurrent. Many of our patients require long-term maintenance treatment . . . [There is evidence supporting] the hypothesis that some forms of affective illness are a chronic condition with periodic clinical manifestations, similar to hypertension or diabetes . . . [There is] compelling evidence that depression is a long-term illness, and that a substantial number of people suffer from chronic or recurrent depression.[23]

The depressed people of whom Dr Mendels was speaking would have been treated largely or only by drugs, chiefly the antidepressant drugs. In 1999 Sam Forshall, Senior Registrar, and David Nutt, Professor of Psychopharmacology at the University of Bristol, wrote a short paper for the *Psychiatric Bulletin* reviewing the 'current evidence and opinion with regard to the long-term treatment of unipolar depression.' They wrote:

> Formerly, major depression was viewed as having a relatively good prognosis, however, long-term naturalistic community surveys have indicated that this is not the case as there is a high risk of recurrence and chronicity. Of those who have suffered one episode of depression 50–85 per cent will have a subsequent episode, while of those who have two episodes 80–90 per cent will develop a third. With each recurrence a further recurrence becomes more likely and the period in remission tends to become shorter.

Many psychiatrists prescribe an antidepressant drug as a prophylactic treatment to prevent a recurrence of depression. Sam Forshall and David Nutt wrote, 'In trials 20–70 per cent of patients have a recurrence despite prophylactic treatment.'[24]

In September 2001 the *British Journal of Psychiatry* published a supplement devoted to research papers about the use of antidepressants in the treatment of depression. Dr Robert Hirschfeld wrote:

> Concepts of depression have changed markedly over the last century. In the early part of the 20th century, Kraepelin described depression as a long-term affliction, characterised by recurrences and chronicity. In the 1960s and 1970s came a pharmacological revolution. Newly developed medications for depression – monoamine oxidase inhibitors (MAOIs) and tricyclic antidepressants (TCAs) – caused dramatic improvement within weeks. These developments led to a reformulation of depression as an illness that could be 'cured' quickly, like a bacterial infection . . .

Research findings emerging in the 1980s challenged this view. For example, the National Institute of Mental Health Collaborative program of the Psychobiology of Depression involved a multi-year follow-up of over 400 patients. After 15 years, only one in eight of these patients had recovered from their original episode and stayed well. Over 80% had suffered at least one recurrence, and 6% had remained chronically depressed throughout the entire 15-year period.

These and other findings, as well as experience with antidepressant pharmacology, have led physicians to return to the Kraepelinean notion of depression as a long-term, recurrent and often chronic illness.[25]

In other words, the antidepressant treatment of depression produces results little different from those produced by the methods of treatment which were available before the 'pharmacological revolution'. This might lead us non-psychiatrists to conclude that treatments other than drugs need to be used, but no. The advice from the psychiatrists writing in this supplement and the policy-makers in the Royal College of Psychiatrists is that more, not fewer, antidepressants should be prescribed, and for longer – in some cases, for life. Moreover, the drugs prescribed should be the new SSRIs such as Prozac and Seroxat.

Joanne Moncrieff, Senior Lecturer in Psychiatry at University College, London, and David Cohen, Professor, School of Social Work, Florida International University, have pointed out that increased prescribing of antidepressants has not resulted in any diminution in the incidence of depression. They wrote, 'Recent sharp increases in antidepressant use have been accompanied by increased prevalence and duration of depressive episodes and rising levels of sickness absence. Naturalistic studies have also shown that depressive episodes are more frequent and last longer among antidepressant users than nonusers, and that sickness absence is more prolonged, although severity is likely to explain some of this effect (i.e. it is likely that patients are on antidepressants because they have more severe disease.) Follow-up studies of people treated for depression indicate high levels of nonrecovery or relapse.' They went on to say that the evidence seems to suggest that antidepressants themselves cause abnormal states 'which may coincidentally relieve psychiatric symptoms. Alcohol's disinhibiting effects may relieve symptoms of social phobia, but that does not imply that alcohol corrects a chemical imbalance underlying social phobia. Sedation may lessen high arousal, present in many acute psychiatric conditions. Drugs that induce indifference, such as neuroleptics or opiates, may help reduce the distress of acute psychotic symptoms. Low-dose stimulants may help improve attention and concentration in the short term.' These effects may be amplified by that most effective drug, placebo. If the antidepressants did have a curative effect on a disease process then the people taking these drugs would enjoy a long-term elevation of mood, but that is not the case.[26]

At this point I must stress that if you are taking an antidepressant you must not stop taking it abruptly. You must come off the drug very slowly. David Taylor, Chief Pharmacist at the Maudsley Hospital, London, wrote about his experience of coming off an antidepressant drug. He said:

> The real truth is that, for many people, antidepressant withdrawal syndrome is neither mild nor short-lived. For six weeks or so, I suffered symptoms which were at best disturbing and at worst torturous. This was despite following a cautious, decremental withdrawal schedule. Whilst I did not experience headache or paraesthesia, the severity of other symptoms certainly made up for it. The dizziness I felt varied from a slight wobbliness to a frightening inability to stand up without support. For most of the time, I could not turn my head without inducing a paralysing nausea. Alongside this, I endured a more-or-less continuously pounding heartbeat and a close facsimile of influenza. When all of this subsided, I was short-tempered and moody, and remained so for a further two weeks or more. None of my conversations with others who have withdrawn from antidepressants leads me to believe that my experience is unique or even unusual.[27]

A new, and real, disorder is serotonin syndrome, which can occur when two different kinds of antidepressant drugs are taken, though it can occur with just one drug. According to Shameem Mir, Senior Clinical Pharmacist, and David Taylor at the Maudsley Hospital, symptoms of serotonin syndrome include confusion, hypomania, agitation, shivering, tremor, diarrhoea, inco-ordination, and fever. The symptoms can be mild but they can be more severe and even fatal.[28]

Serotonin syndrome seems to be related chiefly to monoamine oxidase inhibitors (MAOIs) such as Parnate and the SSRIs such as Prozac. Over the past few years the addictive MAOIs have been phased out, but a number of people, having taken them for many years, are dependent on them and cannot cope with the withdrawal symptoms.

The UK Committee on the Safety of Medicines (CSM) was considering revoking the licence for the large drug company SmithKline Beecham to make Parnate while allowing some smaller companies to produce it so that it would be available to people who cannot do without it. The MAOIs fell out of favour with psychiatrists because they were addictive, though this fact was never publicized. Coming off an MAOI must be done in tiny incremental steps in the same way as coming off benzodiazepines and amphetamines.

One of the advantages of the SSRIs which was widely publicized was that they were not addictive. Now it is clear that their withdrawal symptoms are far from minor problems, and for some people Prozac dissolves the barriers they had constructed against suicidal thoughts and actions, in much the same way that alcohol can remove our inhibitions so that we relinquish reason and good sense and behave in outrageous and often dangerous ways.

Charles Medawar, who has studied the history of the wonder drugs used in psychiatry, each of which in turn proved to be addictive,[29] pointed out that the drug 'is prescribed not just for mild depression but for a range of anxiety and mood disorders, such as obsessive compulsive disorder and "social anxiety disorder" – for people who feel panicky at the thought of mixing at parties. But crucially, he said, the problems show up when people stop taking Paxil/Seroxat because it has a shorter half-life than most of the other SSRIs. That means it clears the body faster and so it is more obvious that fatigue and pains are related to quitting the drug. With SSRIs that linger in the system for longer, by the time the symptoms appear it may seem that depression has set in again – and so the doctor's answer is another SSRI prescription.'[30] Not surprisingly, GlaxoSmithKline denied that there is any problem.

Meanwhile, many depressed people have found relief with a herb, St John's wort. What is reliably known about St John's wort is that it contains a serotonin-like substance which could improve a person's mood, and that it is not a good idea to take this herb along with a prescribed drug. In fact, it is never a good idea to take any herbal preparation along with prescription drugs because very little is known about the interactions between herbal preparations and prescription drugs and very little research has been done on this.

Antidepressant drugs can relieve the heaviness and stuckness of being depressed. Gwyneth Lewis told how it took three weeks for her to feel any effect of the antidepressants she had been prescribed. She then found that the drugs 'affected the quality of my depression but without changing its nature. What they gave me was some psychic space, a small but crucial distance between me and the horrors. Like a line of crustacean riot police, they pushed back the nightmares clamouring for my attention. This gave me a narrow cordon sanitaire in which to move, some room to breathe. The mental crowds were still there, of course, but they had less power over me, as if the anarchists had turned into paparazzi. The lighting of the intrusive cameras was blinding but at least I was free to move out of their way and into sleep's foyer.'[31] Such a reaction can be very useful in helping you to get started on finding those activities and people that will help you to change, but, if you do not use the relief the drug gives you, such relief will dissolve and leave you still in the prison.

Whenever I have sat with a severely depressed person I have longed for some magic pill which would dissolve in a trice such pain and suffering, but experience has taught me that no such pill exists or ever will exist. There is only one way to get out of the prison of depression and to stay out, and that is to gain the wisdom that allows you to leave the prison and never need its defence again.

The Way out of the Prison

Over the past fourteen years the number of therapists and counsellors has burgeoned, as have the different kinds of therapy. The differences between all these therapies are not as great as their practitioners may make out, and most of the differences relate to the jargon used by each kind of therapist. One useful way of categorizing therapies is to divide them into prescriptive and exploratory therapies. Prescriptive therapies tell you what to do; exploratory therapies explore how you think and feel. Most therapists use a combination of both, which is necessary because, if a therapist does not know what the client thinks and feels, he does not know what to prescribe. There has been a great deal of research into the effectiveness of different therapies, and all the results show that the effectiveness depends on the nature of the relationship between the therapist and the client.

Defining just what that relationship is is difficult. It has the qualities of friendship – trust, truthfulness, reliability, affection – but it is different from a friendship in that it is not reciprocal as a friendship must be. In a friendship both people are equal in power, but in the therapeutic relationship the therapist is more powerful than the client. The therapist looks after the client; the client does not look after the therapist. Moreover, the relationship between a therapist and a client is set within well-defined limits of how and when the two people meet.

The one therapy that has been well researched is cognitive behaviour therapy. There is no doubt that cognitive therapy does help depressed people, and what they can learn from it can give them the tools of thought with which they need never again fall back on the defence of depression. However, in the hands of some cognitive therapists the technique can be remarkably shallow and fatuous, because the therapist is afraid to confront the major issues of life and death which the depressed person is confronting.

Moreover, cognitive therapy is still closely attached to psychiatry. Aaron Beck, who devised cognitive therapy, is a professor of psychiatry, and he has taken great care not to confront his colleagues with the research findings lest he be cast into outer darkness along with the heretics Thomas Szasz, Ronald Laing, Loren Mosher and Peter Breggin.

Psychiatrists have become increasingly interested in cognitive therapy, but the language they use is based on the assumption that depression is a chronic illness. According to the pamphlet published by the Andrew Sims Centre for Professional Development, advertising a training event called Overcoming Depression, the workshop was for 'Psychiatrists and other health professionals who manage patients with depression'. After this workshop a participant would be able to

- Offer this cost and time effective form of CBT to depressed patients within a 15–20 minute consultation.
- Appreciate how patients can use the jargon-free booklets to understand their illness, learn new coping skills and better self-manage their condition.

The fee for this event was quite modest and included a copy of the book written by the presenter, Dr Chris Williams, all additional learning materials, lunch and refreshments. As the pamphlet explained, 'The course is supported by an educational grant from SB Pharmaceuticals,' but 'Delegates are advised that there will be no commercial influence on the content of the event.'[32]

It is not possible for any or us, whether depressed or not, to give an adequate account of our past life and present situation in just fifteen to twenty minutes, much less learn and consistently apply a very different way of thinking. Even more important, therapists can come in all shapes and sizes and espouse all kinds of theories, but if a therapist is going to be of any use to us, he must believe that we are capable of changing and releasing ourselves for ever from our misery. A therapist who believes that the best we are capable of is to live quietly with our misery (self-manage our condition) is nothing more than a human tranquillizer, bottled and sold by the drug companies.

Most cognitive therapists are far more than human tranquillizers. Many believe that we can change how we think and thus make our lives far happier. However, cognitive therapists have never created a model of depression in solely cognitive terms. It would be easy to do so, and it would be very similar to what I have created. Instead, they hang on to the usual psychiatric jumble of causes and do not attempt to explain how such a ragbag of causes could lead to the experience of depression. Even though cognitive therapy is concerned solely with how a person interprets himself and his world, this does not form the basic assumption of the theory and practice of cognitive therapy. The ragbag of causes makes it impossible to explain why a particular individual became depressed. The website of the British Association for Behavioural and Cognitive Psychotherapies (BABCP) no longer talks about 'an imbalance of several brain chemicals' as being one of the causes of depression, but an equally vague term, 'vulnerability', is used and not explained.

There is no one single cause of depression. Several factors can act together to cause it. Depression does appear to run in some families and therefore some people are vulnerable to depression throughout their lives because of this. Others are vulnerable because of the surroundings in which they live. For example those who have difficulties with raising young children or those who are isolated and don't get support from others, are much more at risk of developing depression. Vulnerability to depression also comes from having suffered from disruptive childhood experiences such as abuse, bullying or loss. In addition depression often comes about as a clear reaction to a major event in their lives, such as a relationship break-up, loss of a job, or the loss of a loved one.[33]

The above paragraph is a rewriting of the list of causes of depression given by the Royal College of Psychiatrists in their pamphlet on depression for the general public. These causes are: things that happen to us in our lives, circumstances, physical illness, personality, alcohol, gender (i.e. being a woman), genes (depression can run in families). Having for many decades presented as an incontrovertible fact that the cause of depression is a chemical imbalance in the brain, the Royal College has quietly dropped all reference to it on its website.[34]

Cognitive therapists used to describe their task as one of identifying their client's 'dysfunctional cognitions' and teaching the client to use 'functional cognitions'. Now the term used in the BABCP's pamphlet on depression is 'negative style'. 'The sufferer learns to fight the negative styles of thinking which in so many cases makes their mood even lower. Techniques that fight some of these unhelpful thinking styles will be tried out.'[35] Whatever the words used, it still seems that cognitive therapists do not recognize that the ideas which led the person to become depressed were not the result of perversity or stupidity but were the best ideas that the person could create at the time. If, as a small child, you discover that your parents are not perfect, indeed that they are dangerously imperfect, and that you have a choice of seeing yourself as being utterly alone, weak and helpless, or of blaming yourself for your parents' imperfection and hoping that you can keep yourself safe by being good, then obviously the second choice is the better one to make. Of course, as time goes by and circumstances change, you would be wise to review your earlier conclusions and see whether these still apply to your situation. What therapy should be about is helping a person review the conclusions drawn in childhood to see whether they are still a good fit for the person's present circumstances. If they are not, then the therapist and client can explore all the possible conclusions which may now apply. Therapy should not be about labelling and denigrating the client.

In recent years an increasing number of cognitive therapists have been incorporating the concept of Mindfulness into their work. Of course, the value of mindfulness, that is, paying attention to the present and not thinking about the past and the future, has been known for many centuries, but it would probably surprise the Buddha to learn that it is now possible to take an MA or MSc in Mindfulness at the University of Wales. This reminds me of the American publication which a friend assured me did exist called *Yoga to Win*.

At Oxford University's Centre for Suicide Research 'Mindfulness-based Cognitive Therapy has been developed with the aim of reducing relapse and recurrence for those who are vulnerable to depression.' The account of this work given on their website[36] is couched in the language of medicine – 'relapse', 'recurrent', 'episode of depression', 'symptoms'. In a fashion similar to the accounts by academic psychiatrists of mental disorder, these academic cognitive therapists give little sense that what is being described is the experience of real, living people. They separate mood from thinking as if these exist separately when in real experience they do not. Mood – emotion – is our interpretation of how safe or unsafe we are as a person, while thoughts are also interpretations. The answer given on the website to the question, 'Why do people remain vulnerable to relapse?' is

New research shows that during any episode of depression, negative mood occurs alongside negative thinking (such as 'I am a failure', 'I am inadequate', 'I am worthless') and bodily sensations of sluggishness and fatigue. When the episode is past, and the mood has returned to normal, the negative thinking and fatigue tend to disappear as well. However, during the episode a connection has formed between the mood that was present at that time, and the negative thinking patterns.

This means that when negative mood happens again (for any reason) a relatively small amount of such mood can trigger or reactivate the old thinking pattern. Once again, people start to think they have failed, or are inadequate – even if it is not relevant to the current situation. People who believed they had recovered may find themselves feeling 'back to square one'. They end up inside a rumination loop that constantly asks 'what has gone wrong?', 'why is this happening to me?', 'where will it all end?' Such rumination feels as if it ought to help find an answer, but it only succeeds in prolonging and deepening the mood spiral. When this happens, the old habits of negative thinking will start up again, negative thinking gets into the same rut, and a full-blown episode of depression may be the result.

The discovery that, even when people feel well, the link between negative moods and negative thoughts remains ready to be re-activated, is of enormous importance. It means that sustaining recovery from such depression depends on learning how to keep mild states of depression from spiralling out of control.[37]

Anyone who has been depressed on more than one occasion can see what these psychologists are driving at but it is not an accurate account of experience. To arrive at such an account these psychologists have had to change what their clients told them into the concepts of the psychologists' theory. If their clients had used their experience of cognitive therapy to learn what, in Gwyneth Lewis's words, depression had to teach them, they would have been able to describe how their life had been going along unremarkably when suddenly a disaster loomed before them. They knew how to deal with this disaster without becoming depressed again, but that was hard work. They could not help thinking, 'If I get depressed again I won't have to deal with this.' Having learnt how to get depressed, they could do it again. The question was, could they manage to resist temptation?

The mindfulness which we can learn through meditation can help us resist temptation, whether it is the temptation of another drink, another cream cake, another affair with some unsuitable person, or another term in the prison of depression. If you want to resist any such temptations you need to ask yourself, 'What advantages do I get out of doing all these things?' If you have the honesty to identify exactly what you get out of being depressed and the courage to give up these advantages, then you can free yourself from the prison.

Freeing yourself from your prison highlights aspects of yourself and of your life that you would prefer not to acknowledge. Many depressed people as adults do not want to review the attitudes that originated in childhood because that will mean remembering the events that gave rise to these attitudes. They dare not criticize their parents, and so they seize on any terminology or therapy that renders self-exploration irrelevant. Seasonal Affective Disorder or SAD has been a boon to many such people because it requires no self-exploration and is based on an idea with which most of us can agree. Bright, sunny weather is more pleasant than dark, cold weather. Sunlight, so this theory goes, acts on our brain, releasing chemicals that cheer us up, while darkness depletes these chemicals and we become depressed. If this were the case, depression would be most prevalent in northern climes and rare in sunny places. The Scandinavians certainly are a gloomy lot, plagued by depression and suicide, but darkness is not the cause. Their culture is dominated by Lutheran Protestantism with its creed of the virtues of suffering. In the south, Australians do not seem to find their sunny weather a protection from depression. There the rates of depression are the same as in the rest of the world, and large numbers of young men, who have spent most of their lifetime playing in the sunshine, kill themselves. This is a national tragedy.

The cure for SAD, sitting for periods each day in front of a bright light, seems to depend for its effectiveness on the beliefs the user has about the use of the light. A study of the relative effectiveness of a bright white light and a dim red light found no differences between the two, but noted that the participants' expectations about the effectiveness of the light treatment were 'generally high'.[38]

When a person decides to take time each day to sit in front of a bright light to rest or to read, that person has made a decision to do something pleasant for themselves. Deciding to care for yourself is the first step out of the prison of depression.

Many people have made such a decision and have joined a self-help group. One woman, Andrea, wrote:

For me depression has always meant locking myself away in silence, shutting out the world to withdraw into this grim dark space where nothing can reach me or hurt me any more, dreaming of death as the ultimate refuge from everything that is painful. To me this is where the main strength of a self-help group lies; it is a space where you are allowed to be depressed. For the first time you find out that there is nothing wrong with feeling depressed, that you are not this unique monster that has to feel guilty for his dark thoughts and feelings. . .

Listening to other members of the group I always think that all these people are really nice; none of them is ugly and horrible. How can they possibly have a low opinion of themselves? Then I think that maybe the others feel the same about me; perhaps I am not this ugly, horrible and worthless person I am often convinced I am.[39]

Andrea's decision to go to a self-help group led to an experience which challenged an idea which she had held for most of her life and which was central to how she saw herself and her world. She had begun to learn the lesson which her depression had to teach her.

Depression always begins with the discovery that there is a serious discrepancy between what we thought our life was and what it actually is. We have created a story about ourselves which is not actually true. We may have been telling ourselves that the people we love will never do anything which would hurt us, or that if we work hard to be good nothing bad will ever happen to us. Of course you know that even the most loving people can deal out hurts. People often love themselves far more than they love others, and you only have to look about you to see that no amount of goodness prevents disaster. But you lock this knowledge away inside you, pretend it is not there, and over the years your secret becomes, as Gwyneth Lewis said, a monster 'you're afraid to look at. Once recognised, it's comic rather than horrific. If you're not too proud to suffer this humiliation – that the reason you've been putting off living your real life is, at base, foolish – then you will never have to face up to anything worse. I had, over the years, become used to thinking of myself as a perfectionist Tragic Queen.

In order to make this true and prove I wasn't the bitch I thought I was, I was quite prepared – no, driven – to follow a career I didn't want, to have children for the wrong reasons and not do the one thing that gives me more pleasure than anything else [write poetry]. Far from being heroic, this self-denial was just phoney and more than a little silly.'[40]

What depression has to teach us is that our story is not true. We have to abandon that story and create another one which is as true as we can make it. At the beginning of our depression we are like a person who has been seized by the police and flung into a cell without an explanation as to why this is happening. We bang on the door of the cell and demand to be released. We can go on banging and protesting, and stay locked up, or we can start to think that perhaps we have something to do with our imprisonment. We begin to doubt our story. Gwyneth wrote, 'People in the middle of a depression are beings who have to live, for a while, without a story, which is why it feels as though you've lost your soul. But this period is a dark room where you're developing the next chapter of your life before living it. The work will be all the more vivid if you're patient and let it take its own course.'[41]

People get into all kinds of difficulties, of which getting depressed is one, because they believe that they are incapable of change and that everything about them and their life is fixed and real. They need to learn that all their perceptions, ideas, beliefs, attitudes, opinions, feelings are interpretations which they have created. Understanding this is what the Buddhists call enlightenment, but it has to be more than an intellectual understanding. It has to be an understanding which becomes your whole way of being. Gwyneth was acquainted with Buddhist thinking before she became depressed, and this seems to have helped her learn the lessons which her depression had to teach her. In the time she had spent in a Buddhist retreat she had learned about mindfulness, but a better understanding of what mindfulness actually means came to her as she stopped *trying* to be good, *trying* to get better, *trying* to achieve something each day, and just lived. Some days she rested, and some days she did a few simple things. She wrote,

'Life in the present was suddenly vivid. I started listening as I cut vegetables and enjoying the different degrees of crunch. I hadn't been aware of these sounds for a very long time. It was as if they could, at last, get through to my body. A layer of plastic between me and the world had dissolved. In the supermarket I walked past the freezer section twice, just to feel the cold pressing on me from both sides. I was back in the present, not living in the past, with its hall of mirrors.'[42]

Philip Martin, who wrote about the Zen path through depression, said:

We have not realized it, but we have been the jailer who has kept us imprisoned. We have lived within a small life, where we believe we are safe, and where we believe we can force our circumstances to comply with our desires.

We can give up on this attempt to force things to be the way we believe they should be – and in doing so we can leave our prison behind. Like an inmate coming into the light and fresh air, we can find a larger and more spacious world. It is not limited by the confines of our suffering, nor even by our ideas of freedom.[43]

Chapter Nine

Turning Fear into Anxiety, Panic and Phobias

Everyone gets anxious. Whenever we feel that something is about to happen which we may not be able to deal with, we feel anxious. Anxiety is the anticipation of events that we believe are likely to be beyond our control. This may be an accurate interpretation of our situation, or it may be an interpretation based on our idea that we are inadequate and incapable of dealing with whatever happens to us. Some people get anxious for periods in their life, and some people make being anxious their way of life. For these the world is a dangerous place no matter how peaceful it may appear to be, and there is no situation about which they cannot worry.

Expert worriers value worrying. If they did not they would not do it so much. Some believe that worrying about something prevents it from happening. Some believe that worrying about someone shows that you love that person. The one great advantage of worrying is that while you concentrate on feeling anxious about some trivial matter, or something that may never happen, you can ignore the major issues in your life which, if you acknowledged them, would show only too clearly that your meaning structure was a not an accurate representation of what was actually going on.

Some people manage for all their lives to put off facing the reality of their situation. Steadfastly denying to themselves that things are not as they wish them to be, they never become who they might have been: they never know who they are. They feel false, even an impostor, and, though they may love others with a passion and intensity, they can never feel that the love they are given is actually for themselves. If you cannot be yourself, how can anyone know who you are?

Some people have the truth of their situation forced upon them, and with that the terror of annihilation overwhelms them, and they feel themselves to be falling apart, crumbling, disappearing. They cast around for something that will hold them together. Introverts go inward, into the internal reality of their thoughts and feelings. Extraverts, fearing the fear inside them, try to deal with it in their external reality. Some extraverts locate the cause of their fear in their external reality. They call their fear panic, and they identify certain places, situations, people, animals, insects or objects as the source of their fear.

In the terror of annihilation there is both the feeling that the sense of being a person is falling apart *and* the bodily feelings that accompany the physiological changes of fear with the preparation for fight or flight. The sense of being a person is in internal reality. We experience our body as being in both our internal and external realities, so it is easy to regard our body as being in external reality and to locate in it all the sensations we are feeling in our internal reality. We can then interpret these sensations, not as the effects of adrenaline on the body, but as the forerunners of some catastrophic event, the outcome of which will be that we shall be left utterly and completely alone. The catastrophic event may be seen as death, and we all die alone. Or it may be that we will vomit or faint, whereupon every onlooker will reject us. Once the panic subsides, we do not ask, 'What led me to feel so frightened?' but instead we attach the fear to the place where it occurred. We resolve never to be in that place ever again. This resolution has far-reaching effects on our life because the places where the panic may occur increase in number until they encompass the whole world and the sky.

Some people attach the fear they call panic to social situations where, if they panic, everyone present will reject them. In social situations they do not need a full-blown panic to be rejected. Their nervousness alone turns social situations into torture.

For some people the focus of their fear of panic becomes one activity such as flying, or going in a lift, or up high in a building or on a mountain or cliff. Such people do not ask themselves why this specific fear has developed, and if they are asked why they are frightened they will say, 'I don't know. I just am.' They will talk about how they refuse to fly, or are willing to do so only in a drugged stupor, how they always climb the stairs instead of using the lift, no matter how many flights there are, or how, when up high, they fear that they may be impelled to plunge into space, or that the solid plate glass between them and space will dissolve and they will fall. I have found that if at this point in the conversation I point out that they do not trust other people – pilots, lift operators, engineers and builders – and themselves, they look utterly bored and wait for me to stop talking. I ought to know better than to point out to them what they fear the most, that the people on whom they depend for their existence, not just nameless technicians but family and friends, cannot be trusted. Nor can they trust themselves not to let their need for excitement, which means so much to them, overcome their need for safety.

Most of us, extraverts and introverts, have some specific situation which makes us anxious but which clearly connects to our past. I, an introvert, am very sensitive to any situation where I might suffocate. I have had many near-suffocation experiences, not just in terms of malfunctioning lungs, but in terms of being overwhelmed by water. When surfing I have many times been dumped by enormous waves, and as a small child I was often pushed and held underwater by older children. My husband, an extravert, refused to eat where there was little light. He liked to see the food he was eating because once, when he was stationed in Darwin, the army cook served a meal in the dark. Halfway through the meal a lantern was brought and the men discovered that the stew they were eating was infested with cockroaches. These kinds of experiences teach us to be careful of possible, real dangers. If you grow up in Australia you have to learn to be wary of spiders and snakes because there many of the snakes and spiders can kill you, but nevertheless Australia is not a country of spider and snake phobics. A specific fear of spiders or snakes stands for something other than real and possible danger.

I have a young woman friend who is terrified of spiders. Although she loves flowers she refuses to help her husband garden. She had a very religious upbringing in the Catholic Church, and, although she is no longer a practising Catholic, the strict Catholic view of the world as a dangerous place permeated with evil is still her vision of the world. Other people are a mystery to her because they do not behave in the ways she knows they ought to behave. She sees herself as having little power or competence, and, even though she is very beautiful, she feels that she is fat and ugly. Her fear-soaked vision of everything that exists is extremely difficult for her to live with, so she tries to encapsulate it in one small object, a spider. A spider is real. She can call for help and some fearless person will remove it. The spider is her scapegoat, the bearer of all her sins and fears.

Do I explain this to her? No. Fearing spiders seems to be a small price for avoiding the terror of her world. But what will happen to her as she gets older? Strong men will rush to remove spiders from the path of a young, beautiful woman, but will they be so keen when she is middle aged or old? Will they not dismiss her as a silly old woman?

So I tell her about the Friendly Spider Programme at the London Zoo, which offers a one-day course and has an 80 per cent success rate. She looks as impressed with this advice as my friend with the fear of flying does whenever, in answer to his question about how to overcome his fear, I tell him about the course run at Heathrow airport for people like him, and how, if he does not want to mix with hoi polloi, there are many competent psychologists who would be pleased to take his money and teach him how to fly without fear. Somehow, this information always slips his mind.

There is another set of fears which extraverts can develop in order to locate their internal terror in their external environment. Here the person expresses his need for relationships with others in terms of needing to be needed and therefore needing to be responsible for other people. However, instead of feeling a generalized sense of responsibility for people at large, the person focuses on one special group that could suffer injury through the person's own incompetence, or by being unaware of a special danger of which the person himself is keenly aware. While such anxieties can have a real basis, the person develops the fear without reference to any kind of probability except that of 'If any disaster can happen it will'. These exaggerated anxieties have clear links with the person's past experiences, and these experiences can suggest that the exaggerated concern for others is not so much fear as unadmitted anger, but these matters are usually of little interest to the person. If you are running away from your internal reality you do not want to stop and interrogate it.

Cognitive therapy, which asks people to observe their thinking without asking them why they came to such conclusions, has had considerable success in the treatment of panic and its consequences. However, for this therapy to work the person has to want to change.

Panic and the Fear of Panic

What extraverts – people persons – fear most of all is being left completely and absolutely alone, so they try to lead their lives so that there is always a group of people around them. If they know themselves to be lovable and likable, they can feel sure that there will always be people wanting to be around them, but if from their childhood they have believed that they are basically not lovable and likable, then they are always frightened that they will be rejected. One way to keep people around you is to be unfailingly loving and kind, always putting other people's needs before your own, always doing everything perfectly, but, even so, people can still leave you, or be physically present but isolate you by being indifferent to your needs and wishes, or not bothering even to try to understand your point of view.

Helen was a very sensible woman. She was practical, down to earth, full of common sense. She ran her home, brought up her children, taught part time, and organized the household to fit in with the demands of her husband's business, all with great efficiency and success. She could not understand why one evening, as she was standing beside the kitchen table, serving the children their supper, she was suddenly swept by terrible fear.

The feeling began in her stomach, a sense of falling away. She tried to stop it, but it rose, enveloping, shaking, drenching. There was a thundering in her ears, a pounding in her chest, a tightening in her throat. She thought it was death.

No one was there to call. Her husband was away. Her next-door neighbours were on holiday. She was amazed to see that the children went on eating and noticed nothing.

Gradually the terrible feeling ebbed away. She stood beside the sink watching the children eating, then sent them off to change for bed, having reminded them that she was going out and they should behave themselves when the baby-sitter was there. Then she tidied herself and was collecting her books when the baby-sitter arrived. Helen gave her the usual precise instructions and set off to take her class in Children's Books.

The class went well. She was, as usual, well prepared, and her students responded with their usual curiosity and enthusiasm. However, all the time she was in dread that that terrible feeling of panic would return.

And it did. Three days later, as she was transferring her husband's supper to plastic containers for freezing (Gordon had just phoned to say he would not be home until late and would eat out) and thinking about what shopping she needed to do for the weekend when her mother was visiting, the terrible panic came again.

She was alone. Afterwards, as she thought about it, she was sure that anyone watching would have seen a peculiar sight. She must have looked as if she were going mad.

She became afraid to go out. What if someone saw her like that? She tried to reassure herself that the panics had occurred only at home. Perhaps there was something there she was allergic to. Then, one day, just as she had finished arranging the flowers in the church, she overheard the vicar's wife saying to the vicar that the summer flowers were really beautiful, but didn't he think that the vase of red and yellow roses near the altar was a little, well, *gaudy*. Helen felt her hands shake, and then the full panic was upon her.

She wanted never to set foot in that church again, but to do that she would have to explain to her husband why, and that meant telling him about the panics. He listened sympathetically and said, 'It's probably got something to do with your hormones. Why don't you see Dr Trent?'

So she went down to the clinic and talked to Dr Trent. She was surprised that he was so matter-of-fact. He did not seem to think that what was happening to her was anything special or unusual. What surprised her even more was that he suggested that she talk to a psychologist. She did not understand that at all. He did give her some pills, but with so many warnings about not taking them too often that she dared not take any at all. She left his surgery feeling very puzzled.

Gordon listened to her account of the visit and said, 'Well, you'd better do what he suggested. Go and see this psychologist.'

Helen decided that she would. Not because she wanted to, but because she did not want to upset Dr Trent and Gordon by not doing what they said.

So a few weeks later she was sitting very nervously in my office. She told me how it had started and how by now the fear of having a panic attack was almost as bad as the panic attack itself. She did not want to give up doing things, but it was getting harder and harder to leave home. She dreaded going to places where she had had an attack, and she just had to force herself to go. Being with other people worried her most, especially people she did not know very well. Yet she hated to be alone. Every day was a struggle.

She told me how helpful her husband was. He did not really understand what she felt like, but he was sympathetic and kind. Whenever he could he went with her to places – she could not manage the supermarket on her own – but of course he could not be with her all the time. Anyway, that was no way to live.

I asked her whether she had talked about this to anyone else.

'No, no one.'

'Why not?'

'Well, people wouldn't understand.'

'What about your mother? Would you tell her?'

402

'Oh, no, never.'

'Why not?'

'She would say it was weakness. She always expects me to cope.'

'With everything?'

'Yes. My housework, the children, teaching. She expects me to do everything perfectly every time. Even the clothes I wear. She's always been very particular about the way I dress.'

She went on to describe how, when she was a little girl, she was not allowed to get dirty. 'She'd put me in a white starched frock and heaven help me if I got it dirty. I could only play in the back garden. Not in the front garden, and never outside in the street. I wasn't allowed to play at all on Sunday. When I went to school she always checked on my friends. She was . . . she still is . . . a . . . I suppose you could call her a snob. I'm lucky I married someone she approved of. She approves of anyone with a university degree. That is, if they're white. Not if they're black, or Indian, or anything like that. When she comes to stay, Gordon and I just try to keep off any subject that might have anything to do with racial matters. And television. There's so much on that she disapproves of that when she's staying with us we just don't put the TV on. She thinks the world of the children, but she's always telling them what a hard life she had as a child and how they have to be grateful for all the things they've got. She doesn't think I'm grateful enough for all she did for me. I am grateful to her. I know things weren't easy for her. Dad was a teacher, and teachers weren't paid much. But she felt she had a position to keep up. So she expected me to be perfect all the time.'

'What happened to you when you weren't?'

'I'd get a telling off, or if I'd done something really bad, I'd be sent to my room. She didn't hit me much. I'd have to stay in my room until she said I could come out. Or she wouldn't speak. If she was annoyed with Dad she wouldn't speak to him for weeks.'

'How did you feel about being sent to your room and not spoken to?'

'Terrible. I hated it. I'd rather have a slap or a telling off and get it over with.'

'If you hurt yourself or felt upset, what would your mother do? Would she give you a cuddle?'

'Oh, good heavens no. She never cuddled me or sat me on her knee. Don't get me wrong – if I was ill she'd look after me very well, but I was never allowed to cry. She didn't approve of tears.'

'Would she allow you to get angry with her?'

'Angry? Absolutely not. That's unthinkable. I still wouldn't dream of getting angry with her. I often get annoyed with her – she still talks to me as if I'm three years old – but I wouldn't dream of saying anything to her. I know she loves me and I wouldn't want to upset her.'

I asked her what she meant by 'upset'. She thought that what she had said was a self-evident truth, but as we unravelled her meaning for 'upset' we found that it meant for her making the other person feel angry, worried or guilty.

'Why', I asked, 'is it important to you not to upset people?'

Again, a self-evident truth, but one which could be unravelled to reveal that she needed to be needed. She needed to be part of a group.

'So when you were naughty and your mother locked you in your room, that must have been the very worst thing that could happen to you. You were all alone. The fear you felt then must have been like the fear you feel now.'

'Yes, I suppose it was.' Helen sat silently thoughtful, and then said, 'I guess I've always felt insecure. I hadn't really thought about it. Are you saying that what happens to us in childhood affects us in our adult life?'

She was genuinely amazed at this idea. As a teacher and mother who had spent much time and energy trying to influence children, she was surprised to find that I thought that children had experiences that influenced them all their lives.

However, in our subsequent conversations Helen came to see that there is indeed a connection between our experiences in childhood and adulthood. As we went painstakingly through the events of the night of the first panic, not just the external events, what she was doing, but the internal events, what she was thinking and feeling, we found that she had been feeling increasingly alone. Gordon was becoming more and more wrapped up in his business. All her children were now at school and seemed to need her less and less. Gordon was talking of moving house to somewhere more convenient for him, and she did not like to tell him how much she felt attached to their house. She did not like being in strange surroundings. She hated change.

On that particular evening she was worried about whether she had prepared enough material for her students. They were all mature students and inclined to be critical, especially one woman who was older than her.

'Old enough to be your mother?' I asked.

'Not quite. But she can be critical like my mother. I try to make sure that she doesn't criticize me.'

'What's so bad about being criticized?'

'I can't take criticism. I just flare up.' It was dangerous to 'flare up' because if you got angry with people they would reject you, and being rejected – cast out of the group – meant that you were annihilated for ever and ever.

So she tried to be perfect in everything she did to avoid criticism and thus survive. However, there was one person whose criticism she could not avoid.

'My mother criticizes me all the time. I just have to switch off. You can't get angry with a seventy-five-year-old woman.'

There was no way she could talk to her mother about how, all those years ago, she had been frightened and her mother had not comforted her. Any readjustments she might make to her feelings about her childhood had to be done without her mother's help.

The panics we experience in adulthood – that is, the terror of annihilation – remind us of the experiences of annihilation we had in childhood, often at the hands of those people who should have cared for us.

Rosa's husband had died suddenly several years earlier and her sons had grown up and left home. Even before she was widowed, Rosa took Valium to help her cope with her family problems – money worries and the responsibility of caring for two sick old women, her mother and mother-in-law. Now she was alone, always anxious and often swept by waves of panic.

As she told me about herself it was clear that she was a 'people person', someone who was happiest and most secure when part of a group. She told me that what she had enjoyed most was amateur dramatics and singing. 'We used to go as a concert party to hospitals like this one,' she said. 'I loved that.'

So she could understand what her panics meant. I described to her how 'people persons' need other people around them and suffer dreadfully when they feel they have been abandoned or rejected.

Rosa nodded. 'When I was a child my sister died. It affected my mother terribly. She got very depressed and suicidal. She used to say that she was going to take me with her – she was going to kill me and then kill herself. She had some photos of my sister and me, standing side by side. One day, when I was a child, I found them among my mother's things. She'd blotted me out. I wasn't in the photos any more. There was just my sister and a black smudge where I had been.'

I said, 'Would I be right in thinking that the terror you feel now is just like the terror you felt then, when your mother said she'd kill you and when you found yourself blotted out in the photos?'

'Yes,' said Rosa, 'yes, it is.'

The terror of annihilation is far greater when we dare not protest about the behaviour of the person who has inflicted possible annihilation upon us. When this happens in childhood we may be left with a lifelong distrust of other people. They may appear to be charming and pretend to like you, but behind their smiling masks you know they are criticizing and rejecting you.

Assaults upon a child's sense of being a person come in many ways. As a teenager Megan had always enjoyed company, and when she met Tim, a young naval officer, the social life of a navy officer's wife appealed to her, but as she got older she found the round of social engagements more and more difficult. She was so frightened of panicking and having everyone looking at her that she kept making excuses not to go. Tim tried to understand and to help her with her anxiety in a logical, sensible way, but, somehow, his suggestions never seemed to work.

Megan knew that her childhood had something to do with her problems. She told me first about how her parents had led busy lives with little time for their daughter. Her mother never even took the time to see that she had enough clothes. Megan described to me how at thirteen her breasts were so well developed that she needed a bra. For once her mother noticed Megan's need, but she met it by taking her to a shop that sold old-fashioned, matronly underwear and buying her an ungainly cotton brassière, 'two huge cotton circles', as Megan called it.

While Megan's mother was showing her that she regarded Megan's body as unattractive and of no value, her father was creeping into Megan's bedroom at night when he thought she was asleep and fondling her breasts.

I asked Megan why she had not protested to her parents about their treatment of her – why had she pretended to be asleep when her father came into her room, why she had not demanded decent clothes – and she said that she loved her parents and did not want to hurt them. They were splendid people, especially her father, and she was broken hearted when he died.

Megan could remember and talk about the events that had brought her such pain, helplessness and total fear, but the conclusion she drew from them was not 'How dare my parents treat me in this way' but 'I must have deserved their bad treatment'. She had already learned to construe herself as bad and her parents as good. To construe them as bad would have meant that she was entirely alone, and that too would have meant annihilation.

Whenever Lucy came to see me her husband Gavin came too. Someone else is always involved whenever we resort to a desperate defence, but, unlike Gavin, our nearest and dearest often refuse to recognize this.

Lucy remembered the event that made her realize that her parents were not pillars of wisdom and goodness who held up the sky so she could play safely beneath. At the most terrifying moment of her young life they failed her.

She remembered the event, but she did not want to talk about it. One day, when I had said something about how young children suffer sexual assaults and how these experiences, though they may not be remembered consciously, have long-term effects, Lucy said, 'That's happened to me.'

She would not tell me what happened, except to say that she was four at the time and that she had run home crying and told her father what had happened. He was standing there shaving, and when she finished telling him he went on shaving. Her mother said to him, 'Don't you think you ought to do something?' and he did not reply. Nothing further was said or done.

Many months later Lucy told me the rest of the story, and then only in the briefest, baldest terms. I shall add one detail, something which Lucy would not have said. At forty she was very pretty. At four she must have been breathtakingly beautiful.

All she told me was that she had been playing in the park and a man had come by and picked her up and sat her on a ledge. Then he urinated into her mouth.

I commented on how devastated she must have been by this, not just by the ugly act perpetrated upon her, which must have rendered her helpless and frightened, but by her parents' failure to find and punish her traducer, to protect her from further assaults, to comfort her and to reassure her that no matter what filth had been flung upon her body it was nothing that could not be washed away, and she was, as ever, their dearest, sweetest, much-beloved daughter. Instead, they had shown her that they did not think she was worth any special effort or concern. They might be prepared to give her food and a roof over her head, but where her survival was concerned she was on her own. And if they did not value her, how could she value herself?

There were many other events in her childhood and adolescence which proved to her, time and time again, that she was of little value. Her father was a domineering man who demanded, and got, obedience from his wife and children. The household was run for his benefit and no one else's. Her mother would not dare stand up for herself or protect the children from him. Lucy tried to help her mother, but often found her efforts unappreciated. Moreover, she was regarded as the stupid one of the family. At school her anxiety about not being able to do her schoolwork prevented her from doing it, so school was a misery, and she left as soon as she could. It was not until years later, when she and her husband had started their own business, that she came to realize that she was not stupid at all.

Whenever Lucy talked about her childhood and her family, she always interspersed her narrative with comments like 'Don't get me wrong, Dorothy. Dad thinks the world of me,' and 'Mum's a wonderful person. She'd do anything for anybody.' Thus must the child protect the parents.

But at what price? The price Lucy paid was panic attacks and the fear that the constrictions in her throat and chest and the dizzy, muzzy feelings in her head were the symptoms of a serious illness. She would have preferred to have had a physical illness, for if she did not, if all these strange feelings were the result of 'tension' and 'nerves', then she was mad, and mad people ended up in psychiatric hospitals, despised and rejected by everyone, and being rejected and alone was the fate she feared most of all.

So coming to see me in my office in a psychiatric hospital was a risky business. She dared not let anyone know she came. She often said to me that she would love to meet someone else who had panic attacks, and I could have granted her wish and arranged such a meeting – with some difficulty, though, since so many of her fellow sufferers also feared being found out – but her curiosity could not overcome her fear.

The only way she could risk coming to see me was to attend with her husband Gavin. Our sessions, which were usually of at least two hours' duration, always began with a discussion of Lucy's symptoms, out of which I would try to develop some further mutual understanding of how Lucy experienced herself and her world, and from that would come some revelations of how Lucy and Gavin got on together.

All the physical things that Lucy complained of were always vague, shifting, confused and confusing unpleasantnesses, difficult to describe and define. She never complained of sharply delineated pain. Indeed, whenever she did feel sharp physical pain, such as when she fell over her son's bike left standing in a dark hallway, thus banging and scraping her shins quite severely, she would say, in passing, 'The pain, that was nothing.'

One day I asked her about this. She said, 'I don't mind pain,' and when I questioned her further, I found that she valued physical pain, for it showed her that she was alive and existing. Sometimes, she said, when the muzziness and her sense of unreality were at their strongest, she would pinch herself to produce a sharp, distinct pain.

When she said that, I valued Gavin's presence even more. So many women like Lucy, bereft of someone to love them, find themselves in psychiatric hospitals where they are no more than just another patient to the nurses and doctors. Nothing in the monotonous, impersonal hospital routine has any personal significance for them, and they feel their fragile sense of being a person dissolving, emptying into a nothingness. In desperate terror, they seize a razor blade to slit open their arms, or matches to set fire to their clothes, and in the ensuing pain they feel once more the basis of a human being's existence, the sense of existing as a person.

There were times when Lucy hated herself so much that she felt that everyone – Gavin, her children, her parents, me, even her dog – was tired of her and wanted to be rid of her, and with this feeling the black tide of depression would rise and envelop her. When that happened she found it even harder to follow the rule she had set herself of getting out of the house and doing something. She was determined not to give in completely and hide herself away. She took the dog for a walk every day, although she always had to follow the same route each time, clinging close to the houses at the edge of the playing fields and never venturing into the vast open space of the fields beyond, never going so far from home that she could not get back there in a few minutes. She had become a very efficient shopper, knowing what she wanted, no browsing, in and out in minutes. She had given up going to most social events, but she could manage church or a visit to the cinema with Gavin, as long as she sat right beside the aisle. She could travel in the car with Gavin driving or driving herself over short, familiar distances, but she was always terrified of being caught in a traffic jam. She could not travel with another driver and she would not even think of travelling by bus, train or plane.

'Why not?' I would ask, and each time the answer was the same.

'I might faint.'

What was so terrible about fainting?

Shame. That terrible, draining, annihilating fear. All those hostile, uncaring, rejecting eyes on her, and she alone, small, weak and disgusting.

It was no use pointing out to Lucy that, in all the places she feared, people are usually very sympathetic and helpful when someone becomes ill or faints. Lucy knew this, but she felt that the kindness of strangers was reserved for others, not for her. She was not worthy of their concern.

She knew this was so because she had had one terrifying experience of breathlessness and fainting, so bad that at the time she was sure she was dying, and this had ended with what felt to her as rejection. One summer day, when she and Gavin were on holiday, they had been driving along, and suddenly Lucy found that she could not breathe. Her throat had constricted tightly. She fought to get her breath and could not. She collapsed. Gavin rushed her to hospital, where she was admitted. Three hours later the doctor came and told her that the problem was hyperventilation and there was nothing to worry about. She was discharged from hospital.

She felt rejected. The doctor obviously thought she was mad, getting herself into such a state that she could not breathe. He could not be bothered with her, so much so that he did not examine her properly, and so, she worried, had missed discovering what was really wrong with her. That inability to breathe was, perhaps, a sign that there was something seriously wrong with her heart and lungs.

She did not think a great deal about dying, not as much as she had done earlier in her life. She told me, 'I used to worry a lot about dying. It's funny, since I've had these panic attacks I've stopped worrying about dying.'

Not that dying itself promised a relief from panics. When I asked her what she wanted when she died, to be buried or cremated, she answered immediately, 'Cremated. I couldn't bear to be shut in a coffin under the ground. That would be terrible.'

Dying is the ultimate in being alone. If panic attacks stop you thinking about it, then panic attacks are useful.

On the first occasion they came to see me Lucy told me how she had been upset recently because they were having problems with one of the small firms that supplied their business. Gavin said that he thought she was worrying unnecessarily. Businesses always had problems like this. It was just one of the challenges that running a business always presented. He said that he liked challenges.

I asked him why a challenge was important to him, and he said that that was what life was about – meeting a challenge and winning. This was the reply of an introvert, committed to extending and developing himself.

However, Gavin set some very real limits on what he responded to as a challenge. He never entered a contest or responded to a challenge unless he was sure of winning. He never spoke out or argued unless he was sure that some positive achievement would follow. He saw no point in arguing with their suppliers. He could call them selfish and crooked, and all they would do, so he said, would be to agree with him that they were and then challenge him to do something about it. There was nothing he could do about it. The sums of money involved were too small for it to be worthwhile for them to take the suppliers to court. Lucy thought that he should speak out. She believed in plain speaking. He did not.

Then, after nearly two hours' discussion, the reason for Lucy's terrible panic in the car on holiday became clear. It had occurred as they were in the car driving away from her cousin Martin's home. While they were there they had witnessed Martin treating his daughter in a vile and despicable way. Lucy was horrified. She hated cruelty. She wanted Gavin to say something to Martin, but

Gavin would not let her say anything and he would not speak out himself. After all, he did not know the full facts. He did not know what the girl had done. It was best not to interfere.

I pointed out the similarity of that situation with the situation in Lucy's childhood, when she had been the victim of cruelty and no one had come to her defence. Lucy seemed unconvinced by what I said. Six months later she still said she did not know why she had had such a terrible panic attack while on holiday. We had by then talked of how authoritarian her father had always been and how frightened she was of him. I reminded her how the scene she witnessed must have awakened her memories of harsh treatment at the hands of her father. She brushed this aside. Her niece, she said, was very badly behaved.

There was one challenge that Gavin often wondered whether he should accept. One day, when we were talking about how meaningless and empty Lucy found her life to be, she turned to Gavin and said, 'Sometimes I think, if only you'd make me do something. If you'd just say to me, "We're going for a drive, I've booked a table for dinner. Get your coat on." I think I might be able to manage that.'

Gavin asked me whether I thought this would work. 'If you say so, I'll do it.'

I demurred. 'I'm not going to be responsible for your most monumental row.' I could just imagine the scene, but I knew it would not take place.

Gavin knew that if he confronted her with such a challenge she would refuse to accept it. She would make some excuse, like she hadn't washed her hair, and she couldn't go out with unwashed hair.

However, it would not happen just because Lucy would produce excuses as to why she could not go out. Gavin was scared even to try to push Lucy into anything that would lead to a row because he was frightened she would leave him.

'That's silly,' she said. 'You know I wouldn't leave you.'

He reminded her that when they did have a row she would often say that she would leave him.

'But I don't mean it,' she protested. 'I just say that because I'm angry.'

Gavin looked stricken. She patted his hand (they always sat side by side) and said to him, 'I know you get worried you'll be left again, like you were when you were a child. But I won't leave you. You know that.'

Gavin saw very clearly that Lucy's panics and depression were not just inside her, but linked to her family, past and present, and to him. He not only searched for and found these links, but appreciated them in the context of the ridiculousness of human endeavour, something we often laughed about together.

One day, when Gavin was talking about the severe migraine attacks he had had, he said, 'I don't get them now. I always used to get them when we had to go to some social do. It's only lately I realized that that was when I got them.'

I asked, 'If Lucy gives up having panic attacks does that mean that you'll have to go back to having migraines?'

He laughed and said that he would have to give that some considered thought.

Many husbands, I found, were not like Gavin. They saw their wife's panic attacks, and her fear of all situations where a panic attack could occur, as nothing but her own weakness and stupidity. They would not dream of going along with her to talk to a therapist. It was her problem, and she had to solve it alone.

However, being alone was the one thing that she could not bear. Marjorie told me how 'We used to do things as a family' but now her children had withdrawn from her into the self-absorption of adolescence and her husband into his work. Night-time was very difficult for her. She said, 'I was upset and crying and he turned over and went to sleep.'

Even concerned and caring husbands do not always see what is happening between themselves and their wife, especially in terms of how anger is expressed and received. It is not just that the phobic person (male or female) is afraid to express anger because that may lead to rejection but that within the family the phobic person's anger may not be accepted by the partner, the 'sensible' one.

One day, when Gordon came with Helen to see me, we got on to the subject of arguments between them, and what became clear was that even if Helen felt secure enough with Gordon to express her anger with him, he did not accept her anger as real and legitimate. She was just being silly.

Helen said, 'I get angry and you go quiet and just walk away.'

'I'm just waiting for you to get over it,' he said.

Helen felt strong enough to ignore this put-down and continued, 'I have supper ready and then you phone and say you're going to be two hours late. You know earlier than that that you're going to be late. You could let me know.'

'You know I'm not always near a phone,' said Gordon, sweet reason itself. However, he did admit, as we talked about it, that in the home he grew up in and the school he went to, expressions of anger were severely punished. It was not so much that he was being reasonable in refusing to accept the reality and legitimacy of Helen's anger, but that her anger frightened him.

Lorna's husband had his own way of invalidating Lorna's anger. If she overcame all her inhibitions about expressing her anger and actually did give vent to it in an outburst, he would say, 'Do you feel better after that?'

If another person will not accept our anger then it means that that person will not accept us. We are belittled and humiliated, and we can lose confidence in ourselves. This is what happens to so many women. They have been taught that anger is unfeminine, and if you are unfeminine you will not be loved. We all need love, whether we are men or women, extraverts or introverts.

Anger may be frightening to an extravert who fears that the expression of it will result in rejection, but it can be equally frightening to an introvert, who sees in the expression of anger a dangerous, uncontrollable emotion which threatens chaos. Since extraverts so often marry introverts, this means that many of their misunderstandings and arguments are not so much about the couple's anger as about their fear of anger.

Sometimes it is not just the problem of anger and the fear of anger between two people which has to be resolved if the one who has panic attacks is to be able to give up the attacks. Sometimes it is the problem of love and the fear of love.

Bill, whose panic attacks were destroying his life, was desperate for love. He knew that he needed to be loved, but he shut himself off from his wife and parents.

'Your mother would love you to kiss her and give her a hug,' his wife Felicity said, 'but you never do.'

'I can't help it,' he said to us both, 'I always put up a shield. It's a defence mechanism.'

I put to him the alternatives he was facing. 'If you keep the shield then you will always be frightened and lonely. If you drop the shield and open yourself to other people, you run the risk of being hurt, but you have the possibility of the closeness you desire.'

Bill did not seem ready to make the choice that meant no longer going on being frightened and lonely. I asked him how long he had had this shield, and he said for as long as he could remember. He did not know why. His parents had always been kind and loving to him.

'His mother's told me that Bill was always a good child. Never any trouble. Not like his sister,' said Felicity.

'She's seven years older than me,' said Bill, 'and she's always been spoilt. She'd have terrible temper tantrums when she couldn't get her own way. My parents never hit me, but I can remember my father taking the dog lead to her.'

It was not until much later in our conversation that Bill gave the reason for the barrier he kept up against his wife. 'It's so I can keep her in control. If I dropped it, she'd just go crazy, spending money, doing what she wants.'

'Don't be silly,' said Felicity. 'I'm not like that.'

'You feel that she's just like your sister,' I said.

'I never thought of that,' said Bill, 'her being like my sister.'

We are always in the business of creating meaning, of linking one part of our past experience with our present experience, but we are not always aware that this is what we are doing, simply because we have always done it and no one has ever pointed out to us that this is what we all do *and*, because it is something that we have done from our earliest days and never questioned, we take our construction of our reality as the one and absolute truth. The way we see reality is the way reality is and everyone else in their right minds sees reality just as we do. Unaware and unquestioning, we do not see the bars of the cage we have built for ourselves.

If we want to believe that our way of seeing the world is the right way we have to limit how much of the world we actually observe, because the more we see of the world around us, the more likely we are to have our ideas disconfirmed. This is a major reason why so many people take no interest in politics and current affairs.

Don's GP asked me whether I could help Don out of the terrible tangle he had got himself into. He had started having panic attacks some two years before. He had lost his job, and now here he was, a family man, with little chance of getting another job in a town where there were a lot of unemployed people, and he was still panicking.

Don described the panic attacks as a complete mystery to him. He had always been an anxious sort of person – 'highly strung', he said – but he had been a good worker, learned a trade, and had a reasonably well-paid job, with overtime, in a large factory. He earned enough to support his wife and two children, he was buying his own home, he had a car, and they could afford a decent holiday each year. Then things started changing. He was not quite sure how, but there was not as much overtime and he found that they could not afford a holiday that year. This disappointed him a lot. He always looked forward to a fortnight away with friends whom he was not otherwise able to see for the rest of the year because they lived a long way away. There were other treats that disappeared – days at the seaside for the children, a meal out for his wife and him. When he found that it would be a struggle to buy the children the Christmas presents they wanted, it felt like the last straw. Then he found that he was getting more and more anxious, especially so in the mornings on weekdays. He would wake up with a feeling of dread, and he would have to force himself to get out of bed and get ready for work. He rode a bike to work, and sometimes on the way there he would suddenly be completely overwhelmed with panic. He would have to get off his bike and stand on the side of the road until the shaking diminished and his heart stopped pounding. Sometimes it was so bad he had to go back home and take the day off work. Even if he did force himself to go on it meant he was late for work, and soon he was in trouble for poor time-keeping. He could not explain what was happening, and so, after a lot of unpleasantness with his foreman and others at work, he was dismissed.

He was not too keen to tell me the next part of the story. From what he said it sounded as if he had gone into a sort of manic, defiant state, in which he ceased to be the good, responsible person he had always been and instead indulged himself in some riotous living. However, neither his family nor his conscience could cope with this for long, and the realization that he had wasted what little money he had saved brought him to the stage where he knew he had to do something to get himself out of this mess. But how, especially as his anxiety was ever present and ready to turn into a full-blown panic?

We talked about the changing economic conditions in the town and he showed himself to be like so many good people, caught up in the shifting and diminishing of industry, who blame themselves rather than the political and economic circumstances. Many good people prefer to blame themselves and so feel guilty because that way they preserve an illusion of control ('If I had behaved differently, then the world would be different') rather than see themselves as a helpless victim of huge forces totally beyond their control. Many such people take good care not to inform themselves about economic and political matters because that way they have no knowledge that might challenge their belief that had they been a better person, wiser, more hard working, with greater foresight, they could have avoided the disaster that was upon them. Don had carefully avoided informing himself of the vast economic and political forces that were changing the lives of most people in Britain. He gave himself the excuse that he was not bright enough to learn about these things.

His belief that he was not bright was revealed when we were

discussing how he felt about work. He had always worked hard. His father had owned a village shop and post office, and he had expected Don to work ever since Don had been old enough to do anything useful. He did not know what it was like to go out playing after school. He always had to help in the shop, or run errands, or look after the vegetable garden. His whole life had been one of hard work.

This had not given him the feeling that he was good at doing things. Whenever he had a job to do he worried about whether he would be able to do it. This was the problem about getting another position. Even if he were offered a job, his problems would not be solved. He would feel he was under stress, and under stress he would not cope.

I asked, 'What do you mean, ''under stress''?'

'There'll be something new, something I don't know about, and I'll feel I ought to know about it. I ought to know these things.'

'That sounds like your father or one of your teachers talking.'

He went on to tell me how nervous he got if he had to do mental arithmetic in public, such as when he was playing darts. He always tried not to be the one who kept the score. 'I ought to be able to do it,' he repeated, 'and I can't. I don't want the others to know I can't do it.'

He did not realize that many people cannot do mental arithmetic. I pointed out the immense popularity of pocket calculators to support my argument. I told him I was one of those people who never do mental arithmetic in public. When I was in primary school my teacher would put a column of figures on the blackboard, then point with her long, thin cane at a child who had to stand and add up the figures aloud. If the child faltered or made an error, the cane would be brought down sharply on the child's hand. My hands often felt that cane, for when I was ordered to stand and perform, my mind would become a complete blank, a response I still produce whenever something has to be done with numbers in public. For me mental arithmetic has to be a completely private act.

All this came as a great surprise to Don. He was equally surprised to find that millions of people share his inability to fill in

419

forms. He had no idea that it is a major function of government departments to produce forms that are totally incomprehensible to everyone but the initiated. That way the form-makers feel more powerful and elite and the form-fillers-in feel more powerless and inadequate, and thus are more easily governed. When the first election for the London mayor and Assembly was held a Spoiled Ballot Paper candidate would have romped home.

This kind of political analysis was right outside his experience. He still thought, 'I ought to be able to do these things.'

Where had this belief come from? His childhood. His father had expected him to do things straight off. If Don could not – after all, nobody is born knowing how to do every possible thing, although there are plenty of people who would lead you to believe that they *were* born in this omniscient state – his father would not take the time to show him what to do but, with a 'Here, give that to me', he would impatiently take the task away from Don and do it himself.

Don never had the chance to make mistakes and so learn. He had grown up pretending he could do things and fearing that he could not. When he worked in a factory where everything was laid out for him he could pretend that he could do things.

'Now I feel I've been found out.'

When I asked him why it was important for him to appear to be able to do everything, he said that it made him feel popular. He thought people would reject him, as his father had done, if he could not do things. It had not occurred to him that people who claim to know everything are not always popular. In fact, people who admit to ignorance and inadequacy are often regarded as charming and are very much liked.

Panic attacks produce the fear of panic attacks, and to defend against this fear a person will develop all kinds of patterns for avoiding problem situations. Sometimes as well the person can find himself involved in anxious ruminations that go on and on. Such ruminations can be very wearing, producing all the signs of physical exhaustion, which, of course, the person can then interpret as symptoms of a fatal disease.

If your sense of existence depends on having people around you, then the best way of gathering people around you is for them to see you as being lovable and likable. However, if you doubt that anyone could see anything in you that was lovable or likable, you have to find another way to keep people near you. One most effective method is to get people to need you. Look after other people, meet their needs, be friendly, trustworthy and reliable, and you will not be left on your own. There are some drawbacks to this strategy. Many people who use it fear growing old because then they will not be capable of meeting other people's needs. Many such people come to feel burdened by the responsibilities they have taken on, especially when their interpretation of responsibility is such that there is no limit to the extent of their responsibility.

Ken needed to be needed. That was how he kept people around him. However, he doubted his ability to carry out his work as an electrical engineer perfectly, and so he constantly worried about every task he undertook. When he first came to see me he had all the symptoms of anxiety and tiredness that go with such ruminations, though, fortunately, they occupied so much of his thought he did not have time to worry too much about a fatal illness. He talked of the terrible anxiety he felt over whether he had carried out his tasks correctly or whether he had made a mistake and left the technical work for which he had been responsible in some dangerous state. He worried about jobs he had done many years before and in places where, if there had been any fault, that fact would by now have been discovered. The jobs he worried about most were those where, if there were an electrical fault, people's lives would have been put at risk.

The first few times we met he was grey and drawn and totally serious, but as the months passed he became more relaxed. One day he arrived looking happier than I had seen him before, and during our conversation he frequently smiled and laughed. However, he still had great difficulties. He was waking at 5 a.m. and was unable to get back to sleep. The lack of sleep made his head ache in a most unpleasant way. When he was tired he found it much harder to resist the questions from the Judge.

On previous occasions, when he had described how he would

worry about whether he had carried out some electrical work correctly, he had talked in terms of asking himself questions like 'Did you set that switch correctly?' Now he spoke of these questions coming not from himself but from the Judge.

'I see this Judge sitting up high, and he's asking me these questions, and I'm down here and I'm responsible. I've got to answer these questions. He picks on one thing I did and if I answer that question then he asks another question and on and on. If I can't answer, or if I got it wrong, I'll be responsible. I'll have hurt someone and everyone will know.'

'You'll be shamed in front of everyone?'

'Yes. I'll be blamed for everything. It's the sort of thing . . . suppose I had two balls, a black one and a white one, and I put the black ball in a drawer and locked it and went out of the room and locked the door. The Judge would say to me, "Which ball did you put in the drawer?" and if I say, "The black one," he'd say, "Are you sure? Are you sure you didn't put the white one in the drawer?" I'd have to go back and unlock the door and the drawer and look. He'd go on and on, and at last I'd get to a point where I couldn't answer his questions. It's amazing how much I remember about jobs I did years ago, but even with how much I remember there comes a point where it's impossible to answer, and then it's just terrible. Now I try to stop the Judge. I won't answer his first question, because if I do he'll go on and on. If I ignore him he'll be quiet for a bit, and then he'll start again on something else. He's always up there, looking down on me.'

Ken's mother had always dominated him and everyone else. Her family was her whole life. She wanted the best for them and she would do everything she could to make sure that they got the best and that they did their best. So shop girls would hide when she came into the shop and greengrocers would suffer her critical inspection of their fruit and vegetables. Her son submitted to her demands and tried to please her. If he did not she would shame him.

'That's the way it was. I didn't know any different. That was the way things always were,' he said. However, later he said, 'I let my sons please themselves. I don't tell them what to do.'

'So you did know, and you wouldn't do to your sons what your mother did to you.'

'I must have, I suppose.'

It had not occurred to him that the Judge might be his mother, demanding that he justify his existence, measure up to her standards and achieve what she wanted him to achieve. The critical parent of our childhood can become our conscience, the eye that is always upon us, making us aware that we are ourselves and filling us with shame that we are as we are, the judge that sees everything we do and finds us guilty of our actions.

The next time Ken came to see me he said, 'I've realized that in my life I've made only two decisions who I'd marry and what car I'd buy. Everything else my mother has decided for me.'

Three months later Ken returned after a holiday. It had been a good holiday, but often, as he had stretched out in the sun, the Judge would start his questioning. Ken said, 'I get very careful in what I say to people. For instance, I might notice that you had a bald tyre on your car. I might say to you, "You ought to get that changed." Then later I'd think, "She'd better make sure she's tightened the nuts properly," and then this would start on me. I'd be worrying about whether you'd tightened the wheel nuts. Next time I saw you I'd have to ask you about the tyre, and I'd say, "Did you tighten the wheel nuts?" I'd make a joke of it, mind, but I'd have to say it.'

He told me how some time ago he had given an old car to the local technical college for their Youth Training Scheme and then spent months worrying that the students might have an accident and that he would be blamed. He said, 'It didn't matter that their teachers are trained. If something went wrong, it would be my fault.'

We talked about his sense of responsibility, which went far beyond what would ordinarily be expected. He took upon himself responsibility for others, and then punished himself for failing, or perhaps failing to meet his responsibilities. He could not leave others to be responsible for themselves but had to take all responsibility on himself.

'It's like I'm God,' he said, 'responsible for everybody.'

When we feel shame we feel that we are powerless in the eye of the beholder. To overcome the powerlessness and passivity of shame we can totally deny that we are so, and claim complete power and freedom of activity. However, the advantage of being powerless is that we are not responsible for what happens. The disadvantage of being completely powerful is that we are totally responsible. Poor Ken. He had tried to overcome his sense of powerlessness, and, without ever once enjoying the heady delights of complete power (as an extravert using the defence of mania will do), he went straight to the great disadvantage of power, total responsibility.

Now he had to find a point somewhere between a sense of complete helplessness and a sense of complete power, and from that confront the analysis that is presented to all human beings: 'What in life are my responsibilities and what responsibilities belong to other people?' People who had parents who dominated them as children always have difficulty in understanding what responsibility is and in defining the limits of their own responsibility. As children they often heard their parents telling them to be responsible, and they did not realize that what their parents called responsibility was really obedience. The only way parents can give their children a sense of responsibility is to give them the freedom to make choices, and, with those choices, mistakes. Parents who need to be dominant are people who are so frightened of themselves and their world that they cannot give their children the freedom to learn courage.

Ken's anxieties and responsibilities were focused on objects in external reality that were in some way mechanical. All his attention was directed outward. Someone who knew him and knew he was coming to see me told me that his house contained not one book, magazine or newspaper. His sense of himself was based on being a practical person. His way of relating to people was to solve their practical problems. His sense of being a person had always been threatened by his mother, and she lived inside him as the Judge, but rather than acknowledge that the source of his anxiety was inside him he located it outside himself in practical, mechanical matters.

In an article in the *Observer*, a psychology student, Melanie Wiseman, described the problem she had developed of being touched. She said,

'I had a problem having my blood pressure taken, and then it spread. Then I couldn't have the insides of my wrists touched, or my arms, or the backs of my knees, or the insides of my feet, or my armpits, or my neck.' Her boyfriend simply knew what he could and could not touch.

Wiseman kept her arms covered at all times. But then summer would come along, and suddenly everybody would be baring their arms and legs. 'I could see the backs of other people's legs and the insides of their arms, which was quite traumatic. You worry about what might happen: what if they fell over something sharp, that would really hurt, and there are lots of blood vessels close to the surface and you'd bleed a lot. Because they didn't fold themselves up or cover themselves up, I felt they were really vulnerable.'

Just talking about her phobia to her mother caused her to black out, and when she joined a new practice and the doctor insisted she have her blood pressure taken, she had a full-blown panic attack in the waiting room: 'I nearly passed out. I could hardly breathe, and I was crying uncontrollably.'[1]

Melanie Wiseman came to feel that she could no longer live her life in that way, and so she consulted a psychologist, Linda Blair, at the University of Bath, who had found that a short series of cognitive therapy sessions could be very successful in these cases. Linda said, 'It doesn't matter if these people have been having these phobias for twenty years or one month. If they're motivated to get over it, that's all it takes.'

Being motivated to change – that is the starting point.

Relinquishing Panic, Phobias and Fear

Cherie was so pretty and so charming that it seemed inconceivable that she would have any problems in meeting people and going out. If you had met her you would have thought that to give herself confidence all she needed to do was to look in the mirror. However, if I said anything like that to her, as I sometimes did, she would look at me as if I were crazy. I suspected that she thought that I said such things, not because I meant them, but because it was my job to make her feel better. She was too kind a person to put such ungracious thoughts into words.

She told me of terrible panics and of her fear of such panics. She could not possibly travel by bus, so she bought a car and learned to drive. This solved some of her practical problems, but even if she could drive into town she still found it well nigh impossible to get out of the car and go into the shops. Also, she was running out of excuses as to why she could not meet for the first time her boyfriend's family and friends. She could manage visiting people she knew very well, but visits to acquaintances and strangers were a torture she could no longer inflict upon herself. It was getting into these places which was so difficult. If she achieved it and did not make a fool of herself by shaking or going red, then she might manage. However, more and more those first few minutes of shopping and visiting became like some high unscalable wall. The social things she could actually manage to do were becoming fewer and fewer.

There were other things she could not do as well, such as standing up for herself. When the electricity bill for the flat she shared with two other girls was extra large because one of the girls had insisted on keeping the radiator on in her bedroom all night that winter, Cherie dared not argue that a three-way split of the bill was not fair. She paid more than she thought she should have, and despised herself for doing so. She despised herself too because she was so pitifully grateful that her boyfriend had come back to her after they had split up and he had started going out with someone else, but along with her gratitude to him was the belief that when he said he loved her he was lying and that one day he would leave her for good. Sometimes she found herself wishing that he would go now so that the agony of waiting for his defection would be over.

She told me these things about herself simply because of the relief of being able to talk about them to someone. She did not think her fear of getting angry and her belief that anyone who said he loved and admired her was either a fool or a liar had anything to do with her panics. She rather liked the psychiatrist's definition of the panics as an illness, something that had come upon her like a bad attack of flu and which, if she was lucky, would, like flu, go away. She did not know whether or not to be grateful when I pointed out to her something which the psychiatrist had failed to tell her – that the benzodiazepine he had prescribed for her was addictive and that she should use it sparingly.

She was surprised when I asked her about her childhood. Surely I did not think things that had happened all that long ago (when you're twenty, childhood is a long time ago) had any effect on her now?

She said that she remembered very little of her childhood and supposed it to have been quite ordinary. She then went on to tell me of a childhood far from ordinary, of one fraught with pain and suffering and great uncertainty. It was only over many months that the story emerged. She told me of her father's painful death from cancer when she was fourteen, and how, on what proved to be his last day, she was rude to him, and he died, without her having the chance to say goodbye and ask for his forgiveness. Not that she would have dared to ask, or even think (consciously, that is) that he owed her this. But he did. For, when she was a tiny girl, he and her mother had inflicted on her the most terrible pain.

Her parents may have loved one another, but any sign of their affection was blotted out by their fights. It would begin with her mother starting to nag and criticize her father and him becoming silent. Quick to recognize the beginning of a fight, Cherie would try to stop them, to deflect their attention to something else. Sometimes she was successful, sometimes not. Then she would hide under the table while the fight raged over her head. Her mother would goad her father until, in violent anger, he would turn on her and hit her. Her mother would fight back, until he would leave, slamming out of the house, declaring that he would not return.

Even when he had not left the house in a rage her father was often away because of his work. Alone with her daughter, Cherie's mother would frequently vent her frustration and anger and her disappointment with her life onto her small daughter. It was not her mother's blows which frightened Cherie so much as her mother's oft-repeated words 'If it wasn't for you I wouldn't be here'. Cherie felt that she had no right to be in her parents' house. Indeed, she had no right to exist at all.

When Cherie and I had a look at the practical dimensions of her panic problem, where she could not go and what she could not do, it became apparent, at least to me, that the territory which she saw as dangerous was territory that belonged to other people, especially people whom she did not know very well. She was all right in her own home, in her mother's home (she and Cherie got along very well together once she had grown up), in the small office where she worked, where she knew everybody, in her own car and in what might be called common property like a street. Where she felt in danger was in territory that belonged to other people who could tell her that she had no right to be there and who could throw her out. It did not matter whether the shop assistants and her boyfriend's relatives and friends were pleasant to her. She knew that pleasantness could hide an uncontrolled rage, and that the most loving of people could become violently rejecting. When she went into territory that she knew was dangerous, she did not need, or want, to bring to mind the reasons why she knew it was dangerous. All she felt was the fear and the need to escape. When she could not escape, she panicked.

Cherie listened to my description of the meaning of her fear with great interest. I did not know whether it made any great difference to her. There was something else I said which she remembered and reminded me of the next time she came to see me. There was a gap of more than six months between these two visits. Cherie had not found it necessary to make another appointment in that time. We worked on the understanding that, as it was hard for her to get time off work, she would phone and make an appointment whenever she felt the need and could fit it in with the demands of her job.

On this occasion she looked more relaxed and free than I had ever seen her. She said, 'Do you remember, you said to me that if I changed I might find that my boyfriend wasn't as important to me as I thought? Well, I didn't believe you at the time, but you were right.'

Then she told me how she had decided to take an evening job working in the local sports centre as a receptionist. There she had met this wonderful man. She was still very fond of her boyfriend, but this man, well, he was different. And he thought she was wonderful too. The problem was not just that she had to decide between her boyfriend and this wonderful man, but that he was working here for just a few months. His home was in London. She had never been to London.

Cherie had already decided what she was going to do. All she wanted from me was support, and some advice about driving to London. She had worked out that the horrors of driving on the motorway to London were as nothing compared to the horror of letting your life slip away and doing nothing of significance and meaning with it.

To retrieve the devastating childhood experiences that laid the foundations for anxiety and panic attacks in later life, and to reassess them in the light of adult knowledge and experiences, it is very helpful if some of the adults who played a part in the childhood experiences also take part in the retrieval and reconstructing of the past, sometimes simply by supplying more information and sometimes by sharing in mutual reconciliation and forgiveness. Unfortunately, this is not always possible.

Sometimes our parents have died before we reach the stage of reassessment. Sometimes our parents are not prepared to help us reassess, for it involves a reappraisal of their own past actions. A friend told me how, having reached a point in her therapy where she could understand and accept her mother's actions towards her which had caused her great pain, she went to her mother and said,

'Mother, I forgive you.' Whereupon her mother flew into a rage and said, 'How dare you forgive me! I've never done anything which requires forgiveness.'

Sometimes we are lucky. Our parents are alive and they are prepared to help us reassess.

Bill had such good fortune, although it took him many months to realize that it was necessary to talk to his mother.

When Bill first came to see me all he could talk about was the terrifying physical symptoms of a major panic attack. He had had several, the worst being when one day, far from home, he had collapsed on the grass verge beside the road where he had been driving. Everything he had ever dreaded – a heart attack, total helplessness, death – seemed to him to be happening there. Friends got him home, and after that he dared not go very far from his house. He could no longer tolerate crowded rooms without an easy exit. He gave up playing squash, running, and going for a drink at his local, all things that he used to enjoy very much. He had always been convinced that he would die of a cardiac arrest, and now he feared that a panic attack would result in such a fatal outcome. So he tried to avoid all the situations that might provoke one, but he was not always successful, and even when he went for days without an attack, he was waiting anxiously for the next one to occur.

At first Bill thought my interest in his life was quite pointless. All he wanted me to do was to produce the magic word, or wave the magic wand, and all his panics would disappear. He got somewhat irritated with me for not doing this, but, on the other hand, I did sit and listen to him, and this was more than his wife and parents would do. Felicity found his complaining very wearisome, especially when he was also so bad tempered and unapproachable. He did not like to talk to his parents about his problems, because he did not want to worry his mother (she had high blood pressure) and he did not want to let his father know just how weak he was. 'He's twice the man I am,' he would say, as he told me of how active and determined his father was, even though he was well into his seventies.

Bill admired his father tremendously and would never dream of criticizing him, even when he told me of one vivid memory he had of his childhood, when his elder sister was very angry and disobedient and his father thrashed her with the dog lead. He remembered her afterwards lying on the floor and crying, but he felt no sympathy for her. His father had done the right thing. It was at that time that Bill resolved never to get angry or to disobey his father. He never linked this episode with his belief that he was weaker than his father. Yet, as his father had never let him win an argument, Bill could only grow up with the belief that he could never measure up to his father, a truly wonderful man.

Bill found his mother to be equally wonderful. She was always loving, always kind. 'I was spoilt,' he said, as a way of explaining how such perfect parents could have such a weak man as a son. They had loved him too much. He wished his marriage was as idyllically happy as his parents' marriage had always been.

He spoke of his childhood as being extremely happy, yet, when I asked him about it, there was remarkably little that he could remember. He was uncertain about which schools he went to and when he went to them. This forgetting of childhood, which I come across often in my work, never fails to amaze me. I can run the memories I have of my childhood through my mind like a film, I can remember the names of people from fifty years ago more easily than the names of people I met fifty minutes ago, and if I want to remember when some event took place all I have to do is bring a picture of it to mind, judge where I was and how tall I was within that picture, and I can arrive at a date and a place and a memory of what went on and how I felt. These are certainly not all happy memories, but they are important to me, and if I woke up one morning and found that they had gone I would be bereft. Yet so many of the people who report that they do not remember their childhood seem indifferent to this situation. Most people, extraverts and introverts, remember their childhoods, but those who do not are usually extraverts who rely heavily on the defence of repression. Some introverts say they do not remember their childhood, but when they talk about it they discount, rather than fail to remember, traumatic events by saying that these events did not affect them in any way and therefore did not need to be remembered. What is being denied here is emotion.

Bill and I went on talking over a number of months. Then Bill's mother took ill and went into hospital. Bill was ashamed that he could not overcome his fear of hospitals to go and visit her, but as soon as she was home again he could return to his usual habit of calling in to see her every day. One day he decided to ask her about his early childhood. He had started to feel curious about the events he could not remember. He began by telling her a little bit more about his 'nerves' and about his visits to me.

Bill's mother shocked and amazed him by saying that when she was pregnant with him she had suffered with her nerves just like him. Further, she said that her marriage then had been far from happy.

Bill came to see me soon after this conversation and told me about it with a mixture of surprise and pleasure. As we were talking he started to remember scenes from his childhood. They came into his mind like new events, yet he recognized them with all the joy and amazement we feel when we find some long-lost treasure hidden in a trunk.

First, he remembered walking down the garden, looking over the fields and feeling the strange sensations that he now knew to be panic, and wondering what these feelings were. He could only have been about eight, for when he was nine they had moved to another house.

Then he remembered walking home from school and feeling that he and everything he saw was somehow unreal. He knew that feeling only too well in his adult life, but he had never thought that he could have known it all those years ago.

He remembered, when he was about six, seeing a man on the bus on the way to school each day and wanting this man to be his father. He described a kindly, gentle, fatherly man. This memory puzzled him. He could not yet see that when he was six he knew his own father to be harsh, dangerous and powerful, and he longed for a father who was loving and kind.

Having retrieved these memories and more, Bill was then able

432

to tell me what it was that really terrified him about death. Up till then, in many conversations about his panic attacks and his belief that he would die of a heart attack (the form of death that terrified him the most), he had never been able to answer my question 'What's so terrible about dying?' Now he could speak of 'a sense of impending doom' and the panics as being a reaction to this. He had always sensed 'a force of evil' which was much more effective than 'the force for good'. He feared death because he felt that beyond death lay 'hellfire and damnation'.

That conversation with his mother was the turning point for Bill. It freed him to get on with his life. He could distinguish between the parents of his childhood and the parents he had now, and see that while they had not been the wisest and kindest of parents then, they had gained in wisdom and kindness. He did not have to see them as bad, just human. He had no need to protect their reputation at the expense of his own. It was all right to feel good about himself.

Often, in the negotiations that go on at the beginning of therapy, a client will ask, 'How long is this course of therapy going to last? How long will it take for me to get better?' Different therapists have different answers. My truthful answer is that I just do not know, and that is because I do not know what part luck will play in it. It was none of my doing that Bill's mother had the courage to confront what must have been a very painful part of her life and talk about it with Bill. Also, a client's strengths are not apparent in a first interview, when the client is busy talking of all his deficits and weaknesses. I did not know that, for all his uncertainty about himself, Bill never felt that his panic attacks were something so shameful that he could not talk about them with other people whom he met in the course of his work. Over the time he was coming to see me he met a large number of people who proved to be suffering from some form of anxiety and depression. He would enter into conversations with them, recommend my book on depression (something I approved of enormously) and discuss ways and means of coping and becoming more confident. He seemed to be running a continuous therapy group across the town.

Clearly all this helped him to change. At our last meeting he told me that Felicity had said that he was now like a stranger to her. She would have to get to know him all over again. Fortunately, or so it seemed from what he told me about the change in their relationship (they no longer lay without touching side by side in bed), he had become the kind of stranger she approved of very much.

When we are children we experience threats to our sense of being a person, and sometimes these threats can all but overwhelm us. Often such threats are of being abandoned and rejected, something all children fear, but for extravert children these are the greatest threats of all. In adult life situations can arise which seem like action replays of childhood experiences. Our emotional response to the adult situation is then multiplied many times by our emotions from the past. Such experiences can be entirely pleasurable, such as when we meet a person who seems to us to be like someone we once loved. We feel a rush of affection for that person, or even the magical rush of falling in love. Far less happily, the new situation can instantly remind us of once being abandoned and rejected, and we relive the terror we felt then. We can experience this terror as the aloneness of dying, as the shame and the humiliating rejection that we believe would follow some disgraceful behaviour, such as fainting or vomiting in public. Or it can be experienced as disappearing into a vast nothingness, as is felt by those who fear to go into an open space or even face an open window for fear of being swallowed up by the sky.

In this case, because the first experience was so painful, the memory of it has been repressed, although the effects of it, which are a loss of self-confidence and a persistent anxiety, continue into adult life.

Because the memory of the original situation has been repressed, the person has not developed the ability to link all the past and present events of his life into one continuous, meaningful story, and to see the significance of present events in the context of his whole life and thus gain mastery over them. So when a situation arises which is reminiscent of the earlier, annihilating one, he cannot master it by recognizing that he is now an adult, not a child, and that he is no longer helplessly dependent on powerful and dangerous adults whom he is not allowed to see as bad.

Because he cannot name the fear he feels in the context of his personal life, he experiences it as alien, which makes it all the more frightening. The fear has to be named and explained, so he looks for a name and an explanation where extraverts always look, in external reality that is – in his body and in the place where the fear arose. Thus he interprets the physical concomitants of fear as the symptoms of a fatal illness, he avoids the places where the fear arose, he becomes sure that other people despise and reject him, or he identifies an animal, insect or object that bears some intrinsic but slight danger as being capable of immense, incalculable harm. The careful monitoring of bodily sensations, the anxious thoughts about the physical sensations which are observed, and the avoidance rituals that are developed all act as a defence against overwhelming fear.

This form of defence can rapidly lead the person into living a severely circumscribed life, as more and more places are identified as 'no-go' areas. To gain the courage to leave this defensive position, the person needs to do two things simultaneously.

One is to retrieve the hidden memories, so as to construct the continuous story of his life, to see his childhood from two perspectives, that of himself as a child and as an adult, and thus to understand the meaning of the great fear which he sees as threatening to overwhelm him.

At the same time he needs to integrate this new experience with his experiences in his external reality by entering the 'no-go' areas of his territory. He can do this gradually (perhaps a slightly longer journey each day) or all at once (doing what he fears most to do), but whichever option he takes, by acting differently in his external reality he changes his internal reality by coming to perceive himself as stronger and more capable.

However, to achieve all this he needs his loved ones to change. They have to be prepared to see him differently and to support his efforts to find increased autonomy and independence. They also have to inspect their own attitudes to anger and to recognize their own anxieties about its expression.

The changes in his internal reality which will allow him to relinquish his rigid defences altogether is the understanding that *'Just because I am alone it doesn't mean that that will be the end of me'*.

Changing is not easy because to change the person has to confront the fear that he is running away from. He may, under gentle questioning, admit to himself that his great fear is behaving in such a way that people reject him, and he may be able to admit that there is an even greater fear, and that is being rejected and abandoned, because that would mean the annihilation of his sense of being a person. However, he can tolerate such questioning only when the subject under discussion concerns his being afraid of something, be it dying, vomiting, social situations or spiders. What he finds hard, even impossible, to tolerate is examining any situation in which his dominant emotion was not fear but anger. When a therapist, keen to establish the connections between past experiences and present difficulties, becomes interested in some anecdote concerning an experience in which he was angry but dared not admit his anger even to himself he becomes bland, feigns boredom, and dismisses any interpretation the therapist may make. This was what Lucy did when I linked an incident with her cousin's daughter with an incident in her own childhood. She had not dared be angry with her parents, and she dared not be angry with her cousin. As she saw it, anger always destroyed relationships.

Yet anger is pride's response to insult.

People who have to resort to a desperate defence have been insulted again and again throughout their life. Their problem is not that they are angry but that they are frightened of their anger. Fear of anger leads us to lie and dissemble. Adrian Wells, a leader in the field of cognitive therapy in the treatment of social phobia, wrote, 'The person with social phobia may censor information, engage in subtle avoidance in the therapy situation, or act in a manner that is distracting to the therapist.'[2]

When psychologists first took an interest in people with phobias they used simple behavioural methods to help them overcome their fear. These methods were probably as old as our species is, and were developed to ensure our physical survival. There are two basic methods of overcoming fear of a situation or object – the sudden method and the slow. The sudden method is: If your horse throws you, get back in the saddle immediately. The slow is: If you are afraid of deep water, enter the water each day and each time go a little farther out. The early behaviourist psychologists were utterly uninterested in what their clients thought and felt. In those days I found that if I offered an explanation about why behaviour therapy worked with some people and not with others in terms of how the person saw the situation, the behaviourists reacted with scorn and anger.

Some of these behaviourists abandoned this field of endeavour, and some, like Isaac Marks at the Institute of Psychiatry, kept on working, refining and elaborating their techniques, and achieving impressive results. Some years ago I heard Isaac Marks speaking modestly, as he always did, about his work but regretting that, while the drug companies gave lavishly to research looking at the effects of drugs on manifestations of anxiety, these companies would not assist in funding his kind of research, even though cognitive behavioural methods achieved long-lasting improvements while the anti-anxiety drugs, the benzodiazepines, achieved little more than dependence on the drug. But then turkeys don't vote for Christmas, do they?

As time went by many behaviourists took a gradually increasing interest in their subjects' point of view and transformed themselves into cognitive behavioural therapists. Now some cognitive therapists are even becoming interested in what they once dismissed as unscientific Freudian nonsense. Chris Brewin and Bernice Andrews wrote, 'After many years of neglect, cognitive behaviour therapists are becoming more and more interested in defence mechanisms, particularly the conscious suppression or avoidance of threatening thoughts and feelings.'[3]

Adrian Wells, in developing effective treatments for social phobia, categorized a person's thoughts, feelings and behaviour according to categories of negative automatic thoughts, self-processing and safety behaviours. Thus one person reported that in a social situation she would always think, 'I don't know what to say. People will think I'm stupid.' Self-processing for this person was described as 'self-conscious; image of self as a plain, unintelligent, "bimbo"'. She described her safety behaviours as 'Avoid eye contact, don't draw attention to yourself, let partner do the talking, plan what to say, pretend to be interested in something.'[4]

Cognitive therapists talk about 'schemas', sets of ideas that the person treats as absolute, unquestionable beliefs which inform the decisions the person makes. Adrian Wells divided the schemas in social phobia into unconditional beliefs, e.g., 'I'm weird', 'I'm unlikable', 'I'm a failure/unacceptable'; conditional assumptions, e.g., 'If people see I'm anxious they will think I'm weak and pathetic', 'If I get my words wrong people will think I'm stupid'; and rigid rules, e.g., 'I should always be able to cope', 'I need to be liked by everyone'.[5]

Setting such thoughts out in these ways makes it easy for the person to look at them objectively, assess their probability of being an accurate representation of the situation, and to devise alternative, less self-defeating ways of thinking. Such self-examination can be continued for the rest of his life.

Anyone who is using a desperate defence is completely self-involved. If you are alone in a fortress that is besieged by a clamorous army determined to destroy your defences and kill you, you do not spend any time observing the soldiers disinterestedly, wondering how they see things. Similarly, if you are trying to survive a cocktail party without making a complete idiot of yourself, you are too busy trying not to sweat or tremble or stammer to be interested in the people around you.

Adrian Wells came to the conclusion that if in a social situation you focused your attention on the people around you instead of on yourself, you would discover that, not only were you mistaken in your assumption that they were all busy noticing you in order to reject you, but they were not noticing you at all. In fact, they were not interested in you. This may be a discovery you do not wish to make. A great many people, if offered the choice of being held in the hostile gaze of another person or being completely ignored, choose the hostile gaze because they fear that if they are ignored they will disappear.

Yet the hard truth is that most people are so wrapped up in themselves that they observe very little of the people around them. In 1936 Dale Carnegie wrote a book, *How to Win Friends and Influence People*, that remains a bestseller to this day. In this he pointed out that if you want people to like you you have to show them that you are interested in them. Ask them about themselves and listen with obvious interest to their answers, and they will love you. They may not take an interest in you – indeed, your interest in them may be so satisfying that they will not relinquish it for a second – but you will at least find that your being interested in them passes the time, and soon the social situation you feared will come to an end. If you feel insignificant then recognizing that people are not interested in you can be disheartening, but remember that, when you get confidence in yourself, as you will if you work at it, you will find that you do not need other people to notice you. You discover just how much you can get away with if you are simply yourself without any pretence or anxiety.

Attention training, as developed by Adrian Wells and his colleagues, can help you gain this wonderful liberating understanding.[6] If Adrian could get us all to pay careful attention to other people instead of being absorbed in ourselves, how very different our society would be!

The number of people needing help for chronic anxiety and various phobias is far greater than mental health resources can provide. Some psychologists have developed group and individual self-help methods whereby people can learn to understand the physical symptoms they experience and to use relaxation and other methods for reducing and managing their anxiety.

Jim White and his colleagues in Glasgow developed what they call 'large group didactic anxiety management' courses and reported good results.[7] Jim also created what he called Stresspac, a seventy-nine-page booklet and a relaxation tape. A three-year follow-up of individuals using Stresspac showed that it was effective in teaching people ways of managing and overcoming their anxiety.[8] More recently Jim and colleagues developed a cognitive behavioural computer therapy program for anxiety disorders. Six months after the pilot study was held in a GP clinic the results showed that 'This approach was effective and was welcomed by patients.'[9]

There are now quite a number of self-help books, tapes and computer programs dealing with anxiety and phobias. They can be extremely helpful, but it is a matter of finding something in which the language and general tone are right for you. No one wants to be preached at or talked down to, and some of these authors are relentlessly cheerful and seem never to have discovered that there really is a nasty, dangerous world out there, as well as a very delightful one.

Our ability to experience fear helps us survive, but for a happy life we need to be able to assess the dangers realistically, to understand why we get frightened, and to develop flexible, effective strategies for dealing with the dangers. Often it is wise to run away from external dangers, but it is never wise to run away from the fear within us.

Chapter Ten

Turning Fear into Mania

'Sean is everything I'm not. He's warm, outgoing, exciting, wonderful company, marvellous with other people. He's got hosts of friends. People love him. He's so creative. He gets things done. And so easy going. Nothing upsets him. He never gets angry – well, not until now.' Jill twisted her handkerchief and looked out of the window, blinking back tears. She was elegantly, very expensively dressed. Sean must be doing well, I thought.

I had known Sean slightly for nearly twenty years. He had been a student in business studies when I first knew him, and we had a mutual friend who kept me informed of his exploits. He added to his income by gambling and was extraordinarily successful. He put some big winnings into a vending-machine business which gave him a good income, but then, apparently, he had expanded too rapidly, did not consolidate, and went bust.

Sean bounced back remarkably quickly, going into a paper towel business with a partner. He was doing well – I remember him calling to see my friend and driving a large, flashy, expensive car – when suddenly he vanished abroad. There was talk of something shady, but all seemed well when he returned a few years later. I had heard astonishing tales of his capacity for hard work and hard play, but all his activity had apparently paid off. I had also heard tales of a dark undercurrent in his life – a suicide attempt in his late teens, a charge of attempted murder in Hong Kong, something to do with a woman. A good lawyer had got him off.

I had not met Jill until now. She had come on my friend's recommendation to ask for help for Sean. She told me that Sean had changed. Instead of being the warm, outgoing, loving person that she had known him to be, he had turned on Jill, abusing her, telling her he was tired of her continual nagging. He had taken to staying away from home, not telling her where he was, but leaving evidence lying around the house which made it clear that he was with other women. He was also buying things.

'There are three new cars sitting in the driveway at home,' Jill said, 'and this morning a white grand piano was delivered. Neither of us can play the piano.'

'Does Sean think there is anything wrong with him?' I asked.

'No,' said Jill. 'He thinks everything he is doing and saying is perfectly all right.'

Sean did agree to talk to me but there was no way he was going to acknowledge that his excesses of spending and his cruelty to Jill had anything to do with the terror he felt when Jill began to press him to agree to her wish to have a baby, though in a joking way he explained why he did not want a child. A baby, he felt, would make demands and usurp his place in Jill's affections. He joked about her being a nagging wife, but his complaints showed that he regarded her demands as unjustified and unfair, as he did the demands that his mother made on him as a child. He wanted to be free of all demands. However, he knew that if he rejected the demands that people made on him he himself was likely to be rejected, and that he could not live with.

He sought a solution to this conflict by action in his external reality. He vented his anger and hate on Jill, while becoming increasingly active in reassuring himself of his attractiveness to other people, especially women, and of his belief that the possession of objects was as satisfactory as the possession of relationships with people. As each of these reassurances failed to satisfy him, his activity increased.

People who use the defence of phobias turn their backs on their internal reality, concentrate on external reality and locate their fears there. People who use the defence of mania do not simply turn their backs on their internal reality; they run as fast as they can into their external reality. By doing this they hope to leave behind not only their fear but their anger, envy, jealousy, murderous rage and hate.

To understand this we need to know how we all operate in the two realities we live in, the reality of what goes on around us and the reality of what goes on inside us. When we are born we are immediately presented with the task of making sense of what is happening. In the first few months of life we gradually become aware that we live in these two realities. Learning to differentiate the two is difficult. Young children have to learn how to distinguish between a dream, a daydream, and what is actually going on. Even as adults we can make mistakes in this. We may feel that a dream we had actually happened, or that an actual event is in a dream. If as children we do not lay the foundations for knowing ourselves to be valuable and acceptable, we find it harder in later life to maintain the distinction between internal and external reality. We may, as extraverts, see our external reality as being dark and dangerous, without recognizing that such a perception of darkness and danger comes from within us; or we may, as introverts, hear voices that we think are in our external reality when in fact these are memories of voices we once heard.

Even if we succeed in performing the tasks of identifying internal and external reality and of creating considerable self-confidence, we still perceive a difference in the degree of reality in our internal and external worlds. For introverts, internal reality is more real than external reality. They do not doubt the reality of what they think and feel, but they can easily doubt the reality of what they are seeing and hearing. For extraverts, external reality is more real than internal reality. They can easily doubt the reality of what they think and feel, but they do not doubt the reality of what they see and hear. Under stress, we retreat to the reality in which we feel more secure. Introverts retreat into themselves. Extraverts retreat from themselves into their external reality.

Those of us who cope with life, more or less, have spent considerable time increasing our competence in our less real reality. As introverts we have consciously acquired social skills, and as extraverts we have, equally consciously, familiarized ourselves with our internal world. However, there are many introverts who regard external reality in the way that sixteenth-century Europeans regarded the Antipodes – an upside-down world inhabited by monsters – and many extraverts who regard their internal reality as a mystery, and not a mystery that they wish to unravel.

Spike Milligan's books about his wartime experiences and his fantasies about those experiences are very funny, but they are concerned with events and actions, not about thoughts, feelings and reflections. He describes events in minute detail, recounting names and places and conversations, but what he does not describe in any detail at all are the terrible periods of mania and depression which often came close to destroying him. He mentions them in passing only when necessary for the description of another event. Even less does he try to describe and analyse his internal reality so as to understand it and to link it to the events in his life. In the volume *Where Have All the Bullets Gone?*, which covers the period when he was in a military psychiatric hospital, there are only two sentences concerning his internal reality. In 1944 he was on leave in London with his girlfriend:

> We sat at night and listened to Harry Parry and the Radio Rhythm Club with Benny Lee. I also remember how her mother made sensational roast beef and Yorkshire pudding for Sunday lunch. I now know that I was, in my mind, living in a dream. I was floating on other people's emotions, and only concerned with my own which were very childlike, naive, and basically, deep down, there was a yearning for recognition.[1]

We all fantasize, extraverts and introverts, and many of these fantasies are aimed at compensating us for what we have suffered and lost. The greater our suffering and loss, the greater and more omnipotent our fantasies. The opposite of annihilation can be conceived of not as survival but as omnipotence. This is the opposite chosen by the child who is under major threat, and thus the child goes on to create fantasies of omnipotence and to plan to gain through admiration what he cannot gain through love. Both introvert and extravert children have such fantasies, but in the execution of them extraverts are more likely to succeed. Because they feel alone and threatened, introvert children retreat into the safety of their internal reality, and so may not develop a good understanding of what the world regards as success. Unless they have some special talent which some adult recognizes and fosters, thus giving the child a direction to follow, the introvert child may develop fantasies and practices that take him farther and farther from ordinary life and into the life of a proud but isolated eccentric.

Whether we are under threat of annihilation or not, introvert fantasies are about achievement. The introvert may dream of an achievement that leads to many people looking at him with admiration and awe, but such a response from other people is not essential because the introvert is his own judge of achievement. Extravert fantasies may also be about achievement, but it is the audience that adores and admires the extravert which is essential. Extravert fantasies are about surrounding the dreamer with people who admire and adore him. Shy extraverts, who like to think of themselves as loners, often develop elaborate games and pastimes which people their life with fantasy figures.

Melvyn, a self-described loner, very depressed and anxious, told me how in his childhood he spent many hours playing a game called 'Owzat', where the player (it could be played by two people, but he played it on his own) threw a dice to represent the runs being made by two cricket teams. The results of matches won or lost were recorded in score books. He created a league of cricket teams, a host of men who became as real to him as his parents (and much nicer) and he enjoyed the omnipotent power of being the high-scoring batsman, the powerful bowler, the intrepid fieldsman, the sagacious umpire, while at the same time controlling all the play and determining its outcome (when we play games on our own we often cheat).

By fourteen, David Wigoder was putting his fantasies into action.

Every experience excited me and it seemed unimportant whether the excitement was fearful or pleasurable, provided that something, anything, was happening. Until I was fourteen, apart from outings with my sister, I did most things on my own. At school I told lies, describing an imaginary circle of friends, because none of the boys I knew appeared to spend as much time on their own as I did. At home, when I went out, I often told more lies, telling my parents that I was meeting a friend when mostly I went alone to the cinemas or parks. Some days, during school holidays, I bought a ticket on the Underground, and for a few pennies I travelled for hours from the beginning to the end of each separate route. Provided that I never left the stations, and merely crossed from one platform to another, it seemed like an interesting way to cure boredom. I forced myself to believe that it was exciting, travelling for five hours in different directions, ending up where I'd begun. I created a private existence, silently entertaining myself, and fantasized about each small event until it developed into a big, exciting drama.[2]

If the extravert fears that no one could possibly adore and admire him, then his fantasy will concern controlling many people. He will look after them in wonderful, though conventional, ways, and, though they may not love him, they will feel for him an undying gratitude which will ensure they will never leave him. Matthew, an accountant, told me about his fantasy of becoming financial adviser to a rich aristocratic family who had little idea how to look after their wealth and possessions. He would not simply sort out their finances but guide them in all their decisions so they could live more orderly, happy lives. For this the family would be eternally grateful.

Extravert fantasies are about actions. The psychoanalyst Donald Winnicott, in describing omnipotent fantasies that the extravert using the manic defence creates, wrote:

In the ordinary extrovert book of adventure we often see how the author made a flight to day-dreaming in childhood, and then made use of external reality in this same flight. He is not conscious of the inner depressive anxiety from which he has fled. He has led a life full of incident and adventure, and this may be accurately told. But the impression left on the reader is of a relatively shallow personality, for this very reason, that the author adventurer has had to base his life on the denial of personal internal reality. One turns with relief from such writers to others who can tolerate depressive anxiety and doubt.[3]

That Donald Winnicott was an intellectual introvert is shown by his last sentence. Many people relax with and enjoy tales of adventure that do not require great thought on the part of the reader.

Extraverts who are comfortable in themselves usually believe that the best way to deal with anxiety is to be busy. If you can, act to solve the problem that is troubling you, and, if this is not possible, keep busy. However, if the anxiety increases and self-confidence diminishes, the person may become busier and busier, and sooner or later reach a stage where he is no longer taking sensible account of what needs to be taken account of. Even so, he enjoys the excitement of being so busy. The flight into mania is seductive to the extravert because it is so exciting. Kay Jamison wrote:

There is a particular kind of pain, elation, loneliness, and terror involved in this kind of madness. When you're high it's tremendous. The ideas and feelings are fast and frequent like shooting stars, and you allow them until you find better and brighter ones. Shyness goes, the right words and gestures are suddenly there, the power to captivate others a felt certainty. There are interests found in uninteresting people. Sensuality is pervasive and the desire to seduce and be seduced irresistible. Feelings of ease, intensity, power, well-being, financial omnipotence, and euphoria pervade one's marrow. But, somewhere, this changes. The fast ideas are far too fast, and there are far too many; overwhelming confusion replaces clarity. Memory goes. Humour, and absorption on friends' faces are replaced by fear and concern. Everything previously moving with the grain is now – against you are irritable, angry, frightened, uncontrollable, and enmeshed totally in the blackest caves of the mind. You never knew those caves were there. It will never end, for madness carves its own reality.

447

It goes on and on, and finally there are only others' recollections of your behavior – your bizarre, frenetic, aimless behaviors – for mania has at least some grace in partially obliterating memories. What then, after the medications, psychiatrist, despair, depression, and overdose? All those incredible feelings to sort through. Who is being too polite to say what? Who knows what? What did I do? Why? And most hauntingly, when will it happen again? Then, too, are the bitter reminders – medicine to take, resent, forget, take, resent, and forget, but always to take. Credit cards revoked, bounced checks to cover; explanations due at work, apologies to make, intermittent memories (what did I do?), friendships gone or drained, a ruined marriage. And always, when will it happen again? Which of my feelings are real? Which of the me's is me? The wild, impulsive, chaotic, energetic, and crazy one? Or the shy, withdrawn, desperate, suicidal, doomed, and tired one? Probably a bit of both, hopefully much that is neither.[4]

Kay Jamison was an American psychologist who saw her periods of mania as a genetic illness which must be managed by taking lithium. Her book *The Unquiet Mind*, published in 1995, received much publicity and is often quoted, but it is an entirely conventional view of manic-depression. Her only objection to the traditional psychiatric model was the way the DSM had replaced the term 'manic-depression' with 'bipolar disorder'. She wrote, 'As a person and a patient I find the word "bipolar" strangely and powerfully offensive: it seems to me to obscure and minimize the illness it is supposed to represent. The description "manic-depressive", on the other hand, seems to capture both the nature and the seriousness of the disease I have, rather than attempting to paper over the reality of the condition.'[5]

Kay Jamison's book is very much an extravert's tale of action, of what she did, not why she did it. She described runaway feelings and thoughts without any attempt to discover what they were running away from. The other people in her story had walk-on parts. They were all wonderful. All the men in her life were wonderful.

She idolized her parents and her brother and sister, and, while the account of her childhood would suggest to anyone aware of the effects of certain childhood experiences that she must have experienced a plethora of fear, anger and jealousy in her family, she did not even hint at this. Instead, she skated over it, and presented a romantic picture of a loving and exciting family. If we cannot bring ourselves to acknowledge what happened to us in childhood, how can we ever reach a point where we are no longer angry with our parents and might even come to forgive them?

In his account of his life, his periods of mania and the crimes he committed in that mania, David Wigoder struggled with his anger and fear. His life had been devoted to finding excitement. His choice of a career as an accountant may not appear to be an exciting one, but he made it so.

However much I earned – and once I had qualified, my earnings were always high – I never *had enough*. I could advise clients wisely and, when necessary, cautiously, but I could not exercise self-discipline. I wanted to accumulate capital, but as my income increased, so, too, did my dashes into material possessions. If a month passed and I displayed no new award for my home, I felt defeated. Every month, when my well-trained bank statements or credit card accounts overtook me, I made a fresh start, determined to save, not to spend; but then, to thrash worry, I dashed out and bought something else.

It was not uncommon for me to work until three or four o'clock in the morning on a thrilling idea for expansion, or a demanding client's latest urgent request for advice, gulping a couple of pain-killing tablets every hour to relieve my tension. At night, secreted away with my over-activity while most of the world slept, I became increasingly desperate for continual change. There had to be something new happening. If there was not, life seemed to stand still; and when it stood still, I did not know what to do with myself. Yesterday's success was quickly forgotten. I wanted to be the firm's star, radiating brilliance. When I knew that I needed to 'consolidate', to take time off to enjoy what I had, I did not know how to. Always, at the back of my mind, was the fear that if I did not do immediately what I wanted to do, a dark bout of depression might engulf me in physical and mental isolation.[6]

David Wigoder made and lost a fortune, he stole large sums from his firm, and he attempted to kill his wife. I met him when his book *Images of Destruction* was published in 1987. By then he was a quiet, unassuming man. What changed him was not being in prison but a six-month stay in a psychotherapy unit, which he called Shipley Grange, where he was challenged again and again to look into himself and discover why he behaved as he did. When he left the unit he so valued his journey inward that he continued in therapy. In his book he told his story as truthfully as he could. He did not spare himself nor his parents, who had created such a devastating childhood for him.

David Wigoder accepted that the excesses of his mania necessarily invited the attention of the law, but for Kate Millett it was not the law but her family and friends who objected to her behaviour and had her incarcerated as an involuntary patient in a psychiatric hospital. I have never met Kate Millett but I feel as though I have known her for years, because she was one of the great figures in the Women's Movement in the 1970s. She acquired a farm in Poughkeepsie, Connecticut, where she and her friends could write and paint, but she came close to losing it after she decided in 1980 to stop taking lithium. In her book *The Loony Bin Trip* she told the story of her mania and depression and the treatment she received from family and friends and the psychiatric system. She knew why her nearest and dearest had taken her liberty from her. She wrote, 'Mystical state, madness, how it frightens people. How utterly crazy *they* become, remote, rude, peculiar, cruel, taunting, farouche as wild beasts who have smelled danger, the unthinkable . . . How crazy craziness makes everyone, how irrationally afraid. The madness hidden in each of us, called to, identified, aroused like a lust. And against that the jaw sets. The more I fear my own insanity the more I must punish yours: the madman at the cross road, the senile old woman, the wild-eyed girl, the agitated man talking to himself on the subway. But they are at a distance; we are close.'[7]

Family, friends and the law are interested in mania because it disturbs other people's peace. What does not interest them is depression. The American poet Robert Lowell said, 'Mania is sickness for one's friends, depression for oneself.'[8] Kate Millett wrote of how her family ignored her when she was depressed. Depressed, she wrote, 'Now, only now, are you crazy to yourself. Depression is death, the very tinge and certainty of decay. Paradoxically, depression is when you finally contract the sickness they accused you of as a manic. A delayed reaction, if you will; the internalisation of all the crimes of your high-and-mighty time in the suffering of your fallen, dying time. Depression is when you agree with them all and surrender.'[9]

Mania is a social issue. Phobic people, obsessional people and depressed people keep to themselves. Most schizophrenic people do so too. It is the rare schizophrenic person who kills. But manic people are a nuisance. They make a fuss. They embarrass family, friends and strangers. They must be silenced. Kate Millett wrote, 'It is mania which interests the doctors, that must be stamped out. Depression is your own problem; get out of it however you can. Wait out the months, a year maybe, before it goes away. Only you must not commit suicide – that is absolutely forbidden. Your life does not belong to you but to the doctors, the relatives, the state; the social circle. Show any symptoms of suicide and they'll pick you up like a thief.'[10]

It is in dealing with mania that the psychiatrist's role as agent of social control becomes clear. The manic person must be kept off the streets and silenced. Arraigned before the psychiatrist, the person must confess, repent and accept the punishment. Kate Millett, deeply depressed, agreed to see the eminent psychiatrist Dr Foreman. She felt 'too tired and humbled and broken, too sick to fight back'.

Capitulate and get a prescription. I was mad to stop taking lithium, yes, manic as they say. There's no point in arguing it;

it no longer applies. What applies now is the descent of the one illness I have never questioned – depression. I feel it descending hourly, daily, recognize the vertigo. I am certain of the onset because of the panic, the great heightened fear – which is both imaginary in its monstrous proportions and real as well, since it is the last attempt of the psyche to struggle free before being buried alive in inertia. Panic is a haste in emergency that finds the dime but drops it while scrabbling for the telephone number.

Foreman would be more than right; he is merciless, laying down the law about my disease, infirmity, blight: 'No doubt about it, no way around it, Kate, you're a manic-depressive, that's you, Kate.' How I hate his use of my first name in this condescending sentence. He calls me Kate. I call him doctor. 'Get used to that, you're just going to have to live with it,' he says, leaning back in his chair, smiling. 'Of course we've got a new name for it now: bipolar affective illness.'[11]

To exert social control, psychiatrists must insist that mania is a disease caused by chemical changes in the brain. Kate Millett might once have agreed with him because in her book she is loath to criticize her parents and sister, though she cannot tell her story without revealing how horrible they were to her, but, after what she had been through, she cannot lie to herself.

My sickness is chemical, they say, and the cure is also chemical. They say that depression follows mania as the night the day, though at some indeterminate time. But what if I were only broke and deflated, censured by others and unsure of myself in my art? At odds with my friends, sad over losing my lover, scared of my future without anything in the bank or the prospect of a job? Then I would not be chemically and fatefully overcome by disease – just blue. Maybe with something real to complain about, even if without solutions: new lovers, better publishing prospects, and so forth. Then my depression would be what Foreman himself used to call reactive – a reaction to the real world. Why go to a doctor if what you need is a good publisher and a lover? Because you have been manic, he insists.

So you accept this reproach for your shameful, eccentric behavior – craziness, the flower of insanity, the ugly root of it in your very genetic structure; constitutional, perhaps even inherited. Foreman has decided it's genetic. I wince. 'Afraid so, Kate, we're just about certain of it now. Wasn't your father an alcoholic?'[12]

Dr Foreman's use of the fact that Kate Millett's father may have drunk excessively as proof of the genetic inheritance of mania is typical of the thinking that underlies the popular assertion that manic-depression is clearly a genetic disease. Psychiatrists who believe this refer to family trees in which people in successive generations are assumed to have had manic-depression. They ignore the concern that if psychiatrists cannot agree on the diagnosis of a live person standing in front of them, how can they be certain of the diagnosis of a person long dead and known only through second- and third-hand reports? Such psychiatrists never match a family tree with an account of the difficulties and unhappiness each generation encountered and how they dealt with one another. They would ignore the cruel treatment David Wigoder received from his parents, but they would seize on the fact that his mother killed herself. They would ignore the fact that she had had a very unhappy childhood as the eldest of seven children in a poor family in London's East End. Her parents had had a very difficult life as Jewish immigrants from Poland, escaping poverty and pogroms. What her father's childhood must have been like can only be guessed at, because he would never speak of any events in his life before he was sixteen. In such a family it would be harder to account for a child growing up to be self-confident and happy than for one becoming manic and depressed. Psychiatrists wedded to the genetic hypothesis respond to such accounts of family unhappiness by arguing that such events are not the cause of mental illness. They simply provoke the latent madness gene into action.

Psychiatrists who believe that manic-depression is a genetic disease also quote twin studies in which identical twins, separated at birth and thus having different environments to grow up in, still go on to develop manic-depression. However, only a proportion of these twins do so, and just what proportion varies from study to study. In these studies no attempt is made to determine just how different the environment of each twin is. Some twins would have gone to a completely new family and environment, and some would have gone to Granny around the corner or Aunty across the road. Twin studies do not look at the possible incidence of child sexual abuse, nor at what expectations the adults in the child's life have for him. Many twins report that they were expected to be the same even though they knew that they were quite different people. Psychologists have established that if you want your child to be intelligent, treat that child as if he is intelligent. The same applies to madness.

Recent research seems to have undermined the Royal College of Psychiatrists' belief that manic-depression is a genetic disorder. This increased doubt appears to have occurred at the same time as the Royal College has quietly dropped all reference to a chemical imbalance being the cause of depression. In 2006 the Royal College removed its pamphlet on manic-depression from its website and after some months replaced it with a new one in which the causes of manic-depression or bipolar disorder were presented very tentatively. It says:

We don't have a complete answer to this, but:

- Research suggests that it runs in families – it seems to have more to do with genes than with upbringing.
- There seems to be a physical problem with the brain systems which control our moods – this is why the symptoms of bipolar disorder can often be controlled with medication.
- Episodes of illness can sometimes be brought on by stressful experiences or physical illness.

'The brain systems that control our moods' – what could be more vague and non-scientific? Neuroscientists do not talk about 'brain systems', but they do say that complex behaviour is accompanied by very complex changes in the brain. Talk about 'brain systems' is a nonsense. However, research has certainly made clear that episodes of mania, depression and psychosis are preceded by significant events in the individual's life.

When manic-depression was still called manic-depression the received wisdom was that the best drug to treat the illness was lithium carbonate, a drug which takes the colour out of a person's life by reducing the highs and lows of emotion. However, manic-depression fell victim to a marketing procedure now known by its opponents as 'disease mongering'. This has been defined as 'the selling of sickness that widens the boundaries of illness and grows markets for those who sell and deliver treatments. It is exemplified most explicitly by many pharmaceutical-funded disease-awareness campaigns – more often designed to sell drugs than to illuminate or educate about the prevention of illness or the maintenance of health . . . Drug companies are by no means the only players in this drama . . . Informal alliances of pharmaceutical corporations, public relations companies, doctors' groups, and patient advocates promote these ideas to the public and policymakers – often using the mass media to push a certain view of a particular health problem. While these different stakeholders may come to the alliance with different motives, there is often a confluence of interests – resulting in health problems routinely being framed as widespread, severe, and treatable with pills.'[13]

The designers of the DSM are key players in disease mongering. Thus in 1980 manic-depression became bipolar disorder, which in turn became

Bipolar I Disorder characterized by one or more Manic or Mixed Episodes, usually accompanied by Major Depressive Episodes.

Bipolar II Disorder characterized by one or more Major Depressive Episodes accompanied by at least one Hypomanic Episode

Cyclothymic Disorder characterized by at least 2 years of

numerous periods of hypomanic symptoms that do not meet the criteria for a Manic Episode and numerous periods of depressive symptoms that do not meet the criteria for a Major Depressive Episode.

Bipolar Disorder Not Otherwise Specified – bipolar symptoms about which there is inadequate or contradictory information.[14]

With the arrival of these new disorders estimates of the prevalence of bipolar disorders have risen from 0.1 per cent of the population having bipolar I disorder (this must involve an episode of hospitalization for mania) to 5 per cent or more when all the other kinds of bipolar disorder have been included. Originally lithium was regarded as being the only drug which could prevent further episodes of mania but it was not referred to as a mood stabilizer. As David Healy noted, 'The term ''mood stabilizer'' had barely been heard before 1995 when Abbott Laboratories got a licence for using the anticonvulsant sodium valproate (Depakote) for treating acute mania ... The first group of drugs to colonize this new mood stabilizer niche was anticonvulsants. Anticonvulsants are beneficial in epilepsy and were until quite recently thought to be beneficial by quenching the increased risk of succeeding epileptic fits brought about by fits that had gone before.'[15] Despite the fact that having an epileptic fit and being manic are two very different experiences, psychiatrists argued that if anticonvulsants stopped the first they might stop the second.

In the extremes of mania a person loses touch with everyday reality, so lost is he in the most grandiose delusions. In a state deemed to be psychotic he would be prescribed the antipsychotic drugs which are used in schizophrenia. David Healy wrote, 'Against a background of epidemiological studies indicating that the prevalence of bipolar disorders might be greater than previously thought, and growing academic interest in that condition, Lilly, Janssen, and Astra-Zeneca, the makers of the antipsychotic drugs olanzapine, risperidone and quetiapine respectively, marched in on the new territory to market these drugs for the prophylaxis [prevention] of bipolar disorder. There was, however, no consensus on a theoretical rationale that would lead the average clinician to think that these three drugs might "quench" the propensity to further affective episodes, as opposed to simply assist in the management of acute manic states . . . With the possible exception of lithium for bipolar I disorder, there are no randomized trials to show that patients with bipolar disorders in general who receive psychotropic drugs are better in the long term than those who receive no medicine.'[16]

Antipsychotic drugs do not seem to prevent episodes of manic-depression. However,

(1) a consistent body of evidence indicates that regular treatment with antipsychotics in the longer run increases mortality: and
(2) there is evidence in placebo-controlled trials of antipsychotics submitted in application for schizophrenia licences [licences for manufacturing drugs for use in schizophrenia] that there is a statistically significant excess of completed suicides on active treatment. A range of problems associated with antipsychotics, from increased mortality to tardive dyskinesia, never show up in the short-term trials aimed at demonstrating treatment effects in psychiatry.[17]

An increasing number of people are being diagnosed as having a bipolar disorder and prescribed the drugs which are known to do severe damage to the cortex of the brain. This is the disease called tardive dyskinesia. In the USA children under five are being diagnosed as having paediatric bipolar disorder, even though they do not meet the traditional criteria for bipolar I disorder. 'Drugs such as Zyprexa [olanzapine] and Risperdal [risperidone] are now being used for preschoolers in America with little questioning of this development.'[18] Risks associated with both these drugs are tardive dyskinesia and diabetes.

If we use the defence of mania our difficulties multiply a thousandfold. Even if you manage to avoid being diagnosed as bipolar and given dangerous drugs, family and friends are alienated, jobs lost, money squandered. When the depression eases, the fear of becoming depressed again joins the other fears. At such a time it is extremely difficult to ask oneself the question 'How did I get into this situation?' and to set out to find the answer. Events have piled upon other events, and feelings becomes more and more chaotic. Such a situation could well lead an introvert to lose contact with his external reality and retreat into an idiosyncratic world which few could share, but for an extravert escape is into external reality and into activity that becomes less and less connected to what is actually going on. Both states are psychotic, out of touch with reality, and it is often difficult for an outside observer to distinguish one from the other, though from the inside the experiences are very different. Both experiences are defences, the most desperate defences we can create.

The Manic Defence

When I first arrived in England in 1968 I went to work in Sheffield, where the head of my department, Alec Jenner, was researching into the metabolic basis of mood change. He had a research clinic where people with a diagnosis of mania came from across the UK, and sometimes from across the world, to stay for a few days or months. They patiently and co-operatively allowed their blood and urine to be sampled and many aspects of their physical functioning, along with their moods, whether they were 'up' or 'down', to be observed and recorded.

According to the theory, periods of mania, followed by depression, followed again by mania, and so on, were the result of cyclical changes in the functioning of the body. That certain cycles did exist was well documented. All that needed to be done was to find the cyclical physiological changes which produced the cycles of mania and depression. I was not a doctor, a physiologist, a biologist, or a chemist, so there was no part I could play in this research. Except, perhaps, to elaborate the descriptions we already had of the behaviour of these people when they were manic or depressed. This meant that instead of wearing a white coat and doing important things in the laboratory, or recording data on the report sheets in the office (this was before computers), I sat on the sidelines, usually in my office or in the garden or in the patients' day room where I talked to them and observed the goings-on in the ward.

At this stage, at the end of the sixties, I knew very little about depression and mania except what I had read in textbooks, so I was quite ready to accept the theory of the metabolic basis of these extremes of mood change. However, through my observations and conversations, I began to wonder.

One of the people who visited the unit every few months was a man called Jimmy who, in his youth, had wreaked havoc on himself and his family through the wild excesses of his behaviour when he was in a manic state. He had ended up in a hospital where Alec, then a consultant psychiatrist, was beginning his researches, and Jimmy came to play a major part in this work. His mood changes lasted twenty-four hours each. For twenty-four hours he was in the depths of depression; and then, suddenly, like Cinderella turning into a princess, he became manic. However, when the clock struck twelve, or thereabouts, like Cinderella he was stripped of all his finery and plunged into a depression again. So he and Alec, himself no mean worker when he was in an expansive mood, entered upon a series of investigations which included, at one time, being shut up together in a large box in which each day was no longer twenty-four hours but varied according to the experimental design. Alec would often talk of the importance in science of 'dotting the i's and crossing the t's', and this work dotted a lot of i's and crossed a lot of t's.

Jimmy was still having quite large mood swings which made it difficult for him to plan a life outside the hospital. Alec by then was due to move to Sheffield as Professor of Psychiatry, so he decided to see if a new drug, lithium, would help Jimmy. It did, most remarkably. When I met Jimmy he had been living outside the hospital for some time, and to all intents and purposes was an ordinary man. However, those people who knew him had no difficulty in identifying whether today was an up day or a down day for Jimmy. There was a difference, and each change came every twenty-four hours. One day there was a liveliness and the next a stillness. Proof, if proof were needed, that these mood changes were the result of physiological changes, and that these changes could be controlled by lithium.

And yet. My 'and yet' came one day when I was sitting in the garden with Jimmy and he was telling me about his life. He expressed regret for the hurt and damage he had done to different members of his family, and then he said, 'When I think about my family and what I've done to them, and about all the chances I've had and I've thrown away, I could feel that I've wasted my life altogether. The only thing that stops me and that makes me feel that it hasn't been entirely wasted is that I've been a good research subject for Professor Jenner. He's a wonderful man.'

I shared (and still share) Jimmy's admiration for Alec, so I could understand how he could endure all the indignities, unpleasantness and boredom that can be part of being a research subject, but I could not help wondering whether a desire to please and to make recompense on the part of the subject might confound some of the research results.

My misgivings were increased when I sat with Geraldine in the day room. The nurses' office was next door, and I could often hear the nurses' conversation there and in the corridor quite clearly. Perhaps, though, I could hear them because I was not a patient, and no good patient (hospital patients must aspire to a level of goodness higher than that of people outside hospital) listens to the conversations between his betters, the nurses and doctors. I did not know what Geraldine heard or did not hear, but I would often be aware of the nurses discussing which of the patients was, according to the charts kept in the office, due to have a mood change. 'Geraldine', I might hear them say, 'should go up later this week,' meaning that she should change from her near-immobile depressed state to an active manic state. Meanwhile, Geraldine might be saying to me, 'Do you think Professor Jenner will let me go home this weekend? Do you think, if I'm good, he'll let me go home?' I did not tell her what I thought, except to say that she should ask him. What I did wonder was whether she was being good by being deaf, or being good by dutifully going 'up' before the end of the week.

When an element of behaviour has entered our repertoire, whether it was caused by a physiological change, as in epilepsy, or by something in our environment, like going to an acting class and learning how to fall, we can always produce it again. We may not do it so well – we may still not be able to swim a hundred metres flat out – but we do not forget how to do it. This was often one of the issues I would have to tackle at the end of therapy, when I was asked, 'Will I get depressed again?' The answer is 'If you choose to do so', for once you have learned how to be depressed, you can always choose to do it again, if you want to, just as you can always choose to do the tango if you have ever learned how.

Once you have learned the behaviours of mania and depression (and all the other defences) you can always use them again to your advantage. The manic phases of one of the patients at the clinic, Christopher, included wild spending sprees, often involving Alec and the other staff. I remember Christopher going to Alec and telling him that he had bought him, as a birthday present, a large organ which would be delivered that afternoon. This was just a tease, and Christopher was delighted with the way Alec's face went white. Momentarily Alec believed that Christopher was manic and that he had again become involved in one of Christopher's disastrous escapades. Then he saw Christopher grinning and realized that it was a joke and laughed with him. There were some staff there who considered that teasing the professor was itself an example of manic behaviour, but there was none who would have wondered what lay behind this joke – not merely a desire to make people laugh, but also a desire to hurt. In those days at that clinic, no such questions were ever given serious consideration.

By this time I had begun exploring the possible uses of a new technique in psychology called the repertory grid, which was a structured way of asking people about themselves and how they saw their world. It was possible to devise different kinds of grids, and I experimented with quite a number. One of my favourites was one I called the Dyadic Relationship Grid because I wanted to write about it in some articles for academic journals whose editors I wished to impress. This grid was a structured way of asking a person about how he saw important people in his life and how he felt they perceived him. I could ask a person, 'How much do you love your mother?' and if it was the most he could love anyone he would say, 'Seven,' and if he did not love his mother at all he could say, 'One,' or he could use 2, 3, 4, 5, or 6 to indicate gradations in love between 7 and 1. I could then ask, 'How much does your mother love you?' and get a similar numerical reply.

The result of such questioning was a matrix of numbers which my friend and colleague Patrick Slater at the Institute of Psychiatry would analyse using a statistical method called principle components analysis. If I gave one person the same grid on two occasions, Patrick could measure how much the second grid differed from the first.

A twenty-three-year-old graduate called Susan was admitted to the university clinic in a hypomanic state. She agreed to talk to me and do some tests. We did a grid where the relationships she assessed were those with her mother, father, sister, brother and a friend. Each of these relationships she rated in terms of friendship, happiness, anger, wanting to be liked, trust, fear, admiration, guilt, kindness, her ability to talk to the person, affection and patience. Four weeks later, just before Susan was discharged from the clinic, as she was now much calmer, we did the grid again.

The two grids were quite different, and these differences were not random but related to feelings of fear, guilt and anger. In my research report I wrote:

When we perceive that another person is angry with us, we recognize that we are in danger of being hurt. When we perceive that another person is frightened of us, we recognize that we are isolated from that person, who will retreat or retaliate if we advance, and that there is something frightening about us which we cannot control. When we perceive that another person feels guilty about us, we recognize that there is something wrong with us, caused, perhaps irreparably, by actions or failure of actions of the other person. The pain of fear, guilt and anger within ourselves is something we can perhaps learn to deal with, but to be the object of fear, guilt and anger is to be in a position of dangerous isolation where there is little choice or control.

One way of dealing with such a situation is to deny that it exists. Thus Susan insisted that the significant relationships in her life were always warm and secure. To maintain the defence of denial it is often necessary to be very active and talkative, since meditation may allow what is being denied to become conscious. . .

The comparison of grids done in the hypomanic and calm state shows that the greatest changes on the constructs concern Susan's perception of fear, guilt and anger. . . Changes in feelings of fear and guilt relate to changes in her relationship to her mother and father, and in the relationship of her parents, her psychiatrist and her friend to her. Thus in a hypomanic state she experienced feelings of fear and guilt towards her parents and perceived her parents, her psychiatrist and her friend as feeling fearful and guilty about her.

As well as giving Susan the grid, I had also asked her to fill in a child's Report on Parental Behaviour Inventory.[19]

The relationship of the mother to Susan needs to be looked at separately. There is little change in the perception of this relationship. In the first grid Susan showed her mother as being somewhat guilty about and frightened of her, but in the second grid they share a perfect relationship. But from Susan's answers to the Parental Behaviour Inventory there emerges a picture of a mother who at times is cold and rejecting of her daughter. Perhaps more significant is the fact that on the first grid Susan stated that the person who frightened her most, at the upper limit of the scale of fear, was her mother.

It seems that in a hypomanic state Susan is fighting against the fear aroused by her perception of her world where she sees herself as isolated, worthless and in danger. In a calm state she wants to see her world of relationships as warm and loving, but it seems that this perception is maintained by denial of some aspect of reality, especially in her relationship with her mother.[20]

I was well aware that Freud and other psychoanalysts had described mania as a defence against fear. Susan's repertory grids seemed to support their view.

I would sometimes go over to the main psychiatric hospital to see patients who seemed to get depressed at regular intervals. The first of these was Maude, a gentle, unassuming woman in her sixties who was a patient on one of the women's wards. She had begun her career as a psychiatric patient in the university clinic, but as her depressions returned year after year, for longer periods and responding more and more slowly to the antidepressant drugs and ECT, she was transferred to the big psychiatric hospital. I was horrified to see her – indeed, to see any woman – on such a ward, which could have been designed and built only by men (I do not imagine there were too many women architects in the 1930s in England) who regarded psychiatric patients as no more than sheep to be herded, fed and watered. For any woman who was concerned both about personal cleanliness and privacy, this ward must have been a nightmare. There was Maude, enduring it, feeling that she deserved it, because she was such a wicked person. Wicked because she felt feelings like anger and jealousy which she should not feel, and wicked for causing shame and grief to her family because she was depressed.

Maude was originally thought to be a victim of her cyclical body rhythms because she got depressed every August. By now her depressions lasted much longer than the month of August. They stretched over much of the year. However, that was her history. Every August she became depressed.

I suppose she talked to me because she did not have many visitors, and I suppose she told me about her marriage because I told her about mine – how I had come to England after my husband and I had separated and he had remarried. She told me something which she had never told her consultant or any member of staff.

She explained why she became depressed. When she was first depressed she had gone with her husband to the clinic to see the consultant psychiatrist. Her husband had gone in first to talk to the consultant, and she had been left sitting outside in the hallway, while these two men talked about her. Then her husband came out and said to her, 'He wants to see you now. I have told him that we are happily married.'

So she went into the consultant's office, and when he asked her, 'Has anything happened recently which has upset you?' she said, 'No, nothing,' and when he said, 'How do you and your husband get on?' she said, 'We get along very well.' He asked, 'What about in bed?' and she said, 'I'm happily married.' She did not say, 'My husband had an affair with one of his colleagues at work and it broke my heart.' It had been her little daughter who had innocently told her about this, not her husband.

There were other tragedies in her life, and many burdens, and sometimes these were associated with autumn. So it was in autumn that she became depressed. What had looked like a cyclical event in her physiology was an anniversary reaction.

With all these and other observations I lost faith in the idea that some special cyclical physiological rhythm can explain the periods of depression and mania that some people experience. From then on, whenever a person told me that she had been diagnosed as hypomanic, as one woman did, I was more interested in exploring her statement that when she was depressed 'I feel that I am not worth the air I breathe' than in looking for a calendar on which to plot her mood changes.

Mania begins, as all desperate defences do, with a loss of self-confidence and self-worth, and the discovery that there is a serious discrepancy between what you thought your life was and what it actually is. All of this is in Kay Jamison's story, though she did not identify it as such.

Her father was an air force officer, and the family moved around the world with each of his postings. In Lincolnshire, in the years I worked there, there were a number of Royal Air Force bases still in operation. In our psychology department we saw a disproportionate number of RAF families in comparison with the number of Lincoln-shire families we saw – air force wives, husbands and children.

The RAF wives were depressed and anxious. They would talk of how helpless and inadequate they felt. They had to live their lives according to RAF rules and discipline, and they had no control over when and where the family had to move to. On one occasion I was invited to talk to a group from a charitable organization in which there were a number of air force wives. As part of my talk I told them about some research undertaken with pairs of rats. Each rat was put in one of two cages, stacked one on top of the other and linked by an electric wire. This wire delivered electric shocks to each rat. The rat in the bottom cage had a switch which it could learn to stop the electric shock, but the rat in the top cage was totally dependent on the other rat for the swiftness with which its torture was ended. I did not have to describe to these RAF wives how the rat in the top cage reacted to this situation. They knew it was the rat in the top cage that became extremely neurotic because they immediately recognized this as their own situation. Kay Jamison's mother was in similar circumstances. She had to cope with many upheavals over which she had no control. She told her daughter how, as a young wife, she had been instructed by the commanding officer's wife how she should conduct herself socially, and how pilots should 'never be angry or upset when they fly. Being angry could lead to a lapse in judgement or concentration: flying accidents might happen; pilots could be killed. Pilots' wives, therefore, should never have any kind of argument with their husband before the men go flying. Composure and self-restraint were not only desirable characteristics in a woman, they were essential.'[21] It was not just her own temper which the woman had to keep under control, it was her children's temper. Squabbling among themselves is part of siblings' life, but the Jamison children could not do this when their father was due to go to work.

In Lincolnshire the RAF men who came to the psychology department were usually at the point of leaving or had just left the RAF. These men had found that they could not cope with the uncertainties of civilian life, and they became depressed and anxious.

When Kay Jamison's father left the air force he and his wife, 'although still living together became essentially estranged'.[22] 'Colonel Jamison' became increasingly manic and then plunged into a deep depression.

The RAF children who were referred to us had as their problem a father who expected the instant obedience he got from recruits. A young man joins the military knowing that he will have to give up much of himself in order to fit into military life, but children do not know that this will be expected of them. They are shocked to discover that they are being forced to deny even more of themselves than they would have done in an ordinary home. Kay described her life on an air force base as lively and interesting, but her energy and various enthusiasms, and her desire to be herself and not conform to ridiculous rules, such as learning to curtsy to adults of high social rank, conflicted with what her father expected of her. She learnt that she was not acceptable as she was. She had to learn to be good. 'Good' meant obeying the rules. In elementary school she had seen an air force plane crash, and later she was told that the young pilot was a hero because, while he could have bailed out and saved his life, he stayed with his plane to prevent it crashing into her school. Thus she discovered not just death and the aloneness of that but also that such a sacrifice could be demanded of her. She went with her family to church every Sunday, and so she learned to believe in the Just World. She wrote, 'There was a time when I honestly believed that there was only a certain amount of pain one had to go through in life. Because manic-depressive illness had brought such misery and uncertainty in its wake, I presumed life should therefore be kinder to me, in more balancing ways.'[23]

The serious discrepancy in Kay's life developed when her father left the air force. The family moved to California, and for the first time in her life Kay had to go to an ordinary school, what she called 'a civilian school'. She was bereft of all her security.

For a long time I felt totally adrift. I missed Washington terribly. I had left behind a boyfriend, without whom I was desperately unhappy: he was blond, blue-eyed, funny, loved to dance, and we were seldom apart during the months before I left Washington. He was my introduction to independence from my family, and I believed, like most fifteen-year-olds, that our love would last forever. I also had left behind a life that had been filled with good friends, family closeness, great quantities of warmth and laughter, traditions I knew and loved, and a city that was home. More important, I had left behind a conservative military lifestyle that I had known for as long as I could remember . . . It was a small, warm, unthreatening, and cloistered world. California, or at least Pacific Palisades, seemed to me to be rather cold and flashy. I lost my moorings almost entirely, and despite ostensibly adjusting rapidly to a new school and acquiring new friends – both of which were made relatively easy by countless previous changes in schools that had, in turn, bred a hail-fellow-well-met sort of outgoingness – I was deeply unhappy. I spent much of my time in tears or writing letters to my boyfriend. I was furious with my father.[24]

Her brother had gone to college, 'leaving a huge hole in my security net. My relationship with my sister, always a difficult one, had become at best fractious, often adversarial, and, more usually, simply distant. She had far more trouble than I did in adjusting to California, but we never really spoke about it. We went almost entirely our separate ways, and, for all the difference it made, we could have been living in different houses.' Her father became manic and then depressed. 'After a while, I scarcely recognized him. At times he was immobilized with depression, unable to get out of bed, and profoundly pessimistic about every aspect of his life and his future. At other times, his rage and screaming would fill me with terror. I had never known my father – a soft-spoken and gentle man – to raise his voice. Now there were days, and even weeks, when I was frightened to show up for breakfast or come home from school. He was also drinking heavily, which made everything worse. My mother was bewildered and frightened as I was, and both of us increasingly sought escape through work and friends.'[25]

Such an escape was not enough to bridge the serious discrepancy between what she thought her life was and what it actually was. Her secure world had disappeared, never to return. She had believed that if she was good nothing bad would happen to her. Someone so keen to conform and to be accepted and loved could not blame those on whom she relied for lying to her and letting her down, so she blamed herself for not being good enough.

By the time I was sixteen or seventeen, it was clear that my energies and enthusiasms could be exhausting to the people around me, and after long weeks of flying high and sleeping little, my thinking would take a downward turn toward the really dark and brooding side of life. . . I was a senior in high school when I had my first attack of manic-depressive illness; once the siege began, I lost my mind rather rapidly. At first everything seemed so easy. I raced about like a crazed weasel, bubbling with plans and enthusiasms. . . The world was filled with pleasure and promise; I felt great. Not just great, I felt *really* great. My mind seemed clear, fabulously focused. . . Not only did everything make perfect sense, but it all began to fit into a marvellous kind of cosmic relatedness. . . I did finally slow down. In fact, I came to a grinding halt . . . then the bottom began to fall out of my life and mind.[26]

Matthew came to see me very much as a last resort. The psychiatrist on whom he had depended for so long had left the district, and shortly after his departure Matthew had plunged into a deep depression. He was a senior accountant, very honest, upright and conscientious. He did not see how I could help him, but expected that I would impart some facts to him and give him some advice. He intended to learn what I taught him as diligently as he had studied at school and college and to carry out my advice, and then, if I was any good at my job, he would no longer be depressed.

He had three anxieties about this. The first was that I was very remiss about giving advice. I gave none, or very vague and woolly stuff like 'Be kind to yourself' or, worse, immoralities like 'Why not take some time off and do something frivolous and unnecess-ary?' (People who have to resort to mania and depression in order to survive either never play or play only to win.)

His second anxiety was that what I said was obviously nonsense. I seemed to think that his childhood had something to do with his present state. His psychiatrist had never come out with this sort of nonsense. A ten-minute interview, with an exchange of pleasantries and a check of his drug prescription, was all that that wise doctor needed to do. Why go into these things which happened so long ago?

His third anxiety was that whenever he emerged from his depression he would go along for a while on an even keel, and then he would gradually become more active until he reached a state that he called manic. Dare he risk coming out of this depression?

It was only with difficulty that I got him to tell me of his experience of depression. He described being depressed as feeling that inside him was a hollow space. 'On the outside', he said, 'I look the same and I can go around doing the things I always do, but inside is this empty space.'

He went on, 'When I'm manic the hollow space is filled in. Then I've got lots of good ideas and things to do.'

Anger to Matthew was complete anathema. He prided himself not only on never losing his temper but on his skill in reasoned argument. All disputes, he considered, could be resolved if people met together and argued calmly and logically. He made no allow-ance for emotions which, no matter what they are, never fit into neat, logical boxes. He described his depression only in the physical terms of bodily weakness and a tiredness that forced him to stay in bed for days at a time.

It was only when he described something of those periods which his psychiatrist called manic that he gave some hint of the volcano of rage inside him. He enjoyed the start of such a period, when he felt whole and full of creative ideas. However, he would then find himself doing some things which, in retrospect, he felt were quite worrying.

He described to me how, if he saw other drivers going too fast and so wasting petrol, he would wave at them to stop, and then would speak to them sternly, reminding them of their duty to conserve petrol. He did not tell me how many of these drivers threatened physical violence in response to such good advice. I wondered whether the person he was really reprimanding was not the other driver but himself, for 'speeding up'.

I did not offer this interpretation, for he would have found it strange and offensive. He would have found my interpretations of two other things he did in this period of mania even more so. An IRA bomb left him with the feeling that he should be looking out for suspicious people. This he did. Sometimes he would stop a person he thought suspicious and question him about his activities. He uncovered no Irish terrorists, any more than he uncovered and recognized his own anarchic impulses, which were close to breaking through and disrupting the peaceful pattern of his life. Again, although ordinarily very careful where money was concerned, he found himself taking the precaution, before going on holiday, of joining both the main motoring organizations, the AA and the RAC, even though membership of one is ample protection. His explanation to himself of his action was that he wanted to be sure of getting his wife and children to safety if his car broke down in the wilds of Scotland. Here I felt it inappropriate to question whether such an action was a denial of the resentment and hate he felt for his family, who placed such onerous demands upon him.

Matthew's childhood, so he would tell me, had been happy. There was one event when he was three which his mother still remembered but he did not, so it could not be important. This was when he had been admitted to hospital with scarlet fever. In those days parents were not allowed to visit their sick children in hospital. When his mother came to collect him she found that he had lain so long sucking his thumb that a sore had developed inside his mouth. Not long after he had returned home his mother gave birth to his sister.

I tried to put these events into the context of a child's experience. Leaving his parents and going into hospital would have been beyond his comprehension. It would have felt like total abandonment, complete annihilation. The nurses there had obviously made no effective attempt to assuage this sense of overwhelming loss, but left him to lie in the passive state of a child who has given up hope. On his mother's arrival he would have observed her distress, which clearly had to do with something being wrong with him, and probably her distress was exacerbated by his initial lack of response to her, as children in this abandoned state react when reunited with their mother. To this picture I could add only the knowledge that both parents were, in their own way, dominant people. Possibly there was some friction between them about what had happened and what should be done. Without understanding why, he would have felt that he was the cause of this friction.

The violence Matthew experienced was probably not as physically immense as that which David Wigoder experienced, but in terms of psychic pain it was very great. After being the centre of his parents' attention, Matthew was supplanted by another. His mother had betrayed him. Matthew dismissed this interpretation. 'My sister and I get on very well,' he said. He was very glad to have assumed full responsibility for his widowed mother's financial affairs, even though she was not always prepared to follow his advice.

By the time he was fifteen, David Wigoder had suffered three bouts of depression. He told no one, and his parents, engaged in battle and each locked into their own misery, did not notice. He first withdrew into the prison of depression when he was thirteen. He did not know it was depression. He thought he was going mad. He had already developed a pattern of living whereby he escaped from himself into activity in his external reality. He developed this with great skill, working hard to achieve fame and admiration and creating exciting, but solitary, adventures for himself. However,

At night, when I reluctantly switched off my bedroom light, or my torch battery became too dim to read by, nothing felt exciting. I just felt alone. If I'd spent an afternoon with a friend I worried that he, or she, might not want to see me again; or, if

I hadn't spent an afternoon with one, why I had no friends. I could not understand why each adventure – whatever it was, even when it made me happy at the time – quickly turned into sad disappointment. The answer seemed to keep finding more things to do.[27]

David's account of his childhood shows that from the beginning he was the victim of violence. His mother was a violent woman, prone to shouting and hurling things, striking her children and threatening to kill herself. She was addicted to barbiturates and this reduced her self-control even further. When David, as a toddler, showed the usual aggressiveness that all toddlers show he was not guided by his parents into better ways of dealing with anger and envy but punished harshly for his own violence. When he was three, he was also punished by a teacher, who washed out his mouth with soap because he had bitten another child. When he was older he stole a pound note from his mother and destroyed it without understanding why. Later, in a moment of closeness, he confessed to his mother, and she promised to keep this as their secret. However, she betrayed him to his father, who tied him to the bed and belted him until he bled.

David had repressed memories of his childhood but group therapy brought them back. He wrote:

When those memories, and feelings, returned, I knew that I had distrusted my parents many years before my teens. It was a startling discovery. Uncountable, fearful memories flashed through my mind and magnified my feelings: the day I fell into a river and was scared to go home because my mother would scream at me for dirtying my clothes; the afternoon I ate some grapes which she had bought for my father, and she made me stand up on a chair for what seemed like hours; a Sunday, when my father was wallpapering our dining room, and my mother had shrieked at him and then collapsed on the floor, prostrate and unmoving, drenched in water spilled from the bucket he was using; a bowl of cereal tipped over my head after I shouted that I could not hear *Dick Barton* on the radio because my mother would not stop talking. These seemed tiny memories to be recalling, but the fear and guilt I felt had been immense. I realized that I had been terrified of my mother for as long as I could remember. Destruction acquired a new meaning.[28]

The damage done to children by violence is not simply that caused by the actual infliction. We all carry inside us representations of our parents, so that in one sense our parents never die. If our parents have been kind and loving, their representations inside us strengthen and comfort us, but if they have been violent towards us, we can go on suffering this violence long after they are dead. The poet A. E. Housman wrote about this:

> *They cease not fighting, east and west,*
> *On the marches of my breast.*
>
> *Here the truceless armies yet*
> *Trample, rolled in blood and sweat;*
> *They kill and kill and never die;*
> *And I think that each is I.*
>
> *None will part us none undo*
> *The knot that makes one flesh of two,*
> *Sick with hatred, sick with pain,*
> *Strangling – When shall we be slain?*
>
> *When shall I be dead and rid*
> *Of the wrong my father did?*
> *How long, how long, till spade and hearse*
> *Put to sleep my mother's curse?*[29]

Long before he began his journey into self-discovery, David had refused to have anything more to do with his mother. He was ashamed and frightened of her, and even when he was in the depths of depression and longed for her, he made no attempt to contact her. The last time he saw her was in a shop, and he passed by without speaking. Four years later she died alone of an overdose of barbiturates.

Matthew, David and Kay Jamison represent the extremes of a response to parents which has not gone through the maturing process, needed by all of us, of observing our parents with an adult's eye: judging them, ceasing to be angry with them, and perhaps forgiving them. The extremes are to idealize them, or to treat them with total contempt. They are, in their way, the same response. 'Contempt for parents', wrote Alice Miller, 'often helps to ward off the pain of being unable to idealize them.'[30] Both responses are a refusal to go beyond idealizing parents and to reach an understanding and acceptance that our parents are fallible human beings who inflict pain on us for which there is no recompense. With such understanding we are no longer filled with hate for our parents' failure to be perfect, and so we may feel sad and mourn our loss.

In group therapy David realized that 'For many years I believed that my childhood experiences had been good for me. Because of them, I reasoned, I had thrown myself energetically into my school work, and become ambitious. If I had not had such misery at home, I told myself, I may not have had the motivation to work hard and succeed, so that I could leave home. Had I not felt the need to get out of the house as often as I could, perhaps, I would not have met so many interesting people, and learned how to mix socially.'[31]

In his school years, he wrote, 'I consciously divided my life into separate compartments. One of me lived at home, the mad one; the other, the normal one, went to school. Whatever happened, I used to tell myself guiltily, no one must know about the mad me. To ensure that my secret remained hidden, throughout my years at school I never took a friend home, unless my parents were out of the house, or I was enjoying a brief reconciliation with my mother. I never told any of my friends about my home life; and I rarely told my parents anything about school which I did not have to.'[32]

When he went to high school, David encountered 'the infamous

Dr Dory', whom he determined to impress. When he left school Dr Dory told him:

> I had gained the highest pass mark in Ordinary Level GCE of any boy whom he had ever taught, and the highest awarded that year by the University of London – 92 per cent. He also told me that it had been a pleasure to have me as a pupil, and invited me to join him at the local library so that he could show me how he was preparing research documentation for a newly-commissioned book. I could not understand why, when I expected to be glowing with pride at my success, the first thing I did after leaving him was to rush to the lavatory and cry. For years after that final meeting I felt angry that my success had only been at Ordinary Level – why not Advanced Level? 'A boy of excellent character' the headmaster had written. I was pleased to have such a commendation, although nobody ever asked to see it, but what about the *me* who was omitted from my glowing report?[33]

The extravert child, fleeing into his external reality, gains a very good idea of what the world regards as success and sets out to achieve it. He has a keen eye for convention and orthodoxy. At school, if he has sufficient intelligence, he can do well simply by carrying out the teachers' instructions. He is not distracted from incorporating the set syllabus by doubt and wonder, as introvert children are. If he cannot shine academically he can become a spectacular member of a sports team, or, if all that fails, he can abandon the conventions of school and shine instead in the conventions of street life and crime.

The fantasies of omnipotence that a child develops to overcome the threat of annihilation gradually create a sense of grandiosity. This sense, often bolstered by real achievements, can become one of the main characteristics of the person, who may be unaware of its significance. As Alice Miller wrote, 'Grandiosity is the defence against depression, and depression is the defence against the deep pain over the loss of the self.'[34]

She went on:

The person who is 'grandiose' is admired everywhere and needs this admiration; indeed, he cannot live without it. He must excel brilliantly in everything he undertakes, which surely he is capable of doing (otherwise he would not attempt it). He, too, admires himself – for his qualities: his beauty, cleverness, talents; and for his success and achievements. Woe betide him if one of these fails him, for then the catastrophe of a severe depression is imminent. It is usually considered normal that sick or aged people who have suffered the loss of much of their health and vitality, or, for example, women at the time of the menopause, should become depressive. There are, however, other personalities who can tolerate the loss of beauty, health, youth, or loved ones, and although they mourn them, they do so without depression. In contrast, there are those with great gifts, often precisely the most gifted, who suffer from severe depression. One is free from depression when self-esteem is based on the authenticity of one's feelings and not on the possession of certain qualities.

The collapse of self-esteem in a 'grandiose' person will show clearly how precariously that self-esteem had been hanging in the air 'hanging from a balloon', a female patient once dreamed. That balloon flew up very high in a good wind but then suddenly got a hole in it and soon lay like a rag on the ground... For nothing genuine that could have given strength and support later on had been developed...

It is thus impossible for the grandiose person to cut the tragic link between admiration and love. In his compulsion to repeat he seeks insatiably for admiration, of which he never gets enough because admiration is not the same as love. It is only a substitute gratification of the primary needs for respect, understanding, and being taken seriously – needs that have remained unconscious. The grandiose person is never really free, first, because he is excessively dependent on admiration from the object, and, second, because his self-respect is dependent on qualities, functions and achievements that can suddenly fail.[35]

Extraverts who believe that they are unlovable can seek admiration instead. They can also try to get the attention and gratitude of others by controlling them. David found it hard to accept that he tried to control others.

> My behaviour in the group seemed to indicate that I acted out a role which I had inherited from my mother. Like her, I wanted to powerfully control other people. I wanted to dominate them. I insisted on being the centre of attention. If they refused to satisfy my demands, then I wanted to hurt them. I wanted to be the best resident, best able to understand my past, best able to communicate, best able to begin a new life, best able to forgive – best able to control.[36]

Often the person creates a fantasy which, if implemented, would fulfil this need to control others. The fantasy that would appeal most to a lonely, rejected child who desperately wants to be a loved and admired member of a group is that of being a parent in a happy family. David described his fantasy:

> I idealized married love into a cosy, comfortable relationship; as cosy and comfortable as the apparently ideal families I had met through friends at the Circus Club, or fanciful visions which I created in waking dreams. Love, the love I wanted, possessed a private key which opened a door leading into a private home, where nobody could disrupt my blissful tranquillity, and where I could offer and receive protection. The protection I wanted to offer, and to have accepted, was to be a provider of care and financial security. I wanted to work hard and prove that I could do what my parents could not. I wanted to be respected and admired for my efforts, and in return I expected to assume all the conventional responsibilities of a Victorian husband. My wife, the one who would help me understand love, would give me what I had never known – a stable home, where I would not be frightened to use my key when I reached the front door, and

478

inside which would be certainty, the certainty that there was always someone who wanted me.[37]

This passage illustrates how sentimentality is the denial of hate, for here a sentimental account denies the fact that family life, no matter how loving the parents and children are, contains plenty of frustration, anger and disappointment. Victorian fathers as envisioned by David were tyrants. They damaged and destroyed their wives and children, and they usually ended up as lonely, selfish, feared and unloved old men.

In the grip of such a sentimental fantasy a person may be oblivious of the fact that if we control people we become responsible for them, and many people, especially partners and children, will gladly hand over their responsibilities to the person who wishes to manage their lives. Thus before long the controller becomes weighed down with burdens, and with awareness of the burdens comes resentment and hate.

We may often relieve our own resentment to some degree by complaining and being irritable, and our family has to put up with our behaviour. However, hate is a powerful emotion. It shows us that we are not the good, civilized person we thought ourselves to be. We hate, and we wish to destroy. We have to have a detailed knowledge of ourselves in order to be able to recognize and cope with our own hate. To do this we need to have had a mother who tolerated our hate and hers when we were a baby. Failing that, we need to learn how to tolerate and cope with our own hate.

If you were born an extravert, and if you have come to believe that you are not acceptable as you are, if you were not helped to develop an understanding of your internal reality but were rather shown that you contained a dangerous emotional darkness from which you must flee into external reality, then hate becomes the danger that you must never recognize but from which you must always flee.

When, in the first weeks of group therapy, David discovered that 'my childhood had been bad for me' he thought: 'If I could put my bad feelings into something uncertain called "the past", where they belonged, then I would be on the road forward. During my early days at Shipley Grange, I was convinced that, if I could learn how not to hate my parents for what they did to me during my teens, my depression would vanish; I would stop being incapacitated by tension headaches, and start sleeping properly. If I did all that, then I would kill off the part of me that was mad.'[38] However, inside him was a time bomb.

In art therapy he painted a self-portrait.

I painted an angry, active volcano; a rough, destructive triangle inside which oranges and reds fought each other, and molten, purple rock spewed upwards, breaking into great chunks of black, gaseous debris which tumbled down the sides. It reminded me of the excitement I felt when seeing pictures of erupting volcanoes in full spate. Volcanoes, like earthquakes, hurricanes, tornadoes, tidal waves and thunderstorms, had always excited me.

That painting, and accumulated talking and acting out, began another journey at the unit, the journey which was to provide me with more self-knowledge about my emotional state stranger than I had ever known. I began to understand that I existed in two extreme emotional states: when something dramatic was happening I felt dynamic and hyperactive; when I felt dormant and useless I fantasized about death.[39]

When David and I met he told me of the rage he felt with people who did not obey the rules. 'When we had electricity cuts, I insisted that my family turn off all the lights in the house except the ones they absolutely needed. When I drove home at night and saw other houses with their lights blazing, I felt furious.'

He went on to say, 'When someone makes a mistake I exult. I'm always watching my therapist to see if I can catch him out.'

I asked him what lay behind this.

He said, 'Whenever I see the order and security that someone else has, I feel envious and I want to destroy it. I am filled with destructiveness, terrible destructiveness. I used to think that I was doing everything to preserve my family, but I wasn't.'

480

Here he echoed Alice Miller when she said of the grandiose person:

He is envious of healthy people because they do not have to make a constant effort to earn admiration, and because they do not have to do something in order to impress, one way or the other, but are free to be 'average'.[40]

David spoke of how, through therapy, he was gaining an understanding of himself, but he still found within himself a torrent of emotion which he could neither understand nor control. He described himself as being a very good predictor of other people's behaviour. These observational skills, combined with a greater knowledge of how a person's internal reality functions, while increasing his skills in getting along with people, had also increased his skill in finding how to hurt people. He said, 'I pick up something in what a person says and then I say something to that person which hurts. I intend it to hurt. But it's only with people with whom I can have that kind of conversation, when I see things in that other person that I recognize, that I feel there's a real relationship. My family don't like to enter into conversations with me. They say, "Don't psychoanalyse me." I can't be bothered with superficial conversation. It's a waste of time. The only people now I can communicate with are my wife and my therapist.'

What David showed here was how, for him, a close relationship must still contain hate and hurt as well as love. Children who have been involved in violence always have difficulty in separating love and hate. In adulthood they may be violent towards others, or they may hide their violence under a guise of caring and controlling and inflict their hurts in the name of love, or they may, like David, do all these things.

David began his book with an account of his attempted suicide when he was in California. After some treatment he was allowed to return to England provided he sought psychiatric help. Unwillingly, he accepted an appointment at a psychiatric hospital where he met a psychiatrist, 'a calm, neatly-dressed grey-haired man in his early sixties'. David told the psychiatrist he did not need drugs. He needed to go home. 'Like a host politely offering his guest a cup of tea, he ignored my words and asked, "Are you angry?" That was when my mind went blank.'

Later, 'When I tried to remember what had taken place at that meeting, I kept hearing his question – "Are you angry?" I wrestled mentally with the puzzle for days. Throughout my life, until then, I had believed that I controlled what little anger I felt.'[41]

It was this psychiatrist who persuaded David to go to Shipley Grange, and there he learned about his anger, hate and violence. He discovered and acknowledged these emotions, and he came to see that they were not some alien, incomprehensible, frightening force which took him over against his will but were part of him. They were his truth, not a pleasant truth, but the truth. He was all of one piece. Recognition, acknowledgement and acceptance of responsibility for these emotions did not dissipate them, but having now recognized his ownership he could decide how he would deal with these passions. This is the best that any of us can do.

Kay Jamison did not reach this point of understanding. She continued to be frightened of what lay in her internal reality. All she had was a name for it – a madness, manic-depression and a drug – lithium. She was estranged from herself.

When she was fifteen she visited a large psychiatric hospital with some fellow students. She wrote, 'Despite the fact that I had no obvious reason to believe that I was anything but passably sane, irrational fears began to poke away at my mind. I had a terrible temper, after all, and although it rarely irrupted, when it did it frightened me and anyone near its epicenter. It was the only crack, but a disturbing one, in the otherwise vacuum-sealed casing of my behaviour. God alone knew what ran underneath the fierce self-discipline and emotional control that had come with my upbringing. But the cracks were there, and they frightened me.'[42] She failed to learn that, when we refuse to recognize our anger and hate but bottle them up and pretend they do not exist, they do not dissipate but grow more and more powerful because they are our truth and demand to be expressed. We have a choice as to just how they should be expressed, but, if we refuse to exercise that choice, our truths will find some way of expressing themselves.

Kay's truths expressed themselves in her depressions and manias. She wrote:

> Both my manias and depressions had violent sides to them. Violence, especially if you are a woman, is not something spoken about with ease. Being wildly out of control – physically assaultive, screaming insanely at the top of one's lungs, running frenetically with no purpose or limit, or impulsively trying to leap from cars – is frightening to others and unspeakably terrifying to oneself. In blind manic rages I have done all of these things, at one time or another, and some of them repeatedly; I remain acutely and painfully aware of how difficult it is to control or understand such behaviors, much less explain them to others. I have, in my psychotic, seizurelike attacks – my black, agitated manias – destroyed things I cherish, pushed to the utter edge people I love, and survived to think I could never recover from the shame. I have been physically restrained by terrible, brute force: kicked and pushed to the floor; thrown on my stomach with my hands pinned behind my back; and heavily medicated against my will.[43]

Hate is part of what it is to be human. It is one of the functions of pride. When we feel utterly powerless and helpless we can hold ourselves together by hating the people we see as responsible for our desperate state. In this way many of the dispossessed and powerless people in the Middle East came to hate the USA and Israel, and some children have come to hate their parents. However, the first kind of hatred can be expressed by forming groups, attacking those they hate, and feeling virtuous for so doing, but children who hate their parents are likely to believe that it is wicked to do so. This belief prevents them from acknowledging and thus mastering their hatred.

An immediate way of solving this problem, of not so much mastering hate as running away from it, is to flee into activity in our external world. However, when we do this we prevent ourselves from developing the only safeguards human beings have against their own destructiveness, a knowledge and acceptance of ourselves and the impetus to develop effective methods of managing our hate and destructiveness.

Without these safeguards we destroy those things which we perceive as unconnected with us and as not being human like ourselves. Thus we can chop down trees, blow up mountains, pollute the seas and the atmosphere, eradicate whole species of animals, birds and fish because we do not understand that we are connected to everything on our planet, and therefore need to be careful about what and how much we destroy. We can see ourselves as free to destroy not only animals but creatures who may bear a passing resemblance to us. They may walk and talk and live in groups just like us, but, if we do not perceive them as human like us, we can bomb and maim them, exploit them, starve them, and inflict hurt upon them without feeling shame or guilt. We can perceive other people as being human like ourselves only when we can make that special leap of the imagination which takes us from our own internal world into theirs.

We are all born with a capacity to hate and to destroy. We are also born with the capacity to know our internal world and to empathize with others. A child brought up in love and acceptance develops all these capacities and can balance one against the other. Empathy balances the hate and keeps the destructiveness in check. We can feel immense hatred for another person and we can desire to harm him, but at the same time we know how it would feel to be the victim of that hatred and harm.

However, the less we value and accept ourselves, the more powerless and helpless we feel, thus the less we value and accept ourselves and the more likely we are to use hatred as a defence. If we do not understand that we are using hatred as a defence, and if we see such hatred as justified and virtuous, our hatred becomes boundless and such a part of us that we cannot relinquish it, no matter what peaceful compromises our enemies may offer us. Hence the continuing hatred between some Protestants and

Catholics in Northern Ireland and between many Israelis and Palestinians.

If we use hatred as a defence but see hatred as wicked, we have to prevent ourselves from being aware that we are using such a defence and that we need a defence. We can do this by turning the hate and destructiveness against ourselves and becoming depressed. When that becomes too terrifying, we may flee from depression and our internal reality to an external reality which may offer temporary shelter but never release from turmoil, because the key to this release lies not in the outside world but in ourselves.

Finding Yourself

When, in the 1970s, a wonderful and extraordinary woman called Janet Stevenson set up the first self-help group for depressed people, I was drawn into Depressives Associated almost immediately. However, I had no contact with another group formed later, called the Manic-Depression Fellowship. This fellowship was based on the assumption that manic-depression was a physical illness best treated by psychiatrists with lithium. Time went on, and by the early 1990s the Fellowship was changing markedly. David Guinness, then the chair, asked me to speak at a public meeting on manic-depression. Like a number of people with a diagnosis of manic-depression, he had experienced the limitations of lithium and had come to feel that there was a place for psychotherapy in the care of people with manic-depression.

I have spoken at far too many public meetings to remember them all, but this one I shall never forget. It was in London, and drew such an immense crowd that the hall was filled to capacity and the overflow installed in an adjacent hall. The atmosphere was quite stormy because three differing points of view were well represented. There were the people who believed that manic-depression was a biological illness, and they resented the fact that a psychologist had been invited to speak; there were people who were angry that their years of taking lithium had proved to be no more than a miserable existence; and there was a group who wanted to explore whether manic-depression could best be understood in psychological terms. I stood on the stage in front of a microphone, spoke for thirty minutes or so, and then answered questions for what seemed to me an interminable period. I felt that something very important was happening. People were questioning what they had been told and the treatment they had been given. I knew that many of these people had colluded with their psychiatrists in their diagnosis of a manic-depressive illness, so as to avoid a journey into what for both psychiatrist and patient was the most dangerous territory of all, their internal reality, and many had never been given the opportunity to make this journey. Some of the people who read my books write to me, and among those who had been given the label of manic-depressive many said, 'I have never been offered psychotherapy.'

The changes in the Manic-Depression Fellowship which followed from that meeting were quite profound. Even those members who were wedded to the medical model of manic-depression knew that they could not go on being just a support group for patients with a particular illness who were dutifully doing what their doctor told them to do. They had to do something for themselves.

The Manic-Depression Fellowship (MDF) now has a very informative website[44] but its content shows that the organization is still trying to satisfy those members who believe that they have a physical illness best treated in physical ways, professionals who share their view, and members and professionals who see the best way forward as that of self-knowledge and self-management. The organization is now called MDF The BiPolar Organisation. The website gives as the causes of bipolar disorder the usual mishmash of genetics, stressful life events and 'the brain's chemistry' but much of the website is devoted to showing people how they can learn to become aware of the situations which make them so frightened that they are tempted to use mania or depression as their defence. Thus they can deploy the tactics they have learned in order to keep their fear in check and so continue to behave in ordinary ways. Below is an outline of the MDF programme as given on their website.

MDF The BiPolar Organisation works to enable people affected by bipolar disorder/manic depression to take control of their lives. We aim to fulfil this mission by:

- Supporting and developing self-help opportunities for people affected by manic depression;
- Expanding and developing the information services about manic depression;
- Influencing the improvement of treatments and services to promote recovery;
- Decreasing the discrimination against, and promoting the social inclusion and rights of people affected by manic depression;
- Being an effective and efficient organisation with sufficient resources to sustain and develop our activities, thereby ensuring members receive a unique, high quality service.

MDF offers its members not just a network of self-help groups across the country but self-management training.

Self management training is designed to give people diagnosed with bipolar disorder a thorough and comprehensive understanding of the concepts, tools and techniques involved in learning to self manage extreme mood swings.

Research has shown that learning to self manage bipolar disorder (manic depression) is an invaluable part of stabilising the condition. It can significantly improve an individual's affective perception of areas such as self-esteem and reduction in suicidal thoughts.

Programme

The programme aims to teach the individual with bipolar disorder how to recognise the triggers for, and warning signs of, an impending episode of illness. Participants learn to take action to prevent or reduce the severity of an episode. The programme, which is delivered in various formats and in locations all over the UK, is continuously improved and updated as participants provide us with feedback and details of their experiences.

These self-management courses are tremendously important. As anyone who has experienced periods of mania can describe, that sudden burst of happiness that can brighten the dullest or most miserable of days can be something that they dare not allow themselves to enjoy because they fear that they cannot hold it in check. Recently two intelligent, educated professional men separately described to me how something I had done, something I regarded as a trivial act of helpfulness, produced in them a burst of happiness which was followed by a stream of increasingly grandiose fantasies about the wonderful things that would happen to them in the near future. Both knew enough about themselves to stop the fantasies in their tracks, but doing so also ended that lovely feeling of being happy. In the social conversation I had with each of these men (people tell me all sorts of things about themselves in a social conversation) I discovered that one of them had made a major effort to understand the significance of certain traumatic events in his childhood, while the other was still wary of such an exploration.

The same kind of wariness is evident in the advice the MDF website gives about those kinds of psychotherapies which explore the conclusions we have drawn from our experiences. The website seems to imply that cognitive behavioural therapy is the therapy of choice. Unfortunately a cognitive therapist can collude with a manic-depressed person in a reluctance to examine internal reality, and thus the person will do no more than dip a toe into his internal reality and then hastily withdraw from its murky waters.

Consequently, the machinations of primitive pride, intent on maintaining the meaning structure without regard to the consequences and to what is actually going on, are never challenged. One of the results of this is that the high value which extraverts place on excitement is never examined and, where necessary, modified. The lives of those people who go from mania to depression and back again in what seems like an endless cycle of trauma are full of pain and catastrophe. In their extremes they will ask for help, but, even in their extremes, if you said to them, 'I have a magic formula which will ensure that you never get into an emotional state again. You will live the rest of your life on an even keel,' many of them would say, 'No, I don't want it.' They consider that a life without its highs and lows is not worth living.

When Peter was asked if his therapy was worthwhile, he said:

I think that when I came out of it, it was much better in the sense that one understood the guilt. One's behaviour didn't promote shame, or indeed guilt either, which was nice. But in a curious sort of way it balanced the books. On the one hand there was a great deal more tranquillity, a great deal more contentment, one felt more even, less bizarre, less of a freak, but on the other hand, the lows had been cut off and so had the highs. A lot of the sparkle had gone. A lot of the excitement. I was, and still am, quite resentful that the upper sort of peaks, of having great enjoyment and perhaps being a bit excessive, if you like, in one's pleasures and so on are no longer there. I suppose I feel less of a person in some ways because a lot of what was there which was me has gone. I think it needed to go and I don't regret it. I mourn it, but I don't regret it. It needed to go, but I'm also resentful of the fact that it has gone because part of me is missing, and it's like part of me has been cut out. And it needed to be and it was right that it should be, but the operation still hurt.

Many of the people who take lithium regularly to limit the extent of their mood change feel, as Peter feels, a loss of a vital, creative, lively part of themselves. If, unlike Peter, they have not made their journey into self-understanding, they resent this loss, thus adding to their mountain of resentments, without being able, at the same time, to recognize the necessity of the loss and thus mourn it.

One of the conceits that many people allow themselves to enjoy is that of believing that madness and creativity belong together:

you cannot have one without the other. This belief can have tragic consequences. Both Virginia Woolf and Sylvia Plath believed that their creativity had the same source as their madness. Each of these women had extremely difficult childhoods, which a perusal of their biographies and their writings shows clearly. However, they feared that therapy might render them happy, and in this untroubled state, rather than use their genius to the full, they would be unable to write. So they stayed troubled, and, when events turned against them, they boxed themselves into a corner from which suicide seemed to be the only escape.

Kay Jamison enthusiastically embraced the idea that manic-depressive illness is intimately linked to what she called 'the artistic temperament'. She wrote a very large book, *Touched by Fire*, in which she listed eighty-three poets, forty-one writers, twenty-three composers, seven non-classical composers and musicians, and forty-one artists as having had manic-depression. She quoted the DSM's long lists of criteria for 'major depressive episode', 'manic episode', 'cyclothymia' and 'hypomania', criteria which can easily be stretched to include us all. Some of the people she listed had been given the diagnosis of schizophrenia, but she dismissed this as 'often misdiagnosed manic-depression'.[45] She did not mention the extensive research by American and British psychiatrists into their respective diagnostic predilections which showed that American psychiatrists tended to see manic-depression where British psychiatrists tended to see schizophrenia.

Kay Jamison did not compare the incidence of manic-depression, depression, alcoholism and suicide in writers, musicians and artists with that in people in other occupations. The medical profession, not noted for its artistic temperament, has a high incidence of drug addiction and suicide, but this is usually explained by doctors' easy access to drugs. Farmers in the UK have a high incidence of suicide, but this is usually explained in terms of the changes in agriculture, isolation, and a proud refusal to ask for help. Jamison made much of Virginia Woolf's troubled family, but she did not mention that as a child Virginia was sexually abused by a cousin of whom she said years later, 'George ruined my life.' Similarly Jamison made much of Ernest Hemingway's suicide, but she did not mention the famous incident when Hemingway was asked what was needed to become a great writer and replied, 'An unhappy childhood'.

An unhappy childhood certainly provides a deep mine of material which can be reworked again and again. Writers tell their life story many times over, but some writers are better than others at doing this. Such writers have a good understanding of how language works, and they have distanced themselves sufficiently from their past to be able to see it from a multitude of perspectives. Less talented writers do not have the same feel for language, and often they have not distanced themselves at all from their story, hence they tell it in a rush of uncritical emotion or in self-aggrandizing fantasies.

The belief that creativity and madness have the same root is a comforting delusion. I have met quite a number of would-be writers who are sure they would be great writers if only creativity's partner, depression, did not prevent them from being famous. They may indeed not be famous, but at least they had spared themselves the rebuffs and disappointments that are part of all writers' lives. The great benefit of lacking self-confidence is that, while you may never win, you never lose.

Then there are the people who, having demonstrated their creativity, give as an excuse for their bad behaviour the inevitability of it because they are creative. In the days of William Faulkner, Scott Fitzgerald, Ernest Hemingway and Tennessee Williams, it seemed that any man who aspired to write the great American novel had to be a drunk. In more recent years many film stars and entertainers saw it as an essential part of their career, and proof that they were great artists, to take illegal drugs, followed by a period in a fashionable clinic, then to have a much-publicised come-back. This, reworked for the drug era, is the old revivalist theme of the sinner now repenting and proving by his remorse his virtue.

Many people who would regard themselves as being not at all creative like the idea that creativity and madness are inseparable because it shows the workings of the Just World. They are comforted by knowing that those who are touched by genius and enjoy fame, wealth, position, and are loved by all, will inevitably be humbled by madness.

Madness – the desperate defences – wastes time and energy that no one can afford. The only benefit these defences can bring is that through them we can learn wisdom, but we cannot gain this wisdom if we refuse to try to understand why we suffer.

Gaining self-knowledge is hard work, and most of the hard work you have to do on your own. Other people, through books, friendship and therapy, can be helpful. Finding a therapist who suits you is not easy. Kay Jamison spoke highly of the therapy she received, but it seems to have been framed in terms of helping her live with her illness in much the same way as someone with multiple sclerosis may find it helpful to talk to a therapist about the difficulties of living with that terrible illness. David Guinness discovered a particular form of therapy called Focusing. He wrote:

Undoubtedly my system undergoes biochemical changes when I am high or low but my experience is that these do not occur without cause. In the pre-lithium days, authors used to write at length about the psychology of manic-depression, particularly the notion that mania is a defence against the underlying depression. I concur with this; my depressions always contain feelings of failure and my highs are triggered by success. Anyone guess I had high parental expectations also?

He went to a Focusing workshop where the group was encouraged to make contact with 'a place that we would normally keep at arm's length – a ''habit-protected place'' '.

Before long I was in touch with a very old, very deep-seated sense of failure. I felt at the time and I still feel that this is the mainspring of my MD. If it gets on top of me, I feel submerged in it and get depressed; if I protect myself from it by running away into fantasy, then I go high. It seems we can 'process skip' in all sorts of ways; mania is trying to do it by changing one's identity. There's a saying in MD 'If there's a light at the end of a tunnel it's the light of an oncoming train'. But the workshop finished three weeks ago and I'm still in touch with my sense of failure. If I can continue to own it, make friends with it and let it tell its story, then maybe it just won't bother me any more.[46]

Guinness was not alone in his sense of failure. One woman, having read the original edition of *Beyond Fear*, wrote to me saying, 'I identified with the manic phase very much, doing things just to prove I am worthy to exist.'

Robert, a very successful professional man, contacted me after his beloved wife, unable to endure the excesses of his behaviour any longer, left him. Like David Wigoder, Robert had discovered that writing was an excellent way of exploring his internal reality and integrating it with his external reality. In a letter to me he wrote, 'I don't know who I am. I was suffocating, frightened to death of my internal world. For here was I, imprisoned on the outside by my so-called success, or what I prefer to call "my ritual accumulation of materialistic bric-a-brac". And, on the inside, lost, unable to thread a knowing path through my internal chaos. I am frightened of being alone – not physically but emotionally. I so need someone to understand me.'

Robert had to confront the despair of the small boy who loved the father who whipped him unmercifully for every transgression. He tried to talk to his mother about what had happened to him as a child, but she refused to acknowledge that such a childhood could affect him adversely. When he pressed her about one particular incident – when, aged six, he had attempted to climb out of a second-floor window in order to escape from his father, but his father had hauled him back and whipped him – all she would say was that he was a bad child and deserved the whipping. Robert told me, 'I don't expect her to make it right – that's not possible – but if she could say yes, it happened and I'm sorry, I would feel so much better.' It is much easier to change if our nearest and dearest allow us to change, and even easier if such people accept some responsibility for our predicament.

David found life in a therapeutic community quite different from what he had expected. It was far from easy, yet, after a while, he began to realize just how valuable it was. He wrote:

> There, at the unit, if I could work out what I did, and how I felt, and try not to explain it away by blaming my past, was the answer I wanted. Through the members residents – more than the staff – I could understand myself. They were facing the same problems, experiencing the same angry feelings, and reacting as I did. If I stopped trying to escape from them, perhaps I would feel better. . . I still could not control my feelings, but I was learning to recognize them, and that helped. Bit by bit, despite feeling bad most of the time, I felt I was 'getting there'.[47]

He believed that his overriding emotion was sadness, and when he was told he was angry he got angry. Years later, 'I realized I was not sad. I was angry; angry at losing what I needed. I had always wanted my aunt to be my mother.'[48] His aunt had married and left. When a nurse he had come to depend on later left suddenly it was a loss like that of his aunt. And there was an earlier loss, that of the mother he had wanted instead of the one he had.

David also started to learn about complex emotions.

> I began to understand that the complex emotions I felt could not be isolated. The effort of accepting each emotion as truth made me wish I could isolate them. 'That's anger,' I wanted to say. 'That's jealousy.' And so on. It was hard to say that. It was harder to accept that 'that' could be anger and jealousy; or that one twinge of feeling might include anger, jealousy, rejection, and most of the other feelings I was beginning to think about – and feel.[49]

When David left Shipley Grange he and his wife Helen separated and divorced. He had changed so much he was no longer the person Helen had married. She had stood by him even though he had attempted to kill her and had injured her quite badly in doing so. However, she had come to feel that he was much closer to his group at Shipley Grange than to her, and indeed this was so. Therapy may present us with some very hard choices.

Three years after leaving the Grange, he found that his need of possessions had vanished and he had far better relationships with his family. However, what remained was his fear of loss. He found it hard to believe that those he loved would not leave him. This was not an irrational fear but one we all have to learn to live with. Life can and does take away those we love. However, David felt able to write:

> I hate being alone. I need people, not many, perhaps only one, with whom to share my feelings and aspirations. Depression, or whatever else it may be called – emotional disturbance, personality problems or any other label – is a lonely business. But occasionally, because of the isolation, I enjoy a wondrous experience – a day when after a good night's sleep I wake up refreshed, my head clear of worrying thoughts, my body supple and relaxed. There are not many of them – perhaps one in two months – but when they arrive, unexpectedly, I want to shout out with joy that there aren't two of me at all, just one person who sometimes believes that he can come to terms with himself.[50]

He was no longer the mad one and the normal one. He was simply himself.

Kate Millett had never seen any reason to consult a therapist, but alone in New York, badly treated by the psychiatrist Dr Foreman, with little money and in the very depths of depression, she went to a public hospital to ask for a prescription for lithium. She waited her turn in a grim little waiting room. 'Finally, a very young man, boyish in fact, calls my name. In the lottery of life I've drawn a kid, I think, following him. Maybe I can get a substitute; perhaps it's a different one each time. But the frenzy I bring him doesn't discriminate. I used up Foreman's stuff. Now if I could get more lithium from this guy here, and if the lithium works, I could climb out of this state.'

But: 'They not only give out lithium here, he says, they do a bit more therapy than I've been used to – how do I feel about that? Not terribly cordial, I admit, but at this point I am very depressed, and simply grateful for his patience with me. He saw me three times a week thereafter, tense, dreadful sessions wherein I remained nearly speechless – wanting to reveal as little of my life as possible and in any case deprived of language by the silence of depression. Below that speechless lassitude the mind races from one imminent disaster to another, each of them a foregone conclusion, all very real.'[51]

Dr Benfield wanted to see some of her writing but she refused. 'I regard what I'm working on sacred or magical enough never to be discussed.' This seemed to hurt his feelings, but 'otherwise he was kindness personified, merely being himself and concerned. . . We got along. My days are spent, many of them, walking across town to get my blood levels drawn for lithium and in the hour with Benfield, the one being who seems to care whether I live or die. An odd relationship to have formed with a stranger, a good fortune that hardly seems credible. [He] was completely necessary at first, then both of us cutting down on the visits until that great moment when his mere existence in a certain room on Thursdays is no longer all there is between me and death or isolation or despair. I cannot help be grateful, and tell him so. Even that first day. He smiled. ''Accepting help is the hardest thing of all.'' '[52]

Kate was then able to keep her farm, re-establish her relationships, get work and, between 1982 and 1985, she wrote *The Loony Bin Trip*. In 2000 a second edition was published, and to this Kate added a conclusion. She found, as I have found, that it is a curious experience rereading a book you wrote ten or twenty years before. You realize how differently you now see things. Kate wrote, 'Now, when I reread it, I find something in it rings false. True, it describes depression: the giving in, the giving up, an abnegation so complete it becomes false consciousness. But typing it over I want to say, Wait a moment – why call this depression? – why not call it grief? You've permitted your grief, even your outrage, to be converted into a disease. You have allowed your overwhelming, seemingly

496

inexplicable grief at what has been done to you – the trauma and shame of imprisonment – to be transformed into a mysterious psychosis. How could you?'[53]

Then she was invited to attend a conference of the National Association for Rights, Protection and Advocacy, professionals authorized by the federal government to protect the rights of person with mental illness. Through this group she met the 'veteran organizers of the anti-psychiatric movement'. She made friends within this group, and with their support she gradually reduced her intake of lithium until for the first time in seven years she took none at all. 'Nothing happened. Nothing ever happened. None of the anger I had feared; indeed it seemed that lithium had created a stifled fury in me for years which abated and fell away. To my surprise I had a new patience now, and serenity, was more tolerant and open, even able to fall in love again.'[54]

Kate finished her book in Paris, at a window looking out at the spire of Sainte Chapelle. She wrote:

Let us stop being afraid. Of our own thoughts, our own minds. Of madness, our own or others'. Stop being afraid of the mind itself, its astonishing functions and fandangos, its complications and simplifications, the wonderful operation of its machinery – more wonderful because it is not machinery at all or predictable. As ingenious and surprising and uncertain of result as the first stroke of a painting, as various in possibility. As full of ornament and invention as the spire of the Sainte Chapelle outside my window, a really crazy steeple full of frills, and balls, and cuckoos.[55]

Chapter Eleven

Turning Fear into Obsessions and Compulsions

At one point in my life I was living in a house that had a large kitchen whose floor was covered with green linoleum which showed every footmark. There were plenty of footmarks as my five-year-old son and his friends ran in from the garden and the beach. If I had been sensible I would have ignored the floor, but I could not do that. Every day I washed and polished it. As soon as a mark appeared I hurried to remove it. I was very busy. I was working full time and studying for my clinical diploma, as well as looking after a husband, a child and a large house. Yet the floor had to be kept clean and spotless. At the time I could not see why this floor was so important, but later I understood. In the years during which I lived in that house the pattern that I called my life, present and future, slowly disintegrated. As I began to feel it slipping from my control, I looked for some part I could hold on to and keep ordered, clean and perfect. Only the kitchen floor was willing to meet my requirements.

I was an introvert doing what all introverts do – perceiving the threat to my sense of being a person as coming from my external reality and trying to deal with it by establishing order and control in that external reality. Like an army under attack, I retreated to an area I thought I could defend, and, like an army close to defeat, I pitched my standard – the symbol for the meaning and purpose of that army – and prepared to defend it against all onslaughts as the world I once governed dissolved into chaos. Fortunately for me, I did not have to defend my standard (the kitchen floor) to the death. I did not have to go on cleaning it day after day, for it did not

498

become an obsession, a defence against the threat of the annihilation of myself. Instead, it proved to be what Donald Winnicott called a transitional object, something I could hold on to like a comfort blanket, while I made the transition from one way of life to another. For, while I dreaded the chaos of change and was angry at losing many of the things I valued, I could see the possibility that through this chaotic change in my life something better would emerge, as it did.

One thing I did gain was a better understanding of myself and, as a consequence, of other people. It was during this time that I experienced so very clearly the threat of annihilation and felt myself shattering and falling through infinite space. This experience was both terrifying and enlightening. For introverts, understanding is all. If introverts can understand – that is, see some clear pattern as to why things happen as they do – they feel much better, even though the pattern they see and the events they study can be quite horrific. Extraverts like to know why, but knowing means for them going into action. Many extraverts prefer not to ask why but, when they see something wrong, they like to spring straight into action to put it right.

Extraverts and introverts may behave in much the same way, but they do what they do for very different reasons. Many extraverts are passionate about keeping things clean, but they do this in order to maintain and strengthen relationships rather than to bring order into the world as introverts wish to do. Many extraverts, like many introverts, are careful.

Most of us are careful. We turn off gas taps, lock outside doors before we go to bed, put sharp knives out of the reach of children, wash our hands after we go to the toilet, and try not to knock anyone down when we are driving. We do all these things because we want to look after ourselves and other people.

Some of us are *very* careful. We have a system for making sure that gas taps are turned off, doors locked, sharp knives put away, that ourselves and our possessions are always clean, and that we are careful, law-abiding drivers. However, good though our systems of organization and control may be, we do need to check that we did do what we are supposed to do. As we are getting into bed at night, we may think, 'Did I lock the back door?' and we go downstairs to check. We would say that we are careful and well organized because we want to look after other people and ourselves. When our systems break down, or something happens to stop them working properly, we feel annoyed and anxious. We do not like being upset because emotion is so disorganized and uncontrolled. *Very* careful people are quite likely to be introverts.

A few of us are *extremely* careful, so careful in fact that we spend most of our time being careful. We do not just turn off gas taps. We go back twenty or thirty times to make sure that we did turn them off. Sometimes we have to turn them on again to prove to ourselves that we did turn them off. Then we have to keep going back to make sure we turned them off the second time, and so we turn them on again to prove that we had turned them off, and so on and on. We work out various rituals for making sure the taps are turned off, and then we have to create a ritual to make sure that we are doing the first ritual properly, and then a ritual to make sure we are doing the second ritual properly, and so on and on.

It is the same with checking that we have locked the house doors and the car doors, until our loved ones scream at us in exasperation. We have a system for locking away sharp knives which means that no one can get to them. We do not just wash our hands after going to the toilet. We wash them forty or fifty times, so many times that the skin on our hands cracks and bleeds. We see how contamination could spread from the toilet bowl, and we work out a systematic ritual to prevent this which we have to follow every time we go to the toilet. We know, too, that contagion can come from the floor. Outside the house there are dogs and dog dirt and we can see how the contagion could spread from where we walk and what we touch. Part of our house becomes a no-go area, and we wash and wash and wash. Driving, we pass a cyclist or pedestrian, and then think, 'Did I knock that person over?' We go back and look, and again never satisfy ourselves that we have done no harm. We wake in the night filled with terror and guilt.

This is how introverts think when their self-confidence and self-acceptance have dwindled away and the world around them becomes increasingly unreal. Some extraverts become keenly aware of the possibilities of contagion, and they may, as one friend of mine does, boil tea towels and dishcloths and discard any that become stained. Or they may, as another friend of mine does, feed their family nothing but organic food. However, the sole aim of their obsessional habits is to keep their family alive. They are not engaged in *saving the universe and themselves from chaos*.

The obsessions and compulsions which introverts may develop can seem to an outside observer indistinguishable from phobias about open spaces, spiders and the like. However, if we go beyond behaviour and ask why someone behaves as he does, obsessions and compulsions can be seen to be very different from phobias. In their book *Obsessive-Compulsive Disorder: the Facts*, Padmal de Silva and Stanley Rachman wrote:

> The ritualistic behaviour of the obsessive-compulsive is absent in the phobic. Many of the former may describe their feeling, when affected by an obsession or exposed to a triggering situation, such as contact with dirt, not so much as 'fear' but as 'discomfort', 'uneasiness', or 'disgust'. A further important difference is that someone with a phobia usually can, if he successfully avoids the object or situation he is afraid of, feel safe and be unaffected by the problem in his day-to-day life. Someone with a phobia of elevators, for example, will avoid using elevators and be able to live a perfectly happy life as long as he is not forced to use an elevator, and someone with a phobia of spiders can lead a normal life as long as he avoids encounters with spiders. In contrast, an obsessive-compulsive patient cannot escape from his problems as easily; even if he keeps away from things that trigger his obsession or compulsive urges, he does not feel free. For example, a woman with this disorder may totally avoid knives, scissors, and other sharp objects, which she fears she may use to attack people, but still frequently worry that she may commit these acts, or indeed even wonder whether she has actually attacked someone.[1]

A person in the grip of obsessions and compulsions does feel fear, but it is the fear we describe as a dread of the unknown. This is a far worse fear than the fear of something visible – an open space, or a spider, or an onlooker. Obsessions and compulsions can start very early in life, and the fear that provoked them, the fear of annihilation, not acquire any name that brings it into ordinary experience. Marc Summers, a popular American television presenter and the author of *Everything in Its Place: My Trials and Triumphs with Obsessive Compulsive Disorder*, began his book with:

> From the time I was six years old, everything in my world had to be perfect. My clothes had to be folded a certain way. The shirts hanging in my closet had to be a quarter-inch apart, no more, no less, with all the hangers facing in the same direction. My books were organized alphabetically and lined up so that they were exactly the same distance from the lip of the shelf. I shined my shoes each day until they glowed and I could see my face in them. If I erased something in a homework paper and left the slightest smudge or, God forbid, a hole, I'd redo the assignment on a fresh sheet of paper because I thought my failure to do so would result in something bad happening to me or to my parents. One of us would have a freak accident or contract a deadly disease. I thought I was the only kid in the world who felt this way. I thought I was crazy, so I kept the secret of my bizarre behaviors to [myself]. . . From the time I was eight years old until I was sixteen, every single Sunday of my life I cleaned everything [in my room] in exactly the same order.

As a small child Summers was entranced by television, and he worked occasionally on a children's television programme. He wrote, 'Even at the time, television was the only place where I felt totally comfortable. At school, in the playground, at home, I always felt slightly on edge, as though I was on the verge of disaster: a drink spilled on my pants, my father coming home late, dust behind my bureau.' About his adult life he wrote, 'I had been tormented since I was a child with the constant anxiety of living in an inherently chaotic, imperfect world where I needed everything in its place. Most of the time the anxiety was at a low pitch. At other times it shrieked inside me like a siren. It was always there, lurking in the background.'[2]

Those introverts who are *extremely* careful would say that they are like this because they are extremely concerned about safety, their own and other people's. They can see danger and death in everything that happens. They see their boss about to sit down and they think, 'That chair could break and he'd smash his head.' They pick up a knife and think, 'I could plunge this into my baby.' They see some children and imagine doing to them something too grossly sexual and murderous to be described. Curiously, with all these thoughts there is no emotion. No anger or sexual impulse. Just the thought. Then, afterwards, comes the doubt, 'I didn't do that, did I?', and then the guilt. Dreadful, obsessive, mind-gripping guilt. Reassurances from sensible people are of no avail. No absolute reassurance is possible because they can always doubt.

Doubting is something that introverts are extremely good at. While we all operate in the two realities that every person knows – the reality of the world around us, our external reality, and the reality inside us, our thoughts and feelings, our internal reality – introverts find that their internal reality is more real than external reality. They have many doubts about external reality and how they act in it. Introverts act in external reality by treating it *as if* it is real. When they are full of self-confidence the *as if* quality of external reality fades into the background, but if they make a mistake, or something happens completely unexpectedly, the as-if-ness of external reality suffuses the scene around them.

The only way of keeping external reality looking as if it is real is to keep it organized and under control. If they do not do this, external reality will become so chaotic it will threaten to overwhelm them. Keeping everything progressing in some way gives introverts a sense of achievement, and that, they feel, is what life is about. People who find external reality more real than internal reality –

that is, extraverts – are not continually concerned with organizing external reality and achieving some result. For instance, they may be indifferent to doing the washing up and tidying the kitchen before going to bed, while to an introvert a clean and tidy kitchen can be both a necessity and an achievement. On the other hand, some introverts are indifferent to kitchens and can leave them to fester while they get on with organizing some other part of the universe, while some extraverts diligently tidy the kitchen before retiring to bed, but they do so not in order to organize the universe but to ensure that their family has a proper breakfast and a packed lunch. If you want to keep your family around you, you have to keep them alive.

Extraverts see practical, everyday things as having the potential to harm themselves and those they love, and so they strive to do practical, everyday things to keep their loved ones alive. They may read about crop-spraying leaving a poisonous residue on fruit and vegetables, and so they wash and peel with extra diligence the fruit and vegetables they buy. Or they may hear about the dangers of microwaves emitted by the pylons used for mobile phone transmissions, and they protest most vigorously when such pylons are built near their homes. Their fears may be excessive in view of the actual danger, but they do relate to actual disasters that have a certain probability, though very small, of occurring.

The line of thinking of an obsessional introvert is very different. It begins with someone close to the introvert doing something that is an extreme threat to the introvert as a person. This provokes the rage and the hate that we all have experienced, and which leads us to wish that the person who enraged us was dead. If thinking murderous thoughts could by itself effect practical results, we would all be orphans. For many years now I have tried to kill the people I regard as monsters of evil not just by thinking murderous thoughts but by shouting at them every time they appear on television, 'Die! Die!' but, alas, each of them continues to enjoy a healthy, accident-free life.

However, some children fail to learn that thought alone is powerless without action. Consequently, when they wish their parents dead, their hate quickly turns to fear that they have killed their parents. They know that in external reality some action can be undone. Writing can be erased and dirty clothes made clean. Hence they think that certain thoughts can undo certain earlier thoughts. This second kind of thought has the power to turn certain actions into magical actions, and this magic acts as a shield to protect the hated person from the murderous hate winging towards him.

All this murderous thinking might be fine, except for the introvert's infinite capacity for doubt. What if the ritual did not work, or if it was not carried out properly? With such a thought the introvert becomes very afraid.

Marc Summers described how he feared that he had killed his parents. These fears '. . . began when I empathized with my mother's fear that, when my father was late, it meant he'd had an accident'.

> But my anxieties began to escalate. I thought that my parents would die if I didn't do everything in exactly the right way. When I took my glasses off at night I'd have to place them on the dresser in exactly the right way. Sometimes I'd turn on the light and get out of bed seven times until I was comfortable with the angle. If the angle wasn't right, I felt my parents would die. The feeling ate up my insides.
>
> If I didn't grab the moulding on the wall in exactly the right way as I entered or exited my room; if I didn't hang up a shirt in the closet perfectly; if I didn't read a paragraph a certain way; if my hands and nails weren't perfectly clean, I thought my incorrect behaviours would kill my parents. . .
>
> The rare occasions when I failed to perform a ritual or complete a task were sheer hell. I would wake up in the middle of the night and lie there, consumed by fear. I'd sneak out of bed, careful not to wake my brother, and tiptoe down the hall. I'd stand in the doorway of my parents' room, listening for their breathing. . . I wouldn't leave there until I heard them both breathing. Often I would fall asleep standing up, leaning against the doorframe, and my father would catch me and say, 'What are

you up to? Go to bed!' He always thought I was sleepwalking, but I was making sure that Mom and Dad were both still alive. When I saw they were, and that my 'failure' didn't have terrible consequences, for a brief time – perhaps a week or two, sometimes longer – the fears would decrease.[3]

For the organizers and doubters of external reality, the difference between being ordinarily careful, very careful and *extremely* careful is one of self-confidence and valuing oneself. The less self-confidence we have and the less we like ourselves, the greater the dangers we see and the more helpless we feel in the face of them. The kind of childhood experiences that robbed us of our self-confidence and taught us that we were bad and unacceptable were also the kind of experiences that made us feel helplessly angry – an anger we were not allowed to express. Over the years this anger, with the other frustrations that come when we do not value ourselves, turned to murderous hate, and this is a doubly dangerous, forbidden, chaotic emotion. Denied, it returns as perceptions of danger to other people, and in terrible fantasies.

Those of us whose life is a round of doubt, guilt, obsessions and compulsions harbour childish beliefs – namely, that thoughts can kill and that anger is endless and shattering. Thought alone does not murder, any more than it scrubs the kitchen floor. Anger, like all emotions, is self-limiting. We cannot go on and on being possessed by anger any more than we can go on and on being possessed by laughter. However, if in childhood we never have a chance to learn that anger is self-limiting and that angry thoughts alone cannot destroy, we grow up believing that anger is evil, and that thought can kill.

Introverts find it easy to separate thought from feeling, and so they can readily deny that they experience the emotions that cause chaos. Introverts feel comfortable with thought, and so they easily come to overvalue it and believe that it can do more than it actually can. Extraverts also find it easy to separate thought and feeling, but it is thought – that is, memory – which they deny. They easily come to overvalue feelings and believe that they can do more than they can. Introverts think that thoughts can kill; extraverts think that love alone can save the world. Neither is right.

Extraverts often think introverts are crazy, always wanting to know why, and coming up with all kinds of ludicrous explanations which change nothing. Extraverts prefer to get on and *do* something without waiting for an explanation. As long as they get their feelings right – plenty of excitement and enthusiasm, warmth and closeness – they feel fine. Introverts like to keep their heads in order, extraverts their hearts.

For introverts, keeping your head in order – that is, thinking clearly and logically, though not necessarily sensibly – is the only way of keeping your external reality in order, which you must do, since an excess of stimulation is very painful and chaos is terrifying.

There are three things which create chaos in external reality – objects, people and feelings. Introverts are very good at keeping objects in order, whether it is keeping the kitchen clean or developing a management system for a multinational company. Objects can be put in perfect order, but then along come human beings, and they ruin the system. So introverts try to deal with human beings by controlling them. Extraverts are keen on controlling others too, but the aim of their control is different. Extraverts want to control others so as to keep them in the extravert's group. Introverts want to control others so as to keep everything orderly. However, as every extravert parent desperate to keep the children from leaving home finds, and every introvert dictator committed to creating the perfect society has found, human beings are very adept at slipping out of another person's control.

The reason that human beings are so difficult to control is that they have their own individual way of seeing things. They have feelings, and feelings are spontaneous. They happen. They are our own, instantaneous truths. If we interpret a situation or a person as frustrating us, getting in our way, we respond with anger because anger can give us the strength and power, physical or verbal, to remove the source of the frustration, or at least to attempt to do so. If we interpret a situation or a person as insulting or belittling us, we respond with angry pride, 'How dare that be done to me!' Either or both of these reactions can occur within a second, but all we may be conscious of is the feeling of anger. We may try to deny that we have certain feelings, but that is like trying to deny that the rain falls and the sun shines.

Feelings, our own and other people's, make external reality very difficult to control, and that is why introverts are always very wary of feelings. Introverts are very skilled at separating feelings from thought, and then minimizing their experience of their feelings, or denying their feelings altogether. If you let go of your feelings you will stir up trouble for yourself in your external reality.

Doubt, Hate and the Denial of Feeling

Simon's journey from work to home by car should have taken no more than thirty minutes. Most nights it took him three hours. It would have taken longer, only he would become too exhausted to go on driving, and even then he was not certain that along the way he had not injured or killed a fellow traveller. Every evening he set off from work determined to drive straight home. On the way he would pass someone, a boy on a bike, a woman with a pram, or an old man getting off a bus, and then he would think, 'Did I hit that person?'

There had been no bump, no sound of a body hitting the car, no reason at all for him to be anxious, but the doubt remained. He turned the car around and went back to check. The fact that there was no sign of an injured person did not reassure him. He set off for home again, and on the way he thought about how he could have missed seeing a body lying in a ditch or behind a hedge. He returned, again and again, to the spot, but, no matter how often he returned and how thoroughly he searched, he could not satisfy himself that he had not killed someone. When he finally arrived home exhausted he discounted his parents' reassurances, and woke in the night in a sweat of terror and guilt.

Psychiatrists call what Simon did a symptom of obsessive-compulsive disorder, and they prescribe antidepressants and tranquillizers. They advise the person to relax his high standards of morality, organization and cleanliness, but, while the person may agree that this is a good idea, secretly he thinks that his standards and performance in work, in cleanliness or in driving are not high enough. He checks and rechecks his work, and he is meticulous about cleanliness, even to the point of washing his hands far more often than is necessary. In every aspect of his life he, or she, is concerned with order, control, achievement and cleanliness.

The psychiatrist will get from his patient a life history in meticulous detail, but what will usually be missing from it is an account of feelings. The patient will speak of guilt – he is an expert on guilt – but feelings like rage or fear of loss of security are likely to be omitted from the account. This omission means that his story is just a string of unrelated events. Often when I sat in a case conference and listened to a junior doctor reporting a patient's case history I would think, 'This isn't a story. It's just a collection of events in chronological order with nothing to explain why one event led to another.' Only the patient's reasons, and the feelings involved in those reasons, can explain why one event led to another and an ordinary life led to a dominating obsession.

Simon's account of the beginning of his obsession was simple. One day he was driving home from work and he passed a middle-aged man who was crouching, on the side of the road, his back to oncoming traffic, beside a powerful motorbike. Simon thought, 'That's a stupid place to fiddle with your bike,' and then, 'I could have hit him.' He worried about this all the way home, and the next evening, driving home and passing a boy waiting to cross the road, he began his endless search.

An account of Simon's feelings changes the story. The day he passed the man with the motorbike should have been his day off from a temporary job he particularly disliked. That morning his boss had phoned to ask him to work after all but Simon, having planned to do something that day in connection with setting up his own business, had refused.

Hearing this, Simon's father intervened. He told Simon that he must go to work. 'You must do what your boss tells you to do,' he said. 'You don't want people thinking that you're lazy.'

Simon always did what his father told him. He did not argue. His father expected obedience and respect, and saw that he got them. Inwardly, though, Simon seethed. Actually he felt more than rage. For the first time in his life he was sure that his father was wrong, and this realization both exhilarated and terrified him.

All his life Simon had accepted his father's power and discipline because he believed that his father knew everything and so could keep organized a world that Simon feared was changeable and dangerous. His parents had always told him that this was so. Now Simon was trying to take his first steps towards independence, and his father, still treating him as a child, was blocking him. Simon was furious. He tried to quieten his rage by telling himself that his father was only thinking of his best interests, but the meaning of his rage could not be denied. He knew that his father wanted to maintain his power over him. It was a war in Simon's head between what is and what ought to be. 'What is' said, 'You'll never be free while your father is alive,' and 'what ought to be' said, 'You must not kill your father.'

Like many introverts, Simon found it difficult to distinguish 'what is' from 'what ought to be' because 'ought' can dominate an introvert's thinking. When 'what is' pressed itself on Simon, he usually dismissed it with a 'what ought to be', but on this occasion he could not because this 'what is' was telling him that he would be wiped out as a person if he went on letting his father dominate him.

On the edge of the road a middle-aged man tinkering with a powerful motorbike, a symbol of male potency, focused all Simon's rage and fear into one image. Another young man, driving by such a scene, may have said to himself, 'Stupid old goat. I should have run the bugger down,' and not given the scene another thought. Simon, however, had never let himself feel such aggression. All his life he had backed away from confrontation, and prided himself on his lack of aggression.

Simon's obsession was both an expression and a denial of his hate. The ever-present hate demanded the obsession's repetition, and the denial of the hate prevented the hate ever being recognized and resolved.

Many people, trapped like Simon in a sorry round of sin ('I could have injured that person') and expiation ('I'll check that I didn't and by checking I'll show I'm repentant'), and finding that the psychiatrist's drugs do little to relieve their misery, change their way of living in order to avoid the conditions of their obsession. They may give up driving altogether, and explain this with specious excuses, or they may place on their partners the responsibility for preventing them from searching, and so strain and sometimes ruin their relationship. However, the obsession stays with them. Even when walking down the street, Simon worried that his mere presence on the pavement might cause harm.

We are all taught that it is permissible to hate the enemies of the group to which we belong, but it is not permissible to hate the members of our group, especially our family. Yet it is our family who are most likely to provoke our hate because they can frustrate us and threaten to wipe us out as a person. We can hate, and at the same time seek to protect the object of our hate.

On one occasion, when I was preparing dinner, I had finished peeling the potatoes and was wrapping up the peelings in newspaper when I thought, 'I never wrap up the sharp knife with the rubbish.'

This was a memory from my childhood. In our house we had one sharp knife which did all the jobs that sharp knives have to do. However, frequently it would go missing. Someone, usually Mother, could not find it – it was not in the cutlery drawer, or on the draining board, or on the kitchen table – and there would be a great hue and cry. Then Mother would ask herself the question she always asked us when we could not find anything, 'Where did you have it last?', and she would hurry down the back stairs to the space under the veranda where the garbage can was kept. There she would unwrap the neatly rolled newspaper packages of rubbish and in one of them, along with the peelings, would be the knife.

I took this to be one of those regular events in family life which had no particular significance. After all, it is easy to lay a knife down among the peelings and not notice it later when you clear away. However, forty years later, I saw the significance of this.

I still remember vividly the occasions – not many, but enough to frighten and anger me – when my mother would beat me and shout that she was going to kill me and then kill herself. Now I could see why the sharp knife had to be wrapped up and thrown away to protect me, and my sister and father. Mother hated us so much that she wanted to kill us, but she cared for us and had to protect us. She hated herself so much that she sometimes wanted to kill herself, but she had too much pride to show such weakness to the world. It was better to hide herself, and the knife, right away.

Well before we are conscious of being a person our meaning structure comes into being along with the functions of pride, anger and hate which protect it. As babies we formed a picture of our world, and usually this picture included the expectation that when we felt hunger pangs or physical pain our good mother came and took these discomforts away. Whenever that did not happen our meaning structure was disconfirmed, but we did not accept this quietly. Our pride told us that we should be looked after. We made angry protests, and, if our protests were ignored, our anger turned to hatred. We screamed, kicked and bit the bad mother who had failed us.

However, as time passed we gradually came to realize that we did not have a good mother who looked after us and a bad mother who failed to relieve our pain, but just one mother who might be good to us or bad to us. Thus we discovered that the people we love can also be the people we hate.

This is another of the problems in life for which there is no once-and-for-all solution, other than death, or an acceptance that the people we love the most can provoke in us the greatest hate, simply because they may possess and refuse to give us that which we need the most. We can, as small children, arrive at this acceptance provided the people we love and need do not present us with too many occasions to hate them and, when we do hate them, they tolerate our hate because they are able to tolerate their own.

If we are fortunate we are born into such a family. However, if we are not fortunate, then hate remains a problem and a threat for the rest of our lives. The people who have to defend their sense of being a person from annihilation by using one of the desperate defences had, in their first years of life, a multitude of experiences that provoked their hate and adults around them who refused to accept their hate.

In not accepting the child's hate adults teach the child that it is wicked to hate the person who threatens your sense of being a person. Believing himself to be wicked, the child feels guilty and sees himself as being intrinsically bad. He can fail to make the distinction between feeling hate and giving expression to that hate, and thus fail to see that feeling hate is what people do but giving expression to that hate can be exceedingly wicked. The feeling of hate serves some very useful purposes. Hating, we strengthen our sense of individuality, whether we are an infant needing to develop a separate identity from our mother, or an adult needing to redis-cover a separate identity when a relationship such as a marriage comes to an end. For instance, a couple may have a relationship that has been reasonably harmonious but, perhaps through an act of infidelity or the feeling that they have grown apart, they decide to separate. Then they are suddenly surprised by the intensity of hate they feel for each other. It frequently happens that the man who has always been generous with his money turns on his wife and accuses her of being greedy and unscrupulous. She, surprised and hurt, turns on him. Mutual hatred, painful though it is, helps them break the bonds they have built up over the years together.

Hate sensitizes us to danger. Instead of our going blithely on and running the risk of allowing ourselves to be harmed, hate warns us to beware and points out the dangers that can lie behind the most innocent of façades. Hate makes us aware, too, of those things in our environment which we can use to defend ourselves from attack. Hate helps us to survive.

Even though we deny that we feel hate we can still enjoy its benefits. We can turn our denied hate into a strong sense of jus-tice, or into national, racial or religious pride, or into humanitarian zeal, and allow ourselves to feel outrage with those who are unjust, or who denigrate our nation, race or creed, or who are cruel and uncaring.

However, we can deny our hate because we believe that it is wrong to hate. If we catch a glimpse within the darkness of our internal reality of the hate that hides there, we can feel great shame and guilt. Intimations of the hate within can make an extravert flee into external reality and deny the hate with an excess of activity. Such intimations can provoke in an introvert a sense of guilt which, in the chaos such fear brings, threatens to annihilate their sense of being a person. An introvert thus threatened becomes an expert on guilt and in ways of atoning for such guilt.

When the threat of annihilation becomes very strong, the introvert creates many ways of dealing with the guilt. These are the traditional ways of sacrifice, propitiation, atonement and reparation. Freud noted the similarity between the defences of obsessions and compulsions and the rituals of religion. All religions have rituals of washing. Hindus find salvation by bathing in the Ganges. Muslims wash before praying. Christians are baptized in water or have water sprinkled on them and are then brought into church, where they believe they are bathed in the Blood of the Lamb. Buddhists purchase gold leaf to press on a statue of the Buddha, Muslims give alms to the poor, Christians pay a tithe or purchase candles, all of which are aimed at making reparation for their sins. Catholics confess their sins, while Protestants hope that through faith and good works the treasure they build up in heaven will praise God and absolve them of their sins. The person carrying out his obsessions and compulsions is saying to himself, 'If I sacrifice something which is important to me, or if I sacrifice myself, then I shall atone for my sin and be protected from harm,' or 'If I carry out this ritual then I shall propitiate the gods and I won't be punished,' or 'If I cleanse myself of sin (dirt) then I shall be safe,' or 'If I make good or undo the harm I have done, then I shall be safe.'

Seeing oneself as guilty and so seeking forgiveness is a fruitless task, because then unacknowledged hate can never be confronted, experienced and assessed, understood and brought to a conclusion. Thus the guilt grows, and the rituals aimed at moderating and controlling it become more elaborate, and the demand for their repeated performance becomes more and more pressing. What began as a cleansing ritual to prove to God (mother) that you are a good child who would not even *think* of hurting her by being dirty becomes a ritual washing of hands performed over and over again, until the skin is cracked and bleeding, and the tasks and responsibilities, and pleasures, of life are left ignored outside the bathroom door.

Painfully repetitious though the various actions of obsessions and compulsions may be, they are only the tip of the iceberg. The major part of obsessions and compulsions is *thought*.

This is thought without emotion. An introvert in the grip of an obsession can think with emotionless clarity, 'There is a knife. I could pick that knife up and plunge it into my child's heart,' and only afterwards, when the possibility of this action has been clearly and calmly acknowledged, comes the realization that the action could have been carried out and the person most dear and valuable to him would be lying bleeding and dead. Then comes the fear. The whole process may take no more than a second, but it is always emotionless thought followed by fear.

So now sharp knives must be wrapped up and put away. No reparation is possible. Only a turning against yourself. You are wicked even to have thought the thought. You might have acted upon the thought – spontaneous, so easy, so dangerous. So, you must not act until you have thought and thought again. Spontaneity is dangerous. Spontaneity is forbidden. Observe, consider, plan, think and think again before you act. Only when you have thought everything through and considered every possibility can you act.

In thinking such thoughts the obsessional introvert may not use much visual imagery. He may not actually see himself, say, seizing the knife and plunging it into his child (whom he loves but hates because the child reminds him of himself). The thought is in words. This is very much in contrast to the extravert, whose day-dreams are dramatically visualized. The obsessional introvert's thoughts come in the clarity of the child's first use of language and the simple, uncomplicated attitudes of that time: 'Knife – strike – kill'.

'No,' says the obsessional introvert. 'No, I didn't do that vile act.' And then, doubt. 'I didn't do it, did I?'

The trouble is that if we rely on thought alone, stripped of emotion, we are always prey to doubt. Without emotion we cannot be sure that something actually happened. Emotions are interpretations which concern whether we are safe or in danger, and thus they give us a solid centre when all around us is in flux – provided, of course, we are truthful with ourselves about what we are actually feeling. Extraverts destroy this solid centre of themselves when they tell themselves that they are frightened when in fact they are angry. Introverts destroy this solid centre when they tell themselves that they do not feel any emotion. When extraverts destroy their solid centre they feel themselves being blown this way and that by whatever happens. When introverts destroy their solid centre they are consumed by doubt. Confronted by someone's words or actions, introverts may be very calm. Afterwards they think the matter over, and then ask themselves, 'Did that really happen?' If they are unafraid of their emotions their answer to this question becomes, 'Yes, it did,' because they can let themselves feel the emotion they have kept under control, and this truth – the emotion – confirms the matter. If they are afraid of emotion they cannot use their emotions to check the reliability of their memory, and so they are plagued by doubt. No matter how much an obsessional introvert plans, organizes, considers, reviews, the doubt will appear. *Did I do what I ought not to have done, or fail to do what I ought to have done?*

To deal with doubt, he checks. Over and over again. He may wash his hands. (No one will die from my filth.) He may check the locks, the gas taps and the power points. (No one will murder my loved ones or destroy their possessions. My loved ones will not die from gassing, electric shocks or fire.) He may retrace again and again his path from office to home. (No motorist, cyclist or pedestrian will die at my hands.) But such actions performed over and over again do not erase doubt.

Years ago there was a television advertisement with the slogan *Wipe away doubt with Dettox*. It was an advertisement made by an introvert for an introvert.

516

Persistent doubt leads some obsessional introverts to be unable to make decisions, even the most unimportant decisions. Padmal de Silva and Stanley Rachman, being psychologists devoted to behaviourism, outlined in their book what people do but not why they do it. They described a young woman who 'found getting dressed in the morning impossible because she could not decide what clothes to wear. She would put on, then take off, several dresses. Eventually, her mother had to decide each night what the woman should wear the next day and all her clothes except these were locked away at night.'[4]

Doubt can be seen to reside in imperfection, so then the only acceptable standard becomes complete perfection. Setting the standard of perfection can be a source of great pride. When Marc Summers went looking for his first job in television he was rebuffed. He wrote, '. . . I had been taught that walking into a meeting with confidence always impressed people. But I guess I took it too far. . . Far from believing I had anything messed up in my head, I thought I was the "rightest" person in the world. Always on time, always correct, always neat – I wasn't odd, the rest of the world was sloppy, slow, and negligent.'[5]

Many people, not just those who resort to obsessions and compulsions, set themselves this impossible standard and condemn themselves to miserable lives. Padmal de Silva and Stanley Rachman told of a woman student who was working on her doctoral thesis on which she was making no progress. She felt that 'every sentence was imperfect, and she could not proceed until she got a "perfect" sentence, a "perfect" paragraph, and so on. She had been "writing" this thesis for years, yet there was little she could show as a tangible product.'[6]

This demand for perfection is just one aspect of a kind of grandiosity very different from the grandiosity of the extravert who resorts to mania as a defence. Both extraverts and introverts may inflate their own importance by claiming responsibility for other people's actions, but, in fact, we can be responsible only for those matters over which we have control. Thus the head of a hierarchy of managers in a business is responsible for the actions of his employees while they are at work. He issues orders, and any employees who do not obey those orders he can chastise or sack. However, there are limits to his responsibility. He does not control what his employees do in their own time, so he is not responsible for their private lives. Parents start off having a large amount of control, though not total, over their baby, and so their responsibility is great, but once the child ventures into the world to go to school the parents' control, and therefore responsibility, decreases.

The only matter over which we have total control is the interpretations we make. We are responsible for very little of what happens, but we are always totally responsible for how we interpret what happens.

Whenever we feel guilty we are claiming that we were responsible for the event in which we failed to act correctly. Thus it can be appropriate to feel guilty if, through your inattention, your two-year-old child falls down a flight of stairs, but it is not appropriate to feel guilty if your twenty-two-year-old child takes up climbing and falls off a mountain. Upset, yes, but guilty, no. A parent cannot control a twenty-two-year-old, and therefore responsibility and guilt are inappropriate. The appropriate response is the recognition of the helplessness that makes being the parent of adult children so very difficult.

Many people fear helplessness more than they fear guilt, and so they will claim responsibility, with its consequent guilt, for matters over which they have no control. Extraverts usually confine their guilt to matters concerning family and friends. If they feel guilty about climate change or the plague of AIDS in Africa, they identify the home destroyed by floods, or the orphaned child dying of AIDS, with their own home or children. Introverts may feel guilty because they believe they have let their family down by failing to achieve or by failing to help others to achieve, but they may also feel guilty because they have failed to make the world what it ought to be – that is, how they think it ought to be. Introverts who become obsessional may see themselves as being totally responsible for strangers. When Simon searched for the body of the person he thought he had knocked down, not for one minute did he think that person had some responsibility for what he did on or near a busy road. Claiming responsibility for matters far beyond our control is pride defending us from knowing what little control we have over events and how helpless we are.

Pride also enables the obsessional introvert to see thought as having extraordinary power. Thought becomes magical. By thought alone the introvert can influence the world. St Paul taught that the thought was as evil as the deed. Thinking about sex is as wicked as indulging in sex (though not so much fun). Mohammed taught that, in judging whether an act is a sin, what must be considered is the intention. Thus a thought that encapsulates a wicked intention is as sinful as the act itself.

One of the tasks of infancy is to discover the difference between internal and external reality and to understand that our thoughts are private. This task may take a long time, for there may be many events in a child's life which suggest that thoughts are not private, and that thought alone can influence the environment. An infant does not know that his mother is not actually reading his thoughts when she responds to what he is thinking, but is simply observing the expression on his face, or using her knowledge of children generally to interpret his needs and wishes. Some parents may be so insistent that they are able to read their child's mind that such children grow up still believing that their mother knows what they are thinking and saying, even though she may be many miles away, or even dead. Some parents insist that their child reveal to them what he is thinking, and then punish the child for thinking the wrong thoughts. This is an effective way of teaching your child how to lie. Sadly, even parents who respect their child's privacy may be misunderstood by the child, who expects that his parents *should* read his thoughts and thus know what he wants without his telling them.

The realization that thought alone does not affect the environment may be delayed because sometimes our wishes are fulfilled without us having to act. We may feel hungry and fantasize about food, and, lo, food appears. Or we may fantasize about murder, and the mother who failed to meet our needs disappears. It may take the child a long while to realize that while the first event was a result of his mother's empathy, the second had no causal connection. His thought did not cause her to take ill and go to hospital, or to leave her family, or to die.

The understanding that our thoughts are private and their power limited has an advantage and a disadvantage. The advantage relates to how we can then, freely and securely, use the privacy of our thoughts to express and master our most selfish and dangerous wishes. We can expend our hate in fantasized murder, and, when the hate vanishes with the fantasy, continue to enjoy the company of the person we have just killed in our thoughts. The disadvantage is that we can think all kinds of marvellous thoughts, but such thoughts have no effect upon the real world until we put them into action. We have to find some way of linking our internal reality with our external reality.

The obsessional introvert cannot appreciate the privacy and limited power of thought. He has been taught that he can sin by thought alone. Thinking murder is as evil as doing murder. Such teaching gives an immense power to thought, and an introvert will accept that, because we like to have power within our preferred reality. Moreover, if the child has suffered many traumas and indignities, he will try to shore up his confidence and to comfort himself by vowing to inflict similar punishments on those who have harmed him. The frightened, weak child dreams of becoming the most powerful and dangerous person in the world by thought alone. The adult obsessional introvert still believes that thought is magic.

Of course, thought *is* magic in one way. Through thought we can experience many more things than we could ever perform in our external world. These can be wonderful things; these can be terrible things.

Thought can conjure into being endless obsessions and compulsions.

George was a parson, just like his father. I went to talk to him in his vicarage in a small village. He told me:

I can say that I'm very much a person that likes tidiness. If you want to hear about obsessions I could keep you here till teatime. They're all concerned with 'Am I doing any harm to anybody else?' I don't think this is a virtuous thing. It has to do with guilt in me. There's a whole range of hygiene ones. When I go to the toilet, I wash my hands for hours, and when I've finished I'm under a terrific compulsion to do it again. This is particularly strong if I'm going to church to take communion service where I'm handling bread. There are all sorts of ramifications of this. If I pick up the bowl with the cat's meat, I have to wash my hands after that. If I'm out on the road and I pull something out of my pocket and I drop a ten-pence piece on the pavement, now I'll pick it up and I'll have an absolute horror that it's dropped into some dog dirt. There's nothing on the pavement, but I've got to walk back to make sure there's nothing there, and this coin feels almost deadly to anybody else. If I put it in my pocket I wonder if I've got something infectious in my pocket. I might pick up my briefcase to take to church and because the gate's padlocked I might put the case down to open it, and I'll wonder if I've put it in some dog dirt again.

He went on:

Then there's a whole range to do with money. If I go to the post office and pay for something, when I come out I wonder, 'Did I give that chap the right amount?' I wonder if I've done him. And this happens many, many times. There's a whole range of other ones. If I'm driving a car – it's not as bad as it used to be – I overtake a cyclist and I wonder if I've touched him or not. This was awful one time, when, many times on a journey, I had to stop and turn round and go back. Until the psychiatrist I was under said whatever you do you mustn't go back. Generally speaking now, if I don't check up it goes. It could happen even as a pedestrian. I cross the road and I might be thinking of something else and when I get to the other side I think, I wonder if I looked. Has a car, in order to avoid me, crashed into the side or something? I'll go back and look, and see if the road's clear. As a rule, it's to do with money – have I cheated someone? Or on the road or as a pedestrian – have I caused an accident? Or hygiene things – am I passing on to someone some infection?

I opened my mouth to ask a question but George swept on.

Another one is glass. If I'm washing some glasses and I tap the glass and it goes ping, I've got to make sure it isn't chipped, but if it's chipped, where's that bit of glass gone? – if someone were to drink it and harm themselves. . . Perhaps the chip has bounced into some food. Those are the main things. You mentioned panic. I'm not aware of panic, although if I give way to checking I'll go on and on and on, and that feels almost like panic. But, if I can stop myself, after a bit it will disappear. Some of these obsessions, like the road ones, they'll last for a week. Once, I rang the police and asked if there'd been an accident there. I would always rather work to clear a backlog than have the feeling 'I haven't done it, I haven't done it'. It worries me if things aren't done in time. I like planning ahead and know that I've got things organized before I get there. I'm concerned to keep the bit that's my responsibility under control, and then when someone takes over from me that's his fault, not mine. I'm always frightened that I haven't got everything right that I'm not going to be there on time, or when I'm in church, something'll go wrong. I always feel guilty in case I've harmed somebody.

George's obsessions concerned keeping chaos at bay and proving that he was good. He would not wish harm on anyone, anywhere, at any time. The harm that he wished not to inflict was death. He was a Christian given by God the duty of teaching that belief in Him overcame death, and that those who believed would find eternal life. Yet he spent a great deal of time thinking about how people could die.

When we hate we fantasize about murder, and then, in fear of punishment for our evil thoughts, we see ourselves threatened with death. As I described in my book *The Courage to Live*, we can construe death in many different ways, and our personal constructions of death have profound effects on the way we live our lives. In this book I wrote about Jill, who came to see me hoping that I could cure her of her obsessional habits of excessive washing of clothes, hair and hands, and of refusing to touch certain objects or to go into certain parts of her house. She involved her young son in these rituals, which now occupied so much of her day that a normal family life was no longer possible. Jill was a beautiful, well-educated, intelligent young woman brought up in a family where, she told me, 'My father expected us to do what he said and I always did.' Her mother was 'a worrier'.

When Jill was first married she worked in the office of a chemical firm. One day, when she was walking through the laboratory, a small quantity of a chemical compound was accidentally squirted on her skirt. She went to the first-aid room where, she said, 'They looked it up in a book and said, oh, well, there's nothing we can do. There's no antidote. If you're still alive by nine o'clock tonight you'll be all right. I was very worried. Someone since told me they were joking because they thought it wasn't very serious, but I didn't realize this at the time. I went home and took the skirt off and put it aside because I was a bit scared to wash it and I didn't want to throw it away because it was brand new. I don't know how it got into the back of the cupboard where it was when we moved.'

The skirt became the source of the contagion. As Jill saw it, the contagion spread to all the objects in the cupboard where the skirt was. When Jill and her husband and child moved house, the contents of the cupboard were shifted and the contagion spread to every object and person that touched them or even just came into close proximity to them. The only way the contagion could be removed was by washing. Some things, like books, could not be washed, and while Jill was washing what she could, the contagion spread to her hair and clothes. She drew lines of demarcation in the house and made rules for her husband and child to follow, and when they transgressed the lines and rules she panicked and washed everything again. Even when all the rules and rituals were kept she would look at something and doubt. 'I opened a cupboard door and saw a cup which I hadn't used for ages. I suddenly didn't want to touch it. Anything that hasn't been in circulation or is unusual, I get worried. There seems to be no end to it.'

I asked Jill whether she saw this contagion as being able to harm her. She said, 'I don't really know what I think will happen if I touch them. If they're small things I lick them if they're suitable to be licked to prove to myself that nothing will happen. I get this feeling that I don't want to touch them. If I do touch them I have to wash my hands or my hair as well. I washed it four times yesterday. I don't know why I have to do it, but I can't relax until I've washed my hands and my hair.'

Jill would come and sit nervously on the edge of her chair, her scaly, over-washed hands clasped tightly in her lap, and look at me, waiting for me to produce a practical solution which she could then show me by words or deeds was no solution at all. She would talk about her obsession, but questions about other topics – childhood, relationships with husband and parents – received guarded and conventional replies. She could see no reason to discuss her childhood – it was quite ordinary – and when I explained how we carry the image and metaphor of our childhood into our adult life she said that this could not apply to her since 'I'm not an imaginative person'. Nevertheless, I thought I would try to get her to imagine the contagion as being a person, and then to describe the attributes of that person.

Not without difficulty, Jill described the contagion as minute particles of a grey and deadly dust which spread by touch or drifting. She could imagine it as a person, 'a bit like a ghost that doesn't want to be seen or touched. I think it wants to be left alone.' However, if she did not keep a close eye on the shape it might come after her, surround her and annihilate her. Proving to her that one object did not have the grey dust on it only led her to the thought that the dust had moved on to something else. In one conversation Jill and I worked out that in all areas of her life except one she deferred to her husband and her mother. Only in her relationship to the contagious shape did she make her own decisions. If she gave up her obsession she would be doing what her husband and mother wanted her to do. It is sad when all we can see ourselves owning is our death.[7]

As with Simon, Jill's way of obediently deferring to her father and mother and then to her husband meant that she was constantly facing the threat of annihilation as a person. She could not assert her independence even by considering her childhood and the conclusions she had drawn from her experiences. Her obsession served several purposes. She could prove to herself again and again that she really was a good person by striving to protect her family from contagion. She could assert her independence by having to attend to the contagion before she attended to her family. And, in a delicious enjoyment of power without responsibility, she could punish her family by making them endure countless inconveniences. It was no wonder she resisted someone like myself who might, as her GP wished me to do, take away her obsessions. Moreover, her defence was not just against hate but against altogether losing her grip on external reality. She would not have seen it in those terms. For her, her obsession was a defence against madness.

Steve's wife Madeline phoned me. 'I'm sorry to trouble you,' she said in a voice breathless and shaky. 'Our GP told me he's written to you about my husband to ask you to see him.'

I explained that I did not have a vacancy until early February, some eight weeks ahead. She said, 'That's all right. Just to know that something's going to be done. Such a comfort.'

So I sent him an appointment card, and duly the day, and Steve, arrived. He was very composed. He explained that he had had no difficulty in getting time off work for the appointment because he was already off work with a bout of flu.

The flu had more significance than I first realized. Later in our conversation he told me about his interest in running. He had been impressed with one well-known runner who said that he trained every day. So, said Steve, he had made a New Year resolution to train every day. He had kept his resolution for five years. Irrespective of the weather or how he felt, he had run a mile or two, or more, every day. However, when he got this flu and was very ill, and went to the doctor and the doctor said, 'Go home, go to bed and stay there,' he thought about going for a run before going to bed, and then decided against it. He went home, went to bed, and had not trained for five days.

'I was surprised how well I took it,' he said. 'I thought I would have a bad time but I didn't.'

What he meant by 'a bad time' was what he did to himself when he failed to meet one of the challenges he set himself. 'I have a guilt complex,' he said, and meant that cruel, persecuting conscience which drove him on relentlessly. He justified his existence by setting himself challenges and meeting them.

'Why is it so important to set yourself challenges?' I asked.

'It's important to achieve. People are like that. It's an instinct.'

His very existence was a striving for clarity and perfection. The threat of chaos came with any falling away from this striving.

He spoke of how sometimes, when he woke in the morning, just for a moment everything was 'clean, empty, peaceful'. Then suddenly the guilt would come crowding in and he was in misery.

I picked up on the word 'clean'. 'Is cleanliness important to you?'

'Yes. Very. I wash my hands too much. When I was in my teens, when I was doing my O-levels and working very hard, I used to be always washing my hands. I was washing away germs. I think it's crazy now, but then I thought I had something on the back of my shoulder and I'd always be rubbing it on something.' He demonstrated this on the back of the chair. 'I was working very hard. I'd do a paper round first thing in the morning, then some study, then school, homework when I got home, and then to evening college for more study.'

We talked about his family. He had been adopted. His adoptive parents, well into their thirties when they took him, were Methodists. When he was three they had a child of their own, a boy who, so Steve said, was able to have an easy and full social life and still do well at school. Not like him, for whom everything was a hard slog.

Sex was never mentioned in his home. He remembered being scolded by his mother for walking from his bedroom to the bathroom with no clothes on. His parents had told him that he had been adopted when he was about nine months old, but they told him nothing about his real parents except, he said, that they were a very young couple who could not marry and raise a family.

Anger was expressed in his family home, but only as the anger of parents expressed against the child. He was beaten for certain misdemeanours. He remembered his mother beating him with a poker. He and his brother would fight, but at school he avoided fights as much as possible. 'I was a coward,' he said.

Now anger and sex had come together in terrible, frightening impulses. He was a schoolteacher, teaching mathematics and physics, but was often called upon to help train the children in athletics and swimming. He described, in very general terms, the impulse to thrust his hips towards a child in an act of sexual aggression, and the terrible guilt which followed. He spent much time going over and over these matters in his head, trying, and failing, to prove to himself that he had not given vent to this impulse.

I spoke of how some people find driving a car difficult because they may fear that they have knocked someone down and not noticed it at the time. He nodded, understanding the pain of this, and said that he too suffered in this way.

Steve found it very hard to talk about feelings, or anything that was not simple and practical. He did not reminisce. Often, when he spoke of something that anyone might imagine would result in a great deal of emotion, he would say, 'I never thought anything of it.'

He did talk directly about feeling when he described the time when one of their cats was killed on the road outside their house. This distressed him greatly. 'Our cats are like our family,' he said. 'It's hit me more than when my grandfather died.'

I spoke of the strange sense of emptiness a loss brings, an emptiness as real and palpable as a presence.

He agreed that this was so. Afterwards, when he began again to talk about his obsessional thoughts, he talked more about his

527

feelings, how he felt no desire to act sexually to a child, but how the thought without the emotion would come, followed by the doubt about whether or not he had done something, accompanied by an enormous sense of guilt. 'It happens quickly, but I think about it in slow motion.'

He often spoke of guilt. I asked him how far back in his life he could remember this sense of guilt.

He said that he could not remember, and then he suddenly recalled when 'I was seven or eight, I was given a watch – for birthday or Christmas. I looked at this watch' – he placed the thumb and fingers of his right hand carefully round the watch on his left wrist – 'and I thought, "I mustn't scratch it, I must keep it perfect." Then I suddenly got this urge to scratch it. And I did, and then I felt terribly guilty.'

Like many introverts, Steve treasured an image of perfection as 'clean, empty, peaceful'. When such introverts were small children this image was very clear to them, in their mind, in their body, in their person. Then, when they were rejected, or betrayed, or disappointed, or made to feel that they were filthy, ugly and bad, their image of perfection was besmirched and damaged. When rejection, betrayal, disappointment, and the feeling of being filthy, ugly and bad, became the norm for them rather than the exception, they feared that anything they encountered that was perfect would inevitably be besmirched and damaged. When Steve had been given what, to him, was a perfect watch, he was certain that sooner or later it would be robbed of its perfection. He could not bear the tension of waiting for this to happen. He damaged the watch and his waiting was over. In the same way some children, unable to bear the tension of waiting for some punishment, punish themselves by falling off their bicycle, or, running, trip and fall and hurt themselves. Then, like Steve, they have to feel guilty for causing such damage.

Children often feel guilty for something an adult has done. I asked Steve whether, as a child, he had experienced a man exposing himself to him. 'Children often have this experience,' I said.

'No,' he said immediately, without reflection.

On another occasion, when Steve was telling me about his recent obsessive ruminations about whether he had splashed some orange juice on a little girl, an event that had a sexual connotation for Steve, I asked him how a child who was sexually assaulted would feel. He could not answer this, but when gently pressed said that children did not remember such things.

Nowadays, many therapists would want to probe further to see whether Steve had suffered sexual abuse as a child. This may have been so, but, if one takes into account the kind of upbringing Steve had, it is not necessary to hypothesize sexual abuse to explain why Steve blocked any exploration in this area. In his family a child's ordinary exploration of sexual matters, both on his own and with his brother and other children, would have been regarded by his parents as being filthy, disgusting and utterly evil, deserving great punishment. In this case, Steve would hope that children did not remember such events because this would mean that his brother and his playmates had forgotten, even if he had not.

In Steve's obsessional ruminations was the voice of a little child.

He said, 'My arm turned just a fraction. That's natural, isn't it? I thought, if it did turn, the drink I was holding, it could have splashed. But I wasn't that close to the girl, was I?' And there was the little child saying to himself, 'Did that really happen, or didn't it?'

He went on, 'When I'm walking up the street and I see children coming towards me I turn away. I know I wouldn't do anything, but still . . .', and, 'I think I didn't flick any stones up, but there were some at the edge of the road and I did drive the car a bit fast across the intersection. So I went back to look. There was an old man getting off a bus. I couldn't see him when I went back. He might have got on the bus. I don't think the stones would have hurt him,' and there was the voice of the little child saying, 'It wasn't my fault, was it?'

Those introverts who are forced to defend themselves with obsessions and compulsions go to extreme lengths not to be aggressive. George stressed to me how conventional and obedient he was, but he was prepared to defy convention and risk the disapproval of many of his parishioners and clergy colleagues by promoting the cause of the Campaign for Nuclear Disarmament and challenging the necessity for a nation to defend itself with weapons of total destruction. Except for her persisting in her obsessions, Jill would not defend herself against the demands of her family. Steve called himself 'a coward'.

One obsessional young man, Russell, abhorred all kinds of fighting and argument. He had attended a secondary school where fighting among the boys was taken as a way of life, but in six years there he had avoided all fights except one, and he still felt guilty about this. Some evenings it would take Russell three hours to complete a journey of four miles, for whether he drove a car, rode a bicycle, or walked, he would become convinced that he had injured someone on his journey, and he would have to keep going back to check and check again. However, all his efforts to be completely unaggressive and to undo any harm he might have inadvertently inflicted on another person could not prevent grotesquely cruel fantasies of injury and death to others, especially children, coming again and again into his mind. There was nothing I could say which would assuage his guilt at thinking such thoughts, and nothing could persuade him that these thoughts were not evidence of his inherent wickedness but rather the outcome of childhood traumas. He had had, he insisted, a perfectly happy childhood.

I have kept in touch with Russell since that time. In the early years when I knew him, Russell was diligent and hard working in jobs that required him to travel extensively. Now he has settled, with a responsible job, a wife and family, and a keen interest in the betterment of his community. People who know him would commend him, but they may not know that he is a man of tremendous courage to have achieved all that he has. Courage is possible only when we are afraid. To be courageous we have to overcome our fear, and Russell had immense fear to overcome.

When an introvert resorts to obsessions and compulsions as a desperate defence, that person is frightened of the hate he finds inside himself. To deal with the fear he denies the hate. If hate has to be denied, then the events that gave rise to that hate must be forgotten, or, if remembered, their significance must be denied.

George said, 'I accept the fact that there's a massive amount of anger buried in me, but I'm not aware of feeling any anger, so obviously there's a lot of repression there. Occasionally I get angry with my wife Heather, and on rare occasions I explode, but not very often.'

I asked, 'Do you remember as a child being angry?'

'No, I can't actually. I was sent away to a boarding school when I was not quite eight. I don't think I can remember – I've got a rotten memory anyhow. I remember calling my aunt an old so-and-so, but I don't think this was really anger. It was because she was just so blooming bossy. I went straight from boarding school to the Services. It was a great relief to go into the army.'

I asked, 'What were the rules in your family about anger?'

'What do you mean? Could you be more explicit?'

I explained that every family has its rules, and there are always rules about anger. These rules may never be put into words, but children always know that in their families there are rules like 'No one gets angry ever', or 'Only Father is allowed to get angry'.

George said, 'My sister's description of my father would be entirely different from mine. We used to call him the vicarage policeman, but Father was Father. I'm not aware when I was at home that it was anything but a fairly relaxed atmosphere.'

Heather explained, 'His sister describes him as fairly authoritarian, but George has no memories of this.'

George added, 'If I thought I was going to be late for lunch I would come back like hell for leather. You weren't allowed to be late for meals, though if you were you'd get a disapproving stare. I think as a youngster I would always stick to the rules. I always had an exaggerated respect for anybody older than me, which was reinforced by the public schools, until it was shattered when I got in the army and saw that older people weren't so wise after all. Perhaps it's my nature, not to be rebellious. I don't think I felt rebellious. My main impression of childhood is of happiness. I was much more of a loner than my brother, but I think I was happy.'

I explained that for children to have a happy childhood they have to learn to follow the family's rules. 'If we have parents who expect obedience, we have a happy childhood if we are obedient. If we have parents who expect cleanliness, we have a happy childhood if we learn to be clean. You learned your family's rules very well. You were good at being good.'

George said, 'On the other hand, I had a great deal of freedom. I could get on my bike and disappear. I quite liked my own company.'

'Both you and your sister are most uncritical of other people,' said Heather.

'Underneath is the feeling of anything for a peaceful life,' said George wryly.

I commented that as a child he could protect himself by escaping from his home, away and free on his bikes, but as an adult he had no such freedom. A vicar is always being observed by his parishioners.

'We've taken life much too seriously. All we've done is work, work, work,' said Heather.

George said, 'I know that we all put on a front to the outside world, but, no, I don't know who I am.' What he meant was that, while he knew only too well what he *ought to be*, he never dwelt on who he actually *was* except to feel again and again that what he was fell far short of what he ought to be. This is a very different experience from that of those extraverts who know so little of what goes on inside them that they will say, 'I don't know who I am.' They have little sense of being a person who has certain attributes. If pressed further to explain what they mean, they will talk of being nothing but a role or a series of roles, all without an actor, or they will say, 'I'm always scared that if I look in the mirror there'll be no one there.'

Through George's childhood and youth he had been and done what he thought he ought to have been and done. He said, 'I think certainly in my teenage years to some extent, when I was thirteen and went on to public school, I didn't enjoy life as I should have done because of what I saw as the constraints of conscience. I was a very priggish Christian. Before communion on a Sunday morning I'd go through a long list of things and check that I'd obeyed every one – they were all written down, things like masturbation and thinking wrong thoughts. Looking back now I can see how ridiculous it was – but it turned you in on yourself. As long as I hadn't done any of these, to hell with anybody else, but, as long as I hadn't, that was fine and therefore I suppose I worried more about trivial things.'

He went on:

I was brought up in the tradition of making a confession before major festivals. Now, I used to do that to my father, and I think, looking back, some of the things which disturbed me most, like masturbation, those sort of things . . . There must have been lots of other petty little things. I have learned now that that is the kind of religion which cripples a person. It's not the sort of thing which enriches but sort of cripples. Now to what extent that affected me I don't know. I suppose it was the kind of thing one did. I would think, once this is behind me I can enjoy Christmas. Almost a ritual in a sense, almost a connection between that and my obsession about hygiene. It does show how much a conformist I was. My conscience would demand that I told my father everything. So there can't have been anything very important to tell him. I must have been a one for the rules. When I went to the Services I began to grow up and I almost dropped out of Christianity altogether. Then when I became a parson I started this confession business again, but then I stopped because I found it wasn't doing me the slightest bit of good. It was a negative thing.

'Had it helped you as a child?' I asked.

'I don't think so. I thought of it as one of the hurdles you had to get over if you're a Christian.'

'It gave your father tremendous power.'

'I don't think so. To me it was one of the things you had to do.'

Making a ritual confession to your father, a priest who is vested with God's power to punish and to absolve you of your sin, takes from the child the privacy of thought and action that is a necessary part of being and becoming the person you are. Melanie Klein psychoanalysed her three children when they were small, and at least one of them, Melitta Schmideberg, as she once told me, never forgave her. Melitta, like most psychoanalysts today, felt this to be a terrible misuse of a parent's power. However, at least she did feel she was allowed to be angry with her mother. George dared not criticize the man who had demanded to know the secrets of his soul.

'I remember before I was eight I was away at school two-thirds of the year. In this British stiff-upper-lip tradition you didn't tell your parents, not because you were frightened to tell them, but because you were taught to keep your trouble to yourself. There were lots of things I just didn't tell them. You had to keep yourself to yourself.'

George and Heather told me about George's grandmother, how her son had been killed in the First World War and how she had said, 'I've now got nothing to live for,' thus leaving her daughter, George's mother, to cope by herself. George's mother had not coped very well. She had periods of deep depression and, finally, when George's children were small and Heather was ill, she committed suicide.

George said, 'It wasn't just my mother who had a breakdown. When I came out of the Services at the end of the war, my father had a breakdown. I thought it was because he'd had so much worry with Mother he'd just folded up. Eventually I persuaded him to retire. He was depressed, and then he eventually slipped into senility.'

'It's one of the things which is worrying George. That he'll go the same way,' said Heather.

George added, 'I've always felt because I was sent away to school I had great attachment to my home county Cornwall, but my attachments are very much more to the place than to people. I'm ashamed to say I didn't grieve particularly when my parents died. When I came home from overseas, if I could have got off that plane and got on another and gone straight back I'd have done so gladly. The war ended when I was still overseas. I was offered an early release to go to university, and then my brother wrote to me and said, "Look, you've been enjoying yourself for long enough. Time you came home and took up your responsibilities." So very reluctantly I accepted the opportunity to come home. If I hadn't I'd have stayed out in East Africa.'

'You knew that going back home wasn't good for you,' I said.

'I don't know why particularly.'

I told George how, when I was in India, I met Sri Madhava Ashish, born Alexander Phipps, whose ashram was high in the Himalayas. Ashishda was an Englishman who, so he told me, had been sent to India during the war. At the end of the war he decided not to return home because, if he did, his sister and widowed mother would expect him to allow them to depend on him for support and care. This, Ashishda said, would have destroyed him. So he stayed in India to seek his own enlightenment, and this had led him to the ashram and hill farm of which he became the much-loved and respected leader.

George said, 'I would have been finished by that kind of decision. I wouldn't have got over it. I would have had it on my conscience all the time.'

Whenever Steve came to see me I became aware, yet again, of how he was not fully experiencing his emotions. It was not that he did not have emotions. His passions were strong, but he thought that if he did not acknowledge and name them they did not exist.

Slowly, though, it seemed that we were getting to know one another. One day we were discussing how he could not talk to his mother, a topic regarding which he would make a statement like 'I can't talk to my mother' and not elaborate on it. When I asked him what attitude his mother had to men in general he, as usual, could not answer the question. He had no idea what she thought about men. I ran through some of the attitudes women have to men. Some like men and think them wonderful; some are frightened of men, especially of their sexual power; some are very envious of men and seek to bring them down; some hate men and want to destroy them. Of course, men have a range of generalized attitudes to women. He nodded when I mentioned the way some men divide women into the Madonna and the Whore, the asexual, idealized woman and the sexual, bad woman. Steve had had a Methodist upbringing and was well acquainted with the Virgin Mary and Mary Magdalene, the supposed whore.

I asked him how he thought I saw men. He turned to me, his face alive with interest. He had plenty of ideas about this. He spoke of me expecting men 'to do their whack', not waiting on them, expecting them to do their share. At the same time, I liked men. 'But you'd have to, wouldn't you, to do this job?'

Steve went on to talk about his mother and said more than he had said in all the months we had been meeting. His mother had been a powerful woman. Now, at sixty-five, she was mellowing, but she had always been an obsessional, religious woman who dominated her husband and sons. Her husband would always go along with what she wanted, and her natural son might be rebellious in her absence but was always obedient in her presence. Only Steve dared to argue with her and disobey her.

However, he never won an argument with her. If he did disobey her and insist on doing what she forbade him to do she would 'whinge and whine' so much that his victory became a defeat. He spoke with passion of the petty restrictions and rules she imposed.

'We weren't allowed to play football on the lawn. We'd wear the grass out. We used to wait until they went to church and then we'd go and kick a ball around. Sunday was the most boring day of the week. I hated Sundays. You weren't supposed to do anything except go to church. I stopped going as soon as I could.' However, when we have an upbringing in a particular religion, even though we might cease to practise that religion, we still have as an important part of our meaning structure the concepts of that religion, particularly the way it defines good and bad, rewards and punishments. An obsessional introvert with a religious upbringing may lose his faith but still retain a belief in virtue and vice as absolute and unforgiving as that held by the most fundamentalist believer.

He spoke with scorn of the obsession his mother had with keeping the house clean and tidy. 'On Sunday afternoon she'd be complaining about how tired she was and how much she had to do. I'd tell her she didn't have to do it. They used to go to church in the evening, and sometimes they'd invite people back for coffee. If I was at home – this was when I was at university – I'd go for a run then, but when I got back she wouldn't let me have a bath. She said it steamed up the bathroom. I'd tell her that when visitors came they didn't go in the bathroom and give you a mark out of ten for neatness.' She never appreciated his humour. He spoke, too, of how inhibited his mother was about sexual matters. 'Her generation didn't know about these things.'

As he spoke he was revealing the picture of a boy who was often isolated in his family, rejected by his mother and deserted by his father. He had been rejected and deserted by his natural parents whom he never knew. If he fought to defend himself he was defeated. His parents never allowed him to win a battle. It was no wonder that he was filled with rage and hate.

Even so, he could feel some sympathy for his mother. 'My father handled all the money. He didn't say much, but in the end he made all the decisions. She couldn't do anything without him. She never learned how to look after the bills. She never learned how to drive a car.'

His mother had shown none of the contentment that a happy woman would reveal. Instead, her behaviour suggested that she was in the grip of helpless rage, just like her son.

In early summer Steve and Madeline visited his parents. Later he told me, 'Except for one thing that happened, it wasn't too bad a time.'

He described the 'one thing'. They had gone on a day's outing to Scarborough. 'My parents and Madeline and me were walking along the front, the four of us. I saw this family up ahead of us – the parents and two small girls. Just as we came up near them, one of them – 'she wasn't very tall, just up to here' – he indicated his waist – 'ran across in front of us and leaned on the rail. In a flash, you know how you can think these things in a millisecond, I thought, ''She's going to turn round and run back just in front of me,'' and I thought if I thrust – but I didn't. Afterwards, Madeline said it was nothing, I didn't do anything wrong. I mean, we were just walking by. I didn't look at the girl, but you know how you can know there's someone there. But I didn't do anything wrong, did I?'

He looked agonized. All that had happened on that seafront had gone on in his mind. Anyone surveying the scene would have seen four people strolling down the front and passing a little girl who was looking over the rail. Madeline, with her arm through Steve's, saw or felt nothing untoward, and knew nothing of what Steve saw and felt until, later that evening, he told her what had happened and asked her, repeatedly, to reassure him that nothing he had done was wrong.

I tried to understand what had happened. Steve described how everything seemed to happen very slowly, as action can seem very slow in a situation of great danger. He did not have a visual image of what he might do, just the thought of it, followed by the terror that he might have carried out the impulse. He had seen that the little girl's head was the same height as his pelvis, and had thought of pushing his penis into her mouth.

As soon as the thought had entered his mind he had been filled with terror and guilt, and immediately began the endless questioning of himself. 'Did I move my hip? Did I do anything wrong?'

It took us some time to talk about this. Steve had difficulty in putting these matters into words, and I had difficulty in coming to feel sure that I understood what he was telling me.

'Did I do anything wrong?' he asked.

'That's the wrong question,' I said. 'Of course you didn't do anything wrong. The question is why these thoughts come into your mind.'

Until Steve had come to talk to me he had not considered that his childhood had been in any way different from other children's.

'Well, you don't know, do you?' he said. 'You think your family's just like that.'

Now he was beginning to see that perhaps his childhood had

not been the easiest. Now he was puzzling over why his mother could laugh at sexual innuendos on television but still would not accept anything but the most correct behaviour from him.

I was saying something about the way a small child can be punished for doing things that are quite natural when he interrupted to inform me that he had just remembered something. When he was about ten his mother had washed out his mouth with carbolic soap because he had been swearing.

I suggested that there was a connection between his thought about the little girl and the resurgence of this memory of having his mother wash out his mouth.

Such an action by his mother suggested that what he had in his mouth – his words – was filthy and dangerous. In powerless rage and hate at such injustice, a small boy could give vent to his feelings only by fantasizing a terrible revenge upon his mother. What could he imagine pushing into his mother's mouth that was as filthy as that which she had washed out of his? And what would cause him the greatest guilt?

Both introverts and extraverts assess themselves as good or bad in terms of what other people will think of them and in terms of what they think of themselves. However, when they perceive themselves as failing to be good enough, extraverts are more likely to react with *shame* and introverts with *guilt*. Shame for the extravert is 'Every one will know and they will reject me'. Guilt for the introvert is 'I know that I am failing to achieve clarity and to keep chaos at bay'. At the root of the extravert's panic attack is shame at being exposed to the rejecting gaze of others. At the root of the introvert's obsessions and compulsions is guilt at having transgressed the Law, a Law that may reside in the introvert's conscience and nowhere else. When he transgresses this Law by failing to behave correctly, the introvert feels that there is now a breach in the defensive wall he has built around himself with his organization and control. Through this breach will pour the forces of chaos, bearing the punishment for his wickedness.

Shame is about the whole person or the sense of identity. In shame we think, 'How could *I* have done that?' Guilt is about specific actions and involves remorse about what we have done. In guilt we think, 'How could I have done *that*?'[8]

The ancient Greeks saw shame as *fate,* something that comes upon us and which we can do nothing to avert, and guilt as *hubris,* the sin of challenging the gods. Feelings of shame are associated with helplessness, impotence and weakness. Feelings of guilt are associated with a sense of having overstepped some limit, to have transgressed, to have acted as an individual out of pride and selfishness.[9]

Ken's battle with the Judge, in Chapter 9, concerns the avoidance of shame. The Judge constantly tried to shame him in the way his mother had shamed him, and all his obsessional thoughts and checking were aimed at proving that he had *acted rightly* and that he had no reason to feel ashamed. Whereas the obsessions and compulsions that people like George, Steve, Jill and Russell carry out are concerned with guilt. They fear that they have *acted wrongly* and must atone for their guilt.

Ken, feeling helpless in the eyes of his Judge/mother, tried to overcome this weakness and terror which threatened to destroy his sense of being a person by moving from the position that his mother forced him as a child to adopt, 'I have no responsibility for my life. Other people make my decisions,' to 'I have total responsibility for everyone'. Such a move strengthened his sense of being a person by giving him a sense of power, but it also meant that, in addition to striving to avoid shame, he had to feel considerable guilt. If we are responsible, then when we fail we must feel guilty.

The great attraction of guilt is that it supports our pride. Guilt helps us preserve the illusion that we can actually control our environment, ourselves and others. Immense personal pride is present in the belief that we can live within the continuity of our physical world and not collect and pass on noxious substances, or not inadvertently cause objects to move in ways dangerous to other people. Immense personal pride is present in the belief that we can control the natural spontaneity of thought, or that we have more knowledge and power than other people and so must be responsible for them. Guilt is impossible without pride. It always contains the belief 'I could have acted otherwise'. Terrible though guilt may be, many people find it better to hang on to guilt than to look behind it for those early childhood experiences of shame in which the young child, helpless, weak, humiliated and friendless, felt the terror of annihilation.

This is one of the reasons why obsessional introverts resist therapy. Guilt and the obsessional rituals to atone for the guilt may be terrible, but they are preferable to complete vulnerability.

Moreover, if your conscience will not allow you to attack your loved ones directly, you can inflict pain and discomfort on them by demanding that they conform to your rituals, answer your endless questions, and by not rewarding them by giving up your obsessions.

The obsessional introvert takes great pride in his awareness of the importance of morality. However, the moral rules that he has created for himself are harsh and the punishments for their infringement very severe. 'An eye for an eye, and a tooth for a tooth.' Or, as in the Spanish proverb, 'Take what you like, says God, and pay for it.' There is little room in his moral world for understanding and forgiveness. Some obsessional introverts may be understanding and forgiving of others, making allowances and bending the rules in ways they would never do for themselves, but others apply their rules strictly to all, and so place themselves in a dangerous isolation from which it is easy to fall into depression.

For a therapist working with an obsessional introvert it is very easy to see why Freud created the concepts of id, ego and superego. These three aspects of the person are clearly delineated in the client's behaviour. The id, the wild, childlike wishes and feelings, is present by default, so to speak, by always being denied. The ego, the rational self, and superego, the conscience, are there so clearly that the therapist gets the impression of talking to two people at once. This makes for a difficult conversation, for there is very little the therapist can say which will please the introvert's ego and superego simultaneously. The introvert's ego will be on the lookout for anything the therapist may say which could be interpreted as criticism and as siding with the punitive superego. The ego will have nothing to do with the superego's allies. However, if the therapist tries to argue that the introvert should be kinder to himself, the superego will be shocked at the immorality of the therapist and refuse to join an alliance with him.

I tried not to get caught in this trap by bringing it out into the open and pointing out what an impossible situation my client had placed me in, but as an introvert myself I know that, no matter how much I want to believe the wonderful things someone may be telling me, the rational, sceptical critic in my head, so often allied to my conscience, will be saying, 'You're not going to believe that rubbish, are you?' and I do not.

Where a rational, sceptical critic is so valuable is that it helps me sort out within my internal reality what is valuable and what is just the tinsel of vanity. This is a very necessary exercise for introverts, for there is always the temptation to give too much power to thought, just as for extraverts there is always the temptation to give too much importance to action.

To live wisely we have to knit together our internal and external realities. A flight into either is a flight into madness. When an introvert fails to check his thoughts against his experience of external reality, or refuses to accept the consensus of other people's opinions (for instance, most of us would think that if you do knock someone off their bike as you drive by, it is highly likely that the police will tell you about it), he is letting his vanity override his common sense. He does this because he is still trying to comfort the frightened child within, but, as he will not acknowledge why the child is frightened, he cannot understand why he does what he does, much less choose to change it.

To live peacefully within ourselves we have to be able to accept and love and feel sorrow for the child we once were, and to regard our conscience not as an adversary but as a good friend, someone who is on our side and telling us that we are doing well and, if we make a mistake, that next time we will do better. If you feel that it will take a long time for you to develop such a relationship with your conscience, you might draw comfort and strength, as one of my friends does, from the words of Gerard Manley Hopkins:

542

My own heart let me more have pity on: let
Me live to my sad self hereafter kind,
Charitable; not live this tormented mind
With this tormented mind tormenting yet.[10]

To make our conscience our friend we have to come to realize that we cannot control our thoughts. We have to accept that thought is spontaneous. To make our conscience our friend we have to be able to accept our anger and our hate and to realize that we do not have to feel frightened and guilty when we think angry, murderous thoughts. However, to accept our thoughts as being spontaneous we have to be able to experience helplessness, not as something potentially annihilating, but as the way we float in and are part of the ever-changing cosmos. It is possible to be helpless, not in control, but still safe and strong.

Gaining Freedom

All introverts try to keep some part of the universe organized and under control. Apart from some completely power-mad exceptions, they do not try to keep the entire universe organized and under control, just that bit of it which bothers them most if it tends towards chaos. Some introverts have spotless kitchens but their wardrobes are a jumble. Some have messy kitchens but their collection of two thousand CDs is in alphabetical order. Some work in a study that looks chaotic, but ask them for a file or a book and they can put their hand on it straight away because what appears to be chaos is a system which the creator of the system, the introvert, understands.

Every introvert has a system and standards that are applied to the bit of the universe being kept under control. Introverts are proud of their system and their standards. As I watched my builder with brush and dustpan sweep up every wisp of sawdust from his perfectly built shelves, I commented on his need for perfection. 'Well,' he said, 'someone has to set the standards.'

If you question an introvert about why he or she chose one part of the universe rather than another to keep in order, and why a particular standard of order was regarded as an absolute necessity, you do not have to probe the unconscious to find the answers. A few childhood reminiscences will provide answers. These reminiscences will involve not just a threat but a virtue of which the introvert is proud.

As a child the part of the universe I chose to keep in order was my personal cleanliness, the tidiness of what living space I was responsible for, and my handwriting and my spelling. I chose these areas because it was here that I experienced the most danger. In every aspect of my life I received no praise, either from my family or my teachers, but I did receive endless, carping criticism. My father was largely oblivious to what I did, though if he felt I had misbehaved he could easily make me feel extremely guilty; my sister criticized everything I did; my mother concentrated on criticizing my appearance, every aspect of my personal cleanliness (this included the fact that I coughed) and the state of my bedroom whenever it deviated in the slightest from the perfect order that she had imposed. In the days before computers and blessed spellchecks, imperfect handwriting and misspelled words were regarded as sins by parents and teachers. To preserve my sense of being a person I had to try to keep myself and my room perfectly clean and tidy, to do nothing that would provoke criticism (a hopeless task), and to spell and write perfectly – another hopeless task since I was left handed and forced by school rules to write with my right hand. Like many left-handed people, I found spelling very difficult. As much as I felt frightened, I could take pride in my efficiency in creating tidiness and cleanliness, and, although my handwriting and spelling improved only a little, I had an ability with words which my teachers had to acknowledge.

In my childhood and early adulthood I knew that I was using my obsessions to hold myself together because I was afraid that I could lose my grip on myself and my world, although I would not have been able to describe this as I do now. I never felt that my obsessions controlled me. It is when the obsessions and compulsions take over the control of a person's life that the ordinary defences of establishing order and control turn into the desperate defences that hold the person together at the expense of ruining his life.

From early childhood Marc Summers had been using obsessions and compulsions as a desperate defence. As an adult, even when his life was going well, his obsessions about orderliness, and his rituals to ward off death, took up much of his time, but when life went badly they dominated his every waking minute. He was presenting a talk show which he loved but, in the way of show business, the show was cancelled and he was out of a job. He could not cope with unemployment. He wrote:

> . . . I became obsessed with keeping the house straight, and con-stantly arranged and rearranged paintings, vases, furniture, pillows, curtains, glasses, window blinds, photographs, rug fringes. If it could be moved, adjusted, or rearranged, I was powerless to resist. Every couple of hours I'd have to go through the house, straightening everything, although nothing had been touched since my last round. I'd feel anxiety start to well up. It was like a maddening itch that I couldn't quite scratch. The straightening and restraightening made the itch better for a little while, calmed it, but then it would catch fire again, crawling under my skin, and I'd have to go back and do the whole bloody thing again, moving cushions only by millimeters, making sure the vase with flowers was placed in the exact center in the foyer. . . My work life was a mess, but if I could make the house perfect, at least something would be right.[11]

It did not matter to Marc that he embarrassed his teenage children and made it extremely difficult for them to bring friends home, or that, when he could be spending time with his family, he was engaged in making his house perfect. He felt that he was fighting for his life.

Before he lost his job one of the people Marc interviewed on air was Dr Eric Hollander, who was a specialist in obsessional-compulsive disorder. Up till then Marc had thought of his obsessions and compulsions as peculiar ways of behaving, but when he read the preparatory notes for his interview it occurred to him that he might have this disorder. On air, as Dr Hollander described what he called the symptoms of the disorder, Marc said, 'Dr Hollander, I think I have this.'

At the end of the programme Dr Hollander gave Marc his card and assured him that something could be done to help him, but Marc did nothing until after he had lost his job, and his wife, unable to bear his behaviour any longer, ordered him to phone Dr Hollander.

Some time later Dr Hollander wrote the foreword to Marc's book, in which he said, 'We can now effectively treat the disorder with medication and behaviour therapy, and we have a startlingly high success rate. Seventy per cent of OCD sufferers who undergo treatment report a substantial improvement in their symptoms and their quality of life.'[12]

Note that Dr Hollander did not speak of cure, only improvement, and of those treated in this way, 30 per cent did not improve. Nevertheless, Marc seized happily on the theory that Dr Hollander presented. Now, he thought, his behaviour was explicable, and he was not responsible for what he did because it was something he had inherited. His parents were not so keen on this explanation, and they felt shamed by their son's public revelations. It is no comfort to parents to be told that they have unwittingly passed a dread disease on to their child. They may feel guilty for not being aware of what they were doing, and helpless because their body has betrayed them.

The alternative explanation, that Marc's obsessions and compulsions had developed out of his upbringing, would have been equally upsetting. Marc did not want to consider this, and he was supported by Dr Hollander, who believes that, in our brain, those pesky neurotransmitters create meaningless thoughts and are thus the cause of many problems. Dr Hollander warned him that the only other alternative treatment, traditional psychoanalysis, was likely to make him worse. Marc seemed to be unaware that a great deal has happened in psychology since Freud was writing a hundred years ago. Over the last fifty years psychologists have been examining how we make sense of events and how we remember. How our brains make sense of events is now much better understood than it was in Freud's day, and the sense that we make is now seen as having developed from our interpretations of events since, or even before, birth. Cognitive psychologists interested in the role of memory and forgetting in trauma are now finding parallels between their work and Freud's work on repression and suppression.

In his book Marc said little about his family, but enough to show connections between his childhood experiences and his obsessions and compulsions. He said of his father, 'His closet is perfect, impeccable, like a fancy men's clothing shop. It's amazing, a work of art. Every suit, every tie, every shirt is in perfect order. It looked like my own closet! . . . Our entire house was pretty much like that. I used to joke in my comedy routines that when I got up in the night and went to the bathroom, I'd come back to find that my bed had been made. I'd also joke that my mother would put paper under the cuckoo clock.'[13]

It is bad science to assume that if a child behaves in ways similar to a parent then the child has inherited the genetic cause of this behaviour. If this were the case, there must be a voting-Labour gene, which I inherited from my father and my son inherited from me. No doubt the New Labour gene is a mutation. Of course, we do get a great deal from our parents, but by observing what they do and learning to do likewise. What we learn about our relatives, even if we have not met them, can influence our behaviour. Many a child who has been told, 'You'll turn out to be a scoundrel just like your father was!' resolves to do exactly that.

Neither of Marc's parents questioned their son's cleaning rituals. No doubt his father saw them as right and proper, and his mother benefited from the way Marc helped her with her cleaning. Many mothers of sons would have envied her as he helped her clean. She enjoyed a closeness with Marc, what Marc called 'a special bond'. This would have been a comfort to her because she was a very anxious woman. Marc described how his mother expected her husband home from work each evening on the dot of 9 o'clock. If he had not arrived by 9.20 her increasing anxiety would turn to panic and she would want to call the police. When her husband, delayed by traffic, arrived home soon after, he would be quite unsympathetic. Marc wrote, '. . . My mother's hysterics turned me into a complete wreck. I agonized about my father. Was he okay? Had something happened? As my mother paced, I paced right behind her. I prayed that Dad wasn't dead.'[14]

Marc's relationship with his elder brother Mike seems to have played a significant part in how he experienced his need for achievement. He wrote, 'My mother's special attention was very important to me because I was intensely competitive with my brother Mike. His IQ was off the charts, and he had a photographic memory. . . It wasn't his intelligence I envied, however. He had played the drums from a very early age and was a child prodigy . . . I envied him because he was closer to show business than I was.'[15]

The effects that siblings have on one another has been little studied, yet all of us who are blessed or cursed with siblings know how much we have influenced one another. An older sibling, through experience and size, can threaten a younger sibling with both death and annihilation. Marc did not seek to understand the nature of his relationship with his brother, but he wrote, 'I'm very competitive. To this day my kids hate to play Monopoly or Scrabble with me. I'm a *pain*. I tell them I'm going to crush them. I rag them to death. I do whatever it takes to win. Whether playing Monopoly or climbing the show business ladder, I have to be the best.'[16] He explained his competitiveness as being a symptom of obsessional-compulsive disorder, but he took great pride in it. He described the day his teenage son beat him at basketball as 'the hardest day of my life'.[17]

In his book, Marc mentioned behaviour therapy but did not describe in any detail what it entailed. Padmal de Silva and Stanley Rachman wrote, 'Rather than attempt to unravel an assumed root cause, behaviour therapists work directly on the problem behaviour itself. They concentrate on the problem as it is now, and what factors are associated with it, rather than its past history.'

They went on, 'In recent years, the scope of behaviour therapy has been expanded to include aspects of what is known as "cognitive therapy". Cognitions are thoughts, ideas, beliefs, and attitudes. Cognitive therapists focus their treatment on elicitation of the patient's cognitions that are relevant to his problems and on helping him modify them. . . In the case of obsessive-compulsive disorder, there is a clear role of cognitive therapy techniques – that is, to prepare the ground for the implementation of behaviour therapy, and to prevent a return of the problem once the treatment is over.'[18]

This kind of therapy usually involves the person in some way limiting the repetitive behaviours and in some way doing what he is afraid to do. There is no one programme that suits everyone, but rather each person works out with the therapist a programme tailored to their needs. Regular homework is set and later discussed with the therapist. Sometimes the therapist accompanies the person to supervise and take part in certain activities. A friend or family member may be co-opted to work with them.

However, whether we think of obsessions and compulsions as a defence or a disorder, they do not reside solely and completely inside the person. These behaviours are part of the relationship between the person and his family. All the desperate defences can be part of the game that Eric Berne called 'See What You Made Me Do, Ma'. Without actually accusing the parent of causing his suffering, the adult child may enact the accusation by resorting to a desperate defence, or taking up drink or drugs, or becoming a criminal, anything that will embarrass the parent. It is possible to play this game while at the same time feeling guilty for causing the parent distress. The same game can be played in a marriage. If at some level the obsessional person gets satisfaction from his parent's or partner's discomfiture, then getting the parent or partner to participate in the therapy may not turn out well.

In any case, the person who resorts to a desperate defence acts selfishly, as we all do when we are in fear of our lives. Marc Summers commented, 'People with OCD have a hard time compromising and putting the needs of others before their own needs. The disorder makes you selfish – your mission is to get rid of your intense feelings of anxiety, and you take immediate action. It's hard to worry about anyone else who's in the way.'[19]

There is considerable research which shows that obsessive-compulsive disorder, as Susan Simpson reported, 'can have deleterious effects on couples' relationships, leading to a build up of anger and frustration over time. Difficulties such as financial burden, and the disruption of family routine, leisure and interactions have been noted, particularly in married couples. A recent study found that disruption of the personal life of family members was reported in four-fifths of their sample.'[20]

Susan Simpson found that one wife who acted as a co-therapist for her husband believed that, to be a good wife and mother, 'I must meet all the demands of my family, and always put their needs before my own, or I will be a failure as a wife and mother', and 'I must be in complete control of my thoughts and feelings at all times, or I will go mad'.[21] Not surprisingly, Simpson found that trying to work with her husband in his therapeutic programme led to the wife becoming exceedingly anxious.

Cognitive behaviour therapy can be very helpful, much more helpful than drugs, in enabling the person to gain some control over his obsessions and compulsions, but the person resorting to this desperate defence cannot fully relinquish his defence and free himself from the power of the obsessions and compulsions until he recognizes the factors that made the defence necessary.

Tim Lott, the novelist, wrote about his obsessions in a newspaper article. These obsessions had to do with people, often women for whom he developed a passion that was more than simple love. Tim told of one such woman.

When it comes to obsessions with people, I experienced the classic pattern when I became obsessed with a woman 15 years ago. I was, and am, an introvert albeit a very outgoing one. I felt my world spinning out of control when my girlfriend – let's call her Jane – left me.

So far so bad. I became very miserable and resolved to get over it. For a while I couldn't get her out of my head. Then, however slightly, she began to fade. I woke up one morning realising that she was not the first thing I thought of.

Suddenly something disastrous happened – at least for someone in my situation and with my personality. She told me that she still loved me and that she might, at some unspecified later date, come back to me. Although this at first filled me with excitement, it took a while to dawn on me that I was now trapped. To be an ex-lover is bad enough; to be a pseudo ex-lover is worse, for the opportunity to grieve and move on is taken away.

From time to time, over several subsequent years, we would speak on the phone, and she would always suggest that she was still in love with me or at least never make any effort to disabuse me of the notion. And as anyone who has studied behavioural science will know, this pattern of occasional unpredictable reward or 'partial reinforcement' can have a terrible effect on anyone who is susceptible.

Give a rat an amount of food at a predictable time, and they will turn up to eat then and spend the rest of their time interesting themselves in other activities. Give them the same amount of food, but make the delivery unpredictable, and they will stand obsessively by the place where the food is delivered and take little interest in any other activity.

Gambling casinos all over the world exploit this simple equation with fruit machines and roulette wheels. But with that you only lose money. Eventually, I lost my very sense of self. For me the break-up with Jane began a process that ended three years later with me suffering a nervous breakdown.

The obsession came out of nowhere. One moment I was living a life in which I assumed I was a stable, reasonably well-adjusted 27-year-old. Over a brief period of weeks, I was hurled into a world of mental turmoil which stayed with me for years.

Every day I thought of her. Every day I hoped that she would come back. I was too weak and immature to dump her, especially since my love fed on her unavailability. And instead of this fading, it just stayed with me. And stayed with me and stayed with me.

Tim wanted to discover why this had happened. He also wanted to discover why his mother killed herself and why he had become depressed. He sought answers, and out of these 'whys' and the answers he found came Tim's remarkable biography of his mother, *The Scent of Dried Roses*.[22]

In his article Tim wrote:

> I was vulnerable because I was not only an introvert, but also in a difficult and stressful situation. Studying as a mature student at university, I would spend five or six hours a day by myself in a library . . . There was another possible reason for my state of mind – although I am half prepared to dismiss it as an inadequate excuse for such destructive behaviour. I was born with cancer as well as a cleft lip. For my first few months I was very close to death, and had a (presumably painful) operation in which one of my kidneys was removed.
>
> My first impression of my mother's face, then, instead of the normal smiles and cooing, would probably have been fear, and possible revulsion. So to experience as an adult a greater than normal fear of abandonment would not be an unusual reaction, I imagine. Whatever the reason, after Jane left me, I was left feeling very different from my 'normal self'. I think for a brief while I indulged in a very mild form of stalking. It wasn't persistent or long-lasting, but I certainly felt I was unable to control my behaviour (one of the clinical definitions of obsession). On two occasions I went to the houseboat where she lived and simply stood there, like a fool, staring at it, compelled to be in her orbit. I idealised her; she became the love I would never again recapture.

Tim's answers to his 'whys' were extensive, but such answers are rarely complete. I had met two of the women he had loved and they, like his mother, had beautiful dark hair. As a young woman his mother had been very beautiful but, when she was a young married woman going through a stressful time, all her hair had fallen out, never to grow again. It seems that she never came to tolerate her loss because she allowed no one, not even her husband with whom she shared a bed, to see her without either her wig or a scarf tied around her head.

One day, when Tim had phoned me to discuss some current problem, I asked him whether all the women he had fallen in love with had dark hair. There was silence at the other end of the phone. He was shocked by his discovery that he had never fallen in love with a blonde.

It would be impossible to establish every connection between Tim's childhood experiences and his later obsessions, but to dismiss such connections and not try to understand them would be foolish in the extreme. Only by understanding our past can we free ourselves from it.

His obsession with Jane came to an end, but some years later another very similar situation arose. Tim was able to deal with it differently. He wrote:

Eventually, I managed to grieve and the pain began to pass. I was determined not to make the same mistake I had before, and I succeeded. But it was very, very tough. It was as if I had to kill her psychologically in order to live myself.

Most of us are capable of non-pathological obsessions of one kind or another. Mothers can be obsessed with their children. Lovers can be obsessed with their partners. One can be obsessed with enemies or friends. At the root of all these obsessions, I suppose, is that most mysterious of phenomena: one's relationship with oneself, and one's attitude to the past – how you visualise it, how you relate to it, how you process it. Once something has happened, if you have the courage to let go of it and let it pass through you, as it were, obsession withers and dies.

But if you hold on to something, if you become fixated on the subject of your love or hate – and both are inseparable –

then obsession flowers, and its roots and branches slowly strangle your inner life.

I have learned a bitter lesson through my own experience and I feel reasonably sure that I will never go down that path again. For obsession is a kind of choice, born out of fear, and in the end it can be avoided – but that takes courage. Yet courage does not come in pills and cannot even be parcelled out by therapists. Thus some people simply never find it. They are the ones that become dangerous, either to others or, much more frequently, to themselves.[23]

The courage of which Tim speaks is the courage to overcome our greatest fear, the fear of annihilation. Annihilation is the experience of falling apart, which is what we feel when we discover that a major part of our meaning structure is no longer an accurate picture of what is actually going on. If we do not understand this we see the falling apart as madness. Extraverts, especially the extraverts who resort to the desperate defence of phobias, fear getting overexcited and going completely out of control. Introverts, especially those introverts who resort to the desperate defence of obsessions and compulsions, fear losing touch with what goes on around them, finding it impossible to understand external reality in the ways that other people do, and being overwhelmed by chaos. Extraverts will hold on to their phobias to defend themselves against mania, and introverts will hold on to their obsessions and compulsions to defend themselves against the chaos of the psychosis called schizophrenia.

Chapter Twelve

Turning Fear into Schizophrenia

Schizophrenia is the madness that everyone fears. People who are manic can be extremely difficult to get along with, and their anger can be dangerous, but we can understand what they are on about, even though we may deplore its lack of common sense. We just want them to slow down and behave more reasonably. However, people in a state of psychosis are strange, unreachable in any ordinary way, and because they are so strange and unpredictable, we are afraid of them.

It is very difficult to write simply and clearly about schizophrenia because it is impossible to separate the individual's schizophrenic experience from the economics and politics of the society in which the individual lives. You can indulge in your anxiety and panics, your obsessions and compulsions, your depression, and even your mania, provided you do not break the law or become a public spectacle, but, once you choose schizophrenia as your defence, society will not let you be. Whether you emerge unscathed from your schizophrenic experience depends as much on what society decides to do with you as on what you decide to do for yourself.

Those two profound experiences, depression and schizophrenia, are more than just the experiences of troubled individuals. Just as the experience of depression addresses itself to all the moral issues of life, so the experience of schizophrenia addresses all the issues of becoming and being an individual in relation to a group.

Yet, while being depressed has become fashionable, being psychotic never has. Joanne Chambers, who has known both psychosis and depression, wrote:

Depression, we are constantly reminded, is suffered by one in four people at some point in their lives . . . Many famous celebrities have been there and back: Freddy Starr, Caroline Aherne, Paul Merton, Tony Hancock, Patsy Kensit, Sarah Lancashire and countless others. These people, many of whom are comedians by profession, prove that those who suffer from depression are not socially inadequate, self-pitying loners or failures. Many of them are confident and social creatures, at the top of their professions.

Now one star after the other comes out with their story of their personal battle against depression, or anorexia, or drug addiction, or alcoholism, to grace the pages of a *Hello!* exclusive. Just as often as they go in and out of the famous Priory clinic as if it were a five star hotel rather than a psychiatric hospital.

But where are the psychotics? Where are the stars revealing their experience of delusions, thought disorders, paranoia, hallucinations? No one is so quick to reveal this side of mental illness. Why? Because it seems to be the misunderstood, the most feared and the unacceptable face of mental illness.

I have admitted to many people that I have suffered from depression, and they have responded in a sensitive, kind and respectful way to me, saying they are glad to see that I am so well, and that their friend's daughter's piano teacher's mother once suffered from it too.

But pop the P-word into the conversation and you might as well have put the F-word in instead; mouths hang open and awkward silences ensue.[1]

Frequently, the words 'schizophrenia' and 'schizophrenic' are used in conversations and in the media quite incorrectly, as meaning a split personality or being inconsistent. People will say, 'He's schizophrenic about it,' when the person simply cannot choose between two alternatives, or 'He's schizophrenic, he's got a split personality.'

The kind of person who might be described as having a 'split personality' – that is, acting in one role or as one person for a time and then switching to another role, like Dr Jekyll and Mr Hyde, but without the aid of a mysterious potion – is not the sort of person who is likely to have the experiences that are rightly called schizophrenic. Rather, this way of experiencing yourself as several apparently separate people who are in themselves ordinary and everyday is the defence called multiple personality disorder. The notion of 'splitting' contained in the word 'schizophrenic' comes from Eugene Bleuler, who coined the word 'schizophrenia' to reflect the way a person enduring the schizophrenic experience seems to be separating his emotions from his ideas. For instance, such a person may say, 'My mother died recently,' and instead of looking appropriately sad may giggle and make a joke, while another event – say, a broken plate – may produce tears. Psychiatrists call this 'inappropriate affect' and regard it as a symptom of the illness of schizophrenia. What Eugene Bleuler and his successors did not realize is that while the schizophrenic person's emotional reactions may appear inappropriate to the observer, such reactions are appropriate to and consistent with the way in which that person gives meaning to his world.

We are always in the business of trying to make sense of our world. To do this, we need the events we are trying to understand to have some consistency and regularity. When our external reality seems to us to be inconsistent and incomprehensible we feel helpless, and our sense of being a person is threatened with annihilation. Extraverts react to such a situation by springing into action to sort matters out. Introverts retreat into their internal reality. Fleeing into their more real reality, extraverts and introverts then attempt a reconstructing and ordering of their world.

Extraverts under immense threat may reconstruct by using massive denial. For instance, instead of grieving for her family destroyed without warning by a terrorist bomb, an extravert woman may say, and believe in the face of all evidence, 'My family have gone away on holiday. They will be home tomorrow,' and go on living a life quite ordinary in every respect, except for her denial that her family are dead.

An introvert woman in the same situation may attempt a similar reconstruction of her world, but, having retreated to her internal reality, she finds her external reality so unreal and inconsistent that she can no longer distinguish it from her internal reality of dreams and fantasies. Suppose such a woman has had from her earliest childhood a strong religious faith which includes the belief that she has her own guardian angel looking after her, and that if she is good then this angel will protect her from all harm. She may never have told anyone that she has held fast to this belief all her adult life. However, now that disaster has befallen her, she has to ask herself whether her guardian angel has failed her, or whether she has lost the protection of her angel because she has sinned. To prove to herself that her family has not been destroyed by her own wickedness, and that her guardian angel is still there caring for her, she may fantasize that her family has been miraculously restored to her by the angel. This fantasy seems, as she develops it, amazingly real, but she has lost the ability to distinguish her fantasy from her external reality. The needs and fears contained in this fantasy are immensely powerful and demand confirmation. Suddenly the woman knows, beyond all shadow of a doubt, that the postman, delivering her letters, is her guardian angel in disguise, and that the letters, masquerading as sympathy cards and electricity bills, like the voices she hears from her broken television set, are messages of love and hope from her family, as well as warnings from her angel's alter ego, the Devil, about how she should behave if she is to escape a terrible fate. Knowing that her mother is safe in the care of her angel, she may laugh happily at any mention of her mother's death. If she believes that breaking a plate will earn the Devil's displeasure, she may cry in penitence and fear when she breaks a plate. Such fantasies are to her no stranger than the events that have already overtaken her, but more, they bring her comfort, and she cannot bear to recognize them as fantasies, for to do so would plunge her back into the hell of total helplessness. So she insists, against all argument and evidence, that her fantasies are total and immutable reality. Such fantasies are called the delusions and hallucinations of schizophrenia.

For some people this kind of defence is necessary only for a short period, following a crisis that gradually subsides into something less threatening, but for others, external reality never becomes sufficiently safe for the defence to be relinquished, and so the person goes on living in a world that bears little resemblance to the external reality that people generally share. This experience of an extremely idiosyncratic world may be called schizophrenia.

Brian Davey was well acquainted with his own idiosyncratic world. He also knew what it is like to have control of your life taken over by psychiatrists and the staff of a large psychiatric hospital. Some years ago he decided to take charge of his own life, and from then on he went from strength to strength, but to do that he had to come to understand what was happening to him. Later he wrote:

> When you are psychotic your inner concerns are so dominant that they structure your interpretation of your incoming perceptions. The relationship between one's internal world of thoughts and feelings and the external world is dominated by the internal world. This internal world of extreme feelings and strange thoughts seems to be utterly bizarre and not to match the external reality at all. I believe, however, that it is possible to make sense of this strange internal world. The way to do this is to see oneself as reliving the concerns, responses and feelings of the earliest stages of one's life – when one was a baby, infant and small child; to put it in the jargon, one has regressed. But one has regressed to the concerns, feelings and responses one made in conditions of fear and powerlessness of that time, to feelings of horror or to one's 'slave feelings' . . . I call them 'slave feelings' because they are associated with the powerlessness the baby or small child feels if it cannot find the appropriate matching response to the expression of its feelings or if it finds it always has to do what the big people want, irrespective of its feelings.[2]

Brian's understanding of slave feelings and their link to the experience of psychosis came, in part, from his exploration of his experiences in his early childhood. He told me about this at the time, and more recently he expanded on this in an e-mail to me. He wrote:

A good few years ago I talked to my mother who told me things about my infancy which helped me develop my understanding of my regressions. This did require courage on both our parts, but it proved valuable. In particular, my mother told me about how my sister bullied me. She was much older and jealous at attention directed at me. Also, when I was about three I became very distressed, stopped eating, and lost a lot of weight. My father had taken me to a slaughter house and the reality of death, meat, as well as what happened to the chickens in the back garden and to the kittens drowned in a sack . . . The chickens and kittens were my friends. 'Mr Pig doesn't mind being eaten' didn't seem credible because Mr Pig had screamed before he was stunned by the slaughter worker. This incident came out time and time again in my psychoses. My mother showed me a photo taken of me before my visit to the slaughter house. I looked well fed, confident and secure. Later, a photo of a family group on their way to a wedding showed me looking thin and anxious. This helped me remember the difference in size between my sister and me.

However, the years can heal if it's possible to get back into your mind as a child and understand what happened then. My relationship with my mother and sister is better now than it has ever been. I have never talked to my sister about the past and it's probably unnecessary now. My father died a few years ago, but I made my peace with him before he died. I think I would have been troubled if that had not happened.

Reconciliation with his family was a special blessing, but Brian also devoted himself to making his understanding of his own experiences available to other people through his teaching and writings. He explained the connections between early childhood experience and the experience of psychosis in terms of the meanings we create. He wrote:

Our structure of thought will reflect the nature of our early experiences. In this respect thinking is the use of symbols of human communication, chiefly words, to form an inner picture of the world and our place in it, that guides our responses and interpretations. We are likely to grow up with systems of interpretations that reflect or are maybe mirror rejections of our parents' thinking. Perhaps if we grow up unloved and we seek an understanding for this we take for our explanation their account that we are bad. They say this because we ignored or rejected their demands on us. In our thinking we construct strategies that will enable us to survive.

Breakdown is the collapse of our defences, it is the return of feelings we learned to cut off from or not notice; it is return to the starting point, the horrors and fear and powerless we felt at the beginning.

If we are stressed with negative feelings for long enough, breakdown is inevitable. In madness we return to the original experience of powerlessness. If in our original experience of powerlessness there was no one there to support and comfort us then we find nothing but an incoherent awareness of endless terror and horror. The experience seems as if it will be endless, for the baby has, as yet, no experience of time, no notion that it has a future in the adult world.[3]

In babyhood our meaning structure is trying to set itself up as a coherent whole. Only when it has can the infant begin to acquire that sense of being a person which is part and parcel of consciousness. Slowly we wake to consciousness and become a person. Consciously knowing ourselves to be a person comes later, but our defences are operating well before that. In breakdown, as Brian describes it, we go back to having to create defences, just as the infant created defences, but the defences that an introvert in breakdown creates are those of delusions and hallucinations. 'Madness,' wrote Ron Coleman, 'far from being an illness is for many a desperate attempt to preserve the self.'[4]

Ron was brought up in a working-class Catholic family. When

he was eleven he went through a religious phase and wanted to become a priest. He met with his priest once a week for instruction, but the priest became ill and was replaced by another who abused him while they were praying side by side. Ron wrote, 'I was there but I was not there (those who have been abused will know what I mean). Much later in my life I discovered that this was called dissociation and it is the most common form of self-preservation of those who have been abused. . . Experience has taught me that the failure to deal with abuse means that the abuse will stay with you throughout your life and in many ways shape your life in terms of future relationships. This is especially true when it comes to trusting friends or life partners. This event more than any other was to shape my life or should I say my illness.'[5]

Time passed. Ron grew up, worked, played rugby, and fell in love with Annabelle.

Our relationship developed quickly from the torrid passion of new lovers to the passion that consumes those who are indeed soul mates. We spent as much time as we could in each other's company. Often we would sit up through the night talking and planning as couples do. We were planning our life together, this was normality at its best. But like all normality, madness was lurking, waiting its chance to pounce and consume us, and then one day it did.

Like the day I met Annabelle the day our relationship ended was a Saturday. I had been playing rugby and went home with something for both of us to eat. When I got in I called to Annabelle asking her if she wanted tea or coffee. She didn't reply. I went into the living room and she was lying on the couch. I asked her again and still got no reply. I gave her a shake but she would not wake up. I rushed out of the house to a neighbour and asked them to phone an ambulance. They rushed her to hospital and put her on a life support machine. She did not make it, and three days later she was pronounced dead. Annabelle had taken her own life. I never really found out why but I know that I blamed myself. I don't know why I blamed myself, though it was to be many years before I stopped doing so.

When she died a large slice of me died also. I swore that never again would I get emotionally involved with anyone. Like many others I suppressed all of my emotions about Annabelle and her death. I continued on with a semblance of existence that others called life. Like the abuse, I chose to pretend it never happened and like the abuse my feelings of grief and loss and hatred of the world festered inside, growing and growing, waiting for their chance to devour me.

The time came for my emotions to overcome me when I had an accident on the rugby pitch that put me out of the game for ever. Barely weeks had passed since I was discharged from hospital (still on crutches) when I heard a voice for the first time. I was in my office waiting for the computer to deliver the results of some data I had inputted when a voice behind me said that I had done it wrong. I looked behind me but there was nobody there. I stopped what I was doing immediately, went to the pub and got drunk. I remember thinking that I was stressed and needed a break.

Within a short six-months period the voice had been joined by other voices that spent most of the day screaming at me. I could not focus on my work and the only relief I got was when I had drunk myself into oblivion. Eventually my boss told me I had four weeks to get my act together. Four weeks later I was out of work, losing my home and on my way (though I didn't know it then) to my first encounter with the psychiatric services. In double quick time I became a pitiful sight with an unkempt beard, more often than not dirty clothes and more and more frequently drunk rather than sober.

Eventually I could not take any more and I phoned the Samaritans and after much talking went to see my GP. He ended the consultation with the words 'I am going to arrange for you to see a specialist.' Fine, I thought, that will take a while. What a surprise I was in for. He took me out of his consulting room and asked me to wait in a small side room in the surgery. A few minutes later he returned with a nurse who he told me was going to look after me while he arranged an appointment with the specialist. The only thing I remember about that wait with the nurse was how little she spoke. It was as if she was frightened to be in the same room as me.[6]

Ron spent six of the next ten years as an in-patient of a psychiatric hospital, almost all of that time on Section 3, which is a treatment order allowing him not only to be kept in hospital without his agreement but also to be medicated, forcibly if necessary. It took him ten years to escape from the system.

Brian and Ron, like many thousands of people, struggled with psychosis for a significant part of their life. For other people the period of psychosis is brief, having arisen when the person discovered that there was a serious discrepancy between what he thought his life was and what it actually was, and along with this suffered a considerable loss of self-confidence. Jessica was one of these.

Jessica's partner was Andy, whom I first met fifteen years before when he was referred to me by his GP. Andy was a passionate man, passionate about life, love and music, an extravert who could not live with or without other people, especially women. However, as time passed, he got older and wiser, and he seemed to have found a peaceful and satisfactory life with Jessica. Then one Sunday evening Andy phoned me at home. 'Something's happened to Jessica. She's started acting very strangely. She's hearing voices, I think, I can't make sense of what she's saying. Our GP came to see her and he got a psychiatrist and now she's going into hospital.'

He was very upset. I tried to reassure him that she would be well looked after. I described the hospital procedures and told him how best to find out how she was and what decisions the staff had made about Jessica. Over the next few weeks he kept in touch with me, and when Jessica was discharged, having had the usual treatment for schizophrenia, he phoned to ask whether Jessica and he could come to see me. I agreed, and some time later phoned him to arrange a time. Jessica answered, her old self. Yes, she would like to come and talk. She thought it could be very helpful.

They arrived, a handsome couple in their late forties. They had been together for just five years, and each had a personal history of various relationships, marriages and alliances. Jessica now occupied her time with various small tasks which supplemented their income, but she still spoke with all the authority of a woman who had held senior posts in a large organization and had discharged her duties there competently and responsibly.

'When I was working,' she said, 'I would see how inefficient the firm was because people didn't work together co-operatively. I would draw up plans to overcome these problems – models of co-operative organization – but I could never get them implemented. My colleagues would say, ''You can get people to work together because you're you, but your plans won't work generally.'' So eventually I decided to get out and I came here to live.'

I was interested in Jessica's emphasis on co-operation. Was this more than an interest in sensible social organization? Was it a denial of aggression within herself?

'Only to a certain extent,' she said. 'I'm a fighter when I have to be. When I was a child I fought my father all the time. I remember it caused a laugh at the time one day when he'd made me so angry I said that when I grew up I'd come back and murder him.'

She spoke of herself as being a passionate woman, full of strong sexual feelings. She spoke of affairs, and how hurt she was that although Andy shared her house he did not share her bed. Nevertheless, she had thought that they had a good relationship. They shared lots of interests and enterprises, they talked together a great deal, they pooled their knowledge and experience in ways that she found delightful and stimulating. She judged that all these benefits outweighed the times they argued.

An argument with Andy could be a dangerous activity for a woman. Even though he was now a much more peaceful, contented man than he had been in his youth, he had, he felt, been pursued and unjustly tortured by a monstrous regiment of women – his mother, wives, girlfriends, female colleagues – and he had developed a fine line of abuse about women generally which any woman standing within earshot could not help but feel was directed at her. So Jessica, over the years of being at the receiving end of Andy's sharp tongue, had gradually lost confidence in herself.

'In the five years we've been together,' she said, 'I've come to feel increasingly bad about myself.'

However, despite this she had felt that she could see and assess their relationship quite clearly and she had confidence in her judgement. Then something happened which showed her that she could not. She discovered that Andy was having an affair with a woman neighbour. Each day when he was supposed to be going about his various tasks, he was disappearing into this woman's house. Jessica told me she was shattered.

'I felt I could no longer trust my judgement in anything. This is what is so important. I have to be able to trust my judgement and to act on it. My judgement isn't just from my head, my intellect, but from here,' she pressed her hands against the region of her heart and stomach. 'It has to come from here out, on what is out there, and I have to be able to trust it so I can act. If I don't trust my judgement I don't know how to act. When Andy criticized me he would attack my judgement and that was what was so devastating. He would say that I was wrong in my judgement of other people – people who were important to me. He'd question my motives. He'd make out that my motives were bad, that I wanted to hurt him, when I knew they weren't. I didn't want to injure him, but he said I did. My father did the same to me as a child. He wanted to tell me that I was bad, wicked. I would tell him that I wasn't but he wouldn't believe me.'

The news of Andy's defection brought more than the pain of rejection. Her confidence in her judgement, the process whereby she structured and evaluated her world, was shattered. Now she was in danger of annihilation.

'I was filled with the most terrible sense of dread. It was the most horrible experience. I felt that something terrible was about to happen. It was something I was going to do, or something was going to happen to me. I thought I had killed Andy and buried him in the garden. I thought that Andy and Alex were going to live together in my house and I would have to live with her husband. I went out into the garden and stayed there because I thought nothing bad could happen to me there. Then I went next door. My neighbour there is a very good woman and I thought nothing bad could happen if I stayed with her. Then I felt that that wouldn't work, so I went out into the marketplace. I thought if I was in such a public place then people would see and nothing terrible could happen to me there. To others all this running about seemed quite crazy, but to me it made sense at the time.'

Along with these desperate attempts to avoid the greatest danger came thoughts of omniscient power. 'I thought I understood the most complex mathematical concepts. It frightened me having so much knowledge. In the past I felt I was blocked in every direction. Now I felt I had changed. I had got rid of all the blocks. I was free to go in any direction.'

'Is that how you feel now, that you've changed?' I asked.

Jessica looked at me, her lips tightening. 'There are some things which I see now are not important. But, no, nothing's changed.'

Eighteen months later she had revised her opinion. She said that it had 'not been a bad experience. Just what I needed really. You have fixed pictures in your unconscious and you don't have access to them, although they exert a strong influence. In that experience of madness everything gets well and truly mixed up. That was good for me.'

She contrasted this experience in which her structures had fallen apart with other experiences in her life in which all her structures came together in a complete and wonderful whole, and she entered into periods of what mystics call 'union' or 'enlightenment'. The experience of feeling at one with everything around you, that the common barriers that separate you from the rest of the world have melted away and you know yourself to be part of everything that exists, is very common. Studies by Alistair Hardy[7] and by David Hay[8] have shown that this experience can occur in a multitude of settings and profoundly, and usually happily, affects the people who experience it. Many others seek it through meditation.

The link or contrast between psychosis and mystical union adds another complication in our understanding of schizophrenia. The relationships between psychosis and mystical union can be understood in terms of the meanings or structures we create. All that we know of what actually exists is that it is a seamless, ever-changing whole. This is the description that physicists arrive at in their study of the subatomic world of quantum physics. These physicists impose their structures on this subatomic world by talking about particles and giving them quaint names like muon and charm, just as we in our everyday lives impose our structures on the seamless, ever-changing whole. We see divisions where none exists. We like to think of our body as being separate and distinct, but it and the atmosphere around it are in constant interaction, as is everything that we see and name. Physically we are connected to everything that exists. Only our ideas appear to be separate, but our ideas are constructions that can change and disappear.

The thought of being an integral part of everything that exists can be terrifying or comforting. We can see it as losing our sense of being a person, something we defend against all the time, or as choosing to give up our sense of being a person, something we desire when the effort to make sense of everything becomes a burden. The first is terrifying, the second is a wonder beyond words. Whether in the tradition of Christian meditative prayer or the Buddhist tradition of meditation, or in simple communion with nature, those who have experienced such unity have struggled to find words to describe it. Many people who practise meditation would say that, although they have never experienced anything like what the mystics have tried to describe, they find that the lower foothills of meditation create a sense of calm and peace that greatly enhances their life.

The difference between psychosis and mystical union can be likened to the difference between being seized by someone and thrown off a high diving-board into dangerous deep water and choosing oneself to execute a perfect dive into a deep, transparent pool. In both cases the person, once in the water, soon bobs to the top because water always bears us up. Similarly, whether our structures break and crumble or whether we choose to relinquish our structures, we sooner or later return to the ordinary world that our structures create for us. Communing with nature and meditating are time limited and soon we return to ordinary life. However, many of those whose structures have broken and crumbled do not return to ordinary life because they are prevented from doing so. Society traps them in a kind of halfway house, a purgatory from which there is no escape, no redemption, no reward.

This entrapment by society arises out of conflicting sets of ideas, the fear of madness, and the power and pride of vested interests, all of which are connected to an idea, not an entity: the idea called schizophrenia.

An Idea Called Schizophrenia

There is no doubt that some people have psychotic experiences similar, but not identical, to those described by Brian, Ron and Jessica. The question is whether all these experiences can validly be seen as evidence of an underlying mental illness or disorder called schizophrenia. Psychosis can be described very loosely as being out of touch with external reality, but this 'out of touch' covers an extremely wide range of experiences, far too wide to be the symptoms of one single illness.

There are a number of statistical methods that will show if certain phenomena cluster together. Such methods have been applied to psychotic symptoms and to people diagnosed with schizophrenia. The British Psychological Society report *Recent Advances in Understanding Mental Illness and Psychotic Experiences* summarized the results of these studies:

Another way of examining the validity of diagnostic categories involves using statistical techniques to investigate whether people's psychotic experiences actually do cluster together in the way predicted by the diagnostic approach. The results of this research have not generally supported the validity of distinct diagnostic categories. For example, the correlation amongst psychotic symptoms has been found to be no greater than if the symptoms are put together randomly. Similarly, cluster analysis – a statistical technique for assigning people to groups according to particular characteristics – has shown that the majority of psychiatric patients would not be assigned to any recognisable diagnostic group. Statistical techniques have also highlighted the extensive overlap between those diagnosed with schizo-phrenia and those diagnosed as having major affective disorder.[9]

What are called psychiatric symptoms are descriptions only of what people in the midst of a psychotic experience *do*, not the reasons why they so behave. Consequently much of what such people experience is not examined. Thus the parallels between psychotic experience and mystical union have not been examined by psychiatrists who see a psychotic person as suffering from a mental illness. Any mystical experience reported by a patient would be seen by the psychiatrist as no more than evidence of the illness. Nor have psychiatrists examined the ability that some introverts, whether psychotic or not, have of knowing about something occurring in the internal reality of another person and about which that person has not spoken.

It is quite disconcerting to a therapist when a client who seems to be entirely wrapped up in his own internal reality comments on what the therapist is thinking or doing, something that the therapist thinks that no one else could possibly know. The second time Harry came to see me, when he was talking to me in highly abstract terms which were often difficult for me to follow, he suddenly said, 'This room is your haven'. This hit straight home. My office was not a particularly attractive or comfortable room, but it was my own territory. At that time I was feeling under great threat from some powerful people outside my office, so I was often glad to retreat to its safety. Moreover, the threat and anxiety concerned Harry, because in previous years I would have been able to give him a great deal of time and perhaps would have been able to work with the counsellors at his university so he could continue his career, but the threats to the future of our psychology service now meant that we could not give Harry the help he needed. All the time I was listening to Harry and trying to understand what he was telling me I was angry and grieving that this gentle young man had entered upon a path which, without adequate intervention, would mean that he would either die by his own hand or spend his days like those strange automatons who were heavily drugged and who I saw walking past my window every day. Harry knew that this room was my haven, and he tried to comfort me.

While Harry saw this in me, and while he tried to help me, he did not realize that making such a comment would shake me. Many people do not like being surprised and shaken like that. Many people prefer that certain aspects of the truth should not be noted and commented upon. Truth is very important to many introverts, for it is only by striving to know the truth, no matter how unpalatable it may be, that any sort of structure and certainty can be found in their external reality. However, truth is not a commodity much valued in a conforming society, and introverts like Harry are often punished for their truth-telling.

Harry's life had been spent at home and at school and nowhere else. This was why going to university far away from home had been such an unsettling shock to him. In his close-knit family he had not been able to acquire much knowledge of the outside world. He certainly did not have any concepts like 'the structure and reorganization of the National Health Service', or 'the functions of a psychology department', so he would have had no tools for comprehending and assessing my situation in a way that would have been comprehensible to most other people. If you have this ability to perceive what is going on in another person's internal reality, in order to make good use of it you need to have both strong self-confidence and an array of concepts through which to organize what you discover – concepts that are shared with other people. For instance, if I sense that the person to whom I have just been introduced is, under a guise of friendliness, really very angry, I can organize this subtle information into, say, a question to myself like 'I wonder what he's angry about?' and, if I feel confident in myself, decide that his anger has nothing to do with me, or, if it has, that he is a fool to get angry with such a wonderful person as me. However, if I do not have these concepts, and I have no confidence in myself, what I perceive is anger, danger and confusion.

Gerda de Bruijn told how one of her clients, Walter, who had never given any indication of hearing voices, had greatly surprised her once when he came to see her.

My conversation was not going smoothly that day, mainly because I was giving him only half of my attention; the other half was still preoccupied with a recent, unrelated incident and a person with whom I had been very angry. In the course of my conversation, Walter became more and more withdrawn, until eventually it was almost as if he was listening to his own inside. Suddenly he said with great feeling that behind the real, ordinary world of our conversation there was another, a frightening world, and that he heard voices coming from this other world. I did not hear these voices, but it was clear from Walter's trembling that he was genuinely scared by what he heard. After a while he agreed to tell me what the voices were communicating: violent curses.

On the face of it, there may appear to be nothing remarkable about this story. But the words Walter heard spoken coincided exactly with the curses that I, during our conversation, had been phrasing in my mind with the other half of my attention. It was as if Walter's voices were literally saying what I had been thinking in silence.[10]

De Bruijn later discovered that other therapists reported having similar experiences. She wrote about her experience in the context of the paranormal and, like many of the people who explain events in terms of the paranormal, she did not look for other possibilities.

Thought occurs in our brains. Scanning techniques have revealed that different kinds of thinking take place in different parts of the brain. The thought 'Damn you!' would occur in the part of the brain dedicated to subvocalizations – that is, words which we hear in our heads but do not say out loud. If a particular subvocalization carries a lot of emotion, the vocal cords and throat muscles are likely to move in a measurable and perhaps noticeable way. Often subvocalizations are involuntarily spoken aloud, especially when we are alone or wrapped up in our own thoughts.

Walter would have seen that his therapist was distracted and angry, and he could have picked up enough of her subvocalizations to have a good idea of what she was thinking. Most of us are not inventive enough to think up new kinds of curses. He had come into his therapist's room expecting her full attention, and he would have been disappointed when he did not get it. He dared not confront her because she was more powerful than he, and other people's anger would have frightened him. So he seems to have made use of the one advantage that being seen as mad gives. He could have told her that he knew what she was thinking, but, since she might react aggressively, he could protect himself by talking about hearing voices. He was saying 'I know what you're doing' without actually saying so. As Helen Reddy sang, 'It's so nice to be insane, no one asks you to explain.'[11]

I had been shaken when Harry commented accurately on what my room meant to me but I already knew how he could do that. As far back as I can remember I have been able to pick up what is going on inside another person – not words, as Walter did, but complex feelings and attitudes. I certainly do not do this all the time because, like most people most of the time, I am so involved with my own concerns that I am only marginally aware of what is going on with other people. This ability – or disability – starts functioning when I am in a situation that makes me anxious (a state I was in most of the time in my childhood) or when it becomes important to me to know what is happening to the other person, and then I focus my attention. It may sound as if this would be a boon to a therapist, but actually it is an impediment because, though I might know something about the person which I had not been told, I have no idea whether the person is able to admit to himself what is happening to him, much less to me. This knowledge does not tell me anything about the person's past or future. I am not privy to that person's secrets. All I get is a glimpse of what the person is thinking and feeling at that moment. I can see that, while a person appears to be calm, he is not, or he appears happy but is sad, or is saying one thing but not meaning it.

As a child this kind of knowledge was of use to me when it showed me that I should make myself physically safe by getting out of the room (or even the house) when my mother was brewing up one of her rages, but, in other situations, what I knew paralysed me with fright or uncertainty because I did not know what to do with what I knew. I soon learned not to talk about anything connected to what I knew because this would make me even more peculiar in my family's eyes, but years later when I was working in Sydney with psychotic adolescents, I discovered that I was not the only person who laboured under the possession of this ability. I have yet to come across a psychotic young person who grew up in an ordinary, happy home, so I came to think of this ability as a skill that a small child might have to learn in order to survive both physically and as a person. This is not an example of the paranormal in action. It is a matter of being able to detect a certain posture, a tone of voice and a look in the eyes which together form a certain pattern. It is a skill analogous to the skill whereby an Australian Aboriginal tracker can look at what, to others, is an ordinary piece of ground and know who has passed by and when. He has learned how to see certain patterns and to know what they mean.

I suspect that introverts and extraverts, in seeking to know what is going on inside another person, gather evidence and marshal it in different ways. My friend Jill Tweedie, a very perceptive extravert, once told me how, when she was a small child, she perceived the emotions her parents were feeling as colourful auras around their bodies. When they were miserable the aura was blue, and when the aura was red she knew they were angry and that she had better get out of their way. There are many things that introverts know about internal reality, particularly their own internal reality, but which they find hard to assemble and present in an understandable way to other people. This is partly due to a lack of appropriate words in our language to describe internal events, and partly due to the fact that certain ways of perceiving which are ordinary to the introvert sound most peculiar when described to another person. I have often tried and failed to explain to an extravert what I mean when I say 'external reality becomes unreal'.

However, while some introverts have an immediate and alarming apprehension of another person's internal reality, others are very much oblivious to people, instead focusing on machines or abstract systems like mathematics or computer programming. Others are more fortunate and grow up with a nice balance of interest in people, objects and theories.

If we live solely in our internal reality we soon become confused, for in our internal reality we can create many ideas, and there is no way of making our ideas reliable and true to life because we do not test them against our external reality. However, for an introvert, especially an introvert who lacks confidence in himself, it is not always easy to go out and do this testing.

When your internal reality is more real than your external reality, you always have a sense of looking out upon the world. It is like living in a room and looking at the outside world through a window. To act upon the world you have to go through this window, and sometimes, especially when you lose confidence in yourself, the window is there like a barrier, so you hesitate, doubting whether you can act because what is actually beyond the window may be very different from what you see. The only way to move is to act as if what you see is real. If you have the courage to suspend your disbelief in what you *see*, what you *do* may then become real. You may feel a marvellous exhilaration at having acted upon external reality and found that it was there and real.

However, crossing the barrier is very difficult. Pretending that you believe in the reality of something whose existence you do not trust is very risky. It is much safer to stay inside yourself and not act. If the acting upon your suspension of disbelief is not followed by exhilaration but by pain and punishment and more confusion (the chaos that threatens to annihilate you), then you will withdraw even more and not risk action. Introvert children who are constantly criticized and punished may find that the safest way to behave is to do nothing and to say nothing. Such a decision can lead to the complete immobility called catatonia.

When I did my clinical training in the early 1960s we were taught that there were three kinds of schizophrenia: paranoid, hebephrenic and catatonic. Anyone who was not clearly paranoid or catatonic was classed as hebephrenic. (The DSM calls it the 'disorganised type'.) Someone who was catatonic did not move at all. Sometimes the person would become immobile in some strange position. Catatonia was the ultimate in not daring to move or speak. If the person did speak at all it was only to echo the words of whoever had just spoken. That way the person could not be accused of saying anything wrong. Catatonia is nowhere near as prevalent as it once was, probably because conditions in psychiatric hospitals gradually improved and patients no longer lived under such a harsh, even brutal, regime. What sometimes happens now is that a patient will take up a position in a certain place on a ward or in a corridor and have to be coaxed to go into the dining room or to bed, but such patients have, in the logic of their internal reality, a good reason to behave in this way. One young woman I knew took up a position in the middle of the day room on a ward and would not budge, but she did tell me that, if she went outside, the ward would burn down. I knew that she hated being on that ward so much that she felt like burning it down. By positioning herself on guard in the ward she was preserving herself and others from her anger.

Learning how to knit together internal and external reality and how to act successfully upon external reality begins at birth. The first six months of life are when the child gains his first impressions of what the world is like and how he can engage the interest of the world and act effectively in it. Babies who receive what Donald Winnicott called 'good enough' mothering have no difficulty in attracting the attention of their mothers, who behave with sufficient regularity and predictability for the baby to come to experience his external reality as something he can rely on. Such mothers give the baby the opportunity to succeed, or to feel that he has succeeded, in his activities directed towards external reality. The exchanges between a good enough mother and her baby are finely tuned and complicated to describe, but they do not require 'book learning' to acquire. Studies of mothers with their babies in many different cultures show remarkable similarities in the interactions between the mother and baby when the mother is encouraging the baby to be confident in himself and in his actions.

Introvert babies do not want to be over-stimulated, so they may be quiet babies, often taken for being 'good' by their mothers, who may then leave them alone for longer periods than they would a more noisy and demanding baby, as extravert babies often are because they want lots of company. Thus right from the start the baby may not have sufficient opportunity to discover his external reality. Or it may be that the mother is ill or depressed and does not have the energy or enthusiasm to play with her baby and talk to him, and give him those little experiences which leave him with the impression that he can act effectively in his external reality. For a baby 'a win' is anything that has a happy outcome, from catching hold of a rattle to having his nappy changed. Again, for reasons right outside the mother's control, she may be unable to provide her baby with a sufficiently regular and predictable environment to give the baby confidence in his external reality.

It is during this phase of life, when the baby is learning how much he can trust his external reality, that he begins to put together his meaning structure. If something happens which overwhelms this fragile sense of being a person, the infant is flooded with fear, the most terrible experience of his life, so terrible that he spends the rest of his life trying to defend against a repetition of this experience. As Donald Winnicott said:

What is common in all cases [of schizophrenia] is this, that the baby, child, adolescent or adult *must never again experience* the unthinkable anxiety that is the root of schizoid illness. This unthinkable anxiety was experienced initially in a moment of failure of the environmental provision when the immature personality was at the stage of absolute dependence.[12]

This 'failure of environmental provision' need not be deliberate or even ignorant neglect on the part of the parents. It may be crises quite beyond their control, or some developmental lag on the part of the child. Thus a combination of factors, none in itself devastating, could create a situation in which the infant is unable to cope.

The 'unthinkable anxiety' is the breaking down of all structures and a falling into chaos. The infant who has suffered this builds up another set of structures, but these may not have firm foundations. The infant no longer trusts the outside world, so the structures he then creates may not relate very closely to his external reality. For instance, studies have shown that infants in hospital who are separated from their parents for long periods are likely to appear not to recognize their parents when they are reunited. An infant whose needs and wishes are overridden or ignored by his mother is in a situation in which his nascent meaning structure is constantly under threat. This is what Brian Davey called 'slave feelings' of helplessness and powerlessness. The infant may create a set of structures which are totally idiosyncratic, as does the child who earns the diagnosis of autistic. Or he may construct something that serves him well enough through childhood and early adolescence but fails him when he has to face the stresses of the adult world.

In our first talk Harry said to me, 'I felt that my past and my present and my future didn't make any pattern I could recognize. There were bits, they didn't fit, I couldn't make a pattern.'

He spoke of a law that said it was evil to make barriers between people. I asked him if he was a committed Christian and he said he was 'a committed theologian'. He was well equipped to be a theologian. Later he told me, 'When I was young I read the Bible under the bedclothes every night.'

Now he said, 'I hate being scrutinized.'

I said, 'It hurts to be scrutinized when the person is also criticizing you. But we need to scrutinize others in order to understand them.'

'I don't scrutinize others.' He put his head down. 'I want them to be free.'

He spoke of the need for stability and purity, which led on to the immense power of God. Stability was pattern; instability was chaos, pain and loss. I included aggression here, in response to fear, but he said he became aggressive only when he was trying to break free. He said, 'I had to forget that loss,' but did not explain what loss he meant. I said, 'When we lose something that was important to us we always feel the pain of that loss,' and he agreed.

He kept talking of how 'I need to have a schedule to organize my time. Then I can sort myself out.'

On the next occasion we met I asked him whether I could jot down some of the things he said. These are the notes I made.

'It's like everything all at once and you can't control it.'

'The Jews say that to know everything at once is certain death.' (If he becomes totally powerful and spiritually pure he will die, but the opposite is to be like mud.)

'We can become anything we want to be.'

'The fear is that we don't know what the fear is.' (This is the theme of *Beyond Fear*, the original edition of which I was writing at the time, but I had not told him about it.)

'As far as I know I could be anybody at any place at any time.' (If you give up the structures of space and time and person you could indeed be anybody at any place at any time.)

'It's like there's no beginning. We construct the time and the place. We construct the scene and we act in it.'

'It's like fears are invented by something that should be there.' (The longing for the security we once knew but now have lost?)

'There must be a written code.' (He sees the need to have some firm, authoritarian rules to keep some order within the freedom to structure. He would not dare overthrow his father's rules.)

'There's no true beginning.'

'I feel very polluted within myself.'

'I long for the things I've lost – my poetic sense, my basic rhythm. I never had them much, that's why I lost them so easily. That's what carries people along.'

I noted that 'All his utterances are in abstract terms. He ignores my attempts to interpret one of his statements as a metaphor for a real-life situation.'

The next time Harry came he looked a lot better. He had had his hair washed and cut. He talked about the necessity of structuring his time.

'What's the advantage of having your time structured?' I asked.

'Without structure I'm a shapeless black blob,' he said. He laughed at this, saying that this was what his friend Jim had said of him, but he went on to explain that as a shapeless black blob he would be reviled and criticized and not accepted as a person.

A black blob is vulnerable and valueless. To protect himself Harry needed structures of perfection and purity.

The less real an introvert's external reality becomes, the less he feels that he can deal with it and the more he must retreat from it. However, even when we retreat from our external reality we still have to continue finding some structure for it, some kind of explanation. The farther we retreat into our internal reality, the less our structures for and explanations of external reality actually match its dimensions. We create structures which those people observing us find to be very strange and idiosyncratic. They call these structures 'ideas of reference', 'delusions', 'hallucinations' and 'peculiar ideas'.

The disease theory of schizophrenia treats these structures as no more than symptoms of the illness and not as being meaningful in themselves. Yet they are part of the structure of meaning in which the person lives and breathes and has his being, and so, if he is to be understood, the meaning of these structures has to be understood. This is not easy, for, unlike the manic extravert whose ideas are simply exaggerations of a shared, common external reality, the introvert pushed to this extreme resorts to ideas which have a meaning that is very private and relates to experiences and feelings which he has never disclosed to anyone else. Moreover, where his ideas do relate to an external, shared experience, he may not be prepared to talk about this, for it may involve matters which his loyalty to his family would prevent him from discussing with strangers. This is why so many people diagnosed as schizophrenic and their families collude with the psychiatrist who holds to the belief that the patient is suffering from a disease of the body whose physical cause and course have not yet been discovered but will be. Over the past forty years I have been told, time and time again, that scientists are on the verge of discovering the physiological cause of schizophrenia. Forty years is a very long time to be on the verge.

Introverts, particularly those who resort to the defence of psychosis, may have very peculiar ideas, but so do the psychiatrists who believe that there is a disease called schizophrenia. An immense amount of work by psychiatrists has been devoted to developing methods of classifying mental disorders and of constructing standardized interviews so that psychiatrists working in, say, Los Angeles, Aberdeen and Melbourne will all agree about a diagnosis of schizophrenia, just as physicians expert in respiratory diseases working in such diverse places would all agree about a diagnosis of tuberculosis. However, such scientific precision has not been developed in psychiatry. To distinguish different forms of lung disease, physicians use objective tests such as X-rays, CAT scans and sputum tests, but psychiatrists have no tests to use, only their very subjective 'clinical judgement'. There are no objective, physiological tests for any of the mental disorders listed in the DSM except for those disorders of thinking which are caused by an observable injury to the brain. Consequently, the word 'schizophrenia' refers to an immense range of differing views including whether such a condition actually exists and, if so, what its causes and cures are. A study of the views of some psychiatrists in the UK showed that 'the understanding of schizophrenia is largely individualistic and remains an ill-defined condition despite recent attempts to standardise and delineate it as a diagnosable entity with defined characteristics, treatment and outcome.'[13]

Individualistic understanding can be extremely idiosyncratic. One psychiatrist I used to work with would remark that he could always distinguish a woman who was schizophrenic from one who was not by the fact that the woman who was schizophrenic 'doesn't turn me on'. Another psychiatrist assured me that he knew a certain woman was schizophrenic 'by the shape of her eyebrows'. This woman later told me that she always wore make-up that enhanced her similarity to Elizabeth Taylor, who at the time was extremely famous because of her role as Cleopatra, whose Hollywood version certainly had distinctive eyebrows.

I often observed that the anti-intellectual stance of some psychiatrists resulted in a diagnosis of schizophrenia for any troubled student who happened to be reading philosophy at university. Students are always likely to be the victims of the prejudices that some doctors have against people who are younger than themselves and who have not adopted the conventional attitudes and behaviour that the doctors have assumed as part of their becoming accepted members of the medical profession. Envy is as prevalent in the medical profession as it is in the rest of the population.

A psychiatrist who believes that schizophrenia is a physical illness is unlikely to refer anyone so diagnosed to a therapist, as a friend of mine found only a year ago when she tried to get psychotherapy for her niece, who was psychotic and a patient in a psychiatric unit.[14] Despite the extensive reports by many psychotherapists successfully working with people in psychosis, many psychiatrists still believe that psychotherapy is detrimental to someone with such a diagnosis. The only reason I met Harry was because the psychiatrist considered that all Harry's problems stemmed from his taking drugs at university. As he explained to me, 'If I thought Harry was schizophrenic I would not have asked him to see you.' When it became clear from what Harry and his elder brother told me that he had begun his retreat into his internal world many years earlier, I was placed in a quandary, because if I imparted this information to the psychiatrist he might have insisted that I stopped seeing Harry.

It certainly is not necessary for a patient to display the symptoms of schizophrenia – hallucinations, delusions and changes in thinking and speaking – for that patient to be given a diagnosis of schizophrenia. Some people are given the diagnosis because they have failed to give up being depressed, despite repeated courses of ECT and high doses of the full range of antidepressants and many of the minor tranquillizers. So are those people who are protesting in a not very coherent and orderly way about the injustices in their lives. All too often the diagnosis of schizophrenia means for the psychiatrist 'I don't understand'. The treatment for anyone diagnosed a schizophrenic – doses of the major tranquillizers, the neuroleptics, often by injection – results in the doctors and nurses being no longer so greatly troubled by their patients' grief and protests.

Colleagues have told me that what is happening to some patients who have been given the diagnosis of schizophrenia is that their diagnosis has been changed to that of the popular Borderline Personality Disorder, because this is now the favoured diagnosis for difficult patients. Moreover, now that in a clinical interview a professional is more likely to enquire into questions of childhood sexual abuse, and that many of the people who become psychotic have been so abused, it is more difficult to uphold the view that schizophrenia is a genetic disease.

One of the 'symptoms of schizophrenia' is called 'lack of insight'. This 'lack of insight' occurs when the person reaches a point where he can no longer test his experience of internal reality against his experience of his external reality and arrive at some reliable answer. For instance, if, while waiting for a bus, you say to yourself, 'Is that a bus coming, or did I just imagine it?' you can test the match of your two realities. Either the bus itself arrives, or you see that what you thought was a bus was, say, a large lorry. In ordinary life we are always creating hypotheses in our internal reality and testing them against our external reality (what psychologists call 'reality testing'), but to do this successfully we need confidence in our own powers of judgement and an external reality that is fairly consistent and reliable. If external reality is your more real reality you are better equipped to see its consistencies. If external reality is your less real reality, it is much harder to see it as reliable and consistent, and, under the stress that makes you lose confidence in yourself, you find that external reality becomes more and more strange. So you may choose to retreat to your internal reality and insist, against all arguments by other people, that what you experience there is absolutely and undoubtedly true. This is what is called the symptom of 'lack of insight' in schizophrenia, and what you experience as truth is labelled by others as peculiar ideas, or hallucinations, delusions and paranoia.

There is another 'lack of insight' often diagnosed in psychiatric hospitals. This is where the patient fails to agree with the psychiatrist's assessment of him. The psychiatrist arrives at his diagnosis in a way illustrated by this conversation, which I witnessed.

PSYCHIATRIST: Harry, the nurses tell me that you went home at the weekend and caused a disturbance. Your parents brought you back to the ward, and instead of settling down you made it necessary for the ward doctor to be called to give you an injection. What have you got to say for yourself?

HARRY: I'm sorry I was a trouble to the staff. I would have taken some extra pills but the doctor and the charge nurse insisted I have an injection. That wasn't necessary. And at home, my father got very angry. He tried to strangle me.

PSYCHIATRIST: Your parents are very worried about you. Now, are you going to behave yourself?

HARRY: It wasn't my fault, but I apologize for my behaviour.

PSYCHIATRIST, writing in Harry's case notes: Pt shows lack of insight.

Harry was telling the truth when he told the psychiatrist that his father had tried to strangle him. The psychiatrist dismissed this as a delusion because he was convinced that Harry was an ungrateful, disrespectful son who had gone to university and taken drugs which had made him psychotic. In firm but kindly, paternalistic tones he reminded Harry of his duty to his father. Harry defended himself, but, becoming angry, abruptly left the room. A few minutes later he requested permission to return. The psychiatrist asked him to sit down, but Harry remained standing at a distance, hands by his sides, head bent, and apologized humbly and respectfully for his behaviour and asked for the psychiatrist's forgiveness. The psychiatrist, who came from a country where sons are required to show great respect for their fathers and older men, did not see anything unusual in this scene, but the rest of us present knew that not only was this behaviour not typical of twenty-year-old sons in British working-class families, but that what Harry was doing he had done many times before. In Harry's home the discipline imposed by his father was very strict.

Later, on his own with me, Harry told me a little more about the terrible scene at home when his father had lost his temper and seized him by the throat. Harry had defended himself by hitting his father and then rushing from the room. He did not want to talk about it. He said, 'That's private,' and went on to say of himself, 'They say I'm the black sheep of the family, mother's boy, can't manage on my own.'

When Harry's father came to the hospital he showed great concern for his son. Yet he was clearly a man whom I, for one, would hesitate to cross, and, while he spoke to and of Harry in a kindly way, it was also a subtly belittling way. He did not take Harry seriously, even though Harry's situation – about to drop out of university and enter upon the career of a psychiatric patient – was serious indeed.

The belief that there are such things as mental illnesses and that these have physical causes and are best treated by drugs (this belief is called the medical model) has been examined by many different people coming from many different viewpoints and has been found wanting. Lucy Johnstone, in her book *The Users and Abusers of Psychiatry*, gave a very clear account of the debate about whether it is appropriate to regard psychosis as a mental illness with a physical cause. It is a debate that arouses passionate feelings, especially among psychiatrists who hold fast to the medical model. This debate is not always conducted in edifying terms. When Mary Boyle's erudite book *Schizophrenia: A Scientific Delusion* was published, the editors of the *British Journal of Clinical Psychology* sent it in their wisdom to Dr Anne Farmer (now a professor) of the University of Wales College of Medicine, where a considerable amount of research has been carried out in the search for a genetic basis for schizophrenia.

Anne Farmer began her review with 'Being asked to review this book rapidly induced *déjà vu*. The argument against the notion that schizophrenia is a disease takes one back to the 1960s, when the views of Laing, Szasz and other exponents of the anti-psychiatry movement were fashionable and spawned popular films such as *Family Life* and *One Flew Over the Cuckoo's Nest*. This 1990 reincarnation adds little and one suspects will be heard less.'[15] The rest of the review was in a similar vein.

In her review Farmer failed to give an accurate account of what the book was actually about, and so Mary Boyle requested the opportunity to reply. She wrote:

In fact the book addresses the question of whether schizophrenia is a disease is a valid concept *and* describes in detail why the issue of whether schizophrenia is a disease is unlikely to be thought scientifically meaningful. . . The framework I adopt is drawn from the philosophy of science and medical epistemology. I drew a crucial and often overlooked distinction between the necessary and sufficient conditions for establishing the validity of any hypothetical construct. . . The purpose of the book I did write was to examine why this disarray in research has come about and, more important, given that all science is subject to some disarray, to consider whether things were ever likely to improve. . . One of the book's major aims is to examine the extent to which the common language of medicine and psychiatry might mask important differences between the two groups in relation to concept development: I suggest that this can be best achieved by 'translating' this language into a more general language derived from the philosophy of science.

Anne Farmer was not pleased by this answer. She replied:

Dr Boyle complains that I have misunderstood and misrepresented her book. . . Her arguments reduce to a destructive and unhelpful diatribe against the medical model and disease concept of schizophrenia encased within a veneer of philosophical and epistemological phrasing. . . Schizophrenia is a devastating disorder of the mind's functioning that affects many thousands world wide. . . The condition will not 'go away' because Dr Boyle or anyone else wants it to. Also, in suggesting that the phenomena of schizophrenia are mere extensions of normality as she does in the final chapter, she not only demonstrates a complete misunderstanding of the basic principles of psychopathology but she also does much disservice to sufferers and their families who struggle to cope with the disorder. . . Dr Boyle suggests that my review fails to comprehend the nature of the criticism being levelled at the concept of schizophrenia. Indeed, I think I understand her motives only too well. Despite careful reading, I consider that it is virtually impossible to find anything novel or insightful in this book. Moreover, Dr Boyle's protests sound like those flat-earthers faced with overwhelming evidence that the world is round.[16]

I always feel that in an argument in which one person resorts to personal attack then that person shows that she has lost the argument. It must be very frightening to be shown that your research is based on some very doubtful assumptions. No doubt the alchemists were also scared and affronted when people questioned their assumption that base metal could be turned into gold.

I have been an Associate of the Royal College of Psychiatrists since 1970 and have always read the College's publications, the *British Journal of Psychiatry, Psychiatric Bulletin* and the accompanying papers, very closely. These journals and papers I have come to regard as presenting the best in psychiatric thought. The subjects studied by this leading edge have changed enormously over the last thirty years. In the 1970s virtually all of the content of these journals and papers was based on the medical model, and there were few mentions of anything psychological. That my first academic papers were published in the *British Journal of Psychiatry* owed more to the fact that the then editor of the journal was Eliot Slater, the brother of my colleague and statistician Patrick Slater, than to the editor's interest in Personal Construct Theory and the applications of the repertory grid. Gradually, though, psychological and sociological matter crept into the journal, to the extent that nowadays there are as many, if not more, articles to do with psychology and sociology as there are to do with aspects of the medical model. However, the best of psychiatric thought comes from a handful of thinkers. Many more psychiatrists adhere to the traditional view that there are mental illnesses which are best understood in terms of physiology.

Thus, in the August 2001 volume of the *British Journal of Psychiatry*, Richard Harrington, in the editorial on 'Causal processes in development and psychopathology', wrote:

> It is now widely understood that most mental disorders are not due to single linear causes. Individual risk factors are seldom powerful. More often, psychopathology arises from the complex interplay of multiple risk and protective factors, some genetic and others environmental. A second central concept, which is at the core of much developmental research, is an emphasis on understanding the processes of developmental research and investigating the emergence of patterns of adaptation and maladaptation over time.[17]

No psychologist or critic of the psychiatric system would quarrel with any of that. It is an elegant statement of how we must proceed if we want to understand why we behave as we do. Unfortunately many psychiatrists pay only lip-service to environmental and developmental factors. They focus solely on their belief that schizophrenia is a physical illness with a physical cause. They believe that the schizophrenic gene, or genes, is within a hair's breadth of being discovered. They ignore the major flaws in the methods used to search for these genes.

The search for a genetic cause for schizophrenia uses three methods – namely, studying family trees, looking for a genetic marker, and comparing twins brought up apart. The study of family trees uses extremely doubtful methods of diagnosing members of previous generations and ignores how much one generation learns from earlier generations. In the British Psychological Society report on psychosis, the results of genetic research are summarised with:

> Another, more high-tech, approach is the attempt to identify family patterns of genetic markers for particular diagnoses. Reports of breakthroughs – for example, of an abnormal cluster of genes on chromosome 5 that predisposes to 'schizophrenia' – have not been replicated.[18]

Twin studies are based on the assumption that pairs of separated identical twins were already separated at birth. Professor Michael Howard pointed out that identical twins in the womb share a placenta and 'Even in the postnatal period it is extremely difficult to find identical twins who have been raised entirely separately. That is probably why certain twin pairs are described in published research as having been reared apart when they have actually spent substantial parts of their crucial early years together or in similar environments.'[19]

The British Psychological Society report pointed out that:

> An enormous amount of research has examined possible physical causes of psychotic experiences. This research has yielded some interesting findings, but no definitive conclusions can yet be drawn. Work in understanding biological influences on psychotic experiences may have been hampered by a number of problems:
>
> * The use of unreliable and invalid diagnoses. If diagnoses are misleading, real physical processes that are related to only some of the psychotic experiences might be hidden.
> * The fact the two things happen at the same time does not mean that one has caused the other. Few studies make this distinction.

- The effects of complicating factors (such as medication) have not always been taken into account.
- It has often been assumed from the outset that the reason for these experiences is likely to be a biological one and so other possible reasons have not been investigated.[20]

These errors in the research methods used by those looking for the biological basis of mental illness are widespread and persistent. Yet the people carrying out this research are not novice scientists, so why do these errors persist? Why do these researchers have such a strong belief in the existence of genes that cause mental illness?

We are always in the business of trying to think well of ourselves in order to hold ourselves together as a person. When we or other people behave in ways that threaten our personal pride we try to find some way of explaining this which will restore or strengthen our pride in ourselves. One method we have used throughout history is to believe that there is some separate spiritual or magical realm which is able to influence our world. We use this other realm to explain those activities which we see as strange or wicked. Thus wickedness is ascribed to evil, as represented by the Devil or some force of evil which battles with the force of good. Strange behaviour is ascribed to something paranormal or magical – possession by spirits or the activities of some paranormal force. However, nowadays we like to think of ourselves as rational and scientific, and so, while many people still believe in the Devil or a force of evil and ascribe great powers to the magical or paranormal, others, while wanting to explain wickedness and strangeness in terms of some other realm, also want to appear to be rational and scientific. So these people put their faith in genes. They ignore the fact that all that genes do is express some protein and that this protein interacts with other proteins in complex ways. For them the gene takes on some mystical power. Our destiny, they feel, lies not in our stars but in our genes.

The discoveries of science have often provided matter for those who believe in another realm. The attributes of mercury, discovered by the alchemists, were used as proof of the power of magic. When

Marie Curie discovered radium it was seen as a magical element capable of curing most illnesses. Marie Curie used to carry lumps of radium in her cardigan pockets, and many people copied her, claiming that its magical properties cured their rheumatism or influenza and improved the quality of their lives. In much the same way genes are now seen as the cause of all our problems, and the cure for our problems is to change our genes. Our wickedness and madness come not from our stars nor from the Devil but from our genes. Thus we can appear to be scientific and still enjoy the one great advantage of explaining wickedness and madness in terms of another realm. It is not our fault that some of us are wicked or mad.

Interestingly, when Pat Bracken and Phil Thomas, the founders of Critical Psychiatry, wanted to summarize the traditional psychiatric view of schizophrenia, they used religious concepts to do so. They wrote:

> For psychiatry, schizophrenia remains a sacred relic. It has to attach a great deal of importance to the concept, because it has invested so much time, effort and prestige in a fruitless quest for its causes. Psychiatry claims to be scientific, but scientific approaches to knowledge should be characterized by doubt and scepticism. For psychiatry, schizophrenia is a dogma, an unquestionable article of faith, and to question schizophrenia is to question psychiatry. The failure of biomedical science to reveal the cause of schizophrenia is the ultimate condemnation of the medical model.[21]

There is no doubt that some people have a psychotic experience. How long that experience lasts, the content of that experience, the way each person deals with the experience and its causes vary enormously from person to person. To lump all these experiences together under the one diagnosis of schizophrenia, or even to claim that there are three, six or ten kinds of schizophrenia, is to ignore the wide variety of psychotic experiences. In effect, the diagnosis of schizophrenia is meaningless. The British Psychological Society report argued that what people in any kind of mental distress needed was not the diagnosis of an illness but an individual formulation.

> Psychological formulations are a way of helping people to make sense of their difficulties in a way which is meaningful to them. They comprise a statement of what the person sees as the problem (or problems), how these might have come about and what is keeping them going. Problems will usually be expressed in terms of what the person experiences (such as unhappiness, hearing voices, not functioning well at work, or fearing that people are trying to harm them) rather than in terms of 'symptoms' observed by others.[22]

The belief that schizophrenia is an illness with a physical cause has had some serious consequences. It has been an article of faith that schizophrenia is incurable. Once you have got it, you have it for life. This counsel of despair has prevented most of the people with such a diagnosis from recovering, since the expectation underlying their treatment in the psychiatric system is that they will not recover. Another article of faith held firmly by psychiatrists until recently was that schizophrenia and depression were separate diseases, and if you had one you could not get the other. It gradually became obvious from the research figures that people with a diagnosis of schizophrenia did indeed get depressed. Moreover, some 10 per cent of such people committed suicide.[23]

Theorists among psychiatrists may be highly skilled in hypothesis-saving, which is a kind of shifting of the goalposts in order to prove that you were right all along. Thus the conjunction of schizophrenia and depression was explained by:

a) depression was a side effect of the drugs used in treating the schizophrenia, i.e., the person had no personal reason to be depressed.

b) The 'negative symptoms' of schizophrenia (slowed movement, poverty of speech, loss of pleasure, social withdrawal) were symptoms of depression, i.e., the person had been depressed all the time, while the positive symptoms (hallucinations, delusions) were symptoms of schizophrenia.

Yet even the most cursory inspection of what happens to people given the diagnosis of schizophrenia would show that they have all the necessary requisites to become depressed. Before becoming psychotic they had discovered a serious discrepancy between what they thought their life was and what it actually was, and they had lost confidence in themselves. Research has shown that people who have psychotic experiences are likely to have experienced a considerable number of stressful events in the six months before an episode of psychosis.[24] Next they were told that they had an incurable disease. They were treated as such, and with all the disregard and contempt that people seen as mad have always been treated. They knew that they had lost their place in society and could never regain it, and that they had brought worry and shame upon their family. All they had to do to become depressed was blame themselves for the disasters that had befallen them.

When the belief that schizophrenia is a physical illness teams up with old-fashioned racism, something nasty happens. Ronald Littlewood, along with Maurice Lipsedge, studied the exceedingly high incidence of schizophrenia found among African-Caribbeans living in England.[25] When, in an interview with the *Psychiatric Bulletin*, he was asked, 'Can you say something about the effects of racism on people developing mental illness?' he replied:

The big question is how much psychological alienation contributes towards mental illness . . . The rates of schizophrenia among West Indians in Britain are among the highest which have ever been recorded in the world. If we look at similar groups who have high rates of schizophrenia in the world, that is, in Ireland, among Croatians on the Dalmatian coast, among French-Canadians, among Native Americans, among Australian Aborigines and among the Maori, you can argue that there are certain historical and cultural similarities between these groups. Call it 'internalised colonisation' if you want. I would suggest that there may be something in the neuropsychology of language in which you have to use a dominant language but in which you yourself are objectified. You are alienated by your very process of thought: which goes together incidentally with a curious culture of humour: for these cultures are associated with a great self-deprecating wit, particularly the Irish and the African-Caribbean . . . If schizophrenia is anything to do with the Third World conditions of life – say with nutritional deficit, and obstetric disadvantages and so on, it would be shared by people in Africa – who of course do not have a high rate of schizophrenia. So it is perhaps something to do with post-colonial identity and something to do with racism.[26]

Different cultures have different ways of expressing distress. When we do express our distress we use the metaphors and imagery of our culture. If a doctor does not understand this, when he is examining a person in distress who is from a culture different from his own, he may interpret quite ordinary words and actions as evidence of madness. Thus black people are more likely to receive a diagnosis of schizophrenia than white people, even if the experiences they describe are the same.[27]

The incidence and outcome of schizophrenia seem to relate to matters that have very little to do with biology and genetics. It has been found that the incidence of schizophrenia varies with the degree of unemployment.[28] When the economy is booming and labour is in short supply schizophrenia is more likely to be seen as having social causes and the emphasis in treatment is on rehabilitation and a return to the community, but when the economy slumps schizophrenia is explained as a biological, incurable disease. Moreover, chronic schizophrenia is prevalent in the industrial world but rare in the Third World, because in the Third World people who are psychotic are less likely to be excluded from their society.[29] Professor Julian Leff, who is renowned for his work on families with a member who is schizophrenic, has always been convinced that schizophrenia is an illness with a physical basis. In his book

Advanced Family Work for Schizophrenia: An Evidence-Based Approach he wrote, 'In developing countries like India, the shortage of psychiatric professionals means that only a small proportion of people with psychoses receive biomedical treatment. The rest are probably treated exclusively by traditional healers. Yet the outcome for schizophrenia in India is considerably better than in the West,[30] suggesting that traditional treatments may have a therapeutic effect on the patients.'[31] Julian Leff's use of the word 'may' suggests that he could be one of the doctors David Whitwell was referring to when he wrote, 'It sometimes seems that in psychiatry being right has a higher priority than helping someone get better . . . Doctors tend to have strong beliefs about the world, and people and science. They hold their theories as articles of faith. Things that are thought or assumed to be true are not seen as beliefs but as facts of life.'[32]

Physical illness with a genetic cause occurs in all kinds of families, happy ones and unhappy ones, ordinary and extraordinary. People who become psychotic grow up in families that are unhappy and/or extraordinary. The parents in these unhappy/extraordinary families are rarely wicked people who do not love their children and want to harm them. Usually these parents are simply people who are struggling with their own problems, and this struggle in some way affects the child. Most of these parents mean well. They try to do the best for their children. Oh dear, the crimes we commit when we mean well! When we have a conscience, and most of us do, we mean well, but inadvertently, often through ignorance, often through fear, we hurt the people we mean to help. The fact that we mean well does not necessarily mean that we know what the people we want to help actually need. The history of charitable work is littered with examples of well-meaning people harming, even destroying, the people they came to help. Christian missionaries went to the South Pacific to save souls but they destroyed bodies with the infectious diseases they brought with them. The tragedy for most parents is that when we meant well we did not always help our children.

People who become psychotic may have suffered at the hands

of someone who was not a family member, but their family, for one reason or another, was unable to help them deal with their trauma. Ron Coleman described his sexual abuse at the hands of a priest, but in his account there is no mention of him being looked after by either his family or the Church. Brian Davey wrote about parents who would not accept their child's feelings and who wanted the child's 'well-behaved compliance'.[33] This is what many parents want. They do not realize that a well-behaved, compliant child is often so lacking in self-confidence and so dependent on his parents telling him what to do that when he leaves home for work or university he cannot manage on his own.

A child may find that his anger or his distress is not accepted by his parents. Feelings arise in response to events in external reality, so when a child's feelings are not accepted by the parents, his belief in the validity of his perceptions is undermined. Similarly, a child's perceptions of what is going on around him may be denied. Throughout my life, whenever I presented my mother or sister with any information that did not suit their purposes, they would tell me I was lying. This was an attack both on my perceptions and my worth, and undermined my confidence in both. It was not until I was in my early twenties that I decided that the best thing to do was to act *as if* my perceptions were real, even though I doubted they were so. This decision markedly improved my self-confidence.

I have often pondered why I did not become psychotic in my childhood or adolescence, and I came to the conclusion that what saved me was my mother's laziness. She disliked having to bestir herself any more than she needed to do to run the household, and so, once I had completed the chores she had given me, I could escape from the house and from her influence. Moreover, she was certainly not overprotective, rather the reverse. The parents of children who later become psychotic are often much more energetic than my mother, and so they keep their children close to them by using their authority, or by inspiring guilt, or by overprotecting them.

Some parents think they are acting in the child's best interests by keeping certain matters secret or by denying that something the child knows has happened actually has happened. The parents may hide the fact that the father has been to jail, or a mother may be subjected to her husband's abuse and then, though clearly in a state of distress, insist to the child that she and Daddy are perfectly happy. The child will sense the secret, or become confused about the evidence of his own eyes, and find his confidence in his perceptions undermined. A child needs to be told the truth, but the truth can be far too painful for the parent to utter. What if you cannot bear to say out loud that the man you love, the father of your child, is a liar and a cheat? Or worse, someone who breaks the necessary rules that separate children from adults and children from parents? What do you do when you feel that to tell the truth out loud would destroy you? Parents who are reluctant to tell their child about some family secret are more than likely to be reluctant to talk about such matters to a psychiatrist when the child later becomes psychotic. Such families tend to present a united front to the world and keep themselves very much to themselves. They are a 'close-knit' family.

The media use the term 'close-knit family' as a term of praise, but a close-knit family can be a dangerous place for a child. The child, even in adulthood, cannot break away and become independent. Many depressed, anxious or even manic people find that they greatly improve when they simply put geographical distance between themselves and their family, but people who become psychotic may find this impossible to do. The child who becomes psychotic may feel that he is responsible for the family, that he has to keep the family secret and be the bearer of its woes. He becomes the scapegoat who is sacrificed to save the family.

Perhaps Harry was in the process of sacrificing himself for his family, just as Benjamin had done for his. I first met Benjamin when his psychiatrist, who considered that he had a drug-induced psychosis, referred him to me. Benjamin had just graduated from university. He told me that he had taken some magic mushrooms and had spent a few nights in a tepee in Wales. He did not think that the mushrooms had done him any harm, but who was he to argue with a psychiatrist?

I enjoyed our conversations over the following few weeks, and after he was discharged from hospital we always kept in touch. He would come to see me in my office or phone me for a chat, and on the occasions when he became psychotic I would be called, just as I was called whenever he attempted to kill himself.

Over the years I came to know Benjamin and his family well, but I was not able to help him in any way, except to offer the occasional refuge of my office and a listening ear. I knew that there was more going on in his home than he was prepared to talk about – he was intensely loyal to his family. In his family he was the simple one who had never lived up to his promise, who needed looking after because he had strange thoughts and sometimes did strange things, such as when he sat in a hot bath and slashed his wrist. Yet Benjamin saw his parents, just as he saw me, in all our inadequacies and weaknesses, and he did not reject or criticize us. He smiled at our limitations, just as he smiled when he answered a question about his damaged hand: 'It hurts a lot.' He never recovered the full use of his hand.

Eventually Benjamin organized a life for himself whereby he lived in a bed-sitter but came to the hospital two days a week simply, he told me, to save on his heating bills. He did some teaching and writing, but the drugs he was on interfered with his work.

Benjamin said to me, 'I'm having injections of Haloperidol. It makes my parents feel better.'

'If it wasn't for your parents, would you take it?'

'No. It slows me down. For the first two days after the injection I feel terrible. I perk up a bit after that.'

'You're sacrificing yourself for your parents.'

'That's right. I've given up my life for them.'

Benjamin came to know the members of a group of people who might be called outsiders and who lived in the local town. They were educated but rootless, living on social security and temporary jobs. They shared an interest in drugs, both in using and dealing, and they drank at the same pubs, helped one another when cash was short, and were generally forgiving of one another's short-comings and peculiarities. I knew several of them. There was Terry, who travelled around and bought a bit of this and sold a bit of that, and eased his mind with drugs and drink. He was a gentle, reflective man who had been admitted to the local psychiatric hospital when he was only sixteen and put on a ward with eighty other men. He would come to see me and tell me about his travels and about his friends, like Flora, the glue-sniffer, who had a room in his flat which she never left. Her identity, he told me, was that of a glue-sniffer and nothing else. He said, 'She's the queen of the glue-sniffers. All the other glue-sniffers come round to see her. She's been doing it longer than them and they all look up to her.' Each time, after he talked to me, Terry would go on the wards to visit old friends. He always timed these visits to coincide with meal-times. The kindly nurses on those back wards always fed their ex-patients whenever they appeared in need of a meal. Another member of the group whom I knew was Janice, a beautiful, kind, sweet young woman whose middle-class parents always saw her as the black sheep of the family and punished her for their own failings. She was one of the most anxious people I have ever met, and cannabis was the only drug that took the edge off her anxiety.

Terry and Janice and several other members of the group would give me news of Benjamin, and so I had an idea of how he was actually faring, which was not as well as he had made me believe in the picture he presented to me.

At first Benjamin tried to build a life for himself. He enjoyed teaching and got short-term jobs tutoring schoolchildren in mathematics. He was interested in literature, so he read and tried his hand at writing. His social life was confined to his family and the friends who were as lost and rootless as he was. As time passed, the effects of the psychiatric drugs he was on began to become increasingly obvious. He grew heavy and bloated, he could no longer think clearly enough to teach, write or read, and his behaviour became increasingly erratic and difficult. His friends told me how he tried even their patience on many occasions, and they tried to avoid him.

When a person reaches this stage even the most loving and concerned family finds it impossible to contain him. In one such family the mother told me how she gave up trying to get her son to lead an organized life. He had a room in the family home, and sometimes he would be there and sometimes he would disappear for days and weeks, only to return in a dilapidated state. She tried to train herself not to worry about his absences and wonder whether he was sleeping rough or was injured or dead.

Benjamin saw his situation clearly and knew that everything he had wanted in his life was now beyond his reach. His friends were withdrawing from him, the psychiatric hospital was closing, and I was leaving my job and moving away. The new psychiatric unit attached to the general hospital had no services to offer him. He went back home, but once there he made several suicide attempts. His parents grew exceedingly worried that they could not supervise him closely enough to prevent him killing himself. When, one evening, they discovered that he was in the bath preparing to kill himself, they got him out, dressed him, and drove him to the psychiatric unit. There they impressed on the staff that he needed constant supervision. The staff put Benjamin in a side room on his own. They closed the door, and when someone next went to look at him, he was hanging from a hook behind the door, dead.

Benjamin's story is not unusual. Even more common is the story Tim Parkes told of the conflictive relationship between his brother-in-law Paolo and Paolo's mother, whom the family called Mamma.

Some twenty-five years earlier, when he was a student in the USA, Paolo had been diagnosed as a paranoid schizophrenic. The American authorities repatriated him to Italy, where he lived a very erratic, paranoid life, until he was finally confined to a secure unit where his parents visited him regularly. Mamma's marriage had been very stormy, but she and her husband did not separate. Tim noted that it was one of those families where to talk about anything always meant to talk about everything, because nothing had ever been resolved between them. When her husband died, Tim and his wife Rita had the task of taking Mamma to visit Paolo.

Tim's account of this visit focused on the relationship between Mamma and Paolo. When Paolo met them, 'Immediately Mamma is kissing her son, almost on the lips. She disengages, but only to throw out her arms and embrace him again. Seconds later she's adjusting the collar of one of his shirts. It's not straight. It's not clean. And his hair's too long. He hasn't been eating enough. Has he eaten? She apologizes that we didn't arrive at ten, as she promised. Paolo merely nods amiably, informing us that he's already had his lunch, but that he'll be happy to sit beside us while we eat at our hotel.'

Mamma ordered the waitress to bring a plate, but when Rita and Paolo protested that he had already eaten Mamma accused him of starving himself. When Mamma ordered the waitress to bring him tagliatelle, Tim said, ' ''Mamma, for Christ's sake! The guy's an adult. He knows whether he wants to eat or not!'''

'But exactly as we gang up against Mamma, Paolo turns his head to the waitress and says, ''Yes, do bring me a plate.'' Then immediately he embraces his mother. He begins to caress her wrists and neck and face. One hand is slipped inside the arm of her short-sleeved dress. She is kissing him. ''Mammina,'' he says, ''Mammina, you're all I have left now. There's only the two of us. Just a few years together.'' ''*Povero, povero*,'' she says with immense satisfaction at our expense. But as he pulls away from her, he demands, ''Have you brought my money? I want my money.'' One of the purposes of this trip is to bring Paolo his monthly money. ''We'll have to talk about that later,'' Mamma says. ''But you can't not give me my money,'' he whines.'

Tim had read the psychiatric literature and knew that the psychiatric view was that 'Schizophrenia is basically a result of a biological disorder'. He wrote, 'I begin to notice that Paolo's conversation is mostly normal so long as you don't touch on two key subjects: the reasons for his illness or ''failure in life'', and the possibilities for his future. If this is the result of a virus, it sure is an odd one.'

Then: 'Rita asks: ''Paolo, did they ever suggest you have some therapy with the family?'' Actually, I know she knows the answer to this one. We discussed it with her father once. Paolo nods. He's very matter-of-fact. He did two sessions with Babbo [his father], he says, but Mamma wouldn't come. ''That's not true,'' she exclaims. ''Yes it is.'' Paolo is mild and matter-of-fact, completely convincing. ''I remember you said you didn't want to come.'' Mamma is furious. ''Do you think I wouldn't have come if it could have been useful for you? I can't believe this!'' Immediately he withdraws and we're back to the Mammina routine. Apparently it is impossible for him to comment openly on his mother's contradictory behaviour, her strange mixture of love and recalcitrance. Or could it be that he actually wants things this way, encourages this behaviour? Certainly there's no question here of any one person being solely to blame, it's more the way each person's behaviour complements the other's that's so unhealthy.'

Tim concluded, 'In the 25 years of Paolo's illness no one has suggested to Mamma that she might look for different ways of behaving with her son. No one has suggested that her weirdly intense relationship with him might have anything to do with the unhappy prevarications of her husband. But then, why bother? In the future, when medical research finally gets there, the whole disorder will be cleared with an appropriate medicine and everybody can go on behaving exactly as they please.'[34]

The ambiguities, the conflicts, the intense relationship which Tim Parkes described in this particular family are typical of families in which a child becomes psychotic. It is extremely difficult for an outsider to comprehend what goes on, much less to change this. How much easier it is to say that one individual has schizophrenia and must take the prescribed drugs.

In the early 1950s the sociologist George Brown working with his psychiatrist colleagues discovered that patients diagnosed with schizophrenia who returned home to live with their parents and close family did worse than those who left hospital to live alone or in a hostel. It took many years of investigation by the psychiatrist Julian Leff and his colleagues to establish that, after an admission to hospital with a diagnosis of schizophrenia or depression, patients who go to live with people who are nice to them do better than patients who go to live with people who are nasty to them. Some of us might feel that we already knew that.

In the course of researching what happened when people diagnosed as schizophrenic returned home, Leff and Christine Vaughn developed a way of measuring the amount of emotion expressed in a family. They called this Expressed Emotion and referred to it as EE. The emotions measured include hostility, critical comments, and over-involvement as shown by excessive self-sacrifice, inability to lead separate lives, and overprotectiveness. They found that in families with a high EE the person diagnosed with schizophrenia did badly and in families with low EE the patient did well. From Tim Parkes's description of Paolo's family it would seem that this family would have scored extremely high on EE.

Family members are not always aware that the criticism being flung around is excessive, although the recipient of the criticism feels flayed and frightened. A woman writing about how their schizophrenic daughter had created so many strains and dilemmas in the family said:

My husband is a scientist of – I suppose one can say – national eminence. He thinks that ordinary life has severe enough strains for most people, and an additional strain of a schizophrenic child is almost more than one can take. Whenever Ruth is at home he feels continually irritated by her lack of purpose and idleness, and has to hold himself in check. He says she is not the sort of person he would choose to spend time with, or make a friend of. He thinks a fundamental instinct is involved which causes both animals and human beings to peck at oddity, to rid themselves of the one who does not conform. He resents the effects this situation has had on me, the mother, and says that every time I visit Ruth or she comes home, you can scrub two or three days out of our lives, since it takes time to recover and time to prepare, all like being under a heavy cloud.[35]

It is highly likely that this man's views about idleness and society's misfits are views that he had held for many years, even predating his daughter's birth. Despite momentous events, families tend not to change their style of interaction over the years. I have observed that families whose members were kind and loving to one another remained so over decades, while families whose members were critical and impatient with one another likewise did not change. Thus families who demonstrate high EE with their adult child very likely displayed the same kind of emotion when the child was young. But this is not the case, or so we are told. According to Julian Leff and his colleagues, these families were nice, quiet and ordinary until the child became psychotic and drove them to these extremes. These researchers have developed a technique of family intervention whereby they draw the attention of the family to their emotional, critical ways, and they try to teach family members less emotional, less critical ways of interacting, but all this is done in the context of teaching the family how to look after an ill family member, in the way that parents of children with cystic fibrosis are taught how to keep their child healthy. Julian Leff explained, 'I do not refer to family work as therapy since the family members are not considered to be in need of treatment.'[36] Yet he knows that, 'Recent studies have identified childhood sexual abuse as a risk factor for auditory hallucinations.'[37] He should also know that in the majority of cases of child abuse, the abuser is someone known to the child, usually a family member. In all the years he worked with families he seems not to have noticed that these families are likely to have a family secret. In my experience all the families I knew well had been struggling for many years with issues which made relationships in the family skewed in many ways, yet the family was at great pains to present a normal front to the world. In the 1950s Theodore Lidz and his colleagues studied intensively families which had a schizophrenic member and compared them with families which did not. I found their work invaluable, not just in understanding people who came to me with a diagnosis of schizophrenia but in understanding myself, an introvert who grew up in a very peculiar family. Julian Leff dismissed Lidz's work on the grounds that it did not meet the standards of 'evidence-based medicine' and that, '[Lidz and his colleagues] failed to consider the possibility that the disturbed parental relationships were a response to the development of schizophrenia in an offspring'.[38]

Psychiatry grew out of medicine. All psychiatrists are medical doctors who have done additional training in psychiatry. If mental disorders do not have a physical cause then there is no reason why psychiatrists should be medical doctors. Indeed, there is no reason why psychiatry should even exist as a profession. Some psychiatrists see their medical training as being marginally useful while they operate as psychologists and therapists. Others determined to protect their profession, and so they insist that mental disorders, and certainly schizophrenia, have physical causes and therefore must be treated with drugs.

Are Drugs the Answer?

The drugs used in the treatment of schizophrenia – called neuroleptics or major tranquillizers – do not cure it. Two-thirds of the people who take such medication are likely to experience a recurrence of their psychosis within two years of the original experience. What these drugs do is deaden anxiety without giving any feeling of elation. If the person hears voices, then the drugs may silence the voices or, as some people find, the sound of the voices is turned down, so that they whisper rather than coming through loud and clear.

If the person is agitated, the drugs calm him down, but it is not the calm of peace and contentment. Instead it is, as some people have described it, like having cotton wool in your head. Spontaneity disappears, and the person feels thick and heavy, unable to concentrate or reflect. Even worse, the person may develop tardive dyskinesia, which, 'even in its mild forms, is often disfiguring, with involuntary movements of the face, mouth or tongue. Frequently, the patients grimace in a manner that makes them look ''crazy'', undermining their credibility with other people. In more severe cases, patients become disabled by twitches, spasms, and other abnormal movements of any muscle groups, including those of the neck, shoulders, back, arms and legs, and hands and feet . The muscles of respiration and speech can also be impaired. In the worst cases, patients thrash about continually.'[39]

When arguing in favour of these drugs, psychiatrists point out how, before they were discovered, patients were physically confined in ways that were far from pleasant. Certainly the drugs are an improvement on previous treatments, but people who are given them often describe them as 'a chemical cosh' or 'a chemical straitjacket'.

All these drugs have what psychiatrists call 'side effects'. David Crepaz-Keay, who received a range of psychiatric treatment over ten years and is Head of Patient and Public Involvement at the Mental Health Foundation, and Vice-Chair of the Commission for Patient and Public Involvement in Health, commented, 'The phrase ''side effects'' is carefully chosen to give the impression that the drugs are almost entirely *a good thing* but they may have some marginal consequences that are less desirable. What few doctors are prepared to acknowledge is that negative effects are as likely to occur as the so-called therapeutic effects.'[40]

The latest neuroleptic drugs, called 'atypicals', are considered to produce fewer side effects, but they are not necessarily more effective. Clozapine carries a high risk of agranulocytosis (loss of white blood cells), and thus people taking it must have regular blood tests.

None of the side effects of the neuroleptic drugs has negligible consequences. The person puts on weight, and no amount of dieting will remove it. Memory is impaired, making it extremely difficult for the person to study or work. The inability to reflect and remember prevents the person from making connections between ideas and making deductions from those connections. To act as a coherent person we have to create a coherent picture of the world and ourselves.

Some ten years ago a young woman, Rebecca, wrote to me to say she had read and enjoyed my books. She mentioned having a psychotic experience and afterwards becoming depressed. Some time later we met at a conference. She was slim, pretty, interested in the conference, and, although she was sad, she hoped she had put her psychosis behind her and that she would be able to return to her studies. We kept in touch by letter and phone, and ten years later we met again. In those intervening years Rebecca had been in and out of hospital, quite psychotic, as I knew from many of her phone calls. Now she looked thirty years older. She was stout and her once lustrous hair was reduced to a few wisps. The only thing about her I recognized was her voice. Worst of all, she found it hard to keep her thoughts and actions as a coherent whole. She knew how she wanted to spend her time with me, but the simplest decision – say, where we would eat – meant false starts, changes of mind, anxiety without any cause that I could detect, juxtapositions of ideas that had no logical connection. This was not psychosis but an intelligent brain which was suffering widespread and random breaks in its neuronal connections. Rebecca knew what was happening to her. She knew that other people saw her as a very peculiar old woman. All she could do was try to create some coherent pattern of thought and behaviour, and to keep this in place, even though such coherence was easily lost and the people she met usually lacked the patience to wait until she got it all together again.

The only person who can decide which side effects can be tolerated in order to achieve improvement and which demand too high a price is the person taking the drugs. People who experience psychosis know that there are times when they need these drugs in the absence of any better medication or other help, but they want to be given the right to choose the time to take the drugs and the kind and amount to take. They do not want to have these drugs forced upon them, yet this is what happens to most people.

Dr A. M. Mortimer, writing in the *Psychiatric Bulletin*, summarized the kindly but firm attitude adopted now by many psychiatrists.

Schizophrenia is really no different from any other chronic medical condition: at disease onset the diagnosis must be made promptly and effective treatment begun. Medication is necessary but insufficient: a therapeutic alliance allows the patient to participate actively in his or her treatment and take responsibility for it. Information about the illness, the medication, monitoring of health, accessing services etc is required. Patients need help to accept the limitations imposed by illness, and families need to solve the kinds of problems that arise when a member is ill, especially a young person on the verge of adulthood and independence. To provide this input, the service must back up medication management with appropriate psychosocial interventions. It has been demonstrated that family work reduces relapse rates in schizophrenia, while cognitive-behavioural therapy is useful in coping with positive symptoms.

The superior tolerability of atypicals should obviate treatment cessation because of side effects, which launches the majority of patients on a relapsing career of deterioration: at most, 15% of patients recovering from a first episode of schizophrenia remain well, but nobody can tell who they are. Duration of remission is immaterial to relapse rate on cessation, which is 15% of survivors every month. Very low dose regimes, 'drug holidays' and treatment targeted to imminent relapses are not feasible and cannot be recommended.[41]

Writing in the same issue, Professor Paul Bebbington stressed the importance of taking into account the patient's point of view. He said:

Thus there are arguments for using drugs that seem to bring advances but for using them carefully. This requires a due consideration of the properties of all the available drugs, new and old, in the light of the particular needs and susceptibilities of individual patients. It is morally imperative to involve patients as much as possible in these considerations, but also clinically advantageous. Involving patients can only be done if they are provided with information.

This general approach should, however, be modified in the light of particular and individual considerations: a knowledge of patients' individual preferences and characteristics, and their known or likely susceptibility to given side effects. If discussion with the patient is not possible because of the acute nature of the illness, it should be done later.

Pharmacological treatment of schizophrenia and related psychoses is usually for the long-term, and depends on patients' willingness to take medication when unsupervised. This is far more likely in the context of a good therapeutic relationship. While there are many components in the development of a good relationship, frank discussion about medication is essential. Central to this is a commitment to take seriously, and to respond to, complaints about side effects. The available compounds differ in their side effects. Those particularly incommoding to patients include EPS (extrapyramidal side effects), but also weight gain and effects on sexual function.

My own approach is to avoid EPS as much as possible. In some cases this means accepting the continued experience of positive symptoms: even if they persist, medication usually causes them to be much less intrusive and distressing, and there are other ways of helping patients to deal with residual psychotic symptoms. The overall target of prescribing is improved quality of life and this may sometimes be optimised when some positive symptoms are the price for an absence of side effects.[42]

These statements by two leading academic psychiatrists illustrate what a lottery it is for anyone seeking psychiatric treatment. When we go shopping for a car we can try out different models to see which suits us, but when we go looking for a psychiatrist we do not know what we are getting until we fall into his hands.

The committee that prepared the British Psychological Society's report made their views plain.

If, having considered all the relevant information, the service-user decides not to use medication, this decision should be respected and he or she should continue to be offered support by mental health services. We view with considerable concern the practice adopted by some clinicians of equating such a decision with 'refusing treatment' and withdrawing support as a result.[43]

Some psychiatrists take the view that if a particular drug does not work it is the fault of the patient, not the drug. I once found a heavily underlined statement by her psychiatrist in the notes of a woman I was seeing: 'This woman refuses to accept that she is better on Surmontil.' Ron Coleman wrote, 'If medication does not help a particular individual in any way, how can its continued use be justified? The answer the psychiatrist has to this question is to declare that it is not the medication that is failing the client but the client is failing the medication. It is common within psychiatry to describe someone who is not responding to medication as being drug resistant even when they get adverse effects of the drug.'[44]

Patients often report that they have been punished, or have been threatened with punishment, if they refuse to take the drugs prescribed. Richard Gosden, in his book *Punishing the Patient*, quoted from a personal communication from a woman who had been in an Australian psychiatric hospital. She had demanded that her dopamine levels be tested before she was given a neuroleptic drug, but instead hospital security men held her down while she was injected with it. She wrote:

When the side effects of the drugs started taking effect I told the staff that the side effects were totally unacceptable and that the drugs were toxic. Worse, they were forcing untested drugs on untested patients. The psychiatrist 'treating' me was furious. She said in response that I wasn't to leave the ward with the other patients. I was therefore effectively put in isolation on the ward. I had to endure the side effects etc in silence because there was always ECT down the corridor. Staff then naively believed that I had calmed down because of the drugs. One psychiatric nurse said, 'Look how much better you are now.' This woman honestly believed that I had calmed down because of biological intervention. I hadn't changed my attitudes or feelings one skerrick. It was just that I was too terrified to say anything because the woman treating me was vicious.[45]

Ron Coleman pointed out that the worst side effects of neuroleptics are death and suicide. He wrote, 'National Mind have stated that there are fifty deaths a year in hospital due solely to the use of neuroleptic medication. Indeed, in the twelve-month period there were five deaths directly caused by the re-launched drug clozaril. If this were to occur in any other branch of medicine then the drug would be immediately withdrawn.'[46]

People prescribed neuroleptics often feel that the dose they have been given is too high. Professor Bebbington commented that:

> The general use of high dose antipsychotic medication is under-standable, and arises from a combination of therapeutic optimism and therapeutic caution. Thus it is generally held that the symptoms of psychosis can be controlled by antipsychotics. If a given dose does not work, there is always, therefore, a tendency to increase it in search of the dose that does. Once the dose has been increased, the fact that the patient still has symptoms is virtually never taken as an indication to reduce it. Thus, the impulse to increase doses is always stronger than the impulse to reduce them.
>
> Nevertheless, there are grounds for resisting the urge towards escalating doses. First, not all people have positive symptoms that do respond to antipsychotic medication, a fact more readily acknowledged since 'treatment resistance' became a definable criterion for changing to treatment with clozapine. Second, the analyses of Bollini *et al* (1994) suggest that at a fairly early point increasing doses do not improve treatment response.[47]

The fact that many psychiatrists insist that their patients take their medication continuously and in high doses means that many people develop tardive dyskinesia. Peter Breggin wrote, 'The rates for tardive dyskinesia are astronomical. The latest estimate from the American Psychiatric Association indicates a rate for all patients of five per cent per year, so that 15 per cent of patients develop tardive dyskinesia within only three years. In long-term studies, the prevalence of tardive dyskinesia often exceeds 50 per cent of all treated patients and is probably much higher. The disease affects people of all ages, including children, but among older patients rates escalate. In a controlled study, 41 per cent of patients aged 65 and older developed tardive dyskinesia in a mere 24 months. Hundreds of thousands of older people receive these drugs in nursing homes and state hospitals.'[48]

Peter Breggin was one of the first people to study tardive dyskinesia. He wrote:

In 1983 I published the first in-depth analysis of the vulnerability of children to a particularly virulent form of the tardive dyskinesia that attacks the muscles of the trunk, making it difficult for them to stand or walk. This is now an established fact. In the same medical book, I offered the first detailed documentation showing that many or most tardive dyskinesia patients also show signs of dementia – an irreversible loss of overall higher brain and mental function. Indeed, it was inevitable that these losses would occur. The basal ganglia, which are afflicted in tardive dyskinesia, are richly interconnected with the higher centres of the brain, so that their dysfunction almost inevitably leads to disturbances in cognitive processes. Since my observations, a multitude of studies have confirmed that long-term neuroleptic use is associated with both cognitive deterioration and atrophy of the brain. While defenders of the drugs sometimes claim that this mental and neurological deterioration is caused by schizophrenia itself, their position is untenable. More than 100 years of autopsy studies of patients labelled as schizophrenic failed to show any such deterioration, until the recent advent of neuroleptics.[49]

What can add greatly to patients' problems is the way in which doctors, in response to some event, will abruptly change the dose the patient is taking, either increasing or lowering the dose markedly, or stopping the drug completely without regard to the horrible withdrawal symptoms which can follow. 'Drug withdrawal often causes rebound of the anticholinergic neurotransmitter system, resulting in a flu-like syndrome that includes emotional upset, insomnia, nausea and vomiting. Many patients find themselves unable to stop taking the drugs, suggesting that we should consider them as addictive.'[50]

Moreover, neuroleptics are often taken with other prescribed drugs so the person is taking what is often called a 'cocktail' of drugs. A study by the pharmacists Carol Paton, Stuart Banham and John Whitmore revealed that their results were 'consistent with those of other authors and show that benzodiazepines are frequently used in the long-term in-patients with schizophrenia despite an open acknowledgement of this practice and a paucity of objective data to support its efficacy.' They found that over a quarter of patients had been prescribed benzodiazepines which the ward staff could give out whenever they thought this was necessary (known as a p.r.n. prescription). The pharmacists commented, 'It is possible that staff resorted to medication too easily, and using de-escalation techniques such as talking down, one-to-one attention or "time-out" may have reduced the need for p.r.n.'[51]

Along with tardive dyskinesia may go another related, untreatable neurological disorder called drug-induced akathisia, which 'involves painful feelings of inner tension and anxiety and a compulsive drive to move the body. In the extreme, the individual undergoes internal torture and can no longer sit still. Tardive akathisia often develops in children who have been treated for "hyperactivity", ironically and tragically subjecting them to permanent inner torture. Tardive dystonia involves muscle spasms, frequently of the face, neck and shoulders, and it too can be disfiguring, disabling and agonizing.'[52]

In trying to explain what tardive akathisia feels like, David Healy compared it to seasickness. He wrote, 'Like seasickness, akathisia affects you badly for an hour or two – which seems like an eternity when it's happening – but then it slips away again. It's never gone completely but it's easier to bear for the time being . . . But, just as seasickness can end explosively, maybe just at the time when you thought it was almost all over, so also akathisia can explode into assault, suicide or homicide. Akathisia with antidepressants was unheard of before Prozac (an SSRI). Current evidence suggests that Prozac-induced akathisia may have led to one UK death per week since its launch, and one suicide attempt per day over and above the number that would have happened if the condition had been left untreated.'

David Healy concluded, 'The management of akathisia will one day be seen as the greatest blemish on the record of modern psycho-pharmacotherapy.'[53]

Drug companies are required by law to carry out extensive research into the effects of the drugs they are proposing to market. David Healy is very critical of this research. He wrote, 'The majority of psychotropic drugs trials are business rather than scientific exercises, constructed for the purposes of achieving regulatory approval and thereafter market penetration. . . There are many statisticians who doubt the power of even well-designed randomized controlled trials (RCT) to generalize to the real world. Company-sponsored RCTs invariably recruit samples of convenience, which by definition do not readily sustain an extrapolation to normal clinical practice. In addition, senior investigators on the trials for some of the newer antipsychotics have been jailed, for reasons which leave considerable uncertainty as to how many of the patients in these trials actually existed and how well they were assessed.'[54]

When Peter Breggin's book *Toxic Psychiatry* was published in the UK in 1992, Alec Jenner invited him to give a lecture in the Sheffield Department of Psychiatry. Peter told me he was very touched by this invitation because not one psychiatrist or psychiatric organization in the USA had ever invited him to speak. The psychiatrists in Sheffield listened to him very politely and did not argue with his thesis that neuroleptic drugs caused irreversible damage. However, they were thinking of their patients on the back wards and of the highly disturbed people they were responsible for on the acute wards and in prisons. One of them, a senior lecturer, asked, 'What else can we do but prescribe these drugs?'

The psychiatrists' position was analogous to that of parents faced with unruly children on being told that they should not continue to beat them into submission. Such psychiatrists and parents want to be given some simple, quick solution, but in fact the answer to their question is a tough one – 'You have to change'.

However, if psychiatrists changed their views about schizophrenia and saw what a psychotic person does, not as the symptoms of an illness, but the person's desperate attempts to deal with immense fear, they would also have to change their role as an agent of social control. They might have to relinquish altogether the role of controlling those people who disturb the peace, or, if they retain it, separate it quite unambiguously from that of caring for the individual. The government would have to provide an entirely new system for the care of mentally distressed people. The prime task of the staff in the psychiatric system would not be to restrain and quieten patients but to understand how mentally distressed individuals saw themselves and their world, and how the situation they were in exacerbated their fears. The aim of therapy would be to help restore each person's self-confidence and sense of self-worth. Where a place of safety was needed it would be a place to charm, comfort and delight its inhabitants. All staff would need to be highly skilled, and well able to see the people they care for not as mad people, but fellow human beings suffering from the agonies that life can inflict. For such a system to be developed, politicians would have to change their views about madness, and so would most members of society.

I am hopeful that such changes will come. In my lifetime schools have changed from being institutions where children were over-awed, belittled, chastised, and not understood to being organizations where most of the teachers see children as being people in their own right, to be encouraged and understood. These changes brought protests from the envious, and still do, but the thinking in society about how children should be educated has been transformed enormously, and for the better. There could be similar changes in the thinking about mental distress. Take, for example, how hallucinations are now understood.

Hearing Voices

Psychiatrists have always seen auditory hallucinations – hearing voices – as the primary symptom of schizophrenia. Sometimes in deep depression or in hypomania people hear voices, but these voices are easily understood in terms of the person's mood. For instance, a manic young man may hear a voice telling him he is the world's greatest footballer. If someone reports hearing voices that say nothing the psychiatrist can readily understand, then the voices are deemed to be a symptom of schizophrenia. Ivan Leudar and Phil Thomas, in their study of verbal hallucinations, wrote:

> Received wisdom in psychiatry requires that the clinician should not discuss her patient's abnormal experiences. Hallucinations, being psychotic symptoms, have no inherent value or meaning. They may have a 'worse fear' quality, but in essence they represent little more than the inevitable consequence of disordered brain function which is primarily responsible for the disease. As Thomas Huxley is reputed to have said of the mind, they are of no more significance than the cloud of steam that hangs over a factory. In psychiatry voices have little or no meaning. They are, like mind itself, an epiphenomenon secondary to what are regarded as more important biological processes. The pharmacological management of schizophrenia then becomes the priority, and the subject's preoccupation with and self-reports of voices becomes little more than an index of the extent to which the underlying illness is controlled by medication.[55]

Psychiatrists and nurses are taught not to allow a patient to talk about his voices. Ron Coleman said, 'If you are on a ward and say to a nurse that your voices are bothering you and you want to talk about it, you will receive the time honoured reply of ''Let's play Scrabble''. Scrabble may improve your vocabulary but it will do nothing for your voices. The other option the nurse might take is to see if you are written up for medication PRN, as required. If you are, you are encouraged to take it. Why do they not talk to you about your voices? The answer is understandable. They are taught that to enter into dialogue with one person about their voices is dangerous and should never be done.'[56]

This practice would never have been challenged had not Patsy Hage, a name that should go down in history, managed to interest her psychiatrist in the theory she was developing about her voices. Usually psychiatrists avoid conversations about theories the way cats avoid water, but Marius Romme is no ordinary psychiatrist. He listened and discussed, and from these initial conversations came the Hearing Voices Network and a whole new way of thinking about and working with voices.

Throughout our history, in different times and places, people have listened to and valued their voices. Socrates heard a daemon who guided him like a wise father. The Xhosa of the northern Transvaal still have great faith in their voices. Patsy told Marius about the theory that the American psychologist Julian Jaynes had developed about the origins of consciousness. He had argued that the hearing of voices had been the normal way of making decisions until about 1300 BC, when consciousness began to develop.

Marius wrote:

I began to wonder if [Patsy] might prove to be a good communicator with others who also heard voices, and whether they might find her acceptable or useful. I thought this might have a positive effect on her isolation, her suicidal tendencies and her feelings of dependency on her voices. Together, she and I began to plan ways in which she might share some of her experiences and views.

In due course, we set up one-to-one meetings with others who heard voices. As I sat there listening to their conversation, I was struck by the eagerness with which they recognised one another's experiences. Initially I found it difficult to follow these conversations: to my ears the contents were bizarre and extraordinary, yet all this was freely discussed as though it constituted a real world of and unto itself.

We repeated these meeting on several occasions, and every

session produced a great deal of mutual recognition. However, they also revealed a huge void of powerlessness: in my experience, none of these patients were able to cope with their voices.[57]

To discover whether there were people who coped with the voices they heard, Marius and Patsy appeared on a popular Dutch television programme and asked people to contact them. Of the 700 people who responded, 450 were voice-hearers, and, of these, 150 said that they could cope with their voices.

This provided the basis for Marius's research. He and his colleague Sandra Escher formed a formidable team, both in the quality of their research and in the gentle, easy way they interacted with all the people involved in or interested in their work. They established that:

Hearing voices is not in itself a symptom of an illness, but it is apparent in 2 to 3 per cent of the population. One in three becomes a psychiatric patient, but two in three can cope well and are in no need of psychiatric care and no diagnosis can be given because two out of three are quite healthy and well functioning. There are in our society more people hearing voices who never become patients than there are people who hear voices and become patients.

The difference between patients hearing voices and non-patients hearing voices is their relationship with the voices. Those who never become patients accepted their voices and used them as advisers. In patients, however, voices are not accepted and are seen as evil messengers. . .

Research shows also that hearing voices itself is not related to the illness of schizophrenia. In population research only 16 per cent of the whole group of voices hearers can be diagnosed with schizophrenia. Also therefore it is not right to identify hearing voices as an illness. Psychiatry in our western culture, however, tends unjustly to identify hearing voices with schizophrenia. Going to a psychiatrist with hearing voices gives you an 80 per cent chance of getting the diagnosis of schizophrenia.[58]

Marius and Sandra have been able to demonstrate not only that hearing voices is a common experience but that it is usually related to some kind of stress. People who have been bereaved often report hearing their loved one's voice and perhaps seeing that person. I saw my father sitting in his armchair several days after he died. The loss of my father, though very difficult to bear, was only a part of the high degree of stress I was under at the time. Amnesty International found that some 80 per cent of those tortured hallucinated during their ordeal. The crews of sailing ships and, more recently, people who go ocean racing have reported hallucinatory experiences when they have been at sea, and perhaps alone, for long periods of time. What Marius and Sandra showed was that in the people they studied the voices began after an event that demonstrated, as I would put it, that there was a serious discrepancy between what they thought their life was and what it actually was.

Moreover, they showed that the main differences between patients and non-patients were 'the kind of impact the triggering traumatic event had on them and their future [and] the balance of good and bad experiences the person had in their youth and how this affected their sense of identity, their self-esteem and their defence mechanisms in the face of this triggering episode'.[59]

Whenever we discover a serious discrepancy between what we thought our life was and what it actually is we need people around us who will support and encourage us. If such people are in short supply we have to support and encourage ourselves, but we can do this only if we already value and accept ourselves. If we do not, when we try to deal with the discrepancy by creating some meaning for it, we cannot create a meaning like 'this is a challenge which I shall meet and overcome, just as I met and overcame challenges in the past'. Instead, we arrive at meanings that are concerned with how we deserve the punishment of this disaster and/or how someone else is to blame for it and we are being unjustly punished. We choose either guilt and depression or resentment and paranoia, or we swing backwards and forwards between one and the other. Whichever kind of meaning we create, it is a meaning that serves the function of defending us against being annihilated as a person.

The meaning we create to defend ourselves can come in the form of an instruction to us. Ordinarily our stream of consciousness marshals itself into a command or a comment such as 'Get on with it', or 'How could you be so stupid!' We all hear our own thoughts as a voice in our head, but many of us hear other people's voices in our head as well. I am hopeless at mimicry and at learning to speak a foreign language, but I often hear in my head the voice of someone I know. Usually these are just wisps of sound, but sometimes they come unbidden, as clear as if the person were in the room with me. I know that these are memory traces and that they fade over time, but all that would need to happen for my auditory memories to become voices would be for me to doubt my ability to distinguish what goes on around me from what goes on inside my head.

Nowadays the voices I hear are those of friends whom I see quite often, and my memories of the endless critical comments that assailed me in the first half of my life have mercifully faded. However, I have met many people who would have to live to be as old as Methuselah before their memories of the critical comments directed at them faded away.

Karina Livinstill wrote about the critical comments she had suffered.

I have been called names all my life. Now the names I am called come from within. They sound like people's voices but they are blown on the wind of my inner world.

When I was four I was called 'Goofy', my teeth being prominent . . . Then my Dad called me *lazy, selfish*, my brother called me *ugly*. When I was a teenager it got worse. I was a *bitch,* a *gorp*, a *creep,* and a *cow*. I was the worst person in the world and everybody told me so. My Dad with problems of his own resorted to violence, hitting and strangling and shouting abuse. At school I was very depressed and withdrawn, and I was called a *creep* for knowing the answers to questions. I was bright but it was a crime, it seemed. I was quiet so I got ganged up on by everyone. My Mum told me I should fight my own battles, that I had an inferiority complex and a chip on my shoulder. . .

I had a desperate desire to be loved, for someone to say nice things to me. Falling in love was easy, just hard to find anyone caring enough to reciprocate. I had a couple of boyfriends and then the big one. At first he said all the things I craved, 'You're not ugly, I wouldn't be going out with you if you were,' and he seemed to listen to what I had to say about myself. But he used it to forge a dependent, nervy girlfriend to massage his own ego. He began to undermine me with more words of maliciousness – 'thick as pig shit,' 'stupid,' 'fat arse,' 'prudish,' 'boring'. More bad words to add to the long list.

It is no wonder that I ended up believing all these things. It is no wonder they became carved in the landscape of my brain. Deep etchings of malicious judgemental name-calling, with precious little in my favour. If I did get any positive feedback it was lost amongst the jungle of darkness. So I am left in the dark with the wind blowing the ghostly voices that have made gullies in pathways. The voices of the past I can't escape from, however much I run, wherever I run to.[60]

This woman's story is not unusual among those voice-hearers who find it hard to cope with their voices. Her family was clearly a high EE family. I was amazed when I read an account of EE families by Nick Tarrier. He wrote, 'EE represents a level of stress operating with the home environment which is not necessarily abnormal in any way; it is simply that sufferers from schizophrenia are highly sensitive to even small degrees of stress. If anything, in fact, low EE households could almost be considered abnormal because of their low levels of stress.'[61] His comment reminds me of my mother and sister, who, if I dared to say that what they had said or done had hurt me, would tell me, 'You shouldn't be so sensitive,' which shut me up, but the hurt did not go away. In families like that of Karina Livinstill, answering back is not compatible with going on living.

Ivan Leudar and Phil Thomas pointed out that 'The voices stress the aloneness of the person.'[62] Brian Davey, who has often commented on the loneliness that many introverts feel, wrote, 'Perhaps one of the simplest ways of understanding the hearing of voices is that they are the result of loneliness. But loneliness is not simply the absence of contact with other people; it is the absence of affection arising out of convivial and co-operative joint activity . . . We need a variety of stimulations – sensory and mental – to keep ourselves healthy. If we take a person and put him or her in an artificial environment, deprived of all incoming, sensory information, then that person will begin to hallucinate. This is only to be expected. . . With sensory deprivation only [our] inner reality is still perceivable.'[63]

People become lonely when they cannot converse easily and openly with the people with whom they spend their time. Often they dare not say what they wish to say. The wish to say something, to comment or to answer back, can build up an enormous pressure. A voice can say what you want to say. Richard Bentall and his colleagues noted that 'One patient recognised that her voices tended to become worse following family arguments. She became aware that the content of her voices reflected the things she was feeling and thinking about her family but that she was unable to express.'[64] Avoiding responsibility for what we do is one of our favourite pastimes. Thus this woman was not responsible for what her voices said about her family, just as Socrates was not responsible for what his daemon advised him to do.

Moreover, the voices may speak metaphorically and further distance the hearer from responsibility for what is said. Marius and Sandra found that 'The relationship between the hearer and voices may be a metaphor for the way the person interacts with the outside world.' What the voices say may reflect the hearer's problems, or the way the hearer deals with his problems, or it may show how the hearer cannot cope with his problems.[65]

It can be difficult for a person to give up a defence when it protects him from something he dare not acknowledge. 'When a traumatic event also induces shame or guilt – for example after being raped – the voices act as a shield against them. It may be more acceptable for the person to be haunted by voices than to acknowledge what has happened to them.'[66]

The guide for mental health professionals called *Making Sense of Voices* is a splendid combination of excellent research, simplicity, clarity and organization, all presented with the compassion and quiet authority of Marius and Sandra. I believe that the workshops based on *Making Sense of Voices* which Marius and Sandra run are essential for anyone working, or planning to work, in the mental health field, because in these workshops the participants learn not just how to listen but *what to listen for*.

The workshops and book show how to work within the voice-hearer's frame of reference. Different voice-hearers explain their voices in different ways. Some voice-hearers want to understand their voices in terms of ordinary life. They are pleased to be told that the speech areas of the brain are active when the voices are speaking, and that at the same time the speech muscles become more active, as indicated by an increase in their electrical activity. However, other voice-hearers see their voices as an aspect of the spiritual or paranormal. In this case, all that someone working with the voice-hearer should suggest is that they should concentrate on the inspiring and beneficial aspects of the spiritual or paranormal rather than the persecutory and destructive aspects. For instance, I do not believe in God, but I would not suggest to anyone who came to me for help and who believed in God that they should give up their belief. All I would suggest would be that it is much easier to live with the God of the New Testament, a loving and forgiving God, than the God of the Old Testament, a cruel and punitive God.

Many psychiatric units now have voice-hearing groups, even though the psychiatrists working there still see medication as the essential treatment. Ron Coleman noted that the success of the Hearing Voices Network has meant that some psychiatrists have had to shift the goalposts again. Thus hearing voices has ceased to be a primary symptom and is now just a residual one which a psychologist or nurse running a voice-hearing group can deal with, while the psychiatrist gets on with the important work of medication.[67]

Ron Coleman and Mike Smith have produced an excellent

handbook for people who want to do their own work on their voices. They called it *Victim to Victor*.[68]

The Road to Recovery

When a person becomes psychotic it does not mean that he or she has an incurable mental illness. Rather, it simply means that they have reached a point in their life where they cannot cope with their circumstances, their memories, and the way they have learned to see themselves and their world. They feel themselves falling apart, and they try to defend themselves, but the desperate defence they had at hand was one that led them to behave in ways which society, through its ignorance, regards as mad.

The person chose this defence, but it was not a conscious choice. We all act without conscious choice when we are in danger of being annihilated as a person, and we act in ways aimed at saving ourselves, irrespective of what other people may think. When we are in great physical danger we act without conscious choice, often in the attempt to save ourselves from discarding the moral principles we value. At the beginning of this book I wrote about the fire in a plane at Manchester airport, and how frightened the passengers were. Ten years later I heard one of the survivors of this fire being interviewed about the disaster. She told how the passengers between her and the door were collapsing and blocking the only escape route. She climbed over them, ignoring the fact that they were dying, and managed to squeeze through the small space that was left at the top of the door. Now, she said, she feels ashamed that she acted without any concern for these people, but at the time such moral principles did not enter her mind. All she wanted to do was to save herself by escaping from the plane. Similarly, people who have resorted to one of the desperate defences may later, when they no longer need a desperate defence, look back and feel ashamed of their complete selfishness in the way they acted when they were fighting for their survival, just as the woman passenger was fighting for her life. No doubt in future years we shall hear how people who survived the collapse of the World Trade Center were struggling with their guilt.

Nothing is gained if all we do is look back at our past and feel guilty that we did not act in accordance with the best principles of reason and morality. What we need to do is to learn from our experience. If we have had to resort to a desperate defence we need to recognize the circumstances which led to us doing that, and then we can construct a strategy for either preventing those circumstances from arising again or developing different tactics for dealing with similar circumstances.

We can prevent the circumstances from arising again by changing how we see ourselves and our world, and by separating ourselves from those people who deliberately or inadvertently hurt and harm us. We can deal with similar circumstances differently by recognizing the signs that we are being drawn to use a desperate defence again. This happens when our self-confidence starts to waver. It may be that we have allowed ourselves to become overtired, or that we have not been able to shake off a cold, or that we have encountered some difficulties in our work or social life, but any diminution of self-confidence must be dealt with immediately. Otherwise we have what the medical profession calls a relapse.

The first time we use a desperate defence we learn a skill. We learn how to become agoraphobic, or manic, or depressed, or obsessional, or psychotic, and being each of these is a skill, just as knowing how to ride a bike or dance the tango is a skill. Once we possess a skill we can let ourselves be seduced into using it again. Just as we can let ourselves be seduced by the thought that we have all the energy we need to go for a long bike ride or to impress our friends with our tango, and the next day discover the depth of our folly, so we can be seduced by the thought that trying to live an ordinary life is just too difficult. There is too much hassle, we never get it quite right, we cannot cope with the responsibility. Just as when the night turns cold we pull on an old cardigan, so when life turns cold we can wrap ourselves in the security of an old defence. With the old cardigan and the old defence, we may look odd to others, but we know where we are. Better the devil you know than the devil you don't know.

However, life never repeats itself exactly. The second time we use a desperate defence one of two things can happen. First, once we are locked into the defence we discover that distance had lent enchantment and that we had forgotten what hell it was inside the defence. We now see very clearly that, even though ordinary life is difficult, it is better than this state, and so we get ourselves back to ordinary life as fast as we can. Second, and tragically, once we are locked into the defence the control of our life is taken from us. Perhaps drugs are forced upon us, we are given ECT, made an involuntary patient and locked in a side room. Perhaps our family and friends abandon us, and we are left all alone. Now we are in a perilous situation and we do not know what to do except stick to our desperate defence. We find that the course of events has swept us into what looks like being a long-term career – that of a psychiatric patient.

It is never completely impossible to escape from the career of being a psychiatric patient, but the longer we have been in that career the harder it can be to escape from it, because the psychiatric system forces people into the sick role and tries to keep them there. To escape from the system and to relinquish our desperate defence we have to become experts on ourselves, and out of that knowledge develop a strategy, the aim of which is to lead an ordinary life.

Whatever strategy we develop, central to it must be how we see ourselves. No strategy is going to work if the person still believes that he is unacceptable and worthless. All the accounts given by survivors of the psychiatric system like Ron Coleman and Brian Davey show how they turned themselves from being passive, powerless patients into active, responsible, powerful people. This change meant that they no longer saw themselves as being unacceptable and worthless. Instead, they saw themselves as being acceptable and valuable. Every aspect of the strategy to recover and stay recovered must strengthen the person's ability to care for themselves, to value themselves, and to judge themselves compassionately on reasonable standards.

Fortunately, there are now an increasing number of techniques to assist people in creating successful strategies. The Hearing Voices Network is one of these. Ron Coleman developed a recovery programme called COPS – Choice Ownership People and Self. He set out this programme in his book *Recovery, an Alien Concept*. Cognitive Behaviour Therapy has proved to be invaluable in helping people to be aware of how they see themselves and their world, and to consider whether their ideas are a reasonable reflection of what is actually going on. The techniques of CBT have always been subjected to research, and this has shown that there can be little doubt that CBT can help people make significant, long-lasting changes.

Even with team members who believe that high EE families are simply relaxed, ordinary families driven to distraction by their psychotic member, the techniques of family intervention can lead to changes in the way the family communicates, which means that the member is less likely to become psychotic again. While I tremble at the thought that any family intervention team may have been foolish enough to suggest to my mother that she had not always been the absolutely perfect parent, it seems that there are families who do have the courage to look at the way they interact as a family and, where necessary, to change their ways.

People often discover that changing themselves is quite easy once they resolve to do so, but what proves to be extremely difficult is to persuade their family to see them differently. Lose weight, and every time you visit your mother she gives you cream cakes to eat. Decide to give up being a doormat for your family and instead to stand up for yourself, and your family will pull out all the stops to make you feel guilty about not looking after them properly. Give up being incompetent, useless and psychotic, get yourself a job and an organized life, and your family will spare no effort to show you that they know you are going to break down again because you are ill and you will always be ill. When he was in a psychiatric hospital with a diagnosis of schizophrenia, Rufus May felt that he was seen 'as a failure, a social, moral and genetic outsider... My recovery was about gaining other people's confidence in my abilities and potential. Behind that was the physical recovery which required rest, therapeutic activities and good food. However, the toughest part was changing other people's expectations of what I could achieve.'[69]

Rufus knew that a big factor in recovery was to get a job. 'This was against the consultant's advice. I then had a range of jobs, followed by four months' voluntary work with adults with learning disabilities. Being trusted to carry out responsible and challenging work that I was valued for was a real breakthrough. It gave me the confidence to apply for paid work and make long-term plans to train as a clinical psychologist.'

To be accepted for training as a clinical psychologist, Rufus had to keep silent about his psychosis and time spent in a psychiatric hospital. Once he was qualified and in a job, he decided that he could talk publicly about his experience with a degree of safety, but many people find that public prejudice makes it extremely difficult for an ex-psychiatric patient to get and keep a job. Peter Campbell wrote, 'Discrimination in employment is standard. There are many with psychiatric records who are forced to rinse their talents down the sink and take jobs far below their capabilities. I find it humiliating to have to lie to be in with a chance of work. To be advised to lie, to choose to do so and hereby admit a shame about my past, which is not justified, and which I in no way really feel, has demeaned me more than any other single event of my life outside hospital.'[70]

One of the tasks the Users organizations and Mind have set themselves is to change public attitudes to people regarded as having a mental illness. There is still a very long way to go, but many of the people who belong to a Users group, and certainly those who work as advocates, have found that such work has built up their own self-confidence. Rufus wrote, 'Witnessing inhumane care was a big motivating force for me to want to engage in a political struggle for better, more therapeutic mental health services. This gave my life a clear sense of purpose and meaning.'

Another impediment to being able to work and to carry out the ordinary tasks of day-to-day living is taking neuroleptic drugs. However, coming off drugs is dangerous unless one has a doctor who approves of the project and will supervise it closely. The amount of drugs taken should be reduced in tiny fractions over a long period of time. Coming off drugs must be part of the strategy that includes developing pleasurable interests and activities and building up relationships with friends who give support and encouragement.

The strategy for recovery is a plan for life. It is a plan for the future that draws on what the person has learnt from his past. Many people who have been depressed and learnt from that experience have said that, while the experience was terrible to go through, it was one they came to value greatly because the wisdom they gained from it was priceless. Those people who refused to accept that the occurrence of psychosis meant that they had a lifelong mental illness, some of whom I have mentioned here, might regret the amount of time they spent first in the psychosis and then in trying to escape from the psychiatric system, but they do not regret what they learned about themselves and about life.

Chapter Thirteen

Turning Fear into Courage

Fear is part of life because life has many dangers. However, we can go beyond fear by becoming courageous.

Being courageous means confronting what we fear the most and thus discovering that what we fear does not actually exist. Many of us stumble upon this revelation when we are confronted by a situation which we feel demands that we go beyond our fear. Others, even when confronted with such a situation, feel that they can do nothing but run away from what they fear. In doing so they fail themselves and may also fail the people close to them.

I learnt about such a situation in the aftermath of a tragedy. I had met some friends and colleagues to discuss some work we were doing together, but before we settled down to business we talked about an event that had touched several members of our group. They worked with Colin and his partner Andrew, a couple who had lived together for some ten years. Colin's work took him abroad for short periods, and, while he was away on one trip, some unknown person went to his house and brutally murdered Andrew. When Colin returned to England he did not go home but stayed with a friend. Six weeks after the murder he was still at his friend's home. He had not been back to his own house, and he was stead-fastly refusing to go there ever again. This refusal was causing practical problems for a number of people. The mail arriving at the house needed to be dealt with, and Andrew's elderly parents wanted Colin to wind up their son's affairs and arrange a memorial service, but Colin did not – would not – act. I hardly knew Colin so I sat and listened to the conversation among a group of people, most of whom I knew very well.

Rita said, 'I know just how Colin feels. He can't possibly go back to an empty house. I wouldn't do it, ever.' Rita was highly skilled in making sure that, whatever she did, she was never on her own.

Edgar said, 'I think he's very sensible. There's no point in him getting even more upset than he is now. He can organize everything he needs to organize without him having to go home.' Edgar always liked to talk about the necessity of confronting feelings, but the feelings he preferred to confront were other people's, not his own. His feelings were neatly packaged and explained away. He allowed no chaos or ambiguity into his life.

Niamh said, 'He's got to go home. It's disrespectful to Andrew and it's hurtful to Andrew's parents if he doesn't go. And he's got to face his grief, his loss, sooner or later. The sooner he does it, the easier it will be for him in the long run.' Niamh was no stranger to grief. She had encountered loss, abandonment, rejection, chaos and uncertainty, and she had discovered how to deal with them with courage.

To be courageous we must not let the fear overwhelm us, or else we can do nothing except be afraid. Nor should we run away from the fear by pretending that there is no danger and that we are not afraid. There are times when the best course of action is to make a strategic retreat, but this can be decided upon only after we have made a sensible assessment of what the danger that threatens us is and what we can do to overcome it. We can make a sensible assessment of the danger only on the basis of believing that we have the right to defend ourselves and that we have the self-confidence to do so. If we believe that we are too insignificant, too unworthy, to defend ourselves, or that the danger that threatens us is the punishment we deserve, then we make sure that we are defeated before we start.

If we believe that we have the right to defend ourselves and that we have the self-confidence to do so, we know that we have a purpose in living. The purpose of all living things is to live, but human beings, blessed and cursed with consciousness, interpret this in individual, personal ways. It is the individual purpose in living, armed with the skills of pride and aggression, which has enabled our puny species to survive on this inhospitable planet in a universe indifferent to our existence.

However, when we are frightened we may allow our pride, which takes no account of reality, to mislead us into thinking that we are supremely important and that other people do not matter – indeed, that they are lesser beings, perhaps not people at all but objects that we can harm and destroy. Thus we inflict suffering on the people immediately around us and on the people far away whom we call our enemies. If we understood our fear, all this would be unnecessary.

In the three weeks following the destruction of the World Trade Center in New York on 11 September 2001 we knew that the American government was preparing for military action, though we did not know where. We were told that thousands of Afghans, who were already on the verge of starvation because of the long drought and the conflict in that country, would be fleeing their homeland. A friend phoned me to say that, although she and her family were due to leave for a holiday in Spain, she thought it would be wrong for her to go.

My friend is a woman of great good sense, but a calamity elsewhere usually reminds her of calamities in her own life, times when she suffered a great deal. Also, in her bad old days, when she had little self-confidence, her pride would trick her into feeling guilty about all the woes of humanity. Such guilt implied that she was in some way responsible for all humanity, and such responsibility implied that she had the power to influence and protect all humanity, something that she had failed to do. Now, in a time of great uncertainty, her old, grandiose way of thinking had crept back. Obviously, if by staying home she could avert World War III and feed every one of the starving, she should do so, but, if she understood the limits of her responsibility, she would know that the appropriate response to tragedies that we can neither prevent nor ameliorate is to feel sorrow, not guilt. My friend did have responsibilities – those to herself, her family and her students – and to fulfil these responsibilities a break from routine and a rest were essential so that she would then be able to deal efficiently with the onerous duties winter would bring. No one knew where or how the American government would strike in retaliation, so I reminded her that she could die at any time, and dying in the warmth and sunshine of Spain was preferable to dying in the cold and damp of England.

The day after the tragedy in New York, another friend, an American living in England, phoned me to talk over the events of the previous day. He is a man who always seems very optimistic and self-confident, so he surprised me by saying, 'I just wonder if there's any point in getting out of bed in the morning.'

This was not an idle comment or jest. I thought about our conversation and later in the day I e-mailed him to say that I had a basic philosophy that always ensures that I get out of bed in the morning, no matter what is happening in my life and in the world. If he wanted to know what this philosophy was he could phone me. So he did, and, after some preamble about the necessity of having a philosophy that warmed the heart, I told him what mine was. It is an old Australian saying: 'Never let the bastards win.'

Those people who get out of bed every morning no matter what is happening to them are determined not to let the bastards win. They may not express their determination so crudely. They may say that they intend to achieve this or that, or that they have responsibilities to family, friends, colleagues, or the people they are entrusted to look after, but all these reasons are based upon their often unspoken knowledge that the purpose of life is to live. No one has the right to take that purpose away from us, and we have no right to take it away from ourselves by despairing or deluding ourselves that we would be better off dead.

To go on living we have much to contend with, many people and many events, but most are not bastards, just people and events that lead us to feel hassled and disappointed. By 'bastards' I mean those people and events which threaten to destroy what we hold most dear and see as essential to our life and being.

For many people the great bastard is death. Many people fear death, and their fear of death hangs like a pall over their lives.

They fear dying because, apart from the pain, dying brings us what we fear the most in living – that is, being completely alone and losing all control over ourselves – and they fear death because that brings the annihilation of their sense of being a person. Many people try to overcome their fear of annihilation by believing in some kind of afterlife where their soul or spirit continues on, but such a belief brings with it the fear that they may not be good enough to merit a pleasant afterlife. This fear takes away their freedom to be themselves and to enjoy what life has to offer.

Some people see death as a challenge, a bastard who must not be allowed to win. Neville Crichton is one of the most successful businessmen in Australia and New Zealand. He is also a very successful yachtsman and racing driver. In 1978, when he was thirty-one, he was diagnosed with throat cancer, something totally unexpected as he had never smoked. The first operation left him with one vocal cord and a doubtful future. On leaving hospital he sold his business and took up professional motor racing. In an interview he explained, 'If I was going to die it was going to be in a racing car, not through cancer.'

Despite a number of operations over the next five years the cancer returned. He underwent another operation which left him with a tracheotomy and no voice-box or vocal cords. His doctor told him not to plan to see his next birthday. Neville decided that he was not going to die. He said, 'I never believed that I was sick. I never accepted that there was a problem. I never stopped working.'

However, to work he had to be able to talk. As he said, 'I'm a dealer. My whole life is communication. I buy and sell things.'

He heard of a new method of talking which was being developed and offered himself as a guinea-pig. He learnt the method, which involves vibrating the walls of the throat, and, within an hour, he developed a voice which, though gravelly, carries all the emotional nuances. He explained, 'I had a lot of things I wanted to do in my life, and the fact that I didn't have a perfect voice wasn't going to stop me.'

A tracheotomy creates an uncovered hole at the base of the throat. His doctor warned him to stay away from water but, as

Neville said, 'I'm passionate about yachting. I'm very good at it. One day it might get me, but I don't think about it.'

Having survived twenty-five years and lived life to the full in that time, Neville now talks to people who are about to undergo an operation similar to that which he underwent. He said, 'When people hear that they've got to have the operation the bottom falls out of their world. I tell them to be positive and know that they can live an ordinary life afterwards. I think I'm able to tell whether a person has the drive within themselves, whether they'll be able to pick themselves up and fight it.'

The ideas we bring to a situation determine how we deal with that situation. When Neville was asked how his illness had changed him he replied, 'I think I'm a better person, more tolerant of other people. I've always been aggressive and I'm still aggressive. Whatever I do I like to be successful. I'm extremely aggressive, extremely competitive.'

Neville does not advocate aggression and competitiveness as the means to defeat death but rather being positive in your outlook. A study of a group of nuns begun in 1930 has shown that the nuns who lived well into their old age were usually those who, before they took their final vows in their early twenties, wrote a sketch about themselves in which they expressed many positive ideas and emotions.[1]

For me, death is not a bastard, just something I hope will not happen for a long time. For me bastards are those people who destroy or attempt to destroy other people, not just by killing them but by demeaning, humiliating or ignoring them, treating them as objects, not as people. This book is very much about such bastards, individuals who inflict pain and suffering on others, often on their children, and institutions which, in the guise of looking after people, belittle and hurt them. I rarely feel angry with an individual who belittles and hurts because I usually find that in childhood he has been belittled and humiliated by his parents, and those parents by their parents, and so on back through many generations. This explains his behaviour, though it does not excuse it.

We are all capable of learning and changing how we behave,

but until fairly recently information that might lead an individual to reflect on his behaviour and decide to change it was not generally available. It takes some time for the results of research on behaviour to find their way into books for the general public and for this knowledge to be disseminated widely. However, this kind of information is readily available to those professions concerned with caring for people. Consequently I often feel angry with the big institutions, such as the National Health Service, the social services, the Royal College of Psychiatrists, and educational, legal and prison systems in the UK and Australia, all of which I have had direct contact with. In these institutions information about the necessity of treating other people with dignity and respect has been available for many years, but this has been largely ignored. I am not asking the people in these institutions to behave more virtuously, but to use the findings of science in their work. All the research into effective methods of helping people with mental distress and people who cannot cope with their life, into educating children and teaching people to become law-abiding citizens, shows that the most effective methods begin with coming to understand how the person sees himself and his world. Unfortunately, some people, often powerful people, in these institutions choose to ignore this knowledge in order to maintain their power and prestige. In all these institutions there are many wonderful people doing wonderful work, but it is never easy. They struggle to get funding for their work, and they are always under attack from the forces of unreason.

It is easy to recognize the bastards out there. It can be much harder to recognize the bastardy in ourselves. Pride often tempts us into not giving others the respect and dignity they need. Giving respect and dignity to others is more than being kind and following the golden rule of doing unto others what we would have done unto us. It is a matter of recognizing that we have to understand how another person sees himself and his world. This takes time and effort, and it is so much easier to condemn another person for being mad or bad, or make ourselves seem virtuous by saying in a plaintive tone, 'I don't know why he behaves like that.'

We should treat other people as people and try to understand how they see themselves and their world, not because it is virtuous to do so, but because it is in our own self-interest to do so. When we belittle, demean, humiliate other people and treat them as objects, these people have to protect themselves from being annihilated as a person. Immediately they dislike us. If they have any power they will use that power against us, and, if they have no power, they will strengthen themselves with hatred and vow revenge on us. We saw the result of this process enacted on our television screens on 11 September 2001.

Robert Fisk is a journalist who has lived in the Middle East for many years. His book *Pity the Poor Nation*[2] is essential reading for anyone who wants to understand what led to the events of 11 September. On 20 September he pointed out that theology had played its part in the genesis of those events.[3] The theology that leads a young man to end his life as a suicide bomber or hijacker teaches that suffering is virtuous. Mohamed Atta is believed to be the thirty-three-year-old Egyptian who hijacked American Airlines Flight 11 from Boston and crashed it into the north tower of the World Trade Center. Part of his luggage was not on the plane, and in this was a document in Arabic with instructions about how he should conduct himself on his suicide mission. Among other things it said, 'You will be entering paradise. You will be entering the happiest life, everlasting life . . . A believer is always plagued with problems. . . . You will never enter paradise if you have not had a major problem.'[4] Christianity has always taught that suffering is virtuous. In the early years of the Christian Church hundreds of people sought martyrdom at the hands of a Roman soldier or in a Roman arena because they believed that a martyr went straight to heaven. Once Christianity had become a religion with power and influence, various popes warned against seeking martyrdom, but images of a bleeding Christ on the Cross and saints suffering for their faith strengthened the belief that suffering is virtuous.

Suffering is neither virtuous nor wicked. Suffering is suffering. It is nothing else. Some people suffer and become wiser, more patient and more tolerant, but many do not. Some stay just as they are, and others become mean, self-interested and selfish.

Some suffering is unavoidable. Life is difficult because we all encounter sickness, loss, disappointment and disaster. However, many people seek out suffering because they believe it to be virtuous, and, believing this, they clutch it to their bosom and will not let it go. Believing that we are bad and unacceptable ensures that we suffer. Some people will not let go of their suffering because they believe that to see yourself as valuable and acceptable is wicked.

Suffering is a great waste of time. There are only two advantages to be had from it. The first is that we can learn that we are no different from other people, that we are simply an ordinary member of the human race. The second is that we can learn from our suffering how to appreciate happiness.

We may not be able to avoid sickness, loss, disappointment and disaster, but we make all these much harder to bear when we set ourselves impossible standards to live up to and berate ourselves when we fail to reach them. When Joy discovered that her husband Jack had been sexually abusing their children, she tried to understand the whole complex process which involved all the family and went back into the past and forward into the future. It seemed that the responsibility for all these tragic events lay with Jack, but when Joy examined the process with all the honesty and ruthlessness she could muster she found that an attitude she had adopted early in life in response to the demands her mother had made on her had multiplied her suffering and rendered her less capable to deal with what she had to deal with. Some months after our painful conversations, when I went to visit Joy and Jack, I was surprised to see Joy looking relaxed and calm. She told me, 'All my life I thought I had to make it right for everybody else before I could make it right for myself. Now I've learned that I don't have to be responsible for everyone. I'd always thought that I had to do everything perfectly because I was responsible for everyone. Now I know I'm not, and I can take the time to look after myself. So now, when I need a rest, I go and sit in the garden.'

Joy had chosen to set herself her enormous task when she was a little girl, and the situation she was in seemed to her to be totally chaotic and out of control. To prevent herself from falling apart she now set herself the task of putting everything right and getting everything under control. Many of us have set ourselves this task, though we differ in how we define 'putting right', 'under control' and 'everything'. As small children many of us encountered a situation in which it seemed that everyone in the world had abandoned and rejected us. To prevent ourselves from falling apart we set ourselves the task of making sure that never again would we be threatened by complete isolation. We decided to devote our life to keeping people around us. Different people find different ways of doing this, but all have the aim of never being left completely and utterly alone.

All these people have set themselves the task of controlling every other person and everything in the universe. An utterly impossible task, and an utterly unnecessary task. We may feel ourselves falling apart, we may feel that we are going to shatter, crumble and disappear, but this is not going to happen. *We go on existing*.

We experience this sense of falling apart, shattering and crumbling whenever we discover that there is a serious discrepancy between what we thought our life was and what it actually is. What we thought our life was is simply a set of ideas, a set of guesses about who we are, what our life will be, and what the world is. Events proved our ideas to be wrong. What we feel shattering is our ideas, and these ideas have to shatter in order for us to create new ideas which better reflect our situation. Not all our ideas shatter because they are still a good reflection of what is going on. Water still runs downhill, fire still burns, and the sun still rises in the morning, and we go on existing.

Whenever we discover that there is a serious discrepancy between what we thought our life was and what it actually is we should not let ourselves be overwhelmed by fear. We may feel sad or disappointed if we have lost someone or something we value and if things have not turned out the way we expected, and we may feel uncertain about a large part of our life. The best thing to do in this situation is to trust yourself and live with uncertainty.

Go and sit quietly in the garden and know that things will eventually fall into place. Everything passes, and everything falls into place.

When we have learned to tolerate uncertainty and to trust ourselves, we know how to sit quietly in the garden. Tolerance of uncertainty and trust in ourselves allow new ideas to develop, ideas that are not driven by pride and fear but which allow us to be ourselves and to live our lives fully and freely, beyond fear.

Notes

Introduction

1 *http://www.nice.org.uk/download.aspx?o=502551.*
2 'Mind Your Language', *http://media.guardian.co.uk*, 23 January 2006.
3 *Recovery Beyond Psychiatry*, Free Association Books, London, 2006, pp. 17–21.
4 Oxford University Press, Oxford, 2006, pp. 52, 66.

Chapter One: The Nature of Fear

1 HarperCollins, London, 2000.
2 See R. J. Lifton, *Home from the War*, Simon and Schuster, New York, 1973.
3 See D. Rowe, *The Construction of Life and Death*, Wiley, Chichester, 1982, reissued as *The Courage to Live*, HarperCollins, 1991.
4 Douglas Adams, Pan, London, 1980.
5 Harper Perennial, London, 1994.
6 Charlotte Lessing, July 1985.
7 *Time on Our Side*, op. cit. (note 5), pp. 187–9.
8 P. Mollon, 'Shame in relation to narcissistic disturbance', *British Journal of Medical Psychology*, 57, 1984, pp. 207–14.
9 HarperPerennial, London, 1994.
10 T. Doi, *The Anatomy of Dependence*, trans. J. Bester, Kodansha International Ltd, Tokyo, 1981.
11 Lloyd de Mause, *The History of Childhood*, Bellew Publishing, London, 1991, p. 37.
12 *The Music of Life*, Oxford University Press, Oxford, 2006, p. 139.
13 ibid., p. 140.

Chapter Two: Understanding the Nature of Fear

1 'Primary consciousness: the Interface between Motivation and Cognition', papers delivered at the International Conference on the Evolution of Intelligent Minds, King's College, London, April 2000.

2 Macmillan, London, 2000, p. 10.

3 *Let Them Eat Prozac*, New York University Press, New York, 2004, pp. 12, 291.

4 'Rewriting the Brain', review of Paul Katz (ed.), *Beyond Neurotransmission*, Oxford University Press, Oxford, 2000, in *New Scientist*, 8 April 2000.

5 Penguin Press, London, 2000, p. 165.

6 ibid., p. 13.

7 Dorothy Rowe, *The Real Meaning of Money*, HarperCollins, London, 1998.

8 *The Tao Te Ching*, trans. Stephen Mitchell, Macmillan, London, 1988, p. 48.

9 HarperCollins, London, 1988.

10 Dorothy Rowe, *Depression: The Way Out of Your Prison*, 3rd ed., Routledge, London, 2003, p. 15.

11 ibid., p. 128.

12 HarperCollins, London, 1992.

13 ibid., p. 155.

14 ibid., pp. 260–70.

15 ibid., p. 261. From 'Nothing to Fear', produced by Brendan Hughes, DBA Television, Belfast, Channel 4, 24 March 1990.

16 HarperCollins, London, 2000.

17 *Wanting Everything*, op. cit. (note 12), p. 155.

18 *Friends and Enemies*, op. cit. (note 16), p. 92.

19 *Journal of Personality and Social Psychology*, vol. 75, 1998, p. 617; *New Scientist*, 4 September 1999, p. 49, quoted in *Friends and Enemies*, op. cit., p. 93.

20 'Recent advances in understanding mental illness and psychotic experiences', report by the British Psychological Society, June 2000, p. 46.

21 Everyman series, *The Mind Box*, BBC TV, 2 February 1985.

22 Hans and Michael Eysenck, *Mind Watching: Why We Behave as We Do*, Prion, London, 1989, p. 210.

23 A. T. Beck, *Depression: Clinical, experimental and theoretical aspects*, Harper and Row, New York, 1967.

24 A. T. Beck, *Cognitive Therapy and the Emotional Disorders*, International Universities Press, New York, 1976.

25 B. F. Shaw, 'Stress and depression: A cognitive perspective', in R. W. J. Newfeld (ed.), *Psychological Stress and Psychopathology*, McGraw-Hill, New York, 1982, pp. 125–46.

26 A. T. Beck, N. Epstein, R. P. Harrison and G. Emery, *Development of the Sociotropy-Autonomy Scale: A Measure of Personality Factors in Psychopathology*, unpublished manuscript, University of Pennsylvania, 1983.

27 D. B. Cane, L. J. Linger, I. H. Gotlib, N. A. Kuiper, 'Factor structure of the Dysfunctional Attitudes Scale in a student population', *Journal of Clinical Psychology*, 42, 1986, pp. 307–9.

28 Dorothy Rowe, *The Successful Self*, Harper Perennial, London, 2006.

29 *Family Circle*, July 1985.

30 *Observer*, 14 April 1985.

Chapter Three: Fear Denied

1 R. Scott, 'They hounded him to death', *Daily Mail*, 25 June 1985.

2 *Men*, BBC Books, London, 1984, p. 19.

Chapter Four: Learning How to Deny

1 *The Social Baby*, CP Publishing, Richmond, UK, 2000, pp. 22–30.

2 Alison Gopnik, Andrew Meltzoff and Patricia Kuhl, *How Babies Think: The Science of Childhood*, Weidenfeld and Nicolson, London, 2000.

3 Susie Orbach, *Towards Emotional Literacy*, Virago Press, London, 1999.

4 Daniel Goleman, *Emotional Intelligence*, Bloomsbury, London, 1996.

5 Robyn Davidson, *Tracks*, Ficador, London, 1998, p. 36.

6 *The Child, the Family and the Outside World*, Penguin, Harmondsworth, 1964, p. 62

7 Quoted in Alice Miller, *For Your Own Good*, Faber, London, 1983, p. xviii.

8 Dorothy Rowe, *Wanting Everything*, HarperCollins, London, 1991, p. 81.

9 *Thou Shalt Not Be Aware*, Pluto Press, London, 1985, p. 92.

10 *Friends and Enemies*, op. cit., pp. 191–2.

11 *Sydney Morning Herald*, 24 February 2001.

12 Alice Miller, *Thou Shalt Not Be* Aware, op. cit., p. 130.

13 The Children Are Unbeatable Alliance Briefing, summer 2006, 94 White Lion St, London N1 9PF, *www.childrenareunbeatable.org.uk.*

14 Carolyne Willow and Tina Hyder, *It Hurts You Inside*, National Children's Bureau, Save the Children, 1998, pp. 26–51.

15 *Beating the Devil out of Them*, Lexington Books, Jossey-Bass Inc., San Francisco, 1994.

16 Quoted in *Children Are Unbeatable*, the response to the Department of Health's consultation document on the physical punishment of children by Children Are Unbeatable Alliance, 2000, p. 8.

17 Joan Durrant, *A Generation without Smacking*, Save the Children, London, 1999.

18 'ADHD: Adults' fear of frightened children' in *Making and Breaking Children's Lives*, Craig Newnes and Nick Radcliffe (eds), PCCS Books, Ross-on-Wye, 2005, pp. 71–74.

19 *Sun-Herald*, 18 February 2001.

20 *Guardian*, 22 April 1999.

21 *New England Journal of Medicine*, April 2001, reported on *www.psychport.com*, 28 April 2001.

22 Common Courage Press, Monroe, Maine, 1998.

23 *Changes*, vol. 18, no. 1, 2000, pp. 13–21.

24 *Naughty Boys*, Palgrave Macmillan, London, 2005, p. viii.

25 ibid., p. 111.

26 ibid., p. 110.

27 *Newsday*, 23 September 1999, p. A53.

28 Peter Breggin, *Talking Back to Ritalin*, op. cit. (note 22), p. 87.

29 20 May 2000, pp. 44–5.

30 3 January 2001.

31 HarperCollins, London, 2000, p. 53.

32 Dorothy Rowe, *Time on Our Side*, op. cit., pp. 63–92.

33 ibid., pp. 93–122.

34 ibid., pp. 123–48.

35 Jeffrey Masson, *Freud, the Assault on Truth*, Faber, London, 1984; *Against Therapy*, HarperCollins, London, 1993.

36 Sylvia Fraser, *My Father's House*, Virago, London, 1980; Louise Armstrong, *Rocking the Cradle: What Happened When Women Said Incest*, Women's Press, London, 1996.

37 Lucy Johnstone, *Users and Abusers of Psychiatry*, 2nd ed., Routledge, London, 2000, p. 115.

38 Sheldon Press, London, 2000.

39 D. P. Farrell, unpublished Masters dissertation, Keele University, 1994, quoted in D. P. Farrell, 'Sexual abuse by clergy and the implications for survivors', *Changes*, vol. 17, no. 1, 1999, p. 52.

40 ibid., p. 58.

41 James Joyce, *Guardian*, 17 August 2000.

42 ibid.

43 *Guardian*, 25 November 2000.

44 ibid.

45 'Confusion of tongues between adults and the child', paper read before the International Psycho-analytic Congress, September 1932, quoted in J. M. Masson, *Freud, the Assault on Truth*, op. cit., p. 147.

46 *The Late, Late Show*, Eire TV, 1985.

47 *4.48 Psychosis*, Methuen, London, 2000, p. 43.

Chapter Five: How Society Responds to Mental Distress

1 'Sapping the Spirit: Tory Policy and the people who work for the NHS', paper presented at the annual PPA Conference, 'Work: Curse or Blessing', University of Bristol, April 1995.

2 *Recent Rhetoric in the NHS: Reflections on the Language of Marketed Care*, paper presented at the British Psychological Society Conference on 'Psychotherapy, Psychological Care and Crisis in the NHS', 1998.

3 'Strangers and Enemies' in *Friends and Enemies*, op. cit., pp. 313–87.

4 BBC TV, *Correspondent*, 6 May 2000.

5 *Openmind*, March/April 2000, p. 21.

6 'Pull Yourself Together: A Survey of the Stigma and Discrimination Faced by People Who Experience Mental Distress', The Mental Health Foundation, 2000.

7 'Homicide Inquiries', *Psychiatric Bulletin*, 24, 2000, pp. 6–10.

8 ibid., p. 9.

9 'Newspaper Coverage of Psychiatric and Physical Illness', *Psychiatric Bulletin*, 24, 2000, pp. 104–6.

10 *www.mhmedia.com*.

11 *www.emental-health.com*.

12 *Good Psychiatric Practice 2000*, Royal College of Psychiatrists, Council Report CR33.

13 Lucy Johnstone, op. cit., p. 218.

14 A. Scull, *Museums of Madness*, Penguin, Harmondsworth, 1972, p. 13.

15 'The History of Psychiatry', in Lucy Johnstone, op. cit., pp. 145–65; Craig Newnes, 'Histories of Psychiatry', in *This Is Madness*, vol. 1, eds. Craig Newnes, Guy Holmes and Cailzie Dunn, PCCS Books, Ross-on-Wye, 1999, pp. 7–28.

16 Routledge, London, 1994.

17 'Books for asylum doctors', *Bulletin of the Royal College of Psychiatrists*, 10, March 1986, p. 44.

18 MIND press release, 13 November 2000.

19 *Openmind*, 107, Jan./Feb. 2001.

20 Isabel Goodwin, Guy Holmes, Craig Newnes and Dominic Waltho, 'A qualitative analysis of the views of in-patient mental health service users', *Journal of Mental Health*, 8, 1, 1999, pp. 43–54.

21 *Openmind*, 96, Mar./Apr. 1999, pp. 20, 21.

22 23, 1999, pp. 257–9.

23 Jeannette Copperman, 'The abuse that no one stops', *www.SocietyGuardian.co.uk*, 24 July 2006.

24 *Openmind*, 103, May/Jun. 2000, p. 7.

25 *Guardian*, 10 January 2001.

26 *Openmind*, 97, May/Jun. 1999.

27 *Asylums*, Penguin, Harmondsworth, 1961.

28 Lucy Johnstone, op. cit., pp. 231–2.

29 'Gender, race and the DSM III', *Journal of Health and Social Behaviour*, 29, 1998, pp. 1–22.

30 Routledge, London and New York, 1997, p. 243.

31 Lucy Johnstone, op. cit., p. 234.

32 Maudsley quoted in 'Books for asylum doctors', *Bulletin of the Royal College of Psychiatrists*, 10 February 1986, p. 23.

33 H. Maudsley, *Responsibility in Mental Disease*, Kegan Paul, London, 1984, p. 154.

34 Bailliere, Tindall and Cassell, London, 1970, p. 31.

35 24, 2000, pp. 1–3.

36 Free Association Books, London, 2006, p. 2.

37 ibid., p. 17.

38 ibid., p. 10.

39 ibid., pp. ii, iii.

40 ibid., p. 73.

41 23 December 1977.

42 Unpublished interview by Peter Speedwell and P. G. Virden, 2000.

43 'Training in ''anti-psychiatry''', *Clinical Psychology Forum*, 46, 1992, pp.12–14.

44 Constable, London, 2000.

45 ibid., p. 28.

46 Michele I. Pathe and Paul E. Mullan, 'The Dangerousness of the DSM-R-III', *Journal of Law and Medicine*, vol. 1, July 1993, quoted in Richard Gosden, *Punishing the Patient*, Scribe Publications, Melbourne, Australia, 2001, p. 12.

47 *Diagnostic and Statistical Manual of Mental Disorders* (DSM), American Psychiatric Association, Washington, DC, 1994, p. 327.

48 ibid., p. 332.

49 *The Music of Life*, op. cit., pp. 9, 94.

50 ibid., p. 41.

51 ibid., p. 79.

52 ibid., p. 105.

53 ibid., p. 53.

54 *PLoS Medicine*, vol. 2, issue 12, e392, December 2005.

55 ibid.

56 *www.beyondblue.org.au.*

57 New York University Press, New York, 2004.

58 David Healy, Andrew Herxheimer, David B. Menkes, 'Antidepressants and violence: problems at the interface of medicine and law', *PLoS Medicine*, vol. 3, issue 9, September 2006.

59 'Drugs', in *This Is Madness*, op. cit., vol. 2, p. 92.

60 Lucy Johnstone, op. cit., p. 184.

61 *Guardian*, 2 October 1999.

62 *Time on Our Side*, op. cit., pp. 35–7.

63 Lucy Johnstone, op. cit., p. 189.

64 Whitwell, *Recovery Beyond Psychiatry*, op. cit. (note 36), p. 73.

65 *Changes*, vol. 2, no. 2, 1984, pp. 54–5.

66 'Women and urban community mental health: 20 years on', *Clinical Psychology Forum*, 100, February 1997, pp. 45–7.

67 'Developing a Culturally Appropriate Psychotherapeutic Approach with Indigenous Australians', *Australian Psychologist*, vol. 35, no. 2, 2000, pp. 181–5.

68 Sam Forshall and David J. Nutt, 'Maintenance pharmacotherapy of unipolar depression', *Psychiatric Bulletin*, 23, 1999, pp. 370–3.

69 Chris Brewin, *The Psychologist*, vol. 14, no. 3, 2001, p. 121.

70 322, 24 March 2001, pp. 724–7.

71 A. Jones and C. Schreiber-Kounine, 'Developing a specialist eating disorder service: the trials and tribulations', *Clinical Psychology Forum*, 147, 2001, pp. 39–42.

72 'Controlled bodies, controlled eating', in *This Is Madness*, op. cit., vol. 2, p. 124.

73 *Summer Newsletter*, Issue 33, June 2001.

74 'Developing a survivor discourse to replace the ''psychopathology'' of breakdown and crisis', ibid., pp. 184, 187.

75 BPS Publications, 2000.

76 *Openmind*, 110, Jul./Aug. 2001, p. 16.

77 ibid.

78 ibid., p. 29.

79 Ajay Vijayakrishnan, Joan Rutherford, Steve Miller and Lynne M. Drummond, *Psychiatric Bulletin* 30, 2006, pp. 306–308.

80 24, 2000, pp. 81–2.

81 Dorothy Rowe, *Wanting Everything*, HarperCollins, London, 1991, pp. 32–8.

82 Dorothy Rowe, *Time on Our Side*, HarperCollins, London, 1993, pp. 32–92.

83 *www.mmcinstitute.com*.

Chapter Six: Choosing a Defence

1 BBC2 TV, May 2001.
2 Dorothy Rowe, *The Real Meaning of Money*, op. cit.
3 David Healy, *The Anti-depressant Era*, Harvard University Press, Cambridge, Mass., 1997, p. 212.
4 'Trapped by Trauma: Dissociation and other Responses', the Defence Medical Services Psychological Injuries Unit International Conference, York, 2000, reported in *The Psychologist*, vol. 14, no. 1, 2001, p. 9.
5 DSM, op. cit., pp. 427–9.
6 op. cit. (chapter 5, note 44), pp. 100–25.
7 DSM, op. cit., p. 629.
8 *Making Us Crazy*, Constable, London, 2000, p. 182.
9 'Borderline Personality Disorders', *http://www.stanford.edu*, 20 March 2001.
10 J. L. Herman, J. C. Perry and B. A. van der Kolk, 'Childhood trauma in borderline personality disorder', *American Journal of Psychiatry*, vol. 146, no. 4, pp. 109–12.
11 Personal communication, 30 March 2001.
12 Personal communication, 30 May 2001.
13 Anthony Ryle, *Cognitive Analytic Therapy and Borderline Personality Disorder*, John Wiley, Chichester, UK, 1997.
14 DSM, op. cit., p. 332.
15 ibid., p. 428.
16 Carl Senior et al., 'Depersonalisation', *The Psychologist*, vol. 14, no. 3, 2001, pp. 128–32.
17 John Wiley, Chichester, UK, 1998, p. xiii.
18 *www.voiceofwomen.com/centerarticle.html*, 20 March 2001.
19 *www.dissociation.co.uk*, 20 March 2001.
20 Mollon, op. cit. (note 17), p. 66.

Chapter Seven: A Bodily Solution?

1 3rd ed., Routledge, London, 2003.
2 J. Aubertin, personal communication, 24 August 1985.
3 *Wounded Healers*, ed. V. Rippere and R. Williams, Wiley, Chichester, 1985, p. 168.

4 *www.ibsnetwork.org.uk*.

5 Weidenfeld and Nicolson, London, 2005.

6 ibid., p. 2.

7 ibid., p. 4.

8 ibid., p. 135.

9 ibid., p. 28.

10 ibid., p. 18.

11 ibid., p. 45.

12 ibid., p. 109.

13 ibid., p. 46.

14 Wiley, Chichester, 1978.

15 HarperCollins, London, 1989.

16 ibid., p. 281.

17 Faber and Faber, London, 1958, p. 43.

18 *Openmind* 103, May/Jun. 2000, p. 20.

19 Trio, Gloucester, 1996, p. 30.

20 Spring 2000, p. 5.

21 MIND, 15–19 Broadway, London E15 4BQ, 2000.

22 The Women's Press, London, 1998.

23 University of Chicago Press, Chicago, 1985, p. 119.

24 ibid., p. 18.

25 ibid., p. 8.

26 ibid., p. 115.

27 ibid., p. 13.

28 ibid., p. 51.

29 *Observer* Review section, 21 May 2000.

30 Routledge, London and New York, 1998, p. 72.

31 ibid., p. 106.

32 op. cit. (note 29).

33 ibid., p. 111.

34 op. cit. (note 30).

35 Susie Orbach, *Hunger Strike*, Faber, London, 1986, p. 89.

36 Virago, London, 1984, p. 49.

37 Susie Orbach, *Hunger Strike*, op. cit., p. 69.

38 ibid., p. 69

39 Sheila MacLeod, *The Art of Starvation*, op. cit., p. 25.

40 Raekha Prasad, 'Dispatches from the dinner table', *Guardian*, 12 April 2000.

41 Fay Murphy, Nicholas Troop and Janet Treasure, 'Differential environmental factors in anorexia nervosa: a sibling pair study', *British Journal of Clinical Psychology*, 39, 2001, pp. 193–203.

42 *New Scientist*, 5 February 2000, p. 100.

43 Lucy Johnstone, op. cit., p. 113.

44 S. G. Gowers, J. Weetman, A. Shore, F. Hassain and R. Elvins, 'Impact of hospitalization on the outcome of adolescent anorexia nervosa', *British Journal of Psychiatry*, vol. 176, 2000, pp. 142–9.

45 Denis Campbell, *Observer*, 27 May 2001.

46 *Guardian*, 8 June 2001.

47 *www.rcplondon.ac.uk/pubs/wpnicotinesummary.htm*.

48 *www.nida.nih.gov/ResearchReports/Nicotine/nicotine3.html*.

49 *Living with Drugs*, 5ᵗʰ ed., Arena, Aldershot, 2000, p. 90.

50 Quoted in *Wounded Healers*, op. cit., p. 136.

51 Wiley, Chichester, 1985.

52 G. A. Marlett and D. J. Rohsenow, 'The think-drink effect', *Psychology Today*, 15, 1981, pp. 61–4, quoted in Snyder et al., op. cit. (note 57), p. 226.

53 C. H. McGaghy, 'Drinking and Deviance Disavowal: The case of child molesters', *Social Problems*, 16, 1968, pp. 43–9, quoted in Snyder et al., op. cit., p. 229.

54 *Guardian*, 25 October 2000.

55 Nick Heather and Ian Robertson, *Let's Drink to That*, BPS Books, Leicester, 1996, p. 19.

56 3ʳᵈ ed., Oxford University Press, Oxford, 1998, p. 111.

57 ibid., p. 32.

58 ibid., p. 39.

59 ibid., p. 40.

60 P. C. Naik, J. Lawton and L. W. Brownell, 'Comparing general practitioners and specialist alcohol services in the management of alcohol withdrawal', *Psychiatric Bulletin*, 24, 2000, pp. 214–15.

61 Heather and Robertson, *Problem Drinking*, op. cit. (note 56), p. 205.

62 *Living with Drugs*, op. cit., p. 24.

63 Charles Medawar, *Power and Dependence*, Social Audit Ltd, London, 1992.

64 *Living with Drugs*, op. cit., pp. 58–65.

65 ibid., p. 17.

66 ibid., p. 18.

67 op. cit.

68 op. cit., p. 160.

69 ibid., pp. 160 5.

70 *Guardian*, 14 June 2001.

71 *Living with Drugs*, op. cit., p. 108.

72 C. Heather Ashton, 'Pharmacology and effects of cannabis', *British Journal of Psychiatry*, 178, 2001, pp. 101–6.

73 Andrew Johns, 'Psychiatric effects of cannabis', *British Journal of Psychiatry*, 178, 2001, pp. 116–22.

74 Philip Robson, 'Therapeutic aspects of cannabis and cannabinoids', *British Journal of Psychiatry*, 178, 2001, pp. 107–15.

75 *New Scientist*, 29 July 2006, p. 17.

76 Bloomsbury, London, 1999, p. 7.

77 ibid., p. 17.

78 ibid., p. 173.

79 ibid., p. 176.

80 *Living with Drugs*, op. cit., p. 153.

81 ibid., p. 155.

82 ibid., p. 156.

83 *Observer*, 17 June 2001.

84 *Living with Drugs*, op. cit., p. 144.

85 ibid., p. 143.

86 *Guardian*, 14 June 2001.

87 *Living with Drugs*, op. cit., p. 150.

88 *Sydney Morning Herald*, 7 March 2001.

89 *Living with Drugs*, op. cit., pp. 193, 201.

90 *The Story of Junk*, Headline, London, 1997, pp. 60, 61, 65.

91 *Living with Drugs*, op. cit., p. 191.

92 Dorothy Rowe, *The Real Meaning of Money*, op. cit.

Chapter Eight: Turning Fear into Depression

1 Robert Wainwright, 'Out of the Blue', *Sydney Morning Herald* Good Weekend, 2 July 2006, pp. 20–24.

2 ibid., p. 22.

3 *Sunbathing in the Rain: A Cheerful Book about Depression*, HarperCollins, London, 2002, p. 213.

4 *The Zen Path through Depression*, HarperCollins, San Francisco, 1999, p. 80.

5 ibid., p. 42.

6 Gwyneth Lewis, *Sunbathing in the Rain*, op. cit., p. 205.

7 Philip Martin, *The Zen Path through Depression*, op. cit., p. 1.

8 Robert Wainwright, 'Out of the Blue', op. cit., p. 21.

9 Rippere and Williams (eds), *Wounded Healers*, op. cit., p. 74.

10 *The Anatomy of the Self*, Kodansha International, Tokyo, 1986, p. 149.

11 Gwyneth Lewis, *Sunbathing in the Rain*, op. cit., p. 36.

12 ibid., p. 37.

13 ibid., p. 21.

14 *No Hidden Meanings*, Science and Behavior Books, Palo Alto, California, 1975.

15 *4.48 Psychosis*, op. cit., p. 25.

16 ibid., p. 8.

17 *Modern Times*, BBC2, 29 September 2000.

18 3rd ed., Routledge, London, 2003.

19 Gwyneth Lewis, *Sunbathing in the Rain*, op. cit., p. xiii.

20 Allen Lane, 2005.

21 *http://cep.lse.ac.uk/textonly/research/mentalhealth/DEPRESSION_REPORT_LAYARD.pdf*.

22 *4.48 Psychosis*, op. cit., p. 25.

23 *British Journal of Psychiatry*, vol. 165 (supplement 26), no. 5, 1994.

24 23, 1999, pp. 370–3.

25 'Clinical importance of long-term antidepressant treatment', *British Journal of Psychiatry*, vol. 179 (supplement 42), 2001, pp. 4–8.

26 'Do antidepressants cure or create abnormal brain states?' *PLoS Medicine*, vol. 3, issue 7, e240, July 2006, *www.plosmedicine.org*.

27 *Openmind*, 99, Sept./Oct. 1999, p. 16.

28 *Psychiatric Bulletin*, 23, 1999, pp. 742–7.

29 *Power and Dependence*, Social Audit, London, 1992.

30 *Guardian*, 5 May 2001.

31 Gwyneth Lewis, *Sunbathing in the Rain*, op. cit., p. 73.

32 Leeds Community and Mental Health Services, 15 November 2001.

33 *www.babcp.com/publications*.

34 *http://www.rcpsych.ac.uk*.

35 op. cit.

36 *http://www.psychiatry.ox.ac.uk/csr/mbct.html*

37 *http://www.mbct.co.uk/about.htm#about5.*

38 Samantha Wileman et al, 'Light therapy for seasonal affective disorder', *British Journal of Psychiatry*, vol. 178, 2001, pp. 311–16.

39 *A Single Step*, magazine of the Depression Alliance, no. 3, 1999, p. 13.

40 Gwyneth Lewis, *Sunbathing in the Rain*, op. cit., p. 210.

41 ibid., p. 96.

42 ibid., p. 123.

43 Philip Martin, *The Zen Path through Depression*, op. cit., p. 61.

Chapter Nine: Turning Fear into Anxiety, Panic and Phobias

1 3 December 2000.

2 'Cognitive therapy of social phobia', in Nicholas Tarrier, Adrian Wells and Gillian Haddock, *Treating Complex Cases: The Cognitive Behavioural Approach*, John Wiley and Sons, Chichester, 1998, pp. 1–26.

3 'The example of repression', *The Psychologist*, vol. 13, no. 2, 2000, pp. 615–17.

4 'Cognitive therapy of social phobia', op. cit., p. 7.

5 ibid., p. 9.

6 Adrian Wells and Costas Papageorgiou, 'Social phobia: effects of external attention on anxiety, negative beliefs and perspective taking', *Behaviour Therapy*, 29, 1998, pp. 357–70.

7 Jim White, '''Stress control'' large group therapy for generalized anxiety disorder: two year follow-up', *Behavioural and Cognitive Psychotherapy*, 26, 1998, pp. 237–45.

8 Jim White, '''Stresspac'': three year follow-up of a controlled trial of a self-help package for the anxiety disorders', *Behavioural and Cognitive Therapy*, 26, 1998, pp. 133–41.

9 Jim White, Ray Jones and Eiledh McGarry, 'Cognitive behavioural computer therapy for the anxiety disorders', *Journal of Mental Health*, vol. 9, 2000, pp. 505–16.

Chapter Ten: Turning Fear into Mania

1 M. J. Hobbs in association with Michael Joseph, London, 1985, p. 161.
2 *Images of Destruction*, Routledge and Kegan Paul, London, 1987, p. 132.
3 'The Manic Defence', in *Through Paediatrics to Psycho-analysis*, Hogarth Press and the Institute of Psychoanalysis, London, 1982, p. 130.
4 *An Unquiet Mind*, Picador, London, 1996, p. 68.
5 ibid., p. 181.
6 David Wigoder, *Images of Destruction*, op. cit., p. 147.
7 University of Illinois Press, Urban and Chicago, 1990, 2000, p. 67.
8 Quoted in Kay Jamison, *Touched with Fire*, Free Press, New York, 1993, p. 249, from 'A Conversation with Ian Hamilton', in *Robert Lowell: Collected Prose*, ed. Robert Giroux, Farrar, Straus and Giroux, New York, 1987, p. 286.
9 Kate Millett, *The Loony Bin Trip*, op. cit. (note 7), p. 257.
10 ibid., p. 259.
11 ibid., p. 260.
12 ibid., p. 264.
13 Ray Moynihan, David Henry, 'The fight against disease mongering: generating knowledge for action', *PLoS Medicine*, vol. 3, issue 4, April 2006, p. 0425.
14 *Diagnostic and Statistical Manual for Mental Disorders*, 4th edition, American Psychiatric Association, Washington DC, 2005, pp. 317–318.
15 'The latest mania: selling bipolar disorder', *PLoS Medicine*, vol. 3, issue 4, e185, p. 0441.
16 ibid., p. 0442.
17 ibid., p. 0443.
18 ibid., p. 0443.
19 E. Schaefer, *Child Development*, vol. 36, no. 2, 1965, pp. 413–24.
20 Dorothy Rowe, 'Changes in the perception of relationships in the hypomanic state as shown by the repertory grid', *British Journal of Psychiatry*, 119, 1971, pp. 323–4.
21 Kay Jamison, *An Unquiet Mind*, op. cit., p. 29.
22 ibid., p. 34.
23 ibid., p. 139.
24 ibid., p. 31.

25 ibid., p. 35.

26 ibid., p. 36.

27 David Wigoder, *Images of Destruction*, op. cit., p. 133.

28 ibid., p. 78.

29 'The Welsh Marches', in *The Shropshire Lad*, Jonathan Cape, London, 1972, p. 56.

30 *The Drama of the Gifted Child*, trans. Ruth Ward, Faber, London, 1979, p. 129.

31 David Wigoder, *Images of Destruction*, op. cit., p. 71.

32 ibid., p. 67.

33 ibid., p. 112.

34 Alice Miller, *The Drama of the Gifted Child*, op. cit., p. 56.

35 ibid., pp. 56, 58, 60.

36 David Wigoder, *Images of Destruction*, op. cit., p. 94.

37 ibid., p. 144.

38 ibid., p. 72.

39 ibid., p. 74.

40 Alice Miller, *The Drama of the Gifted Child*, op. cit., p. 59.

41 David Wigoder, *Images of Destruction*, op. cit., pp. 4, 5.

42 Kay Jamison, *An Unquiet Mind*, op. cit., p. 22.

43 ibid., p. 120.

44 *www.mdf.org.uk*.

45 Free Press, New York, 1993, p. 3.

46 *Focusing News*, newsletter of the British Focusing Network, vol. 4, issue 3, 1996, p. 2.

47 David Wigoder, *Images of Destruction*, op. cit., p. 226.

48 ibid., p. 232.

49 ibid., p. 247.

50 ibid., p. 268.

51 Kate Millett, *The Loony Bin Trip*, op. cit., p. 280.

52 ibid., p. 281.

53 ibid., p. 309.

54 ibid., p. 310.

55 ibid., p. 315.

Chapter Eleven: Turning Fear into Obsessions and Compulsions

1 Oxford University Press, Oxford, 1999, p. 26.
2 Jeremy P. Tarcher/Putnam, New York, 2000, pp. 1, 33, 37, 27.
3 ibid., pp. 42, 43.
4 op. cit. (note 1), p. 49.
5 op. cit. (note 2), p. 95.
6 op. cit., p. 49.
7 Dorothy Rowe, *The Courage to Live*, HarperCollins, London, 1991, pp. 185–91.
8 G. Thrane, 'Shame and the construction of the self', *Annual of Psychoanalysis,* 7, 1979, pp. 321–41.
9 P. Mollon, 'Shame in relation to narcissistic disturbance', *British Journal of Medical Psychology*, 57, 1984, pp. 207–14.
10 *Poems,* Oxford University Press, London, 1948, p. 110.
11 Marc Summers, *Everything in Its Place*, op. cit., pp. 157, 160.
12 ibid., p. xvi.
13 ibid., p. 49.
14 ibid., p. 36.
15 ibid., p. 35.
16 ibid., p. 40.
17 ibid., p. 116.
18 Padmal de Silva and Stanley Rachman, *Obsessive-Compulsive Disorder: the Facts*, op. cit., pp. 72, 73.
19 Marc Summers, *Everything in Its Place*, op. cit., p. 208.
20 'Is OCD contagious? The implications of caring for spouse with OCD', *Clinical Psychology Forum*, 144, October 2000, pp. 28–31.
21 ibid,, p. 29.
22 Viking, London, 1996.
23 *Sunday Herald Sun*, 9 July 2000.

Chapter Twelve: Turning Fear into Schizophrenia

1 *Openmind*, 107, Jan./Feb. 2001.
2 In Marius Romme and Sandra Escher (eds), *Accepting Voices*, Mind Publications, London, 1993, p. 184.
3 ibid., p. 186.

4 *Recovery: An Alien Concept*, Hansell Publishing, Gloucester, 1999, p. 54.

5 ibid., p .9.

6 ibid., pp. 10–11.

7 *The Spiritual Nature of Man*, Oxford University Press, Oxford, 1979.

8 David Hay, *Exploring Inner Space: Scientists and Religious Experience*, Penguin, Harmondsworth, 1981.

9 BPS Publications, 2000, p. 17.

10 Romme and Escher (eds), *Accepting Voices*, op. cit., p. 39.

11 A. O'Day, *Angie Baby*, produced by Jo Wissert, Capitol Records, 1987.

12 'Clinical regression compared with defence organization', in Eldred and Vanderpool (eds), *Psychotherapy in the Designed Therapeutic Milieu*, Little, Brown and Co., Boston, 1967, quoted in M. Davis and D. Wallbridge, *Boundary and Space,* Penguin, Harmondsworth, 1983, p. 60.

13 Gavin Cape et al., 'Schizophrenia: the views of a sample of psychiatrists', *Journal of Mental Health*, 3, 1994, pp. 105–13.

14 Dorothy Rowe, *Foreword* in Lucy Johnstone, op. cit., pp. ix–xvi.

15 3, 1991, pp. 30–31.

16 31, 1992, pp. 374–6.

17 179, 2001, pp. 93–4.

18 BPS Publications, op. cit., p. 25.

19 *The Psychologist*, vol. 14, no. 15, May 2001, p. 234.

20 BPS Publications, op. cit., pp. 26–7.

21 *Openmind*, 99, Sept./Oct. 1999, p. 17.

22 BPS Publications, op. cit., p. 20.

23 'Report of the Confidential Inquiry into Homicides and Suicides by Mentally Ill People', Royal College of Psychiatrists, 1996.

24 BPS Publications, op. cit., p. 29.

25 Littlewood and Lipsedge, *Aliens and Alienists*, op. cit.

26 23, 1999, pp. 733–9.

27 S. Fernando (ed.), *Mental Health in a Multi-ethnic Society*, Routledge, London, 1995.

28 R. Warner, *Recovery from Schizophrenia: Psychiatry and Political Economy*, Routledge, London, 1994, p. 139.

29 BPS Publications, op. cit., p. 15.

30 A. Jablensky, N. Sartorius, G. Ernberg et al, 'Schizophrenia manifestations, incidence and course in different countries. A World

Health Organisation ten-country study', *Psychological Medicine Monograph Supplement* 20, Cambridge University Press, Cambridge, 1992.

31 Gaskell, London, 2005, p. 19.

32 *Recovery Beyond Psychiatry*, op. cit., p. 74.

33 *Accepting Voices*, op. cit., p. 18.

34 *Guardian*, 7 October 2000, extracted from *Shrinks*, Granta magazine, London, 2000.

35 Published by the National Schizophrenia Fellowship, Surbiton, Surrey, 1974, quoted in P. Barnham, *Schizophrenia and Human Value*, Basil Blackwell, Oxford, 1984, p. 190.

36 Julian Leff, *Advanced Family Work for Schizophrenia*, op. cit., p. 3.

37 ibid., p. 11.

38 ibid., p. 64.

39 Peter Breggin, 'Should the use of neuroleptics be severely limited?', *Changes*, vol. 14, no. 1, p. 63.

40 'Drugs', in *This Is Madness*, vol. 1, PCCS Books, Ross-on-Wye, 1999, p. 91.

41 25, 2001, pp. 287–8.

42 ibid., pp. 284–6.

43 BPS Publications, op. cit., p. 41.

44 Ron Coleman, *Recovery: An Alien Concept*, op. cit., p. 27.

45 Scribe Publications, Melbourne, Australia, 2001, p. 222; Heather Nolan, personal communication to Richard Gosden, 26 February 1998.

46 *This Is Madness*, op. cit., p. 154.

47 *Psychiatric Bulletin*, op. cit. (note 41), p. 285.

48 Peter Breggin, op. cit., p. 62.

49 ibid., p. 63.

50 ibid. p. 63

51 'Benzodiazepines in schizophrenia', *Psychiatric Bulletin*, 24, 2000, pp. 113–15.

52 Peter Breggin, op. cit., p. 63.

53 *Openmind*, 102, Mar./Apr. 2000, p. 18.

54 *Psychiatric Bulletin*, 25, 2001, p. 290.

55 *Voices of Reason, Voices of Insanity*, Routledge, London, 2000, p. 113.

56 *This Is Madness*, op. cit., p. 156.

57 Romme and Escher (eds), *Accepting Voices*, op. cit., p. 11.

58 *Voices* magazine, Hearing Voices Network, spring 2001, p. 7.

59 *Making Sense of Voices*, Mind Publications, London, 2000, p. 23.

60 *Voices* magazine, op. cit., p. 5.

61 Romme and Escher (eds), *Accepting Voices*, op. cit., p. 182.

62 *Voices of Reason, Voices of Sanity*, op. cit., p. 206.

63 'Upbringing and psychosis', *Changes*, op. cit., p. 52.

64 R. P. Bentall et al., 'Cognitive behaviour therapy for persistent auditory hallucinations', *Behaviour Therapy*, 25, 1994, pp. 303–13.

65 *Making Sense of Voices*, op. cit., p. 28.

66 ibid., p. 33.

67 *This Is Madness*, op. cit., p. 153.

68 *Victim to Victor: Working with Voices*, Handsell Publications, Gloucester, 1997.

69 'Routes to recovery from psychosis: the roots of a clinical psychologist', *Clinical Psychology Forum*, 146, 2000, pp. 6–10.

70 BPS Publications, op. cit., p. 53.

Chapter Thirteen: Turning Fear into Courage

1 D. D. Danner, D. A. Snowdon and W. V. Friesen, 'Positive emotions in early life and longevity: findings from the nuns study', *Journal of Personality and Social Psychology*, 80, 2001, pp. 804–13.

2 Oxford University Press, Oxford, 1992.

3 *Independent,* 20 September 2001.

4 *Guardian*, 29 September 2001.

Books and Websites

Johnstone, Lucy, *Users and Abusers of Psychiatry*, second edition, Routledge, London, 2000.

Kirk, Stuart, and Herb Kutchins, *Making Us Crazy: DSM – The Psychiatric Bible and the Creation of Mental Disorders*, Constable, London 2000.

Lewis, Gwyneth, *Sunbathing in the Rain: A Cheerful Book about Depression*, second edition, Harper Perennial, London, 2006.

Lynch, Terry, *Beyond Prozac*, PCCS Books, Ross-on-Wye, 2004.

Martin, Philip, *The Zen Path through Depression*, Harper Collins, San Francisco, 1999.

Newnes, Craig, Guy Holmes, Cailzie Dunn (eds), *This Is Madness: A Critical Look at Psychiatry and the Future of the Mental Health Services*, PCCS Books, Ross-on-Wye, 1999.

Newnes, Craig, Guy Holmes, Cailzie Dunn (eds), *This Is Madness Too: Critical Perspectives on Mental Health Services*, PCCS Books, Ross-on-Wye, 2001.

Newnes, Craig, and Nick Radcliffe (eds), *Making and Breaking Children's Lives*, PCCS Books, Ross-on-Wye, 2005.

Openmind, openmind@mind.org.uk.

Read, Nick, *Sick and Tired: Healing the Illnesses that Doctors Can't Cure*, Weidenfeld and Nicolson, London, 2005.

Romme, Marius, and Sandra Escher (eds), *Accepting Voices*, Mind Publications, London, 1993.

Romme, Marius, and Sandra Escher (eds), *Making Sense of Voices*, Mind Publications, London, 2000.

Rowe, Dorothy, *Depression: The Way Out of Your Prison*, third edition, Routledge, 2003.

Timimi, Sami, *Naughty Boys: Anti-Social Behaviour, ADHD and the Role of Culture*, Palgrave Macmillan, London, 2005.

Wigoder, David, *Images of Destruction*, Routledge, London, 1987.

British Association for Behavioural and Cognitive Psychotherapies, *www.babcp.com*

British Association for Counselling and Psychotherapy, *www.bacp.co.uk*

British Psychoanalytic Council, *www.bcp.org.uk*

British Psychological Society, *www.bps.org.uk*

Carers UK, *www.carersuk.org*

Eating Disorders Association, *www.edauk.com*

Hearing Voices Network, *www.hearing-voices.org.uk*

Hearing Voices Network Australia, *www.rfwa.org.au/page.php?page=95*

Highland Users Group, *www.HUG.uk.net*

The IBS Network, *www.ibsnetwork.org.uk*

Institute of Family Therapy, *www.instituteoffamilytherapy.org.uk*

MDF The BiPolar Organisation, *www.mdf.org.uk*

MIND, *www.mind.org.uk*

Nafsiyat (an intercultural therapy centre), *www.nafsiyat.org.uk*

National Phobics Society, *www.phobics-society.org.uk*

OCD – UK, *www.ocduk.org*

Richmond Fellowship Western Australia, *www.rfwa.org.au*

Self Help Groups, *www.selfhelpgroups.co.uk*

UK Council for Psychotherapy, *www.psychotherapy.org.uk*

Index

Littlewood, Roland 53, 174
Littlewood, Roland and Lipsedge,
    Maurice
    Aliens and Alienists 174
Livinstill, Karina 620–1
Llewellyn, Sue 52
Lloyd-Jones, Vanessa 164–5
London Zoo
    Friendly Spider Programme 399
loneliness
    finding balance between rejection
        and 13
Loring, M. and Powell, B. 174
Lorna 30–1, 415
Lott, Tim 550–3
lottery winners 230–1
Lowell, Robert 451
LSD 324–5
Lucy 367, 407–14, 436
lunatic asylums 158–60, 161–2,
    168
Lunatics Act (1942/1845) 159
Lundbeck Ltd 156
lung disease 581
Lutz, Beat 327

McGuinness, Martin 129
McHale, Mick 60
MacLeod, Sheila 296
    The Art of Starvation 295–6
McPherson, Conor 129
madness 157–8
    fear of 154
    seen as possession by evil spirits
        157
    see also mania/manic-depression
Mair, Miller 152–3, 305–6
Making Sense of Voices 623
Malson, Helen 294
    The Thin Woman 293
Manchester airport fire 3, 624

mania/manic-depression 441–95
    caused by chemical changes in
        brain theory 452–3
    and cognitive therapy 488
    and creativity 489–92
    and cyclical physiological rhythm
        458, 464
    dealing with by psychiatrists
        451–2
    as defence against fear 442, 464
    defences for 458–85
    finding yourself 485–97
    flight into by extraverts 447–8
    and Focusing 492
    and genetics 448, 454–5
    and metabolic basis of mood
        change 457
    running into external reality
        442–3
    as a social issue 451
    and taking lithium 448, 455, 456
Manic-Depression Fellowship
    (MDF) 485–7
    Self-Management Training
        Programme 487–8
Margaret 24–8, 309–10
Marjorie 414
Marks, Isaac 437
Marlboro cigarettes 302
Martin, Paul 283
Martin, Philip 343–4, 395
    The Zen Path through Depression
        345
Mary 233–4
masculinity 120
Masson, Jeffrey 121
Mathews, Patrick
    Cannabis Culture 327–8
Matthew 446, 469–72
Maude 464
Maudsley, Henry 178, 179